GET THROUGH

MRCPsych Paper A1: Mock Examination Papers

GET THROUGH

MRCPsych Paper A1: Mock Examination Papers

Melvyn WB Zhang MBBS, DCP, MRCPsych
National HealthCare Group, Singapore

Cyrus SH Ho MBBS, DCP, MRCPsych
National University of Singapore

Roger Ho MBBS, DPM, DCP, Gdip Psychotherapy, MMed (Psych), MRCPsych, FRCPC
National University of Singapore

Ian H Treasaden MB, BS, LRCP, MRCS, FRCPsych, LLM
West London Mental Health NHS Trust, Imperial College Healthcare NHS Trust, and Bucks New University, UK

Basant K Puri MA, PhD, MB, BChir, BSc (Hons) MathSci, DipStat, PG Dip Maths, MMath, FRCPsych, FSB
Hammersmith Hospital and Imperial College London, UK

CRC Press
Taylor & Francis Group
Boca Raton London New York

CRC Press is an imprint of the
Taylor & Francis Group, an **informa** business

CRC Press
Taylor & Francis Group
6000 Broken Sound Parkway NW, Suite 300
Boca Raton, FL 33487-2742

Printed in Great Britain by Ashford Colour Press Ltd, Gosport, Hants
Version Date: 20160426

International Standard Book Number-13: 978-1-4822-4742-8 (Paperback)

Visit the Taylor & Francis Web site at
http://www.taylorandfrancis.com

and the CRC Press Web site at
http://www.crcpress.com

MIX
Paper from responsible sources
FSC www.fsc.org FSC® C011748

TABLE OF CONTENTS

INTRODUCTION

The two volumes that comprise this book consist of over 1800 questions. They correspond to the new format of Paper A of the Royal College of Psychiatrists' examinations, which has been revised recently. The questions (a mixture of both multiple choice questions [MCQs] as well as extended matching items [EMIs]) have been set so as to reflect the type and the current standard of the questions of the examinations, at the time of writing.

A good proportion of the questions featured in this book have been set so as to model against the core themes that have been commonly tested in the examinations in recent years. A good proportion of the questions are also being set based on the core domains of knowledge assessed in the examination. The authors have provided detailed explanation for each of the questions included in the mock examination paper. Readers are provided with references to which they could refer to, if they are in doubt with regards to any of the theoretical concepts. The format of the mock examination paper has been organized such that at least a third of the questions are EMIs, and the remaining two-thirds are MCQs.

We welcome any feedback from those of you who are using this book. Please also let us know further the type of questions you would like to see in the next edition of this book.

We wish to thank all the authors who have contributed to this revision guide-book and mock examination series.

Melvyn WB Zhang
Cyrus SH Ho
Roger CM Ho
Ian H Treasaden
Basant K Puri

AUTHORS

Dr Melvyn Zhang, MBBS, DCP, MRCPsych, is a specialist registrar/senior resident at the National Healthcare Group, Singapore. He graduated from the National University of Singapore and received his postgraduate training with the Royal College of Psychiatrists (UK). He is currently working with the Institute of Mental Health, Singapore. He has a special interest in the application of web-based and smartphone technologies for education and research and has been published extensively in this field. He is a member of the Public Education and Engagement Board (PEEB), Royal College of Psychiatrists (UK), as well as a member of the editorial board of the *Journal of Internet Medical Research (Mental Health).* He has published extensively in the *British Medical Journal (BMJ), Lancet Psychiatry* and *BJPsych Advances.*

Dr Cyrus SH Ho, MBBS, DCP, MRCPsych, is an associate consultant psychiatrist and clinical lecturer from the National University Hospital, Singapore. He graduated from the National University of Singapore, Yong Loo Lin School of Medicine and subsequently obtained the Diploma of Clinical Psychiatry from Ireland and Membership of the Royal College of Psychiatrists from the United Kingdom. As a certified acupuncturist with the Graduate Diploma in Acupuncture conferred by the Singapore College of Traditional Chinese Medicine, he hopes to integrate both Western and Chinese medicine for holistic psychiatric care. He is actively involved in education and research work. His clinical and research interests include mood disorders, neuropsychiatry, pain studies and medical acupuncture.

Dr Roger Ho, MBBS, DPM, DCP, Gdip Psychotherapy, MMed (Psych), MRCPsych, FRCPC, is an assistant professor and consultant psychiatrist at the Department of Psychological Medicine, National University of Singapore. He graduated from the University of Hong Kong and received his training in psychiatry from the National University of Singapore. He is a general adult psychiatrist and in charge of the Mood Disorder Clinic, National University Hospital, Singapore. He is a member of the editorial board of *Advances of Psychiatric Treatment*, an academic journal published by the Royal College of Psychiatrists. His research focuses on mood disorders, psychoneuroimmunology and liaison psychiatry.

Dr Ian H Treasaden, MB, BS, LRCP, MRCS, FRCPsych, LLM, is currently an honorary consultant forensic psychiatrist at West London Mental Health NHS Trust and Imperial College Healthcare NHS Trust, as well as a visiting senior lecturer at Bucks New University.

Until 2014, he was a consultant forensic psychiatrist at Three Bridges Medium Secure Unit, West London Mental Health NHS Trust, where he was also the clinical director, College and Coordinating Clinical Tutor for the Charing Cross Rotational Training Scheme in Psychiatry, and tutor in law and ethics and honorary senior clinical lecturer at Imperial College London.

He has authored papers on forensic and general psychiatry, and he is co-author of the books *Textbook of Psychiatry* (3 editions), *Mental Health Law: A Practical Guide* (2 editions), *Emergencies in Psychiatry, Psychiatry: An Evidence-Based Text* and *Revision MCQs and EMIs for the MRCPsych* and the forthcoming *Forensic Psychiatry: Fundamentals and Clinical Practice.*

He qualified in medicine from the London Hospital Medical College, University of London, in 1975 where he was awarded the James Anderson Prize in Clinical Medicine. He undertook training in forensic psychiatry at the Maudsley & Bethlem Royal Hospitals in London and Broadmoor Special Hospital, Berkshire, England between 1982 and 1984.

Basant K Puri, MA, PhD, MB, BChir, BSc (Hons) MathSci, DipStat, PG Dip Maths, MMath, FRCPsych, FSB, is based at Hammersmith Hospital and Imperial College London, United Kingdom. He read medicine at St John's College, University of Cambridge. He also trained in molecular genetics at the MRC MNU, Laboratory of Molecular Biology, Cambridge. He has authored or co-authored more than 40 books, including the second edition of *Drugs in Psychiatry* (Oxford University Press, 2013), third edition of *Textbook of Psychiatry* with Dr Ian Treasaden (Churchill Livingston, 2011) and, with the publisher of the present volume, the third edition of *Textbook of Clinical Neuropsychiatry and Neuroscience Fundamentals* with Professor David Moore (2012).

MRCPSYCH PAPER AI MOCK EXAMINATION I: QUESTIONS

GET THROUGH MRCPSYCH PAPER AI: MOCK EXAMINATION

Total number of questions: 194 (116 MCQs, 80 EMIs)
Total time provided: 180 minutes

Question 1
Vascular dementia has been known to be the second most common cause of dementia. A caregiver of a patient with vascular dementia is now worried about the risk of her acquiring the disorder. You would advise her that the most significant risk is
a. Having an elevated lipid level
b. Having poorly controlled blood pressure
c. Having a previous smoking history
d. Having an underlying heart disease
e. Having a history of chronic alcohol abuse

Question 2
Which of the following would help to reduce the risk associated with acquiring vascular dementia?
a. Low dose of aspirin daily
b. Regular dose of multivitamins
c. Regular dose of thiamine replacement
d. Low dose of antipsychotics
e. Anti-dementia medications

Question 3
Which of the following statements regarding the aetiology of alcoholism is false?
a. Twin studies showed that monozygotic twins do have a higher concordance rate compared with dizygotic twins.
b. Approximately half of the variance in regular drinking habits has been estimated to be genetic in origin for normal twins.
c. Adoption studies support the hypothesis that there is a genetic transmission of alcoholism.

d. Sons of alcoholic parents have an increased risk (three to four times) of becoming alcoholics than the sons of non-alcoholics.
e. The rates of alcohol-related problems are not associated with the severity of the illness.

Question 4

During the lecture on ethics, the Tarasoff case was briefly mentioned. A student, new to psychiatry, has not heard of the key ruling made by the courts and the implications it has for psychiatrists. Which of the following statements about the implications is correct?

a. Psychiatrists now have a responsibility to inform and protect third parties who are at risk from their patients.
b. Psychiatrists should uphold the core principles of ethics and respect the rights of the patients.
c. Psychiatrists need to inform their seniors regarding issues pertaining to safety.
d. Psychiatrists are obliged to disclose information solely to the police for them to take necessary action in terms of protecting the welfare of others around.
e. Psychiatrists should remain focused and act on what is deemed to be in the best interest of their patients.

Question 5

Melanie Klein proposed the following, with the exception of

a. Depressive position
b. Paranoid-schizoid position
c. Projection
d. Introjection
e. Narcissism

Question 6

Which of the following statements is false with regards to the Present State Examination toolkit?

a. Information from the patients is used as a guide in questioning.
b. Information from the patients is used as a guide in scoring.
c. It has good validity.
d. It has good reliability.
e. It has good inter-related reliability.

Question 7

A medical student was puzzled as to why the old age consultant has asked his assistant to help administer the Clifton Assessment Procedures for the Elderly (CAPE). The consultant explains that the CAPE assessment scale is usually used in the assessment of the following:

a. Identification of dementia in the elderly
b. Identification of depression in the elderly

c. Identification of anxiety symptoms in the elderly
d. Identification of late-onset psychosis in the elderly
e. Identification of personality traits in the elderly

Question 8

A 35-year-old male recounts the feelings he has experienced when he lost his wife recently. He mentioned that he went through feelings of denial, anger and bargaining initially. The psychotherapist mentioned to him, 'I'm sorry to be hearing this. It is actually quite common for people to feel the same way as you do when dealing with losses of their loved ones'. This is an example of which interviewing technique?

a. Clarification
b. Encouragement
c. Rationalization
d. Summation
e. Validation

Question 9

The 'cocktail party phenomenon' best illustrates the Gestalt principle. From your understanding of this principle, which of the following would be true?

a. Figures that are separated apart tend not to be automatically visualized as a group.
b. There is a clear figure-ground differentiation and distinction.
c. The principle could only be applicable for visual objects.
d. The principle states that the sum of the whole cannot be greater than the sum of its corresponding parts.
e. The percept usually corresponds to the most complex simulation interpretation.

Question 10

According to the 10th Revision of *International Classification of Disease* (ICD-10) diagnostic classification, which of the following statement is part of the diagnostic criteria for persistent delusional disorder?

a. The delusions must be present for more than 3 months in duration.
b. The delusions are usually not congruent to the mood symptoms.
c. The delusions are not associated with any other psychopathologies.
d. There must be an identifiable stressor preceding the onset of the delusional beliefs.
e. The delusions usually involve multiple themes.

Question 11

Based on your understanding of first-rank symptoms, which of the following presentations is not characteristic of first-rank symptoms?

a. Voices making remarks about the patient
b. Voices performing a running commentary of the patient's symptoms

c. Voices commanding the patient
d. Voices talking amongst themselves
e. Voices addressing the patient in the third person

Question 12

A 30-year-old male, the chief executive manager of a multinational firm, was interested in the differences in leadership styles and how he could adopt them to manage his employees. He feels that laissez-faire leadership might be the most effective in management. You would recommend this if

a. His employees are known to have specialized knowledge of their tasks and could function by themselves independently.
b. His employees, though highly skilled, need constant monitoring to make sure that they would perform their assigned tasks.
c. His employees are not highly skilled.
d. His employees need constant monitoring to make sure that they achieve their assigned tasks.
e. His employees are good at suggesting solutions, but cannot come to a common agreement.

Question 13

A 50-year-old male has heard of genes being involved in Alzheimer's disease. He wonders what would be the increased incidence for an individual who is a heterozygote for apolipoprotein E4.

a. Two times
b. Three times
c. Four times
d. Five times
e. Six times

Question 14

Experiments performed previously by Asch on conformity in a group setting have illustrated that conformity is reduced by the presence of the following factors, with the exception of?

a. Presence of members who are self-reliant
b. Presence of intelligent members
c. Presence of expressive members
d. Presence of socially effective individuals
e. Presence of new members needing guidance from superiors

Question 15

Which of the following statements regarding the ICD-10 is false?

a. The ICD-10 is multi-axial.
b. The ICD-10 has separate categories for neurosis and psychosis.

c. The ICD-10 has a category for culture-bound syndromes.
d. The ICD-10 has a category for organic mental disorders.
e. The ICD-10 takes into account social functioning when establishing a diagnosis.

Question 16

When a 28-year-old female left her child in the clinic consultation room and returned later, it was observed that her child did not cry during her absence and even ignored her when she returned. This is an example of which particular type of attachment?

a. Avoidant attachment
b. Anxious attachment
c. Insecure attachment
d. Secure attachment
e. Separation anxiety

Question 17

A child who is capable of understanding the laws of conservation belong to which of the following stages?

a. Concrete operational
b. Formal operational
c. Operational
d. Preoperational
e. Sensorimotor

Question 18

Which of the following is considered to be a normal development milestone in a child?

a. Tertiary circular reactions at 6 months
b. Constant babbling at 7 months
c. Development of colour vision at 8 months
d. Preoperational stage at 1 year
e. Fear of darkness at 3 years

Question 19

A 20-year-old medical student wondered how cognitive dissonance could affect the dynamics of a group or even individuals in a normal population. It is found out that cognitive dissonance would cause changes in

a. Baseline attitudinal perceptions
b. Degree of conformity to perspectives
c. Group-directed behaviours
d. Attributions within the group
e. Goal-targeted behaviours

Question 20

The four ethical principles (autonomy, beneficence, non-maleficence and justice) were recommended for use in medical ethics by

a. Beauchamp and Childress
b. Benjamin Rush
c. RD Laing
d. Thomas Percival
e. Thomas Szasz

Question 21

There has been increasing numbers of news reports regarding the association between cannabis use and schizophrenia. A 40-year-old mother knows that ever since her son got into university, he has started using cannabis on a regular basis due to the bad company that he mixes with now. What would be the chances of him developing schizophrenia?

a. No increased risk
b. Two times increased risk
c. Three times increased risk
d. Four times increased risk
e. Five times increased risk

Question 22

A 23-year-old male seemed much like a different person after the head injury which he sustained 1 year ago. He currently presents to the mental health specialist clinic and the consultant psychiatrist wishes to perform a detailed cognitive examination. He is intending to use the Wisconsin Card Sorting Test to test for the presence of impairments involving

a. Frontal lobe
b. Hippocampus
c. Parietal lobe
d. Occipital lobe
e. Temporal lobe

Question 23

The key worker, who has known a 25-year-old male, John, a patient with learning disability, has requested to speak to the psychiatrist, because John has been noted to have behavioural changes for the past 2 weeks or so after his scheduled home leave. She mentions to the psychiatrist that when John was well and less emotional, he was only able to communicate with nursing staff using sign language or one-word phrases. He also needed much assistance with his activities of daily living. From the aforementioned information, what level of learning disability would you say John has?

a. Mild
b. Moderate
c. Profound

d. Slightly below norms
e. Severe

Question 24
The following subtypes of schizophrenia could be found within the ICD-10 diagnostic criteria, with the exception of
a. Catatonic schizophrenia
b. Disorganized schizophrenia
c. Hebephrenic schizophrenia
d. Paranoid schizophrenia
e. Simple schizophrenia

Question 25
The consultant psychiatrist asked the core trainee to review a 70-year-old male who had been admitted last night due to behavioural difficulties at home. The core trainee had received some information from the nursing staff. The nursing staff reported based on observations that the patient had been having rapid changes in his consciousness levels. At times, he seemed to respond to both visual and auditory hallucinations. He had some rigidity and gait disturbances as well. Which one of the following might be a likely differential diagnosis for him?
a. Catatonia
b. Delirium
c. Delirium tremens
d. Frontotemporal dementia
e. Lewy body dementia

Question 26
The clinical diagnosis of atypical anorexia nervosa is made when an individual has the following symptoms:
a. Amenorrhea
b. Absence of significant weight loss
c. BMI less than 14
d. Massive and rapid weight loss
e. Marked body image disturbances

Question 27
A 21-year-old male, who was involved in a major road traffic accident, awoke finally after being unconscious for 7 days. The doctors in charge noted that he was unable to recognize familiar faces, like those of his relatives. This is termed as
a. Agnosia
b. Apraxia
c. Colour agnosia
d. Prosopagnosia
e. Visual object agnosia

Question 28
The college is aiming to develop a new programme to prevent suicide amongst patients with schizophrenia. What is the estimated risk of suicide in a patient with schizophrenia?
a. 0.01
b. 0.05
c. 0.08
d. 0.10
e. 0.20

Question 29
Ptosis is a common neurological sign that is present in all of the following clinical diagnoses, with the exception of
a. Myasthenia gravis
b. Horner's syndrome
c. Lambert Eaton syndrome
d. Third nerve palsy
e. Seventh nerve palsy

Question 30
Symptoms that are suggestive of benzodiazepine withdrawal include all of the following except
a. Autonomic hyperactivity
b. Pyrexia
c. Malaise and weakness
d. Tremors
e. Rigidity

Question 31
Pre-traumatic factors that predispose any individual to post-traumatic stress disorder (PTSD) include all the following except
a. Being female in sex
b. Having a previous psychiatric illness
c. Having an internal locus of control
d. Having received lesser education
e. Having experienced previous trauma

Question 32
A woman who has recently been diagnosed with depression is very concerned with regards to the antidepressant that the consultant psychiatrist is going to offer to her. She feels that with her mood symptoms, she is not capable of starting a family. Which of the following antidepressants might affect the efficacy of the oral contraceptive pills that she is taking at the moment?
a. Citalopram
b. Fluoxetine

c. St John's wort
d. Tricyclics
e. Venlafaxine

Question 33

A 22-year-old patient's father was shocked to be informed that his son has developed what seemed to be neuroleptic malignant syndrome (NMS) induced by olanzapine that was started. He wants to know more about NMS. Which of the following regarding NMS is not true?

a. The onset of NMS is much more rapid compared with serotonin syndrome.
b. Patients with NMS usually have an elevated temperature.
c. Patients with NMS might have rigidity and disturbances in gait.
d. Patients with NMS might have raised creatine kinase.
e. The contributing factor for NMS is usually antipsychotics, whereas the contributing factor for serotonin syndrome is usually antidepressants.

Question 34

After understanding the psychopathology of obsessive-compulsive disorder, a group of medical students were debating which would be the most common compulsive behaviour. The correct answer would be

a. Arranging things in a perfect symmetry
b. Checking things
c. Counting and performing rituals a fixed number of times
d. Cleaning things
e. Keeping items even when not needed

Question 35

Which of the following statements about the diagnosis of PTSD is not true?

a. Patients might complain of emotional numbing (inability to experience emotions).
b. Patients might complain of hyper-arousal and being easily startled.
c. Patients might complain of recurrent flashbacks and having nightmares of the previous incident.
d. Patients might have taken measures such as avoidance to prevent re-experiencing any aspect of the event.
e. The onset of symptoms is usually within 2 weeks after experiencing the trauma.

Question 36

An individual with bipolar affective disorder and long-term alcohol dependence develops haematemesis. He is advised by the gastroenterologist to go for an oesophago-gastro-duodenoscopy (OGD) to identify the bleeding site. On assessment, he appears to have the capacity to make that decision and he is not manic. The psychiatrist advises acceding to his wish not to have the OGD. This case illustrates which of the following?

a. The principle of respect for a person's autonomy
b. The principle of beneficence

c. The principle of non-maleficence
d. Paternalism approach
e. Utilitarian approach

Question 37

Which of the following regarding hormonal changes in anorexia nervosa is not correct?

a. Decrease in T3 levels
b. Increase in corticotrophin-releasing hormone (CRH)
c. Increase in cortisol
d. Decrease in growth hormone
e. Decrease in follicle-stimulating hormone

Question 38

A 30-year-old male has been increasingly concerned about his lower back pain. Despite having seen several specialists and having had a detailed investigation, he is still concerned that the doctors might have made a mistake. He is concerned that he might have a malignant tumour. The most likely diagnosis in this case would be

a. Depression with anxiety features
b. Generalized anxiety disorder
c. Hypochondriasis
d. Specific phobia
e. Somatization disorder

Question 39

A 24-year-old male has a long-standing history of alcohol dependence and is currently undergoing recovery. The addiction specialist has proposed that he be started on a course of a medication called acamprosate. Which of the following is not a side effect associated with this medication?

a. Changes in sexual drive
b. Diarrhoea
c. Nausea
d. Renal impairment
e. Rash

Question 40

A 32-year-old female has been started on citalopram 20 mg per day for her major depression following the death of her husband. After 2 weeks, she reports to the psychiatrist that she has noted improvements in the patient's biological symptoms. However, there are times when she still finds the patient's mood to be low. Which one of the following would be the next best approach with regards to the patient's management?

a. Continue the same dose of citalopram
b. Consider augmentation of the antidepressant with lithium
c. Consider electroconvulsive therapy (ECT)
d. Increase the dose of citalopram to 30 mg per day
e. Stop citalopram and consider venlafaxine

Question 41

A 30-year-old male was serving in the military in Syria. Around 6 months ago, he witnessed a traumatic incident in which his colleague was shot dead right beside him. He has seen the mental health specialist and has been diagnosed with PTSD. Which of the following statements is inconsistent with his diagnosis?

a. He reports that he has been experiencing repeated reliving of the trauma.
b. He reports that he has marked hyper-arousal and hyper-vigilance.
c. He reports that he has been sleeping more than usual to avoid thinking of the events.
d. He reports that he has been having intrusive memories of the event.
e. He reports that he feels an emotional detachment occasionally.

Question 42

Which of the following is considered to be the most common disorder of male sexual response?

a. Delayed ejaculation
b. Erectile dysfunction
c. Early ejaculation
d. Male hypoactive sexual desire disorder
e. Substance-/medication-induced sexual dysfunction

Question 43

Which of the following is the most useful tool to help in the diagnosis of dementia?

a. Clinical interview and examination
b. Cognitive assessment (Mini Mental State Examination [MMSE])
c. Cognitive assessment (frontal lobe assessment battery)
d. Computed tomography (CT) scan
e. Magnetic resonance imaging (MRI) scan

Question 44

It is not uncommon that some of the negative cognitions that depressed patients have involve that of learned helplessness. The one who was responsible for proposing the concept of learned helplessness was

a. Beck
b. Freud
c. Mahler
d. Seligman
e. Wolpe

Question 45

A 26-year-old female has been diagnosed with borderline personality disorder and she has been sectioned for admission to the ward following her active ideations of committing suicide. She has been inpatient for the past week, and the nurses are getting very upset with regards to nursing her. Which one of the following factors might be responsible for this?

a. Countertransference
b. Projective identification

c. Splitting
d. Transference
e. Reaction formation

Question 46

A 48-year-old female, the mother of a teenager daughter, is concerned when the consultant psychiatrist recommended antipsychotic treatment for her daughter. She heard that some antipsychotics might cause menstrual cycle disturbances as well as elevated levels of a hormone in the brain. From your understanding, which of the following might have a higher chance of causing the aforementioned?

a. Clozapine
b. Haloperidol
c. Olanzapine
d. Quetiapine
e. Risperidone

Question 47

Bleuler introduced the concept of schizophrenia and further defined the symptoms that schizophrenic patients have. Which of the following did he identify as being of secondary status?

a. Ambivalence
b. Autism
c. Affective incongruity
d. Disturbance of association of thoughts
e. Hallucinations

Question 48

A senior psychiatrist goes to work every day at least 30 minutes early and she needs to get the same parking spot every day. She would be frustrated and irritable if things do not go as she has planned. What is the most likely diagnosis?

a. Anxiety disorder
b. Depressive disorder with anxiety features
c. No mental illness
d. Obsessive-compulsive disorder
e. Obsessive-compulsive personality disorder

Question 49

A psychology intern wonders which of the following would be the most effective in influencing and changing the general public's negative perspectives of mental health illness. The correct answer would be

a. Using propaganda
b. Using persuasive messages
c. Using authority figures to disseminate messages
d. Using authority figures to instill conformity
e. Using authority figures to instill obedience

Question 50

A patient with a long-standing alcohol history has been recently admitted to the inpatient unit for an emergency back operation due to a herniated disc. He currently presents with Wernicke–Korsakoff syndrome. The medical student attempted a bedside cognitive examination, and the patient scored poorly on the MMSE. He wonders what form of memory loss the patient is currently experiencing.

a. Anterograde memory loss
b. Long-term memory loss
c. Procedural memory loss
d. Retrograde memory loss
e. Working memory deficits

Question 51

Which of the following is the diagnosis for a patient who makes up symptoms just to be in the sick role?

a. Conversion disorder
b. Factitious disorder
c. Hypochondriasis
d. Malingering
e. Somatization disorder

Question 52

A 30-year-old female tells her community psychiatric nurse that she has not been feeling good in her mood recently. She claims that she does not feel in control of her mood and shared that others are projecting unhappiness in her. This form of psychopathology is known as

a. Delusional feelings
b. Made emotions
c. Made impulse
d. Hallucinations
e. Somatic passivity

Question 53

A patient who is due for his routine outpatient review shares with the consultant that he does not feel safe in the clinic. He claims that those outside can freely access what he is thinking at the moment. What psychopathology does this refer to?

a. Thought insertion
b. Thought broadcasting
c. Thought block
d. Thought withdrawal
e. Delusional perception

Question 54

A 20-year-old male has been the star player on his team for the last three seasons. However, he missed a goal in the most crucial last match of the season, and now he thinks and feels that he is a burden to the entire team. The specific cognitive error that he is having at the moment might be

a. Arbitrary inference
b. Magnification
c. Minimization
d. Rumination
e. Selective abstraction

Question 55

A trainee who has been working for the past 36 hours tells his colleague at 8 AM the next day that he is feeling depersonalized. Based on your understanding of the terminology 'depersonalization', it also refers to

a. The feeling of 'as if'
b. The feeling of 'if not'
c. The feeling of 'what if'
d. The feeling of 'what next'
e. The feeling of 'why me'

Question 56

You are interviewing the husband of a woman with personality disorder and invite the husband to talk about his feeling towards his wife. He replies, 'frustrated' and does not want to say more. Which of the following interview techniques is most likely to facilitate the interview to continue?

a. Closed-ended questions
b. Long pause
c. Prolonged eye contact
d. Summation
e. Transition

Question 57

A 25-year-old male told the police that he had broken into the house of his ex-girlfriend because people from his workplace had told him to do so. He claimed that he was not in control of his actions, and that his actions were not within his free will. This is an example of

a. Delusion
b. Hallucinations
c. Made impulse
d. Made actions
e. Thought process disorder

Question 58

The following are features of Ganser syndrome except

a. Approximate answers
b. Amnesia
c. Delusional beliefs
d. Pseudo-hallucinations
e. Somatic conversion

Question 59

A joint multidisciplinary team interview was being conducted for a 70-year-old male, named Mr Smith, as the team wanted to recommend to him home help services. During the interview, it was noted that Mr Smith made up false information when asked about the recent events, and he was not at all embarrassed by his lies. Which of the following statements is most likely to be true?

a. He has underlying antisocial personality traits.
b. He has anxious personality traits.
c. He is having Ganser syndrome, and hence he is giving his best approximate answer.
d. He is having memory difficulties, and hence he is confabulating.
e. He is just trying to be funny and is joking with his team.

Question 60

This terminology is commonly used to describe the experience of having a stimulus in one sensory modality producing a sensory experience in another modality. Which of the following would be the most appropriate answer?

a. Extracampine hallucination
b. Functional hallucinations
c. Reflex hallucinations
d. Synaesthesia
e. Visual hallucinations

Question 61

In which of the following personality disorders would one be extremely concerned about rejection and criticism?

a. Anxious avoidant personality disorder
b. Borderline personality disorder
c. Obsessive-compulsive personality disorder
d. Schizoid personality disorder
e. Schizotypal personality disorder

Question 62

Emil Kraepelin was responsible for coining this term during a previous experiment that he had performed. In that experiment, he noted that some patients would repeatedly put out their tongue and allowed their tongues to be pricked, despite the fact that they knew of the consequences. This is an example of

a. Automatic obedience
b. Automatism
c. Echolalia
d. Echopraxia
e. Stereotypies

Question 63

A 45-year-old male has persistent primary insomnia and his doctor has recommended a short course of benzodiazepines. He is very worried about next-day sedation. Which of the following benzodiazepine has the longest half-life and might not be suitable?

a. Alprazolam
b. Lorazepam
c. Nitrazepam
d. Oxazepam
e. Temazepam

Question 64

The mechanism of action of naltrexone, which might be helpful in people who are in abstinence, is by acting as which of the following?

a. Opioid agonist
b. Opioid antagonist
c. Gamma-aminobutyric acid (GABA) agonist
d. Glutamate antagonist
e. Glutamate agonist

Question 65

A core trainee, during his MRCPsych CASC examinations, asks the patient to help spell the word 'World' forwards and then backwards. This is an assessment of

a. Attention and concentration
b. Long-term memory
c. Language abilities
d. Short-term memory
e. Semantic memory

Question 66

Ganser previously described this syndrome that consists of all of the following except

a. Approximate answers
b. Auditory and visual hallucinations
c. Amnesia
d. Anhedonia
e. Clouding of consciousness

Question 67

Schizophrenia has been subclassified into different subtypes. Which of the following has the worst prognosis?

a. Catatonic schizophrenia
b. Hebephrenic schizophrenia
c. Paranoid schizophrenia
d. Simple schizophrenia
e. Undifferentiated schizophrenia

Question 68

A 30-year-old male has been increasingly concerned about his headache after his uncle recently passed away due to a brain tumour. He has been to several general practitioners (GPs) and neurologists, and the necessary investigation has been done. He seems to be reassured for a while thereafter, but gets worried about his headaches again. Recently, he has resorted to checking out the symptoms on the Internet, almost daily. The most likely clinical diagnosis is

a. Conversion disorder
b. Depression with anxiety features
c. Generalized anxiety disorder
d. Hypochondriasis
e. Somatoform pain disorder

Question 69

A 28-year-old female has decided to visit her GP as her mood has been anxious lately. For no reason, over the past 2 months or so, she has been able to listen to conversations from the post office in Manchester, despite the fact that she is living currently in London. This form of psychopathology is termed as

a. Pseudohallucination
b. Extracampine hallucination
c. Hypnopompic hallucination
d. Thought echo
e. Thought broadcasting

Question 70

A consultant psychiatrist was assessing a 20-year-old male in his depression clinic. When asked how his mood was, the patient claimed that he had much difficulty in expressing his current mood state. This form of psychopathology is termed as

a. Alexithymia
b. Apathy
c. Dysphoria
d. Euphoria
e. Affective blunting

Question 71

From your understanding about psychodynamic therapy and the works of Freud, which of the following is not classified as a mature defence mechanism?

a. Acting out
b. Anticipation
c. Altruism
d. Humour
e. Sublimation

Question 72

A 35-year-old female witnessed a fellow shopper being shot dead whilst shopping 3 weeks ago. Currently, she has been experiencing insomnia, poor concentration, as well as tearfulness. She does have occasional nightmares too. Which would be the most appropriate clinical diagnosis?

a. Acute stress disorder
b. Adjustment disorder
c. Depression
d. Generalized anxiety disorder
e. PTSD

Question 73

A 30-year-old male has been admitted to the inpatient unit for first-episode psychosis. The social worker who accompanied him back from his Section 17 home leave noted that he had been tolerating critical comments from his family members for years. Which of the following psychological treatment might be suitable for him and his family in order to prevent a relapse of his underlying psychiatric disorder?

a. Cognitive analytical therapy
b. Cognitive behavioural therapy
c. Family therapy
d. Interpersonal therapy
e. Psychodynamic therapy

Question 74

Which of the following is true with regards to primary attribution error?

a. Making the inference that one is responsible primarily for his or her behaviour
b. Making the inference that other environmental factors are responsible
c. Making the inference that a combination of internal factors and external factors are responsible
d. It refers to a bias made when inferring the cause of another's behaviour – bias made towards situational attributions
e. It refers to a bias made when inferring the cause of another's behaviour – bias made towards internal factors

Question 75

A 55-year-old man is very concerned about dust in the environment. He was seen by various senior psychiatrists who suggested that he suffers from delusional disorder. You think that he may suffer from obsessive-compulsive disorder, and need to defend your diagnosis. Which of the following is expected in this patient if he indeed suffers from delusional disorder?

a. Anxiety
b. Depression
c. Hallucination
d. Normal functioning
e. Somatic passivity

Question 76
A core trainee was wondering which of the following medications would be the safest for treating a patient who is experiencing alcohol withdrawal symptoms, but also has a background of liver disease:
a. Alprazolam
b. Lorazepam
c. Zopiclone
d. Zolpidem
e. Diazepam

Question 77
Which of the following cognitive bias was not part of Aaron Beck's cognitive model of depression?
a. Arbitrary inference
b. Learned helplessness
c. Personalization
d. Magnification
e. Minimization

Question 78
Which of the following individuals proposed that the concept of mental illness has no validity?
a. Bentham
b. Fulford
c. Mil
d. Szasz
e. Williams

Question 79
A 14-year-old girl with Asperger syndrome is referred to the child and adolescent mental health service for quirky movements such as hair twisting. The psychopathology being described is
a. Ambitendency
b. Compulsion
c. Echopraxia
d. Mannerism
e. Stereotypy

Question 80
Which of the following statements about scapegoating is correct?
a. This usually occurs when members of the majority group tend to victimize members of the minority group simply out of frustration.
b. This usually occurs when members of the majority and the minority groups come into direct competition with each other.

c. This usually occurs when members of the minority group make negative remarks to downplay the position of the majority group.
d. This usually occurs when members of the majority group pick on the shortcomings of an individual of the minority group and generalize it to the entire group.
e. This usually occurs when there is a direct conflict of interest amongst members of the majority as well as the minority groups.

Question 81

A 30-year-old woman with a history of depression is in the last term of pregnancy. She complains of an irritating, non-painful sensation in her legs that give her an overwhelming urge to move them. The symptoms occur when she is resting, and get worse from evening onwards. She does not take psychotropic medication, and a recent full blood count shows anaemia. The psychopathology being described is

a. Akathisia
b. Antenatal anxiety
c. Catatonic excitement
d. Mannerism
e. Restless leg syndrome (Ekbom syndrome)

Question 82

An 18-year-old woman presents with auditory hallucination, delusional perception and thought interferences. Psychiatric evaluation established a diagnosis of schizophrenia. She has a history of asthma. She started treatment with haloperidol 10 mg per day because she cannot afford second-generation antipsychotics and cannot tolerate chlorpromazine. Shortly after taking haloperidol, she felt restless with inner tension. Later, her mother reports that she frequently is unable to remain seated, shifts in place and shuffles from foot to foot. The following are appropriate treatments that you might try in order to relieve her symptoms except

a. Reduce the dose of haloperidol
b. Start her on cryproheptadine
c. Start her on propranolol
d. Start her on a benzodiazepine
e. Start her on an antimuscarinic drug

Question 83

The sister of a man with schizophrenia has read about 'simple schizophrenia'. Which of the following symptoms found in her brother do not support a diagnosis of simple schizophrenia?

a. Failure to continue university studies
b. Florid third-person auditory hallucinations
c. Inability to maintain personal hygiene
d. Odd behaviour such as locking himself in the toilet and colouring the water in a bath tub
e. Progressive withdrawal and isolation

Question 84

A 30-year-old man complains that he hears voices from his late mother. Three months ago, his mother died in a car accident when he was driving his car. He feels very sad and guilty. He has not driven the car since the accident and he wants to sell the car. What is your diagnosis?

a. Delayed grief
b. Inhibited grief
c. Normal grief reaction
d. PTSD
e. Prolonged grief

Question 85

A patient is on treatment with psychotropic medications. He wonders which of the following would affect his medications, by acting as an enzyme inducer:

a. Caffeine
b. Grapefruit juice
c. Sertraline
d. Smoking
e. Valproate

Question 86

A 30-year-old man complains of chest pain after his late father died of myocardial infarction 6 months ago. His wife feels that he has become very angry and hostile to her after his father passed away. He has been drinking heavily in the last 3 months. When you ask him the reason of heavy drinking, he wants to be self-destructive. Which of the following abnormal grief reactions is the most accurate diagnosis for this man?

a. Chronic grief
b. Conflicted grief
c. Delayed grief
d. Distorted grief
e. Inhibited grief

Reference and Further Reading: Hooper M (2010). Multiple chemical sensitivity, in Puri BK, Treasaden I (eds), *Psychiatry: An Evidence-Based Text*. London: Hodder Arnold, pp. 811–817.

Question 87

Disorders of self-awareness (ego disorders) usually include the following disturbances except

a. Awareness of self-activity
b. Boundaries of self
c. Continuity of self
d. Immediate awareness of self-unity
e. Subconscious

Question 88

You are teaching depressive disorder to a group of medical students. They want to know the percentage of patients admitted to the university hospital who will have recurrence and require further admission in the long run without committing suicide. Your answer is

a. 20%
b. 30%
c. 40%
d. 60%
e. 80%

Question 89

During an experiment, participants were asked to listen to a speech made by a speaker that supported or opposed World War II. Participants were told that the speech they were about to hear was chosen at random by tossing a coin. After listening to the speech, the participants were asked whether they thought the speaker believed in what he or she said about the war. The results showed that the participants thought the speaker believed in what he or she said even when they knew the positions were chosen at random. Which heuristic best explains the aforementioned phenomenon?

a. Framing
b. Anchoring and adjustment heuristic
c. Availability heuristic
d. Representativeness heuristic
e. Counterfactual thinking

Question 90

A new psychiatric consultant has been appointed by the trust to head a community psychiatric team. He is known to be a 'hands-off' person and not available most of the time. He seldom gives feedback to his team members. Which of the following teams will be effective under his leadership?

a. Assertive team members who request major decisions to be made by voting and thorough discussion amongst the whole team.
b. Team members who are eager to learn and request constant supervision from the consultant psychiatrist.
c. Honest team members who are good at performing routine home visits repeatedly.
d. Humble team members who prefer the consultant psychiatrist to make major decisions.
e. Trustworthy team members who are experienced in community psychiatry and skilful in dealing with complicated issues. They require minimal supervision.

Question 91

A 24-year-old woman is admitted due to elated mood. A core trainee wants to know the differences between hypomania and mania. Which of the following statements is incorrect?

a. Patients with hypomania are not expected to have hallucinations.
b. Patients with hypomania are not expected to have mood-congruent delusions.

c. Patients with mania are expected to have reckless behaviour.
d. Patients with mania and hypomania are expected to have elated mood.
e. Patients with mania and hypomania are expected to have the same level of psychosocial functioning.

Question 92
A 33-year-old female has been diagnosed with PTSD after having witnessing a gun-shot incident in the supermarket that she was shopping at. She wants to get well as soon as possible and is keen on both pharmacological and psychological therapy. From your knowledge about PTSD management, which of the following would be contraindicated in her case?
a. Debriefing
b. Eye movement desensitization and reprocessing (EMDR)
c. Exposure therapy
d. Provision of social support
e. Trauma-focused cognitive behavioural therapy (CBT)

Question 93
A trainee passes the MRCPsych examination Paper 1 having based her revision on past examination questions but other trainees who have studied for long hours and based their revision on textbooks failed Paper 1 despite having gained vast knowledge. The phenomenon being described is
a. Barnum effect
b. Halo effect
c. Practice effect
d. Primacy effect
e. Recency effect

Question 94
A 30-year-old woman is a known case of schizophrenia. She presented to the Accident and Emergency Department with altered mental status, severe stiffness along with rapid eye blinking, unusual head and neck movements, and peculiar behaviour (simulating the doctor's movement). She is afebrile, and creatinine kinase is normal. Which of the following signs is not associated with her condition?
a. Ambitendency
b. Astasia-abasia
c. Automatic obedience
d. Echolalia
e. Gegenhalten

Question 95
The following is a condition that is common in Southeast Asia and China. A Chinese man has extreme anxiety and fear of impending death due to worries that his genitals might retract into his abdomen and would disappear. This condition is known as
a. Amok
b. Dhat

c. Frigophobia
d. Koro
e. Latah

Question 96

A 35-year-old pregnant woman develops depression during the second trimester. Which of the following symptoms is the least reliable in establishing the diagnosis of depression?

a. Anxiety
b. Guilt ruminations
c. Insomnia
d. Lack of interest in the baby
e. Social withdrawal

Question 97

A core trainee has determined that the patient he interviewed has moderate depression and would benefit from an antidepressant. The other medical problems the patient has include that of hypertension and seizure. The core trainee wonders which antidepressant he should avoid, as it might affect his seizure threshold. Which of the following medications should be avoided?

a. Bupropion
b. Citalopram
c. Fluoxetine
d. Mirtazapine
e. Paroxetine

Question 98

Based on the Holmes and Rahe Social Readjustment Rating Scale, which of the following events is considered to be the most stressful event contributing to illness?

a. Death of a close family member
b. Death of a spouse
c. Divorce
d. Marital separation
e. Imprisonment

Question 99

A 40-year-old man with schizophrenia is admitted to the psychiatric ward. The nurse informs you that he lies for hours on his bed with his head raised 10 cm off the mattress. The psychopathology being described is

a. Ambitendency
b. Gegenhalten
c. Mitgehen
d. Psychological pillow
e. Schnauzkrampf

Question 100

In an animal experiment, a rat pressed a lever in the cage and got an electric shock. The rat has never pressed the lever again ever since it was nearly electrocuted. The phenomenon being described is

a. Forward conditioning
b. Negative reinforcement
c. Positive reinforcement
d. Punishment
e. Stimulus discrimination

Question 101

The Nuremberg Code, which was formulated in 1947, is a very important piece of documentation regarding the ethics of medical research. Which of the following statements pertaining to the code is incorrect?

a. The trial involved conducting inquiries about doctors in wartime who performed human experiments in concentration camps.
b. The trial involved Japanese doctors who were deemed unethical.
c. The trial involved Nazi doctors who were deemed unethical.
d. As a result of the trial, this led to a set of 10 research principles.
e. The trial led to doctors recognizing the need to respect the human rights of subjects.

Question 102

In an animal experiment, a rat will get food after it presses a lever. The learning process being described is

a. Cognitive learning
b. Classical conditioning
c. Modelling
d. Operant conditioning
e. Social learning

Question 103

Which of the following can be used to prevent groupthink?

a. An authoritarian leader
b. Isolating the group members
c. A critical evaluator
d. An observer
e. Mindguards

Question 104

A 30-year-old male, Jordon, came to the emergency department, requesting to see Sarah, the psychiatric nurse who treated him 3 weeks ago. He is demanding to see her as he believes that she is in love with him, just from the way she smiled at him previously when he was undergoing treatment. He is keen to take her out for a date and engage in sexual acts with her. Which of the following is the most likely diagnosis?

a. Grandiose delusion
b. Doppelganger
c. Cotard's syndrome
d. Erotomania
e. Couvade syndrome

Question 105

A 50-year-old man suffers from chronic schizophrenia. Three months ago, he developed shortness of breath, numbness, difficulty in handling tools and trouble in walking down the stairs. He came to the Accident and Emergency Department a few times, and the doctors felt that he presented with somatic complaints and then discharged him. His GP urged the doctors at the Accident and Emergency Department to admit this man for further evaluation. He turned out to suffer from cervical cord compression and required urgent operation. After the operation, he developed tetraplegia. His wife is very upset with the hospital. When the Chief Executive meets his wife, he says, 'It is quite acceptable to feel angry at the hospital and perhaps most people would feel angry as you do'. The Chief Executive demonstrates which of the following techniques?

a. Consideration
b. Explanation
c. Reflection
d. Legitimation
e. Negotiation

Question 106

A 29-year-old female has been diagnosed with rapid cycling bipolar disorder, as she has had more than four mood episodes per year. She is currently on pharmacological treatment with valproate. Which of the following factors might have an impact on her condition?

a. Hyperthyroidism
b. Hypertension
c. Usage of alcohol
d. Usage of antidepressants
e. Stressful life events

Question 107

A common cultural-bound syndrome described in North America, in which individuals believe that he or she might have undergone a transformation and become a monster that would practise cannibalism is known as

a. Amok
b. Brain fag syndrome
c. Dhat
d. Koro
e. Windigo

Question 108
Which one of the following terminologies best describes the ratio between the minimum plasma level that would cause a toxic effect and the minimum plasma level that would cause therapeutic effects?
a. Therapeutic index
b. Toxicity
c. Affinity
d. Potency
e. Volume of distribution

Question 109
A 50-year-old woman meets the diagnostic criteria for panic disorder with agoraphobia. Each time she leaves the house, she experiences high levels of anxiety. When she goes back home, her anxiety level goes down. After some time, she learns that by staying at home, she can avoid any possibility of a panic attack in public. This contributes to the maintenance of her disorder. Which of the following statements about the aforementioned phenomenon is incorrect?
a. The reinforcement is contingent upon the behaviour.
b. The behaviour is voluntary.
c. A negative reinforcer positively affects the frequency of response.
d. The reinforcement can occur before the behaviour.
e. An alteration in the frequency of behaviour is possible after reinforcement.

Question 110
A 24-year-old woman is diagnosed with agoraphobia. She attends psychotherapy sessions for the treatment of her agoraphobia. Which of the following statements about the aforementioned phenomenon is incorrect?
a. Shaping can lead to extinction.
b. Spontaneous recovery can occur after extinction.
c. Intermittent reinforcement diminishes the extinction rate.
d. Implosion cannot be used in extinction.
e. Reciprocal inhibition can be used in extinction.

Question 111
Which of the following concepts do not contribute to the aetiology of phobias?
a. Vicarious conditioning
b. Learned helplessness
c. Mowrer's two-factor theory
d. Classical conditioning
e. Biological preparedness

Question 112
Eugen Bleuler proposed the term 'schizophrenia' for what Emil Kraepelin had been calling 'dementia praecox'. The reason was
a. The term 'schizophrenia' refers to a disorder with onset in young adulthood that is different from dementia, which usually occurs in old age.
b. The term 'schizophrenia' refers to a chronic disorder comprising hallucinations and delusions with a downhill course.

c. The term 'schizophrenia' refers to the integration of functional psychiatric disorder and organic disorder (e.g. catatonia).
d. The term 'schizophrenia' refers to a significant deterioration of social functioning and poor long-term outcome that occurred in the era of asylums.
e. The term 'schizophrenia' refers to the 'splitting' of affect from other psychological functions leading to a dissociation between the social situation and the emotion expressed.

Question 113
During a routine physical examination for extra-pyramidal side effects, it was noted that the patient kept stretching out his hands, withdrawing them thereafter and repeating this several times, without allowing the examiner to check for the presence of Parkinson's features in the upper limbs. This form of psychopathology is termed as
a. Ambitendency
b. Automatic obedience
c. Catatonic posturing
d. Mitgehen
e. Perseveration

Question 114
In the United Kingdom, the determinants of social class are based on
a. Education
b. Financial status
c. Occupation
d. Type of residence
e. Geographic area of residence

Extended matching items (EMIs)

Theme: Memory

Lead in: Please identify the correct type of memory applicable to each one of the following situations. Each option may be used once, more than once or not at all.
Options:
a. Declarative memory
b. Working memory
c. Procedural memory
d. Episodic memory
e. Sensory memory
f. Anterograde memory
g. Retrograde memory

Question 115
A 30-year-old male was involved in a road traffic accident. When he awoke post-surgery, he realized that he is unable to recall events leading up to the accident.

Question 116
A MMSE assessment was conducted for a 70-year-old man. He was noted to be unable to recall the three items to which he was presented with.

Question 117
A 70-year-old female with dementia is still able to remember how to sew her dresses as she has been a tailor previously when she was younger.

Question 118
A 50-year-old male was asked to name the capital of the United Kingdom. Which type of memory is he using?

Question 119
A 70-year-old female has Alzheimer's dementia, but she is still able to remember personal events that happened when she was much younger and is still able to share her life story with her grandchildren. Which form of memory is she relying on?

Theme: Lab tests

Lead in: For the below-mentioned drugs please indicate the approximate duration that they could still be detected in the urine. Each option may be used once, more than once or not at all.
Options:
a. 6–8 hours
b. 12–24 hours
c. 24 hours
d. 48 hours
e. 36–72 hours
f. 6 days
g. 8 days
h. 2 weeks

Question 120
Amphetamines

Question 121
Barbiturates

Question 122
Cocaine

Question 123
Heroin

Question 124
Lysergic acid diethylamide (LSD)

Question 125
Methylene-dioxy-methamphetamine (MDMA)

Question 126
Phencyclidine (PCP)

Reference: Puri BK, Hall A, Ho R (2014). *Revision Notes in Psychiatry*. London: CRC Press, p. 529.

Theme: General psychiatry

Lead in: A 28-year-old man has suffered from schizophrenia for 5 years. He is currently stable and has recently got married. He and his wife are planning to have children. He consults you on the genetic risk of schizophrenia.

Each option might be used once, more than once or not at all.

Options:

a. 0%–4%
b. 5%–9%
c. 10%–14%
d. 15%–19%
e. 20%–24%
f. 25%–29%
g. 30%–34%
h. 35%–50%
i. 60%–65%
j. 70%–75%
k. 80%–85%

Question 127
The risk of schizophrenia for his child if his wife also suffers from schizophrenia. (Choose one option.)

Question 128
The risk of schizophrenia for his child if his wife does not suffer from schizophrenia. (Choose one option.)

Question 129
The risk of schizophrenia if he adopted a child with velocardiofacial syndrome. (Choose one option.)

Question 130
The risk of schizophrenia in his half-siblings. (Choose one option.)

Question 131
The risk of schizophrenia in his younger cousin. (Choose one option.)

Theme: Aetiology

Lead in: Match the given aetiological factors to the following clinical scenarios. Each option may be used once, more than once or not at all.

Options:

a. Apolipoprotein E4 gene (homozygous for ε4)
b. Cardiovascular disease

c. Cancer
d. Childhood sexual abuse
e. Death of the mother before the age of 11 years
f. Down syndrome
g. Dysbindin gene
h. Migration
i. Neuregulin gene
j. Old age
k. Streptococcal infection
l. Three children at home under the age of 14 years
m. Unemployment

Question 132
A 10-year-old boy develops obsessions and compulsive behaviour after a sore throat and fever. (Choose one option.)

Question 133
A 19-year-old woman presents with recurrent self-harm following the end of a transient and intense romantic relationship. She has a chronic feeling of emptiness and exhibits binge-eating behaviour. (Choose one option.)

Question 134
A 24-year-old man complains that MI5 is monitoring him and has tried to control his feelings and intentions. He heard the voices of two secret agents talking about him and they issued him with a command. (Choose three options.)

Theme: General adult psychiatry

Options:

a. Specific phobia
b. Adjustment disorder
c. Panic disorder
d. Generalized anxiety disorder
e. PTSD
f. Agoraphobia
g. Mixed anxiety/depression

Select the most appropriate answer for each of the following. Each option may be used once, more than once or not at all.

Question 135
A nurse was involved in a road traffic accident recently, about 3 months ago. Since then, she has been experiencing nightmare, flashbacks as well as irritable mood.

Question 136
A 21-year-old male has been recently enrolled into the military service and he has persistent low mood associated with loss of interest. He finds himself having much difficulty with coping with the demands of the military.

Question 137
A 23-year-old female finds that over the past 6 months she has been increasingly worried about everyday little things.

Theme: General adult psychiatry

Options:

a. Hepatic encephalopathy
b. Wilson's disease
c. Hyperthyroidism
d. Hypothyroidism
e. Cushing's syndrome
f. Addison's disease
g. Syndrome of inappropriate anti-diuretic hormone hyper-secretion
h. Hyperparathyroidism
i. Hypoparathyroidism

Select the most appropriate answer for each of the following. Each option may be used once, more than once or not at all.

Question 138
Patients with this condition usually present with the disease during adolescence; however, the clinical onset may be detected as cognitive impairment, abnormal behaviour and personality change, and renal, haematological and endocrine symptoms.

Question 139
A 45-year-old female is no longer able to meet the demands of her job as she has been complaining of excessive tiredness, lethargy as well as constipation. She has no previous known medical history and has not been on long-term medications.

Question 140
A 25-year-old female has been feeling edgy quite recently and complaining that she has lost a huge amount of weight despite her good appetite.

Question 141
A 23-year-old female has long-standing irregular menses, and now presents with gradually worsening hirsutism and weight gain. She also has been having acnes on her face and feeling depressed.

Question 142
A 25-year-old female presents with weakness, dizziness, anorexia, weight loss and gastrointestinal disturbance. On physical examination, there is noted to be generalized hyper-pigmentation of the skin and mucous membrane. She also has postural hypotension and loss of pubic hairs.

Theme: Diagnostic classification

Options:

a. Paranoid schizophrenia
b. Hebephrenic schizophrenia
c. Catatonic schizophrenia
d. Undifferentiated schizophrenia
e. Residual schizophrenia
f. Simple schizophrenia

Select the most appropriate answer for each of the following. Each option may be used once, more than once or not at all.

Question 143
Based on the ICD-10, this is the most common subtype in which hallucinations and/or delusions are prominent.

Question 144
Based on the ICD-10, the age of onset of this condition is between 15 and 25 years. This particular subtype has been known to be associated with a poor prognosis.

Question 145
Based on the ICD-10 classification system, in this particular form of schizophrenia, psychomotor disturbances may alternate between extremes and violent excitement may occur.

Question 146
Based on the ICD-10 classification system, for individuals with this condition, there is an insidious onset of decline in functioning.

Question 147
In order to make this diagnosis, there must be the absence of depression, institutionalization or dementia or other brain disorders.

Theme: General adult psychiatry

Options:

a. 20%
b. 40%
c. 60%
d. 80%
e. 85%
f. 90%

Select the most appropriate answer for each of the following. Each option may be used once, more than once or not at all.

Question 148
For schizophrenia, the heritability estimate is around this value.

Question 149
For depressive disorder, the heritability estimate is around this value.

Question 150
For bipolar disorder, the heritability estimate is around this value.

Question 151
For panic disorders, the heritability estimate is around this value.

Theme: Basic psychopathology

Options:

a. Stupor
b. Depressive retardation
c. Obsessional slowness
d. Somnambulism
e. Compulsion
f. Psychomotor agitation
g. Ambitendency
h. Catalepsy
i. Cataplexy

Select the most appropriate answer for each of the following. Each option may be used once, more than once or not at all.

Question 152
In individuals with narcolepsy, this refers to the temporary loss of muscle tone.

Question 153
Patients with this psychopathology would make a series of tentative incomplete movements when expected to carry out a voluntary action.

Question 154
Patients with this psychopathology would maintain abnormal postures.

Question 155
Individuals with this psychopathology embark on a series of behaviours when they are asleep.

Question 156
This form of psychopathology is commonly referred to as the motor component of an obsessive thought.

Question 157
This form of psychopathology commonly refers to repeated doubts and compulsive rituals.

Question 158
This form of psychopathology might be seen in catatonic states, depressive states or even manic states.

Theme: Basic psychopathology

Amnesia refers to the inability to recall previous experiences.

Options:

a. Anterograde amnesia
b. Post-traumatic amnesia
c. Psychogenic amnesia
d. Retrograde amnesia
e. Transient global amnesia

f. Hypermnesia
g. Paramnesia

Select the most appropriate answer for each of the following. Each option may be used once, more than once or not at all.

Question 159
A 25-year-old male has just undergone six cycles of electroconvulsive therapy. He claimed to be having problems with his memories – forming new memories as well as recalling old memories. Which terminology correctly describes the pathology that James is experiencing?

Question 160
A 40-year-old male has just been involved in a major car accident. He lost consciousness immediately after the collision. He finds himself having major difficulties recollecting what has happened. Which terminology correctly describes the pathology that Tom is experiencing?

Question 161
A medical student was clerking a psychiatric inpatient, John. He realized that John was unable to recollect his own personal information, but appeared unconcerned about his memory loss. Which terminology best describes this psychopathology?

Question 162
A 25-year-old female's family members brought her into the emergency services. They were concerned about her having a sudden onset of disorientation and being unable to recollect immediate events. Which terminology best describes this psychopathology?

Question 163
A 28-year-old has been a chronic alcoholic. A medical student was assessing his memory and found that Thomas was confabulating at times. Which terminology best describes this psychopathology?

Theme: Neurology

Options:

a. Receptive aphasia
b. Agnostic alexia
c. Pure word deafness
d. Intermediate aphasia
e. Expressive aphasia
f. Global aphasia
g. Jargon aphasia
h. Semantic aphasia

Select the most appropriate answer for each of the following. Each option may be used once, more than once or not at all.

Question 164
In this condition, the person may have difficulties with naming objects or arranging words in the right sequences. Which condition is this?

Question 165
In this condition, the person may have difficulties with comprehending the meaning of words. Which condition is this?

Question 166
In this condition, the person may have difficulties in expressing thoughts in words but comprehension is normal. Which condition is this?

Question 167
In this condition, the person may have difficulties in expressing thoughts in words and also comprehending words. Which condition is this?

Theme: Basic psychology

Learning is defined as a change in behaviour as a result of prior experience. It does not include behavioural change due to maturation or other temporary conditions, such as that mediated by drug effects or fatigue. Two forms of learning have been recognized, which are classical conditioning and operant conditioning.

Options:

a. Delayed conditioning
b. Simultaneous conditioning
c. Trace conditioning
d. Backward conditioning
e. Higher-order conditioning
f. Extinction
g. Generalization
h. Discrimination
i. Incubation
j. Stimulus preparedness

Select the most appropriate answer for each of the following. Each option may be used once, more than once or not at all.

Question 168
This refers to the gradual increment in the strength of the condition response.

Question 169
This refers to a process whereby a response initially evoked by one stimulus could now be evoked by stimulus similar to the original.

Question 170
This refers to a process in which a conditioned stimulus is being paired with a second or third conditioned stimulus which, on presentation by itself, would elicit the original conditioned response.

Question 171
In this form of learning or conditioning, it has been noted that the learning and conditioning becomes less effective as the time interval between the two increases.

Question 172
This process of learning is considered to be optimal when the delay between the onsets of the two stimuli is around half a second.

Theme: Stages of development

Options:

a. Oral stage
b. Anal stage
c. Phallic stage
d. Latency stage
e. Genital stage
f. Trust/security
g. Autonomy
h. Initiative
i. Duty/accomplishment
j. Identity
k. Intimacy
l. Generativity
m. Integrity

Select the most appropriate answer for each of the following. Each option may be used once, more than once or not at all.

Question 173
The failure to negotiate this stage leads to hysterical personality traits.

Question 174
The failure to negotiate this stage leads to personality traits such as obsessive-compulsive personality, tidiness and rigidity.

Question 175
The failure to negotiate this stage might lead to generosity, depression and elation.

Question 176
Which of the aforementioned Erikson's stages is a 5-year-old child undergoing?

Theme: Social psychology

Options:

a. Autocratic
b. Democratic
c. Laissez-faire
d. Authority power
e. Reward power
f. Coercive power
g. Referent power
h. Expert power

Select the most appropriate answer for each of the following. Each option may be used once, more than once or not at all.

Question 177
Which of the aforementioned Erikson's stages is a teenager undergoing?

Question 178
This particular type of leadership is more appropriate for creative and open-ended tasks.

Question 179
For this particular type of leadership, there is a tendency for the tasks to be abandoned in the absence of the leader.

Question 180
This refers to the power derived from assignment to a specific role.

Question 181
This refers to the power derived from the ability to allocate resources.

Question 182
This refers to the power derived from skill, knowledge and experience.

Theme: Models of cognitive development

Options:

a. Sensorimotor
b. Preoperational
c. Concrete operational
d. Formal operational

Select the most appropriate answer for each of the following. Each option may be used once, more than once or not at all.

Question 183
Animism, in which life, thoughts and feelings are attributed to all objects, including inanimate ones, commonly develops during this stage.

Question 184
Primary, secondary and tertiary circular reactions develop during this stage.

Question 185
This is the stage that is characterized by the achievement of being able to think in the abstract.

Question 186
This is the stage in which an understanding of the laws of conservation, number and volume and then weight is normally achieved.

Theme: Psychological test

Options:

a. Mini Mental State Examination
b. Blessed Dementia Scale
c. Geriatric Mental State Schedule

d. Cambridge Examination for Mental Disorders
e. Clifton Assessment Schedule
f. Present Behavioural Examination

Select the most appropriate answer for each of the following. Each option may be used once, more than once or not at all.

Question 187
This particular questionnaire is administered to a relative or friend who is asked to answer the questions on the basis of performance over the previous 6 months.

Question 188
This is an interview schedule that has three components: a structured clinical interview, a range of objective cognitive tests and a structured interview with a relative or informant.

Question 189
Amongst all of the options, this is considered to be a nursing-rated assessment.

Question 190
This particular questionnaire involves interviewing the carer more about the psychopathology associated with dementia.

Theme: Social sciences and stigma

Options:

a. Death of spouse
b. Divorce
c. Marital separation
d. Death of a close family member
e. Marriage
f. Pregnancy
g. Minor legal violation

Select the most appropriate answer for each of the following. Each option may be used once, more than once or not at all.

Question 191
Which one of the aforementioned has the highest life change value based on the Holmes and Rahe (1967) life-change scale?

Question 192
Which one of the aforementioned has the second highest life-change value based on the Holmes and Rahe (1967) life-change scale?

Question 193
Which one of the aforementioned has a life-change value of approximately 50 based on the Holmes and Rahe (1967) life-change scale?

Question 194
Which one of the aforementioned has the lowest life-change value?

MRCPSYCH PAPER A1 MOCK EXAMINATION 1: ANSWERS

GET THROUGH MRCPSYCH PAPER A1: MOCK EXAMINATION

Question 1 Answer: b, Having poorly controlled blood pressure
Explanation: Hypertension has been known to be the most frequent risk factor among those with vascular dementia, and it contributes to as much as 50% of all patients with vascular dementia. Other risk factors known to increase the risk of stroke also increase the risk of vascular dementia, for example cigarette smoking, heart disease, homocystinuria, hyperlipidaemia, metabolic syndrome, low levels of high-density lipoprotein, moderate alcohol consumption, polycythaemia and sickle cell anaemia.

Reference: Puri BK, Hall A, Ho R (2014). *Revision Notes in Psychiatry*. London: CRC Press, p. 699.

Question 2 Answer: a, Low dose of aspirin daily
Explanation: The National Institute for Health and Care Excellence (NICE) guidelines do not recommend the usage of acetylcholinesterase inhibitors (AChEIs) or memantine for cognitive decline in vascular dementia. It is better to try to treat the underlying cardiovascular condition in order to slow down or even halt the progression of vascular dementia. The treatment of hypertension is particularly important. The common risk factors associated with the increased risk of stroke include homocystinuria, hyperlipidaemia, metabolic syndrome, low levels of high-density lipoprotein, moderate alcohol consumption, polycythaemia and sickle cell anaemia.

Reference: Puri BK, Hall A, Ho R (2014). *Revision Notes in Psychiatry*. London: CRC Press, p. 696.

Question 3 Answer: b, Approximately one half of the variance in drinking habits has been estimated to be genetic in origin for normal twins.
Explanation: (b) is wrong. It has been found that in normal twins, approximately one-third of the variance in the drinking habits have been estimated to be genetic in origin. Adoption studies do support the hypothesis of the genetic transmission of alcoholism. The sons of alcoholic parents are three to four times more likely

to become alcoholic than the sons of non-alcoholics, irrespective of the home environment.

Reference: Puri BK, Hall A, Ho R (2014). *Revision Notes in Psychiatry*. London: CRC Press, p. 520.

Question 4 Answer: a, Psychiatrists now have a responsibility to inform and protect third parties who are at risk from their patients.
Explanation: The duty to warn and protect follow Tarasoff's ruling. The duty to warn and protect is indicated when there are sufficient factual grounds for a high risk of harm to a third party, and the risk is sufficiently specified; the risk of danger to the public is imminent; the harm to a third party is not likely to be prevented unless the mental health professionals could make a disclosure; and the third party cannot reasonably be expected to foresee or comprehend the high risk of harm to himself or herself.

Reference: Puri BK, Hall A, Ho R (2014). *Revision Notes in Psychiatry*. London: CRC Press, p. 147.

Question 5 Answer: e, Narcissism
Explanation: Melanie Klein proposed all of the following concepts: object relations, paranoid-schizoid position, aggression and depressive position, and also proposed that the ego and superego developed during the first year of life. Klein believed that the infant was capable of object relations. The paranoid-schizoid position developed as a result of frustration during the first year of life with pleasurable contact with objects such as the good breast. The paranoid-schizoid position, characterized by isolation and persecutory fears, developed as a result of the infant viewing the world as part objects, using the following defence mechanisms: introjection, projective identification and splitting.

Reference: Puri BK, Hall A, Ho R (2014). *Revision Notes in Psychiatry*. London: CRC Press, p. 135.

Question 6 Answer: b, Information from the patients are used as a guide in scoring.
Explanation: The Present State Examination does not use information from patients as a guide in scoring. The Present State Examination has been previously used in the international pilot study of schizophrenia to generate diagnosis.

Reference: Puri BK, Hall A, Ho R (2014). *Revision Notes in Psychiatry*. London: CRC Press, pp. 353–460.

Question 7 Answer: a, Identification of dementia in the elderly
Explanation: The Clifton Assessment Procedures for the Elderly (CAPE) is commonly used to help predict survival, placement and decline in elderly people. The Kew Cognitive Map assesses for parietal lobe function and language functions in the dementing patient. This would help to predict the 6-month survival rates.

Reference: Puri BK, Hall A, Ho R (2014). *Revision Notes in Psychiatry*. London: CRC Press, p. 687.

Question 8 Answer: e, Validation
Explanation: This is an example of validation, which confirms the validity of a prior judgement or behaviour. Another example: 'I just say, if I were in your position, I might have a hard time dealing with those difficult people in your company'.

Reference: Puri BK, Hall A, Ho R (2014). *Revision Notes in Psychiatry*. London: CRC Press, p. 330.

Question 9 Answer: b, There is a clear figure-ground differentiation and distinction.
Explanation: The concept of Gestalt psychology states that the whole perception is different from the sum of its parts. The law of simplicity states that the percept corresponds to the simplest stimulation interpretation. The law of continuity states that interrupted lines are usually seen as continuous. The law of similarity states that like items are usually grouped together. The law of proximity states that adjacent items are grouped together. In figure-ground differentiation, figures are differentiated from their background with contours and boundaries.

Reference: Puri BK, Hall A, Ho R (2014). *Revision Notes in Psychiatry*. London: CRC Press, p. 31.

Question 10 Answer: a, The delusions must be present for more than 3 months in duration.
Explanation: Based on the 10th Revision of *International Classification of Disease* (ICD-10) diagnostic criteria, a delusional disorder is an ill-defined condition, manifesting as a single delusion or a set of related delusions, being persistent, sometimes lifelong and not having an identifiable organic basis. Delusions should be the most conspicuous or only symptom and they should be present for the past 3 months.

Reference: Puri BK, Hall A, Ho R (2014). *Revision Notes in Psychiatry*. London: CRC Press, p. 372.

Question 11 Answer: c, Voices commanding the patient
Explanation: Schneider was the one who proposed the concept of first-rank symptoms. It would include (a) auditory hallucinations – thought echo, in third person or in the form of a running commentary; (b) delusions of passivity – thought insertion, withdrawal, broadcasting, made feelings, impulses and action; (c) somatic passivity and delusional perception. The presence of the aforementioned first-rank symptom makes the diagnosis of schizophrenia highly likely.

Reference: Puri BK, Hall A, Ho R (2014). *Revision Notes in Psychiatry*. London: CRC Press, p. 351.

Question 12 Answer: a, His employees are known to have specialized knowledge of their tasks and could function by themselves independently.
Explanation: For laissez-faire leadership to be effective, it is expected that employees should have specialized knowledge in their tasks and are able to function independently.

Reference: Puri BK, Hall A, Ho R (2014). *Revision Notes in Psychiatry*. London: CRC Press, p. 59.

Question 13 Answer: c, Four times
Explanation: It is essential to note that genetic factors do account for disease only in some patients. In particular, genes such as the *APP* gene on chromosome 21, the Presenilin 1 gene on chromosome 14 and the Presenilin 2 gene on chromosome 1 have been found to be involved. Those who inherit just one allele on ApoE4 would have a two times increased incidence. In this case, given that the individual is a heterozygote, the estimated increased incidence is four times.

Reference: Puri BK, Hall A, Ho R (2014). *Revision Notes in Psychiatry*. London: CRC Press, p. 694.

Question 14 Answer: e, Presence of new members needing guidance from superiors.
Explanation: Self-reliant, intelligent, expressive and socially effective individuals are least vulnerable to group pressure. In addition, two types of conformity have been identified previously. Informational social influence refers to how an individual conforms to the consensual opinion and behaviour of the group both publicly and also in his or her own thoughts. Normative social influence refers to situations in which an individual publicly conforms to the consensual opinion and behaviour of the group, but has a different view in his or her own mind. The individual conforms to the group under social pressure in order to avoid social rejection.

Reference: Puri BK, Hall A, Ho R (2014). *Revision Notes in Psychiatry*. London: CRC Press, p. 60.

Question 15 Answer: e, The ICD-10 takes into account social functioning when establishing a diagnosis.
Explanation: The *Diagnostic and Statistical Manual of Mental Disorders*, 4th Edition, Text Revision (DSM-IV-TR) but not the ICD-10 takes into account social functioning when establishing a diagnosis.

Reference: World Health Organisation (1994). ICD-10 *Classification of Mental and Behavioural Disorders*. Edinburgh, UK: Churchill Livingstone.

Question 16 Answer: a, Avoidant attachment
Explanation: This is an example of an avoidant attachment style. When a child has this form of attachment, a distance is maintained usually from the mother, in

which case the child may sometimes feel ignored. Clinically, avoidant attachment caused by rejection by the mother may be a precursor to future poor social functioning. It might also predict aggression later in life. In contrast, for insecure attachment, there is chronic clinginess and ambivalence towards the mother. Separation anxiety refers to the fear shown by an infant of being separated from his or her caregiver.

Reference: Puri BK, Hall A, Ho R (2014). *Revision Notes in Psychiatry*. London: CRC Press, p. 64.

Question 17 Answer: a, Concrete operational
Explanation: The child is likely to be in the concrete operational stage. This is the third stage of development and usually occurs from the age of 7 years to around 12–14 years of age. During this stage, it is noted that the child is able to demonstrate and use logical thought processes and also make subjective moral judgments. In addition, he is also able to understand the laws of conservation, initially usually of number and volume and then weight.

Reference: Puri BK, Hall A, Ho R (2014). *Revision Notes in Psychiatry*. London: CRC Press, p. 68.

Question 18 Answer: b, Constant babbling at 7 months
Explanation: Tertiary circular reaction (part of sensorimotor stage, Piaget's cognitive model) occurs at 12–18 months. Development of colour vision occurs at 4–5 months. Development of fear of darkness occurs at 8–11 months. Preoperational stage (Piaget's cognitive model) occurs at 2 years.

Further Reading: Puri BK, Treasaden I (eds) (2010). *Psychiatry: An Evidence-Based Text*. London: Hodder Arnold, pp. 119–120, 280–281.

Question 19 Answer: a, Baseline attitudinal perceptions
Explanation: According to the theory on cognitive dissonance, discomfort will occur when two or more cognitions are held but are inconsistent with each other. The individual will be motivated to achieve cognitive consistency and may change one or more of these cognitions. Based on the attitude-discrepant theory, when the attitude and the behaviour are inconsistent, alteration of the attitude helps to bring about cognitive consistency.

Reference: Puri BK, Hall A, Ho R (2014). *Revision Notes in Psychiatry*. London: CRC Press, p. 52.

Question 20 Answer: a, Beauchamp and Childress
Explanation: Rush proposed less confining treatment in the United States. Laing was a psychiatrist who came to hold anti-psychiatry views. He was the author of *The Divided Self*. He saw schizophrenia as a sane response to an insane society. Percival established a code of ethics for Manchester Infirmary.

Szasz was both a professor of psychiatry and a leading proponent of anti-psychiatry. He identified psychiatrists as agents of social control. He also believed that it was unethical to restrict a patient's actions without his consent.

References: Musto DF (1998). A historical perspective, in Bloch S, Chodoff P, Green SA (eds), *Psychiatric Ethics* (3rd edition). Oxford, UK: Oxford University Press; Johnstone EC, Cunningham ODG, Lawrie SM, Sharpe M, Freeman CPL (2004). *Companion to Psychiatric Studies* (7th edition). London: Churchill Livingstone.

Question 21 Answer: b, Two times increased risk
Explanation: Cannabis does lead to a twofold increase in the associated risk of developing schizophrenia. It also leads to a fourfold increase in the associated risk of psychosis. It is important to note that not all cannabis users develop schizophrenia. It depends on the catechol-*O*-methyltransferase (COMT) genotype. People who have homozygous VAL/VAL alleles in the COMT genotype have a relatively higher risk. The usage of cannabis causes amotivational syndrome, flashback phenomena, changes in affect and heart rate, red eyes, motor incoordination, poor concentration and memory problems.

Reference: Puri BK, Hall A, Ho R (2014). *Revision Notes in Psychiatry*. London: CRC Press, p. 361.

Question 22 Answer: a, Frontal lobe
Explanation: The Wisconsin card sorting task is one of the neuropsychological assessment tests of frontal lobe function. Patients are usually given a pack of cards with symbols on them, which differ in form, colour and numbers. Four stimulus cards are available and the patient has to place each response card in front of one of the four stimulus cards. The person is required during the assessment to shift the set from one type of stimulus response to another as indicated by the psychologist.

Reference: Puri BK, Hall A, Ho R (2014). *Revision Notes in Psychiatry*. London: CRC Press, p. 111.

Question 23 Answer: e, Severe
Explanation: In severe mental intellectual disability, the intelligence quotient (IQ) score range is between 20 and 34. It accounts for 3% of all learning disabilities. There would be more marked motor impairment than that in moderate mental retardation, and achievements are at the lower end compared with that in moderate mental retardation. Moderate mental retardation refers to an IQ range of between 35 and 49. There would still be language use and development, and individuals could at least do simple practical work and live independently.

Reference: Puri BK, Hall A, Ho R (2014). *Revision Notes in Psychiatry*. London: CRC Press, p. 663.

Question 24 Answer: b, Disorganized schizophrenia
Explanation: The ICD-10 only includes the following subtypes for schizophrenia: paranoid, hebephrenic, catatonic, undifferentiated and residual. Paranoid schizophrenia is the commonest type with prominent hallucinations and delusions. Hebephrenic schizophrenia is associated with poor prognosis and characterized by marked affective changes. In catatonic schizophrenia, one or more of the following behaviours might be present: stupor, excitement, posturing, negativism, rigidity, waxy flexibility, command automatism and perseveration of words or phrases. For simple schizophrenia, there is an insidious onset of decline in functioning. Disorganized schizophrenia is named as hebephrenic schizophrenia in ICD-10.

Reference: Puri BK, Hall A, Ho R (2014). *Revision Notes in Psychiatry*. London: CRC Press, p. 353.

Question 25 Answer: e, Lewy body dementia
Explanation: The clinical features of Lewy body dementia usually include the following: (1) enduring and progressive cognitive impairment with impairments in consciousness, alertness and attention; (2) apathy, depression, hallucinations (usually complex visual hallucinations, 80%, and auditory hallucinations, 20%) and delusions (65%); (3) extrapyramidal signs and Parkinsonism; (4) neuroleptic sensitivity, falls, syncope and spontaneous loss of consciousness.

Reference: Puri BK, Hall A, Ho R (2014). *Revision Notes in Psychiatry*. London: CRC Press, p. 702.

Question 26 Answer: b, Absence of significant weight loss
Explanation: Based on the *Diagnostic and Statistical Manual of Mental Disorders*, 5th Edition (DSM-5) diagnostic criteria, in atypical anorexia nervosa, there is no significant weight loss but other criteria must be met. The DSM-5 states that for anorexia nervosa, there is restriction of energy and food intake, thus leading to a significantly low body weight in the context of age, sex, development and health status. Significantly low weight is defined as weight that is less than minimally normal. DSM-5 does not specify the percentage of weight loss (i.e. more than 15%) as in DSM-IV-TR. There must also be the presence of intense fear of weight gain or persistent behaviour that interferes with weight gain, even though the weight is significantly low. Body image disturbance is present, and this is a result of repetitive self-evaluation and poor insight of low body weight.

Reference: Puri BK, Hall A, Ho R (2014). *Revision Notes in Psychiatry*. London: CRC Press, p. 589.

Question 27 Answer: d, Prosopagnosia
Explanation: This refers to an inability to recognize faces. Associated with this is what is commonly known as the mirror sign, which may occur in advanced Alzheimer's disease, in which a person may misidentify his or her own mirrored

reflection. Agnosia is defined as the inability to interpret and recognize the significance of sensory information, which does not result from impairment of the sensory pathways, mental deterioration, disorders of consciousness and attention, or in the case of an object, a lack of familiarity with the object.

Reference: Puri BK, Hall A, Ho R (2014). *Revision Notes in Psychiatry*. London: CRC Press, p. 12.

Question 28 Answer: d, 0.10
Explanation: It has been estimated that around 10% of patients with schizophrenia commit suicide. For those who have been recently afflicted with the disorder, it usually happens early in this illness course. Suicide is more likely in the following cases: being male, being young, being unemployed, having chronic illness, relapses and remission, having a high educational attainment prior to onset, abrupt discontinuation of medications and recent discharge from inpatient care.

Reference: Puri BK, Hall A, Ho R (2014). *Revision Notes in Psychiatry*. London: CRC Press, p. 370.

Question 29 Answer: e, Seventh nerve palsy
Explanation: The seventh nerve, also known as the facial nerve, has the following components: the sensory component, the motor component and the autonomic component. None of them are responsible and will result in ptosis. The sensory component helps to detect taste on the anterior two-third of the tongue. The motor component is responsible for facial expression, elevation of the hyoid tension of stapes muscle and corneal reflex. The lesion affects reflex on the ipsilateral side of the face. The autonomic component would cause lacrimation and salivation from the sublingual and submandibular glands.

Reference: Puri BK, Hall A, Ho R (2014). *Revision Notes in Psychiatry*. London: CRC Press, p. 163.

Question 30 Answer: e, Rigidity
Explanation: Withdrawal symptoms might include that of somatic effects such as autonomic hyperactivity, malaise and weakness, tinnitus and grand mal convulsions. There are also cognitive effects with impaired memory and concentration as well as perceptual effects with hypersensitivity to sound, light and touch, besides depersonalization and de-realization. Delirium may develop within a week of cessation, and this is associated with visual, auditory, tactile hallucinations and delusions. It is also essential to note that the onset and intensity of withdrawal symptoms are related to the half-life of the drug used (shorter half-lives lead to a more abrupt and intense withdrawal syndrome). The withdrawal syndrome is also related to the dose used. Onset is usually within 1–14 days after drug reduction/cessation and may last for months.

Reference: Puri BK, Hall A, Ho R (2014). *Revision Notes in Psychiatry*. London: CRC Press, p. 548.

Question 31 Answer: c, Having an internal locus of control
Explanation: The following are psychosocial factors that are responsible for the development of post-traumatic stress disorder (PTSD). This includes female gender, low intelligence quotient at the age of 5 years, previous trauma history, previous psychiatric history: hyperactivity, anti-social behaviour, severity of trauma, perceived life threat, peri-traumatic dissociation, impaired social support and low socioeconomic status. Low education and social class, pre-existing psychiatric problems and female gender are vulnerability factors.

Reference: Puri BK, Hall A, Ho R (2014). *Revision Notes in Psychiatry*. London: CRC Press, p. 427.

Question 32 Answer: c, St. John's Wort
Explanation: It is an inducer of intestinal and hepatic CYP3A4, CYP2c and also intestinal P-glycoprotein, and the hyperforin content is responsible for this induction. According to several case reports, it could interact with other medicines, resulting in serious side effects. Some important drugs may be metabolized more rapidly and therefore become ineffective with serious consequences, for example, increased viral load in human immunodeficiency virus (HIV), failure or oral contraceptives leading to unwanted pregnancy and reduced anticoagulant effect with warfarin leading to thrombosis.

Reference: Taylor D, Paton C, Kapur S (2009). *The Maudsley Prescribing Guidelines* (10th edition). London: Informa Healthcare, p. 242.

Question 33 Answer: a, The onset of NMS is much more rapid as compared to serotonin syndrome.
Explanation: NMS is a life-threatening complication that can occur anytime during the course of antipsychotic treatment. The motor and behavioural symptoms include muscular rigidity and dystonia. The autonomic symptoms include high fever, sweating and increased pulse pressure and blood pressure. Laboratory findings include an increased white blood cell count and increased levels of creatinine phosphokinase. The symptoms usually evolve over 24–72 hours and, if not treated, would last for 10–14 days. Serotonin syndrome has a quicker rate of onset, in comparison.

Reference: Sadock BJ, Sadock VA (2008). *Kaplan and Sadock's Concise Textbook of Psychiatry* (3rd edition). Philadelphia, PA: Lippincott, Williams & Wilkins, p. 474.

Question 34 Answer: b, Checking things
Explanation: The most common compulsions are checking (60%), washing (50%) and counting (36%). Compulsions are defined as repetitive behaviours or mental acts in response to an obsession. The behaviours or mental acts are aimed at preventing or reducing anxiety or distress. Obsessions are defined as recurrent and intrusive thoughts, urges or images that cause marked anxiety or distress. Thus, an individual would resort to attempts to suppress such thoughts, urges or images or attempt to neutralize them using compulsive behaviour.

Reference: Puri BK, Hall A, Ho R (2014). *Revision Notes in Psychiatry*. London: CRC Press, p. 414.

Question 35 Answer: e, The onset of symptoms is usually within 2 weeks after experiencing the trauma.
Explanation: Based on the ICD-10 diagnostic criteria, PTSD arises within 6 months as a delayed and/or protracted response to a stressful event of an exceptionally threatening nature. The typical symptoms include that of repeated reliving of the trauma. Repetitive, intrusive memories (flashbacks), daytime imagery or dreams of the event must be present. Emotional detachment, persisting background numbness and avoidance of stimuli reminiscent of original event are often present, but not essential. Autonomic disturbances (hyper-arousal with hyper-vigilance, enhanced startle reaction and insomnia) and mood disorder contribute to the diagnosis but are not essential. Anxiety, depression and suicidal ideation are not common.

Reference: Puri BK, Hall A, Ho R (2014). *Revision Notes in Psychiatry*. London: CRC Press, p. 423.

Question 36 Answer: a, The principle of respect for a person's autonomy
Explanation: Although this man has a history of bipolar disorder, he has the capacity to make a decision. Hence, his autonomy is respected.

Reference: Puri BK, Treasaden I (eds) (2010). *Psychiatry: An Evidence-Based Text*. London: Hodder Arnold, p. 1231.

Question 37 Answer: d, Decreased in growth hormone
Explanation: The following are changes typically seen in anorexia nervosa. These included a decrease in T3, an increase in corticotrophin-releasing hormone (CRH), an increase in cortisol, an increase in growth hormone, a decrease in follicle-stimulating hormone (FSH), a decrease in luteinizing hormone (LH) and a decrease in oestrogen. The 24-hour pattern of secretion of LH resembles that normally seen in the pre-pubertal individuals. There might be a decrease in oestrogen in women or a decrease in testosterone in men. There are other abnormalities on the full blood count, in the electrolytes, in the arterial blood gas, in the renal and liver function tests as well as in the fasting blood. Radiological imaging such as computed tomography (CT) scan might show the presence of brain pseudo-atrophy, and the bone scan might reveal a reduction in bone mineral density.

Reference: Puri BK, Hall A, Ho R (2014). *Revision Notes in Psychiatry*. London: CRC Press, p. 579.

Question 38 Answer: c, Hypochondriasis
Explanation: In this case, the diagnosis would be hypochondriasis. Based on the ICD-10 diagnostic classification, there is a persistent belief of having at least one

of several illness, despite the fact that multiple repeated investigations have not yielded anything of significance. The patient would not be amendable to the advice of different doctors that he has had previously consulted. Attention is usually focused on one or two organ systems only. Anxiety disorders such as generalized anxiety disorders, obsessive-compulsive disorder (OCD) and depressive disorder are common comorbidities. If depressive symptoms are prominent and precede the onset of hypochondriacal ideas, then depressive disorder may be primary.

Reference: Puri BK, Hall A, Ho R (2014). *Revision Notes in Psychiatry*. London: CRC Press, p. 471.

Question 39 Answer: d, Renal impairment
Explanation: Acamprosate, in combination with counselling, may be helpful in maintaining abstinence. It should be started as soon as possible after the achievement of abstinence. It should be maintained if a relapse occurs. An individual is only allowed to have one relapse while taking acamprosate. If there has been more than one relapse, the psychiatrist should advise the individual to stop the medication. The common side effects will include diarrhoea, nausea, rash, pruritus, bullous skin reactions and fluctuation in libido.

Reference: Puri BK, Hall A, Ho R (2014). *Revision Notes in Psychiatry*. London: CRC Press, p. 522.

Question 40 Answer: a, Continue the same dose of citalopram
Explanation: It would be the most appropriate to continue the current dose of citalopram as the medication has had some effect on the patient. The following are recommendations based on the NICE guidelines: If improvement is not noted with the first dose of antidepressant after 2–4 weeks, it is essential to check that the medication has been taken as prescribed. If the medication is taken as prescribed, then the dose could be titrated upwards. If there is improvement by 4 weeks, it is essential to continue the same treatment for another 2–4 weeks.

Reference: Puri BK, Hall A, Ho R (2014). *Revision Notes in Psychiatry*. London: CRC Press, p. 391.

Question 41 Answer: c, He reports that he has been sleeping more than usual to avoid thinking of the events.
Explanation: PTSD usually occurs within 6 months as a delayed response to an extremely stressful event. The symptoms that are typically experienced include repeated reliving of the trauma and repetitive, intrusive memories of the event. There might also be emotional detachment and avoidance of stimuli that are similar to the original event. There will also be autonomic disturbances such as hyper-arousal with hyper-vigilance. Patients usually present with insomnia.

Reference: Puri BK, Hall A, Ho R (2014). *Revision Notes in Psychiatry*. London: CRC Press, p. 427.

Question 42 Answer: c, Early ejaculation

Explanation: Early ejaculation or premature ejaculation is the most common disorder of the male sexual response. Studies with community samples indicate its prevalence to be around 36%–38%; 13% of attendees at a sexual disorder clinic presents with this problem. The ICD-10 diagnostic criteria state that premature ejaculation refers to the inability to delay ejaculation sufficiently to enjoy sexual intercourse. Ejaculation may occur in the absence of sufficient erection to make intercourse possible.

Reference: Puri BK, Hall A, Ho R (2014). *Revision Notes in Psychiatry*. London: CRC Press, p. 600.

Question 43 Answer: a, Clinical interview and examination

Explanation: A detailed clinical interview and examination is the most useful tool to help in the diagnosis of dementia. The following information should be assessed in a psychiatric interview for an old person: (1) description of the presenting complaints; (2) onset, frequency, intensity, duration and location; (3) antecedents and consequences; and (4) ameliorating and exacerbating factors.

Reference: Puri BK, Hall A, Ho R (2014). *Revision Notes in Psychiatry*. London: CRC Press, p. 687.

Question 44 Answer: d, Seligman

Explanation: Seligman found that dogs given unavoidable electric shocks suffered a number of phenomena, which he considered were similar to depression, such as reduced appetite, disturbed sleep and reduced sex drive. He called this learned helplessness. This is of importance as the cognitive theory of depression is based on this concept. Further studies have found that individuals who believe that they have no personal control over events are more likely to develop learned helplessness, whereas those who believe that nobody could have controlled the outcome are unlikely to do so. Hence, an individual's attribution of what is occurring would influence the likelihood of him developing major depression.

Reference: Puri BK, Hall A, Ho R (2014). *Revision Notes in Psychiatry*. London: CRC Press, p. 53.

Question 45 Answer: a, Countertransference

Explanation: The countertransference usually refers to the therapist's own feelings, emotions and attitudes towards his patient. In this case, the nurses are having countertransference towards the patient with borderline personality disorder.
It is important to differentiate this from transference. Transference refers to an unconscious process in which the patient transfers to the therapist feelings, emotions and attitudes that were experienced and/or desired in the patient's childhood.

Reference: Puri BK, Hall A, Ho R (2014). *Revision Notes in Psychiatry*. London: CRC Press, p. 132.

Question 46 Answer: e, Risperidone
Explanation: Risperidone is the drug that causes the maximum elevation in the level of prolactin. This is due to the fact that dopamine would inhibit prolactin release, and hence dopamine antagonists can be expected to cause an increase in the plasma prolactin levels. Drugs such as clozapine, olanzapine, quetiapine and aripiprazole cause minimal change in the prolactin levels. Hyperprolactinaemia is often asymptomatic. However, persistent elevation in the plasma prolactin levels is associated with a number of adverse consequences. This might include sexual dysfunction, reductions in bone mineral density, menstrual disturbances, breast growth and galactorrhoea, suppression of the hypothalamic-pituitary-gonadal axis and a possible increase in the risk of breast cancer.

Reference: Taylor D, Paton C, Kapur S (2009). *The Maudsley Prescribing Guidelines* (10th edition). London: Informa Healthcare, p. 83.

Question 47 Answer: e, Hallucinations
Explanation: Ambivalence, autism, affective incongruity and disturbances of association of thoughts have been considered to be primary symptoms. He attributed hallucinations and delusions to be of secondary status.

Reference: Puri BK, Hall A, Ho R (2014). *Revision Notes in Psychiatry*. London: CRC Press, p. 351.

Question 48 Answer: e, Obsessive-compulsive personality disorder
Explanation: She is likely to have obsessive-compulsive personality disorder. Individuals with this disorder tend to have perfectionism that would interfere with completion of their tasks. In addition, they are extremely careful and are rigid and stubborn in their thinking. They also have excessive feelings of doubt and caution. Individuals with OCD usually present with clearly defined obsessions and compulsions. People with obsessive-compulsive personality disorder are more ego-syntonic with their behaviour, and hence they lend to be less anxious.

Reference: Puri BK, Hall A, Ho R (2014). *Revision Notes in Psychiatry*. London: CRC Press, p. 453.

Question 49 Answer: b, Usage of persuasive messages
Explanation: Attitudes can be modified either by central pathways, entailing the consideration of new information, or by peripheral pathways, involving the presentation of cues. In persuasive communication, the factors to be considered are concerned with those of the communicator, the recipient and also the message being communicated. It is key to note that message repetition can lead to a persuasive influence resulting in attitude change.

Reference: Puri BK, Hall A, Ho R (2014). *Revision Notes in Psychiatry*. London: CRC Press, p. 58.

Question 50 Answer: a, Anterograde memory loss

Explanation: Korsakoff's syndrome is an alcohol-induced amnestic disorder that is frequently preceded by Wernicke's encephalopathy. It has been described as an abnormal state in which memory and learning are affected out of proportion to the other cognitive functions in an otherwise alert and responsive patient. Clinical features would include retrograde amnesia, anterograde amnesia, sparing of immediate recall, disorientation to time, inability to recall the temporal sequence of events, confabulation and peripheral neuropathy.

Reference: Puri BK, Hall A, Ho R (2014). *Revision Notes in Psychiatry*. London: CRC Press, p. 513.

Question 51 Answer: b, Factitious disorder

Explanation: The diagnosis is that of factitious disorder. In this disorder, the patient intentionally produces the physical or psychological symptoms, but the patient is not conscious about his or her underlying motives. Common presenting signs might include bleeding, diarrhoea, hypoglycaemia, infection, impaired wound healing, vomiting, rashes and seizures. The patient often has poor prognosis and refuses to receive psychotherapy. Factitious disorder is different from malingering. In malingering, the patient intentionally produces physical or psychological symptoms and the patient is fully aware of his or her underlying motives. As a result, the patient does not want to cooperate for further assessment and evaluation due to the discrepancy between the severity of the symptoms reported and the objective physical findings revealed.

Reference: Puri BK, Hall A, Ho R (2014). *Revision Notes in Psychiatry*. London: CRC Press, p. 471.

Question 52 Answer: b, Made emotions

Explanation: Made emotions refer to the delusional belief that one's free will has been removed and an external agency is controlling one's feelings. Made impulse refers to the delusional belief that one's own free will has been removed and that an external agency is controlling one's impulses. Somatic passivity refers to the delusional belief that one is a passive recipient of somatic or bodily sensations from an external agency.

Reference: Puri BK, Hall A, Ho R (2014). *Revision Notes in Psychiatry*. London: CRC Press, p. 7.

Question 53 Answer: b, Thought broadcasting

Explanation: Thought broadcasting refers to the delusion that one's thought is no longer within one's own control, and that one's thoughts are being broadcast out loud so that others can freely access and understand. Thought broadcasting is a subset under thought alienation, in which the individual believes that his or her thoughts are under the control of an external agency or that others are participating in his or her thinking.

Reference and Further Readings: Puri BK, Hall A, Ho R (2014). *Revision Notes in Psychiatry*. London: CRC Press, p. 7; Sadock BJ, Sadock VA (2008). *Kaplan and Sadock's Concise Textbook of Psychiatry* (3rd edition). Philadelphia, PA: Lippincott, Williams & Wilkins, p. 31.

Question 54 Answer: b, Magnification

Explanation: Beck proposed the following cognitive triad in depressed patients. He stated that depressed patients tend to have a negative personal view, a tendency to interpret his or her on-going experience in a negative way and also a negative view of the future. Some of the common cognitive errors in depression include catastrophic thinking, dichotomous thinking, tunnel vision, selective abstraction, labelling, overgeneralization, personalization, should statements, magnification and minimization, arbitrary inference and emotional reasoning.

Reference: Puri BK, Hall A, Ho R (2014). *Revision Notes in Psychiatry*. London: CRC Press, p. 386.

Question 55 Answer: a, The feeling of 'as if'

Explanation: Depersonalization refers to a disturbance in the awareness of self-activity. In depersonalization, an individual might feel that he or she is altered or not real in some way. It also refers to the sensation of unreality concerning parts of oneself, or even one's environment, that occurs usually under extreme stress or fatigue. It is commonly seen in schizophrenia, depersonalization disorder, and also schizotypal personality disorder. This is in contrast to de-realization, to which the individual might feel that the surroundings do not appear real.

Reference and Further Readings: Puri BK, Hall A, Ho R (2014). *Revision Notes in Psychiatry*. London: CRC Press, p. 9; Sadock BJ, Sadock VA. (2008). *Kaplan and Sadock's Concise Textbook of Psychiatry* (3rd edition). Philadelphia, PA: Lippincott, Williams & Wilkins, p. 24.

Question 56 Answer: b, Long pause

Explanation: The husband has gone through a long difficult period by living with his wife and it is difficult to express his difficult feelings all at once. A long pause would be very helpful to give him a chance to organize his thoughts and facilitate the interview. Summation refers to a brief summary of what the person has said and this technique is irrelevant as he has not said much. Transition is a technique used gently to inform the person that the interview is moving on to another topic and it is irrelevant as the interview has not been progressing. Close-ended questions and prolonged eye contact would not facilitate a response from the husband.

Further Reading: Puri BK, Treasaden I (eds) (2010). *Psychiatry: An Evidence-Based Text*. London: Hodder Arnold, pp. 43, 75, 318–319, 1047–1048.

Question 57 Answer: c, Made impulse
Explanation: This is part of the passivity phenomenon. Made impulse refers to the delusional belief that one's free will has been removed and now is under the control of an external agency. In contrast, made actions refer to the delusional belief that one's own free will has been removed and an external agency is controlling one's actions. Made impulse is part of the passivity phenomenon. Other examples of passivity phenomenon includes thought alienation, made feelings, made actions and somatic passivity.

Reference: Puri BK, Hall A, Ho R (2014). *Revision Notes in Psychiatry*. London: CRC Press, p. 7.

Question 58 Answer: c, Delusional beliefs
Explanation: Ganser syndrome is considered and classified under dissociative disorders. It is known as a complex disorder, which is characterized by approximate answers and usually accompanied by several dissociative symptoms, often in circumstances that suggest psychogenic aetiology. The main features of Ganser syndrome include approximate answers, clouding of consciousness, somatic conversion, pseudo-hallucinations and subsequent amnesia.

Reference: Puri BK, Hall A, Ho R (2014). *Revision Notes in Psychiatry*. London: CRC Press, p. 434.

Question 59 Answer: d, He is having memory difficulties and hence is confabulating.
Explanation: He is likely to be having memory difficulties and is confabulating. In confabulation, the gaps in memory are being filled up with false memories. Confabulation is classified under paramnesia, which is a distorted recall thus leading to falsification of memory. Apart from confabulation, others include déjà vu, déjà entendu, déjà pense, jamais vu and retrospective falsification. Retrospective falsification refers instead to how false details are being added to the recollection of an otherwise real memory.

Reference: Puri BK, Hall A, Ho R (2014). *Revision Notes in Psychiatry*. London: CRC Press, p. 9.

Question 60 Answer: d, Synaesthesia
Explanation: Synaesthesia is commonly referred to as a condition in which a stimulation of one particular sensory modality leads to a perception of another sensation in a different sensory modality. A common example of this might be how a musical sound is being perceived as a colour instead. Extracampine hallucination refers to how a hallucination occurs outside an individual's sensory field. Functional hallucination refers to how the stimulus that is causing the hallucination is experienced in addition to the hallucination itself. Reflex hallucination is defined as a stimulus in one sensory field that leads to a

hallucination in another sensory field. Visual hallucinations can be simple or complex in nature.

Reference and Further Readings: Sadock BJ, Sadock VA (2008). *Kaplan and Sadock's Concise Textbook of Psychiatry* (3rd edition). Philadelphia, PA: Lippincott, Williams & Wilkins, p. 31; Puri BK, Hall A, Ho R (2014). *Revision Notes in Psychiatry*. London: CRC Press, p. 8.

Question 61 Answer: a, Anxious avoidant personality disorder
Explanation: Individuals with anxious avoidant personality disorder usually avoid social or occupational activities that might involve significant interpersonal contact, as they are concerned about rejection and criticism. Based on the ICD-10 diagnostic criteria, they tend to have persistent and pervasive tension. They are unwilling to be involved with people unless they are certain of being liked. They have a restricted lifestyle due to the need for physical security. They tend to avoid social or occupational activities that involve significant interpersonal contact because of the fear of criticism, disapproval and rejection. They tend to believe that one is socially inept, personally unappealing and inferior as compared to others. They have excessive preoccupation with being criticized or rejected in social situations.

Reference: Puri BK, Hall A, Ho R (2014). *Revision Notes in Psychiatry*. London: CRC Press, p. 454.

Question 62 Answer: a, Automatic obedience
Explanation: Automatic obedience refers to a condition in which the person follows the examiner's instructions blindly without using his or her own judgement and resistance. For example, when the examiner asks the person to move his or her arm in a different direction and the individual is unable to resist doing it even if it is against his or her own will. Echopraxia refers to the automatic imitation by the individual of another person's movement. Stereotypies refer to repeated regular fixed patterns of movement (or even speech) that are not goal directed in nature.

Reference: Puri BK, Hall A, Ho R (2014). *Revision Notes in Psychiatry*. London: CRC Press, pp. 2–3.

Question 63 Answer: c, Nitrazepam
Explanation: Nitrazepam has the longest half-life and would not be suitable. The usual therapeutic dose is that of 5–10 mg per day, and the time to the onset of action is between 20 and 50 minutes. The guidelines recommend that short-acting hypnotics are better for people who have difficulty falling asleep, but it should be noted that tolerance and dependence would develop quite quickly. Long-acting hypnotics are more suitable for patients with frequent or early-morning awakening. However, it should be noted that for long-acting hypnotics, these drugs

could potentially cause much sedation the next day and there might be associated loss of coordination as well.

Reference: Taylor D, Paton C, Kapur S (2009). *The Maudsley Prescribing Guidelines* (10th edition). London, Informa Healthcare, p. 249.

Question 64 Answer: b, Opioid agonist
Explanation: Naltrexone is still not licensed to treat alcohol dependence in the United Kingdom due to the associated high risk of mortality after overdose and potential withdrawal associated with the usage of the medications. However, it could help people who are in abstinence from alcohol and who are highly motivated. It is known that the opioid receptors are responsible for reward and this would lead to increased craving. Naltrexone works by acting as an opioid antagonist. Hence, alcohol becomes less rewarding when those receptors are blocked.

Reference: Puri BK, Hall A, Ho R (2014). *Revision Notes in Psychiatry*. London: CRC Press, p. 526.

Question 65 Answer: a, Attention and concentration
Explanation: This is part of the Mini Mental State Examination and is largely a test of attention and concentration.

Reference: Puri BK, Hall A, Ho R (2014). *Revision Notes in Psychiatry*. London: CRC Press, p. 685.

Question 66 Answer: d, Anhedonia
Explanation: This is a complex syndrome that has been described by Ganser. It is characterized by approximate answers and usually accompanied by several dissociative symptoms, often in circumstances that suggest psychogenic aetiology. The five main core features of the syndrome include approximate answers, clouding of consciousness, somatic conversion, pseudo-hallucinations and subsequent amnesia. Ganser syndrome is classified as a dissociative disorder. Anhedonia refers to the loss in interest and withdrawal from activities that one usually enjoys.

Reference: Puri BK, Hall A, Ho R (2014). *Revision Notes in Psychiatry*. London: CRC Press, p. 434.

Question 67 Answer: b, Hebephrenic schizophrenia
Explanation: Amongst the various subtypes of schizophrenia, hebephrenic schizophrenia has been considered to have the worst prognosis. The age of onset is usually between 15 and 25 years. Affective changes are prominent. There might be fleeting and fragmentary delusions and hallucinations; irresponsible behaviour; fatuous, disorganized thought; rambling speech and mannerisms are common. Negative symptoms, particularly flattening of affect and loss of volition, are

common and prominent. Drive and determination are lost, goals are abandoned and behaviour becomes aimless and empty. The premorbid personality is usually shy and solitary.

Reference: Puri BK, Hall A, Ho R (2014). *Revision Notes in Psychiatry*. London: CRC Press, p. 353.

Question 68 Answer: d, Hypochondriasis
Explanation: The most likely clinical diagnosis is hypochondriasis. In this disorder, based on the ICD-10 classification system, there is a persistent belief in the presence of at least one serious physical illness, despite repeated investigations revealing no physical explanation of the presenting symptoms, or persistent preoccupation with presumed deformity. There is also persistent refusal to accept the advice of several different doctors that there is no physical illness underlying the symptoms.

Reference: Puri BK, Hall A, Ho R (2014). *Revision Notes in Psychiatry*. London: CRC Press, p. 471.

Question 69 Answer: b, Extracampine hallucination
Explanation: Extracampine hallucinations refer to hallucinations that occur outside of the person's sensory field, and this accounts for her experiences. Pseudo-hallucination refers to a form of imagery that arises from within the subjective inner space of the mind. Thought echo and thought broadcasting are both part of the thought alienation phenomenon, a passivity phenomenon.

Reference: Puri BK, Hall A, Ho R (2014). *Revision Notes in Psychiatry*. London: CRC Press, p. 8.

Question 70 Answer: a, Alexithymia
Explanation: This refers to the difficulty in the awareness of or description of one's emotion. Apathy refers to a loss of emotional tone and the ability to feel pleasure, associated with detachment or indifference. Dysphoria refers to the existence of an unpleasant mood. Euphoria refers to a personal or subjective feeling of unconcern and contentment, usually seen after taking opiates or as a late sequel to a head injury.

Reference: Puri BK, Hall A, Ho R (2014). *Revision Notes in Psychiatry*. London: CRC Press, p. 5.

Question 71 Answer: a, Acting out
Explanation: Acting out is not a mature defence mechanism. Acting out refers to the expression of unconscious emotional conflicts or feelings directly in actions without being consciously aware of their meaning. Sublimation refers to a process that utilizes the force of a sexual instinct in drives, affects and memories in order to motivate creative activities having no apparent connection with sexuality.

Reference: Puri BK, Hall A, Ho R (2014). *Revision Notes in Psychiatry*. London: CRC Press, p. 137.

Question 72 Answer: a, Acute stress disorder
Explanation: The diagnosis in this case is that of acute stress disorder. This is the diagnosis as the onset of symptoms is less than a month in duration. The diagnosis of an adjustment disorder is made when the onset is within 1 month of the stressor, and the duration is usually less than that of 6 months, except for prolonged depressive reaction.

Reference: Puri BK, Hall A, Ho R (2014). *Revision Notes in Psychiatry*. London: CRC Press, p. 432.

Question 73 Answer: c, Family therapy
Explanation: Psycho-educational family programmes to increase medication compliance and coping with stressors are successful in reducing the risk of relapse. Families with high EE were identified using the Camberwell Family Interview. Education and family sessions in the home run in parallel with a relative group. The programme is aimed at teaching problem-solving skills, lowering criticism and over-involvement, and reducing contact between patients while expanding social networks.

Reference: Puri BK, Hall A, Ho R (2014). *Revision Notes in Psychiatry*. London: CRC Press, p. 369.

Question 74 Answer: e, It refers to a bias made when inferring the cause of another's behaviour – bias made towards internal factors.
Explanation: Primary or fundamental attribution error is usually made when asked to infer the cause of another individual's behaviour. There is usually a bias towards dispositional rather than situational attribution.

Reference: Puri BK, Hall A, Ho R (2014). *Revision Notes in Psychiatry*. London: CRC Press, p. 59.

Question 75 Answer: d, Normal functioning
Explanation: If this man suffers from delusional disorder, his delusion is considered to be non-bizarre. Hence, he is expected to have normal functioning. The mean age of onset is 35 years for males and 45 years for females. The onset is gradual and unremitting in 62%. There might be a family history of psychiatric disorder but not of delusional disorder or schizophrenia.

Reference and Further Reading: Puri BK, Treasaden I (eds) (2010). *Psychiatry: An Evidence-Based Text*. London: Hodder Arnold, p. 677.

Question 76 Answer: b, Lorazepam
Explanation: Lorazepam would be the most appropriate medication to be given in this case. This is mainly because it has a short half-life with no active metabolites.

It is important to use low doses, as sedative drugs could potentially precipitate hepatic encephalopathy. Based on the NICE guidelines, both diazepam and chlordiazepoxide have marketing authorization for the management of acute alcohol withdrawal symptoms.

References: Puri BK, Hall A, Ho R (2014). *Revision Notes in Psychiatry*. London: CRC Press, p. 523; Taylor D, Paton C, Kapur S (2009). *The Maudsley Prescribing Guidelines* (11th edition). London: Informa Healthcare, p. 479.

Question 77 Answer: b, Learned helplessness

Explanation: Beck proposed a cognitive model from which cognitive therapy was developed. Based on the cognitive triad, the depressed person has a negative personal view, a tendency to interpret his or her ongoing experiences in a negative way and a negative view of the future. The proposed cognitive bias does not include that of learned helplessness. The common cognitive errors include that of catastrophic thinking, dichotomous thinking, tunnel vision, selective abstraction, labelling, overgeneralization, personalization, should statement, magnification, minimization, arbitrary inference and emotional reasoning.

Reference: Puri BK, Hall A, Ho R (2014). *Revision Notes in Psychiatry*. London: CRC Press, p. 384.

Question 78 Answer: d, Szasz

Explanation: Thomas Szasz (1930–2012), a prominent anti-psychiatrist, identified mental illness as problematic and somatic illnesses as unproblematic. In a society, bodily illness is a genuine illness, and genuine illness is defined as deviation from normal anatomy and physiology of a body organ. On the other hand, Szasz believed that mental illnesses are defined by deviation from social norms in terms of acceptable behaviours. Hence, mental illness is very different in its meaning and nature from a physical illness.

Reference: Puri BK, Hall A, Ho R (2014). *Revision Notes in Psychiatry*. London: CRC Press, p. 157.

Question 79 Answer: d, Mannerism

Explanation: Mannerisms are repeated involuntary movements that are goal-directed. An example would be 'A person repeatedly moving his hand when he talks and tries to convey his message to the examiner'. Stereotypy, on the other hand, refers to non-goal-directed repetitive movements (e.g. rocking forward and backward).

Reference and Further Reading: Rajagopal S (2007). Catatonia. *Advances in Psychiatric Treatment*, 13: 51–59.

Question 80 Answer: a, This usually occurs when members of the majority group tend to victimize members of the minority group simply out of frustration.
Explanation: Scapegoating usually involves members of a majority group targeting and displacing their aggression onto members of a minority group.

Reference: Ciccarelli SK, Meyer GE (2006). *Psychology*. Upper Saddle River, NJ: Pearson Education, p. 444.

Question 81 Answer: e, Restless leg syndrome (Ekbom's syndrome)
Explanation: Restless leg syndrome (Ekbom's syndrome) is an irresistible desire to move the legs when resting with unpleasant leg sensations. It is usually idiopathic. Secondary causes include iron deficiency, uraemia, pregnancy, diabetes, polyneuropathy and rheumatoid arthritis. Dopamine agonists and benzodiazepine such as clonazepam are commonly used for treatment. In psychiatry, Ekbom's syndrome also refers to delusional parasitosis.

Reference and Further Reading: Longmore M, Wilkinson I, Turmezei T, Cheung CK (2007). *Oxford Handbook of Clinical Medicine* (7th edition). Oxford, UK: Oxford University Press.

Question 82 Answer: c, Start her on propranolol
Explanation: This woman suffers from akathisia. Options (a)–(e) are recommended for the treatment of antipsychotic-induced akathisia. Propranolol is contraindicated in patients with asthma.

Reference and Further Reading: Taylor D, Paton C, Kapur S (2009). *The Maudsley Prescribing Guidelines* (10th edition). London: Inform Healthcare.

Question 83 Answer: b, Florid third-person auditory hallucinations
Explanation: Florid third-person auditory hallucinations do not support the diagnosis of simple schizophrenia in this case.

Reference and Further Reading: Puri BK, Treasaden I (eds) (2010). *Psychiatry: An Evidence-Based Text*. London: Hodder Arnold, pp. 593–609.

Question 84 Answer: c, Normal grief reaction
Explanation: This man suffers from normal grief reaction. Sadness, guilt and transient experience of hearing voices of the deceased are common among people with normal grief reaction. The accident occurred 3 months ago, and there is no evidence of prolonged grief. There is not enough clinical evidence to suggest that he suffers from post-traumatic stress disorder.

Reference and Further Reading: Puri BK, Treasaden I (eds) (2010). *Psychiatry: An Evidence-Based Text*. London: Hodder Arnold, pp. 811–817.

Question 85 Answer: d, Smoking
Explanation: Smoking is likely to affect the levels of his medication, as smoking would cause an induction of the CYP4501A2. This is mainly due to the polycyclic hydrocarbons that are present in the smoke itself. This particular enzyme is responsible for the metabolism of many of the common psychotropic drugs. Hence, smoking could thus result in a reduction in the blood levels of some drugs by as much as 50%. Some of the commonly affected drugs include clozapine, haloperidol, chlorpromazine, olanzapine, tricyclic antidepressants, mirtazapine, fluvoxamine and propranolol.

Reference: Taylor D, Paton C, Kapur S (2009). *The Maudsley Prescribing Guidelines* (10th edition). London: Informa Healthcare, p. 506.

Question 86 Answer: d, Distorted grief
Explanation: Distorted grief is associated with intense anger or guilt. The person may develop symptoms that the deceased had prior to death. Other signs of distorted grief are over-activity without a sense of loss hostility towards a specific person and taking self-destructive actions. Since the duration is only 6 months, he does not qualify for chronic grief. Conflicted grief refers to intense ambivalent feeling towards the deceased. Delayed grief refers to a bereaved person who does not show any grief reaction after the deceased person died but grief reaction only comes after a delayed period. Inhibited grief refers to some feelings towards the deceased, which is not expressed.

Question 87 Answer: e, Subconscious
Explanation: Disorders of self-awareness usually include disturbances to the awareness of self-activity, immediate awareness of self-unity, continuity of self and the boundaries of self. Disorders of self-awareness include depersonalization, which refers to the way one feels that one is altered or not real in some way, and de-realization, which refers to how the surroundings do not seem real.

Reference: Puri BK, Hall A, Ho R (2014). *Revision Notes in Psychiatry*. London: CRC Press, p. 9.

Question 88 Answer: d, 60%
Explanation: An old British study showed that approximately 60% of patients had been re-admitted at least once. Only 20% had recovered fully with no further episodes and 20% were incapacitated throughout or died of suicide.

Reference: Lee AS, Murray RM (1988). The long-term outcome of Maudsley depressives. *Br J Psychiatry*, 153: 741–751.

Question 89 Answer: b, Anchoring and adjustment heuristic
Explanation: In this experiment, participants knew that the speaker's position on the war was chosen at random, yet the speaker believed in what he had said. This is

known as fundamental attribution error, defined as the tendency to overestimate the extent to which a person's behaviour is due to internal, dispositional factors and to underestimate the role of external, situational factors. The anchoring and adjustment heuristic is one explanation of fundamental attribution error. Participants use the speech as an initial 'anchor' to base their inference of the speaker's disposition. They then adjust their attributions to account for external, situational factors; this means that the position was chosen at random. Fundamental attribution error arises due to the tendency to insufficiently adjust the initial judgement or anchor.

Further Reading: Jones EE, Harris VA (1967). The attribution of attitudes. *Journal of Experimental Social Psychology*, 3: 1–24.

Question 90 Answer: e, Trustworthy team members who are experienced in community psychiatry and skilful in dealing with complicated issues. They require minimal supervision.
Explanation: This case refers to laissez-faire leadership. Option A is for democratic leadership. Option B applies to both autocratic and democratic leadership. Options C and D are suitable for autocratic leadership.

Further Reading: Puri BK, Treasaden I (eds) (2010). *Psychiatry: An Evidence-Based Text*. London: Hodder Arnold, pp. 292, 118.

Question 91 Answer: e, Patients with mania and hypomania are expected to have same level of psychosocial functioning.
Explanation: Patients with mania are expected to have a lower level of psychosocial functioning compared with patients with hypomania.

Reference and Further Reading: Puri BK, Treasaden I (eds) (2010). *Psychiatry: An Evidence-Based Text*. London: Hodder Arnold, pp. 610, 624–627.

Question 92 Answer: a, Debriefing
Explanation: Based on the NICE guidelines, with regards to the psychological treatment for PTSD, if the onset of the symptoms is less than 3 months after a trauma, it might be beneficial to offer trauma-focused psychological treatment. If the symptoms occur more than 3 months after a trauma, it might be better to offer trauma-focused psychological treatment, which might be trauma-focused cognitive-behavioural therapy (CBT) or eye movement desensitization and reprocessing (EMDR). Debriefing is a technique that is contraindicated for the management of PTSD.

Reference: Puri BK, Hall A, Ho R (2014). *Revision Notes in Psychiatry*. London: CRC Press, p. 424.

Question 93 Answer: d, Primacy effect
Explanation: Practice effect is the influence of test-taking performance due to prior exposure to a test. Practice effect usually results in improved scores.

Barnum effect is the tendency of people to endorse, as an accurate description of themselves. Halo effect is the influence of a positive or negative first impression on subsequent interpretations of a person's behaviour such that it is aligned with the first impression. Primacy and recency effects are the tendencies to remember information at the start and the end more accurately than information in the middle. This phenomenon is collectively known as serial position effect.

References and Further Readings: Collie A, Maruff P, Darby DG, McStephen M (2003). The effects of practice on the cognitive test performance of neurologically normal individuals assessed at brief test-retest intervals. *Journal of the International Neuropsychological Society*, 9: 419–428; Claridge G, Clark K, Powney E, Hassan E (2008). Schizotypy and the Barnum effect. *Personality and Individual Differences*, 44: 436–444; Puri BK, Treasaden I (eds) (2010). *Psychiatry: An Evidence-Based Text.* London: Hodder Arnold, p. 251.

Question 94 Answer: b, Astasia-abasia
Explanation: Her condition is catatonia. Clinical features of catatonia are all of the aforementioned options except astasia-abasia. Other signs of catatonia include stupor, posturing, negativism, stereotypy, mannerism, echolalia, echopraxia and logorrhoea. Causes of catatonia include schizophrenia, mood disorders, organic disorders (e.g. central nervous system [CNS] infection), epilepsy, recreational drugs (cocaine) and medications (ciprofloxacin). Astasia-abasia is a gait disturbance seen in conversion disorder.

Reference and Further Reading: Rajagopal S (2007). Catatonia. *Advances in Psychiatric Treatment*, 13: 51–59.

Question 95 Answer: d, Koro
Explanation: This condition is commonly referred to as Koro. It may occur in epidemic form. It involves the belief of genital retraction with disappearance into the abdomen and this is accompanied by intense anxiety and associated with fear of impending death. The development of Koro has been associated with psychosexual conflicts, personality factors and also cultural beliefs in the context of psychological stress. There have been cases of similar condition being described in non-Chinese subjects. In these cases, the syndrome is often only partial, such as the belief of genital shrinkage, not necessarily with retraction into the abdomen. It usually occurs within the context of another psychiatric disorder, and resolves once the underlying illness has been treated.

Reference: Puri BK, Hall A, Ho R (2014). *Revision Notes in Psychiatry*. London: CRC Press, p. 462.

Question 96 Answer: c, Insomnia
Explanation: Somatic symptoms of depression (e.g. sleep, appetite, energy and libido changes) are not reliable in establishing the diagnosis of depression in

antenatal period because non-depressed pregnant women also experience insomnia, poor appetite, nausea, tiredness and libido changes.

Reference and Further Reading: Puri BK, Treasaden I (eds) (2010). *Psychiatry: An Evidence-Based Text*. London: Hodder Arnold, pp. 715–732.

Question 97 Answer: a, Bupropion
Explanation: It would be recommended for the patient not to be started on bupropion due to the fact that it is contraindicated in seizure disorder. The guidelines state that most of the tricyclic antidepressants are epileptogenic, particularly at higher doses, as well as bupropion and hence should be avoided completely. If antidepressant treatment is necessary, moclobemide and selective serotonin reuptake inhibitors (SSRIs) are good choices. The use of mirtazapine, venlafaxine and duloxetine would require extra care.

Reference: Taylor D, Paton C, Kapur S (2009). *The Maudsley Prescribing Guidelines* (10th edition). London, Informa Healthcare, p. 421.

Question 98 Answer: b, Death of a spouse
Explanation: Death of a spouse is considered to be the most stressful event with 100 life change units (LCU), followed by divorce (73 LCU), marital separation (65 LCU), imprisonment (63 LCU) and death of a close family member (63 LCU).

Reference and Further Readings: Holmes TH, Rahe RH (1967). The Social Readjustment Rating Scale. *Journal of Psychosomatic Research*, 11: 213–218; Puri BK, Treasaden I (eds) (2010). *Psychiatry: An Evidence-Based Text*. London: Hodder Arnold, pp. 155–156; Puri BK, Treasaden I (eds) 2010: *Psychiatry: An Evidence-Based Text*. London: Hodder Arnold, pp. 309–318.

Question 99 Answer: d, Psychological pillow
Explanation: Psychological pillow is a feature of catatonia. The patient holds his or her head a few inches above the bed surface in a reclining posture, and is able to maintain this position for hours.

Reference and Further Reading: Rajagopal S (2007). Catatonia. *Advances in Psychiatric Treatment*, 13: 51–59.

Question 100 Answer: d, Punishment
Explanation: This phenomenon is punishment because it results in a reduction in behaviour. Punishment is any stimulus that is applied after a response and causes a weakening of that behaviour. Punishment is the opposite of reinforcement (both positive and negative). Reinforcement causes a strengthening of the behaviour, whereas punishment suppresses it. In negative reinforcement, an unpleasant stimulus is removed, hence resulting in an increased likelihood of the behaviour occurring again.

Reference and Further Reading: Puri BK, Treasaden I (eds) (2010). *Psychiatry: An Evidence-Based Text.* London: Hodder Arnold, pp. 200–205.

Question 101 Answer: b, The trial involved Japanese doctors who were deemed unethical.

Explanation: The code was developed by the war crimes tribunal against the Nazi German doctors and the main objective was to protect human subjects during experiment and research. An experiment should avoid suffering and injury. Experiments leading to death and disability should not be conducted. Proper preparations should be made to protect research subjects, and the experiments should be conducted by qualified personnel. During the experiment, the research subjects should have the liberty to withdraw at any time and the investigators should stop the experiments if continuation results in potential injury or death of research subjects. The design should be based on results obtained from animal experiments and natural history of the disease. Seeking consent from research subjects is absolutely necessary. Research should yield meaningful results for the good of mankind.

Reference: Puri BK, Hall A, Ho R (2014). *Revision Notes in Psychiatry.* London: CRC Press, p. 147.

Question 102 Answer: d, Operant conditioning

Explanation: Operant conditioning is the learning of voluntary behaviour (pressing the lever) through the effects of positive or negative consequences (obtaining food). This experiment is not an example of classical conditioning because classical conditioning involves involuntary or reflex responses.

Reference and Further Reading: Puri BK, Treasaden I (eds) (2010). *Psychiatry: An Evidence-Based Text.* London: Hodder Arnold, pp. 200–205.

Question 103 Answer: c, A critical evaluator

Explanation: Groupthink is a kind of thinking in which maintaining group cohesiveness and solidarity takes precedence over considering the facts in a realistic manner. This theory of group decision making was developed by Irving Janis. Antecedents to groupthink include options A and B. Option E is a symptom of groupthink. Mindguards are people who shield the group from contrary information. Irving Janis identified seven other symptoms of groupthink, which include illusion of unanimity, self-censorship and stereotyped views of out-group.

Groupthink style of decision making can be avoided by several methods, which include assigning each member the role of a critical evaluator, considering all alternatives and discussing ideas with external experts.

Reference and Further Reading: Aronson E, Wilson TD, Akert RM (2007). *Social Psychology.* Upper Saddle River, NJ: Prentice Hall, pp. 160–162.

Question 104 Answer: d, Erotomania
Explanation: The most likely clinical diagnosis is that of couvade syndrome. This refers to a form of delusion that another person, usually of higher status, might be deeply in love with the individual.

Reference: Puri BK, Hall A, Ho R (2014). *Revision Notes in Psychiatry*. London: CRC Press, p. 6.

Question 105 Answer: d, Legitimation
Explanation: Legitimation is a technique when the therapist allows the patient to describe his or her feelings and indicates to the patient that it is acceptable to feel the way he or she does.

Reference: Poole R, Higgo R (2006). *Psychiatric Interviewing and Assessment*. Cambridge, UK: Cambridge University Press.

Question 106 Answer: d, Usage of antidepressants
Explanation: Rapid cycling bipolar disorder refers to those individuals who have had experience with four or more affective episodes in the last 12 months. It is usually more common in women, and is predictive of poorer prognosis and poorer response to lithium and other treatments. It is known that as much as 20% are induced by antidepressants use. Antidepressants should be avoided and thyroid function tests should be performed 6-monthly. The NICE guidelines also recommend increasing the dose of the anti-manic drug or addition of lamotrigine. For long-term management, the NICE guidelines recommend a combination of lithium and valproate as first-line treatment. Lithium mono-therapy is the second-line treatment.

Reference: Puri BK, Hall A, Ho R (2014). *Revision Notes in Psychiatry*. London: CRC Press, p. 397.

Question 107 Answer: e, Windigo
Explanation: The culture-bound syndrome in this context is Windigo. It is most common amongst North American Indians and usually associated with depression, schizophrenia, hysteria and anxiety. It is a disorder in which the subject believes he or she has undergone a transformation and become a monster who practises cannibalism. It has been suggested that Windigo is in fact a local myth rather than an actual pattern of behaviour.

Reference: Puri BK, Hall A, Ho R (2014). *Revision Notes in Psychiatry*. London: CRC Press, p. 463.

Question 108 Answer: a, Therapeutic index
Explanation: Therapeutic index is the relative measure of the toxicity or safety of a drug and is usually defined as the ratio of the median toxic dose to the median effective dose. The median toxic dose is defined as the dose at which 50% of the patients would experience specific toxic effects. The median

effective dose is defined as the dose at which 50% of the patients would have a specified therapeutic effect. A drug with a high therapeutic index implies that a wide range of dosages of the drug could be prescribed. Conversely, if the therapeutic index is low, closer monitoring of the prescribed medication would be essential.

Reference: Sadock BJ, Sadock VA (2008). *Kaplan and Sadock's Concise Textbook of Psychiatry* (3rd edition). Philadelphia, PA: Lippincott, Williams & Wilkins, p. 915.

Question 109 Answer: d, The reinforcement can occur before the behaviour.
Explanation: This phenomenon is known as operant conditioning, specifically negative reinforcement. Escape and avoidance learning are two examples of negative reinforcement. The removal of the unpleasant stimulus leads to reinforcement of the behaviour. In operant conditioning, the reinforcer (reduction in anxiety levels) is presented only after the behaviour (going home) is executed, which is why Option D is incorrect.

Reinforcements, both positive and negative, work to increase the frequency of the conditioned behaviour. In operant conditioning, this conditioned response is voluntary, whereas in classical conditioning, the conditioned response is involuntary (e.g. salivating in the Pavlov's dogs).

Reference and Further Reading: Puri BK, Treasaden I (eds) (2010). *Psychiatry: An Evidence-Based Text.* London: Hodder Arnold, pp. 200–205.

Question 110 Answer: d, Implosion cannot be used in extinction.
Explanation: Implosion is a behaviour technique used in the treatment of phobias, where the patient is exposed to the feared stimulus all at once, through imagination or visualization. Unlike flooding, implosion does not involve direct contact with the feared stimulus. Reciprocal inhibition is a technique used in systematic desensitization, where the antagonistic response to anxiety (i.e. relaxation) is maintained when the feared stimulus is presented. Shaping involves reinforcement of small approximations to achieve a desired behaviour. It has been used in reducing undesired behaviours such as cocaine addiction.

Reference and Further Readings: Puri BK, Treasaden I (eds) (2010). *Psychiatry: An Evidence-Based Text.* London: Hodder Arnold, pp. 199, 655, 990–991; Preston KL, Umbricht A, Wong CJ, Epstein DH (2001). Shaping cocaine abstinence by successive approximation. *Journal of Consulting Clinical Psychology*, 69: 643–654.

Question 111 Answer: b, Learned helplessness
Explanation: Learned helplessness does not contribute to the aetiology of phobias but can exacerbate the condition of a person with specific phobia. Vicarious conditioning is also known as observational learning. It involves the learning of fear responses by watching the reaction of another person. The concept of

preparedness suggests that fear of certain objects may be evolutionarily adaptive to increase survival and this would make phobias more difficult to treat.

Reference and Further Reading: Puri BK, Treasaden I (eds) (2010). *Psychiatry: An Evidence-Based Text.* London: Hodder Arnold, pp. 195–200, 206, 207, 654.

Question 112 Answer: e, The term 'schizophrenia' refers to the 'splitting' of affect from other psychological functions leading to a dissociation between the social situation and the emotion expressed.
Explanation: Eugene Bleuler proposed the term schizophrenia which refers to the 'splitting' of affect from other psychological functions leading to a dissociation between the social situation and the emotion expressed.

References and Further Readings: Charlton B (2000). *Psychiatry and the Human Condition.* Oxford, UK: Radcliffe Publishing; Shorter E (1997). *A History of Psychiatry.* New York: John Wiley & Sons; Puri BK, Treasaden I (eds) (2010). *Psychiatry: An Evidence-Based Text.* London: Hodder Arnold, pp. 11, 593, 614, 624.

Question 113 Answer: a, Ambitendency
Explanation: In this condition, the person makes a series of tentative incomplete movements when expected to carry out a voluntary action. For example, a woman offers a handshake, then withdraws, and then offers it again 10 times. The examiner cannot make a handshake with her at the end.

Reference: Puri BK, Hall A, Ho R (2014). *Revision Notes in Psychiatry.* London: CRC Press, p. 1.

Question 114 Answer: c, Occupation
Explanation: The determinants of social class include education, financial status, occupation, type of residence, geographic area of residence and leisure activities. In British psychiatry, the Office of Population Censuses and Surveys has traditionally based their classification using occupation. Social class I includes professional, higher managerial and landowners. Social class II includes those with intermediate skills. Social class III includes those who are skilled, or who are doing manual or clerical work. Social class IV includes those who are semiskilled. Social class Y refers to those who are unskilled. Social class 0 refers to those who are unemployed, or who are students.

Reference: Puri BK, Hall A, Ho R (2014). *Revision Notes in Psychiatry.* London: CRC Press, p. 115.

Extended matching items (EMIs)

Theme: Memory

Question 115 Answer: g, Retrograde memory
Explanation: Also known as retrograde amnesia, this refers to the loss of memory for events that occurred prior to an event or condition.

Question 116 Answer: b, Working memory
Explanation: His working memory or short-term memory is clearly affected. The anatomical correlate of auditory verbal short-term memory is the left dominant parietal lobe, while that of the visual verbal short-term memory is the left temporo-occipital area.

Question 117 Answer: c, Procedural memory
Explanation: This is also known as implicit memory. It is recalled automatically without much effort and is learned slowly through repetition. Its storage requires the functioning of the cerebellum, the amygdala, and specific sensory and motor systems used in the learned task.

Question 118 Answer: a, Declarative memory
Explanation: Declarative memory belongs to the subset of explicit memory. Declarative memory involves memory of autobiographical events.

Question 119 Answer: d, Episodic Memory
Explanation: Both declarative memory and episodic memory belong to the sub-set of explicit memory. It is possible to lose one type of memory while retaining the other. Episodic memories involve memories of autobiographical events.

Reference: Puri BK, Hall A, Ho R (2014). *Revision Notes in Psychiatry*. London: CRC Press, p. 103.

Theme: Lab tests

Question 120 Answer: d, 48 hours
Explanation: The length of time for detection of amphetamines in the urine is approximately 48 hours.

Question 121 Answer: c, 24 hours
Explanation: For short-acting barbiturates, the length of time for detection is approximately 24 hours. For long-acting ones, the length of time for detection is approximately 3 weeks.

Question 122 Answer: a, 6–8 hours
Explanation: The duration of detection of cocaine is approximately 6–8 hours.

Question 123 Answer: e, 36–72 hours
Explanation: The duration of detection of heroin is approximately 36–72 hours.

Question 124 Answer: b, 12–24 hours
Explanation: The duration of detection is 12–24 hours.

Question 125 Answer: d, 48 hours
Explanation: The duration of detection is 48 hours.

Question 126 Answer: g, 8 days
Explanation: It could be detected up until 8 days.

Theme: General psychiatry

Question 127 Answer: h, 35%–50%
Explanation: The estimated lifetime expectancy rate when both parents have schizophrenia has been estimated to be around 46%.

Question 128 Answer: c, 10%–14%
Explanation: In this case, given that only one parent has schizophrenia, the rate has been estimated to be around 13%.

Question 129 Answer: e, 20%–24%
Explanation: The estimated incidence should be around 23%. This is a condition that is caused by a micro-deletion in chromosome 22q11.2. More than 50% of patients have mild-to-moderate learning disability. In addition, there is an increased incidence of schizophrenia.

Question 130 Answer: a, 0%–4%
Explanation: The estimated increase in incidence for half-siblings is 4%.

Question 131 Answer: a, 0%–4%
Explanation: The risk of schizophrenia has been estimated to be around 2.4%.

Reference and Further Reading: Puri BK, Treasaden I (eds) (2010). *Psychiatry: An Evidence-Based Text.* London: Hodder Arnold, pp. 474–475, 597, 599.

Theme: Aetiology

Question 132 Answer: k, Streptococcal infection
Explanation: This patient suffers from paediatric autoimmune neuropsychiatric disorders associated with streptococcal infections (PANDAS).

Reference and Further Reading: Puri BK, Treasaden I (eds) (2010). *Psychiatry: An Evidence-Based Text.* London: Hodder Arnold, p. 551.

Question 133 Answer: d, Childhood sexual abuse
Explanation: This patient suffers from borderline personality disorder, and childhood sexual abuse is an important aetiological factor.

Reference and Further Reading: Puri BK, Treasaden I (eds) (2010). *Psychiatry: An Evidence-Based Text.* London: Hodder Arnold, pp. 707, 709.

Question 134 Answer: g, Dysbindin gene, h, Migration, i, Neuregulin gene
Explanation: This patient suffers from schizophrenia, and dysbindin, neuregulin and migration may be the aetiological factors.

Reference and Further Reading: Puri BK, Treasaden I (eds) (2010). *Psychiatry: An Evidence-Based Text.* London: Hodder Arnold, pp. 593–609.

Theme: General adult psychiatry

Question 135 Answer: e, PTSD

Explanation: Based on the current ICD-10 diagnostic criteria, PTSD arises within 6 months as a delayed and/or protracted response to a stressful event of an exceptionally threatening nature. Symptoms include that of repeated reliving of the trauma, emotional detachment and autonomic disturbances.

Question 136 Answer: b, Adjustment disorder

Explanation: These symptoms usually occur within 1 month of exposure to an identifiable psychosocial stressor. The ICD-10 has four sub-classifications, which are brief depressive reaction, prolonged depressive reaction, mixed anxiety and depressive reaction and predominant disturbance of emotions and/or conduct.

Question 137 Answer: d, Generalized anxiety disorder

Explanation: Patients usually report uncontrollable worry. A negative response to the question, 'Do you worry excessively over minor matters?' virtually rules out GAD as a diagnosis. Symptoms of muscle and psychic tension are the most frequently reported by people with GAD.

Reference and Further Reading: Puri BK, Hall A, Ho R (2014). *Revision Notes in Psychiatry*. London: CRC Press, p. 409.

Theme: General adult psychiatry

Question 138 Answer: b, Wilson's disease

Explanation: Wilson's disease is an autosomal recessive disorder of hepatic copper metabolism. The incidence is 1 in 200,000. The gene responsible for this disorder has been located on chromosome 13 and encodes a copper-binding, membrane-spanning ATPase that regulates meta I transport protein. Cirrhosis and fulminant hepatic failure are known complications.

Question 139 Answer: d, Hypothyroidism

Explanation: Hypothyroidism is one of the most common conditions in the United Kingdom with a prevalence of 1.4% in females, but it is less common in males. Thyroxine replacement therapy may help to reverse psychiatric symptoms.

Question 140 Answer: c, Hyperthyroidism

Explanation: This is a condition that affects 2%–5% of all women mostly between the age of 20 and 45 years with a female-to-male ratio of 5:1. Anti-thyroid medication, radioactive thyroxine or thyroid surgery might be able to reverse the psychiatric symptoms.

Question 141 Answer: e, Cushing's syndrome
Explanation: This is a syndrome that is most commonly caused by exogenous administration of steroids. Other causes include ACTH-dependent causes, non-ACTH–dependent causes and alcohol-dependent pseudo-Cushing's syndrome.

Question 142 Answer: f, Addison's disease
Explanation: The aforementioned clinical symptoms are consistent with those of Addison's disease. Fatigue, weakness and apathy are common in the early stage. Around 90% of patients with adrenal disorders present with psychiatric symptoms.

Reference: Puri BK, Hall A, Ho R (2014). *Revision Notes in Psychiatry*. London: CRC Press, p. 477.

Theme: Diagnostic classification

Question 143 Answer: a, Paranoid schizophrenia
Explanation: This is known to be the most common subtype. Auditory, olfactory, gustatory and somatic hallucinations and visual hallucinations may occur. There may also be delusions of control, influence, passivity and persecution.

Question 144 Answer: b, Hebephrenic schizophrenia
Explanation: The aforementioned is true with regards to hebephrenic schizophrenia. The age of onset is generally between 15 and 25 years, and affective changes are usually prominent.

Question 145 Answer: c, Catatonic schizophrenia
Explanation: In this form of schizophrenia, one or more of the following behaviours may dominate: stupor, excitement, posturing, negativism, rigidity, waxy flexibility and command automatism and preservation of words or phrases.

Question 146 Answer: f, Simple schizophrenia
Explanation: There is an insidious onset of decline in functioning. Negative symptoms develop without preceding positive symptoms. Diagnosis requires changes in behaviour over at least 1 year, with marked loss of interest, idleness and social withdrawal.

Question 147 Answer: e, Residual schizophrenia
Explanation: This is a form of schizophrenia that is characterized largely by negative symptoms. There is past evidence of at least one schizophrenic episode and a period of at least 1 year in which the frequency of the positive symptoms has been minimal and negative schizophrenic symptoms have been present.

Reference: Puri BK, Hall A, Ho R (2014). *Revision Notes in Psychiatry*. London: CRC Press, p. 354.

Theme: General adult psychiatry

Question 148 Answer: e, 85%
Explanation: Based on the studies by Farmer et al. (1987) and Cardno et al. (1999), the heritability estimates have been around 80%–85%.

Question 149 Answer: b, 40%
Explanation: Based on key studies by Kendler et al. (1992) and McGulffin et al. (1996), the estimates are around 40%.

Question 150 Answer: d, 80%
Explanation: Based on key studies, the heritability estimates are between 79% and 93%.

Question 151 Answer: b, 40%
Explanation: Based on key studies (Kendler et al., 1992), the estimates are around 44%.

Reference: Puri BK, Hall A, Ho R (2014). *Revision Notes in Psychiatry*. London: CRC Press, p. 290.

Theme: Basic psychopathology

Question 152 Answer: i, Cataplexy
Explanation: This refers to the loss of muscle tone in narcolepsy. For example, a person develops temporary paralysis after emotional excitement.

Question 153 Answer: g, Ambitendency
Explanation: In this condition, the person makes a series of tentative incomplete movements when expected to carry out a voluntary action. For example, a woman offers a handshake, then withdraws and then offers it again for 10 times. The examiner is unable to make a handshake with her even at the end of the interview.

Question 154 Answer: h, Catalepsy
Explanation: Catalepsy refers to the abnormal maintenance of postures. For example, a person holds his or her arm in the air for a long time like a wax statue.

Question 155 Answer: d, Somnambulism
Explanation: This refers to a complex sequence of behaviours carried out by a patient who rises from sleep and is not fully aware of his or her surroundings.

Question 156 Answer: e, Compulsion
Explanation: This refers to a repetitive and stereotyped seemingly purposeful behaviour. It is commonly referred to as the motor component of an obsessional thought. Examples of compulsions include checking, cleaning, counting, dipsomania and dressing rituals.

Question 157 Answer: c, Obsessional slowness
Explanation: Obsessional slowness usually occurs secondary to repeated doubts and compulsive rituals.

Question 158 Answer: a, Stupor
Explanation: The key features of stupor include mutism, immobility, occasional periods of excitement and over-activity. Stupor is commonly seen in catatonic states, depressive states, manic states and also epilepsy and hysteria.

Reference: Puri BK, Hall A, Ho R (2014). *Revision Notes in Psychiatry*. London: CRC Press, pp. 1–2.

Theme: Basic psychopathology

Question 159 Answer: a, Anterograde amnesia and d, Retrograde amnesia
Explanation: Anterograde amnesia refers to the inability to form new memories due to the failure to consolidate or inability to retrieve. Retrograde amnesia refers to the loss of the memory for events that occurred prior to the events (such as intoxication or head injury). It tends to improve with some distant events in the past recovering first. In general, the retrograde amnesia is shorter than the post-traumatic amnesia.

Question 160 Answer: b, Post-traumatic amnesia
Explanation: This refers to the memory loss from the time of the accident to the time that the person can give a clear account of the recent events. It tends to remain unchanged.

Question 161 Answer: c, Psychogenic amnesia
Explanation: This is part of the dissociative disorder consisting of a sudden inability to recall important personal data. It is associated with la belle indifference (lack of concern) of the memory difficulties.

Question 162 Answer: e, Transient global amnesia
Explanation: In this condition, the person presents with a sudden onset of disorientation, loss of ability to encode recent memories and retrograde amnesia for a variable duration. This episode lasts for a few hours and is never repeated. The cause is the transient ischaemia of the hippocampus–fornix–hypothalamus system.

Question 163 Answer: g, Paramnesia
Explanation: Paramnesia refers to a distorted recall leading to falsification of memory. Paramnesias include confabulation, déjà vu, deja extend, dejapense, jamais vu and retrospective falsification.

Reference: Puri BK, Hall A, Ho R (2014). *Revision Notes in Psychiatry*. London: CRC Press, p. 9.

Theme: Neurology

Question 164 Answer: d, Intermediate aphasia
Explanation: Intermediate aphasia includes central aphasia and nominal aphasia. Central aphasia refers to the difficulty in arranging words in their proper sequence.

Nominal aphasia refers to the difficulty in naming objects. The person may use circumlocutions to express certain words, for example the person cannot name the clock but can label the clock as a thing that tells the time.

Question 165 Answer: a, Receptive aphasia, b, agnostic alexia, c, Pure word deafness.
Explanation: Receptive aphasia refers to the difficulty in comprehending the meaning of words. Types of receptive aphasia might include agnostic alexia, which means that words can be seen but cannot be read; pure word deafness, which means that words can be heard but cannot be comprehended and visual asymbolia, which means that words can be transcribed but cannot be read.

Question 166 Answer: e, Expressive aphasia
Explanation: Expressive aphasia is also known as Broca's non-fluent aphasia. This refers to difficulty in expressing thoughts in words whilst comprehension remains.

Question 167 Answer: f, Global aphasia
Explanation: In this condition, both receptive aphasia and expressive aphasia are present at the same time.

Reference: Puri BK, Hall A, Ho R (2014). *Revision Notes in Psychiatry*. London: CRC Press, p. 10.

Theme: Basic psychology

Question 168 Answer: i, Incubation
Explanation: Incubation refers to the gradual increment in the strength of the conditioned response following repeated brief exposure to the conditioned stimulus.

Question 169 Answer: g, Generalization
Explanation: This process refers to generalization. This is a process whereby once a CR has been established to a given stimulus, that particular response could in turn be evoked by other stimuli that are similar to the original conditioned stimulus.

Question 170 Answer: e, Higher-order conditioning
Explanation: In higher-order conditioning, the conditioned stimulus is paired with a second or even a third conditioned stimulus, which on presentation by itself would elicit the original conditioned response. It should be noted that higher-order conditioning is weaker than first-order conditioning, and the higher the order, the much weaker is the conditioning.

Question 171 Answer: c, Trace conditioning
Explanation: In trace conditioning, the conditioned stimulus ends before the onset of the unconditioned stimulus and the conditioning becomes less effective as the delay between the two increases.

Question 172 Answer: a, Delayed conditioning
Explanation: In delayed conditioning, the onset of the conditioned stimulus precedes that of the unconditioned stimulus, and the conditioned stimulus continues until the response occurs. Delayed conditioning is only optimal if the delay between the onset of the two stimuli is around half a second.

Reference: Puri BK, Hall A, Ho R (2014). *Revision Notes in Psychiatry*. London: CRC Press, p. 25.

Theme: Stages of development

Question 173 Answer: c, Phallic stage
Explanation: Phallic stage occurs between the ages of 3 and 5 years. Genital interest relates to own sexuality. The failure to negotiate leads to hysterical personality traits such as competitiveness and ambitiousness.

Question 174 Answer: b, Anal stage
Explanation: This stage occurs between the ages of 1 and 3 years. The anus and defecation are sources of sensual pleasure. Failure to negotiate leads to anal personality traits such as obsessive-compulsive personality, tidiness, parsimony, rigidity and thoroughness.

Question 175 Answer: a, Oral stage
Explanation: This stage occurs between the ages of 0 and 1 year. The failure to negotiate this stage leads to oral personality traits such as moodiness, generosity, depression, elation, talkativeness, greed, optimism, pessimism, wishful thinking and narcissism.

Question 176 Answer: h, Initiative
Explanation: The child is undergoing Erikson's stage of initiative. From the age of 0–1 year, the stage is that of trust and security and from the age of 1–4 years, the stage is that of autonomy.

Question 177 Answer: k, Intimacy
Explanation: The stage that lasts from the age of 15 years to adulthood is that of intimacy.

Reference: Puri BK, Hall A, Ho R (2014). *Revision Notes in Psychiatry*. London: CRC Press, p. 48.

Theme: Leadership and social power

Question 178 Answer: c, Laissez-faire
Explanation: Laissez-faire leadership is more appropriate for creative, open-ended and person-oriented tasks.

Question 179 Answer: a, Autocratic
Explanation: For autocratic leadership, there is a tendency for members to abandon the tasks in the leader's absence. It is good for situations of urgency.

Question 180 Answer: d, Authority power
Explanation: Authority power refers to power derived from a specific role.

Question 181 Answer: e, Reward power
Explanation: Reward power refers to power derived from ability to allocate resources.

Question 182 Answer: h, Expert power
Explanation: Expert power refers to power that is derived from skill, knowledge and experience.

Reference: Puri BK, Hall A, Ho R (2014). *Revision Notes in Psychiatry*. London: CRC Press, p. 59.

Theme: Models of cognitive development

Question 183 Answer: b, Preoperational
Explanation: This is considered to be the second stage of Piaget's cognitive model and occurs from the ages of 2 to 7 years. During this stage, the child learns to use the symbols of language. Thought processes exhibited during this stage include animism, artificialism, authoritarian morality, creationism, egocentrism and finalism.

Question 184 Answer: a, Sensorimotor
Explanation: This is considered to be the first stage and occurs from birth to 2 years of age. Circular reactions are repeated voluntary motor activities, for example, shaking a toy, occurring from around 2 months. Primary circular reaction occurs from 2 to 5 months, and they have no apparent purpose. Secondary circular reaction occurs from 5 to 9 months, and experimentation and purposeful behaviour are gradually manifested. Tertiary circular reactions occur from 1 year to 18 months and include the creation of original behaviour patterns and the purposeful quest for novel experiences.

Question 185 Answer: d, Formal operational
Explanation: Formal operational stage is the final stage and occurs from the age of around 12–14 years. It is characterized by the achievement of being able to think in the abstract, including the ability systematically to test hypotheses.

Question 186 Answer: d, Formal operational
Explanation: This is the third stage and occurs from the age of 7 to around 12–14 years of age. During this stage, the child demonstrates logical thought processes and more subjective moral judgements. An understanding of the laws of conservation of, initially, number and volume and the weight is normally achieved. Reversibility and some aspects of classifications are mastered.

Reference: Puri BK, Hall A, Ho R (2014). *Revision Notes in Psychiatry*. London: CRC Press, p. 68.

Theme: Psychological test

Question 187 Answer: b, Blessed Dementia Scale

Explanation: This particular questionnaire is administered to a relative or a friend of the subject who is asked the questions on the basis of performance over the previous 6 months. There are three sets of questions. The first set deals with activities of daily living, the second set deals with further activities of daily living and the third set is concerned largely with changes in personality, interest and drive.

Question 188 Answer: d, Cambridge Examination for Mental Disorders

Explanation: This is an interview schedule that consists of three sections: (1) a structured clinical interview with the patient to obtain systematic information about the present state, past history and family history; (2) a range of objective cognitive tests that constitute a mini-neuropsychological battery, commonly known as the Cambridge Cognitive Examination; (3) a structured interview with a relative or other informant to obtain independent information about the respondent's present state, past history and family history.

Question 189 Answer: e, Clifton Assessment Schedule

Explanation: This is a nursing rated assessment. Other nursing-rated assessments include the Stockton Geriatric Rating Scale.

Question 190 Answer: f, Present Behavioural Examination

Explanation: The Present Behavioural Examination involves interviewing carers and rates psychopathological and behavioural changes in dementia.

Reference: Puri BK, Hall A, Ho R (2014). *Revision Notes in Psychiatry*. London: CRC Press, p. 99.

Theme: Social sciences and stigma

Question 191 Answer: a, Death of spouse

Explanation: The death of spouse is associated with a life-change value of 100.

Question 192 Answer: b, Divorce

Explanation: Divorce is associated with a life-change value of 73.

Question 193 Answer: f, Pregnancy

Explanation: Pregnancy is associated with a life-change value of 50, with the birth of a child associated with a life-change value of 39.

Question 194 Answer: g, Minor legal violation

Explanation: Minor legal violation is associated with the lowest life-change value of 11.

Reference: Puri BK, Hall A, Ho R (2014). *Revision Notes in Psychiatry*. London: CRC Press, p. 122.

MRCPSYCH PAPER AI MOCK EXAMINATION 2: QUESTIONS

GET THROUGH MRCPSYCH PAPER AI: MOCK EXAMINATION

Total number of questions: 185 (118 MCQs, 67 EMIs)
Total time provided: 180 minutes

Question 1
A 20-year-old male has been brought to the mental health service by his parents as he has been complaining that he has been hearing voices. During the interview with the psychiatrist, he was noted to be repeating particular words with increasing frequency. This form of psychopathology is known as
a. Palilalia
b. Logoclonia
c. Neologism
d. Metonym
e. Punning

Question 2
A dentist proudly mentions that patients in his dental clinic are provided with a relaxing chair, ice cream and magazines to read after that they receive stressful dental procedures. Which of the following best describes the arrangement in his clinic?
a. Avoidance learning
b. Classical conditioning
c. Extinction
d. Operant conditioning
e. Reciprocal inhibition

Question 3
You are posted to work in a new UK-based medical school in Singapore. A nurse is not certain how to keep the following psychotropic drugs in the ward and comes to consult you. The bioavailability of which of the following psychotropic drugs is most likely to be affected by exposure to humid atmosphere?
a. Haloperidol
b. Gabapentin

c. Lithium carbonate
d. Phenobarbital sodium
e. Risperidone

Question 4
A 25-year-old male has been referred by his general practitioner (GP) for a psychiatric assessment. He shared with the psychiatrist that he has been uncomfortable with his gender and is determined to have a gender re-assignment operation to become a woman. Which of the following would be the most appropriate clinical diagnosis?
a. Obsessive-compulsive disorder (OCD)
b. Body dysmorphic syndrome
c. Fetishistic transvestism
d. Transexualism
e. Delusional disorder

Question 5
A medical student asks you the specific type of epilepsy most commonly associated with olfactory hallucination. Your answer should be
a. Medial frontal lobe lesions and complex partial seizure
b. Medial parietal lobe lesions and complex partial seizure
c. Medial parietal lobe lesions and simple partial seizure
d. Medial temporal lobe lesions and complex partial seizure
e. Medial temporal lobe lesions and simple partial seizure

Question 6
Based on your understanding about neurosis and anxiety disorders in general, which of the following phobias has a strong underlying genetic linkage?
a. Agoraphobia
b. Social phobia
c. Blood injection phobia
d. Animal phobia
e. Illness phobia

Question 7
You are posted to work in Kenya. There is a lot of sunlight in the daytime and the hospital does not have an air-conditioned room to keep the psychotropic medications. The bioavailability of which of the following psychotropic drugs is most likely to be affected by exposure to air and light?
a. Carbamazepine
b. Gabapentin
c. Phenobarlatone
d. Topiramate
e. Zonisumide

Question 8
Paramnesia refers to a distorted recall leading to falsification of memory. The feelings of 'being there before' is best described by which of the following terms?

a. Déjà vu
b. Déjà entendu
c. Déjà pense
d. Jamais vu
e. Retrospective falsification

Question 9
A 37-year-old woman is diagnosed with depression. She feels miserable and thinks that her job requires her working long, stressful hours with brash and unfriendly colleagues. Although she is aware of the poor working environment, she does not do anything to better her situation and remains in the same job for many years. Which of the following statements about the above phenomenon is incorrect?

a. This phenomenon occurs when reinforcement is not contingent on behaviour.
b. This phenomenon is the result of a history of repeated failures.
c. This phenomenon is an example of classical conditioning.
d. There is a feeling of having no personal control over events.
e. This phenomenon was described by Seligman.

Question 10
A 25-year-old man suffers from treatment-resistant schizoaffective disorder and takes clozapine. Which of the following psychotropic drugs is contradicted as an augmentation?

a. Carbamazepine
b. Fluoxetine
c. Lithium
d. Valproate
e. Risperidone

Question 11
Which of the following risk factors is associated with the highest risk of developing agranulocytosis in schizophrenic patients taking clozapine?

a. Afro-Caribbean descent
b. Young age
c. Female gender
d. High dose of clozapine
e. Long duration of clozapine use

Question 12
A 45-year-old female has been very concerned about her son Thomas. She has received feedback from his teachers at school that he has been very rigid in his duties and is not able to participate in group work as he cannot delegate tasks.

He consistently seeks perfectionism in all that he does. Which of the following is the most likely clinical diagnosis?
a. OCD
b. Obsessive-compulsive personality disorder
c. No mental illness
d. Schizoid personality disorder
e. Antisocial personality disorder

Question 13
Which of the following is a good prognostic factor for an individual with anorexia nervosa (AN)?
a. Onset younger than the age of 15
b. Lower weight at onset and at presentation
c. Frequent vomiting and the presence of bulimia
d. Long duration of symptoms
e. Male gender

Question 14
A 40-year-old woman complains about generalized headache which has gotten worse over the past 3 weeks. Her GP thought that she suffers from tension headache. Which of the following symptoms suggest an underlying serious pathology?
a. Headache which bands around the head
b. Headache getting worse when lying down
c. Headache and giddiness
d. Pain at the occipital
e. Severity of the headache

Question 15
A 5-year-old boy is brought by his parents for assessment. His parents complain that he has abnormalities in reciprocal social interaction and restricted interest in buses. He was speaking fluently at the age of 2. Physical examination shows stereotyped movement and motor clumsiness. Which of the following is the most likely diagnosis?
a. Autism
b. Asperger's syndrome
c. Attention deficit and hyperkinetic disorder
d. Childhood disintegrative disorder
e. Rett's syndrome

Question 16
Which of the following is true with regards to the psychopathology that a patient is experiencing when he keeps repeating everything that the examiner has been saying?
a. Approximate answers
b. Cryptolalia
c. Circumstantiality

d. Echolalia
e. Flight of ideas

Question 17

Which of the following statements is false?

a. Second-order conditioning is the basis for single-object phobia.
b. Animal phobias have the best prognosis among the various phobias.
c. Punishment is a component of aversion therapy.
d. Second-order conditioning is more easily demonstrated than classical conditioning
e. Forward conditioning is more used than backward conditioning.

Question 18

A 24-year-old man suffers from treatment-resistant schizophrenia and has started clozapine for 1 week. He refuses to have the weekly full blood count but is keen to continue clozapine. His GP is concerned that he will develop agranulocytosis and wants to find out when is the peak period for developing agranulocytosis. Your answer is

a. First month of treatment
b. Second month of treatment
c. Third month of treatment
d. Fourth month of treatment
e. Fifth month of treatment

Question 19

A 1-year-old child should be fearful of

a. Animals
b. Loud noises
c. Death
d. Darkness
e. 'Monsters'

Question 20

A newborn baby possesses all of the following visual characteristics except

a. Ability to discriminate the level of brightness
b. Ability to focus on an object at a distance of 0.2 m
c. Ability to scan objects
d. Depth perception
e. Figure-ground differentiation

Question 21

A 50-year-old man has an infarct in the anterior cerebral artery. Which of the following neurological signs is most likely to be found?

a. Broca's aphasia
b. Ipsilateral lower limb paralysis

c. Contralateral lower limb weakness
d. Contralateral III nerve palsy
e. Nystagumus

Question 22
A concerned mother brought her 5-year-old son for assessment because she worries he has developmental delay. Which of the following development tasks is mainly achieved at 5 years but not in earlier years?
a. The child is able to count age on hand.
b. The child is able to imitate a drawing of a circle and a cross.
c. The child is able to name items at home.
d. The child is able to run on tiptoes.
e. The child knows his name.

Question 23
Which of the following statements regarding the diagnostic criteria for post-schizophrenic depression is false?
a. Based on the *Diagnostic and Statistical Manual of Mental Disorders* (DSM)-IV-TR criteria, post-schizophrenic depression is not a diagnostic entity.
b. Based on the International Classification of Diseases (ICD)-10 criteria, the general criteria for schizophrenia must have been met within the previous 12 months prior to onset of depressive episode.
c. Based on the ICD-10 criteria, a depressive episode instead of post-schizophrenic depression should be diagnosed if the patient no longer has any schizophrenic symptoms for a long time.
d. Based on the ICD-10 criteria, dysthymia is severe enough to meet diagnostic criteria of post-schizophrenic depression.
e. The post-schizophrenic depressive episodes are associated with an increased risk of suicide.

Question 24
Which of the following types of schizophrenia is not found in the DSM-IV-TR?
a. Catatonic type
b. Disorganized type
c. Hebephrenic type
d. Paranoid type
e. Residual type

Question 25
Which of the following is not a bad prognostic factor for individuals with AN?
a. Onset at an older age
b. Long duration of AN
c. Previous hospitalization

d. Extreme resistance to treatment
e. Female gender

Question 26

A 40-year-old woman reports that she is the prime minister's sister. When asked what makes her think this, she replies that it is true without further elaboration. Her affect was flat without pressure of speech. Collateral history of her family reveals that she has no relationship with the prime minister and the realization came to her 'out of the blue'. The psychopathology being described is

a. Autochthonous delusion
b. Delusional memory
c. Delusional mood
d. Delusional perception
e. Delusion of grandeur

Question 27

Gestalt principle is based on the following, with the exception of

a. Proximity
b. Similarity
c. Continuity
d. Closure
e. Three-dimensional similarity

Question 28

A 30-year-old schizophrenia man is prescribed with clozapine and the daily dose is 700 mg per day. The consultant psychiatrist worries about the high risk of seizure. Which of the following anticonvulsants is the most appropriate prophylactic agent against clozapine-induced epilepsy?

a. Carbamazepine
b. Lamotrigine
c. Phenytoin
d. Topiramate
e. Valproate

Question 29

A 30-year-old man suffers from third-person auditory hallucination, thought interference and delusion of control for 3 months. Which of the following statements is correct?

a. He fulfils the diagnostic criteria for schizophrenia based on the ICD-10.
b. He fulfils the diagnostic criteria for schizophrenia based on DSM-IV-TR.
c. He fulfils the diagnostic criteria for schizophrenia based on both the DSM-IV-TR and the ICD-10.
d. He does not fulfil diagnostic criteria for schizophrenia based on both the DSM-IV-TR and the ICD-10.
e. None of the aforementioned options.

Question 30

Based on research into conformity and group behaviour, which of the following statements is incorrect?

a. Within the group, member's individual opinions were distorted based on the opinions of others in the group.
b. Conformity was greater in groups that had individuals who were less self-reliant.
c. Conformity was greater in groups that had individuals who were less intelligent.
d. Conformity was greater in groups that had individuals who were less self-expressive.
e. Conformity to the group's decision on a line judgement experiment was greater in a group of 25 members as compared to a group of four.

Question 31

Which of the following statements about the theory of mind is incorrect?

a. In primate research, theory of mind refers to the abilities of primates to mentalize their fellows.
b. In humans, the theory of mind refers to the ability of most normal people to comprehend the thought processes (such as attention, feelings, beliefs and knowledge) of others.
c. At the age of 3, normal human children do not acknowledge the false belief as they have a difficulty in differentiating belief from the world.
d. Cognitive changes occur at the age of 5 for children to adopt the theory of mind.
e. It has been suggested that a failure to acquire a theory of mind is associated with disorders such as autism.

Question 32

Based on the DSM-5 diagnostic criteria, a patient who drinks more than what amount of caffeine is considered to be intoxicated?

a. 80 mg
b. 100 mg
c. 120 mg
d. 150 mg
e. 250 mg

Question 33

The psychological therapy that deals with traps, snags and dilemmas would be

a. Cognitive behavioural therapy
b. Cognitive analytical therapy
c. Interpersonal therapy
d. Psychodynamic psychotherapy
e. Rational emotive therapy

Question 34

There have been multiple aetiologies accounting for the development of personality disorders. In particular, which of these personality disorders has the strongest genetic relationship?

a. Schizoid personality disorder
b. Schizotypal personality disorder

c. Borderline personality disorder
d. Dependent personality disorder
e. Obsessive-compulsive personality disorder

Question 35

A 70-year-old man has a tumour in the frontal lobe. Which of the following neurological signs is most likely to be found?

a. Amusia
b. Anosmia
c. Anterograde amnesia
d. Apraxia
e. Bitemporal hemianopia

Question 36

Previous research has demonstrated that when there are more people around during an emergency, the participants are less likely to help. Which of the following best describes this?

a. Social dilemma
b. Moral dilemma
c. Bystander effect
d. Groupthink
e. Conformity to the norm

Question 37

A 25-year-old male has treatment-resistant schizophrenia and has been sectioned for inpatient hospitalization on multiple occasions. He has just been started on clozapine, but he has been complaining of a change in the tone of his upper limbs. Which of the following terminology best describes the psychopathology that he has been experiencing?

a. Cenesthesia
b. Delusional perception
c. Made feelings
d. Somatic passivity
e. Visceral hallucinations

Question 38

A 40-year-old African man is referred to you for psychiatric assessment after he attempted to attack his wife. He believes that his wife has been unfaithful to him and she is having an affair with a Caucasian man. He has been trying for 1 year to prove this belief despite her repeated denial and reassurance from friends and relatives. His attempts included following her, searching her mobile phone, confronting her and checking her clothes. Which of the following aetiological factors is least likely to be associated with his condition?

a. Alcohol dependence
b. Amphetamine misuse

c. Delusional misidentification
d. Depression
e. Paranoid schizophrenia

Question 39
Based on Bandura model of learning, all of the following are crucial steps in the modelling process, with the exception of which of the following?
a. Attention
b. Retention
c. Reproduction
d. Motivation
e. Insight

Question 40
Which of the following is not considered to be a theory of interpersonal attraction?
a. Reinforcement theory
b. Conditioning theory
c. Social exchange theory
d. Equity theory
e. Proxemics

Question 41
An examiner asks a person to move his arm in different directions and the person is unable to resist even if it is against her will. This phenomenon is known as
a. Automatic obedience
b. Gegenhalten
c. Mitmachen
d. Mitgehen
e. Waxy flexibility

Question 42
A 32-year-old female has just given birth to a baby boy 5 days ago. She has been afraid to care for her newborn, as she has been hearing voices of the devil telling her nasty things about her child. She believes that the child has been placed under a curse by the devil. Which of the following would be the most appropriate clinical diagnosis for her?
a. Postnatal depression
b. Postnatal psychosis
c. Postnatal blues
d. Depression with psychotic features
e. Schizophrenia

Question 43
A voluntary organization is attempting to recruit more volunteers to help them. They first started by asking the new volunteers to help out in a once-off charity

event. Thereafter, they started to ask the volunteers to commit more of their time in helping out the organization. Which of the following techniques best describes this?

a. Door in the face technique
b. Foot in the door technique
c. Reinforcement technique
d. Conditioning technique
e. Gradual approximation technique

Question 44

When the examiner is attempting passively to move the arm of an 80-year-old man with dementia, the examiner feels that the patient is applying the same amount of force in resisting the passive movement. This phenomenon is known as

a. Ambitendency
b. Gegenhalten
c. Mitmachen
d. Mitgehen
e. Waxy flexibility

Question 45

A medical student was asked to examine a patient and determine what pathology he has. On neurological examination, it was noted that the patient is unable to cooperate and looks downwards and laterally. He complains of double vision when attempting to do so. This is most likely due to a lesion involving

a. Second cranial nerve
b. Third cranial nerve
c. Fourth cranial nerve
d. Fifth cranial nerve
e. Sixth cranial nerve

Question 46

Aggression has been described as a behaviour intended to harm others. There are various explanations for aggressive behaviours. Which of the following is incorrect?

a. Aggression is perceived to be a learnt response, from previous observation, imitation and operant conditioning.
b. Victim suffering and material gains will reinforce subsequent aggressive behaviour.
c. The consequences of aggression usually play a role in determining future aggression.
d. Behaviours such as maintaining a distance, evoking a social response incompatible with aggression and familiarity will help to inhibit aggression.
e. Emotional arousal might or might not increase aggression.

Question 47

A 30-year-old man was brought to the Accident and Emergency Department. He suddenly fell down after hearing a loud sound at a party. There was no loss of consciousness. The psychopathology being described is

a. Catalepsy
b. Cataplexy
c. Catatonia
d. Posturing
e. Waxy flexibility

Question 48

Which of the following movement disorders is not typically associated with schizophrenia?

a. Ambitendency
b. Mannerism
c. Mitgehen and mitmachen
d. Negativism
e. Stupor

Question 49

A 50-year-old man suffers from schizophrenia and he has been taking chlorpromazine for the past 20 years. You are the consultant psychiatrist and reviewing his drug list because you are concerned of drug interaction. Which of the following drug interaction is the most significant?

a. Amitriptyline decreases the serum concentration of chlorpromazine.
b. Chlorpromazine decreases the serum concentration of amitriptyline.
c. Chlorpromazine increases the serum concentration of amitriptyline.
d. Chlorpromazine decreases the serum concentration of valproate.
e. Chlorpromazine increases the serum concentration of valproate.

Question 50

A 28-year-old female has been diagnosed with a previous psychiatric condition. Her symptoms have remitted over the past 2 years, but recently due to increased stress at work, she has been resorting to measures to cope with stress. One of the methods she has been using is to restrict her diet, in order to reduce her body mass index from the current of 20 to 15. What form of psychological therapy would be the most useful and beneficial for her?

a. Cognitive behavioural therapy
b. EDMR
c. Trauma-focused therapy
d. Dialectic behavioural therapy
e. Supportive therapy

Question 51

Which of the following aphasia resembles speech disturbances that schizophrenic patients have?

a. Intermediate aphasia
b. Expressive aphasia
c. Global aphasia
d. Jargon aphasia
e. Semantic aphasia

Question 52
Schemas help to influence the way people organize knowledge about the social world and also help them to interpret new situations. All of the following about schemas are incorrect with the exception of
a. Schemas tend to slow down the rate of mental processing.
b. Schemas are not likely to be helpful when dealing with an ambiguous situation.
c. Schemas usually require more effortful thinking.
d. Schemas tend to persist even after evidence for the schema has been discredited.
e. Schemas play a part in maintaining prejudice.

Question 53
A 40-year-old man with schizophrenia is admitted to the psychiatric ward. The nurse informs you that he always protrudes his lips, which resemble a snout. The psychopathology being described is
a. Ambitendency
b. Gegenhalten
c. Pout
d. Rooting
e. Schnauzkrampf

Question 54
A 30-year-old male, Thomas, was at his father's funeral, helping to carry his father's coffin when he developed an acute onset of bilateral blindness. The medical team doctors have seen him, and they have found nothing medically wrong. He has also been seen by the on-call psychiatrist, to which he reports feeling indifferent to the blindness. What is the most likely clinical diagnosis?
a. Somatoform disorder
b. Conversion disorder
c. Body dysmorphic disorder
d. Generalized anxiety disorder
e. Malingering

Question 55
All of the following are known clinical features of Wernicke's encephalopathy, with the exception of
a. Ophthalmoplegia
b. Nystagmus
c. Hypothermia

d. Ataxia
e. Clouding of consciousness

Question 56

Which of the following correctly describes fundamental attribution error?

a. Attributing others mistakes to the context in which the mistakes occur
b. Attributing one's own mistakes to one's character and personality
c. Refusing to accept one's own errors
d. Denying the fundamental flaws behind one's own negative behaviour
e. Attributing others' mistakes to their personal dispositions

Question 57

A 60-year-old man suffers from prostate cancer and was admitted to the hospital for chemotherapy. He developed nausea and vomiting after chemotherapy. Whenever he sees the hospital building, he feels nauseated. He has completed chemotherapy and is not required to return to the hospital. The nausea feeling disappears. The disappearance of nausea feeling is known as

a. Discrimination
b. Extinction
c. Generalization
d. Inhibition
e. Recovery

Question 58

A 60-year-old man suffers from prostate cancer and he was admitted to the hospital for chemotherapy. He developed nausea and vomiting after chemotherapy. Two months later, he feels nausea when he sees the hospital building. The nausea feeling associated with the hospital building is known as

a. Conditioned response
b. Conditioned stimulus
c. Unconditioned response
d. Unconditioned stimulus
e. Second order conditioning

Question 59

A 35-year-old man sets a daily alarm on his mobile phone to remind him to take his medication, Drug A. He constantly experiences side effects whenever he takes Drug A, which includes nausea. After some time, when he hears a similar alarm from his alarm clock, he also experiences nausea. This phenomenon is known as

a. Discrimination
b. Extinction
c. Generalization
d. Inhibition
e. Recovery

Question 60

A 25-year-old woman meets the diagnostic criteria for schizophrenia and exhibits first-rank symptoms. First-rank symptoms include the following except

a. Delusional perception
b. Delusion of passivity
c. Delusion of persecution
d. Thought insertion
e. Thought withdrawal

Question 61

A 65-year-old woman with a history of depression presents with bilateral ptosis. Which of the following condition is least likely?

a. Levator palpebrae muscle paralysis
b. Myasthenia gravis
c. Myotonic dystrophy
d. Ocular dystrophy
e. Guillain–Barre syndrome

Question 62

Which of the following is not true about fundamental attribution error?

a. Seen in adults in western societies
b. Primarily an attribution error
c. Overestimation of personal factors
d. Bias towards attributing a behaviour to situational causes
e. Overestimation of dispositional factors

Question 63

A public health official wants to consult you on the use of APOE alleles as a screening test to identify individuals with a high chance to develop Alzheimer's disease and offer early intervention. Which of the following is true about APOE screening test?

a. Low positive predictive value; low negative predictive value; low sensitivity and low specificity
b. Low positive predictive value; high negative predictive value; low sensitivity and low specificity
c. Low positive predictive value; high negative predictive value; high sensitivity and low specificity
d. Low positive predictive value; high negative predictive value; high sensitivity and high specificity
e. High positive predictive value; high negative predictive value; high sensitivity and high specificity

Question 64

A medical student attached to the Consultation–Liaison team asked the consultant psychiatrist which of the following would be the earliest and most reliable sign to differentiate between dementia and delirium. The correct answer would be

a. Presence of focal neurological signs on clinical examination
b. Presence of short-term memory deficits

c. Presence of long-term memory deficits
d. Presence of hallucinations
e. Presence of altered consciousness

Question 65
Which of the following is the best way to prevent dementia?
a. Offer genetic testing to older adults
b. Prescribe oestrogen to older women
c. Prescribe nonsteroidal anti-inflammatory drugs
d. Supplement with vitamin E
e. Treat systolic hypertension (>160 mm Hg) in older people (age >60 years)

Question 66
The consultant psychiatrist shows his medical students a video on interviewing a schizophrenic patient, and mentions to them that the patient in the video has the full set of all the first-rank symptoms. Which of the following should the consultant psychiatrist clarify with the students and tell them that it is not considered as a first-rank symptom?
a. Thought insertion
b. Thought block
c. Thought broadcast
d. Thought withdrawal
e. Auditory hallucinations

Question 67
Peri-trauma factors that predispose and cause an individual to develop post-traumatic stress disorder (PTSD) include all the following except
a. Being female in sex
b. Perceived lack of social support during the trauma
c. Perceived threat to life
d. Peri-trauma dissociation
e. Severity of the trauma

Question 68
Which of the following best defines social psychology?
a. The scientific study of the way in which people's thoughts, feelings and behaviours are influenced by the real, imagined or implied presence of other people
b. The scientific study of how people's behaviours, thoughts and feelings are influenced by the social environment
c. The scientific study of how people's behaviours, thoughts and feelings are influenced by society
d. The scientific study of behaviour and mental processes
e. The scientific study of how behaviours are influenced by mental processes

Question 69

A 30-year-old woman is referred by her dermatologist to see you. She complains of pruritus as a result of an infestation with parasites. She shows you her debris contained in plastic wrap and claims that it contains the parasites. The patient is most likely suffering from

a. Capgras syndrome
b. Cotard syndrome
c. De Clerambault's syndrome
d. Ekbom syndrome
e. Fregoli syndrome

Question 70

A 35-year-old man sets a daily alarm on his mobile phone to remind him to take his medication, Drug A. He constantly experiences side effects whenever he takes Drug A, which includes nausea. After some time, when he hears a similar alarm from his alarm clock, he also experiences nausea. However, this phenomenon disappears after a few days. This phenomenon is known as

a. Discrimination
b. Extinction
c. Generalization
d. Inhibition
e. Recovery

Question 71

A 35-year-old man sets a daily alarm on his mobile phone to remind him to take his medication, Drug A. He constantly experiences side effects whenever he takes Drug A, which includes nausea. After changing his medication to Drug B, he stops experiencing nausea. However, after a few days, he again starts to feel nauseated when he hears his mobile phone alarm. This phenomenon is known as

a. Discrimination
b. Extinction
c. Generalization
d. Inhibition
e. Recovery

Question 72

A 50-year-old man has a lesion in the left occipital lobe. Which of the following sign is most likely to be found?

a. Dyslexia without agraphia
b. Homonymous hemianopia
c. Left eye papilloedema
d. Loss of pupillary reflex
e. Quadrantanopia

Question 73
Which of the following trails or tests led to public outrage and request from Queen Victoria to clarify the legal standard in the 1840s?
  a. Bifurcated trial
  b. First right versus wrong test
  c. Daniel M'Naghten trial
  d. The irresistible impulse test
  e. Wild beast test

Question 74
A 25-year-old male presented to the mental health services as he has been feeling low for the past 2 months. The low mood is associated with diminished interests, feelings that life is not worth going on and biological symptoms such as poor sleep and appetite. Which of the following descriptors best describes the severity of his underlying depression?
  a. No depression
  b. Mild
  c. Moderate
  d. Severe
  e. Prolonged

Question 75
A 38-year-old father is diagnosed with schizophrenia. His wife does not have any psychiatric illness. He wants to know the risk of his son developing the disorder. Your answer is
  a. 5%
  b. 10%
  c. 15%
  d. 20%
  e. 25%

Question 76
A 55-year-old male is extremely upset that his son has been sectioned for admission for psychosis. He knows that it might be due to the drugs – cannabis which his son has been using. Cannabis is known to increase the incidences of psychosis by approximately how much percent?
  a. No increased risk
  b. Two times increased risk
  c. Three times increased risk
  d. Four times increased risk
  e. Six times increased risk

Question 77
A 40-year-old female Sally is concerned whether her brother who has Down's syndrome would develop psychosis. Based on the current research evidence, the risk of her brother developing schizophrenia has been estimated to be

a. Two percent increased risk.
b. Four percent increased risk.
c. Six percent increased risk.
d. The same as the normal population.
e. There has been found to be an association, but there is no strong evidence to support the estimated increment in risk.

Question 78

A 6-year-old girl has a fear of injections but requires frequent injections. She has to consult with a doctor before getting her injection. She recognizes her doctor by his white coat. After her consultation with the doctor, she has to wait for her turn in the waiting area before proceeding to another room for her injection. Soon, whenever she sees a doctor's white coat, she reports feeling scared and anxious. This phenomenon is known as

a. Backward conditioning
b. Delayed conditioning
c. Simultaneous conditioning
d. Temporal conditioning
e. Trace conditioning

Question 79

The term 'schizoaffective psychosis' was introduced by Kasanin in which of the following decades?

a. 1910s
b. 1920s
c. 1930s
d. 1940s
e. 1950s

Question 80

Based on the Driver and Vehicle Licensing Agency (DVLA) guidelines in the UK, how long must a bipolar patient be stable and well before being allowed to drive again?

a. 2 weeks
b. 1 month
c. 3 months
d. 6 months
e. 1 year

Question 81

The relative risk of developing Alzheimer's disease in a 55-year-old patient with Down's syndrome has been estimated to be

a. 10%–15%
b. 20%–25%
c. 35%–40%
d. 45%–50%
e. More than 50%

Question 82

Deinstitutionalization peaked in the 1970s. Which of the following statements is not associated with deinstitutionalization?

a. Availability of antipsychotic medications.
b. People with mental illnesses are not at a higher risk of offending compared to general population.
c. Increase in awareness of civil rights of people with mental illnesses.
d. Increase in costs of institutionalization care.
e. Reduction in availability of hospital beds.

Question 83

An 8-year-old girl has a phobia of spiders. When she is presented with a spider, it elicits high levels of fear and anxiety. The experimenter plays a ringing sound at the same time and for the duration of the presentation of the spider. The experimenter is hoping to elicit similar feelings of fear and anxiety when the girl hears the ringing sound without the presentation of the spider. This phenomenon is known as

a. Backward conditioning
b. Delayed conditioning
c. Simultaneous conditioning
d. Temporal conditioning
e. Trace conditioning

Question 84

Based on your understanding about the history of schizophrenia, the concept that schizophrenia developed from a split mind was proposed by

a. Bleuler
b. Kraeplin
c. Morel
d. Hecker
e. Kahlbarum

Question 85

Schizoaffective disorder was a disorder introduced by the following individual:

a. Hecker
b. Sommer
c. Kurt Schneider
d. Kasanin
e. Cooper

Question 86

Which of the following statements is false with regards to the consequentialist approach?

a. An action is moral if it makes the greatest number of people happy.
b. Different treatment options can be measured by foreseeable consequences such as quality-adjusted life years (QALYs).

c. In managed mental health care, the consequentialist approach may lead to discrimination of individual patients and moral dilemmas owing to factual uncertainties.
d. It is based on an obligation of fidelity (including a pledge for confidentiality), deontological theory and virtue ethics.
e. Under the consequentialist approach, confidentiality is an absolute condition in psychiatric practice.

Question 87

You are assigned to provide tutorial to four medical students. Each student needs to write a case report for a psychiatric patient. One student is confused about the meaning of mental state examination (MSE). Which of the following statements is true?

a. The Mini Mental State Examination (MMSE) is a shorter version of the Mental State Examination.
b. MSE provides important information in establishing a psychiatric diagnosis.
c. MSE should be conducted after history taking.
d. The student does not need to report any physical finding because MSE has replaced physical examination in psychiatry.
e. When there is a discrepancy between information from the history and findings at the MSE, the student should establish the diagnosis based on the information from the history.

Question 88

You are interviewing a woman who was diagnosed with schizophrenia. You think that she may suffer from other psychiatric disorders as her first-rank symptoms are inconsistent. Which of the following features is not typically associated with schizophrenia?

a. Catatonia
b. Delusional perception
c. Emotional liability
d. Passivity
e. Negativism

Question 89

A 50-year-old man with chronic schizophrenia says, 'The community psychiatric nurse syringerisperidone me fortnightly'. This psychopathology is known as

a. Asyndesis
b. Cryptolalia
c. Metonym
d. Neologism
e. Vorbeigehen

Question 90

Based on the ICD-10 diagnostic and classification criteria, the diagnosis of delusional disorder could be made only if the symptoms have lasted for at least the past

a. 1 week
b. 1 month

c. 3 months
d. 6 months
e. 1 year

Question 91

Which of the following statements about the genetics of AN is correct?

a. Heritability of AN is around 50%.
b. Less than 5% of first-degree relatives are usually affected.
c. Linkage genes on chromosome 3 have been found.
d. The ratio for monozygotic (MZ) to dizygotic (DZ) concordance is around 56:5.
e. Research has found the concordance rates for monozygotic twins to be the same as that for dizygotic twins.

Question 92

The mother of a 21-year-old male, who has just been diagnosed with OCD, wonders which of the following compulsions is the most common amongst adults. Which of the following is true?

a. Checking
b. Counting
c. Doubting
d. Symmetry
e. Washing

Question 93

A 45-year-old female has been dependent on medications to help her with her anxiety condition. Recently, her psychiatrist removed one of the chronic medications that she used to be taking. This has resulted in the following withdrawal symptoms: autonomic hyperactivity, malaise and weakness, tinnitus and grand mal convulsions. Which of the following is the most likely clinical diagnosis for her?

a. Neuroleptic malignant syndrome
b. Serotonin syndrome
c. Serotonin discontinuation syndrome
d. Benzodiazepine withdrawal syndrome
e. Organic causes

Question 94

The Folstein's MMSE includes all of the following items except

a. Drawing an intersecting pentagon
b. Drawing the face of a clock, indicating 10 past 11
c. Orientation to time, place and person
d. Serial subtraction or spelling 'WORLD' backwards
e. Three-stage command

Question 95

A Greenland Inuit woman suddenly strips off her clothes and rolls in the snow followed by echolalia and echopraxia. She has no recollection of the episode afterwards. This woman suffers from which of the following culture-bound syndromes?

a. Amok
b. Latah
c. Pibloktoq
d. Uqamairineq
e. Windigo

Question 96

What was the implication of Tarasoff I (1974)?

a. Duty to assess
b. Duty to protect
c. Duty to respect
d. Duty to treat
e. Duty to warn

Question 97

What was the implication of Tarasoff II (1976)?

a. Duty to assess
b. Duty to protect
c. Duty to respect
d. Duty to treat
e. Duty to warn

Question 98

An Inuit living in the Arctic Circle complains of sudden paralysis when he slept. He recalls that he was very agitated during the paralysis. The day before the attack, he could hear transient and unusual sound in his neighbourhood. He attributes the unusual experience to spirit possession. This man suffers from which of the following culture-bound syndromes?

a. Amok
b. Latah
c. Pibloktoq
d. Uqamairineq
e. Windigo

Question 99

A 6-year-old boy has phobia of snakes. When he is presented with a snake, it elicits high levels of fear and anxiety. The experimenter plays a ringing sound after the presentation of the snake. The experimenter is hoping to elicit similar feelings of fear and anxiety when the boy hears the ringing sound without the presentation of the snake. This phenomenon is known as

a. Backward conditioning
b. Delayed conditioning
c. Simultaneous conditioning

d. Temporal conditioning
e. Trace conditioning

Question 100
Which of the following is not a feature of pseudobulbar palsy?
a. Donald Duck speech
b. Emotional incontinence
c. Normal jaw jerk
d. Spastic tongue
e. Upper motor neuron lesions as a result of bilateral lesions above the mid-pons

Question 101
Which of the following statements regarding Montreal Cognitive Assessment (MoCA) is correct?
a. A score of 21 or above is considered normal.
b. MoCA has lower sensitivity compared to the MMSE in identifying mild cognitive impairment.
c. MoCA is available in English and French only.
d. The short-term memory recall task involves two learning trials of ten nouns and delayed recall after approximately 20 minutes.
e. Visuospatial abilities are assessed using a clock-drawing task and a three-dimensional cube copy.

Question 102
A 20-year-old African university student has been preparing for a pharmacology examination and presents with a burning headache, blurred vision, difficulty in understanding the meaning of the textbook and an inability to remember the drugs he studied. This man suffers from which of the following culture-bound syndromes?
a. Amok
b. Brain fag
c. Dhat
d. Koro
e. Latah

Question 103
The most common defence mechanism seen in paranoid personality disorder is
a. Denial
b. Projection
c. Reaction formation
d. Sublimation
e. Undoing

Question 104
The case *Tarasoff v. Regents of the University of California* is related to which of the following ethical principles:

a. Autonomy
b. Capacity
c. Confidentiality
d. Consent
e. Equality

Question 105

A 20-year-old Chinese national serviceman in Singapore is referred by the army doctor. He complains that his penis is getting shorter and that it will continue to retract into his abdomen. He measures his penis every day and he cannot concentrate on his work. This man suffers from which of the following culture-bound syndromes?

a. Amok
b. Brain fag
c. Dhat
d. Koro
e. Latah

Question 106

A 22-year-old female has had a previous episode of depression 2 years ago. Currently, she presents to the mental health service with hypomania. Which one of the following clinical diagnosis would you label her with?

a. Bipolar disorder type I
b. Bipolar disorder type II
c. Bipolar disorder type III
d. Rapid cycling bipolar disorder
e. Cyclothymia

Question 107

A core trainee wants to know more about the Addenbrooke's Cognitive Examination—Revised (ACE-R). Which of the following statements is correct?

a. The ACE-R does not incorporate MMSE.
b. The ACE-R is available in Cantonese for Hong Kong patients.
c. The cut-off score gives rise to high sensitivity and 100% specificity for diagnosing dementia.
d. The cut-off score gives rise to high specificity and 100% sensitivity for diagnosing dementia.
e. It is a cognitive test commonly used for screening delirium.

Question 108

A 50-year-old woman was admitted to the ward and the nurses are having difficulty with her. She appears to be arrogant, refuses to follow ward rules and insists to drink alcohol in the ward. She believes that she is a 'special' patient and requests first-class treatment. Her husband mentions that she tends to exploit others and that most people try to avoid her. Which defence mechanism is the least commonly used by people with such a disorder?

a. Denial
b. Distortion
c. Projection
d. Rationalization
e. Suppression

Question 109

A 60-year-old man suffers from prostate cancer and was admitted to the hospital for chemotherapy. He developed nausea and vomiting after chemotherapy. Whenever he sees the hospital building, he feels nausea. Today he needs to see an oncologist in the clinic. When he sees the doctor's white coat, he feels nausea. The nausea feeling associated with white coat is known as

a. Conditioned response
b. Conditioned stimulus
c. Unconditioned response
d. Unconditioned stimulus
e. Second order conditioning

Question 110

Based on the ACE-R scale, which of the following cut-off scores is the most specific?

a. 80
b. 82
c. 84
d. 86
e. 88

Question 111

A 43-year-old man is angry at being caught speeding by the traffic police. He goes home and yells at his wife and children. Which of the following defence mechanisms best describes the aforementioned phenomenon?

a. Denial
b. Reaction formation
c. Displacement
d. Projection
e. Sublimation

Question 112

Based on previous research studies, it has been demonstrated that patients with schizophrenia would relapse if they were discharged back to their families with high expressed emotions for more than

a. 20 hours per week
b. 23 hours per week
c. 30 hours per week

d. 33 hours per week
e. 50 hours per week

Question 113
The anatomical correlate of this form of memory is either in the visual association cortex or in the auditory association cortex. Which of the following terminologies best describes this form of memory?
a. Declarative memory
b. Episodic memory
c. Implicit memory
d. Sensory memory
e. Short-term memory

Question 114
A 50-year-old businessman was killed in a road traffic accident when he crossed the road. His son turns his anger and plans to take revenge on the negligent driver into the energy of taking over his father's business. Which of the following defence mechanisms best describes the aforementioned phenomenon?
a. Denial
b. Reaction formation
c. Displacement
d. Projection
e. Sublimation

Question 115
A 5-year-old girl is scared of monkeys. When she goes to the zoo, she behaves aggressively on seeing a monkey, as if she is about to attack the monkey. Which of the following defence mechanisms best describes the aforementioned phenomenon?
a. Denial
b. Reaction formation
c. Displacement
d. Projection
e. Sublimation

Question 116
You are seeing a 60-year-old woman who is referred by her GP for depression. She complains of 6-month history of worsening progressive dysphagia and there has been no improvement. Her husband confirms her history. This patient is most likely suffering from
a. Cerebrovascular accident
b. Moderate depressive episode with somatic complaints
c. Myasthenia gravis
d. Motor neuron disease
e. Hypochondriasis

Question 117
When a 25-year old female was asked to describe her premorbid personality, she claimed that she is someone who always finds it tough to make decision. Which particular personality disorder is she likely to have?
a. Schizoid personality disorder
b. Schizotypal personality disorder
c. Borderline personality disorder
d. Dependent personality disorder
e. OCD

Question 118
Patients with catatonia tend to present with the following symptoms, with the exception of
a. Ambitendency
b. Echopraxia
c. Specific mannerisms
d. Echopraxia
e. De-personalization

Extended matching items (EMIs)

Theme: Cognitive testing

Lead in: Please select the most appropriate answer for each one of the following. Each option may be used once, more than once or not at all.

Options:
a. Mini Mental State Examination
b. Cambridge Neuropsychological Test Automated Battery
c. Blessed Dementia Scale
d. Geriatric Mental State Schedule
e. Clifton Assessment Schedule
f. Vineland Social Maturity Scale

Question 119
This is a test which could be used for the assessment of dementia as well as in the assessment of childhood development and learning disability.

Question 120
This is a nursing rated assessment scale.

Question 121
This is a questionnaire that is usually administered to a relative or friend of the patient.

Question 122
This is a semi-structured interview that assesses the subject's mental state.

Question 123
This is a questionnaire that consists of 13 computerized tasks.

Question 124
This is a brief test that could be used to rapidly detect possible dementia, to follow up on the course of cognitive changes over time and to differentiate between delirium and dementia.

Theme: Executive function tests

Lead in: Please select the most appropriate answer for each one of the following. Each option may be used once, more than once or not at all.

Options:

a. Stroop Test
b. Verbal fluency test
c. Tower of London Test
d. Wisconsin Card Sort Test
e. Cognitive Estimates Test
f. Six elements test
g. Multiple errands task
h. Trail making test

Question 125
Some frontal lobe damaged patients may occasionally give grossly incorrect answers to known phenomena.

Question 126
This is a strategy application test that helps to uncover evidence of organization difficulty that might have occurred as a result of frontal lobe damage.

Question 127
The following abilities are tested in this test: sequencing, cognitive flexibility, visual scanning, spatial analysis, motor control, alertness and concentration.

Question 128
This is a test that helps to pick up perseverative errors.

Question 129
Left frontal lobe lesions are usually associated with poor performance on this particular test that tests for planning ability.

Question 130
This is a test that involves asking the subject to articulate as many words as possible over a fixed duration of time.

Question 131
This is a test that tests the interference that may occur between reading words and naming colours.

Theme: Clinical interview

Options:

a. Acting-out
b. Ambivalence
c. Anger
d. Disinhibition
e. Dysphoric mood
f. Euphoric mood
g. Failure of empathy
h. Fatuousness
i. Flat affect
j. Good rapport
k. Guardedness
l. Humour
m. Humiliation
n. Incongruous affect
o. Labile affect
p. Resistance
q. Restricted affective range

Lead in: A 30-year-old woman was admitted to the neurosurgical ward after she was hit on her head after a fight in the pub. The neurosurgeon refers her for psychiatric assessment. When a male trainee interviews her, she exhibits the following phenomenon. Identify which of the aforementioned terminology resembles her clinical presentation. Each option might be used once, more than once or not at all.

Question 132
She copes with her memory impairment by making jokes. (Choose one option.)

Question 133
She laughs and jokes with the trainee. Then she suddenly bursts into tears and asks for forgiveness. (Choose one option.)

Question 134
When a male trainee interviews her, she touches his inner thigh and wants to take off her blouse. (Choose one option.)

Theme: Basic psychology

Options:

a. Context-dependent forgetting
b. Cue-dependent forgetting
c. Decay theory
d. Displacement theory
e. Motivated forgetting
f. Proactive interference
g. Retrieval failure
h. Retroactive interference

i. State-dependent forgetting
j. Storage failure

Lead in: Identify which of the above terms best explains the following scenarios. Each option might be used once, more than once or not at all.

Question 135
A patient is busy sending a SMS message while the psychiatrist is talking to him. When the psychiatrist asks the patient to recall what he has just said, the patient cannot recall. (Choose one option.)

Question 136
A 50-year-old man hears a gunshot when he is walking in a city centre park. He suddenly remembers a long forgotten memory of witnessing an armed robbery. (Choose one option.)

Question 137
A 25-year-old woman from Canada visits her brother who lives in the UK. When she is about to get in his car, she always finds herself getting into the driver side despite multiple reminders from her brother. (Choose one option.)

Theme: Classification systems

Options:

a. ICD-6
b. ICD-11
c. DSM-1
d. DSM-II
e. DSM-III
f. DSM-III-R
g. DSM-IV

Lead in: Select the most appropriate answer for each of the following. Each option may be used once, more than once or not at all.

Question 138
This was a classification system developed and based upon the mental disorders section of ICD-6.

Question 139
This was considered to be an innovative psychiatric classification system that tried not to appear to favour any theories and included the multi-axial classification.

Question 140
Revisions were done and this was published in 1987.

Theme: Learning theories and behavioural change

Options:

a. Positive reinforcer
b. Negative reinforcer

c. Punishment
d. Primary reinforcement
e. Secondary reinforcement
f. Continuous reinforcement
g. Fixed interval schedule
h. Variable interval schedule
i. Fixed ratio schedule
j. Variable ratio schedule

Lead in: Select the most appropriate answer for each of the following. Each option may be used once, more than once or not at all.

Question 141
Escape conditioning is an example of this.

Question 142
This refers to a situation in which an aversive stimulus is presented whenever a given behaviour occurs.

Question 143
This refers to reinforcement that is occurring through reduction of needs driving from basic drives.

Question 144
This refers to reinforcement that is derived from association with primary reinforcers.

Question 145
In this particular schedule of reinforcement, reinforcement occurs only after a fixed interval of time.

Question 146
In this particular schedule of reinforcement, reinforcement occurs only after variable intervals.

Question 147
This particular schedule of reinforcement is generally considered to be good with regards to maintaining a high response rate.

Theme: Attachment abnormalities

Options:

a. Insecure attachment
b. Avoidant attachment
c. Separation anxiety
d. Acute separation reaction
e. Stranger anxiety
f. Maternal deprivation

Lead in: Select the most appropriate answer for each of the following. Each option may be used once, more than once or not at all.

Question 148
This form of attachment would predispose individuals towards childhood emotional disorders and disorders such as agoraphobia.

Question 149
This form of attachment would predispose individuals towards poor social functioning in later life, which might include aggression.

Question 150
As a result of this, an infant may hold a comfort object or a transitional object.

Question 151
Developmental language delay, shallow relationships and lack of empathy might arise due to this.

Theme: Clinical assessment and neuropsychological processes

Options:

a. Lexical dysgraphia
b. Deep dysgraphia
c. Neglect dysgraphia
d. Dyspraxic dysgraphia
e. Alexia without agraphia
f. Alexia with agraphia

Lead in: Select the most appropriate answer for each of the following. Each option may be used once, more than once or not at all.

Question 152
A patient breaks down the word's spelling and has much difficulty in writing irregular words. This is an example of

Question 153
A patient is unable to spell non-existent words. This is an example of

Question 154
A patient tends to misspell the initial part of words. This is an example of

Question 155
Three months after suffering a stroke, a patient develops a new technique to help himself recognize words. He reads letter by letter and spells the word out loud. Then he recognizes the word after hearing himself spell it out. This is an example of

Theme: Psychology

Options:

a. Aversive conditioning
b. Chaining
c. Flooding

d. Habituation
e. Insight learning
f. Latent learning
g. Penalty
h. Premack's principle
i. Reciprocal inhibition
j. Shaping
k. Systematic desensitization
l. Token economy

Lead in: Select the aforementioned behavioural techniques to match the following examples. Each option might be used once, more than once or not at all.

Question 156
The staff of a hostel for learning disability patients wants to train her clients to clean up the tables after meals. She develops a successive reinforcing schedule to reward her clients. The clients will be rewarded successively over time for putting their utensils away from the dining table back to the pantry. Then they need to clean the utensils and put them back to the cupboard. (Choose one option.)

Question 157
A 2-year-old son of a woman is scared of dogs. His mother tries to reduce his fear by bringing him to see the dogs in the park. The fear-provoking situation is coupled and opposed by putting him on her lap and allowing him to drink his favourite juice. (Choose one option.)

Question 158
A 40-year-old woman staying in London develops fear of the tube and she sees a psychologist for psychotherapy. The psychologist has drafted a behavioural programme where the patient is advised to start with travelling between two tube stations with her husband and gradually increase to more stations without her husband. At the end of the hierarchy, she will travel from the Heathrow terminal station to the Cockfosters Station along the Piccadilly line. (Choose one option.)

Question 159
A 40-year-old woman staying in London develops fear of the tube. She is instructed to start with the most fearful situation by taking a train from the Heathrow terminal station to the Cockfosters Station along the Piccadilly line on her own. (Choose one option.)

Question 160
An 11-year-old girl is referred to the Child and Adolescent Mental Health Service (CAMHS) as she refuses to do her homework. She prefers to stay in her room and plays piano for the whole day. The team has advised the parents to adopt the following plan: The girl is allowed to play her piano for 30 minutes only after spending 1 hour on her homework. (Choose one option.)

Question 161
A 9-year-old girl is referred to the CAMHS as she refuses to do her homework. The case manager advises the mother to reward her child with a sticker every time she has completed her homework. Once she gets 20 stickers, she can use them to exchange for a present. (Choose one option.)

Question 162
In the prison, the psychologists have developed an *in vivo* exposure programme for the prisoners to expose themselves to the images of being arrested and other social sanctions on their criminal behaviour. Some prisoners find that their urge to commit crime reduces after repeated exposures. (Choose one option.)

Theme: Psychology

Options:

a. Aversive conditioning
b. Chaining
c. Flooding
d. Habituation
e. Insight learning
f. Latent learning
g. Penalty
h. Premack's principle
i. Reciprocal inhibition
j. Shaping
k. Systematic desensitization
l. Token economy

Lead in: Select the above behavioural techniques to match the following examples. Each option might be used once, more than once or not at all.

Question 163
A 6-year-old boy is put in a maze to look for the toy box. After a few trials, he learns the cognitive map of the maze and getting shorter time to find the toy box. (Choose one option.)

Question 164
A 2-year-old child is undergoing toilet training. The complex behaviour is broken down into simpler steps. She is rewarded with a sticker if she informs her mother of her urge to urinate. The positive reinforcement continues until she can inform her mother reliably without failures. Then the contingencies are altered and she needs to go to the toilet on her own before the sticker is given. (Choose one option.)

Question 165
A patient with moderate learning disability has aggressive tendency and tends to assault the other residents in the hostel. The staff has devised a plan in response to his aggressive behaviour. His main pleasurable activity is watching television. He

will be removed from the TV room and put in a single room for a 2-hour time-out period if he assaults any resident. (Choose one option.)

Question 166
A 14-year-old anorexia nervosa patient with body mass index (BMI) of 11 was admitted to the eating disorder unit for inpatient treatment. Initially, she was hostile to the staff and resistant to feeding. She did not like the ward environment. She has decided to comply with the treatment programme. She also wants to reach the target weight as soon as possible as she wants to get out of the ward. (Choose one option.)

Question 167
A 10-year-old boy was taught by his parents not to respond to the TV sound when he is doing homework as the stimulus is not significant. (Choose one option.)

Question 168
A 20-year-old man was sacked by his company. His partner had criticized him. He suddenly realized that he had been lazy and irresponsible. He decided to change and wanted to demonstrate his competency to his partner. The next day, he went to the career centre to look for a job. (Choose one option.)

Theme: History of psychiatry

Options:

a. Bleuler
b. Kahlbaum
c. Kasanin
d. Kraepelin
e. Langfeldt
f. Leonard
g. Hecker
h. Griesinger
i. Kane
j. Andreasson
k. Crow
l. Liddle
m. Mayer–Gross
n. Kendler

Lead in: Select one person who is associated with each the following terms.

Question 169
Catatonia. (Choose one option.)

Question 170
Cycloid psychosis. (Choose one option.)

Question 171
Dementia praecox. (Choose one option.)

Question 172
Hebephrenia. (Choose one option.)

Question 173
Schizophrenia. (Choose one option.)

Question 174
Schizoaffective disorder. (Choose one option.)

Theme: General adult psychiatry

Options:

a. 0%–4%
b. 5%–9%
c. 10%–14%
d. 15%–19%
e. 20%–24%
f. 25%–29%
g. 30%–34%
h. 35%–50%
i. 60%–65%
j. 70%–75%
k. 80%–85%

Lead in: A 28-year-old man has suffered from schizophrenia for 5 years. He is currently stable and recently got married. He and his wife are planning to have children. He consults you on the genetic risk on schizophrenia.

Each option might be used once, more than once, or not at all.

Question 175
The risk of schizophrenia in his child if his wife also suffers from schizophrenia. (Choose one option.)

Question 176
The risk of schizophrenia in his child if his wife does not suffer from schizophrenia. (Choose one option.)

Question 177
The risk of schizophrenia if he adopted a child with velocardiofacial syndrome. (Choose one option.)

Question 178
The risk of schizophrenia in his half siblings. (Choose one option.)

Question 179

The risk of schizophrenia in his younger cousin. (Choose one option.)

Theme: Basic pharmacolog

Options:

a. 1
b. 2
c. 5
d. 15
e. 25
f. 35
g. 45
h. 55
i. 65
j. 75

Lead in: A 17-year-old man was referred to the early psychosis team for the first episode of schizophrenia. You gave him risperidone 1 mg nocte. His mother requests an answer from you on the following questions. Each option might be used once, more than once or not at all.

Question 180

His psychotic symptoms are not controlled. His mother wants to know the minimum effective dose (in mg) of risperidone in his case. (Choose one option.)

Question 181

His psychotic symptoms are under control. His mother wants to know the duration of antipsychotic treatment (in months) in his case. (Choose one option.)

Question 182

After 18 months of treatment, the patient has decided to stop the medication. His mother wants to know the risk of relapse in percentage. (Choose one option.)

EMI on aetiology

a. Apolipoprotein E4 gene (homozygous for ε4)
b. Cardiovascular disease
c. Cancer
d. Childhood sexual abuse
e. Death of mother before the age of 11 years
f. Down syndrome
g. Dysbindin gene
h. Migration
i. Neuregulin gene
j. Old age

k. Streptococcal infection
l. Three children at home under the age of 14 years
m. Unemployment

Lead in: Match the aforementioned aetiological factors to the following clinical scenarios. Each option may be used once, more than once or not at all.

Question 183
A 10-year-old boy develops obsessions and compulsive behaviour after a sore throat and fever. (Choose one option.)

Question 184
A 19-year-old woman presents with recurrent self-harm following the end of a transient and intense romantic relationship. She has a chronic feeling of emptiness and exhibits binge eating behaviour. (Choose one option.)

Question 185
A 24-year-old man complains that MI5 is monitoring him and has tried to control his feelings and intentions. He heard the voices of two secret agents talking about him and they issued him with a command. (Choose three options.)

MRCPSYCH PAPER A1 MOCK EXAMINATION 2: ANSWERS

GET THROUGH MRCPSYCH PAPER A1: MOCK EXAMINATION

Question 1 Answer: a, Palilalia
Explanation: This is known as palilalia, which means that a patient repeats a word with increasing frequency. It is important to differentiate this with logoclonia, which occurs when the person repeats just the last syllable of the last word. Both of these terms are examples of preservation of speech. In perseveration, mental operations are continued beyond the point at which they are relevant.

Reference: Puri BK, Hall A, Ho R (2014). *Revision Notes in Psychiatry*. London: CRC Press, p. 4.

Question 2 Answer: e, Reciprocal inhibition
Explanation: Reciprocal inhibition is a technique used in systematic desensitization, where the antagonistic response to anxiety (i.e. relaxation) is maintained when the feared stimulus is presented.

Reference and Further Reading: Puri BK, Treasaden I (eds) (2010). *Psychiatry: An Evidence-Based Text*. London: Hodder Arnold, pp. 655, 990.

Question 3 Answer: d, Phenobarbital sodium
Explanation: This question is asking which of the aforementioned psychotropic drugs is hygroscopic. A hygroscopic drug is one which attracts moisture from the atmosphere. Phenobarbital sodium is hygroscopic. Even in the absence of light, phenobarbital sodium is gradually degraded on exposure to a humid atmosphere. The other psychotropic medications are coated and they are very stable compounds because no degradation is observed by the action of heat and light.

Reference: Church C, Smith J (2006). How stable are medicines moved from original packs into compliance aids? *Pharmaceutical Journal*, 276: 75–81.

Question 4 Answer: d, Transsexualism
Explanation: The clinical diagnosis is that of transsexualism. In this condition, there is the desire to live as a member of the opposite sex, with marked discomfort

with one's own anatomic sex and with an intense desire to change the body into that of the preferred sex. It is important to differentiate this from transvestism, which refers to the wearing of the clothes of the opposite sex to obtain sexual excitement. More than a single item is worn, often an entire outfit. It is clearly associated with sexual arousal; there is no wish to continue cross-dressing once orgasm occurs, distinguishing this from dual-role transvestism.

Reference: Puri BK, Hall A, Ho R (2014). *Revision Notes in Psychiatry.* London: CRC Press, p. 603.

Question 5 Answer: d, Medial temporal lobe lesions and complex partial seizure
Explanation: Seizures are associated with medial temporal lobe lesions, and complex partial seizures are known as uncinate seizures which can give rise to olfactory hallucinations.

Reference and Further Reading: Cummings JL, Mega MS (eds) (2003). *Neuropsychiatry and Behavioural Neuroscience.* New York: Oxford University Press; Puri BK, Treasaden I (eds) (2010). *Psychiatry: An Evidence-Based Text.* London: Hodder Arnold, p. 532.

Question 6 Answer: c, Blood injection phobia
Explanation: The blood injection phobia (usually associated with needles, injections, medical procedures) has a strong underlying genetic linkage. In defining a phobia, the following need to be considered: It is considered to be out of proportion to objective risks; it cannot be reasoned or explained away; it is beyond voluntary control and it leads to avoidance behaviour.

Reference: Puri BK, Hall A, Ho R (2014). *Revision Notes in Psychiatry.* London: CRC Press, p. 406.

Question 7 Answer: a, Carbamazepine
Explanation: This is another version of a multiple-choice question (MCQ) about storage of psychotropic medications. Among all the options, carbamazepine is most likely to be affected by exposure to air and light. In these circumstances, the psychiatrist should recommend the nurses to keep carbamazepine in a sealed container and avoid sunlight.

Reference and Further Reading: Puri BK, Treasaden I (eds) (2010). *Psychiatry: An Evidence-Based Text.* London: Hodder Arnold, pp. 532, 538, 910.

Question 8 Answer: a, Déjà vu
Explanation: This refers to déjà vu, which is when the individual feels that the current situation has been seen or experienced before. Option (b) refers to the illusion of an auditory recognition. Option (c) refers to the illusion of recognition of a new thought. Option (d) refers to the illusion of failure to recognize a familiar

situation. Option (e) refers to how false details are being added to the recollection of an otherwise real memory.

Reference: Puri BK, Hall A, Ho R (2014). *Revision Notes in Psychiatry*. London: CRC Press, p. 9.

Question 9 Answer: c, This phenomenon is an example of classical conditioning.

Explanation: This phenomenon is learned helplessness. It is the tendency to fail to escape from a situation due to repeated failures in the past. Seligman first described learned helplessness. The classic experiment involved delivering electric shocks to dogs that were harnessed so that they could not escape the shock. Subsequently, these dogs did not try to escape the shocks even when unharnessed. Learned helplessness was applied to the cognitive theory depression. One's vulnerability to depression is dependent on one's attribution style, that is one's habitual pattern of explaining life events. Learned helplessness is not an example of classical conditioning.

Reference and Further Reading: Puri BK, Treasaden I (eds) (2010). *Psychiatry: An Evidence-Based Text*. London: Hodder Arnold, pp. 206, 298, 614.

Question 10 Answer: a, Carbamazepine

Explanation: Combination of clozapine and carbamazepine will lead to blood dyscrasia. Lithium is sometimes added to clozapine to treat clozapine-induced neutropenia. Risperidone is sometimes added to clozapine in patients who do not respond to clozapine alone. There is no contraindication to add fluoxetine or valproate onto clozapine.

Reference and Further Reading: Puri BK, Treasaden I (eds) (2010). *Psychiatry: An Evidence-Based Text*. London: Hodder Arnold, pp. 425–457, 603.

Question 11 Answer: c, Female gender

Explanation: Female gender, Ashkenazi Jewish descent and older age are associated with a high risk of developing agranulocytosis. The risk of developing agranulocytosis is not directly proportional to dose and duration of treatment.

Reference: Alvir JMJ, Lieberman JA, Safferman AZ, Schwimmer JL, Schaaf JA (1993). Clozapine-induced agranulocytosis. Incidence and risk factors in the United States. *N Engl J Med*, 329:162–167. http://www.nejm.org/toc/nejm/329/3/.

Question 12 Answer: b, Obsessive-compulsive personality disorder

Explanation: The clinical diagnosis is as aforementioned. Individuals with this disorder tend to have feelings of excessive doubt and caution. They are obsessed with perfectionism that would interfere with tasks. They tend also to be very rigid and stubborn in their cognitions.

Reference: Puri BK, Hall A, Ho R (2014). *Revision Notes in Psychiatry*. London: CRC Press, p. 453.

Question 13 Answer: a, Onset younger than the age of 15
Explanation: The earlier onset, especially below the age of 15, is indicative of a good prognostic factor. The good prognostic factors include that of onset prior to the age of 15, higher weight at onset and at presentation, those who have received treatment within 3 months after the onset of the illness, those who recovered within 2 years after the initiation of treatment, those with supportive family, good motivation to change and good childhood social adjustment.

Reference: Puri BK, Hall A, Ho R (2014). *Revision Notes in Psychiatry.* London: CRC Press, p. 581.

Question 14 Answer: b, Headache getting worse when lying down
Explanation: Postural trigger of headache may suggest raised intracranial pressure.

Reference: Fuller G, Manford M (2003). *Neurology – A Illustrated Colour Text.* Edinburgh, UK: Churchill Livingstone.

Question 15 Answer: b, Asperger's syndrome
Explanation: Autism and Asperger's syndrome are similar except that delayed speech is found in autism but not in Asperger's syndrome. In autism, performance IQ is higher than verbal IQ. In contrast, verbal IQ is higher than performance IQ in Asperger's syndrome. Rett's syndrome occurs in girls with sudden arrest of development at 6 months. Children with childhood disintegrative disorder have normal development up to 2 years and have loss of skills in language, play, social skills, bladder or bowel controls and motor skills.

Reference and Further Reading: Puri BK, Treasaden I (eds) (2010). *Psychiatry: An Evidence-Based Text.* London: Hodder Arnold, pp. 1066–1067, 1088–1090.

Question 16 Answer: d, Echolalia
Explanation: Echolalia refers to the automatic imitation by the person of another person's speech. Approximate answers refer to an approximate answer that, although clearly incorrect, does demonstrate that the is known. Cryptolalia refer to speech in a language that no one could understand. Circumstantiality refers to thinking that appears slow with the incorporation of unnecessary trivial details. The goal of thought is finally reached, however. Flight of ideas refers to speech that consists of a stream of accelerated thoughts with no central direction.

Reference: Puri BK, Hall A, Ho R (2014). *Revision Notes in Psychiatry.* London: CRC Press, p. 3.

Question 17 Answer: d, Second-order conditioning is more easily demonstrated than classical conditioning.
Explanation: Option (d) is false. Classical conditioning is more easily demonstrated than second-order conditioning because second-order conditioning requires an initial learning of associations between conditioned and unconditioned stimuli

before learning an extra association, which would constitute second-order conditioning. Option (a) is true. Objects resembling fear-provoking stimuli can elicit fear themselves through second-order conditioning. Option (b) is true. Animal phobias have the best prognosis, social phobias are likely to improve gradually and agoraphobia has the worst prognosis. Option (e) is true. Forward conditioning is also known as delayed conditioning. Backward conditioning produces little learning.

Reference and Further Reading: Puri BK, Treasaden I (eds) (2010). *Psychiatry: An Evidence-Based Text*. London: Hodder Arnold, pp. 198–199, 653–656.

Question 18 Answer: c, Third month of treatment
Explanation: The hazard rate for agranulocytosis peaked during the third month of treatment.

Reference: Alvir JMJ, Lieberman JA, Safferman AZ, Schwimmer JL, Schaaf JA (1993). Clozapine-induced agranulocytosis. Incidence and risk factors in the United States. *N Engl J Med*, 329: 162–167. http://www.nejm.org/toc/nejm/329/3/.

Question 19 Answer: b, Loud noises
Explanation: From 6 months, children develop a fear of loud noises. Fears of animals, darkness and 'monsters' begin at 3–5 years. The fear of death begins in adolescence.

Reference and Further Reading: Puri BK, Hall AD (2002). *Revision Notes in Psychiatry*. London: Arnold, p. 73; Puri BK, Treasaden I (eds) (2010). *Psychiatry: An Evidence-Based Text*. London: Hodder Arnold, pp. 119–120.

Question 20 Answer: d, Depth perception
Explanation: Depth perception is developed at 2 months.

Reference and Further Reading: Berk LE (2006). *Child Development* (7th edition). Boston: Pearson, pp. 152–160.

Question 21 Answer: c, Contralateral lower limb weakness
Explanation: The neurological signs and lesions of specific branches of anterior cerebral arteries are summarized as follows:

- Orbital branch: apathy and memory impairment
- Medial striate artery (supplying cranial V, VII and XII nerves): dysarthria and dysphagia
- Callosomarginal brain (supplying the supplementary motor area): contralateral hemiparesis (leg > arm), incontinence as a result of weakness in pelvic floor and mutism
- Pericallosal branch (suppling corpus callosum): ideomotor apraxia and tactile anomia

- Left anterior cerebral artery: mixed aphasia
- Right anterior cerebral artery: dysapraxia
- Bilateral anterior cerebral artery: akinetic mutism

Lesions in unilateral posterior cerebral artery cause contralateral III nerve palsy. Lesions in vertebral and basilar arteries cause nystagmus.

Reference: Malhi GS, Malhi S (2006). *Examination Notes in Psychiatry: Basic Sciences* (2nd edition). London: Hodder Arnold.

Question 22 Answer: d, The child is able to run on tiptoes.
Explanation: A child is able to walk a few steps on tiptoe by age two, 10 feet by age four and run on tiptoes by age five. Option (c) and (e) are achieved by age two. Options (a) and (b) are achieved by age three.

Reference and Further Reading: Berk LE (2006). *Child Development* (7th edition). Boston: Pearson, p. 175.

Question 23 Answer: d, Based on the ICD-10 criteria, dysthymia is severe enough to meet diagnostic criteria of post-schizophrenic depression.
Explanation: The depressive symptoms must be severe and extensive to meet criteria for at least a mild depressive episode.

References: American Psychiatric Association (2000). *Diagnostic Criteria from DSM-IV-TR*. Washington, DC: American Psychiatric Association; World Health Organisation (1994). *ICD-10 Classification of Mental and Behavioural Disorders*. Edinburgh, UK: Churchill Livingstone.

Question 24 Answer: c, Hebephrenic type
Explanation: Both hebephrenic and simple schizophrenia are found in the ICD-10 but not in the DSM-IV-TR. Hebephrenic schizophrenia is characterized by flattening of affect, aimless behaviour, disjointed thought and less prominent hallucinations and delusions. Simple schizophrenia has a slow but progressive development over a period of at least 1 year. There is a significant change in the overall quality of personal behaviour, deepening of negative symptoms and a marked decline in performance.

References: American Psychiatric Association (2000). *Diagnostic Criteria from DSM-IV-TR*. Washington, DC: American Psychiatric Association; World Health Organisation (1994). *ICD-10 Classification of Mental and Behavioural Disorders*. Edinburgh, UK: Churchill Livingstone.

Question 25 Answer: e, Female gender
Explanation: All of the aforementioned are considered to be bad prognostic factors for anorexia nervosa (AN), with the exception of female gender. The other bad prognostic factors include onset at an older age, lower weight at onset and at presentation, very frequent vomiting and presence of bulimia, very severe weight loss, long duration of anorexia nervosa (AN), previous hospitalization, extreme resistance to treatment, continued family problems, neurotic personality and male gender.

Reference: Puri BK, Hall A, Ho R (2014). *Revision Notes in Psychiatry*. London: CRC Press, p. 581.

Question 26 Answer: a, Autochthonous delusion

Explanation: Primary delusion is a fully formed delusion that arises without any discernible connection with previous events. Primary delusions (e.g. delusional perception and delusional memory) do not start with an idea and can occur out of the blue or may be preceded by delusional mood, which is a feeling that something unusual and threatening is about to happen.

Reference and Further Reading: Puri BK, Hall AD (2002). *Revision Notes in Psychiatry*. London: Arnold, p. 152.

Question 27 Answer: e, Three-dimensional similarity

Explanation: All of the aforementioned are based on the principles of Gestalt psychology, with the exception of option (e). It proposes that the whole perception is different from the sum of its parts. It also proposes the law of simplicity, the law of continuity, the law of similarity, and the law of proximity and figure-ground differentiation. The law of simplicity states that the percept would correspond to the simplest stimulation interpretation. The law of continuity refers to how interrupted lines are being perceived as continuous. The law of similarity refers to how like items are being grouped together. The law of proximity refers to how adjacent items are grouped together.

Reference: Puri BK, Hall A, Ho R (2014). *Revision Notes in Psychiatry*. London: CRC Press, p. 31.

Question 28 Answer: e, Valproate

Explanation: An audit performed in the South London and Maudsley National Health Service (NHS) Trust in 2007 suggests that valproate actually prevents clozapine-induced seizures. Carbamazepine is contraindicated in this case.

Reference: Sparshatt A, Whiskey E, Taylor E (2008). Valproate as prophylaxis for clozapine-induced seizures: Survey of practice. *Psychiatric Bulletin*, 32: 262–265.

Question 29 Answer: a, He fulfils the diagnostic criteria for schizophrenia based on the ICD-10.

Explanation: Based on the ICD-10, a period of at least 1 month is required before a diagnosis of schizophrenia could be made. Based on the DSM-IV-TR, a period of at least 6 months is required.

Reference and Further Reading: American Psychiatric Association (2000). *Diagnostic Criteria from DSM-IV-TR*. Washington, DC: American Psychiatric Association; World Health Organisation (1994). *ICD-10 Classification of Mental and Behavioural Disorders*. Edinburgh, UK: Churchill Livingstone; Puri BK, Treasaden I (eds) (2010). *Psychiatry: An Evidence-Based Text*. London: Hodder Arnold, pp. 594–596.

Question 30 Answer: e, Conformity to the group's decision on a line judgement experiment was greater in a group of 25 members as compared to a group of four.
Explanation: Previous research has demonstrated that as the size of the group increases, the impact of one's decision decreases, thus leading to lesser pressure to conform. It should be noted that self-reliant, intelligent, expressive, socially effective individuals are least vulnerable to group pressure.

Reference: Puri BK, Hall A, Ho R (2014). *Revision Notes in Psychiatry.* London: CRC Press, p. 60.

Question 31 Answer: d, Cognitive changes occur at the age of five for children to adopt the theory of mind.
Explanation: Cognitive changes usually occur at the age of four for children to acquire a theory of mind. It has been suggested that a failure to acquire such a theory of mind is associated with disorders such as autism.

Reference: Puri BK, Hall A, Ho R (2014). *Revision Notes in Psychiatry.* London: CRC Press, p. 59.

Question 32 Answer: e, 250 mg
Explanation: Based on the DSM-5, individuals who consume more than 250 mg per day of caffeine is considered to be intoxicated. This might result in anxiety, restlessness, nausea, muscle twitching and facial flushing. It is important to note that at levels of intake in excess of 600 mg per day, dysphoria will replace euphoria, anxiety and mood disturbances become prominent, and insomnia, muscle-twitching, tachycardia and sometimes cardiac arrhythmias might occur.

Reference: Puri BK, Hall A, Ho R (2014). *Revision Notes in Psychiatry.* London: CRC Press, p. 544.

Question 33 Answer: b, Cognitive analytical therapy
Explanation: Cognitive analytical therapy is a combination of cognitive and analytical therapy. It helps in the identification of faculty procedures such as traps (which are repetitive cycles of behaviour and their consequences that become perpetuation), dilemma (false choice or unduly narrowed options) and snag (extreme pessimism about the future and halt a plan before it even starts).

Reference: Puri BK, Hall A, Ho R (2014). *Revision Notes in Psychiatry.* London: CRC Press, p. 337.

Question 34 Answer: b, Schizotypal personality disorder
Explanation: Schizotypal disorder has been demonstrated to have the strongest genetic linkage. Almost all the studies of the families of schizophrenic pro-bands

have found an excess of both schizophrenia and schizotypal personality disorder among relatives (22% in the biological relatives of schizophrenics as compared to 2% of the adoptive relatives and control).

Reference: Puri BK, Hall A, Ho R (2014). *Revision Notes in Psychiatry.* London: CRC Press, p. 440.

Question 35 Answer: b, Anosmia
Explanation: Tumour of frontal lobe is a known cause of anosmia (loss of olfactory function). Other common causes include injury to olfactory nerve, Alzheimer's disease and Parkinson's disease. Amusia is caused by lesions in the superior temporal lobe. Anterograde amnesia is caused by lesions in the medial temporal lobe. Apraxia is caused by lesions in the non-dominant parietal lobe. Bitemporal hemianopia is caused by tumours in the pituitary gland.

Reference: Malhi GS, Malhi S (2006). *Examination Notes in Psychiatry: Basic Sciences* (2nd edition). London: Hodder Arnold.

Question 36 Answer: c, Bystander effect
Explanation: This refers to the phenomenon where individuals are less likely to extend help during an emergency in the presence of others.

Reference: Puri BK, Treasaden I (2010). *Psychiatry: An Evidence-Based Text.* London: Hodder Arnold, p. 290.

Question 37 Answer: a, Cenesthesia
Explanation: Cenesthesia refers a change in the normal quality of feeling tone in a part of the body.

Reference: Sadock BJ, Sadock VA. (2008). *Kaplan and Sadock's Concise Textbook of Psychiatry* (3rd edition). Philadelphia, PA: Lippincott, Williams & Wilkins, p. 23.

Question 38 Answer: c, Delusional misidentification
Explanation: This condition is known as morbid jealousy (or pathological jealousy or Othello syndrome), which is the delusional belief of infidelity of the spouse or sexual partner. Patients with morbid jealousy go to excessive lengths to test their partner's fidelity and make accusations based on insignificant evidence. The condition is more common in men. Some aetiological factors include psychoactive substance use disorders, paranoid schizophrenia, depression, neurosis or personality disorders and organic disorders such as dementia.

Reference and Further Reading: Puri BK, Hall AD (2002). *Revision Notes in Psychiatry.* London: Arnold, p. 381.

Question 39 Answer: e, Insight
Explanation: Attention, retention, reproduction and motivation are all involved in the modelling process. Successful observational learning is more likely when there

is optimal arousal, the presence of an attractive, prestigious, colourful and dramatic model. Reproduction also helps to ensure what has been remembered have been translated into behaviour. It is important to note that unsuccessful observational learning is more likely to occur in association with the following factors including low arousal, over-arousal and in the presence of distracting stimuli.

Reference: Puri BK, Hall A, Ho R (2014). *Revision Notes in Psychiatry.* London: CRC Press, p. 27.

Question 40 Answer: b, Conditioning theory
Explanation: All of the aforementioned are theories that explain interpersonal attraction. Reciprocal reinforcement of the attraction occurs with rewards in both directions. Based on the social exchange theory, people tend to prefer relationships that appear to offer an optimum cost–benefit ratio. Equity theory states that the preferred relationships are those in which each feels that the cost–benefit ratio of the relationship for each person is approximately equal. Proxemics relates to interpersonal space and body buffer zone.

Reference: Puri BK, Hall A, Ho R (2014). *Revision Notes in Psychiatry.* London: CRC Press, p. 59.

Question 41 Answer: a, Automatic obedience
Explanation: Automatic obedience refers to a condition in which the person follows the examiner's instructions blindly without judgement and resistance.

Reference and Further Reading: Puri BK, Treasaden I (eds) (2010). *Psychiatry: An Evidence-Based Text.* London: Hodder Arnold, pp. 294–295.

Question 42 Answer: b, Post-natal psychosis
Explanation: She is likely to be having post-natal psychosis. Post-natal psychosis usually has an abrupt onset, usually within the first 2 weeks after childbirth. In addition, it is characterized by marked restlessness, fear and insomnia. There might be delusions, hallucinations and disturbed behaviour, which develop rapidly. There might be marked perplexity, but with no detectable cognitive impairment. Usually, there is noted to be rapid fluctuations in the mental state, sometimes from hour to hour.

Reference: Puri BK, Hall A, Ho R (2014). *Revision Notes in Psychiatry.* London: CRC Press p. 568.

Question 43 Answer: b, Foot in the door technique
Explanation: This is an example of the foot in the door technique. Foot in the door technique involves asking for a small commitment, followed by a bigger commitment after gaining initial compliance.

Reference: Puri BK, Tresaden I (2010). *Psychiatry: An Evidence-Based Text.* London: Hodder Arnold, pp. 290–291.

Question 44 Answer: b, Gegenhalten
Explanation: Gegenhalten is a form of paratonia consisting of uneven resistance of the limbs to passive movement.

Reference and Further Reading: Campbell RJ (1996). *Psychiatric Dictionary.* Oxford, UK: Oxford University Press.

Question 45 Answer: c, Fourth cranial nerve
Explanation: The fourth cranial nerve is likely to be affected, as it supplies the superior oblique muscle of the eye, which has been affected in this clinical example.

Reference: Puri BK, Hall A, Ho R (2014). *Revision Notes in Psychiatry.* London: CRC Press, p. 159.

Question 46 Answer: e, Emotional arousal might or might not increase aggression.
Explanation: Emotional arousal would potentially increase aggression. In addition, the frustration–aggression hypothesis proposes that preventing a person from reaching their goal will induce an aggressive drive resulting in a behaviour intended to harm the one causing the frustration. Expressing this aggression will reduce the aggressive drive.

Reference: Puri BK, Hall A, Ho R (2014). *Revision Notes in Psychiatry.* London: CRC Press, p. 60.

Question 47 Answer: b, Cataplexy
Explanation: Cataplexy refers to the temporary paralysis and loss of antigravity muscle tone without loss of consciousness. Cataplexy is often precipitated by emotional excitement and associated with narcolepsy.

Reference and Further Reading: Campbell RJ (1996). *Psychiatric Dictionary.* Oxford, UK: Oxford University Press.

Question 48 Answer: b, Mannerism
Explanation: Mannerisms are repeated involuntary movements that are goal directed. An example would be 'A person repeatedly moving his hand when he talks and tries to convey his message to the examiner'.

Reference and Further Reading: Rajagopal S (2007). Catatonia. *Advances in Psychiatric Treatment*, 13: 51–59.

Question 49 Answer: e, Chlorpromazine increases the serum concentration of valproate.
Explanation: Chlorpromazine inhibits the metabolism of valproate and decreases its clearance. Hence, chlorpromazine increases the serum level of valproate. Option A is incorrect. A significant increase in the serum chlorpromazine concentration was observed when administered with amitriptyline.

Reference and Further Reading: Rasheed A, Javed MA, Nazir S, Khawaja O (1994). Interaction of chlorpromazine with tricyclic anti-depressants in schizophrenic patients. *J Pak Med Assoc*, 44: 233–234; Puri BK, Treasaden I (eds) (2010). *Psychiatry: An Evidence-Based Text*. London: Hodder Arnold, pp. 12, 893, 901–902, 903.

Question 50 Answer: a, Cognitive behaviour therapy
Explanation: Generally for outpatients, cognitive analytical therapy, cognitive behaviour therapy, interpersonal therapy and focal dynamic therapy would help. The main aims of psychotherapy would be to reduce the risk, enhance patient's motivation, encourage healthy eating and reduce other symptoms related to AN. In particular, CBT is able to target specific cognitive distortions and also behaviours that are related to weight, body image and eating. The minimum duration for outpatient psychological treatment is 6 months. It should be noted that psychotherapy is difficult for patients with severe emaciation. It has been advised that psychotherapy should wait until the weight has increased.

Reference: Puri BK, Hall A, Ho R (2014). *Revision Notes in Psychiatry*. London: CRC Press, p. 580.

Question 51 Answer: d, Jargon aphasia
Explanation: In jargon aphasia, the patient utters incoherent meaningless neologistic speech. There are two forms of intermediate aphasia: In central aphasia, in which there is difficulty in arranging words in the proper sequence; and nominal aphasia, in which there is difficulty with naming objects. In expressive aphasia, this refers to the difficulty in expressing thoughts in words whilst comprehension remains. In global aphasia, both receptive aphasia and expressive aphasia are present at the same time. Semantic aphasia refers to the errors in using the target words due to deficits in semantic memory.

Reference: Puri BK, Hall A, Ho R (2014). *Revision Notes in Psychiatry*. London: CRC Press, p. 10.

Question 52 Answer: d, Schemas tend to persist even after evidence for the schema has been discredited.
Explanation: Schemas have been known to persist after evidence for the schema has been discredited because the old schema has been activated more times than the new, modified schema and will be reactivated when there are little cognitive resources or time to activate the new schemas.

Reference: Aronson E, Wilson TD, Akert RM (2007). *Social Psychology*. Upper Saddle River, NJ: Prentice Hall, pp. 58–72.

Question 53 Answer: e, Schnauzkrampf
Explanation: Schnauzkrampf is a feature of catatonia and described as a protrusion of the lips such that they resemble a snout.

Reference and Further Reading: Roper P, Grad B (1968). A sign of schizophrenia: Clinical response of possible significance observed during electroconvulsive therapy. *Can Med Assoc J*, 99: 798–804.

Question 54 Answer: b, Conversion disorder
Explanation: The clinical diagnosis is likely to be that of conversion disorder. In conversion disorders, there is no evidence of physical disorder that may explain the symptoms. Instead, there is evidence for psychological causation, and usually there is a clear association in time with related stressful events. There might be calm acceptance known as la belle indifference. Conversion disorders are presumed to be psychogenic in origin. They are associated with traumatic events, insoluble problems or disturbed relationships.

Reference: Puri BK, Hall A, Ho R (2014). *Revision Notes in Psychiatry*. London: CRC Press, p. 433.

Question 55 Answer: c, Hypothermia
Explanation: All of the aforementioned are features of Wernicke's encephalopathy, with the exception of hypothermia. It is usually caused by the deficiency of thiamine, which is due to prolonged alcohol abuse in the Western countries. There are also other medical causes that need to be excluded as well. An estimated 10% of patients with the condition have the classical triad. Peripheral neuropathy may also be present in some individuals.

Reference: Puri BK, Hall A, Ho R (2014). *Revision Notes in Psychiatry*. London: CRC Press, p. 517.

Question 56 Answer: e, Attributing others' mistakes to their personal dispositions
Explanation: Fundamental attribution error is the tendency to overestimate the extent to which a person's behaviour is due to internal, dispositional factors and to underestimate the role of external, situational factors.

Reference and Further Reading: Aronson E, Wilson TD, Akert RM (2007). *Social Psychology*. Upper Saddle River, NJ: Prentice Hall, p. 109.

Question 57 Answer: b, Extinction
Explanation: Extinction is the gradual disappearance of the conditioned response (i.e. nausea) following repeated presentations of the conditioned stimulus (i.e. hospital) without the unconditioned stimulus (i.e. chemotherapy).

Reference and Further Reading: Puri BK, Treasaden I (eds) (2010). *Psychiatry: An Evidence-Based Text*. London: Hodder Arnold, p. 199.

Question 58 Answer: a, Conditioned response
Explanation: In this scenario, the unconditioned stimulus is chemotherapy and the conditioned stimulus is hospital building. The nausea feeling associated with the hospital building is a conditioned response.

Reference and Further Reading: Puri BK, Treasaden I (eds) (2010). *Psychiatry: An Evidence-Based Text*. London: Hodder Arnold, pp. 197–200.

Question 59 Answer: c, Generalization
Explanation: Stimulus generalization refers to a stimulus (i.e. alarm from the alarm clock) that is similar to a conditioned stimulus (i.e. mobile phone alarm) spontaneously causing a conditioned response (i.e. nausea).

Reference and Further Reading: Puri BK, Treasaden I (eds) (2010). *Psychiatry: An Evidence-Based Text*. London: Hodder Arnold, p. 199.

Question 60 Answer: c, Delusion of persecution
Explanation: Schneiderian first-rank symptoms include auditory hallucinations (audible thoughts, voices heard arguing and voices giving a running commentary), delusion of passivity (thought insertion, withdrawal and broadcasting; made feelings, actions and impulses), somatic passivity and delusional perception. Other delusions such as delusion of persecution, hallucinations and emotional blunting are second-rank symptoms.

Reference and Further Reading: Puri BK, Hall AD (2002). *Revision Notes in Psychiatry*. London: Arnold, p. 368.

Question 61 Answer: a, Levator palpebrae muscle paralysis
Explanation: Levator palpebrae muscle paralysis, Horner's syndrome and III nerve palsy are common causes of unilateral ptosis. Options (b) to (e) are common causes of bilateral ptosis.

Reference and Further Reading: Ward N, Frith P, Lipsedge M (2001). *Medical Masterclass Neurology, Ophthalmology and Psychiatry*. London: Royal College of Physicians; Puri BK, Treasaden I (eds) (2010). *Psychiatry: An Evidence-Based Text*. London: Hodder Arnold, pp. 336–338, 351, 525–527.

Question 62 Answer: d, Bias towards attributing a behaviour to situational causes
Explanation: The fundamental attribution error is best viewed as a bias towards attributing an actor's behaviour to dispositional causes rather than as an attribution error towards situational causes. It has been found that people in individualistic, Western cultures prefer dispositional attributions compared to those in collectivistic cultures, who take situational factors into account when making attributions.

Reference and Further Reading: Aronson E, Wilson TD, Akert RM (2007). *Social Psychology*. Upper Saddle River, NJ: Prentice Hall, pp. 109–110

Question 63 Answer: a, Low positive predictive value, low negative predictive value, low sensitivity and low specificity
Explanation: APOE screening is not recommended as a result of low positive predictive value, low negative predictive value, low sensitivity and low specificity.

Reference: Puri BK, Treasaden I (eds) (2010). *Psychiatry: An Evidence-Based Text.* London: Hodder Arnold, p. 473.

Question 64 Answer: e, Presence of altered consciousness
Explanation: Delirium is commonly defined as a state of fluctuating global disturbance of the cerebral function, which is abrupt in onset and of short duration, usually arising as a consequence of physical illnesses. Awareness is always impaired. Alertness tends to change and can be either increased or decreased. Orientation is always impaired, particularly for time. Recent and immediate memory is impaired with poor learning and lack of recall for events occurring during the delirious period. However, the knowledge base remains intact.

Reference: Puri BK, Hall A, Ho R (2014). *Revision Notes in Psychiatry.* London: CRC Press, p. 707.

Question 65 Answer: e, Treat systolic hypertension (>160 mm Hg) in older people (age >60 years).
Explanation: Option (e) is based on good evidence. Option (a) is recommended in first-degree relatives of Alzheimer's disease but not for the general population. There is insufficient evidence to support options (b), (c), and (d). High-dose vitamin E is associated with excess mortality and should not be recommended.

Reference: Puri BK, Treasaden I (eds) (2010). *Psychiatry: An Evidence-Based Text.* London: Hodder Arnold, pp. 511–513, 1100–1108.

Question 66 Answer: b, Thought block
Explanation: The classical first-rank symptoms include auditory hallucinations (thought echo, in third person, in the form of a running commentary), delusions of passivity (thought insertion, withdrawal and broadcasting and made feelings, impulses and actions) and somatic passivity and delusional perception. Second-rank symptoms include perplexity, emotional blunting, hallucination and other delusions. First-rank symptoms could occur in other psychosis and, although highly suggestive of schizophrenia, are not pathognomonic.

Reference: Puri BK, Hall A, Ho R (2014). *Revision Notes in Psychiatry.* London: CRC Press, p. 351.

Question 67 Answer: b, Perceived lack of social support during the trauma
Explanation: The following are psychosocial factors that are responsible for the development of PTSD: female gender, low intelligence quotient at the age of five, previous trauma history, previous psychiatric history, hyperactivity, anti-social behaviour, severity of trauma, perceived life threat, peri-traumatic dissociation, impaired social support and low socioeconomic status.

Reference: Puri BK, Hall A, Ho R (2014). *Revision Notes in Psychiatry.* London: CRC Press, p. 427.

Question 68 Answer: a, The scientific study of the way in which people's thoughts, feelings and behaviours are influenced by the real, imagined or implied presence of other people.
Explanation: Social psychology is the scientific study of the way in which people's thoughts, feelings and behaviours are influenced by the real, imagined or implied presence of other people. Option (d) defines psychology.

Reference and Further Reading: Puri BK, Treasaden I (eds) (2010). *Psychiatry: An Evidence-Based Text.* London: Hodder Arnold, p. 131.

Question 69 Answer: d, Ekbom's syndrome
Explanation: This woman suffers from delusions of parasitosis or Ekbom's syndrome, which is the belief that one is infested with parasites that live on or under the skin. The primary symptom is a cutaneous pruritus. This itch causes continuous picking of the skin to extract the suspected parasites. Patients often present with foreign objects or debris from their skin in small containers. This is called the 'matchbox sign'.

The syndrome is associated with bipolar disorder, paranoia, schizophrenia, depression as well as abuse of drugs, such as cocaine, ritalin and amphetamines. Risperidone or olanzapine are the current treatments of choice.

Reference and Further Reading: Edlich RF, Cross CL, Wack CA, Long WB 3rd (2009). Delusions of parasitosis. *American Journal of Emergency Medicine*, 8: 997–999.

Question 70 Answer: a, Discrimination
Explanation: Stimulus discrimination refers to the tendency to stop responding to the stimulus similar to the conditioned stimulus, as the similar stimulus is not paired with the unconditioned stimulus. The man learns to differentiate or discriminate between the two alarm sounds and learns to respond differently to each alarm.

Reference and Further Reading: Puri BK, Treasaden I (eds) (2010). *Psychiatry: An Evidence-Based Text.* London: Hodder Arnold, p. 199.

Question 71 Answer: e, Recovery
Explanation: Spontaneous recovery is the recurrence of a conditioned response after extinction. Extinction is the weakening of the conditioned response after the removal of the unconditioned stimulus (i.e. Drug A).

Reference and Further Reading: Puri BK, Treasaden I (eds) (2010). *Psychiatry: An Evidence-Based Text.* London: Hodder Arnold, pp. 199, 208.

Question 72 Answer: a, Dyslexia without agraphia
Explanation: Dyslexia without agraphia refers to word blindness with writing impairments and is caused by lesions in the left occipital lobe. Homonymous hemianopia occurs in optic tract, radiation and cortex lesions. Papilloedema and loss of pupillary reflex are caused by optic nerve lesions. Quadrantopia is caused by optic radiation lesions.

Reference: Malhi GS, Malhi S (2006). *Examination Notes in Psychiatry: Basic Sciences* (2nd edition). London: Hodder Arnold.

Question 73 Answer: c, Daniel M'Naghten trial
Explanation: Daniel M'Naghten suffered from delusions of persecution for years and stalked Prime Minister Sir Robert Peel. He mistook Edward Drummond, Peel's secretary, for Peel and shot him. Drummond 'languished' for 4 months and then died while M'Naghten was found not criminally responsible in 2 minutes. The M'Naghten trail led to public outrage, and Queen Victoria requested clarification of the 'not criminally responsible' standard. M'Naghten rule tests criminality of murder committed by a person who is deemed to be mentally insane. For option (a), bifurcated trial means that the person must be proven guilty of each offence first and the 'not criminally responsible' issue is the second part of the trial. For option (b), the first right versus wrong test is associated with the Bellingham trial in 1812. For option (e), the wild beast test is associated with the trial Rex versus Arnold in 1724.

Reference and Further Reading: Puri BK, Treasaden I (eds) (2010). *Psychiatry: An Evidence-Based Text.* London: Hodder Arnold, pp. 1162, 1163, 1168.

Question 74 Answer: c, Moderate
Explanation: Based on the ICD-10 diagnostic classification system, he is likely to be suffering from moderate degree of depression. Duration of 2 weeks of symptoms is required for the diagnosis. This applies to the first episode only. Severity is classified into mild depressive disorder, moderate depressive disorder, severe depressive episode without psychotic symptoms and severe depressive episode with psychotic symptoms.

Reference: Puri BK, Hall A, Ho R (2014). *Revision Notes in Psychiatry.* London: CRC Press, p. 378.

Question 75 Answer: b, 10%
Explanation: His son has 10% risk of developing schizophrenia.

Reference and Further Reading: Puri BK, Treasaden I (eds) (2010). *Psychiatry: An Evidence-Based Text.* London: Hodder Arnold, pp. 474–475, 597, 599.

Question 76 Answer: d, Four times increased risk
Explanation: Cannabis would cause an estimated fourfold increment in the risk of psychosis.

Reference: Puri BK, Hall A, Ho R (2014). *Revision Notes in Psychiatry.* London: CRC Press, p. 361.

Question 77 Answer: e, There has been found to be an association, but there is no strong evidence to support the estimated increment in risk.
Explanation: Previous research has found that patients with Down's syndrome are at a higher risk to develop Alzheimer's disease. Other psychiatric co-morbidities include

obsessive-compulsive disorder, depression, autism, bipolar disorder and psychosis. There has not been strong evidence to support the estimated increment in risk.

Reference: Puri BK, Hall A, Ho R (2014). *Revision Notes in Psychiatry*. London: CRC Press, p. 665.

Question 78 Answer: e, Trace conditioning
Explanation: This phenomenon is known as trace conditioning. In trace conditioning, the conditioned stimulus is removed before the onset of the unconditioned stimulus. In this example, the conditioned stimulus is the doctor's white coat. As the girl has to wait for her turn before she receives her injection (i.e. the unconditioned stimulus), there is an interval between the conditioned stimulus and the unconditioned stimulus, which is why this phenomenon is trace conditioning and not delayed conditioning. The conditioned response in trace conditioning is usually weaker than that in delayed conditioning. Trace conditioning becomes less effective as the delay between the two stimuli increases.

Reference and Further Reading: Puri BK, Treasaden I (eds) (2010). *Psychiatry: An Evidence-Based Text*. London: Hodder Arnold, p. 198.

Question 79 Answer: c, 1930s
Explanation: The term schizoaffective psychosis was introduced by Kasanin in 1933 in order to describe a condition with both affective and schizophrenic symptoms, usually with sudden acute onset after good premorbid functioning and with almost complete recovery.

Reference: Puri BK, Hall A, Ho R (2014). *Revision Notes in Psychiatry*. London: CRC Press, p. 373.

Question 80 Answer: d, 6 months
Explanation: Based on the advice given by the DVLA to doctors, it has been stated that patients with bipolar disorder requiring admission should be placed off the road for 6–12 months.

Reference: Puri BK, Hall A, Ho R (2014). *Revision Notes in Psychiatry*. London: CRC Press, p. 150.

Question 81 Answer: c, 35%–40%
Explanation: Research has found that people with Down syndrome are at a higher risk of developing Alzheimer's disease. For those who are between the ages of 50 and 59 years, the increased incidence has been estimated to be around 36%–40%. For those between the ages of 60 and 69 years, the increased incidence has been found to be around 55%. Research has shown that as age advances, there is a higher incidence of neurofibrillary tangle and plaques being deposited.

Reference: Puri BK, Hall A, Ho R (2014). *Revision Notes in Psychiatry*. London: CRC Press, p. 665.

Question 82 Answer: b, People with mental illnesses are not at a higher risk of offending compared to general population.
Explanation: Since the peak of deinstitutionalization in the 1970s, the proportion of inmates in prisons with serious mental illnesses has increased significantly. People with mental illnesses are at a higher risk of offending compared to the general population, and the rates of mental illness among prisoners have increased steadily since deinstitutionalization.

Reference and Further Reading: Puri BK, Treasaden I (eds) (2010). *Psychiatry: An Evidence-Based Text.* London: Hodder Arnold, pp. 3–15.

Question 83 Answer: c, Simultaneous conditioning
Explanation: In simultaneous conditioning, the onset and termination of the conditioned and unconditioned stimuli occur at the same time. In this example, the spider (i.e. unconditioned stimulus) and the ringing sound (i.e. conditioned stimulus) are presented at the same time, and this elicits fear (conditioned response) in the girl.

Reference and Further Reading: Puri BK, Treasaden I (eds) (2010). *Psychiatry: An Evidence-Based Text.* London: Hodder Arnold, p. 198.

Question 84 Answer: a, Bleuler
Explanation: It was in 1911 that Bleuler introduced the term schizophrenia and applied it.

Reference: Puri BK, Hall A, Ho R (2014). *Revision Notes in Psychiatry.* London: CRC Press, p. 349.

Question 85 Answer: d, Kasanin
Explanation: The term 'schizoaffective psychosis' was introduced by Kasanin in 1933 to describe a condition with both affective and schizophrenic symptoms, with sudden onset after good premorbid functioning and usually with complete recovery.

Reference: Puri BK, Hall A, Ho R (2014). *Revision Notes in Psychiatry.* London: CRC Press, p. 373.

Question 86 Answer: e, Under the consequentialist approach, confidentiality is an absolute condition in psychiatric practice.
Explanation: Confidentiality is recognized as a *prima facie* obligation. An action is morally right only if it promotes the best consequences for the greatest number of people.

Reference: Green SA (1998). The ethics of managed mental health care, in Bloch S, Chodoff P, Green SA (eds) *Psychiatric Ethics* (3rd edition). Oxford, UK: Oxford University Press.

Question 87 Answer: b, MSE provides important information in establishing a psychiatric diagnosis.
Explanation: The Mini Mental State Examination (MMSE) is a cognitive assessment and is not a shorter version of the Mental State Examination. The MSE should be conducted as soon as the interview begins, and the mental state of the patient is observed throughout the process of history taking. Physical examination is required in psychiatric assessment, and the MSE cannot replace physical examination. Information obtained from history taking is affected by the patient's subjective views and defence mechanisms. Observations during the MSE are more objective and reliable.

Reference and Further Reading: Puri BK, Treasaden I (eds) (2010). *Psychiatry: An Evidence-Based Text.* London: Hodder Arnold, pp. 92, 515, 786, 1101.

Question 88 Answer: c, Emotional liability
Explanation: The presence of emotional labiality suggests the diagnosis of bipolar disorder.

Reference and Further Reading: Puri BK, Treasaden I (eds) (2010). *Psychiatry: An Evidence-Based Text.* London: Hodder Arnold, pp. 593–609.

Question 89 Answer: d, Neologism
Explanation: The person exhibits neologism while condensing words such as 'syringe' and 'risperidone'. It is defined as a new word that is constructed by the person or an everyday word is being used in a special way by the person.

Reference and Further Reading: Puri BK, Hall AD (2002). *Revision Notes in Psychiatry.* London: Arnold, p. 4.

Question 90 Answer: c, 3 months
Explanation: According to the ICD-10, a delusional disorder is an ill-defined condition, manifesting as a single delusion or a set of related delusions, being persistent, sometimes life-long and not having an identifiable organic basis. Delusions are the most obvious or are the only symptoms that are present for at least 3 months. For the diagnosis to be made, there must be no evidence of schizophrenia symptoms or brain diseases.

Reference: Puri BK, Hall A, Ho R (2014). *Revision Notes in Psychiatry.* London: CRC Press, p. 370.

Question 91 Answer: d, The ratio for MZ to DZ concordance is around 56:5.
Explanation: The ratio of MZ to DZ concordance has been found to be 56:5 (Holland et al.). Twin studies have found higher concordance rates for monozygotic twins than for dizygotic twins. Five per cent of the first-degree relatives are usually affected. The heritability of AN has been estimated to be around 80%. Linkage genes controlling serotonin function on chromosome 1 and AN have been found.

Reference: Puri BK, Hall A, Ho R (2014). *Revision Notes in Psychiatry.* London: CRC Press, p. 575.

Question 92 Answer: a, Checking
Explanation: Checking is the most common compulsion, followed by washing and counting. Symmetry and doubting are associated obsessions. Compulsions are defined as repetitive behaviours or mental acts in response to an obsession. The behaviours or mental acts are aimed at preventing or reducing anxiety or distress. Obsession is defined as recurrent and intrusive thoughts, urges or images that cause marked anxiety or distress. Thus, an individual would resort to attempts to suppress such thoughts, urges or images or attempt to neutralize them using compulsive behaviour.

Reference: Puri BK, Hall A, Ho R (2014). *Revision Notes in Psychiatry*. London: CRC Press, p. 418.

Question 93 Answer: d, Benzodiazepine withdrawal syndrome
Explanation: She is likely to be experiencing benzodiazepine withdrawal syndrome. This would include withdrawal symptoms such as autonomic hyperactivity, malaise and weakness, tinnitus and grand mal convulsions. There are cognitive effects with impaired memory and concentration. There are also perceptual effects with hypersensitivity to sound, light and touch; depersonalization and derealization. Delirium may develop within a week of cessation, associated with visual, auditory and tactile hallucinations and delusions. Affective effects such as irritability, anxiety and phobic symptoms may also occur.

Reference: Puri BK, Hall A, Ho R (2014). *Revision Notes in Psychiatry*. London: CRC Press, p. 548.

Question 94 Answer: b, Drawing the face of a clock, indicating 10 past 11
Explanation: Folstein's MMSE does not include drawing a clock face, which requires intact frontal lobe and parietal lobe function.

Reference and Further Reading: Puri BK, Treasaden I (eds) (2010). *Psychiatry: An Evidence-Based Text*. London: Hodder Arnold, pp. 92, 515, 786, 1101.

Question 95 Answer: c, Pibloktoq
Explanation: Pibloktoq is characterized by prodromal fatigue, depression or confusion followed by a 'seizure' including stripping off clothes, frenzied running, rolling in snow, glossolalia or echolalia, echopraxia, property destruction and coprophagia.

Reference and Further Reading: Puri BK, Treasaden I (eds) (2010). *Psychiatry: An Evidence-Based Text*. London: Hodder Arnold, pp. 309–318; World Health Organisation (1994) *ICD-10 Classification of Mental and Behavioural Disorders*. Edinburgh, UK: Churchill Livingstone.

Question 96 Answer: e, Duty to warn
Explanation: There were two court hearings of Tarasoff's case. After the first hearing in 1974, the California court held that the mental health professionals bear a duty to use reasonable care to give threatened persons such warnings because warnings are essential to avert foreseeable danger arising from a patient's condition.

Reference and Further Reading: Puri BK, Treasaden I (eds) (2010). *Psychiatry: An Evidence-Based Text*. London: Hodder Arnold, pp. 1228–1229.

Question 97 Answer: b, Duty to protect
Explanation: There were two court hearings of Tarasoff's case. After the second hearing in 1976, the California court held that the mental health professionals have a duty to protect potential victims by reasonable means if their patients have plans to harm the others. The protective privilege ends where the public peril begins.

Reference and Further Reading: Puri BK, Treasaden I (eds) (2010). *Psychiatry: An Evidence-Based Text*. London: Hodder Arnold, pp. 1228–1229.

Question 98 Answer: d, Uqamairineq
Explanation: Uqamairineq is characterized by sudden paralysis associated with borderline sleep states. It is accompanied by anxiety, agitation or hallucinations.

Reference and Further Reading: Puri BK, Treasaden I (eds) (2010). *Psychiatry: An Evidence-Based Text*. London: Hodder Arnold, pp. 309–318; World Health Organisation (1994) *ICD-10 Classification of Mental and Behavioural Disorders*. Edinburgh, UK: Churchill Livingstone.

Question 99 Answer: a, Backward conditioning
Explanation: In backward conditioning, the conditioned stimulus is presented after the unconditioned stimulus has been terminated. In this example, the ringing sound is the conditioned stimulus (i.e. ringing sound) and it is presented after the unconditioned stimulus (i.e. the snake).

Reference and Further Reading: Puri BK, Treasaden I (eds) (2010). *Psychiatry: An Evidence-Based Text*. London: Hodder Arnold, p. 198.

Question 100 Answer: c, Normal jaw jerk
Explanation: Candidates are advised to be familiar with the differences between bulbar and pseudobulbar palsies. The differences are summarized as follows:

	Bulbar palsy	Pseudobulbar palsy
Lesions	Lower motor neuron	Upper motor neuron
Causes	Motor neuron diseases, Guillain–Barré syndrome, polio, syringobulbia, brainstem tumours and central pontine myelinolysis in people with alcohol misuse	Bilateral lesions above the mid-pons, for example, in the corticobulbar tracts in multiple sclerosis, motor neuron disease and stroke. It is more common than bulbar palsy
Tongue	Flaccid and fasciculating	Spastic
Jaw jerk	Normal	Increased
Speech	Quiet, hoarse and nasal	Donald Duck speech Inappropriate laughter or emotional incontinence

Reference and Further Reading: Longmore M, Wilkinson I, Turmezei T, Cheung CK (2007). *Oxford Handbook of Clinical Medicine* (7th edition). Oxford, UK: Oxford University Press; Puri BK, Treasaden I (eds) (2010). *Psychiatry: An Evidence-Based Text*. London: Hodder Arnold, pp. 544, 554.

Question 101 Answer: e, Visuospatial abilities are assessed using a clock-drawing task and a three-dimensional cube copy.

Explanation: MoCA was designed as a rapid screening instrument for mild cognitive dysfunction. Hence, option (b) is incorrect. Option (a) is incorrect because a score of 26 or above is considered normal. The total possible score is 30 points. MoCA assesses different cognitive domains: attention and concentration, executive functions, memory, language, visuoconstructional skills, conceptual thinking, calculations and orientation. Time to administer the whole MoCA is approximately 10 minutes. Hence, option (d) is incorrect.

The short-term memory recall task involves two learning trials of five nouns and delayed recall after approximately 5 minutes.

Reference: http://www.mocatest.org/pdf_files/MoCA-Instructions-English_2010.pdf.

Question 102 Answer: b, Brain fag

Explanation: Brain fag refers to brain fatigue from too much thinking demanded of students. Brain fag is a culture-bound syndrome in West Africa.

Reference and Further Reading: Campbell RJ (1996). *Psychiatric Dictionary*. Oxford, UK: Oxford University Press; Puri BK, Treasaden I (eds) (2010). *Psychiatry: An Evidence-Based Text*. London: Hodder Arnold, pp. 309–318.

Question 103 Answer: b, Projection

Explanation: A person with paranoid personality disorder often projects the tendency to harm other people and believes that others are trying to harm him or her. This results in suspicion and lack of trust. Other common defence mechanisms include projective identification and splitting.

Reference and Further Reading: Puri BK, Hall AD (2002). *Revision Notes in Psychiatry*. London: Arnold, pp. 168–169.

Question 104 Answer: c, Confidentiality

Explanation: This case occurred in the 1960s. Prosenjit Poddar was a university student and he fell in love with a female student called Tatiana Tarasoff. Poddar told the university psychologist that he wanted to kill Tarasoff in a psychotherapy session. Without any precedent, the psychologist decided to maintain the confidentiality of Poddar's homicidal plan. Poddar eventually murdered Tarasoff. The Tarasoff family sued the psychologist from the University of California for not informing Tatiana Tarasoff and the police about Poddar's homicidal plan. In 1976, the California Supreme Court concluded that the mental health professionals have to breach confidentiality in such situations.

Reference and Further Reading: Puri BK, Treasaden I (eds) (2010). *Psychiatry: An Evidence-Based Text.* London: Hodder Arnold, pp. 1228–1229.

Question 105 Answer: d, Koro
Explanation: Koro refers to acute panic or anxiety reaction involving fear of genital retraction.

Reference and Further Reading: World Health Organisation (1994) *ICD-10 Classification of Mental and Behavioural Disorders.* Edinburgh, UK: Churchill Livingstone; Puri BK, Treasaden I (eds) (2010). *Psychiatry: An Evidence-Based Text.* London: Hodder Arnold, pp. 309–318.

Question 106 Answer: b, Bipolar disorder type II
Explanation: The clinical diagnosis should be bipolar disorder type II. This disorder lasts for a minimum of 4 days. There is at least one major depressive episode and at least one hypomanic episode. Individuals usually have no impairments in terms of their functioning. It is important to note that the number of symptoms required to diagnose hypomania is similar to that of a manic episode.

Reference: Puri BK, Hall A, Ho R (2014). *Revision Notes in Psychiatry.* London: CRC Press, p. 378.

Question 107 Answer: c, The cut-off score gives rise to high sensitivity and 100% specificity for diagnosing dementia.
Explanation: The cut-off score of 82 gives rise to high sensitivity (84%) and 100% specificity for diagnosing dementia. The ACE-R incorporates MMSE and frontal lobe assessment. The Addenbrooke's Cognitive Examination Revised (ACE-R) is available in Mandarin for people in Mainland China but not in Cantonese for Chinese people in Hong Kong. It is used to screen for dementia but not delirium.

Reference: Mioshi E, Dawson K, Mitchell J, Arnold R, Hodges R (2006). The Addenbrooke's Cognitive Examination Revised (ACE-R): A brief cognitive test battery for dementia screening. *Int J Geriatr Psychiatry*, 21: 1078–1085.

Question 108 Answer: e, Suppression
Explanation: This person suffers from narcissistic personality disorder. Options A to D are common narcissistic defence mechanisms.

Reference: Gabbard GO, Beck JS, Holmes J (2005). *Oxford Textbook of Psychotherapy.* Oxford, UK: Oxford University Press.

Question 109 Answer: e, Second-order conditioning
Explanation: In this scenario, the white coat is new conditioned stimulus. This new conditioned stimulus is learnt through the original conditioned

stimulus (i.e. the hospital building or hospital environment) but not the original unconditioned stimulus (i.e. the chemotherapy). The nausea feeling associated with white coat is known as second-order conditioning.

Reference and Further Reading: Puri BK, Treasaden I (eds) (2010). *Psychiatry: An Evidence-Based Text.* London: Hodder Arnold, pp. 198–199.

Question 110 Answer: b, 82
Explanation: The two cut-offs were defined in ACE-R (score 88: sensitivity = 0.94, specificity = 0.89; score 82: sensitivity = 0.84, specificity = 1.0). Hence, the cut-off at 82 is the most specific.

Reference: Mioshi E, Dawson K, Mitchell J, Arnold R, Hodges R (2006). The Addenbrooke's Cognitive Examination Revised (ACE-R): A brief cognitive test battery for dementia screening. *Int J Geriatr Psychiatry*, 21: 1078–1085.

Question 111 Answer: c, Displacement
Explanation: Displacement is the redirecting of feelings from a threatening target to a less threatening one. Projection involves placing one's unacceptable or threatening thoughts onto others. Sublimation is the turning of unacceptable impulses into socially acceptable behaviour.

Reference and Further Reading: Puri BK, Hall AD (2002). *Revision Notes in Psychiatry.* London: Arnold, pp. 168–169.

Question 112 Answer: d, 33 hours per week
Explanation: Schizophrenic patients are more likely to relapse if they have been discharged back to their families in which their relatives displayed highly critical comments and over-involvement. Changes in physiological arousal might account for this. This is especially so for families with highly expressed emotions for more than 33 hours per week. Previously, it was also found that schizophrenics had experienced more independent life events in the 3 weeks prior to the onset of a relapse as compared to controls.

Reference: Puri BK, Hall A, Ho R (2014). *Revision Notes in Psychiatry.* London: CRC Press, p. 360.

Question 113 Answer: e, Short-term memory
Explanation: With regards to short-term memory, the anatomical correlate of auditory verbal short-term memory is in the left (dominant) parietal lobe, while that of the visual verbal short-term memory is possibly in the left temporo-occipital area. The anatomical correlate of non-verbal short-term memory is possibly in the right (non-dominant) temporal lobe.

Reference: Puri BK, Hall A, Ho R (2014). *Revision Notes in Psychiatry.* London: CRC Press, p. 103.

Question 114 Answer: e, Sublimation
Explanation: The son has transformed the unacceptable and destructive impulse into acceptable and constructive form. This defence mechanism is known as sublimation.

Reference and Further Reading: Puri BK, Hall AD (2002). *Revision Notes in Psychiatry*. London: Arnold, pp. 168–169.

Question 115 Answer: b, Reaction formation
Explanation: This girl behaves in an opposite manner to hide her underling fear of the monkey and she exhibits reaction formation.

Reference and Further Reading: Puri BK, Hall AD (2002). *Revision Notes in Psychiatry*. London: Arnold, pp. 168–169.

Question 116 Answer: d, Motor neuron disease
Explanation: Depression does not cause progressive worsening dysphagia and her history is supported by her partner. The attending psychiatrist must rule out underlying neurological conditions because progressive dysphagia may indicate a worsening mechanical lesion. Motor neuron disease is associated with progressive dysphagia. Myasthenia gravis is associated with fluctuating dysphagia, and cerebrovascular accident is associated with static dysphagia.

Reference and Further Reading: Ward N, Frith P, Lipsedge M (2001). *Medical Masterclass Neurology, Ophthalmology and Psychiatry*. London: Royal College of Physicians; Puri BK, Treasaden I (eds) (2010). *Psychiatry: An Evidence-Based Text*. London: Hodder Arnold, pp. 441, 527, 543–544, 441.

Question 117 Answer: d, Dependent personality disorder
Explanation: The most appropriate diagnosis would be dependent personality disorder. Individuals with dependent personality disorder usually have tremendous fear of being left alone, and their expression of disagreement is limited. They tend to avoid decision making and taking on responsibilities. Their relationship is sought urgently with other relationships' end. For individuals with dependent personality disorder, they tend to lack self-confidence as well.

Reference: Puri BK, Hall A, Ho R (2014). *Revision Notes in Psychiatry*. London: CRC Press, p. 453.

Question 118 Answer: e, De-personalization
Explanation: The clinical features of catatonia include all of the following: ambitendency, automatic obedience, mitegehen, mitmachen, mannerism, negativism, echolalia, echopraxia, logorrhea and stereotypy. The common etiological causes for catatonia include schizophrenia, depression of manic (more common than schizophrenia), organic disorders, epilepsy, medications, recreational drugs and psychogenic catatonia.

Reference: Puri BK, Hall A, Ho R (2014). *Revision Notes in Psychiatry*. London: CRC Press, p. 369.

Extended matching items (EMIs)

Theme: Cognitive testing

Question 119 Answer: f, Vineland Social Maturity Scale
Explanation: This is a scale that consists of 117 items that assess different aspects of social maturity and social ability. It can be used for the assessment of dementia, childhood development and learning disability.

Question 120 Answer: e, Clifton Assessment Schedule
Explanation: Both the Clifton Assessment Schedule and the Stockton Geriatric Rating Scale are scales that are used by nurses for assessment.

Question 121 Answer: c, Blessed Dementia Scale
Explanation: This is a questionnaire that is usually administered to a relative or friend who is asked to answer the questions on the basis of performance over the previous 6 months. The first set of questions deals with activities of daily living, the second set deals with further activities of daily living and the third set deals with changes in personality, interest and drive.

Question 122 Answer: d, Geriatric Mental State Schedule
Explanation: The Geriatric Mental State Schedule is a semi-structured interview which assesses the subject's mental state.

Question 123 Answer: b, Cambridge Neuropsychological Test Automated Battery
Explanation: This is an automated computerized task that offers sensitive and specific cognitive assessment, using a touch screen. It consists of 13 computerized tasks.

Question 124 Answer: a, Mini Mental State Examination
Explanation: The answer is Mini Mental State Examination. It in itself has a clear advantage over a combination of cognitive testing and informant questionnaire.

Reference: Puri BK, Hall A, Ho R (2014). *Revision Notes in Psychiatry*. London: CRC Press, p. 98.

Theme: Executive function tests

Question 125 Answer: e, Cognitive Estimates Test
Explanation: In the absence of a reduction of intelligence quotient (IQ), some frontal lobe damaged patients may give outrageous incorrect cognitive estimates of commonly known phenomena. For example, when asked to estimate the length of an adult elephant, they might reply 100 yards.

Question 126 Answer: f, Six elements test
Explanation: In this test, the subject is asked to carry out six different tasks (in two groups of three) during a quarter of an hour. In order to maximize their score, the subject needs adequately to plan and schedule these tasks while also monitoring the time that has elapsed.

Question 127 Answer: h, Trail making test
Explanation: The aforementioned test evaluates all of the above-mentioned abilities. Difficulties with cognitive flexibility or complex conceptual thinking may manifest as much longer times being required for Trail B than would be expected from the Trail A time score.

Question 128 Answer: d, Wisconsin Card Sorting Test
Explanation: This helps to pick up perseverative errors (such as continuing too long to sort the cards by number, well after the indexing rule has changed to colour) and non-perseverative errors. Poor performance on this task is particularly associated with dysfunction of the left dorsolateral prefrontal cortex.

Question 129 Answer: c, Tower of London Test
Explanation: The Tower of London Test is based on the Tower of Hanoi game and test planning. The subject is asked to move coloured discs of varying sizes between three columns, either using a model or via a computer program, in order to achieve a given result. Left frontal lobe lesions are associated with poor performance on this test.

Question 130 Answer: b, Verbal fluency test
Explanation: A typical verbal fluency test involves asking the subject to articulate as many words as possible, during a 2-minute interval, starting with the letters F, A, S and in turn. Proper nouns and derivatives such as plurals and different verb endings are not allowed to count together with the root words. Verbal fluency is impaired in left (dominant) frontal lobe lesions.

Question 131 Answer: a, Stroop Test
Explanation: The aforementioned is true with regards to the description of this test. Inference may occur between reading words and naming colours. Left dominant frontal lobe lesions are associated with poor performance on the Stroop test.

Reference: Puri BK, Hall A, Ho R (2014). *Revision Notes in Psychiatry*. London: CRC Press, p. 96.

Theme: Clinical interview

Question 132 Answer: l
Explanation: This is an example of humour.

Question 133 Answer: o
Explanation: This example demonstrates labile affect.

Reference and Further Reading: Puri BK, Hall AD. (2002). *Revision Notes in Psychiatry*. London: Arnold, p. 150.

Question 134 Answer: d
Explanation: This illustrates disinhibition. If such scenario occurs in the CASC examination, a male candidate should inform the examiner to call in a chaperon.

Reference and Further Reading: Puri BK, Treasaden I (eds) (2010). *Psychiatry: An Evidence-Based Text*. London: Hodder Arnold, p. 510.

Theme: Basic psychology

Question 135 Answer: j
Explanation: The patient has storage failure and cannot recall.

Question 136 Answer: i
Explanation: The cue of the anxiety provoked by the gunshot in the park helps him to remember things he forgot in the past.

Question 137 Answer: f
Explanation: In proactive interference, old learning affects new learning.

Reference and Further Reading: Puri BK, Treasaden I (eds) (2010). *Psychiatry: An Evidence-Based Text*. London: Hodder Arnold, pp. 256–262.

Theme: Classification systems

Question 138 Answer: c, DSM-I
Explanation: DSM-I was written and produced in 1952 and was essentially based on the mental disorders section of the ICD-6.

Question 139 Answer: e, DSM-III
Explanation: The DSM-III, launched in 1980, was essentially an innovative classification system that tried not to appear favourably disposed to competing aetiological theories and introduced the operational diagnostic criteria as well as a multi-axial classification system.

Question 140 Answer: f, DSM-III-R
Explanation: The DSM-III was revised, corrected and published as the DSM-III-TR in 1987.

Reference: Puri BK, Hall A, Ho R (2014). *Revision Notes in Psychiatry*. London: CRC Press, p. 18.

Theme: Learning theories and behavioural change

Question 141 Answer: b, Negative reinforcer

Explanation: It refers to an aversive stimulus, whose removal would increase the probability of occurrence of the operant behaviour. Escape conditioning is an example of this, as the response learnt provides complete escape from the aversive stimulus.

Question 142 Answer: c, Punishment

Explanation: Punishment is the situation that occurs if an aversive stimulus is presented whenever a given behaviour occurs, thereby reducing the probability of occurrence of this response. The removal of the aversive stimulus then allows it to act as a negative reinforcer rather than a punisher.

Question 143 Answer: d, Primary reinforcement

Explanation: This is the reinforcement that occurs through reduction of needs deriving from basic drives such as food and drink.

Question 144 Answer: e, Secondary reinforcement

Explanation: This is reinforcement derived from association with primary reinforcers such as money and stress.

Question 145 Answer: g, Fixed interval schedule

Explanation: This form of reinforcement has been known to be particularly poor at maintaining the conditioned response; the maximum response rate typically occurs only when the reinforcement is expected.

Question 146 Answer: h, Variable interval schedule

Explanation: In a variable interval schedule, reinforcement occurs after variable intervals. It is considered to be very good at maintaining the CR.

Question 147 Answer: i, Fixed ratio schedule

Explanation: In a fixed ratio schedule, reinforcement occurs after a fixed number of responses. It is good at maintaining a high response rate.

Reference: Puri BK, Hall A, Ho R (2014). *Revision Notes in Psychiatry*. London: CRC Press, p. 28.

Theme: Attachment abnormalities

Question 148 Answer: a, Insecure attachment

Explanation: In insecure attachment, there is chronic clinginess and ambivalence towards the mother. Clinically, this may be relevant as it is a precursor towards childhood emotional disorders (including school refusal) and disorders (such as agoraphobia) starting in adolescence and adulthood.

Question 149 Answer: b, Avoidant attachment
Explanation: In avoidant attachment, a distance is typically kept from the mother, who may sometimes be ignored. Clinically, avoidant attachment caused by rejection by the mother may be relevant as it may be a precursor to poor social functioning in later life (including aggression).

Question 150 Answer: c, Separation anxiety
Explanation: Separation anxiety refers to the fear an infant shows of being separated from his or her caregiver. Holding a comfort object or a transitional object would help to deal with these feelings. The rate of disappearance of separation anxiety varies with the child's experiences of previous separations, handling by mother, perception of whether the mother will die or depart and temperament.

Question 151 Answer: f, Maternal separation
Explanation: Following a failure to form adequate attachments, for example due to prolonged maternal separation or rejecting parents, can lead to the development of language delay, indiscriminate affection seeking, shallow relationships, lack of empathy, aggression and social disinhibition.

Reference: Puri BK, Hall A, Ho R (2014). *Revision Notes in Psychiatry*. London: CRC Press, p. 63–65.

Theme: Clinical assessment and neuropsychological processes

Question 152 Answer: a, Lexical dysgraphia
Explanation: This is caused by lesion in the left temporo-parietal region. The person breaks down the word's spelling and has difficulty in writing irregular words.

Question 153 Answer: b, Deep dysgraphia
Explanation: This is caused by extensive left hemisphere lesion and a breakdown of the sound-based route for spelling.

Question 154 Answer: c, Neglect dysgraphia
Explanation: Neglect dysgraphia is caused by right hemispheric lesions and leads to misspelling of the initial part of the word.

Question 155 Answer: e, Alexia without agraphia
Explanation: This is due to the occlusion of the left posterior cerebral artery that leads to infarction of the media; aspect of the left occipital lobe and the splenium of the corpus callosum. The explanation for the clinical presentation is as follows: after the stroke, the patient starts off with right hemianopia and he cannot read in the right visual field. Then, the words have to be seen on the left side, which are projected to the right hemisphere. There is a lesion in the splenium that prevents the transfer of visual information from the right to the left side. The primary language area is

disconnected from incoming visual information. As a result, he cannot comprehend any written material, although he can write. As times goes by, he develops a strategy of identifying the individual letters in the right hemisphere. Saying each letter aloud enables him to access the pronunciation of word in the left hemisphere.

Reference: Puri BK, Hall A, Ho R (2014). *Revision Notes in Psychiatry*. London: CRC Press, p. 107.

Question 156 Answer: j, Shaping
Explanation: In shaping, successively closer approximations to the desired behaviour are reinforced in order to achieve the latter. It finds application clinically in the management of behavioural disturbances in people with learning difficulties and in the therapy of patients suffering from psychoactive substance use disorder.

Reference and Further Reading: Puri BK, Hall A, Ho R (2014). *Revision Notes in Psychiatry*. London: CRC Press, p. 29; Puri B, Treasaden I (eds) 2010: *Psychiatry: An Evidence-Based Text*. London: Hodder Arnold, p. 204.

Question 157 Answer: i, Reciprocal inhibition
Explanation: Reciprocal inhibition is a concept developed by Joseph Wolpe. Opposing emotions cannot exist simultaneously. It can be used in treating conditions associated with anticipatory anxiety.

Reference and Further Reading: Puri B, Treasaden I (eds) (2010). *Psychiatry: An Evidence-Based Text*. London: Hodder Arnold, pp. 655, 990; Puri BK, Hall A, Ho R (2014). *Revision Notes in Psychiatry*. London: CRC Press, p. 28.

Question 158 Answer: k, Systematic desensitization
Explanation: Systemic desensitization was developed by Wolpe.

During this process, the patient is successfully exposed (in reality or in imagination) to these stimuli in the hierarchy, beginning with the least anxiety-evoking one, each exposure being paired with relaxation.

Reference and Further Reading: Puri B, Treasaden I (eds) (2010). *Psychiatry: An Evidence-Based Text*. London: Hodder Arnold, p. 990; Puri BK, Hall A, Ho R (2014). *Revision Notes in Psychiatry*. London: CRC Press, p. 28.

Question 159 Answer: c, Flooding
Explanation: Flooding involves exposure to the top stimulus in the hierarchy *in vivo*, while implosion involves exposing to the top stimulus by imagination.

Further Reading: Puri B, Treasaden I (eds) (2010). *Psychiatry: An Evidence-Based Text*. London: Hodder Arnold, pp. 665, 991.

Question 160 Answer: h, Premack's principle
Explanation: Premack's principle uses high-frequency behaviour in this case (e.g. playing piano) to reinforce the low-frequency behaviour (e.g. doing homework).

Premack's principle is useful when it is difficult to identify reinforcers. The high-frequency behaviour does not need to be pleasurable.

Question 161 Answer: l, Token economy
Explanation: Token economy or behavioural therapy has been used to reinforce behaviours.

Reference: Puri BK, Hall A, Ho R (2014). *Revision Notes in Psychiatry*. London: CRC Press, p. 501.

Question 162 Answer: a, Aversive conditioning
Explanation: This type of aversive conditioning is known as convert sensitization as the prisoners imagine the adverse outcomes.

Reference: Puri BK, Hall A, Ho R (2014). *Revision Notes in Psychiatry*. London: CRC Press, p. 25.

Question 163 Answer: f, Latent learning
Explanation: Latent learning shows that learning can take place in the absence of reinforcement.

Further Reading: Puri B, Treasaden I (eds) (2010). *Psychiatry: An Evidence-Based Text*. London: Hodder Arnold, pp. 207, 222.

Question 164 Answer: b, Chaining
Explanation: In chaining, the components of a more complex desired behaviour are first taught and then connected in order to teach the latter. Chaining may be conceptualized in the following two different ways: responses that function as discriminative stimuli for subsequent responses or responses that produce stimuli that function as discriminative stimuli for subsequent responses.

Reference: Puri BK, Hall A, Ho R (2014). *Revision Notes in Psychiatry*. London: CRC Press, p. 29.

Question 165 Answer: g, Penalty
Explanation: Penalty refers to the removal of pleasant stimulus following undesirable behaviour. It is different from punishment which gives an unpleasant outcome, for example canning.

Further Reading: Puri B, Treasaden I (eds) (2010). *Psychiatry: An Evidence-Based Text*. London: Hodder Arnold, p. 949.

Question 166 Answer: a, Aversive conditioning
Explanation: This example demonstrates escape conditioning, an example of aversive conditioning.

Further Reading: Puri B, Treasaden I (eds) (2010). *Psychiatry: An Evidence-Based Text*. London: Hodder Arnold, p. 949.

Question 167 Answer: d, Habituation
Explanation: Sensitization is opposite to habituation. In sensitization, the strength of response is increased as the subject is told that the stimulus is significant.

Further Reading: Puri B, Treasaden I (eds) (2010). *Psychiatry: An Evidence-Based Text*. London: Hodder Arnold, p. 990, 949.

Question 168 Answer: e, Insight learning
Explanation: Insight learning involves a spontaneous and sudden gaining of insight and solution to the problems.

Further Reading: Puri B, Treasaden I (eds) (2010). *Psychiatry: An Evidence-Based Text*. London: Hodder Arnold, p. 949.

Question 169 Answer: b, Kahlbaum
Explanation: In 1882, Karl Kahlbaum, who was a German psychiatrist, coined the terminology cyclothymia.

Question 170 Answer: f, Leonard
Explanation: In this condition, the psychotic symptoms appear suddenly a few days before menstruation, resolve with the onset of menstrual bleeding and reappear with the next cycle. Between psychotic episodes, the woman appears largely asymptomatic. Most cases do not show familial psychiatric comorbidity. The first psychotic episode usually occurs at a young age. The psychiatric picture is nonspecific and changes with every menstruation. Some common features include psychomotor retardation, anxiety, perplexity, disorientation and amnestic features.

Reference: Puri BK, Hall A, Ho R (2014). *Revision Notes in Psychiatry*. London: CRC Press, p.559.

Question 171 Answer: d, Kraepelin
Explanation: In 1896, Emil Kraepelin grouped together catatonia, hebephrenia and the deteriorating paranoid psychosis under the name of dementia praecox.

Further Reading: Puri B, Treasaden I (eds) (2010). *Psychiatry: An Evidence-Based Text*. London: Hodder Arnold, pp. 11, 593, 614, 624.

Question 172 Answer: g, Hecker
In 1871, this was described by Hecker.

Question 173 Answer: a, Bleuler
Explanation: In 1911, Bleuler introduced the term schizophrenia, applied it to Kraepelin's cases of dementia praecox and expanded the concept to include what today may be considered to be schizophrenia spectrum disorders.

Further Reading: Puri B, Treasaden I (eds) (2010). *Psychiatry: An Evidence-Based Text*. London: Hodder Arnold, p. 593.

Question 174 Answer: c, Kasanin

Explanation: Oneiroid state consists of a strange, dream-like, psychotic experience with narrowing of consciousness. It can occur in catatonia.

Reference: Puri BK, Hall A, Ho R (2014). *Revision Notes in Psychiatry.* London: CRC Press, p. 351.

Question 175 Answer: h (36%–50%)

Question 176 Answer: c (13%)

Question 177 Answer: e (23%)

Question 178 Answer: a (4%)

Question 179 Answer: a (2.4%)

Explanation: The concordance rate for monozygotic twins is approximately 45%, and for dizygotic twins, it is approximately 10%. The approximate lifetime risks for the development of schizophrenia in the relatives of patients with schizophrenia are as follows:

a. Parents: 6%
b. All siblings: 10%
c. Siblings (when one parent has schizophrenia): 17%
d. Children: 13%
e. Children (when both parents have schizophrenia): 46%
f. Grandchildren: 4%
g. Uncles, aunts, nephew and nieces: 3%

Reference and Further Reading: Puri B, Treasaden I (eds) (2010). *Psychiatry: An Evidence-Based Text.* London: Hodder Arnold, pp. 474–475, 597, 599; Puri BK, Hall A, Ho R (2014). *Revision Notes in Psychiatry.* London: CRC Press, p. 358.

Question 180 Answer: b

Question 181 Answer: d (12–24 months)

Question 182 Answer: j

Explanation: The following facts should be remembered:

5%–25% of schizophrenics remain unresponsive to conventional neuroleptics.

40%–60% of patients are known to be noncompliant with medications. The possible reasons include having limited insight into the disease, limited beneficial effect, unpleasant side effects, pressure from family and friends and poor communication with the medical team. Depot would help to increase compliance and reduce the relapse rates.

Of patients who have stopped medications, 60%–70% of them would relapse within 1 year and 85% of them within 2 years. This is in comparison to 10%–30% of those who are continued on treatment.

Reference: Puri BK, Hall A, Ho R (2014). *Revision Notes in Psychiatry*. London: CRC Press, p. 365.

EMI on aetiology

Question 183 Answer: k

Explanation: This patient suffers from paediatric autoimmune neuropsychiatric disorders associated with streptococcal infections (PANDAS).

Reference and Further Reading: Puri BK, Treasaden I (eds) (2010). *Psychiatry: An Evidence-Based Text*. London: Hodder Arnold, p. 551.

Question 184 Answer: d, Childhood sexual abuse

Explanation: This patient suffers from borderline personality disorder, and childhood sexual abuse is an important aetiological factor.

Reference and Further Reading: Puri BK, Treasaden I (eds) (2010). *Psychiatry: An Evidence-Based Text*. London: Hodder Arnold, pp. 707, 709.

Question 185 Answer: g, Dysbindin gene, h, Migration, i, Neuregulin gene

Explanation: This patient suffers from schizophrenia, and *dysbindin*, *neuregulin* and migration may be aetiological factors.

Reference and Further Reading: Puri BK, Treasaden I (eds) (2010). *Psychiatry: An Evidence-Based Text*. London: Hodder Arnold, pp. 593–609.
This question has been modified from the 2008–2010 examination.

MRCPSYCH PAPER AI MOCK EXAMINATION 3: QUESTIONS

GET THROUGH MRCPSYCH PAPER AI: MOCK EXAMINATION

Total number of questions: 194 (119 MCQs, 75 EMIs)
Total time provided: 180 minutes

Question 1
Which of the following statements about delusion is false?
a. It is a false belief based usually on incorrect inference about external reality.
b. It is firmly sustained despite what almost everyone else believes.
c. It is firmly sustained despite what constitutes as obvious proof or evidence to the contrary.
d. It is usually not preceded by a delusional mood.
e. The belief is not accepted by other members of the person's culture or subculture.

Question 2
A man with a phobia of open spaces is made to draw up a hierarchy of situations, from the least anxiety provoking to the most anxiety provoking. He is then taught relaxation techniques and gradually exposed to the hierarchy of situations that he has previously drawn up. This is known as
a. Classical conditioning
b. Operant conditioning
c. Systematic desensitization
d. Punishment
e. Flooding

Question 3
In order to determine whether a client is suitable for intensive psychotherapy, which one of the following needs to be assessed?
a. Analysis of transference
b. Analysis of countertransference
c. Analysis of personality and intelligence
d. Assessment of client's family
e. Assessment of dreams

Question 4

An electrocardiogram (ECG) tracing was done as part of the annual assessment for a schizophrenia patient who is on follow-up with the outpatient service. The corrected QTC was noted to be 750 ms. Which of the following medications is most likely to be responsible for this?

a. Risperidone
b. Olanzapine
c. Quetiapine
d. Abilify
e. Clozapine

Question 5

A 22-year-old male has been feeling increasingly troubled by his neighbours, as he believes that they are spying on him consistently. He does not report any other perceptual abnormalities and there has not been any decline in terms of his functioning. The most likely clinical diagnosis would be

a. Paranoid schizophrenia
b. Hebephrenic schizophrenia
c. Delusional disorder
d. Simple schizophrenia
e. Paranoid personality disorder

Question 6

A core trainee has been asked to obtain collaborative history from the family members of a patient who has just been admitted. According to the family members, the patient has been having behavioural changes for the past 6 months. At times, he would be laughing to himself, and he has shown a general decline in his personal functioning. He does have delusional beliefs and auditory hallucinations. Which subtype of schizophrenia would this be?

a. Paranoid schizophrenia
b. Hebephrenic schizophrenia
c. Undifferentiated schizophrenia
d. Residual schizophrenia
e. Post schizophrenia depression

Question 7

An elderly old man looks into the mirror and is shocked that he is unable to see himself in the mirror. What form of psychopathology is this?

a. Autoscopy
b. Negative autoscopy
c. Extracampine hallucination
d. Functional hallucination
e. Reflex hallucination

Question 8

A 25-year-old man, John, has just been discharged from the ward following treatment for first-episode psychosis. He is followed up closely by his community psychiatric nurse. She is concerned that when John is at home, he is being subjected to critical and harsh remarks from his father. She is asking the multi-disciplinary team to consider other interventions that might be appropriate for John. Which of these interventions would be the most appropriate?

a. Interpersonal therapy
b. Cognitive behavioural therapy
c. Psychodynamic therapy
d. Cognitive analytical therapy
e. Family therapy

Question 9

A 20-year-old male has been recently diagnosed with first-episode psychosis. He started on an antipsychotic risperidone around 4 weeks ago. The community psychiatric nurse reports that there has not been any improvement in his symptoms. As a core trainee, what would you want to consider?

a. Increasing the dose of the medications
b. Switching to another antipsychotic
c. Augmentation with another medication
d. Switching to clozapine
e. Exploring potential non-concordance to medications

Question 10

With regards to the treatment of Wernicke's encephalopathy, which of the following should be administered first?

a. Intravenous saline
b. Intravenous glucose
c. Intravenous thiamine and vitamin B
d. Intravenous potassium
e. Intravenous phosphate

Question 11

Based on the *International Classification of Diseases* (ICD)-10 and *Diagnostic and Statistical Manual of Mental Disorders* (DSM)-5 classification system, which of the following psychiatric disorder is believed to be part of a continuum between schizophrenia and mood symptoms?

a. Depression with psychotic features
b. Bipolar affective disorder type I
c. Bipolar affective disorder type II
d. Schizoaffective disorder
e. Post-schizophrenia depression

Question 12

Which of the following statements about persuasion is incorrect?

a. Audience identification with the communicator plays a key role in persuasion.
b. Views of reference groups usually do not play a role if the communicator is credible and has expertise.
c. High self-esteem and intelligence of the recipient increase the likelihood that complex communications will be persuasive.
d. Simple message repetition can be a persuasive influence leading to attitude change.
e. A low anxiety recipient is more influenced by a high fear message and vice versa.

Question 13

A 30-year-old Malaysian man is referred by police for psychiatric assessment. Few days ago, he was arrested by police for shoplifting in the supermarket. Then, he became mildly depressed because he 'lost face' after the incident. This morning, he took a knife and tried to kill pedestrians who walked across his path. He is amnesic for the episode. This man suffers from which of the following culture-bound syndromes?

a. Amok
b. Brain fag
c. Dhat
d. Koro
e. Latah

Question 14

All of the following are considered to be part of the normal stage of grief with the exception of

a. Denial
b. Anger
c. Bargaining
d. Depression
e. Agitation

Question 15

A 22-year-old male has been diagnosed with paranoid schizophrenia and sectioned for treatment in the mental health service three times since the onset of his schizophrenia. He has had an adequate trial of haloperidol and olanzapine, which did not help with his symptoms. It is now decided that he start on a trial of clozapine. Which one of the following investigations should be considered before starting him on clozapine?

a. Full blood count
b. Renal panel
c. Liver function test
d. Thyroid function test
e. Metabolic markers

Question 16

A patient presents with catatonia to the outpatient clinic and a joint decision was made for inpatient admission for further treatment. The trainee should expect to find the following signs of catatonia, with the exception of

a. Neologism
b. Ambitendency
c. Mitgehen
d. Negativism
e. Mannerism

Question 17

A 22-year-old male came for his routine outpatient clinic follow-up and he reported that he had been troubled by voices recently. He shared that he was worried about the voices, as the voices seemed to be commenting on what he is doing. The psychopathology being described would be

a. Command hallucination
b. Running commentary
c. Pseudohallucination
d. Functional hallucination
e. Hallucinosis

Question 18

A 40-year-old man suffers from alcohol dependence. His general practitioner (GP) asked him to take disulfiram but no clear instruction was given. Every time he drinks alcohol, he takes disulfiram. He develops flushing of the face, headache, vomiting, chest pain and sweating when he drinks alcohol. He attributes the unpleasant experiences to alcohol and he has decided not to drink alcohol in his life. This phenomenon is known as

a. Aversive conditioning
b. Backward conditioning
c. Classical conditioning
d. Forward conditioning
e. Systematic desensitization

Question 19

A 21-year old male has a history of bipolar disorder and he has been previously admitted thrice for manic episodes and just recently for a depressive episode. During his routine outpatient review, the core trainee noted that the patient has pervasively low mood with reduced interest and fulfils the criteria for bipolar, depressive episode. Which of the following medications would be most suitable for him?

a. Doxepin
b. Fluoxetine
c. Sertraline
d. Mirtazapine
e. Lamotrigine

Question 20

This is a particular subtype of schizophrenia in which there might be marked psychomotor disturbances that might alternate between extremes. In addition, the patient might also report experiencing a dream-like state with vivid scenic hallucination.

a. Paranoid schizophrenia
b. Simple schizophrenia
c. Residual schizophrenia
d. Post-schizophrenia depression
e. Catatonic schizophrenia

Question 21

A 75-year-old woman has suffered from a recent cerebrovascular accident (CVA). After the CVA, her family members note that she has global dementia and associated frontal lobe personality changes. Which of the following might be implicated?

a. Infarction of the anterior cerebral arteries
b. Infarction of the middle cerebral arteries
c. Infarction of the posterior cerebral artery
d. Subarachnoid bleed
e. Subdural bleed

Question 22

A medical student being attached to the addiction specialty wonders how long an individual needs to have symptoms of alcohol dependence in order for a diagnosis to be made. The correct answer, based on the ICD-10 classification system, would be

a. 1 month
b. 2 months
c. 6 months
d. 1 year
e. 2 years

Question 23

There are five types of social powers that have been proposed. Which of the following types of social power best describes someone who is often being looked up to as a role model, is well liked by many and has the ability to make people around them feel good?

a. Authority
b. Reward
c. Coercive
d. Referent
e. Expert

Question 24
The following defence mechanism is commonly used in borderline personality disorder:
a. Splitting
b. Reaction formation
c. Rationalization
d. Humour
e. Sublimation

Question 25
A patient with obsessive-compulsive disorder (OCD) tends to make use of this particular defence mechanism:
a. Projection
b. Acting out
c. Splitting
d. Reaction formation
e. Projective identification

Question 26
Which of the following medications would be the most helpful for patients diagnosed with catatonia?
a. Benzodiazepines
b. Nonsteroidal anti-inflammatory drugs (NSAIDs)
c. Antipsychotics
d. Antidepressants
e. Mood stabilizers

Question 27
A welfare organization decides to hire a man with schizophrenia for vocational training. This man will be paid £400 at the end of each month if he can make 100 key chains per month. This phenomenon is known as
a. Classical conditioning
b. Fixed interval schedule
c. Fixed ratio schedule
d. Variable interval schedule
e. Variable ratio schedule

Question 28
The following best describe auditory hallucinations that psychotic patients experience, with the exception of
a. Command voices
b. Demeaning voices
c. Voices doing a running commentary
d. Voices telling them that they are useless
e. Voices arguing amongst each other

Question 29

Which of the following factors account for the lower incidence of alcoholism in Orientals?

a. Presence of isoenzyme aldehyde dehydrogenase
b. Absence of isoenzyme aldehyde dehydrogenase
c. Presence of isoenzymes alcohol dehydrogenase
d. Absence of isoenzyme alcohol dehydrogenase
e. Presence of ultra-rapid metabolizing CYP 450 enzymes

Question 30

Which of the following personality disorders might be present in someone who presents with the psychiatric diagnosis of malingering?

a. Schizoid personality disorder
b. Schizotypal personality disorder
c. Antisocial personality disorder
d. Borderline personality disorder
e. Dependent personality disorder

Question 31

On examination of a patient's visual field, the examiner would ask the patient to cover one eye and fixate on the examiner's opposite eye. Mapping of the visual field is then carried out by the examiner. The objective of this examination is to check for

a. Weakness of the extraocular muscles
b. Checking for presence of organic disorders (myasthenia gravis or thyroid eye disease)
c. Lens dislocation
d. Assessment for lesions involving the central visual pathway
e. Myopia

Question 32

A 20-year-old university student presents with delusions, hallucinations, disorganized speech and grossly disorganized behaviour for 3 weeks. He failed an examination 3 weeks ago. Which of the following statements is correct?

a. This patient does not fulfil both DSM-IV-TR and ICD-10 diagnostic criteria for brief and acute psychotic disorders respectively.
b. This patient fulfils the DSM-IV-TR diagnostic criteria for brief psychotic disorder.
c. This patient fulfils the ICD-10 diagnostic criteria for acute and transient psychotic disorder.
d. This patient fulfils both DSM-IV-TR and ICD-10 diagnostic criteria for brief and acute psychotic disorders respectively.
e. DSM-IV-TR diagnostic criteria for brief psychotic disorder do not consider the person's culture.

Question 33

Colon cancer patients have a tendency to compare themselves with other patients who are deemed to be more ill than them. Which of the following terminology best describes this phenomenon?

a. Downward social comparison
b. Upward social comparison
c. Normative social comparison
d. Relative social comparison
e. Absolute social comparison

Question 34

Attitudes are made up of which of the following components?

a. Motivational only
b. Motivational and emotional only
c. Motivational, emotional and perceptual
d. Motivational, emotional, perceptual and cognitive
e. Motivational, emotional and cognitive

Question 35

A 30-year-old female has been too afraid recently to step out of her house. She feels that other people around her can know what she is thinking just by looking at her. This form of psychopathology is known as

a. Thought insertion
b. Thought withdrawal
c. Thought broadcast
d. Thought interference
e. Delusion of reference

Question 36

A talented child believes that he will get the highest marks in class if he wears a red watch on the day of examination. When he does not have an examination, he usually wears a blue watch. The interval for him to get the highest mark varies. Nevertheless, his habit of wearing a red watch during examination remains stable over the years. He tends to wear the red watch more often if he has not obtained the highest marks in class for a long time. This phenomenon is known as

a. Classical conditioning
b. Fixed interval schedule
c. Fixed ratio schedule
d. Variable interval schedule
e. Variable ratio schedule

Question 37

A 30-year-old man suffering from schizophrenia used to take chlorpromazine 100 mg orally per day. He wants to change antipsychotics and requests a list of drugs. Which of the following lists indicate the correct dosage which is equivalent to oral chlorpromazine 100 mg per day?

a. 0.5 mg/day for haloperidol, 0.5 mg/day for risperidone, 2.5 mg/day for olanzapine, 37.5 mg/day for quetiapine, 15 mg/day for ziprasidone and 3.75 mg/day for aripiprazole
b. 1 mg/day for haloperidol, 1 mg/day for risperidone, 2.5 mg/day for olanzapine, 37.5 mg/day for quetiapine, 30 mg/day for ziprasidone and 3.75 mg/day for aripiprazole
c. 1.5 mg/day for haloperidol, 1.5 mg/day for risperidone, 2.5 mg/day for olanzapine, 37.5 mg/day for quetiapine, 30 mg/day for ziprasidone and 3.75 mg/day for aripiprazole
d. 2 mg/day for haloperidol, 2 mg/day for risperidone, 5 mg/day for olanzapine, 75 mg/day for quetiapine, 60 mg/day for ziprasidone and 7.5 mg/day for aripiprazole
e. 4 mg/day for haloperidol, 4 mg/day for risperidone, 10 mg/day for olanzapine, 150 mg/day for quetiapine, 120 mg/day for ziprasidone and 15 mg/day for aripiprazole.

Question 38

Which of the following is considered to be a poor prognostic factor for patients with schizophrenia?

a. Being male
b. Being married
c. No ventricular enlargement on computed tomography (CT) imaging
d. Affective component to the illness
e. Good initial response to treatment

Question 39

A 60-year-old male sustained head injuries, after being involved in a major road traffic accident about one year ago. Recently, his wife has noticed marked changes in his behaviour. She is concerned especially about him making inappropriate, rude sexual remarks when he is out. The symptoms that he is currently experiencing suggest an injury to which part of his brain?

a. Frontal lobe
b. Temporal lobe
c. Parietal lobe
d. Cerebellum
e. Hippocampus

Question 40

A 25-year-old woman develops brief psychosis following childbirth. In order for her to fulfil the diagnostic criteria for postpartum psychosis, which of the following statements is incorrect?

a. The DSM-IV-TR specifies the onset of her psychotic episode has to be within 4 weeks postpartum.
b. The ICD-10 states that her psychotic episode should commence within 6 weeks of delivery.

c. The DSM-IV-TR provides postpartum onset specifier associated with brief psychotic disorder.
d. In the ICD-10, her condition is classified under schizophrenia.
e. There is no specific diagnostic criterion for postpartum psychosis in the DSM-IV-TR and the ICD-10.

Question 41

A 28-year-old specialist registrar was at the annual Royal College of Psychiatrist academic conference. There were a lot of participants and she was having a discussion with Professor Brown regarding her latest research. She was able to identify Professor Wilson, who called out for her. Which form of attention process was Jane using?

a. Selective/focused attention
b. Divided attention
c. Sustained attention
d. Non-sustained attention
e. Differentiated attention

Question 42

A 30-year-old motorcyclist suffers from head injuries after a road traffic accident. His partner comments that his memory has become very poor. Which of the following is not a standardized test to assess his memory?

a. Auditory–Verbal Learning Test (AVLT)
b. California Verbal Learning Test (CVLT)
c. Recognition Memory Test (RMT)
d. Wechsler Memory Test (WMT)
e. Weigl Colour–Form Sorting Test (WCFST)

Question 43

A 35-year-old male has a diagnosis of narcissistic personality disorder. He is rejected from further admission to the ward because he has made the nurses very upset by making unreasonable complaints. The nurses are begging the consultant not to admit him, although he is highly suicidal. This is an example of

a. Acting out
b. Countertransference
c. Displacement
d. Irresponsibility
e. Narcissistic injury

Question 44

All of the following are immature defence mechanisms except

a. Denial
b. Humour
c. Hypochrondriasis
d. Repression
e. Somatization

Question 45

A 60-year-old man is admitted to the gastroenterology ward because of abdominal pain. He has been complaining for the past 6 months that his intestines have stopped working, and said to the gastroenterologist, 'My intestines are rotten and you can smell it.' He has also told the doctor that he could hear his neighbours saying bad things about him. What is the most likely ICD-10 diagnosis?

a. Acute and transient psychosis
b. Late onset schizophrenia
c. Persistent delusional disorder
d. Schizophrenia
e. Severe depressive episode with psychotic features

Question 46

Which of the following statements with regards to the respective delusions is incorrect?

a. Delusional jealousy – Othello syndrome
b. Delusion of doubles – i'illusions de sosies
c. Delusion of infestation – Ekbom's syndrome
d. Doppelganger – Cotard's syndrome
e. Delusion of pregnancy – Couvade syndrome

Question 47

A gambler thinks that the more often he gambles, the more often he will win. He is not certain about the number of times gambling resulted in winning. The time interval between two episodes of winning is also unpredictable. His wife complains that he often has emotional outbursts when he pursues to win. This phenomenon is known as

a. Classical conditioning
b. Fixed interval schedule
c. Fixed ratio schedule
d. Variable interval schedule
e. Variable ratio schedule

Question 48

The following are findings from the Clinical Antipsychotic Trials of Intervention Effectiveness (CATIE) study, except

a. More patients taking second-generation antipsychotics continue the antipsychotic treatment compared with patients taking conventional antipsychotics.
b. Olanzapine was the most effective in terms of the rates of discontinuation.
c. The efficacy of the conventional antipsychotic agent perphenazine appeared similar to that of quetiapine, risperidone and ziprasidone.
d. Olanzapine was associated with greater weight gain and increases in measures of glucose and lipid metabolism.
e. Perphenazine was associated with more discontinuation for extrapyramidal effects.

Question 49

A medical student reading up on the history of psychiatry found out that lactate infusion was given in the late 1960s. From his reading, the intravenous infusion of lactate caused patients to have several symptoms, which included sudden onset of palpitations, chest pain, choking sensations, dizziness, depersonalization and also a significant fear of losing control and dying. What is the psychiatric condition that has resulted from intravenous lactate infusion?

a. Specific phobia
b. Generalized anxiety disorder
c. Panic disorder
d. Post-traumatic stress disorder
e. Lactic acidosis

Question 50

A trainee wants to start a research about attitudes. He has only basic understanding that attitudes are usually based on pre-existing beliefs. Which one of the following statements associated with the measurement scale is incorrect?

a. Thurstone Scale – Dichotomous scale indicating agreement or disagreement
b. Thurstone Scale – Ranking is unbiased
c. Likert Scale – More sensitive in comparison to the dichotomous Thurstone Scale
d. Semantic Differential Scale – Easy to use and has good test-retest reliability
e. Semantic Differential Scale – Positional response bias might occur

Question 51

A 50-year-old woman has received six sessions of electroconvulsive therapy (ECT). She complains of significant recent memory loss while remote memories remain intact. This phenomenon is known as

a. Gestalt's law
b. Marr's law
c. Ribot's law
d. Tarasoff's law
e. Weber–Fechner law

Question 52

This particular ethical principle emphasizes minimization of the risks and maximizing the benefits for the greatest number of individuals. This ethical principle is referred to as

a. Utilitarian
b. Deontology
c. Virtue
d. Paternalism
e. Beneficence

Question 53

Based on your understanding of the basic ethical principles in psychiatry, deontology refers to

a. Providing a duty-based approach.
b. Acting in the patient's best interest.
c. Ensuring that the action performed is considered to be morally right if it would lead to the greatest human pleasure, happiness and satisfaction.
d. Ensuring that all individuals receive equal and impartial consideration.
e. A doctor's native motive is to provide morally correct care to his or her patients and focus solely on the rightness and wrongness of the actions themselves, and not on the consequences of the actions.

Question 54

The following are ICD-10 diagnostic criteria for delusional disorder, except

a. There is a set of related delusions (e.g. persecutory, grandiose, hypochondriacal, jealous or erotic delusions).
b. The minimum duration of delusions is 6 months.
c. There must be no persistent hallucination.
d. The general criteria for schizophrenia and depressive disorder should not be fulfilled.
e. There must be no evidence of primary or secondary organic mental disorders.

Question 55

A 40-year-old man wants to transfer from another NHS trust to your trust. He is admitted to the psychiatric ward because of low mood. He complains to the ward manager that the inpatient service is not up to standard. After discharge, he has written 15 letters to the chief executive about the delay in psychologist appointment. Which of the following personality disorders is the most likely diagnosis?

a. Anankastic
b. Anxious (avoidant)
c. Antisocial
d. Borderline
e. Narcissistic

Question 56

A patient was called into the interview room. Throughout the interview process, he was noted to be moving his hand repeatedly whenever he talks. This form of psychopathology is known as

a. Automatic obedience
b. Catalepsy
c. Cataplexy
d. Mannerism
e. Echopraxia

Question 57

A 35-year-old patient with schizophrenia previously on olanzapine was diagnosed by his GP to suffer from diabetes mellitus. Her GP has written a letter to consult you on the most suitable antipsychotics to prescribe in this case. Which of the following antipsychotics would you recommend in this case?

a. Amisulpride
b. Chlorpromazine
c. Clozapine
d. Risperidone
e. Quetiapine

Question 58

Individuals usually tend to feel uneasy when cognitive dissonance occurs and this might lead to increased anxiety. There is always a motivation to achieve internal cognitive consistency. All of the following help with the reduction of anxiety associated with cognitive dissonance, except

a. Changing one or more of the thought processes involved in the dissonant relationship
b. Changing the behaviour that is considered inconsistent with the cognition
c. Addition of new thoughts that are consistent with pre-existing thought processes
d. Altering attitude
e. Challenging negative automatic thoughts

Question 59

During routine outpatient review, a patient with a diagnosis of schizophrenia, who has been concordant to his medications and has not had a relapse in the last decade, informs the psychiatrist that he wishes to stop medical treatment. The psychiatrist is concerned and cautioned him about the risk of relapse as well as the advantage and benefits of staying on the medications. The patient has mental capacity to understand and formulate a decision. However, his decision in this case would not be the best option. The psychiatrist feels compelled to go along with the wishes of the patient. This is an example of the ethical principle of

a. Utilitarianism
b. Deontology
c. Nonmaleficence
d. Autonomy
e. Beneficence

Question 60

A 40-year-old female teacher suffering from depression has been on sick leave for the past 6 months. She has asked the core trainee to continue giving her sick leave. The core trainee is concerned and consults you. Which of the following is an indicator for not issuing a medical certificate to this patient?

a. She is willing to continue the antidepressant as suggested by the core trainee.
b. She is keen to see a psychologist for psychotherapy as suggested by the core trainee.

c. She wants to be in a depressive state because her husband gives her more support when she is sick.
d. She is very depressed and cannot focus on teaching. She needs to be exempted from her normal social role.
e. She is very depressed and worries that the school will blame her for being responsible for causing her own depression.

Question 61

A concerned sister brought her 50-year-old brother to see you. She feels that he suffers from obsessive-compulsive personality disorder based on the information available on the Internet. Which of the following clinical features highly suggest that he indeed suffers from anankastic personality disorder?

a. He was asked to leave a church because he said obscene things to fellow church members.
b. He was fined by the traffic police for illegal parking because he tends to park anywhere on the street.
c. He was penalized by the HM Revenue & Customs for delay in filling up income tax form because he could not make up his mind what to report and feared making mistakes.
d. He was sued by his ex-wife for refusing to pay maintenance fee because he believes that she can support herself.
e. He was suspended from school when he was young because he vandalized school properties.

Question 62

Which of the following statements correctly defines what is meant by delusional perception?

a. It means that an abnormal perception has taken on delusional significance.
b. It refers to a delusional mood with delusional significance.
c. It means that a normal perception has taken on a delusional significance.
d. It means that a normal perception has been misinterpreted.
e. It arises due to the recall of an abnormal memory.

Question 63

A 3-year-old boy was playing with his toy car when it rolled under the sofa. He attempted reaching for the toy car with his hands but it was too far in. After several tries at using his hands, he picked up an umbrella and succeeded at using the hook of the umbrella to reach for his toy car. Which of the following learning theories best describes the aforementioned phenomenon?

a. Cognitive learning
b. Mowrer's two-factor theory
c. Psychological imprinting
d. Observational learning
e. Operant conditioning

Question 64

Which of the following phenomenon is the most common extrapyramidal side effect associated with the first generation antipsychotics?

a. Akathisia
b. Acute dystonia
c. Galactorrhoea
d. Pseudo-parkinsonism
e. Tardive dyskinesia

Question 65

A 45-year-old doctor wakes up at 6.00 AM every day and goes to the hospital to ensure that the parking lot closest to the hospital main entrance is not occupied. She is easily upset with other doctors who occupy this parking lot. She could only buy fish and chips from the same store in the last 10 years and she usually declines to try other foods during lunch. She is a very clean person and likes to document in great details. Her colleagues consult you about her personality. Your answer is

a. Anankastic personality
b. Anxious avoidance personality
c. Normal personality
d. Schizoid personality
e. Schizotypal personality

Question 66

A 14-year-old teenager is experiencing and undergoing which stage, based on Erikson's stage of development?

a. Initiative
b. Accomplishment and duty
c. Identity
d. Intimacy
e. Generativity

Question 67

In an experiment, it was found that when there were more people around during an emergency, the participants were less likely to help. Which of the following best describes the aforementioned phenomenon?

a. Propinquity effect
b. Overjustification effect
c. Bystander effect
d. Social dilemma
e. Moral dilemma

Question 68

A psychotherapist, on knowing the difficulties that his patient has had experienced recently (being dismissed from work and working through the grief associated with the loss of his loved ones), mentioned to his client that 'You have indeed coped extremely well despite the circumstances that you have been in'. This is an example of

a. Summarizing
b. Reflective listening
c. Affirmation
d. Normalization
e. Empathetic statement

Question 69

A medical student was shown a list of symptoms during his psychiatry examinations and he was asked which one of the following would be helpful towards arriving at a psychiatric diagnosis for schizophrenia. What would the correct answer be?

a. Diminished interest
b. Short-term memory difficulties
c. Long-term memory difficulties
d. Attention and concentration difficulties
e. Thought withdrawal

Question 70

A 35-year-old man suffering from treatment-resistant schizophrenia is treated with clozapine. He wants to know the most common side effect. Your answer is

a. Agranulocytosis
b. Hypersalivation
c. Sedation
d. Seizure
e. Weight gain

Question 71

A 30-year-old woman with a history of depression complains of 1-week history of worsening diplopia. During physical examination, her left eye is medially deviated giving a diplopia best prevented by closing her left eye. On attempted left lateral gaze, her right eye achieves full adduction but her left eye remains static, producing a widely separated image horizontally. Which of the following conditions is the most likely?

a. IV nerve palsy
b. Left VI nerve palsy
c. Left III nerve palsy
d. Right VI nerve palsy
e. Right III nerve palsy

Question 72

A neurosurgeon was concerned about the cognitive deficits after he operated on a 23-year-old driver who had recently been involved in a traumatic road traffic accident. He referred him to the psychiatrist for further evaluation. It was found that the driver had impaired parietal lobe functioning. Which one of the following is NOT a test of parietal lobe functioning?

a. Left and right orientation
b. Acalculia
c. Dysgraphia
d. Cognitive estimates
e. Ideomotor apraxia

Question 73

You are performing a risk assessment on a 20-year-old man suffering from paranoid schizophrenia. Which of the following factors is least likely to be associated with violence?

a. The person has well-planned violence.
b. The person has access to weapons.
c. The person retains the ability to plan.
d. The person is staying in the community.
e. The person is totally losing touch with reality.

Question 74

You are performing a risk assessment on a 22-year-old man suffering from acute psychosis. Which of the following conditions is least likely to be associated with violence?

a. He experiences hallucinations causing positive emotions.
b. He feels dominated by forces beyond his control.
c. He feels that there are people wanting to harm him.
d. He feels that his thoughts are being put into his head.
e. He reacts in despair by striking out against others.

Question 75

A 40-year-old man is referred by his GP because he needs to drink one bottle of beer first thing in the morning, two bottles of beer during lunch time and at least few glasses of hard liquor in the evening. He needs to drink to calm his nerves as he finds his job is very stressful. According to his wife, he was previously diagnosed with personality disorder. Which of the following personality disorders is most likely?

a. Antisocial personality disorder
b. Anxious avoidant personality
c. Borderline personality disorder
d. Dependent personality disorder
e. Narcissistic personality disorder

Question 76

Which of the following is not considered to be a formal thought disorder?

a. Asyndesis
b. Condensation

c. Derailment
d. Fusion
e. Perseveration

Question 77
A 23-year-old female has just been recently diagnosed with an anxiety condition known as agoraphobia. The consultant has recommended that she be started on a course of medication (antidepressants) and also a course of psychological therapy. She has been concordant thus far and has improved such that she is now able to leave home independently. Which of the following psychological interventions has helped her?
a. Classical conditioning
b. Operant conditioning
c. Habit reversal
d. Exposure and response prevention
e. Extinction

Question 78
A 24-year-old female patient comes for review to your outpatient clinic. The inpatient consultant prescribed olanzapine and she has taken this medication for 3 months since discharge. She complains of a weight gain of 10 kg and increased appetite. She has a family history of diabetes. She requests a change in antipsychotic. Which of the following medications would you recommend?
a. Aripiprazole
b. Paliperidone
c. Quetiapine
d. Risperidone
e. Ziprasidone

Question 79
A medical student new to her posting wonders at roughly what age newborns will acquire skills of accommodation and colour vision. Which of the following would be correct?
a. Immediately at birth
b. 2 months
c. 4 months
d. 6 months
e. 1 year

Question 80
Psychiatry is the only specialty whose diagnoses are not confirmed by investigations but rests upon history taking. Which of the following statements regarding history taking is the most incorrect?

a. Assessment proforma such as admission sheets which could be found in the case notes of long-stay patients in large mental hospitals is not a good example of psychiatric history taking.
b. Clinical errors often occur because the clinical history itself is inadequate.
c. Continuing history taking is sometimes neglected because the patient is 'well-known' to a psychiatrist.
d. History taking should not be a passive process of information collection.
e. The standard schema of psychiatric history taking is a good guide to the structure of the psychiatric interview.

Question 81

A core trainee-1 resident was interviewing an elderly man in his clinic. He decided to perform a bedside Mini Mental State Examination on the patient in view of his recent difficulties with his memory. He asked the man to copy intersecting polygons. This is a test of which part of the brain functions?

a. Frontal lobes
b. Parietal lobes
c. Temporal lobes
d. Corpus callosum
e. Hippocampus

Question 82

A 30-year-old woman with a history of depression complains of 1-week history of worsening diplopia. When her right eyelid is lifted, her right eye is looking down and out and the pupil is fixed and dilated. When she is asked to gaze to the left, her right eye remains in position while her left eye achieves full abduction. Which of the following conditions is most likely?

a. IV nerve palsy
b. Left VI nerve palsy
c. Left III nerve palsy
d. Right VI nerve palsy
e. Right III nerve palsy

Question 83

A 40-year-old man needs to drink alcohol immediately after he wakes up in the morning, again a few pints of beer during lunch time and again at least 8 units of alcohol in the evening. He annoys his family members who always ask him to cut down his alcohol intake. He claims that he is not an alcoholic and he needs to drink to keep himself calm. Based on the clinical information, which of the following is your diagnosis?

a. Anankastic personality disorder
b. Antisocial personality disorder
c. Alcohol-dependent syndrome
d. Generalized anxiety disorder
e. OCD

Question 84

Which of the following statements with regards to delusional perception is incorrect?

a. Delusional perception is a primary delusion.
b. Delusional perception is a secondary delusion.
c. It might be preceded by a period of delusional mood in which the person might be aware that something strange and threatening might be happening.
d. It is considered to be one of the first-rank symptoms.
e. It usually arises fully formed without any discernible connections with prior events.

Question 85

A 20-year-old man agreed to participate in a research project. He was first given Drug A, which caused tachycardia. Five minutes later, he was given Drug B, which was supposed to cause bradycardia. Drug B was not strong enough to overcome the tachycardia associated with Drug A. The subject still had tachycardia after administration of Drug B. The administration of Drug A and Drug B was repeated 12 times over the 3 days. On the fourth day, the investigator only gave the subject Drug B and was surprised to find that he developed tachycardia. The tachycardia associated with administration of Drug B on the fourth day is known as

a. Conditioned response
b. Conditioned stimulus
c. Unconditioned response
d. Unconditioned stimulus
e. Second-order conditioning

Question 86

A 30-year-old man suffers from treatment-resistant schizophrenia and he is on clozapine. He also suffers from post-schizophrenia depression. Augmentation with which of the following antidepressants is the safest option in view of the potential risk of epilepsy?

a. Amitriptyline
b. Bupropion
c. Clomipramine
d. Fluoxetine
e. Venlafaxine

Question 87

Who was responsible for discovering the use of lithium?

a. John Cade
b. Maxwell Jones
c. Viktor Frankl
d. Carl Rogers
e. Joseph Wolpe

Question 88

The individual who was responsible for the development of existential therapy was

a. Maxwell Jones
b. Viktor Frankl
c. Jacob Kasanin
d. Cerletti
e. John Bowlby

Question 89

Which of the following terms best describes 'the presence of clearly demarcated total memory loss, with no recovery of this lost memory over time', for individuals who have experienced alcoholic blackouts?

a. State-dependent memory
b. Fragmentary blackouts
c. En bloc blackouts
d. Episodic memory impairments
e. Declarative memory impairments

Question 90

A 30-year-old woman with a history of depression complains of 1-week history of worsening diplopia. She describes difficulty looking down, often notable when reading or walking down stairs. Which of the following conditions is most likely?

a. II nerve palsy
b. III nerve palsy
c. IV nerve palsy
d. VI nerve palsy
e. VII nerve palsy

Question 91

A 55-year-old male who has a history of alcohol dependence was admitted just 2 days ago for an emergency hip operation following a fall. He now reports that he is troubled by visions of multiple small spiders running around the room. Which of the following correctly describes his experience?

a. Lilliputian hallucination
b. Functional hallucination
c. Reflex hallucination
d. Macropsia
e. Micropsia

Question 92

A 39-year-old man with a history of cocaine dependence continues taking the drug to avoid experiencing withdrawal symptoms. This phenomenon is known as

a. Aversion
b. Negative reinforcement
c. Partial reinforcement

d. Positive reinforcement
e. Punishment

Question 93
A medical student wants to know the most common sign of neuroleptic malignant syndrome. Your answer is
a. Altered mental state
b. Hyperhidrosis
c. Incontinence
d. Labile blood pressure
e. Rigidity

Question 94
Based on Piaget's theory, which stage would a child be in if he is able to recognize that containers, even though they are of different shapes, contain similar amounts of water?
a. Sensorimotor
b. Preoperational
c. Operational
d. Concrete operational
e. Formal operational

Question 95
A 30-year-old woman with a history of depression complains of a 3-month history of worsening diplopia and ptosis in the evenings. Which of the following conditions is the most likely?
a. Cavernous sinus thrombosis
b. Guillain–Barre syndrome
c. Mitochondrial diseases
d. Myasthenia gravis
e. Multiple sclerosis

Question 96
A 60-year-old retired naval officer with depression believes that he is in danger of imminent arrest and life imprisonment for stealing a uniform from the Royal Navy 30 years ago. The psychopathology being described is
a. Delusional mood
b. Delusional perception
c. Delusion of guilt
d. Delusion of reference
e. Nihilistic delusion

Question 97
A 25-year-old woman with a history of methamphetamine abuse reports that she continues smoking the drug because of 'euphoria' she experiences. This phenomenon is known as
a. Aversion
b. Negative reinforcement
c. Partial reinforcement
d. Positive reinforcement
e. Punishment

Question 98
There are reported differences in the development of boys versus girls. In particular, the average age of onset of puberty of boys is much later. Which of the following is the average age of puberty for boys?
a. 10 years old
b. 11 years old
c. 12 years old
d. 13 years old
e. 14 years old

Question 99
There are several theories that explain interpersonal attraction. Which of the following is not a theory of interpersonal attraction?
a. Proxemics
b. Social exchange theory
c. Equity theory
d. Reinforcement theory
e. Mutual attraction

Question 100
Please choose the most appropriate statements with regards to schizophrenia:
a. Afro-Caribbean immigrants to the United Kingdom have a much lower risk of developing schizophrenia.
b. The winter excess of births in schizophrenics is due to a seasonal prevalence of a viral infection or other perinatal hazard.
c. Males have generally a later onset of schizophrenia as compared to females.
d. It has been found that there is a reduction in the relapse rates of schizophrenia in those who have lived with families in which the relatives displayed high EE.
e. Obstetric complications are less likely in individuals with schizophrenia.

Question 101

A mother worries that her daughter will develop depression because of the family history of depressive disorder. Which of the following genes is associated with increased risk?

a. APO E4 gene on chromosome 21
b. Catechol-*O*-methyltransferase (COMT) gene on chromosome 21
c. Presenilin-2 gene on chromosome 1
d. Presenilin-1 gene on chromosome 14
e. Serotonin transporter gene

Question 102

During a clinical examination, a core trainee was asked what terminology would best describe 'memories for events occurring while intoxicated are lost when sober, but returns when next intoxicated'. Which of the following would the most appropriate terminology?

a. State-dependent memory
b. Fragmentary blackouts
c. En bloc blackouts
d. Episodic memory impairments
e. Declarative memory impairments

Question 103

A 22-year-old male, Jack, is usually not an aggressive person. However, in 2011, while participating in a large-scale riot in London that turned violent, Jack found himself engaged in violence as well. Which of the following best explains Jack's behaviour?

a. Social loafing
b. Social facilitation
c. Social norms
d. Deindividuation
e. Social tuning

Question 104

At what age does a British child start to have early comprehension of English grammar?

a. 1–2 years
b. 2–3 years
c. 3–6 years
d. 6–9 years
e. 9–12 years

Question 105

A 65-year-old man presents with unequal pupils, right-sided ptosis and anhidrosis of the right half of the face and body. The patient is most likely suffering from?

a. Argyll Robertson pupils
b. Diabetic neuropathy

c. Holmes–Adie syndrome
d. Horner's syndrome
e. Pupillary defect

Question 106
A 23-year-old man meets the diagnostic criteria for schizophrenia and exhibits passivity phenomena. Passivity phenomena include the following, except
a. Made feelings
b. Made impulses
c. Thought blocking
d. Thought broadcasting
e. Somatic passivity

Question 107
A 14-year-old girl was disallowed to meet her friends over the weekend as she was caught lying to her parents. This phenomenon is known as
a. Aversion
b. Negative reinforcement
c. Partial reinforcement
d. Positive reinforcement
e. Punishment

Question 108
A 40-year-old man has been prescribed with lithium, haloperidol and fluoxetine. A trainee consults you because the patient has developed a tremor. Which of the following features suggest that the tremor is caused by haloperidol?
a. Coarse tremor
b. Dysdiadochokinesis
c. Fine tremor
d. Parkinsonism
e. Wide-based gait

Question 109
Attention refers to an intensive process in which information selection takes place. Which one of the following statements is true?
a. Dichotic listening studies test for selective attention.
b. With divided attention, performance is enhanced.
c. Attention is the equivalent of working memory.
d. Attention involves information retrieval from the short-term memory storage.
e. Attention involves information retrieval from the long-term memory storage.

Question 110
You are the trainee psychiatrist in the child and adolescent mental health service (CAMHS). An anxious mother brings her 2-year-old daughter for developmental assessment. She is concerned about her daughter's language and speech

development. Which of the following developmental milestones is expected of her daughter?
a. Cooing
b. Repetitive babbling
c. Grammatical morphemes
d. Vocabulary of five words
e. Telegraphic speech

Question 111
Autochthonous delusions are
a. ego-dystonic
b. ego-syntonic
c. secondary to hallucinations
d. shared with a partner
e. starting with an idea

Question 112
The case of Phineas Gage describes which of the following syndrome?
a. Frontal lobe syndrome
b. Temporal lobe syndrome
c. Parietal lobe syndrome
d. Vascular dementia
e. Alzheimer's dementia

Question 113
Which of the following will predispose the child to emotional problems later in life?
a. Thumb-sucking at age 4
b. Transitional object for more than 6 months in the first year of life
c. Nocturnal enuresis
d. Upbringing in an authoritarian family setting
e. Adoption after 2 months

Question 114
A core trainee presents a list of symptoms for neuroleptic malignant syndrome (NMS). The following are symptoms of NMS, except?
a. NMS presents within 48 hours after the initiation of a new antipsychotic
b. Dysphagia
c. Labile blood pressure
d. Leucocytosis
e. Mutism

Question 115
A drug company wants to promote its new antidepressants. Patients will get one box of antidepressants free of charge if they purchase three boxes of antidepressants at one time. This phenomenon is known as
a. Classical conditioning
b. Fixed interval schedule

c. Fixed ratio schedule
d. Variable interval schedule
e. Variable ratio schedule

Question 116
Morbid jealousy is not
a. a misidentification phenomenon
b. associated with erectile dysfunction
c. associated with violence
d. encapsulated
e. more common in men than in women

Question 117
A 60-year-old man has had a stroke recently. He is concerned about developing dementia and wants to find out which medication could prevent vascular dementia. The correct answer is
a. Low-dose aspirin
b. High dose of statins
c. Low dose of hypoglycaemic agents
d. Thiamine
e. Vitamin E

Question 118
Previous research has found which of the following to be an important protective factor for Alzheimer's dementia?
a. High level of education
b. Occasional physical activities
c. Early retirement
d. Smoking
e. Previous history of depression

Question 119
Which of the following is not a primary prevention strategy in children and adolescents?
a. Easing the impact of traumatic milestones and transitional events in school and family
b. Preventing vulnerable population from succumbing to psychiatric disorder
c. Preventing the onset of carefully defined psychiatric disorder
d. Promoting and enhancing adaptability and healthy functioning
e. Measuring intelligence at regular intervals from children to adolescence

Extended matching items (EMIs)

Theme: Attention

Options:
a. Selective/focused attention
b. Divided attention

c. Sustained attention
d. Controlled attention
e. Automatic attention
f. Stroop effect

Lead in: Select the most appropriate answer for each of the following. Each option may be used once, more than once or not at all.

Question 120
In this particular type of attention, at least two sources of information are attended to simultaneously and the performance is inefficient.

Question 121
This particular type of attention is commonly described as the cocktail party effect.

Question 122
In this particular type of attention, the environment is monitored over a long period of time.

Question 123
In this particular type of attention, the subject becomes so skilled with the task that little conscious effort is now required.

Theme: Memory tests

Options:
a. Benton Visual Retention Test
b. Rey–Osterrieth Test
c. Paired Associate Learning Test
d. California Verbal Learning Test
e. Rivermead Behavioural Memory Test
f. National Adult Reading Test
g. Raven Progressive Matrices

Lead in: Select the most appropriate answer for each of the following. Each option may be used once, more than once or not at all.

Question 124
This is a memory test that could be utilized in clinical settings to estimate the premorbid intelligence quotient.

Question 125
This is a test that tests for the perception of relations between abstract items.

Question 126
This is a memory test battery that has an emphasis on tests related to skills required in daily living.

Question 127
This particular test is effective in testing for brain damage as well as early cognitive decline.

Question 128
Non-dominant temporal lobe damage can lead potentially to impaired performance on this test, whereas dominant temporal lobe damage tends not to.

Theme: Social sciences and stigma

Options:

a. Stereotype
b. Enacted stigma
c. Felt stigma
d. Prejudice
e. Discrimination

Lead in: Select the most appropriate answer for each of the following. Each option may be used once, more than once or not at all.

Question 129
This is the dogmatic belief that one race is superior to another one and that there exist identifiable racial characteristics which influence cognition, achievement and behaviour.

Question 130
This terminology refers to the enactment of prejudice.

Question 131
This terminology refers to the experience of discrimination of an individual who bears a stigma.

Question 132
This terminology refers to the fear of discrimination of an individual who bears a stigma.

Theme: Dynamic psychopathology and theories

Options:

a. Unconscious
b. Preconscious
c. Conscious
d. Primary process
e. Secondary process
f. Pleasure principle
g. Id
h. Ego
i. Superego

Lead in: Select the most appropriate answer for each of the following. Each option may be used once, more than once or not at all.

Question 133
This is the operating system of the preconscious and the conscious.

Question 134
This is deemed to be the operating system of the unconscious.

Question 135
This contains memories, ideas and affects that are typically repressed.

Question 136
This is the part of the mind that develops during childhood and serves to maintain repression and censorship.

Question 137
Based on the structural model of the mind, this is considered to be unconscious. It contains primordial energy reserves derived from instinctual drives.

Question 138
Based on the structural model of the mind, this helps to fulfil the task of self-preservation.

Theme: Clinical psychiatry – old age psychiatry

Options:

a. Alzheimer's dementia
b. Vascular dementia
c. Binswanger's disease
d. Fronto-temporal dementia
e. Dementia with Lewy bodies
f. Parkinson's disease dementia

Lead in: Select the most appropriate answer for each of the following. Each option may be used once, more than once or not at all.

Question 139
Antipsychotics are usually not indicated for mild-to-moderate non-cognitive symptoms because of the risk of severe adverse events.

Question 140
Patients with this form of dementia tend to have a younger age of onset, with more severe apathy, disinhibition, reduction in speech output, loss of insight and coarsening of social behaviour.

Question 141
This form of dementia is characterized by a stepwise deteriorating course with a patchy distribution of neurological and neuropsychological deficits.

Question 142
In this form of dementia, on CT scan, there is noted to be progressive subcortical vascular encephalopathy with CT scan revealing markedly enlarged ventricles secondary to infarction in hemispheric white matter.

Question 143
This is a form of dementia that is more common in males.

Theme: Clinical psychiatry – somatoform and dissociative disorder

Options:

a. Somatization disorder
b. Somatoform autonomic dysfunction
c. Persistent somatoform pain disorder
d. Hypochondriacal disorder
e. Conversion disorder
f. Factitious disorder
g. Malingering

Lead in: Select the most appropriate answer for each of the following. Each option may be used once, more than once or not at all.

Question 144
This is a condition in which the patient intentionally produces physical or psychological symptoms and the patient is fully aware of his or her underlying motives.

Question 145
In this condition, the patient intentionally produces physical and psychological symptoms but the patient is unconscious about his or her underlying motives.

Question 146
Patients with this condition usually presents with persistent, severe, distressing pain, which cannot be explained by physical disorder.

Theme: Clinical psychiatry – women's mental health

Options:

a. Premenstrual syndrome
b. Cyclic psychosis
c. Depressive disorder in pregnancy
d. Bipolar disorder in pregnancy
e. Puerperal psychosis
f. Postnatal blues
g. Postnatal depression

Lead in: Select the most appropriate answer for each of the following. Each option may be used once, more than once or not at all.

Question 147
This occurs usually on the third to the fifth day after pregnancy and occurs in about 50% of women.

Question 148
Poor social adjustment, marital relationship and fear of labour are predisposing factors leading to the development of this condition.

Question 149
This condition has an abrupt onset, usually within the first 2 weeks after childbirth, and there might be rapid changes in mental state, sometimes from hour to hour.

Question 150
This condition occurs in 10%–15% of postpartum women usually within 3 months of childbirth.

Question 151
This is a condition that a higher prevalence in those around the age of 30 years, and the prevalence increases with increasing parity.

Theme: History of psychiatry

Options:

a. Phineas Gage
b. Wilhelm Griesinger
c. Benedict Morel
d. Jacob Mendes Da Costa
e. Paul Broca
f. Carl Wernicke
g. Emil Kraepelin
h. Sigmund Freud
i. Carl Jung
j. Henry Maudsley

Lead in: Select the most appropriate answer for each of the following. Each option may be used once, more than once or not at all.

Question 152
This is one of the best-known psychiatrists during the Victorian era. He was the first person to propose the abolishment of physical restraints in England.

Question 153
He was first to develop the technique of psychoanalysis.

Question 154
This led to the formation of the terminology 'Soldier's heart' during the American Civil War.

Question 155
Broca's aphasia was coined by which one of the aforementioned individuals?

Question 156
This individual proposed the degeneration theory that states that mental illness affecting one generation can be passed on to the next generation in ever-worsening degrees.

Theme: Ethics and psychiatric research

Options:

a. Nuremberg code
b. Declaration of Helsinki
c. Belmont report

Lead in: Select the most appropriate answer for each of the following. Each option may be used once, more than once or not at all.

Question 157
This code emphasizes that all experiments should avoid suffering and injury.

Question 158
This code emphasizes that seeking consent from research subjects is absolutely necessary.

Question 159
This code states the importance of formulation in research protocol and informs the subjects of the protocol details.

Question 160
This code emphasizes on the importance of justice.
Answer: (c) Belmont report

Theme: Clinical psychiatry – personality disorder

Options:

a. Paranoid personality disorder
b. Schizoid personality disorder
c. Schizotypal personality disorder
d. Antisocial personality disorder
e. Histrionic personality disorder
f. Narcissistic personality disorder
g. Avoidant personality disorder
h. Obsessive-compulsive personality disorder
i. Borderline personality disorder

Lead in: Select the most appropriate answer for each of the following. Each option may be used once, more than once or not at all.

Question 161
These patients tend to have marked emotional coldness and have little interest in activities that provide pleasure or in relationships.

Question 162
These patients tend to have unusual perceptions, are friendless and have odd beliefs and speech. They might also have ideas of reference.

Question 163
These are individuals who bear grudges without justification and are excessively sensitive to attacks.

Question 164
The age of onset of this disorder is usually from adolescence or early adulthood. This disorder is associated with a suicide rate of 9%.

Question 165
Patients with this disorder usually have very low tolerance to frustration and a low threshold for discharge of aggression, including violence.

Theme: Clinical psychiatry – substance misuse disorders

Options:
a. Alcoholic blackouts
b. Withdrawal fits
c. Wernicke's encephalopathy
d. Korsakoff's syndrome
e. Alcoholic dementia
f. Alcoholic hallucinosis
g. Pathological jealousy

Lead in: Select the most appropriate answer for each of the following. Each option may be used once, more than once or not at all.

Question 166
Individuals with this condition usually present with the following clinical symptoms: ophthalmoplegia, nystagmus, ataxia and clouding of consciousness.

Question 167
Approximately 10% of patients with this condition have the classical triad, but for others, peripheral neuropathy might also be present.

Question 168
This is commonly described as an abnormal state in which memory and learning are affected, out of proportion to other cognitive functions in an otherwise alert and responsive patient.

Question 169
This usually occurs within 48 hours of stopping drinking.

Question 170
Intoxication of alcohol usually leads to episodes of short-term amnesia and blackouts.

Theme: Basic psychopharmacology

Options:
a. Carbamazepine
b. Diazepam
c. Electroconvulsive therapy
d. Haloperidol
e. Lamotrigine
f. Lithium
g. Olanzapine
h. Quetiapine
i. Sodium valproate
j. Sertraline

k. St John's wort
l. Topiramate

Lead in: Choose the appropriate physical treatments for the following clinical scenarios. Each option might be used more than once or not at all.

Question 171
A 45-year-old man suffers from bipolar disorder. He has had five episodes of depression and one episode of hypomania over the past 5 years. He had hypothyroidism 20 years ago. He prefers to take medications. (Choose one option.)

Question 172
A Foundation Year 2 doctor consults you regarding which anticonvulsant is not recommended for routine use in the prophylaxis in bipolar disorder. (Choose one option.)

Question 173
A 40-year-old man suffers from bipolar disorder. He has had two episodes of depression and three episodes of mania over the past 1 year. He has not responded well to the monotherapy with lithium. You suggest augmentation therapy with another medication. (Choose one option.)

Question 174
A 35-year-old man who suffered from bipolar disorder was treated by the psychiatrist in a tropical country. He was referred by the urologist to review his psychotropic medication as he has developed renal calculi after coming back to the UK. Which medication is associated with the development of renal calculi? (Choose one option.)

Question 175
A 45-year-old man suffers from bipolar disorder and hypertension. His GP prescribes angiotensin-converting enzyme (ACE) inhibitor to treat his hypertension. The ACE inhibitor increases the serum level of one medication. (Choose one option.)

Theme: Basic psychopharmacology

Options:

a. Carbamazepine
b. Diazepam
c. Electroconvulsive therapy
d. Haloperidol
e. Lamotrigine
f. Lithium
g. Olanzapine
h. Quetiapine
i. Sodium valproate
j. Fluoxetine
k. St John's wort
l. Topiramate

Lead in: Choose the appropriate physical treatments for the following clinical scenarios based on the NICE guidelines. Each option might be used more than once or not at all.

Question 176
A 35-year old woman with rapid cycling bipolar disorder was admitted to the hospital due to severe depressive symptoms. She takes Lithium CR 800 mg nocte and has been adherent to lithium. Which medication would you consider to add onto the lithium? (Choose one option.)

Question 177
A 35-year old woman with rapid cycling bipolar disorder is being managed in the community. She does not respond to monotherapy. The GP consults you on the long-term management. Combination of which two medications is recommended? (Choose two options.)

Theme: Cultural psychiatry

Options:

a. Amok
b. Brain fag
c. Dhat
d. Koro
e. Latah
f. Pibloktoq
g. Susto
h. Taijin Kyofusho
i. Windigo

Lead in: Identify which of the aforementioned resembles the following clinical scenarios.

Question 178
A 20-year-old African university student preparing for pharmacology examination presents with burning headache, blurring eye sight and difficulty in understanding the meaning of the textbook, and cannot remember the drugs he studied. (Choose one option.)

Question 179
A 20-year-old Chinese national serviceman in Singapore was referred by the army doctor. He complains that his penis is getting shorter and it will go into his abdomen. He measures his penis every day and he cannot concentrate on his work. (Choose one option.)

Question 180
A 25-year-old Malaysian woman becomes dissociative after a road traffic accident, followed by echopraxia, echolalia, command obedience and utterance of obscene words. (Choose one option.)

Question 181
A 30-year-old indigenous Indian staying near Yellowknife, Canada, complains that he is possessed by a spirit to eat human flesh of the tribe leader after long-term conflict with him. (Choose one option.)

Theme: Psychopathology

Options:

a. Acting-out
b. Ambivalence
c. Anger
d. Disinhibition
e. Dysphoric mood
f. Euphoric mood
g. Failure of empathy
h. Fatuousness
i. Flat affect
j. Good rapport
k. Guardedness
l. Humour
m. Humiliation
n. Incongruous affect
o. Labile affect
p. Resistance
q. Restricted affective range

Lead in: A 58-year-old woman is admitted to the psychiatric ward for the treatment of depression. The consultant psychiatrist worries that she does not simply suffer from depression because she walks with short shuffling steps and exhibits bradykinesia. During the interview, the consultant psychiatrist observes the following clinical features. Identify which of the aforementioned terminology resembles her clinical features. Each option might be used once, more than once or not at all.

Question 182
She has a mask-like face and shows no feelings at all. (Choose one option.)

Question 183
She stands perplexed at the door, putting one hand forward and then taking it back. (Choose one option.)

Question 184
She shouts and damages the door after she knows that she cannot go for home leave this weekend. (Choose one option.)

Theme: Basic psychology

Options:

a. Bandura, Albert
b. Pavlov, Ivan

c. Seligman, Martin
d. Skinner, Burrhus Frederic
e. Thorndike, Edward
f. Watson, John

Lead in: Which of the aforementioned researchers is most strongly associated with the following experiments? Each option may be used once, more than once or not at all.

Question 185
In this experiment, an 11-month infant was allowed to play with a white rat. At this point, the infant showed no fear of the rat. The investigator made a loud sound whenever the infant touched the rat. Two weeks later, the infant showed fear of the rat and rabbit eventhough there was no loud sound. (Choose one option.)

Question 186
In this experiment, a hungry cat was confined in a puzzle box with food visible on the outside. The cat could manipulate some devices to open the gate of the puzzle box. Foods were placed outside the box, and the food served as an incentive for the cat to open the gate. Initially, the cat first behaved aimlessly as if doing things by trial and error. The presence of food made the opening of gate more likely to occur and the cat took lesser time to get the food after repeated trials. (Choose one option.)

Question 187
In this experiment, a dog was placed in a two-compartment box where there was no escape. After repeated failures to escape, the dog realized that there was an absence of contingency, became withdrawn and stopped jumping from one compartment to another. (Choose one option.)

Theme: Basic psychology

Options:

a. Bandura, Albert
b. Pavlov, Ivan
c. Seligman, Martin
d. Skinner, Burrhus Frederic
e. Thorndike, Edward
f. Watson, John

Lead in: Which of the aforementioned researchers is most strongly associated with the following experiments? Each option may be used once, more than once or not at all.

Question 188
The investigator designed a box that had one or more levers. When a starved rat pressed the lever, a small pellet of food was dropped onto a tray. The rat soon learned that when he pressed the lever he would receive some food. (Choose one option.)

Question 189
In this experiment, a child witnessed the different levels of aggression from an adult towards a doll. The child paid attention to the relevant aspects of aggression and created a visual image of the model in her mind. By repeated observations, the child remembered the aggressive behaviour. The child rehearsed the aggressive behaviour and anticipated similar consequences between herself and the adult. (Choose one option.)

Question 190
In this experiment, the investigator performed a minor operation on a dog to relocate its salivary duct to the outside of its cheek. This allowed easy measurement of saliva. Periodically, a bell was rang, followed shortly thereafter by meat being placed in the dog's mouth. (Choose one option.)

Theme: Basic psychology

Options:

a. Bandura, Albert
b. Kohler, Wolfgang
c. Premack, David
d. Skinner, Burrhus Frederic
e. Tolman, Edward
f. Watson, John

Lead in: Which of the aforementioned researchers is most strongly associated with the following experiments? Each option might be used once, more than once or not at all.

Question 191
This investigator constructed a variety of problems involving obtaining food that was not directly accessible for the chimpanzees. The investigator used chimpanzees because chimpanzees have higher intelligence than cats and dogs. Initially, the chimpanzees spent most of their time unproductively rather than slowly working towards a solution. All of a sudden, they would find a way to obtain the food. (Choose one option.)

Question 192
This investigator designed complex maze running experiments and investigated the role of reinforcement in learning. The rats developed and learned the cognitive map of a maze even when there was no reward. These experiments eventually led to a theory of latent learning, which states that learning can occur in the absence of a reward. (Choose one option.)

Question 193
This investigator conducted experiments using monkeys and found that more probable behaviours would reinforce less probable behaviours. (Choose one option.)

MRCPSYCH PAPER AI MOCK EXAMINATION 3: ANSWERS

GET THROUGH MRCPSYCH PAPER AI: MOCK EXAMINATION

Question 1 Answer: d, It is usually not preceded by a delusional mood.
Explanation: A primary delusion is a delusion that arises full formed without any connection with previous events. It could be preceded by a delusional mood in which the person is aware of something strange and threatening happening.

Reference: Puri BK, Hall A, Ho R (2014). *Revision Notes in Psychiatry.* London: CRC Press, p. 6.

Question 2 Answer: c, Systematic desensitization
Explanation: Systematic desensitization is based on the behavioural concept of reciprocal inhibition. This holds that relaxation inhibits anxiety so that the two are considered to be mutually exclusive. During this treatment, patients are successfully exposed (either in reality or in imagination) to stimuli in the hierarchy, beginning with the least anxiety-provoking event and then to the most anxiety-provoking event, with each exposure being paired with relaxation.

Reference: Puri BK, Hall A, Ho R (2014). *Revision Notes in Psychiatry.* London: CRC Press, p. 28.

Question 3 Answer: c, Analysis of personality and intelligence
Explanation: An assessment and analysis of personality and intelligence is essential to determine whether the client is suitable for psychotherapy.

Reference: Puri BK, Hall A, Ho R (2014). *Revision Notes in Psychiatry.* London: CRC Press, p. 331.

Question 4 Answer: c, Quetiapine
Explanation: The cardiac QT interval is a useful, but imprecise, indicator of risk of torsades de pointes and increased cardiac mortality. Quetiapine has been shown to have a moderate effect on the QTC interval (meaning that it has been observed to prolong the QTC by more than 10 ms on average when given at a normal clinical dose). Clozapine, risperidone and olanzapine have a low effect. Other risk factors

for QTC prolongation include: cardiac history, previous long QT syndrome, bradycardia, ischemic heart disease, myocarditis, myocardial infarction, electrolytes abnormalities and female gender.

Reference: Taylor D, Paton C, Kapur S (2009). *The Maudsley Prescribing Guidelines* (10th edition). London: Informa Healthcare, p. 119.

Question 5 Answer: c, Delusional disorder
Explanation: The answer is a delusional disorder. Based on the ICD-10 classification system, a delusional disorder is largely an ill-defined condition, manifesting as either a single delusion or a set of delusions, being persistent and at times lifelong, and not having an identifiable organic basis. There are occasional or transitory auditory hallucinations, particularly in the elderly. Delusions are the most conspicuous or the only symptoms and are present for at least 3 months. For the diagnosis to be made, there must not be any evidence of schizophrenic symptoms or brain disease.

Reference: Puri BK, Hall A, Ho R (2014). *Revision Notes in Psychiatry.* London: CRC Press, p. 372.

Question 6 Answer: b, Hebephrenic schizophrenia
Explanation: The diagnosis is likely to be hebephrenic schizophrenia. The mean age of onset is usually between 15 and 25 years. It is usually associated with a poor prognosis. Affective changes are usually quite prominent. Fleeting and fragmentary delusions and hallucinations, disorganized thoughts, rambling speech and mannerisms are also common. Negative symptoms such as flattening of affect might also be observed.

Reference: Puri BK, Hall A, Ho R (2014). *Revision Notes in Psychiatry.* London: CRC Press, p. 354.

Question 7 Answer: b, Negative autoscopy
Explanation: In autoscopy, the person sees himself or herself and knows that it is him or her. Negative autoscopy occurs when the person looks into the mirror and cannot see one's image.

Reference: Puri BK, Hall A, Ho R (2014). *Revision Notes in Psychiatry.* London: CRC Press, p. 8.

Question 8 Answer: e, Family therapy
Explanation: Family therapy would be recommended in this case. External indicators for family therapy include the fact that John has just been recently diagnosed with an illness that has caused a significant change in his role within the family; internal indicators for family therapy include the fact that there are communication problems and triangulation within his existing family network. Family therapy, by introducing humour, demonstration of warmth and empathy and through role-playing, would help to modify both verbal and non-verbal communication.

Reference: Puri BK, Hall A, Ho R (2014). *Revision Notes in Psychiatry*. London: CRC Press, p. 343.

Question 9 Answer: e, Considering exploring potential nonconcordance to medications
Explanation: Patients with first-episode psychosis need to be treated with antipsychotics for a minimum duration of at least 6 months. One of the commonest reasons why antipsychotic treatment does not seem effective would be underlying nonconcordance. It would be beneficial to explore potential nonconcordance to medications prior to titrating the dose of the medications. Factors that could help to optimize patient compliance include education, setting reasonable expectations and using alternative medications if there are troublesome side effects.

Reference: Puri BK, Hall A, Ho R (2014). *Revision Notes in Psychiatry*. London: CRC Press, p. 240.

Question 10 Answer: c, Intravenous thiamine and vitamin B
Explanation: It is considered to be a medical emergency, and intravenous thiamine and vitamin B should be given. It should be treated early as 80% of untreated individuals would convert to Korsakov's psychosis if untreated.

Reference: Puri BK, Hall A, Ho R (2014). *Revision Notes in Psychiatry*. London: CRC Press, p. 517.

Question 11 Answer: d, Schizoaffective disorder
Explanation: Schizoaffective disorder is believed to be representative of this continuum. The ICD-10 describes these disorders in which both the affective and schizophrenia symptoms are prominent with the same episode of the illness, either simultaneously or within a few days of each other.

Reference: Puri BK, Hall A, Ho R (2014). *Revision Notes in Psychiatry*. London: CRC Press, p. 373.

Question 12 Answer: b, Views of reference groups usually do not play a role if the communicator is credible and has expertise.
Explanation: This is incorrect. Views of the reference groups are important for persuasive communication. In addition, it is important to note that mere repetition of a message in itself could have a persuasive influence leading to a change in the attitude. Also explicit messages are more persuasive, especially so for less intelligent recipient. Interactive personal discussions and one-sided communications tend to be more persuasive.

Reference: Puri BK, Hall A, Ho R (2014). *Revision Notes in Psychiatry*. London: CRC Press, p. 58.

Question 13 Answer: a, Amok
Explanation: Amok stands for battling furiously in Malay. Amok is a culture-specific syndrome of the Malay consisting of an explosive outburst of homicidal fury, vented

indiscriminately against anyone who happens to cross his or her path. Once the episode is over, the person is amnesic for the episode and may commit suicide.

Reference and Further Readings: Campbell RJ (1996). *Psychiatric Dictionary.* Oxford, UK: Oxford University Press; Puri BK, Treasaden I (eds) (2010). *Psychiatry: An Evidence-Based Text*, London: Hodder Arnold, pp. 309–318.

Question 14 Answer: e, Agitation
Explanation: The normal stages of grief include denial, anger, bargaining, depression and acceptance. Other theories with regards to grief proposed that it has three core phases. The stunned phase usually last for a few hours to a few weeks. This would then give way to the mourning phase, with intense yearning and autonomic symptoms. After several weeks, the phase of acceptance and adjustments takes over. Grief usually lasts for about 6 months.

Reference: Puri BK, Hall A, Ho R (2014). *Revision Notes in Psychiatry.* London: CRC Press, p. 382.

Question 15 Answer: a, Full blood count
Explanation: Given that clozapine is started, it would be important to do a baseline full blood count (FBC) prior to the commencement of treatment. Based on the guidelines of the Clozapine Patient Management System, it is necessary for the patient to be registered and an initial FBC needs to be obtained. Clozapine needs to be started at 12.5 mg once a green blood result is issued by the CPMS.

Reference: Puri BK, Hall A, Ho R (2014). *Revision Notes in Psychiatry.* London: CRC Press, p. 368.

Question 16 Answer: a, Neologism
Explanation: Catatonic typically involves the presence of the aforementioned clinical features: ambitendency, automatic obedience, mitgehen, mannerism, negativism, echolalia, echopraxia, logorrhea, stereotypy, waxy flexibility and verbigeration. Neologism refers to how a new word is being constructed by the person or an everyday word being used in a special way.

Reference: Puri BK, Hall A, Ho R (2014). *Revision Notes in Psychiatry.* London: CRC Press, p. 371.

Question 17 Answer: b, Running commentary
Explanation: This is an example of a mood incongruent complex auditory hallucination. The voices might discuss the person in third place, perform a running commentary on a person's behaviour or even cause an individual to feel that his thoughts are spoken out loud.

Reference: Puri BK, Hall A, Ho R (2014). *Revision Notes in Psychiatry.* London: CRC Press, p. 7.

Question 18 Answer: a, Aversive conditioning
Explanation: Aversive conditioning helps decrease undesirable behaviour by making use of exposure to adverse stimuli while the person is engaging in a targeted behaviour. Escape conditioning, avoidance conditioning and punishments are known collectively as aversive conditioning.

Reference and Further Reading: Puri BK, Treasaden I (eds) (2010). *Psychiatry: An Evidence-Based Text*. London: Hodder Arnold, pp. 197–200.

Question 19 Answer: e, Lamotrigine
Explanation: Lamotrigine has been shown to be effective both as a treatment for bipolar depression and for preventing against further episodes. It has no tendency to induce switching or rapid cycling of the mood states. Previous research has shown that it is as effective as citalopram and it also causes less weight gain as compared to lithium. It is important to note that the main side effect is rash, which is usually associated with the speed of dose titration.

Reference: Taylor D, Paton C, Kapur S (2009). *The Maudsley Prescribing Guidelines* (10th edition). London: Informa Healthcare, p. 164.

Question 20 Answer: e, Catatonic schizophrenia
Explanation: The description is characteristic for catatonic schizophrenia. Catatonic schizophrenia, very often, may be associated with a dream-like state, along with vivid scenic hallucination. One or more of the following behaviours may dominate: stupor, excitement, posturing, negativism, rigidity, waxy flexibility, command automatism and perseveration of words or phrases.

Reference: Puri BK, Hall A, Ho R (2014). *Revision Notes in Psychiatry*. London: CRC Press, p. 354.

Question 21 Answer: a, Infarction of the anterior cerebral arteries
Explanation: This is likely to be due to an infarction involving the anterior cerebral artery. Physical examination might reveal distal and proximal weakness of both legs with impaired pin-prick sensation that spares the arms and the face.

Reference: Puri BK, Hall A, Ho R (2014). *Revision Notes in Psychiatry*. London: CRC Press, p. 494.

Question 22 Answer: d, 1 year
Explanation: The ICD-10 classification system states that the diagnosis of alcohol dependence would be made if there are three or more of the classical symptoms that have been present together at some time over the past 1 year.

Reference: Puri BK, Hall A, Ho R (2014). *Revision Notes in Psychiatry*. London: CRC Press, p. 508.

Question 23 Answer: d, Referent
Explanation: Referent social power refers to someone who is charismatic and is liked by others. Authority refers to power derived from the assignment of a role.

Reward refers to power derived from the ability to allocate resources. Coercive refers to having the power to punish. Expert refers to the power that is derived from skill, knowledge and also experience.

Reference: Puri BK, Hall A, Ho R (2014). *Revision Notes in Psychiatry*. London: CRC Press, p. 59.

Question 24 Answer: a, Splitting
Explanation: Splitting is the most common defence mechanism used. This involves dividing good objects, affects and memories from bad ones. It is often seen in patients with borderline personality disorder.

Reference: Puri BK, Hall A, Ho R (2014). *Revision Notes in Psychiatry*. London: CRC Press, p. 137.

Question 25 Answer: d, Reaction formation
Explanation: Patients with obsessive-compulsive disorder tend to make use of reaction formation. Reaction formation is defined as a psychological attitude that is diametrically opposed to an oppressed wish and constituting a reaction against it.

Reference: Puri BK, Hall A, Ho R (2014). *Revision Notes in Psychiatry*. London: CRC Press, p. 136.

Question 26 Answer: a, Benzodiazepines
Explanation: Benzodiazepines would be indicated for treatment. Intramuscular lorazepam up to 4 mg per day can be given to help with the symptoms. The other alternative treatment would be the use of electroconvulsive therapy. The common causes include schizophrenia, depression or manic (more common than schizophrenia), organic disorders, epilepsy, medications (such as ciprofloxacin), recreational drugs (cocaine), psychogenic catatonia and lethal catatonia.

Reference: Puri BK, Hall A, Ho R (2014). *Revision Notes in Psychiatry*. London: CRC Press, p. 371.

Question 27 Answer: b, Fixed interval schedule
Explanation: Fixed interval schedule has the lowest response rate and is poor at maintaining conditioned response. Fixed interval schedule is also associated with quick extinction. Response rate usually speeds up prior to the next reinforcement. There is a pause after each reinforcement which results in a scallop-shaped reinforcement curve.

Reference and Further Reading: Puri BK, Treasaden I (eds) (2010). *Psychiatry: An Evidence-Based Text*. London: Hodder Arnold, pp. 203–204.

Question 28 Answer: d, Voices telling them that they are useless
Explanation: A hallucination is a false sensory perception in the absence of a real external stimulus. A hallucination is perceived as being located in the objective

space and having almost the same realistic qualities as a normal perception. (d) refers to a mood congruent complex auditory hallucinations, which usually occurs in those with depressive disorder or mania.

Reference: Puri BK, Hall A, Ho R (2014). *Revision Notes in Psychiatry*. London: CRC Press, p. 7.

Question 29 Answer: b, Absence of isoenzyme aldehyde dehydrogenase
Explanation: The absence of aldehyde dehydrogenase would account for the differences in responses. Due to the absence, roughly half of Orientals would develop an unpleasant flushing response when alcohol is ingested, and this is related to the accumulation of acetaldehyde in the system. This intolerance of alcohol protects them from developing alcoholism, since it is much less prevalent in those of oriental heritage.

Reference: Puri BK, Hall A, Ho R (2014). *Revision Notes in Psychiatry*. London: CRC Press, p. 520.

Question 30 Answer: c, Antisocial personality disorder
Explanation: In malingering, the individual usually intentionally produces the physical or psychological symptoms and he or she is usually fully conscious of his or her underlying motives for doing so. Very often, there is a great resistance and reluctance to cooperate for further investigations and examination. There has been an association between malingering and antisocial personality disorder.

Reference: Puri BK, Hall A, Ho R (2014). *Revision Notes in Psychiatry*. London: CRC Press, p. 471.

Question 31 Answer: d, Assessment for lesions involving the central visual pathway
Explanation: This is essentially an assessment for lesions involving the central visual pathway. Candidates need to know the common lesions in the central visual pathway. Lesions in the optic nerve usually result in unilateral visual loss. Lesions at the optic chiasma at the base of the brain would result with bitemporal hemianopia. Lesions when the optic nerves decussate would result in incongruent homonymous hemianopia. Lesions in the Meyer's loop would be associated with superior homonymous quadrantanopia. Lesions in the optic rations are associated with inferior homonymous quadrantanopia.

Reference: Puri BK, Hall A, Ho R (2014). *Revision Notes in Psychiatry*. London: CRC Press, p. 159.

Question 32 Answer: b, This patient fulfils the DSM-IV-TR diagnostic criteria for brief psychotic disorder.
Explanation: The DSM-IV-TR criteria specify that the duration of a brief psychotic disorder is at least 1 day but less than 1 month. The ICD-10 criteria specify that the presentation of the fully developed acute and transient psychotic disorder should

not exceed 2 weeks. DSM-IV-TR further specifies that brief psychotic disorder may not include a symptom if it is culturally sanctioned response pattern.

References: American Psychiatric Association (2000). *Diagnostic Criteria from DSM-IV-TR*. Washington, DC: American Psychiatric Association; World Health Organisation (1994). ICD-10 Classification of Mental and Behavioural Disorders. Edinburgh, UK: Churchill Livingstone.

Question 33 Answer: a, Downward social comparison
Explanation: Based on the social comparison theory, people tend to evaluate their attitudes and abilities by comparing themselves with others. Downward social comparison involves comparing oneself to those who perform worse than themselves.

Reference: Aronson E, Wilson TD, Akert RM (2007). *Social Psychology*. Upper Saddle River, NJ: Prentice Hall, pp. 274–275.

Question 34 Answer: d, Motivational, emotional, perceptual and cognitive
Explanation: Attitude is an enduring organization of motivational, emotional, perceptual and cognitive processes with respect to some aspect of the individual world. Attitudes are largely based on beliefs, a tendency to behave in an observable way, and also have affective components that are the most resistant to change. A change in one of these three components leads to changes in the other two. When predicting behaviour, it is important that situational variables be taken into account. Otherwise, measured attitudes are deemed to be very poor predictors of behaviours.

Reference: Puri BK, Hall A, Ho R (2014). *Revision Notes in Psychiatry*. London: CRC Press, p. 57.

Question 35 Answer: e, Delusion of reference
Explanation: Delusion of reference refers to the fact that events, objects or even people in one's environment have a particular and unusual significance. A delusion in itself is a false belief based on incorrect inference about external reality and that is firmly sustained despite what almost everyone else believes and despite what constitutes incontrovertible and obvious proof or evidence to the contrary. The belief is not one ordinarily accepted by other members of the person's culture or subculture. When a false belief involves a value judgement, it is regarded as a delusion only when judgement is so extreme as to defy credibility.

Reference: Puri BK, Hall A, Ho R (2014). *Revision Notes in Psychiatry*. London: CRC Press, p. 6.

Question 36 Answer: d, Variable interval schedule
Explanation: Variable interval schedule is effective in maintaining conditioned response. Extinction occurs slowly and gradually.

Reference and Further Reading: Puri BK, Treasaden I (eds) (2010). *Psychiatry: An Evidence-Based Text*. London: Hodder Arnold, pp. 203–204.

Question 37 Answer: d, 2mg/day for haloperidol, 2 mg/day for risperidone, 5 mg/day for olanzapine, 75 mg/day for quetiapine, 60 mg/day for ziprasidone and 7.5 mg/day for aripiprazole
Explanation: Chlorpromazine 100 mg orally = 2 mg/day for haloperidol, 2 mg/day for risperidone, 5 mg/day for olanzapine, 75 mg/day for quetiapine, 60 mg/day for ziprasidone and 7.5 mg/day for aripiprazole.

Reference: Woods SW (2003). Chlorpromazine equivalent doses for the newer atypical antipsychotics. *J Clin Psychiatry*, 64(6):663–667.

Question 38 Answer: a, Being male
Explanation: All of the following are considered to be good prognostic factors, with the exception of gender. Those who are female are considered to have good prognosis. Other factors associated with good prognosis include having good premorbid social adjustment, having a family history of affective disorder and short duration of illness prior to treatment. Symptoms predictive of good prognosis include having an affective component to the illness, paranoid (as compared with non-paranoid), lack of negative symptoms and lack of cognitive impairments.

Reference: Puri BK, Hall A, Ho R (2014). *Revision Notes in Psychiatry*. London: CRC Press, p. 370.

Question 39 Answer: a, Frontal lobe
Explanation: It is very likely that Mr Smith has suffered an injury to his frontal lobe. Frontal lobe lesions are associated with personality changes, perseveration, utilization behaviour, impairments of attention, concentration and initiation and aphasia. The personality changes include disinhibition, reduced social and ethical control, sexual indiscretions, poor judgment, elevated mood and lack of concerns for the feelings of other people.

Reference: Puri BK, Hall A, Ho R (2014). *Revision Notes in Psychiatry*. London: CRC Press, p. 110.

Question 40 Answer: d, In the ICD-10, her condition is classified under schizophrenia.
Explanation: Based on the ICD-10, postpartum psychosis is classified under F.53 mental and behavioural disorders associated with the puerperium but not F.20 schizophrenia. In DSM-IV-TR, her diagnosis is classified under brief psychotic disorder with postpartum onset. Both DSM-IV-TR and ICD-10 do not have specific diagnostic criteria for postpartum psychosis.

References and Further Readings: American Psychiatric Association (2000). *Diagnostic Criteria from DSM-IV-TR*. Washington, DC: American Psychiatric Association; World Health Organisation (1994). ICD-10 Classification of Mental and Behavioural Disorders. Edinburgh, UK: Churchill Livingstone; Puri BK, Treasaden I (eds) (2010). *Psychiatry: An Evidence-Based Text*. London: Hodder Arnold, pp. 725–726.

Question 41 Answer: a, Selective/Focused attention
Explanation: This is an example of the cocktail party effect. Jane was making use of selective or focused attention. Selective or focused attention implies that one type of information is attended to, while additional distracting information is ignored. Dichotic listening studies have proved that whilst participants are attending to one channel of information, unattended channel is actually still active and being processed and individuals can switch rapidly if needed.

Reference: Puri BK, Hall A, Ho R (2014). *Revision Notes in Psychiatry*. London: CRC Press, p. 35.

Question 42 Answer: e, Weigl Colour–Form Sorting Test (WCFST)
Explanation: WCFST is a test mainly for executive function. AVLT is a 15-item five-trial test, from which recall (immediate and delayed) and recognition memory can be assessed. CVLT involves a list of 16 words. The list is repeated five times. Then, a second list is given, serving to interfere with the first list, after which recall of the first list is requested. RMT involves recognition of non-verbal material with interference from distracters after the first initial image is presented. The WMT assesses several memory components including concentration and summary indices that can be derived with a mean of 100. Tasks under WMT include assessment of logical memory (subjects are asked to recall the content of two stores read to them with a 30-minute delay); and a verbal paired associates test (learning word pairs, e.g. baby-cries, and to recall the second word when the first word is given).

Reference: Trimble M (2004). *Somatoform Disorders – A Medico-Legal Guide*. Cambridge, UK: Cambridge University Press.

Question 43 Answer: b, Countertransference
Explanation: The nurses exhibit countertransference because of previous unreasonable complaints.

Reference and Further Reading: Puri BK, Treasaden I (eds) (2010). *Psychiatry: An Evidence-Based Text*. London: Hodder Arnold, p. 948.

Question 44 Answer: b, Humour
Explanation: Immature defence mechanisms include denial, fantasy, projection, somatization, hypochondriasis, passive aggressive, acting out, idealization, projective identification and repression.

Reference and Further Reading: Puri BK, Treasaden I (eds) (2010). *Psychiatry: An Evidence-Based Text*. London: Hodder Arnold, p. 948.

Question 45 Answer: e, Severe depressive episode with psychotic features
Explanation: This man presents with nihilistic delusions and mood congruent auditory hallucinations. This suggests that he suffers from severe depressive episode with psychotic features.

Reference: World Health Organisation (1994). *ICD-10 Classification of Mental and Behavioural Disorders*. Edinburgh, UK: Churchill Livingstone.

Question 46 Answer: d, Doppelanger–Cotard's syndrome

Explanation: Doppelganger refers to a delusion that a double of a person or place exists somewhere else. Cotard syndrome refers to a delusion of death, disintegration of organs and nonexistence. Delusions of doubles refer to a delusion that a person known to the person has been replaced by a double. Delusion of infestation refers to a delusion that one is infested by parasites. Delusion of pregnancy refers to a delusion that one is pregnant (usually the husband of a pregnant wife).

Reference: Puri BK, Hall A, Ho R (2014). *Revision Notes in Psychiatry*. London: CRC Press, p. 6.

Question 47 Answer: e, Variable ratio schedule

Explanation: Variable ratio schedule has a quick and steep responding curve. This schedule shows the most resistance to extinction among all schedules.

Reference and Further Reading: Puri BK, Treasaden I (eds) (2010). *Psychiatry: An Evidence-Based Text*. London: Hodder Arnold, pp. 203–204.

Question 48 Answer: a, More patients taking second-generation antipsychotics continue the antipsychotic treatment compared with patients taking conventional antipsychotics.

Explanation: The majority of patients in both groups discontinued their assigned treatment owing to inefficacy or intolerable side effects or for other reasons. Quetiapine had the highest rate of discontinuation for any cause (82%) versus 79% for those on ziprasidone, 75% for those on perphenazine, 74% for those on risperidone and 64% for those on olanzapine. Discontinuation of the drug because of lack of efficacy was the highest among patients on quetiapine (28%) and lowest for those on olanzapine (15%); 19% of patients on olanzapine cited intolerability as the reason for stopping the drug, while intolerability caused 10% patients on risperidone to stop the drug. It was reported that 30% of olanzapine-treated patients gained more than 7% of their body weight during the study, which was significantly greater than weight gain with other study drugs. Predictors of an earlier time to drug discontinuation included higher PANSS score, younger age and long duration of antipsychotic use. CATIE involved 1493 patients with schizophrenia. They were randomly assigned to receive olanzapine (7.5–30 mg per day), perphenazine (8–32 mg per day), quetiapine (200–800 mg per day) or risperidone (1.5–6.0 mg per day) for up to 18 months.

Reference: Lieberman JA, Stroup TS, McEvoy JP (2005). Effectiveness of antipsychotic drugs in patients with chronic schizophrenia. *The New England Journal of Medicine*, 353: 1209–1223.

Question 49 Answer: c, Panic disorder
Explanation: Pitts and McClure (1967) provoked panic attacks in patients with anxiety neurosis through the usage of intravenous sodium lactate. However, it was found that there were no biochemical or neuroendocrine findings that explain lactate-induced panic.

Reference: Puri BK, Hall A, Ho R (2014). *Revision Notes in Psychiatry*. London: CRC Press, p. 414.

Question 50 Answer: b, Thurstone Scale – ranking is unbiased
Explanation: Option b is incorrect. The Thurstone Scale is a scale that indicates either agreement or disagreement with what is being presented. The disadvantages associated with this scale are that different response patterns may still result in the same mean score; the set-up is unwieldy, and the ranking may also be biased. The Likert Scale is a scale that indicates the level of agreement with varying options (five levels). The semantic differential scale is a bipolar visual analogue scale.

Reference: Puri BK, Hall A, Ho R (2014). *Revision Notes in Psychiatry*. London: CRC Press, p. 57.

Question 51 Answer: c, Ribot's law
Explanation: Théodule Ribot proposed that the dissolution of memory is inversely related to the recency of the event in 1881. This is known as Ribot's law and applies to the phenomenon when the recent memories are more likely to be lost as compared to the remote memories in retrograde amnesia. We have noted that not all patients suffering from retrograde amnesia follow Ribot's law. Gestalt's law is related to perception. Marr's law is related to visual perception and three-dimensional perception. Tarasoff's law is related to breach of confidentiality, and Weber–Fechner law is related to stimulus in perception.

Reference: Ribot T (1882). *Diseases of the Memory: An Essay in the Positive Psychology*. New York: D. Appleton and Company.

Question 52 Answer: a, Utilitarian
Explanation: Utilitarian theories emphasize on minimizing the risks and maximizing the benefits for the greatest number. There are two types of this approach: act utilitarian and also rule utilitarian. For example, a patient has thoughts of harming his or her family. In act utilitarian, the psychiatrist may consider disclosing confidential information to his or her family or police by providing good or avoiding harm to the greatest number who stay with him or her or near him or her. In rule utilitarian, the rule of confidentiality may act against the rule of protecting others.

Reference: Puri BK, Hall A, Ho R (2014). *Revision Notes in Psychiatry*. London: CRC Press, p. 145.

Question 53 Answer: e, A doctor's native motive to provide morally correct care to his or her patients, and focus solely on the rightness and wrongness of the action themselves, and not on the consequences of the action.
Explanation: The deontological theories emphasize on a doctor's motive to provide morally correct care to his or her patients. They focus solely on the rightness and wrongness of the doctor's actions and not on the consequences of the actions themselves.

Reference: Puri BK, Hall A, Ho R (2014). *Revision Notes in Psychiatry.* London: CRC Press, p. 146.

Question 54 Answer: b, The minimum duration of delusions is 6 months.
Explanation: The minimum duration is 3 months. Bizarre delusions are not associated with delusional disorders but correspond to the first-rank symptoms of schizophrenia.

Reference and Further Readings: World Health Organisation (1992). *ICD-10: The ICD-10 Classification of Mental and Behavioural Disorders: Clinical Descriptions and Diagnostic Guidelines.* Geneva: World Health Organisation; Puri BK, Treasaden I (eds) (2010). *Psychiatry: An Evidence-Based Text.* London: Hodder Arnold, p. 677.

Question 55 Answer: e, Narcissistic
Explanation: This man suffers from narcissistic personality disorder which is characterised by sense of entitlement and importance.

Reference and Further Reading: Puri BK, Treasaden I (eds) 2010. *Psychiatry: An Evidence-Based Text.* London: Hodder Arnold, pp. 690, 705, 706, 839.

Question 56 Answer: d, Mannerism
Explanation: The psychopathology being referred to here is that of mannerism. Mannerism refers to repeated involuntary movements that appear to be goal directed. Automatic obedience refers to a condition where the person follows the examiner's instructions blindly without judgement and resistance. For example, the examiner might ask the person to move his or her arm in different directions and the person is unable to resist even if it is against his or her will.

Reference: Puri BK, Hall A, Ho R (2014). *Revision Notes in Psychiatry.* London: CRC Press, p. 2.

Question 57 Answer: a, Amisulpride
Explanation: Amisulpride appears not to elevate plasma glucose and seems not to be associated with diabetes. Chlorpromazine, clozapine, risperidone and quetiapine have not been associated with impaired glucose tolerance and diabetes.

Reference and Further Readings: Taylor D, Paton C, Kapur S (2009). *The Maudsley Prescribing Guidelines*. London: Informa Healthcare; Puri BK, Treasaden I (eds) (2010). *Psychiatry: An Evidenced-Based Text*. London: Hodder Arnold, pp. 425–427, 603.

Question 58 Answer: e, Challenging negative automatic thoughts
Explanation: All of the aforementioned options are methodologies, except (e), that could help to achieve cognitive consistency when dissonance is experienced. Hence, in summary, when cognitive dissonance occurs, the individual feels uncomfortable, may experience increased arousal, and is motivated to achieve cognitive consistency. This may occur by changing one or more of the cognitions involved in the dissonant relationship, changing the behaviour that is inconsistent with the cognition or adding new cognitions that are consonant with the pre-existing ones. Cognitive consistency can also be achieved when attitude and behaviour are inconsistent by altering attitude.

Reference: Puri BK, Hall A, Ho R (2014). *Revision Notes in Psychiatry*. London: CRC Press, p. 58.

Question 59 Answer: d, Autonomy
Explanation: This is an example of autonomy. Autonomy refers to the obligation of the doctor to respect his or her patients' rights to make their own choices in accordance to their beliefs and wishes. Non-maleficence refers to the obligation of a doctor to avoid harm to his or her patients. Beneficence refers to the commitment of a doctor to provide benefits to patients and balance benefits against risks when making such decisions.

Reference: Puri BK, Hall A, Ho R (2014). *Revision Notes in Psychiatry*. London: CRC Press, p. 146.

Question 60 Answer: c, She wants to be in a depressive state because her husband gives her more support when she is sick.
Explanation: The patient has an obligation to get well. The others are criteria that a person has to fulfil for Parsons' sick role.

Further Reading: Puri BK, Treasaden I (eds) (2010). *Psychiatry: An Evidence-Based Text*. London: Hodder Arnold, p. 299, 682.

Question 61 Answer: c, He was penalized by the HM Revenue & Customs for delay in filling up the income tax form because he could not make up his mind what to report and feared making mistakes.
Explanation: Patients with anankastic personality disorder have difficulty to make day-to-day decisions because they fear making mistakes.

Reference and Further Reading: Puri BK, Treasaden I (eds) (2010). *Psychiatry: An Evidence-Based Text*. London: Hodder Arnold, p. 657.

Question 62 Answer: c, It means that a normal perception has taken on a delusional significance.
Explanation: A delusional perception means that a normal perception has now taken on a delusional significance. A delusion in itself is a false belief based on incorrect inference about external reality and that is firmly sustained despite what almost everyone else believes and despite what constitutes incontrovertible and obvious proof or evidence to the contrary. The belief is not one ordinarily accepted by other members of the person's culture or subculture. When a false belief involves a value judgement, it is regarded as a delusion only when judgement is so extreme as to defy credibility.

Reference: Puri BK, Hall A, Ho R (2014). *Revision Notes in Psychiatry*. London: CRC Press, p. 6.

Question 63 Answer: a, Cognitive learning
Explanation: Cognitive learning is the acquisition of knowledge through the formation of cognitive or mental maps. Cognitive learning can occur via latent learning and insight learning. This form of learning shows that learning can occur in the absence of a reward.

Reference and Further Reading: Puri BK, Treasaden I (eds) (2010). *Psychiatry: An Evidence-Based Text*. London: Hodder Arnold, pp. 207–208.

Question 64 Answer: a, Akathisia
Explanation: Akathisia is the most common (25%), followed by pseudo-parkinsonism (20%), acute dystonia (10%) and tardive dyskinesia (5%). Galactorrhoea is not an extrapyramidal side effect.

Reference and Further Reading: Puri BK, Treasaden I (eds) (2010). *Psychiatry: An Evidence-Based Text*. London: Hodder Arnold, pp. 901, 903.

Question 65 Answer: a, Anankastic personality
Explanation: According to the ICD-10 criteria, anankastic personality disorder is characterized by (a) feelings of excessive doubt and caution, (b) preoccupation with details, rules, order and organization on schedule, (c) perfectionism that interferes with task completion, (d) pleasure and interpersonal relationships, (e) excessive pedantry and adherence to social conversations, (f) rigidity and stubbornness, (g) unreasonable insistence by the patient that others submit to exactly her way of dealing things, or unreasonable reluctance to allow others to do things and (h) intrusion of insistent and unwelcome thoughts or impulses.

Reference and Further Readings: World Health Organisation (1994). *ICD-10 Classification of Mental and Behavioural Disorders*. Edinburgh, UK: Churchill Livingstone; Puri BK, Treasaden I (eds) (2010). *Psychiatry: An Evidence-Based Text*. London: Hodder Arnold, p. 657.

Question 66 Answer: c, Identity
Explanation: The teenager would be negotiating the identity stage based on Erikson's stages of development model. The age and the corresponding stage that an individual is undergoing are listed as follows: 0–1 (trust/security); 1–4 (autonomy); 4–5 (initiative); 5–11 (duty/accomplishment); 11–15 (identity); 15: adult (intimacy), adulthood (generativity), maturity (integrity).

Reference: Puri BK, Hall A, Ho R (2014). *Revision Notes in Psychiatry.* London: CRC Press, p. 48.

Question 67 Answer: c, Bystander effect
Explanation: Bystander effect is the phenomenon where individuals are less likely to extend help during an emergency when in the presence of others. The most classic example is the murder of Kitty Genovese, during which none of her neighbours called the police despite hearing her cries.

Reference and Further Readings: Puri BK, Treasaden I (eds) (2010). *Psychiatry: An Evidence-Based Text.* London: Hodder Arnold, pp. 290–291; Darley JM, Latané B (1968). Bystander intervention in emergencies: Diffusion of responsibility. *Journal of Personality and Social Psychology*, 8: 377–383.

Question 68 Answer: b, Reflective listening
Explanation: This is an example of reflection and reflective listening. Reflective listening entails repeating the patient's own accounts by paraphrasing and using words that add meaning to what the client has just mentioned.

Reference: Puri BK, Hall A, Ho R (2014). *Revision Notes in Psychiatry.* London: CRC Press, p. 332.

Question 69 Answer: e, Thought withdrawal
Explanation: The presence of thought withdrawal would be of tremendous help in arriving at the diagnosis of schizophrenia. It is part of the first-rank symptoms. The following are first-rank symptoms: auditory hallucinations that either repeat the thoughts out loud, in the third person or performing a running commentary; delusions of passivity which include thought insertion, withdrawal and broadcasting; and somatic passivity and delusional perception.

Reference: Puri BK, Hall A, Ho R (2014). *Revision Notes in Psychiatry.* London: CRC Press, p. 351.

Question 70 Answer: c, Sedation
Explanation: Sedation is the most common side effect, and hypersalivation is the second most common side effect.

Reference and Further Reading: Puri BK, Treasaden I (eds) (2010). *Psychiatry: An Evidence-Based Text.* London: Hodder Arnold, pp. 425–427, 603.

Question 71 Answer: b, Left VI nerve palsy
Explanation: This patient presents with left rectus palsy and horizontal diplopia. This indicates left VI nerve palsy.

Reference and Further Readings: Ward N, Frith P, Lipsedge M (2001). *Medical Masterclass Neurology, Ophthalmology and Psychiatry*. London: Royal College of Physicians; Puri BK, Treasaden I (eds) (2010). *Psychiatry: An Evidence-Based Text*. London: Hodder Arnold, pp. 336–338, 351, 525–527.

Question 72 Answer: d, Cognitive estimates
Explanation: Assessment of the dominant parietal lobe involves the following: finger agnosia (inability to recognize the name of the finger), left and right orientation (inability to recognize left and right), acalculia (inability to recognize number and calculation), dysgraphia, asteroagnosia (inability to recognize the size, shape and texture of an object by palpation), dysgraphesthesia (inability to recognize letters or numbers written on the hand), ideomotor apraxia, Wernicke's or Broca's aphasia as well as impairment of two-point discrimination. Assessment of non-dominant parietal lobe involves asomatognosia (lack of awareness of the condition of all or parts of the body) and constructional dyspraxia (inability to copy double interlocking pentagons). Cognitive estimates is not a test of parietal lobe functioning.

Reference: Puri BK, Hall A, Ho R (2014). *Revision Notes in Psychiatry*. London: CRC Press, p. 114.

Question 73 Answer: e, The person is totally losing touch with reality.
Explanation: Most serious violence is associated with retained ability to plan and reality testing. People with paranoid schizophrenia staying in the community pose higher risk of violence compared to those who are more ill and stay in the hospitals.

Reference and Further Reading: Puri BK, Treasaden I (eds) (2010). *Psychiatry: An Evidence-Based Text*. London: Hodder Arnold, pp. 598, 1175, 1241.

Question 74 Answer: a, He experiences hallucinations causing positive emotions.
Explanation: Hallucinations causing negative emotions such as anger, anxiety or sadness generate more violence. Options B, C and D refer to 'threat/control-override' delusions which appear most risky. Option D is correct because depression is associated with violence.

Reference and Further Reading: Puri BK, Treasaden I (eds) (2010). *Psychiatry: An Evidence-Based Text*. London: Hodder Arnold, p. 1175.

Question 75 Answer: b, Anxious avoidant personality
Explanation: This man needs to use alcohol to calm his nerves and he develops alcohol-dependence syndrome. Hence, anxious personality disorder is the most

likely in this case and this personality disorder can be a maintaining factor in the alcohol dependence.

Reference and Further Reading: Puri BK, Treasaden I (eds) (2010). *Psychiatry: An Evidence-Based Text.* London: Hodder Arnold, p. 653.

Question 76 Answer: e, Perseveration
Explanation: All of the aforementioned options are considered to be part of formal thought disorders, with the exception of (e). Asyndesis refers to the juxtaposition of elements without adequate linkage between them. Condensation refers to combining ideas to make the incomprehensible. Derailment refers to how the thought processes are being derailed into a subsidiary thought. Fusion refers to how different elements of the thought are being interwoven with each other. Other features of formal thought disorder include omission and substitution.

Reference: Puri BK, Hall A, Ho R (2014). *Revision Notes in Psychiatry.* London: CRC Press, p. 4.

Question 77 Answer: e, Extinction
Explanation: Extinction refers to the gradual disappearance of a conditioned response (avoidance of going out of the house). This is achieved when the conditioned stimulus (in this case going out of the house) is repeatedly presented without the unconditioned stimulus.

Reference: Puri BK, Hall A, Ho R (2014). *Revision Notes in Psychiatry.* London: CRC Press, p. 25.

Question 78 Answer: a, Aripiprazole
Explanation: The other antipsychotics may produce weight gain.

Further Reading: Puri BK, Treasaden I (eds) (2010). *Psychiatry: An Evidence-Based Text.* London: Hodder Arnold, pp. 425–426, 604, 904.

Question 79 Answer: c, 4 months
Explanation: Accommodation and colour vision take place only at the age of 4 months. At birth, newborns have the ability to distinguish between brightness and also have eye tracking. However, visual acuity is impaired and focusing is typically fixed at 0.2 m. At the age of 2 months, newborns develop depth perception. At the age of 6 months, they would be able to achieve 6:6 visual acuity.

Reference: Puri BK, Hall A, Ho R (2014). *Revision Notes in Psychiatry.* London: CRC Press, p. 33.

Question 80 Answer: e, The standard schema of psychiatric history taking is a good guide to the structure of the psychiatric interview.
Explanation: The standard schema of psychiatric history taking is not a good guide to the structure of the psychiatric interview because it is too rigid. Option A

is correct because assessment proforma signifies the reduction of patient's life to an administrative purpose. Options B and C are correct for obvious reasons. Option D is correct because history taking is an active process which involves understanding and organizing information.

Reference: Poole R, Higgo R (2006). *Psychiatric Interviewing and Assessment.* Cambridge, UK: Cambridge University Press.

Question 81 Answer: b, Parietal lobe
Explanation: This is an assessment of the non-dominant parietal lobe functions. When there is a lesion involving the non-dominant parietal lobe, this would result in constructional dyspraxia, which refers to the inability to copy double interlocking pentagons. Lesions involving the dominant parietal lobe would result in Gerstmann's syndrome, asteroagnosis, dysgraphesthesia, ideomotor apraxia, Wernicke's or Broca's aphasia and impairment in two-point discrimination.

Reference: Puri BK, Hall A, Ho R (2014). *Revision Notes in Psychiatry.* London: CRC Press, p. 114.

Question 82 Answer: e, Right III nerve palsy
Explanation: In right III nerve palsy, there is usually ptosis. The pupil may be dilated and completely nonreactive. The eye is abducted (by the lateral rectus muscle), depressed and looking down and out (by the superior oblique muscle).

References and Further Readings: Malhi GS, Matharu MS, Hale AS (2000) *Neurology for Psychiatrists.* London: Martin Dunitz; Ward N, Frith P, Lipsedge M (2001). *Medical Masterclass Neurology, Ophthalmology and Psychiatry.* London: Royal College of Physicians; Puri BK, Treasaden I (eds) (2010). *Psychiatry: An Evidence-Based Text.* London: Hodder Arnold, pp. 336–338, 351, 525–527.

Question 83 Answer: c, Alcohol-dependent syndrome
Explanation: This is another version of the MCQ which tries to confuse candidates between the concept of alcohol dependence and personality disorders. The man suffers from alcohol dependence syndrome based on the CAGE questionnaire. There is not enough information from this vignette to suggest that he suffers from other psychiatric disorders.

Reference and Further Reading: Puri BK, Treasaden I (eds) (2010). *Psychiatry: An Evidence-Based Text.* London: Hodder Arnold, pp. 782, 1026–1027.

Question 84 Answer: b, Delusional perception is a secondary delusion.
Explanation: Delusional perception is a primary delusion and not a secondary delusion. It is a delusion that arises fully formed, without any discernible connection with previous events. It may be preceded by a delusional mood in which the person is aware of something strange and threatening happening.

Reference: Puri BK, Hall A, Ho R (2014). *Revision Notes in Psychiatry*. London: CRC Press, p. 6.

Question 85 Answer: a, Conditioned response
Explanation: In this experiment, drug A is an unconditioned stimulus and drug B is an unconditioned stimulus. The conditioned response is tachycardia associated with drug B.

Reference and Further Reading: Puri BK, Treasaden I (eds) (2010). *Psychiatry: An Evidence-Based Text*. London: Hodder Arnold, pp. 197–200.

Question 86 Answer: d, Fluoxetine
Explanation: SSRI seems to be the safest option in view of the potential risk of epilepsy.

Reference: Taylor D, Paton C, Kapur S (2009). *The Maudsley Prescribing Guidelines*. London: Informa Healthcare.

Question 87 Answer: a, John Cade
Explanation: John Cade was the one who discovered the properties of lithium. He injected guinea pigs with urine from patients with mania to see if mania was caused by a toxic product. Lithium was used to dissolve the uric acid prior to injection. Guinea pigs injected with lithium were noted to be more stable in mood. Hence, in the late 1940s, Cade decided to inject manic patients with lithium.

Reference: Puri BK, Hall A, Ho R (2014). *Revision Notes in Psychiatry*. London: CRC Press, p. 142.

Question 88 Answer: b, Viktor Frankl
Explanation: Victor Frankl was the one who developed existential therapy.

Reference: Puri BK, Hall A, Ho R (2014). *Revision Notes in Psychiatry*. London: CRC Press, p. 142.

Question 89 Answer: c, En bloc blackouts
Explanation: This is a description of an en bloc blackout. It should be noted that if the memory disturbances carry on for days, it is highly likely that the subject would experience what is deemed as a fugue state, in which he or she may travel some distance before coming around, with no memory of the events occurring during this time.

Reference: Puri BK, Hall A, Ho R (2014). *Revision Notes in Psychiatry*. London: CRC Press, p. 516.

Question 90 Answer: c, IV nerve palsy
Explanation: The common cause of isolated vertical diplopia is superior oblique palsy. This indicates fourth nerve palsy.

Reference and Further Readings: Ward N, Frith P, Lipsedge M (2001). *Medical Masterclass Neurology, Ophthalmology and Psychiatry*. London: Royal College of Physicians; Puri BK, Treasaden I (eds) (2010). *Psychiatry: An Evidence-Based Text*. London: Hodder Arnold, pp. 336–338, 351, 525–527.

Question 91 Answer: a, Lilliputian hallucination
Explanation: Mr Green is experiencing what is commonly termed as lilliputian hallucination. Hallucinated objects tend to appear greatly reduced in size. Reflex hallucination refers to how a stimulus in one sensory field might lead to a stimulus in another sensory field. In contrast, a functional hallucination refers to a stimulus causing the hallucination is being experienced in addition to the hallucination itself.

Reference: Puri BK, Hall A, Ho R (2014). *Revision Notes in Psychiatry*. London: CRC Press, p. 8.

Question 92 Answer: b, Negative reinforcement
Explanation: In negative reinforcement, an unpleasant stimulus (i.e. withdrawal symptoms) is removed, hence resulting in a strengthening of the behaviour (i.e. drug use).

Reference and Further Reading: Puri BK, Treasaden I (eds) (2010). *Psychiatry: An Evidence-Based Text*. London: Hodder Arnold, pp. 200–205.

Question 93 Answer: e, Rigidity
Explanation: Almost all patients would have fever; 90% present with rigidity and 75% present with altered mental state. Hence, rigidity is the most common sign among the options.

Further Reading: Puri BK, Treasaden I (eds) (2010). *Psychiatry: An Evidence-Based Text*. London: Hodder Arnold, pp. 874, 925.

Question 94 Answer: d, Concrete operational
Explanation: Piaget's model of cognitive development has four main stages, which include sensorimotor, preoperational, concrete operational and formal operational. The concrete operational stage is the third stage of development and this usually occurs from the age of 7 to around 12–14 years of age. It is thought that during this particular stage of development, the child would demonstrate logical thought processes and would be able to make more subjective moral judgements. During this stage, there will be an understanding of the laws of conservation of the number and volume and, in the later stages, the concept of weight.

Reference: Puri BK, Hall A, Ho R (2014). *Revision Notes in Psychiatry*. London: CRC Press, p. 68.

Question 95 Answer: d, Myasthenia gravis
Explanation: The severity of symptoms in myasthenia gravis fluctuates during the day, being less severe in the morning and more severe at the day goes on. Myasthenia gravis is associated with other weaknesses such as dysphagia, slurred speech, shortness of breath or limb weakness.

Reference and Further Readings: Ward N, Frith P, Lipsedge M (2001). *Medical Masterclass Neurology, Ophthalmology and Psychiatry.* London: Royal College of Physicians; Puri BK, Treasaden I (eds) (2010). *Psychiatry: An Evidence-Based Text.* London: Hodder Arnold, pp. 533–534.

Question 96 Answer: c, Delusion of guilt
Explanation: Delusion of guilt is the false belief of guilt. Such beliefs may dominate the patient's thoughts and are common in depression. An example of delusion of guilt is the false belief that one committed a crime and needs to be punished. There is usually no logical connection between the situation and the guilt feelings the person perceives.

Reference and Further Reading: Sims A (2003). *Symptoms of the Mind: An Introduction to Descriptive Psychopathology.* London: Saunders, p. 137.

Question 97 Answer: d, Positive reinforcement
Explanation: Positive reinforcement is the strengthening of a response by the addition of a pleasurable stimulus.

Reference and Further Reading: Puri BK, Treasaden I (eds) (2010). *Psychiatry: An Evidence-Based Text.* London: Hodder Arnold, pp. 200–205.

Question 98 Answer: d, 13 years old
Explanation: The onset of puberty in girls would be between 9 and 13 years in 95% of the sample population. The very initial signs include breast formation and also pubic hair growth. The average age of onset in the Western countries has been estimated to be around 13.5 years. For boys, in 95% of them, the onset usually occurs between the ages of 9.5 to 13.5 years. The initial signs include testicular and scrotal enlargement. This is in turn followed by the growth of the penis and also the pubic hair. On average, the mean age of onset is around 13 years.

Reference: Puri BK, Hall A, Ho R (2014). *Revision Notes in Psychiatry.* London: CRC Press, p. 71.

Question 99 Answer: e, Mutual attraction
Explanation: Mutual attraction is a factor that predisposes interpersonal attraction but not a theory. Proxemics relates interpersonal attraction to interpersonal space. Social exchange theory suggests that people prefer relationships that offer optimal cost–benefit ratio. Equity theory states that

preferred relationships are those in which there is equal cost and benefits for both parties. Reinforcement theory states that rewards for both parties reciprocally reinforce interpersonal attraction.

Reference and Further Reading: Puri BK, Hall AD (2002). *Revision Notes in Psychiatry*. London: Arnold, pp. 53–54.

Question 100 Answer: b, The winter excess of births in schizophrenics is due to a seasonal prevalence of a viral infection or other perinatal hazard.
Explanation: Only (b) is correct. Afro-Caribbean immigrants to the United Kingdom would have a higher risk of schizophrenia due to the interaction of multiple factors. Males usually have an earlier onset of schizophrenia as compared to females. Those living in higher EE families tend to have an increased relapse rate of schizophrenia. More obstetric complications are suggested for those with schizophrenia.

Reference: Puri BK, Hall A, Ho R (2014). *Revision Notes in Psychiatry*. London: CRC Press, p. 360.

Question 101 Answer: e, Serotonin transporter gene
Explanation: The serotonin transporter gene is implicated in the aetiology of depressive disorder.

Reference and Further Reading: Puri BK, Treasaden I (eds) (2010). *Psychiatry: An Evidence-Based Text*. London: Hodder Arnold, pp. 476–477, 610–611.

Question 102 Answer: a, State-dependent memory
Explanation: The terminology that would best describe the aforementioned would be state-dependent memory loss. State-dependent memory loss means that memory of events occurring while intoxicated is lost when sober but returns on next intoxication. In fragmentary blackouts, there is no clear demarcation of the memory loss, and islets of memory exist within the gaps. Some recovery occurs with time. In en bloc blackouts, there is a clearly demarcated total memory loss, with no recovery of the lost memory over time.

Reference: Puri BK, Hall A, Ho R (2014). *Revision Notes in Psychiatry*. London: CRC Press, p. 516.

Question 103 Answer: d, Deindividuation
Explanation: Deindividuation is the loosening of social constraints or norms when in a group. This leads to an increase in deviant behaviour, as individuals feel less accountable for their actions when they are carried out as a group. This is because, in a group, it is more difficult to identify and blame an individual. Deindividuation also increases an individual's obedience to group norms. Hence, if an individual is in a group riot where the norm is violence, deindividuation will make the individual act violently.

Social facilitation is the tendency to do better on simple tasks in the presence of other people. Social loafing is the tendency to do worse on a task when working in a group and when performance cannot be evaluated. Social norms are behaviours that are acceptable in a society or group. Social tuning is the process whereby people adopt another person's attitudes.

Reference and Further Reading: Aronson E, Wilson TD, Akert RM (2007). *Social Psychology*. Upper Saddle River, NJ: Prentice Hall, pp. 150–151, 277–286.

Question 104 Answer: c, 3–6 years
Explanation: A child starts to have early comprehension of grammar at the age 6–9 years. Between the ages of 1 and 2 years, the child can master 3 words at 12 months to 40 words at 18 months. Between 2 and 3 years, the child is at two-word stage characterized by telegraphic grammar. Between 6 and 12 years, the speech ability of a child is similar to an adult.

Reference and Further Reading: Puri BK, Hall AD (2002). *Revision Notes in Psychiatry*. London: Arnold, p. 72.

Question 105 Answer: d, Horner's syndrome
Explanation: The triad of Horner's syndrome is classically described as miosis, ipsilateral partial ptosis and sometimes anhidrosis. If anhidrosis affects the entire half of the body and face, the lesion is in the central nervous system. If it affects only the face and neck, the lesion is in the preganglionic fibres. If sweating is unaffected, the lesion is above the carotid artery bifurcation.

Reference and Further Readings: Ward N, Frith P, Lipsedge M (2001). *Medical Masterclass Neurology, Ophthalmology and Psychiatry*. London: Royal College of Physicians; Puri BK, Treasaden I (eds) (2010). *Psychiatry: An Evidence-Based Text*. London: Hodder Arnold, pp. 526, 531.

Question 106 Answer: c, Thought blocking
Explanation: Passivity phenomenon is a delusional belief that one's free will has been removed and the self is being controlled by an outside agency. Examples of passivity phenomena are thought alienation (person believes his or her thoughts are controlled by an external agency: thought insertion, thought withdrawal, thought broadcasting), made feelings (person believes his or her feelings are controlled by an external agency), made impulses, made actions and somatic passivity (the delusional belief that one is passively receiving bodily sensations from an external agency).

Reference and Further Reading: Puri BK, Hall AD (2002). *Revision Notes in Psychiatry*. London: Arnold, p. 153.

Question 107 Answer: e, Punishment
Explanation: This phenomenon is known as punishment, which is any stimulus that is applied after a response and causes a weakening of that behaviour.

Punishment is the opposite of reinforcement (both positive and negative). Reinforcement causes a strengthening of the behaviour, whereas punishment suppresses it.

Reference and Further Reading: Puri BK, Treasaden I (eds) (2010). *Psychiatry: An Evidence-Based Text*. London: Hodder Arnold, p. 205.

Question 108 Answer: d, Parkinsonism
Explanation: Option (c) is a side effect of lithium and option (a) occurs in lithium toxicity. Options (b) and (e) are cerebellar signs.

Further Reading: Puri BK, Treasaden I (eds) (2010). *Psychiatry: An Evidence-Based Text*. London: Hodder Arnold, pp. 541–543.

Question 109 Answer: a, Dichotic listening studies test for selective attention
Explanation: The various types of attention include selective attention, divided attention and sustained attention. For divided attention, performance is impaired. In dichotic listening, studies in which subjects attend to one channel, evidence indicates that the unattended channel is still being processed and the listener can switch rapidly if appropriate.

Reference: Puri BK, Hall A, Ho R (2014). *Revision Notes in Psychiatry*. London: CRC Press, p. 35.

Question 110 Answer: e, Telegraphic speech
Explanation: Telegraphic speech is defined as short two- or three-word sentences using nouns, verbs and adjectives, with some basic form of grammar. An example is 'daddy go', which might represent the child's father going out of the house. This occurs between 19 and 36 months.

Cooing and babbling occur before the age of 1 year. Grammatical morphemes are acquired from 3 to 5 years of age. Morphemes are the smallest units of meaning within a language. Grammatical morphemes or bound morphemes have no meaning in itself but are attached to free morphemes to change its grammatical function. Examples are plurals '-s' and past tense '-ed'. A 2-year-old child should have a vocabulary of around 50–300 words.

Reference and Further Readings: Puri BK, Hall AD (2002). *Revision Notes in Psychiatry*. London: Arnold, p. 72; Puri BK, Treasaden I (eds) (2010). *Psychiatry: An Evidence-Based Text*. London: Hodder Arnold, pp. 115–116.

Question 111 Answer: b, egosyntonic
Explanation: Autochthonous delusions (primary delusions) are egosyntonic and refer to the acceptability of ideas or impulses to the ego, which receives the impulses as constant and compatible with one's own principles. Egodystonic refers to a phenomenon (e.g. obsession) which is unacceptable to the ego and prevented from reaching the ego (e.g. compulsion). Secondary delusions are secondary to

hallucinations. Shared delusions (e.g. folie a deux) are shared with a partner. Primary delusions (e.g. delusional perception and delusional memory) do not start with an idea.

Reference and Further Reading: Campbell RJ (1996). *Psychiatric Dictionary*. Oxford, UK: Oxford University Press.

Question 112 Answer: a, Frontal lobe syndrome
Explanation: This was the earliest case that was described. Phineas Gage suffered from a frontal lobe lesion in 1835, and it was documented that he had changes to his personality, but not his memory or intelligence.

Reference: Puri BK, Hall A, Ho R (2014). *Revision Notes in Psychiatry*. London: CRC Press, p. 109.

Question 113 Answer: d, Upbringing in an authoritarian family setting
Explanation: Parents using authoritarian child-rearing style are high in coercive control and low in warmth, acceptance and autonomy granting. Such parents often criticize, command and threaten to exert control, and use force, punishment or withdrawal of love (psychological control) to ensure compliance to their wishes. These parents make decisions on behalf of their children and their points of view are disregarded. Children brought up in authoritarian family settings are often unhappy and anxious, have low self-esteem and self-reliance, and have a tendency to be hostile when frustrated.

Reference and Further Reading: Berk LE (2006). *Child Development* (7th edition). Boston: Pearson, pp. 564–566.

Question 114 Answer: a, NMS presents within 48 hours after the initiation of a new antipsychotic.
Explanation: NMS can occur at any time during the course of antipsychotic treatment.

Further Reading: Puri BK, Treasaden I (eds) (2010). *Psychiatry: An Evidence-Based Text*. London: Hodder Arnold, pp. 874, 925.

Question 115 Answer: c, Fixed ratio schedule
Explanation: In fixed ratio schedule, there is a pause after each reinforcement. There is a high rate of responding leading to the next reinforcement shortly afterwards. Extinction occurs quickly in fixed ratio schedule.

Reference and Further Reading: Puri BK, Treasaden I (eds) (2010). *Psychiatry: An Evidence-Based Text*. London: Hodder Arnold, pp. 203–204.

Question 116 Answer: a, a misidentification phenomenon
Explanation: Misidentification syndrome refers to Capgras and Fregoli syndrome. Morbid jealousy is a delusional disorder that the marital or sexual partner is

unfaithful, typically accompanied by intense searching for evidence of infidelity and repeated interrogations and direct accusations of the partner that may lead to violent quarrels. Morbid jealousy is more common in men than in women. Morbid jealousy is associated with erectile dysfunction and alcohol misuse.

Reference and Further Reading: Campbell RJ (1996). *Psychiatric Dictionary.* Oxford, UK: Oxford University Press.

Question 117 Answer: a, Low-dose aspirin
Explanation: The NICE guidelines do not recommend the use of anti-dementia drugs in the prevention of cognitive decline. The guidelines recommend that it is worthwhile to try to treat the underlying condition in order to slow or halt the progression of vascular dementia.

Reference: Puri BK, Hall A, Ho R (2014). *Revision Notes in Psychiatry.* London: CRC Press, p. 700.

Question 118 Answer: a, High level of education
Explanation: Protective factors for Alzheimer's dementia include being bilingual, cognitive engagement and late retirement. High level of education of more than 15 years and high level of physical activities are also protective factors.

Reference: Puri BK, Hall A, Ho R (2014). *Revision Notes in Psychiatry.* London: CRC Press, p. 694.

Question 119 Answer: e, Measuring intelligence at regular intervals from children to adolescence
Explanation: Measuring intelligence at regular intervals does not offer primary prevention of any psychiatric illness among children and adolescents. Option (b) works by focusing on children with one or two schizophrenic parents, children of alcohol and drug addicts or those experiencing the death of a parent. Option (c) refers to prevention of poisoning of lead-based plants, neurosyphilis, school phobias in children or addictive behaviour patterns in adolescents.

Reference: Paykel ES, Jenkins R (1994). *Prevention in Psychiatry.* London: Gaskell.

Extended matching items (EMIs)

Theme: Attention

Question 120 Answer: b, Divided attention
Explanation: In divided attention, at least two sources of information are attended to at the same time. Performance is inefficient. The loss of performance is called dual-task interference.

Question 121 Answer: a, Selective/focused attention
Explanation: In selective/focused attention, one type of information is attended to while additional distracting information is ignored.

Question 122 Answer: c, Sustained attention
Explanation: In sustained attention, the environment is monitored over a long period of time. Performance actually deteriorates with time.

Question 123 Answer: e, Automatic attention
Explanation: In automatic attention, the subject becomes skilled at a task and therefore little conscious effort is required.

Reference: Puri BK, Hall A, Ho R (2014). *Revision Notes in Psychiatry*. London: CRC Press, p. 35.

Theme: Memory tests

Question 124 Answer: f, National Adult Reading Test
Explanation: The National Adult Reading Test is a reading test consisting of phonetically irregular words that have to be read aloud by the subject. If a patient suffers deterioration in intellectual abilities, their premorbid vocabulary may remain less affected or unaffected. The NART could thus be used to estimate the premorbid IQ.

Question 125 Answer: g, Raven Progressive Matrices
Explanation: This test of non-verbal intelligence consists of a series of printed designs from each of which a part is missing. The subject is required to correctly choose the missing part for each design from the alternatives offered. The test requires the perception of relations between abstract items.

Question 126 Answer: e, Rivermead Behavioural Memory Test
Explanation: It is actually just another memory test battery. However, it lays emphasis on tests that are related to skills required in daily living. The subtests include orientation, name recall, picture recognition, face recognition, story recall, route memory and prospective memory.

Question 127 Answer: a, Benton Visual Retention Test
Explanation: The subject is serially presented with 10 designs, which he or she has to reproduce from memory. It may be used in subjects aged 8 years and over. It may be used to test for brain damage and early cognitive impairment.

Question 128 Answer: b, Rey–Osterrieth Test
Explanation: In this visual memory test, the subject is present with a complex design. The subject is asked to copy this design, and then, 40 minutes later, without previous notification that this will occur, the subject is then asked to draw the same design again from memory. Non-dominant temporal lobe damage could lead to impaired performance on this test, whereas domain temporal lobe damage tends not to, but that could be associated with verbal memory difficulties.

Reference: Puri BK, Hall A, Ho R (2014). *Revision Notes in Psychiatry*. London: CRC Press, p. 95.

Theme: Social sciences and stigma

Question 129 Answer: d, Prejudice

Explanation: Prejudice is a preconceived set of beliefs held about others who are prejudged on this basis: the negative meaning of the term is the one usually used. It is not amenable to discussion and is resistant to change. Prejudiced individuals may believe in ways that create stereotyped behaviour that sustains their prejudice.

Question 130 Answer: e, Discrimination

Explanation: This refers to the enactment of prejudice. In the case of racism, the enactment is also termed racialism.

Question 131 Answer: b, Enacted stigma

Explanation: This refers to the experience of discrimination of an individual who bears a stigma. Stigma is an attribute of an individual that marks him or her as being unacceptable, inferior or dangerous.

Question 132 Answer: c, Felt stigma

Explanation: This refers to the fear of discrimination of an individual who bears a stigma.

Reference: Puri BK, Hall A, Ho R (2014). *Revision Notes in Psychiatry*. London: CRC Press, p. 125.

Theme: Dynamic psychopathology and theories

Question 133 Answer: e, Secondary process

Explanation: Secondary process is the operating system of the preconscious as well as the conscious.

Question 134 Answer: d, Primary process

Explanation: Primary process is the operating system of the unconscious. It consists of the following: displacement, condensation and symbolization.

Question 135 Answer: a, Unconscious

Explanation: The unconscious contains memories, ideas and affects that are repressed. Characteristic features include it being outside of awareness and that it involves primary process thinking. The motivating principle is the pleasure principle. Access to the repressed contents is difficult and occurs only when the censor gives way, for example, when one is relaxed, fooled, or overpowered.

Question 136 Answer: b, Preconscious

Explanation: The characteristic features of preconscious are that it is outside awareness and the operating system is secondary process thinking. The access can occur through focused attention.

Question 137 Answer: g, Id
Explanation: Most of the Id is unconscious. It contains primordial energy reserves derived from instinctual drives. Its aim is to maximize pleasure by fulfilling these drives.

Question 138 Answer: h, Ego
Explanation: The ego has the task of self-preservation. With regards to external events, it performs the task by becoming aware of the stimuli by storing experiences about them, and by avoiding excessively strong stimuli. With regards to internal events in relation to the id, it performs the task by gaining control over the demands of the instinct, by deciding whether they be allowed satisfaction and by postponing the satisfaction at times.

Reference: Puri BK, Hall A, Ho R (2014). *Revision Notes in Psychiatry*. London: CRC Press, pp. 131–132.

Theme: Clinical psychiatry – old age psychiatry

Question 139 Answer: e, Dementia with Lewy bodies
Explanation: In this condition, there is marked neuroleptic sensitivity for patients. Antipsychotics are not indicated for mild-to-moderate noncognitive symptoms in DLB because of the risk of severe adverse reactions. If it needs to be used, consider 'Quetiapine' and monitor carefully for the extrapyramidal side effects.

Question 140 Answer: d, Fronto-temporal dementia
Explanation: These are the typical symptoms for patients with fronto-temporal dementia. In addition, they might have also primitive reflexes such as grasp, pour and palm mental reflexes.

Question 141 Answer: b, Vascular fementia
Explanation: The aforementioned is true for vascular dementia. In addition, there is usually evidence of vascular diseases on physical examination.

Question 142 Answer: c, Biswanger's disease
Explanation: The aforementioned are characteristic CT scan changes for this disorder. The age of onset is usually 50–65 with a gradual accumulation of neurological signs, dementia and disturbances in motor function.

Question 143 Answer: B, Vascular dementia
Explanation: An excess of vascular dementia has been noted in males, which is likely to be due to the increased prevalence of cardiovascular disease in men.

Reference: Puri BK, Hall A, Ho R (2014). *Revision Notes in Psychiatry*. London: CRC Press, p. 699.

Theme: Clinical psychiatry – somatoform and dissociative disorder

Question 144 Answer: g, Malingering

Explanation: In this disorder, the motivation is usually external gain and the signs and symptoms are usually intentionally produced. There is poor cooperation in evaluation and also treatment.

Question 145 Answer: f, Factitious disorder

Explanation: The primary motivation is to assume the sick role. There is intentional production or feigning the signs or symptoms. Often, these patients provide only a vague and confusing history.

Question 146 Answer: c, Persistent somatoform pain disorder

Explanation: Pain usually occurs in association with emotional conflict and results in increased support and attention.

Reference: Puri BK, Hall A, Ho R (2014). *Revision Notes in Psychiatry*. London: CRC Press, p. 470.

Theme: Clinical psychiatry – women's mental health

Question 147 Answer: f, Postnatal blues

Explanation: Postnatal blues is a brief psychological disturbance, characterized by tearfulness, labile emotions and confusion in mothers occurring in the first few days after childbirth.

Question 148 Answer: f, Postnatal blues

Explanation: Postnatal blues have been associated with poor social adjustment, poor marital relationship, high scores on the Eysench Personality Inventory neuroticism scale, fear of labour and also anxious and depressed mood during pregnancy.

Question 149 Answer: e, Puerperal psychosis

Explanation: It has been shown that the risk of developing a psychotic illness is increased 20-fold in the first postpartum month. Certain distinctive symptoms include abrupt onset, marked perplexity, rapid changes in mental state, marked restlessness fear and insomnia and associated delusions, hallucinations and disturbed behaviour.

Question 150 Answer: g, Postnatal depression

Explanation: Postnatal depression is characterized by low mood; reduced self-esteem; tearfulness; anxiety, particularly about the baby's health; and an inability to cope. Mothers may experience reduced affection for their baby and have difficulty with breast-feeding.

Question 151 Answer: a, Premenstrual syndrome

Explanation: The aforementioned are true with regards to the disorder. There is a higher prevalence in those women who have experienced natural menstrual cycles for longer periods of time.

Reference: Puri BK, Hall A, Ho R (2014). *Revision Notes in Psychiatry*. London: CRC Press, p. 567.

Theme: History of psychiatry

Question 152 Answer: j, Henry Maudsley
Explanation: He was the first person to propose the abolishment of physical restraints in England. He went on to become one of the best known psychiatrists. He believed psychiatric illness to be a physical disorder of the body, much similar to other medical illnesses.

Question 153 Answer: h, Sigmund Freud
Explanation: He initially started studying cases of hysteria using hypnosis. Then he began to develop the technique of psychoanalysis, which was later used to explain the psychological causes of symptoms.

Question 154 Answer: d, Jacob Mendes Da Costa
Explanation: He coined the term Da Costa's syndrome or soldier's heart during the American Civil War. This condition is a functional heart disease and the solders presented with left-sided chest pain, palpitation, breathlessness, sweating and fatigue during exertion.

Question 155 Answer: e, Paul Broca
Explanation: Paul Broca coined the terminology Broca's aphasia, which involves a lesion in the ventro-posterior region of the frontal lobe. This leads to Broca's aphasia that affects speech production but not comprehension.

Question 156 Answer: c, Benedict Morel
Explanation: He proposed the degeneration theory that states that mental illness affecting one generation could be passed on to the next in ever worsening degrees.

Reference: Puri BK, Hall A, Ho R (2014). *Revision Notes in Psychiatry*. London: CRC Press, p. 140.

Theme: Ethics and psychiatric research

Question 157 Answer: a, Nuremberg code
Explanation: The Nuremberg code was developed in wartime tribunal against the Nazi German doctors. The main objective is to protect human rights during experiments and research. An experiment should avoid suffering and injury.

Question 158 Answer: a, Nuremberg code
Explanation: It is stated in the code that proper preparations should be performed to protect research subjects and the experiments should be conducted by qualified personnel. During the experiment, the research subjects have the liberty to

withdraw at any time, and the investigators should stop the experiment if continuation results in potential injury or death of research subjects. The design should be based on results obtained from animal experiments and natural history of disease. Seeking consent from research subjects is necessary.

Question 159 Answer: b, Declaration of Helsinki
Explanation: This declaration states the aforementioned. The principal investigator should balance the predictable risks and the foreseeable benefits, respect integrity and privacy, obtain consent with liberty and free from undue influence, and preserve accuracy in publication of results.

Question 160 Answer: c, Belmont report
Explanation: The Belmont report emphasizes on justice. Individual justice requires the researcher to offer beneficial research to all participants independent of his or her preference. Social justice requires an order of preference in selection of subjects.

Reference: Puri BK, Hall A, Ho R (2014). *Revision Notes in Psychiatry*. London: CRC Press, p. 148.

Theme: Clinical psychiatry – personality disorder

Question 161 Answer: b, Schizoid personality disorder
Explanation: Individuals with schizoid personality disorder tend to have solitary lifestyle, are indifferent to praise and criticism, and have no interest in relationships and sexual experiences. They have few friends and are cold and detached.

Question 162 Answer: c, Schizotypal personality disorder
Explanation: Patients with this disorder tend to have unusual perception, are friendless with the exception of first-degree family, have odd beliefs and speech, have ideas of reference and might also have inappropriate or constricted affect.

Question 163 Answer: a, Paranoid personality disorder
Explanation: They tend to bear grudges without justification, are excessively sensitive to setbacks and tend to read benign remarks into threats with hidden meaning. At times, fidelity of spouse is doubted and the trustworthiness of others are doubted without due course.

Question 164 Answer: i, Borderline personality disorder
Explanation: The aforementioned is true with regards to borderline personality disorder. There are associated clinical signs and symptoms such as identity disturbance, unstable relationships, fear of impulsivity, self-harm, emptiness, dissociative symptoms, affective instability, paranoid ideation, anger, idealization and devaluation and negativistic attitudes towards others.

Question 165 Answer: d, Antisocial personality disorder
Explanation: Patients with antisocial personality disorder usually will have conduct disorder before the age of 15, and tend to engage in antisocial activities.

They tend to lie frequently, are aggressive and do not value the safety of others. They tend to fail to plan and there is denial of obligation.

Reference: Puri BK, Hall A, Ho R (2014). *Revision Notes in Psychiatry*. London: CRC Press, p. 445.

Theme: Clinical psychiatry – substance misuse disorders

Question 166 Answer: c, Wernicke's encephalopathy
Explanation: These are the core clinical features of individuals with the aforementioned condition.

Question 167 Answer: c, Wernicke's encephalopathy
Explanation: Approximately 10% of individuals with the condition have the classical triad. Peripheral neuropathy might be present in some individuals.

Question 168 Answer: d, Korsakoff's syndrome
Explanation: This is a clinical condition that is frequently preceded by Wernicke's encephalopathy. Clinical features include retrograde amnesia, anterograde amnesia, with sparing of immediate recall and disorientation in time. There might be inability to recall the temporal sequence of events, associated with confabulation as well.

Question 169 Answer: b, Withdrawal fits
Explanation: Withdrawal fits may take place within 48 hours of stopping drinking.

Question 170 Answer: a, Alcoholic blackouts
Explanation: This may occur after just one bout of heavy drinking and have been estimated to affect 15%–20% of those who drink. There are three types of blackout, including state-dependent memory loss, fragmentary blackouts and en bloc blackouts.

Reference: Puri BK, Hall A, Ho R (2014). *Revision Notes in Psychiatry*. London: CRC Press, p. 516.

Theme: Basic psychopharmacology

Question 171 Answer: e, Lamotrigine
Explanation: If the patient does not have hypothyroidism, lithium monotherapy is also an option.

Further Reading: Puri B, Treasaden I (eds) (2010). *Psychiatry: An Evidence-Based Text*. London: Hodder Arnold, pp. 532, 536, 906, 910.

Question 172 Answer: l, Topiramate
Explanation: Based on the NICE guidelines, this is not a drug which is recommended for use in the prophylaxis of bipolar disorder.

Further Reading: Puri B, Treasaden I (eds) (2010). *Psychiatry: An Evidence-Based Text*. London: Hodder Arnold, pp. 538, 699, 905, 910.

Question 173 Answer: i, Sodium valproate
Explanation: Sodium valproate could be used as an augmentation strategy.

Further Reading: Puri B, Treasaden I (eds) (2010). *Psychiatry: An Evidence-Based Text*. London: Hodder Arnold, pp. 532, 538.

Question 174 Answer: l, Topiramate
Explanation: Topiramate causes renal stones in poor hydration during the hot weather.

Further Reading: Puri B, Treasaden I (eds) (2010). *Psychiatry: An Evidence-Based Text*. London: Hodder Arnold, pp. 538, 699, 905, 910.

Question 175 Answer: f, Lithium
Explanation: Lithium is increased through sodium depletion.

Further Reading: Puri B, Treasaden I (eds) (2010). *Psychiatry: An Evidence-Based Text*. London: Hodder Arnold, pp. 613, 623, 630, 632, 633, 909–910.

Question 176 Answer: e, Lamotrigine
Explanation: For rapid cycling bipolar disorder, the NICE guidelines recommend to increase the dose of antimanic drug or adding lamotrigine.

Further Reading: Puri B, Treasaden I (eds) (2010). *Psychiatry: An Evidence-Based Text*. London: Hodder Arnold, pp. 532, 536, 906, 910.

Question 177 Answer: f, Lithium and i, sodium valproate
Explanation: For long-term management of rapid cycling bipolar disorder, the NICE guidelines recommend a combination of lithium and valproate as first-line treatment. Lithium monotherapy is the second-line treatment. Antidepressants should be avoided and thyroid function test should be performed every 6 months.

Further Reading: Puri B, Treasaden I (eds) (2010). *Psychiatry: An Evidence-Based Text*. London: Hodder Arnold, pp. 532, 613, 623, 630, 632, 633, 905, 909–910.

Theme: Cultural psychiatry

Question 178 Answer: b, Brain fag
Explanation: This syndrome is commonly encountered among students, probably because of the high priority to education in the African society. Of importance it is particularly prominent during examination times.

Question 179 Answer: d, Koro
Explanation: Koro is common in Southeast Asia and China. It may occur in epidemic form. It involves the belief of genital retraction with disappearance into the abdomen, accompanied by intense anxiety and fear of impending death.

Question 180 Answer: e, Latah

Explanation: This is a condition that usually begins after a sudden frightening experience in Malay women. It is characterized by a response to minimal stimuli with exaggerated startles, coprolalia, echolalia, echopraxia and automatic obedience. It has been suggested that this is merely one form of what is known to psychologists as the hyperstartle reaction and is universally found.

Question 181 Answer: i, Windigo

Explanation: This is described in North American Indians and ascribed to depression, schizophrenia, hysteria or anxiety. It is a disorder in which the subject believes he or she has undergone a transformation and become a monster who practises cannibalism.

Further Reading: Puri B, Treasaden I (eds) (2010). *Psychiatry: An Evidence-Based Text.* London: Hodder Arnold, pp. 309–318.

Theme: Psychopathology

Question 182 Answer: i, Flat affect

Explanation: This is an example of flat affect.

Reference and Further Reading: Puri BK, Hall AD (2002). *Revision Notes in Psychiatry.* London: Arnold, p. 150.

Question 183 Answer: b, Ambivalence

Explanation: This is an example of ambivalence.

Question 184 Answer: a, Acting-out

Explanation: This is an example of acting-out.

Reference and Further Reading: Puri BK, Treasaden I (eds) (2010). *Psychiatry: An Evidence-Based Text.* London: Hodder Arnold, pp. 940, 948–949.

Theme: Basic psychology

Question 185 Answer: f, Watson, John

Explanation: Watson conducted the Little Albert experiment, which demonstrated stimulus generalization.

Reference and Further Reading: Puri BK, Treasaden I (eds) (2010). *Psychiatry: An Evidence-Based Text.* London: Hodder Arnold, p. 199.

Question 186 Answer: e, Thorndike, Edward

Explanation: Thorndike investigated learning in animals by using cats and formulated the law of effect.

Reference and Further Reading: Puri BK, Treasaden I (eds) (2010). *Psychiatry: An Evidence-Based Text.* London: Hodder Arnold, pp. 200–201.

Question 187 Answer: c, Seligman, Martin
Explanation: Seligman demonstrated learned helplessness.

Reference and Further Reading: Puri BK, Treasaden I (eds) (2010). *Psychiatry: An Evidence-Based Text*. London: Hodder Arnold, pp. 206, 298, 614.

Theme: Basic psychology

Question 188 Answer: d, Burrhus Frederic
Explanation: Skinner demonstrated positive and negative reinforcement.

Reference and Further Reading: Puri BK, Treasaden I (eds) (2010). *Psychiatry: An Evidence-Based Text*. London: Hodder Arnold, pp. 200–205.

Question 189 Answer: a, Bandura, Albert
Explanation: Bandura conducted the 'doll experiment' to demonstrate observational learning and vicarious conditioning.

Reference and Further Reading: Puri BK, Treasaden I (eds) (2010). *Psychiatry: An Evidence-Based Text*. London: Hodder Arnold, p. 207.

Question 190 Answer: b, Pavlov, Ivan
Explanation: Pavlov conducted this experiment to demonstrate classical conditioning.

Reference and Further Reading: Puri BK, Treasaden I (eds) (2010). *Psychiatry: An Evidence-Based Text*. London: Hodder Arnold, pp. 197–200.

Theme: Basic psychology

Question 191 Answer: b, Kohler, Wolfgang
Explanation: Kohler used chimpanzees to study insight learning. Insight learning occurs when the animals suddenly realizes how to solve a problem. In the experiment, a banana is placed above the reach of chimpanzees. In the room there were several boxes but none of them was high enough to enable the chimpanzees to reach the banana. Initially, the chimpanzees would run around, jump, and get upset about their inability to get the banana. All of a sudden, they would pile the boxes on top of each other, climb up and grab the bananas.

Reference and Further Reading: Puri BK, Hall AD (2002). *Revision Notes in Psychiatry*. London: Arnold, p. 5.

Question 192 Answer: e, Tolman, Edward
Explanation: Tolman developed the maze running experiment to demonstrate latent learning. Latent learning occurs in the absence of an obvious reward.

Reference and Further Reading: Puri BK, Treasaden I (eds) (2010). *Psychiatry: An Evidence-Based Text*. London: Hodder Arnold, pp. 207, 222.

Question 193 Answer: c, Premack, David
Explanation: Premack's principle was derived from a study of monkeys. It stated that more probable behaviours will reinforce less probable behaviours.

Reference and Further Reading: Mitchell WS, Stoffelmayr BE (1973). Application of the Premack principle to the behavioral control of extremely inactive schizophrenics. *Journal of Applied Behaviour Analysis*, 6: 419–423.

MRCPSYCH PAPER AI MOCK EXAMINATION 4: QUESTIONS

GET THROUGH MRCPSYCH PAPER AI: MOCK EXAMINATION

Total number of questions: 195 (139 MCQs, 56 EMIs)
Total time provided: 180 minutes

Question 1

A 25-year-old male has been taken to the emergency services after hurting himself whilst trying to break the computer in his brother's room. He reports to the doctor that he feels that his thoughts have been controlled and are being taken away by the computer. Which of the following best describes this form of psychopathology?

a. Thought insertion
b. Thought withdrawal
c. Thought broadcasting
d. Made actions
e. Somatic passivity

Question 2

Which of the following statements about 'Stereotypy' is correct?

a. The patient would adopt an inappropriate or bizarre bodily posture continuously for a long term.
b. The patient would have repeated regular fixed patterns of movement that are not goal directed.
c. There is a feeling of plastic resistance resembling the bending of a soft wax rod as the examiner moves parts of the patient's body.
d. The patient would have repeated irregular movements involving a muscle group.
e. The patient would have resting tremors, cogwheel rigidity and postural and gait abnormalities.

Question 3

General practitioners (GPs), though not trained in psychotherapy, could still help patients through the provision of supportive psychotherapy. Supportive psychotherapy's main goal would be to

a. Allow the GP to provide patients with a source of emotional support
b. Allow the patients to have a chance to ventilate their feelings

c. Allow the GP to understand more about the patient's environment and assist in enabling changes
d. Allow the GP to help boost the self-esteem of the patients by agreeing with them
e. Allow the GP to strengthen the patient and help them to stabilize

Question 4

A 21-year-old has been sectioned for admission to the mental health unit as he has been experiencing bizarre delusions as well as auditory hallucinations. The ward team has decided to start him on a low dose of olanzapine for stabilization of his condition. However, it was noted that after the commencement of the medication, he developed a temperature as well as marked rigidity of his limbs. Which one of the following is the most likely clinical diagnosis?

a. Neuroleptic malignant syndrome
b. Serotonin syndrome
c. Lethal catatonia
d. Sepsis
e. Established side effects to olanzapine

Question 5

All of the following statements regarding individuals diagnosed with paranoid personality disorder are true, with the exception of

a. There is a tendency to bear grudges.
b. There is marked suspiciousness.
c. Threats and hidden meanings are read into benign remarks.
d. They confide readily.
e. There is excessive sensitivity to setbacks.

Question 6

Which of the following traits is not seen in individuals with schizoid personality disorder?

a. They tend to lead a solitary lifestyle.
b. They tend to appear indifferent to praise and criticism.
c. They have no interest in relationships.
d. There are times when they desire for the presence of close friends.
e. They usually appear to be cold and detached in their emotions.

Question 7

Based on prior research, it has been established that bulimics are more prone to which of the following psychiatric disorder as compared to anorexics?

a. Substance abuse
b. Personality disorders
c. Dementia
d. Obsessive-compulsive disorder (OCD)
e. Generalized anxiety disorder

Question 8

Which of the following is true regarding higher-order conditioning?

a. The onset of the conditioned stimulus precedes the unconditioned stimulus, and the conditioned stimulus continues until the response occurs.
b. The onset of both stimuli is simultaneous, and the conditioned stimulus continues until the response occurs.
c. The conditioned stimulus ends before the onset of the unconditioned stimulus, and the conditioning becomes less effective as the delay between the two increases.
d. The presentation of the conditioned stimulus occurs only after that of the unconditioned stimulus.
e. The conditioned stimulus is paired with a second conditioned stimulus, which, on presentation, by itself elicits the original conditioned response.

Question 9

An elderly Chinese man complained, 'My guts are rotten and blood stopped flowing to my heart. I am dead.' The psychopathology being described is

a. Acute intestinal obstruction
b. Delirium
c. Delusion of control
d. Nihilistic delusion
e. Hypochondriasis

Question 10

A 24-year-old man covers his head with a helmet because he believes that other people can receive his thoughts. The psychopathology being described is

a. Delusional memory
b. Running commentary
c. Thought broadcasting
d. Thought echo
e. Thought insertion

Question 11

A 10-year-old boy prefers playing computer games to doing his homework. His mother allows him 30 minutes of computer games if he finishes his homework and this motivates him to work on his homework diligently. Which of the following learning theories best describes the aforementioned phenomenon?

a. Backward conditioning
b. Forward conditioning
c. Mowrer's two-factor theory
d. Premack's principle
e. Trace conditioning

Question 12

To which class of antidepressants does duloxetine belong to?

a. Tricyclic antidepressants
b. Selective serotonin reuptake inhibitors

c. Serotonergic and noradrenergic reuptake inhibitors
d. Monoamine oxidase inhibitors
e. Adrenergic type 2 antagonists

Question 13
Which of the following antipsychotics belongs to the class of a substituted benzamide?
a. Amisulpride
b. Haloperidol
c. Clozapine
d. Quetiapine
e. Risperidone

Question 14
A 26-year-old male has a known history of bipolar disorder. He has been concordant with his medications. Recently, he has been experiencing constipation and weight gain, and routine investigation diagnosed him with hypothyroidism. Which one of the following medications might predispose James to have this new clinical condition?
a. Sodium valproate
b. Lithium
c. Carbamazepine
d. Lamotrigine
e. Gabapentin

Question 15
A 35-year-old unemployed woman firmly believes Prince William is in love with her even though she has never met him. Collateral history of her family reveals that she has never contacted him. The condition being described is
a. De Clerambault's syndrome
b. Capgras' syndrome
c. Fregoli syndrome
d. Intermetamorphosis syndrome
e. Othello syndrome

Question 16
A 50-year-old man suffered from prostate cancer 2 years ago. He came to the hospital daily to receive chemotherapy. However, when he received chemotherapy, he threw up because of side effects. From that point forward, whenever he was in the hospital, he felt sick to his stomach. The chemotherapy was stopped 1 year ago, and the nausea associated with hospital environment also disappeared. Which of the following statements regarding the disappearance of nausea associated with hospital environment is correct?
a. This process has no treatment implication.
b. This process only applies to biological responses (e.g. nausea) but not psychological responses.

c. This process was developed in conjunction with both classical conditioning and operant conditioning.
d. The response (i.e. nausea) disappeared suddenly.
e. The response (i.e. nausea associated with hospital environment) would never occur again.

Question 17

A medical student states that a hypomanic episode usually differs from a manic episode in terms of the degree of impairment of baseline functioning and also in terms of the duration of the symptoms. What should be the correct answer with regards to how long the symptoms would need to typically last in a hypomanic episode?

a. 1 day
b. 2 days
c. 3 days
d. 4 days
e. 1 week

Question 18

Theory of mind refers to the ability of an individual to understand and comprehend the thoughts, feelings, beliefs and knowledge about others. In which of the following condition is the development of a theory of mind lacking?

a. Pervasive development disorder
b. Hyperkinetic disorder
c. Depressive disorder in children
d. Anxiety disorder in children
e. Conduct disorder in children

Question 19

Attachment theory is a theory that was proposed by

a. Bowlby
b. Harlow
c. Lorenz
d. Freud
e. Piaget

Question 20

A core trainee has assessed a 70-year-old gentleman to be suffering from depression and is keen to recommend antidepressant treatment. He wonders which one of the following pharmacokinetics parameters would be affected in the elderly. All of the following are likely changes, with the exception of

a. Changes in the serum protein binding of the psychotropic medication
b. Changes in the renal clearance of the medication
c. Changes in the percentage of the total body fat

d. Changes in the gastric pH
e. Increased tubular secretion

Question 21

Which of the following hallucinations typically occurs for patients diagnosed with depression with psychotic features?

a. Somatic
b. Visual
c. Gustatory
d. Auditory
e. Olfactory

Question 22

Which of the following statements regarding eidectic image is false?

a. It typically affects those who are more advanced in age.
b. It is classified as one form of pseudohallucination.
c. It occurs usually in the outer objective space.
d. It is common in depression.
e. It can be considered to be a vivid reproduction of a previous perception.

Question 23

A 20-year-old British soldier was seriously wounded in an attack on troops in a southern Iraqi city in 2004. He returned to the United Kingdom for further treatment. After this episode, he experiences recurrent nightmares and flashbacks. He does not want to return to the army camp in the UK and avoids touching firearms. He does not want to talk about anything related to Iraq. His superior wants to find out from you the underlying reason to explain his avoidance. Which of the following learning theories explains his avoidance?

a. Avoidance conditioning
b. Aversive conditioning
c. Classical conditioning
d. Escape conditioning
e. Operant conditioning

Question 24

A 29-year-old woman undergoes psychotherapy for the treatment of OCD. She has hand-washing compulsions and cannot stand touching any surface that has not been sterilized with antibacterial agents. The psychologist makes her turn the door knob with her bare hands when she enters the room to see the psychologist and she is not allowed to wash her hands throughout the psychotherapy session. Which of the following learning theories best describes the aforementioned phenomenon?'

a. Habituation
b. Simultaneous conditioning
c. Spontaneous recovery

d. Stimulus generalization
e. Stimulus discrimination

Question 25
A man sees a blue car driving past him and he realizes that the terrorists are going to kill him. This is most likely which of the following?
a. Delusion of hypochondriasis
b. Delusion of passivity
c. Delusional perception
d. Delusion of persecution
e. Visual hallucination

Question 26
Which of the following statements about psychological imprinting is correct?
a. An example of this is when a young animal learns the characteristics of its parents.
b. Expression of inheritance is in a parent-of-origin-specific manner.
c. It involves learning that is slow.
d. It involves learning that is dependent on the consequences of behaviour.
e. This concept is studied extensively by Tolman.

Question 27
The latest research findings report that the combination of the first- and second-generation antipsychotics significantly increases the risk of metabolic syndrome amongst people with schizophrenia. Which of the following pharmacodynamic properties of the first-generation antipsychotics is most responsible for the aforementioned research findings?
a. Antiadrenergic
b. Antimuscarinic
c. Antidopaminergic
d. Antihistaminergic
e. Antinicotinic

Question 28
Which of the following statements regarding alcoholic dementia is incorrect?
a. Alcoholics might suffer from mild to moderate degree of cognitive impairment if they have been using alcohol on a chronic basis for some years.
b. Women are more likely to develop cognitive impairment much earlier as compared to men.
c. Brain imaging would show the presence of ventricular enlargement and sulcal widening.
d. Chronic alcoholics might show changes in their personality, likely due to frontal lobe atrophy.
e. The mild or moderate cognitive impairment due to long-term use of alcohol would not improve with abstinence.

Question 29

A 28-year-old female noticed that her friend's 3-year-old son seemed to always keep a distance from his mother, and at times, even ignores his mother. What form of attachment does the child have towards his mother?

a. Secure attachment
b. Insecure attachment
c. Avoidant attachment
d. Anxious attachment
e. Ambivalent attachment

Question 30

The following subtypes of schizophrenia could be found within the 10th revision of *International Classification of Diseases* (ICD-10) diagnostic criteria, with the exception of

a. Catatonic schizophrenia
b. Disorganized schizophrenia
c. Hebephrenic schizophrenia
d. Paranoid schizophrenia
e. Simple schizophrenia

Question 31

Confabulation, pseudologia, and retrospective falsification or false memory all have the following in common:

a. Presence of delusional beliefs
b. Presence of hallucinations
c. Presence of suggestibility
d. Presence of passivity phenomenon
e. Presence of abnormal thought content

Question 32

A medical student is curious about the Folstein's Mini Mental State Examination (MMSE). She wants to know the purpose of the Serial Sevens Test. Your answer is

a. Assess attention
b. Assess mathematical skills
c. Assess memory
d. Assess registration
e. Assess recall

Question 33

A medical student being attached to the addiction specialty wonders how long an individual needs to have symptoms of alcohol dependence in order for a diagnosis to be made. The correct answer, based on the ICD-10 classification system, would be

a. 1 month
b. 2 months

c. 6 months
d. 1 year
e. 2 years

Question 34

A medical student asks the consultant psychiatrist of the addictions service how soon would a chronic alcoholic experience alcoholic withdrawal fits. The correct answer would be

a. 12 hours
b. 24 hours
c. 36 hours
d. 48 hours
e. 72 hours

Question 35

A 50-year-old woman is referred by her GP to you for psychiatric assessment. She sees her son when she looks at various strangers walking down the street. The psychopathology being described is

a. De Clerambault's syndrome
b. Capgras syndrome
c. Fregoli syndrome
d. Munchausen syndrome
e. Othello syndrome

Question 36

A person describes the feeling of familiarity when stored material returns to consciousness. The phenomenon being described is

a. Déjà-vu
b. Jamais vu
c. Recognition
d. Recollection
e. Retrieval

Question 37

A 32-year-old married woman with a history of recurrent depressive episodes takes fluoxetine 40 mg on a daily basis. She wants to conceive in the near future but she is concerned about the safety of fluoxetine during pregnancy. She wants to stop taking fluoxetine but wants to know from the chance of having a relapse of depressive episode. Your answer is

a. 5%
b. 15%
c. 35%
d. 55%
e. 75%

Question 38

A 28-year-old female is seductive and always likes to be the centre of attention. She values her own appearance, and at times, she views certain interpersonal relationships as much closer than what others view. Under which one of the following personality disorders would you classify her?

a. Schizoid personality disorder
b. Borderline personality disorder
c. Paranoid personality disorder
d. Histrionic personality disorder
e. Obsessive-compulsive personality disorder

Question 39

At a certain stage of human development, one is able to process new concepts according to a pre-existing system of understanding. Which of the following concepts from Piaget's theory of cognitive development best describes this phenomenon?

a. Accommodation
b. Animism
c. Assimilation
d. Equilibrium
e. Schema

Question 40

A trainee who is more familiar with DSM-5 wonders where, in ICD-10, neurasthenia is classified. The consultant informs him that neurasthenia is classified under

a. Other mood (affective) disorders F35
b. Other anxiety disorders F41
c. Reaction to stress and adjustment disorders F43
d. Somatoform disorders F45
e. Other Neurotic disorders F48

Question 41

A medical student was asked how best the orientation of an inpatient could be determined. Which one of the following statements is the most accurate?

a. Checking with the patient whether he could remember and recall his own address
b. Checking with the patient whether he could perform serial sevens or spell the word 'World' forwards then backwards
c. Checking whether the patient can name specific objects
d. Checking with the patient whether he is able to tell the occupation or the identity of a doctor or an allied health-care staff
e. Checking with the patient whether he is able to name as many words as possible beginning with the letter 'F' in 1 minute

Question 42

A core trainee-2 is seeing a patient who has an alcohol addiction problem. He wishes to use one of the standardized alcohol assessment questionnaires to help him in his assessment. Please select the questionnaire that is not suitable for him to use.

a. CAGE
b. Alcohol Use Disorders Identification Test (AUDIT)
c. Brief Psychiatric Rating Scale (BPRS)
d. Michigan Alcohol Screening Test (MAST)
e. Clinical Institute Withdrawal Assessment for Alcohol Scale (CIWA)

Question 43

Which of the following statements about memory is incorrect?

a. Both primacy and recency effects are involved in remembering a list of names.
b. Primary memory has been found to have a duration of approximately 7 seconds.
c. Working memory and primary memory are synonymous.
d. Chunking increases the capacity of short-term memory.
e. Short-term memory has a limited capacity.

Question 44

An 80-year-old man says, 'I have a headache because there is too much blood in my head. I feel my throat being blocked and hence, blood cannot leave my head'. The psychopathology being described is

a. Hypochondriasis
b. Nihilistic delusion
c. Passivity experience
d. Somatic delusion
e. Stroke

Question 45

A 32-year-old married woman with a history of recurrent depressive episodes takes fluoxetine 40 mg on a daily basis. She wants to conceive in the near future but she is concerned about the safety of fluoxetine during pregnancy. She wants to know the rate of major malformations in the foetus associated with prenatal exposure to fluoxetine. Your answer is

a. 0%
b. 1%–3%
c. 5%–7%
d. 9%–11%
e. 13%–15%

Question 46

Which of the following statements about the Sequenced Treatment Alternatives to Relieve Depression (STAR*D) trial is incorrect?

a. Approximately one-third of the patients did reach a remission state or has had virtual absence of their symptoms during the initial phase of the study.
b. The remission rate was 20%.

c. Patients who took T3 complained of lesser side effects than those taking lithium.
d. The discontinuation rate for T3 was 10%, whereas the rate for lithium was 23%.
e. The level 4 findings suggested that venlafaxine or mirtazapine treatment would be a better choice than a monoamine oxidase inhibitor (MAO-I).

Question 47

There are known differences between the ICD-10 and the DSM-IV-TR classification system. Which one of the following personality disorders is included in the DSM-IV-TR classification system, but cannot be found in the ICD-10 classification system?

a. Schizotypal personality disorder
b. Paranoid personality disorder
c. Antisocial personality disorder
d. Avoidant personality disorder
e. None of the above

Question 48

An 80-year-old man has been brought in by his family as they are very concerned about his progressive memory loss. The old-age psychiatrist assessing him decided to perform baseline blood investigations, a computed tomography (CT) scan and also a specialized scan. On the specialized scan, multiple protein-like, intra-cytoplasmic inclusion bodies were found in the basal ganglia (which could be visualized only with a microscope). This finding suggests that the aetiology of dementia might be due to

a. Alzheimer's dementia
b. Vascular dementia
c. Frontotemporal dementia
d. Lewy body dementia
e. Alcoholic dementia

Question 49

Which of the following is not part of koro?

a. Illness, exposure to cold and excess coitus are common precursors.
b. Men become convinced that the penis will suddenly withdraw into the abdomen.
c. Onset is usually gradual and slow.
d. Women become convinced that their breasts, labia or vulva will retract.
e. Sufferers expect fatal consequences.

Question 50

Which of the following diagnosis would be the most appropriate to describe a patient who fears that he or she would offend others through inappropriate behaviour or self-presentation?

a. Amok
b. Latah
c. Koro

d. Frigophobia
e. Taijinkyofusho

Question 51

A 14-year-old boy was diagnosed with depression about 1 year ago. He has been receiving intensive psychological treatment. He returns to see the Child and Adolescent Mental Health Service (CAMHS) psychiatrist. Which of the following scales would be the most helpful in determining the diagnosis and symptoms which have been present over the past year?

a. Beck's Depression Inventory (BDI)
b. Hospital Anxiety and Depression Scale (HADS)
c. Montgomery–Asberg Depression Rating Scale (MADRAS)
d. Kiddie Schedule for Affective Disorder and Schizophrenia (K-SADS)
e. Brief Psychiatric Rating Scale (BPRS)

Question 52

Social psychologist Philip Zimbardo designed the Stanford prison experiment where students were randomly assigned to act as either a guard or a prisoner. The 'guards' became abrasive and verbally harassed and humiliated the 'prisoners', and the 'prisoners' became withdrawn and helpless and some were physically ill. This experiment illustrates

a. Social identity
b. Social categorization
c. Social role
d. Social norm
e. Social influence

Question 53

Induced psychosis is a rare delusional disorder, most common amongst which group of individuals?

a. Elderly patients
b. Teenagers
c. Those in a couple relationship
d. Those with blood relationships
e. Any particular group of men or women

Question 54

In a psychological experiment, the subjects find it difficult to remember the following phone number, 18003377924. Which of the following methods would make the phone number most easy to remember?

a. Convert the phone number into two items: 180033-77924
b. Convert the phone number into six items: 18-00-33-77-92–4
c. Convert the phone number into 10 items: 18-0-0-3-3-7-7-9-2-4
d. Remember the phone number, one by one: 1-8-0-0-3-3-7-7-9-2-4
e. Convert the phone number into reverse order: 4-2-9-7-7-3-3-0-0-8-1

Question 55

Hypnagogic hallucinations

a. Are usually visual
b. Occur in slow wave sleep
c. Occur in stage 1 of non-REM sleep
d. Occur in transition to wakefulness
e. Require antipsychotic medication

Question 56

A MRCPsych Paper 1 revision course organizer wants to help the participants accurately retain the information in working memory as long as possible. Which of the following methods is the least useful?

a. The course organizer should keep the number of pieces of information small enough for participants to study.
b. The course organizer should keep attention constantly focused on the information under consideration in each topic.
c. The course organizer should rehearse the information often whilst the student is working on sample MCQs or EMIs.
d. The course organizer should emphasize the participants to store the information in their brain and advise them to reduce access to the information during the course.
e. The course organizer should help participants to move the information to long-term memory as soon as possible.

Question 57

A 50-year-old man perceives his wife has assumed another bodily form, sometimes appearing as a man but sometimes appearing as a young woman. The phenomenon is known as

a. De Clerambault's syndrome
b. Capgras syndrome
c. Fregoli syndrome
d. Reverse Fregoli syndrome
e. Subjective double syndrome

Question 58

A 16-year-old African male was studying for his examination. He suddenly had the following symptoms: headache, blurred vision and amnesia for what he had studied. Which one of the following culture-bound syndromes does the man suffer from?

a. Amok
b. Brain fag
c. Dhat
d. Koro
e. Latah

Question 59

Based on your understanding about defence mechanisms, avoidance is a defence mechanism that is commonly used by patients with the following psychiatric diagnosis:

a. Depression
b. Schizophrenia
c. Schizoid personality disorder
d. Phobias
e. Post-traumatic stress disorder (PTSD)

Question 60

A medical student was interested in psychodynamic psychotherapy and read more about it. He shared with his supervisor who was a psychotherapist several of the defence mechanisms that he read about. Which one of the following defence mechanisms was not described by Melanie Klein?

a. Projective identification
b. Splitting
c. Denial
d. Introjection (internalization)
e. None of the above

Question 61

A medical student doing his psychiatric posting was spending time attached to the psychologist clinic, to learn what the psychologist does in his daily work. He wonders what the psychology would administer as the most evidence-based and gold standard test for assessment of intelligence. Which of the following measures would it be?

a. Wechsler Adult Intelligence Scale
b. Halstead–Reitan Battery
c. Luria–Nebraska Neuropsychological Battery
d. Repeatable Battery for the Assessment of Neuropsychological Status
e. None of the above

Question 62

Which of the following statements about attribution theory is incorrect?

a. Attribution theory involves making inferences.
b. In attribution theory, people tend to attribute their own behaviour to their personality traits.
c. A dispositional attribution is the inference that the cause of behaviour is due to internal factors.
d. Using an internal attribution to explain other people's behaviour is usual.
e. A person's feelings about the event may influence a particular cause attributed to an event.

Question 63

A 28-year-old female, Pamela, migrated from Bulgaria to London months ago. Her mother has noticed that she has been increasingly withdrawn in her behaviour. Just 2 days ago, her mother has noticed that Pamela is refusing to eat or drink and is totally mute. She is very concerned. What is the most likely clinical diagnosis for Pamela?

a. Manic stupor
b. Depressive stupor
c. Dissociative stupor
d. Transient psychotic episode
e. Adjustment disorder

Question 64

Based on your understanding, déjà vu and jamais vu are considered to be disorders of

a. Orientation
b. Memory
c. Attention
d. Self-awareness
e. Intelligence

Question 65

During an outpatient review, a 20-year-old patient who has chronic schizophrenia and is currently on quetiapine shared that he has been feeling increasingly anxious. He feels that others could have access to his thoughts and that, recently, there have been thoughts that arise elsewhere and are inserted into his head. Which of the following terms best describes the psychopathology that James is experiencing?

a. Made feelings
b. Thought insertion
c. Thought withdrawal
d. Thought control
e. Thought broad-casting

Question 66

Your medical colleague is preparing for the magnetic resonance cholangiopancreatography (MRCP) examination and he complains that he keeps on forgetting the information he has learnt. He wants to seek your advice on the underlying reason for forgetting. The following are established factors which could lead to his forgetfulness, except

a. He forgets the information owing to disuse of information after a 1-year period of unpaid leave.
b. He forgets the information as he spent 6 months learning surgery which has displaced his knowledge of internal medicine.
c. When his consultant asks him questions, the answer is almost at the tip of his tongue but he cannot recall it.

d. He can recite his knowledge perfectly in his bedroom with classical music playing but cannot recall it in the examination hall.
e. When he studies, he usually feels sad. In the examination, he often puts down the answer 'don't know' when answering MCQs as he also feels sad during the examination.

Question 67

All of the following statements about anorexia nervosa are true, with the exception of

a. The condition is relatively rare and occurs in around 1–2 per 1000 women
b. Peak age of onset is 20–29 years.
c. The incidence of the condition is 10 times higher in females as compared to males.
d. It is a condition that is more prevalent in higher socioeconomic classes.
e. Twin studies have revealed higher concordance rates amongst monozygotic twins as compared to dizygotic twins.

Question 68

A 30-year-old is referred to see you for unusual experiences. She complains of recurrent episodes of not being at home or in the office, although she is there. She cannot feel emotions towards people who are close to her. In situations where she supposes to feel angry, she feels numb instead. She also complains that her memories seem pale and she is not certain whether past events really happened. The psychopathology being described is

a. Alexithymia
b. Delusional mood
c. Delusional memory
d. Depersonalization
e. Derealization

Question 69

Which of the following statements regarding the diagnostic criteria for bipolar disorder, manic episode is correct?

a. The DSM-IV-TR and ICD-10 classify bipolar disorder into bipolar I and bipolar II disorder.
b. The DSM-IV-TR and ICD-10 do not require the presence of depressive episode in the past.
c. The DSM-IV-TR and ICD-10 require the presence of depressive episode in the past.
d. The DSM-IV-TR requires the presence of at least one major depressive episode but not ICD-10.
e. The ICD-10 requires the presence of at least one major depressive episode but not DSM-IV-TR.

Question 70

Which of the following is not a special feature for DSM-IV-TR bipolar disorder with depressive episode?

a. Atypical features
b. Catatonic features

c. Melancholic features
d. Postpartum onset
e. Seasonal pattern

Question 71
All of the following statements regarding the aetiology of eating disorder are correct, with the exception of
a. Family studies have shown an increased incidence of eating disorders amongst the first- and second-degree relatives of those suffering from anorexia nervosa.
b. Brain serotonin systems have not been shown to be implicated in the modulation of appetite.
c. An excess of physical illnesses in childhood have been found in those with anorexia nervosa.
d. Relationships in families of anorexics are usually characterized by overprotection and enmeshment.
e. Sociocultural factors such as a cult of thinness might affect the development of the disorder.

Question 72
Which of the following statements about memory and ageing is false?
a. Memory loss of recent events is an early feature of Alzheimer's disease.
b. Procedural memory is affected later than spatial awareness in Alzheimer's disease.
c. Procedural memory is affected later than verbal memory in Alzheimer's disease.
d. In an adult life span, performance for free recall is affected earlier than recognition on a word-list learning.
e. Semantic memory may improve with age until the age of 80.

Question 73
A 25-year-old man is referred to you for visual disturbance that causes images to persist even after their corresponding stimulus has ceased. He often uses lysergic acid diethylamide (LSD). The psychopathology being described is
a. Eidetic imagery
b. Pareidolia
c. Palinopsia
d. Panoramic hallucination
e. Peduncular hallucination

Question 74
Which of the following statements regarding diagnostic criteria for rapid cycling disorder is false?
a. Based on the DSM-IV-TR criteria, at least four episodes of a mood disturbance in the previous 12 months meet criteria.
b. Based on the DSM-IV-TR criteria, episodes are demarcated either by partial or full remission for at least 2 months.
c. Based on the DSM-IV-TR criteria, episodes can switch to an episode of opposite polarity.

d. Rapid cycling disorder is a course specifier in DSM-IV-TR.
e. Rapid cycling disorder is a separate entity in ICD-10.

Question 75
Which of the following statements regarding diagnostic criteria for cyclothymia is false?

a. Based on the DSM-IV-TR and ICD-10 criteria, there must have been a period of at least 2 years of instability of mood involving several periods of both depression and hypomania.
b. Based on the ICD-10 criteria, none of the manifestations of depression or hypomania should be sufficiently severe or long-lasting to meet criteria for manic episode or depressive episode.
c. Based on the DSM-IV-TR and ICD-10 criteria, intervening periods of normal mood should not be present.
d. Based on the DSM-IV-TR criteria, the minimum duration of illness is 1 year for children and adolescents.
e. Based on the DSM-IV-TR criteria, there may be superimposed manic episodes after the initial 2 years.

Question 76
Which of the following statements regarding bipolar mood disorder is incorrect?

a. Male to female ratio is the same.
b. It is a condition that is most common in the lower social classes.
c. The average age of onset is around mid-20s.
d. Being unmarried might account for the higher incidence of bipolar disorder.
e. Common comorbidities might include anxiety disorder, substance misuse disorder and antisocial personality disorder.

Question 77
A 30-year old male surrendered himself at the police station as he feels that he is guilty for causing the war between the United States and Iraq by mixing up the mails. In addition, he shared that he knows that the police are monitoring him each time he sees the colour 'red'. What psychopathology is this?

a. Delusional perception
b. Delusion of poverty
c. Delusion of self-accusation
d. Delusion of doubles
e. Nihilistic delusion

Question 78
Which of the following is not one of the techniques that can be used to measure memory?

a. Paired-associate recall
b. Recognition

c. Memory-span procedure
d. Free recall
e. Memory retrieval procedure

Question 79

Rubin's vase, the Necker cube and Boring's old/young woman are examples of

a. Distortions
b. Ambiguous figures
c. Paradoxical figures
d. Fictions
e. Illusions of shading

Question 80

A mother is concerned that her child might develop autism. Based on the diagnostic criteria for autism, the onset of the disorder is usually before the age of

a. 1 year
b. 2 years
c. 3 years
d. 4 years
e. 5 years

Question 81

A 35-year-old man is suing his company for compensation for his cognitive impairment as a result of a head injury that occurred at his workplace 6 months ago. You have referred him for formal neuropsychological assessment. The neuropsychologist has prepared the report. Which of following findings does not suggest feigned amnesia?

a. Impairment of attention or immediate memory is much worse than impairment of overall learning and memory.
b. Standardized scores on tests of recognition memory are higher than standardized scores on tests of free recall.
c. Reports of severe retrograde amnesia together with intact new learning and absence of neurological abnormality.
d. Gross inconsistency across tests or testing occasions.
e. Evasive or unusual test-taking behaviour.

Question 82

A 20-year-old woman has a history of sexual abuse and you worry that she may develop false memory syndrome. Which of the following statements regarding false memory syndrome is incorrect?

a. The interviewer should avoid leading questions.
b. False memory syndrome may lead to medico-legal problems.
c. False memory syndrome is a recognized diagnostic criterion in ICD-10.
d. False memory syndrome is more common in patients who are prone to fantasy.
e. False memory syndrome is relatively common amongst cases of severe childhood abuse.

Question 83
Schemas are cognitive structures representing knowledge about a concept. Schemas influence the way people organize knowledge about the social world and interpret new situations. Which of the following statements about schemas is true?
a. Schemas persist even after evidence for the schema has been discredited.
b. Schemas slow down mental processing.
c. Schemas are not useful in an ambiguous situation.
d. Schemas involve high-effort controlled thinking.
e. Schemas help prevent self-fulfilling prophecy.

Question 84
Which of the following drugs is least likely to cause tremor?
a. Amphetamine
b. B_2 agonist
c. B_2 antagonist
d. Caffeine
e. Risperidone

Question 85
A 23-year-old male John tells the psychiatrist during the clinical interview that there are times when he resorts to wearing clothes of the opposite sex to gain temporary membership and to feel belonged to the opposite sex. He does not have any desire for any active gender reassignment surgery. Which one of the following would be the most likely clinical diagnosis?
a. Dual-role transvestism
b. Fetishism
c. Fetishistic transvestism
d. Paedophilia
e. Exhibitionism

Question 86
Schneider proposed the concept of first-rank symptoms. First-rank symptoms include all of the following, with the exception of
a. Auditory hallucinations
b. Delusions of passivity
c. Somatic passivity
d. Delusional perception
e. Stupor

Question 87
A 22-year-old male has been referred by his GP to see a psychiatrist. He has been insisting that his GP refers him over to a surgeon for a gender reassignment surgery. He claims that he feels like a woman and would prefer to undergo gender reassignment. Which one of the following would be the most likely clinical diagnosis?
a. Dual-role transvestism
b. Fetishistic transvestism

c. Transexualism
d. Exhibitionism
e. Frotteurism

Question 88

Aggression is an intentional behaviour aimed at harming others. There are several explanations of aggression. Which one of the following is incorrect?

a. Aggression is associated with high levels of testosterone.
b. Aggression is a learned response.
c. Aggression is associated with activation of the amygdala.
d. Aggression can be reinforced by operant conditioning.
e. Aggression is associated with high levels of serotonin.

Question 89

A 35-year-old woman has around five episodes of either mania or depression each year and her GP wants to know her diagnosis based on the DSM-IV-TR criteria. Your answer is

a. Bipolar I disorder
b. Bipolar II disorder
c. Bipolar disorder unspecified
d. Rapid cycling bipolar disorder
e. Ultra-rapid cycling bipolar disorder

Question 90

Which of the following conditions is least likely to cause tremor?

a. Degenerative spinal disease
b. Peripheral neuropathy
c. Hypoglycaernia
d. Thyrotoxicosis
e. Wilson's disease

Question 91

Thirty horses galloped out of the riding stables. According to the rescuers, the flock of 20 horses is perceived as together as they are close to each other. There are 10 horses which are far apart and left behind. Which of the following Gestalt's perception theories best describes the rescuers' observation?

a. Closure
b. Continuity
c. Figure ground
d. Proximity
e. Similarity

Question 92

In this clinical condition, the patient actually believes that a familiar person has taken on different appearances. The clinical diagnosis would be

a. Fregoli syndrome
b. Induced psychosis

c. Capgras syndrome
d. Cotard syndrome
e. Erotomania

Question 93
A 20-year-old male has moderate degree of learning disability. Recently, his girlfriend Angela is pregnant and he is increasingly stressed that their baby would be taken away by the social services. He has resorted to exposing his genitalia to others. Which one of the following would be the most appropriate clinical diagnosis?
a. Dual-role transvestism
b. Fetishistic transvestism
c. Transexualism
d. Exhibitionism
e. Frotteurism

Question 94
Which of the following best defines self-fulfilling prophecy?
a. People's expectation of a person causes a person to act in a different way.
b. People's expectation of a person causes a person to act in line with the expectation.
c. People's expectation of a person influences their behaviour towards that person, resulting in an alteration of that person's behaviour.
d. People's expectation of a person influences their behaviour towards that person, resulting in that person acting in line with the expectation.
e. People's expectation of a person influences their behaviour towards that person, causing the person to act in line with the expectation with attempts to modify the expectation.

Question 95
A 24-year-old woman with borderline personality disorder is detained in a gazette ward under the Mental Health Act after a failed suicide attempt. She has politely asked the psychiatrist to discharge her but without success. She suddenly shouted and swore at a health-care assistant with anger. This defence mechanism is known as
a. Displacement
b. Projection
c. Projective identification
d. Reaction formation
e. Splitting

Question 96
A 20-year-old Indian man is referred by an orthopaedic surgeon for psychosomatic complaints. He consulted an orthopaedic surgeon for low back pain and weakness. Physical examination and investigation showed normal findings. When the orthopaedic surgeon tries to explain the normal findings to him, he complains of passage of semen in urine and requests to see an urologist.

On further inquiry, he admits that he is going to get married soon and he fears about sexual performance. This man suffers from which of the following culture-bound syndromes?

a. Amok
b. Brain fag
c. Dhat
d. Koro
e. Khat

Question 97

You were sent to Haiti for volunteer work after the earthquake in 2010. A 30-year-old man is referred to you for sudden outburst of agitation and aggressive behaviour. He had experienced auditory and visual hallucinations for 3 days and then the psychotic experiences disappeared. There is no family history of schizophrenia. Which of the following terms best described his psychopathology in the local context?

a. Folie induite
b. Déjà pensé
c. La belle indifférence
d. La boufféedélirante
e. L'homme qui rit

Question 98

Which of the following statements is true about essential tremor?

a. Early essential tremor is present at rest.
b. Early essential tremor is absent during action.
c. Essential tremor exacerbates with alcohol use.
d. Essential tremor is more common amongst young people.
e. Familial pattern of essential tremor is common.

Question 99

A father is very concerned about his 18-year-old son. He reports to the CAMHS psychiatrist that his son seems to be always withdrawn during social activities. He is not able to partake in a conversation when there are visitors at home. At times, James is noted to be relatively distressed and would be sweating profusely when attending social events. Which one of the following is the most likely clinical diagnosis?

a. Agoraphobia
b. Social phobia
c. Generalized anxiety disorder
d. Obsessive-compulsive disorder
e. Obsessive-compulsive personality disorder

Question 100

A medical student was asked to do a physical examination on a newly admitted psychiatric patient. When the student tried to move the left arm of the patient and asked him to resist against the force applied, he noted that the patient continued to move the arm in the direction of the force applied. The patient later placed his arm back in its original position. This is an example of which of the following psychopathologies?

a. Automatic obedience
b. Mannerism
c. Mitgehen
d. Mitmachen
e. Negativism

Question 101

Thirty horses galloped out of the riding stables. According to the rescuers, a flock of twenty horses is perceived as together as they are heading to town at the same speed. The other ten horses do not seem to be together and run all over the place. Which of the following Gestalt's perception theories best describes the rescuers' observation?

a. Continuity
b. Common fate
c. Figure ground
d. Proximity
e. Similarity

Question 102

The following laboratory parameters are reduced in patients suffering from anorexia nervosa, except

a. Cortisol-releasing hormone
b. Luteinizing hormone
c. Potassium
d. Sodium
e. Triiodothyronine

Question 103

A 15-year-old female failed a Mathematics examination. She blamed her teacher for setting so many difficult questions that she did not have enough time to answer all the questions. Which of the following best describes the aforementioned phenomenon?

a. Self-serving bias
b. In-group bias
c. Actor/observer bias
d. Hindsight bias
e. Fundamental attribution bias

Question 104

Based on your understanding of the basic ethical principles in psychiatry, deontology refers to

a. Providing a duty-based approach
b. Acting in the patient's best interest
c. Ensuring that the action performed is considered to be morally right if it would lead to the greatest human pleasure, happiness and satisfaction

d. Ensuring that all individuals receive equal and impartial consideration
e. A doctor's native motive to provide morally correct care to his or her patients, and focus solely on the rightness and wrongness of the actions themselves, and not on the consequences of the actions

Question 105

During routine outpatient review, a patient with a diagnosis of schizophrenia, who has been concordant to his medications and has not had a relapse in the past decade, informs the psychiatrist that he wishes to stop medical treatment. The psychiatrist is concerned and cautions him about the risk of relapse as well as the advantage and benefits on staying on the medications. The patient does have mental capacity to understand and formulate a decision; however, his decision in this case would not be the best option. The psychiatrist feels compelled to go along with the wishes of the patient. This is an example of the ethical principle of

a. Utilitarianism
b. Deontology
c. Nonmaleficence
d. Autonomy
e. Beneficence

Question 106

This refers to a duty that needs to be always acted upon unless it conflicts on a particular occasion with an equal or stronger duty. Which of the following is the correct ethical theory for the above?

a. Duty-based approach
b. Paternalism
c. Prima facie duty
d. Fiduciary duty
e. None of the above

Question 107

You are on the liaison psychiatry rotation and a gastroenterologist wants to consult you whether a schizophrenia patient has the capacity to refuse urgent oesophogastroduodenoscopy (OGD). Which of the following statements about capacity is false?

a. Capacity implies that the patient understands the relevant information about OGD given by the gastroenterologist.
b. Capacity is a clinical opinion given by a clinician.
c. Capacity is a legal term.
d. Capacity requires the mental ability from the patient to make and communicate a decision.
e. The gastroenterologist is expected to provide all relevant information about OGD.

Question 108

A 30-year-old pregnant woman presents to the hospital at 12 weeks' gestation with an 8-week history of severe vomiting, 15 kg of weight loss, and new-onset weakness, dizziness and blurred vision. Examination of the patient shows confusion, papilloedema, ophthalmoplegia, nystagmus, reduced hearing and truncal ataxia. This patient is most likely suffering from

a. Cerebellar hemisphere haemorrhage
b. Delirium tremens
c. Meningitis
d. Wernicke's encephalopathy
e. Status epilepticus

Question 109

A consultant psychiatrist who is lecturing a group of medical students was explaining the concept of a delusional disorder. Which one of the following is not commonly associated or descriptive of a delusional disorder?

a. Bizarre delusions
b. False belief based on incorrect inference about external reality
c. Firmly sustained despite the beliefs of the normal population
d. Firmly sustained despite there being no obvious proof or evidence against
e. Belief system not accepted by members of one's culture

Question 110

A 20-year-old woman presents with bulimia nervosa. Her height and weight are 160 cm and 60 kg, respectively. What is her body mass index (BMI)?

a. Less than 17
b. 18–19
c. 20–21
d. 22–23
e. More than 23

Question 111

There are several conditions that need to be met in order to reduce prejudice. Which one of the following is not one of those conditions?

a. Equal status
b. Interactions with a member of the out-group
c. Social norms favouring equality
d. Co-operative effort
e. The potential for personal acquaintance

Question 112

The following are criteria for a valid consent, except

a. No misrepresentation of beneficial effects of a proposed treatment
b. No coercion
c. No excessive persuasion
d. No implicit consent
e. No inclusion of information, which is irrelevant to a proposed treatment

Question 113
You are able to assess a 20-year-old man who is aggressive and angry towards the staff at the Accident and Emergency Department. Which of the following measures is least useful?
a. Admit own feelings and inform the patient that the staff are frightened of his aggression and anger.
b. Encourage the patient to verbalize his aggression and anger.
c. Inform the patient that restraint or seclusion will be used if necessary.
d. Inform the patient that physical violence is not acceptable in the hospital setting.
e. Offer the option of using psychotropic medication to calm the patient.

Question 114
A 25-year-old woman presents with asymptomatic unequal pupils. During physical examination, her right eye shows pupillary dilatation with poor constriction to light and accommodation. Examination of lower limbs shows depressed deep tendon reflexes. The patient is most likely suffering from?
a. Argyll Robertson pupils
b. Diabetic neuropathy
c. Holmes–Adie syndrome
d. Horner's syndrome
e. Pupillary defect

Question 115
When interviewing a psychotic patient, it is essential to evaluate for delusions, hallucinations and, most importantly, passivity experiences. Passivity experiences, based on your understanding, include all the following, except
a. Thought insertion
b. Thought withdrawal
c. Thought block
d. Thought broadcast
e. Somatic passivity

Question 116
This is one form of suicide that has been previously proposed by Durkheim, in which the individual commits suicide due to feelings of being increasingly distanced from societal norms.
a. Altruistic suicide
b. Egoistic suicide
c. Acute anomic suicide
d. Chronic anomic suicide
e. None of the above

Question 117
Which of the following statements about mental state examination is correct?
a. During the mental state examination, a psychiatrist should ask a large range of psychopathologies to cover every diagnostic possibility.
b. During mental state examination, probe questions about psychopathology are best framed with technical questions.

c. Mental state examination is best conducted as formal exercise which follows a schema.
d. Serial mental state interrogations are extremely reliable methods of judging the progress of treatment or changes in a patient's mental health.
e. The best clinical approach to mental state examination is in a conversational and informal manner.

Question 118

A 25-year-old schizophrenia patient was admitted to the psychiatric ward under the Mental Health Act. He has not been compliant with oral antipsychotics, and you have proposed depot antipsychotics to prevent relapse since he has not been compliant to the oral medication. He strongly refuses depot injection because he is scared of pain. He does not have psychotic features and understands the risks and benefits associated with depot antipsychotics. Which of the following decisions is the best option based on ethical principles?

a. The doctor should inject him with depot antipsychotics under the Common Law.
b. The doctor should inject him with depot antipsychotics because he was admitted under the Mental Health Act.
c. The doctor should inject him with depot antipsychotics based on his best interests.
d. The doctor should postpone the decision to inject him and consult the guardian board.
e. The doctor should not inject him with depot antipsychotics and respect his wish.

Question 119

According to Durkheim, anomie refers to the social disconnectedness of lack of social norms. All of the following are causes of acute anomie, except

a. Migration
b. Bereavement
c. Redundancy
d. Losses
e. Homelessness

Question 120

Which of the following is most likely to be found in patients with carotid artery stenosis?

a. Amaurosis fugax
b. Bitemporal hemianopia
c. Hemianopia
d. Homonymous quadrantanopia
e. Scotoma

Question 121

The terminology 'institutional neurosis' was previously coined by which one of the following individuals?

a. Hecker
b. Bleuler

c. Goffman
d. Barton
e. Pavlov

Question 122
Which of the following is one of the first SSRIs that was introduced?
a. Zimeldine
b. Fluvoxamine
c. Fluoxetine
d. Sertraline
e. None of the above

Question 123
The following are possible explanations as to why certain psychiatric disorders are more prevalent in each of the social classes, with the exception of
a. Downward social drift
b. Environmental stress
c. Differential labelling
d. Differential treatment
e. Breeder's hypothesis

Question 124
A 25-year-old man with schizophrenia hears his thoughts being spoken aloud whenever he hears the sound of a train whistle. This psychopathological phenomenon is known as
a. Echo de la pensée
b. An extracampine hallucination
c. A functional hallucination
d. Gedankenlautwerden
e. A reflex hallucination

Question 125
A 30-year-old expectant father experiences somatic symptoms when his wife is 3-months pregnant. He complains of morning nausea, decreased appetite, weight gain, constipation and labour pain. The psychopathology being described is
a. Capgras syndrome
b. Couvade syndrome
c. Fregoli syndrome
d. Intermetamorphosis syndrome
e. Othello syndrome

Question 126
A 25-year-old female just went for an interview, hoping to get into Psychiatry as a core trainee. Months later, she was informed that she did not get the position and she believes that it must be because she did not perform well enough during the interview. What kind of attribution is she making?
a. Internal attribution
b. External attribution

c. Primary attribution
d. Secondary attribution
e. Fundamental attribution

Question 127

A medical student wonders what terminology would be more consistent with the following definition 'A set of beliefs about an individual, which is based on prior achievements and other social interactions, and this set of beliefs would interact and influence one's own behaviour'. Which terminology would fit the aforementioned description?

a. Self-concept
b. Self-esteem
c. Self-image
d. Self-evaluation
e. Self-perception

Question 128

This is a form of memory that involves confabulation and reports of false events. Which one of the following terms best describes this form of memory?

a. Anterograde amnesia
b. Retrograde amnesia
c. Post-traumatic amnesia
d. Psychogenic amnesia
e. False memory

Question 129

Which of the following electroencephalogram (EEG) waveforms typically has a frequency between 4 and 7.5 Hz?

a. Alpha wave
b. Beta wave
c. Delta wave
d. Gamma wave
e. Theta wave

Question 130

Two main types of conformity, informational social influence and normative social influence, have been proposed. Based on Asch's conformity theory, normative social conformity would most likely be influenced by

a. Personality traits
b. Presence of cognitive dissonance
c. Type of leadership style
d. Needing to avoid social rejection
e. Highly intelligent and socially expressive individuals

Question 131

Cognitive dissonance theory comprises all of the following, except

a. Selective attention
b. Selective exposure

c. Selective attention
d. Selective perception
e. Selective retention

Question 132
You have been asked to review a 50-year-old man in your dementia clinic for memory problems. Apart from the memory difficulties, the caregivers also vocalized that the patient had been having other difficulties, characterized as abnormal behaviours and movement. Of importance, they shared that one of their close relatives did suffer from a similar movement disorder and passed away at a very young age. It is likely that the patient you are currently assessing has
a. Wilson's disease
b. Early-onset Alzheimer's disease
c. Huntington's disease
d. Fronto-temporal disorder
e. Lewy body dementia

Question 133
A 30-year-old woman is referred by her GP to you for experiencing multiple episodes of unusual experiences at night. She recalls that a sudden loud sound startled her in the middle of the night. Every movement became impossible and she could not speak. She had breathing difficulty and felt her body vibrating. She saw demons staring at her from the ceiling and hands appearing from the wall to strangle her. The psychopathology being described is
a. Cataplexy
b. Nightmare
c. Night terror
d. Sleep paralysis
e. Somnambulism

Question 134
A 40-year-old woman reports that other patients' heads appear to be enlarged as compared to their actual body size. The psychopathology being described is
a. Delusion of doubles
b. Dysmegalopsia
c. Hallucination
d. Hyperaesthesia
e. Xanthopsia

Question 135
You are about to conduct an animal study. The suppliers of animals have a group of mice with reduced expression of glucocorticoid receptors and behavioural

problems. Which of the following psychiatric disorders in humans would this group of mice closely resemble?

a. Anxiety
b. Dementia
c. Depression
d. Learning disability
e. Schizophrenia

Question 136

A 35-year-old woman suffers from a severe depressive episode. She has three young children studying in a primary school. She is unemployed with no confiding relationship. Which of the following works provides an explanation in her case?

a. Brown and Harris: Social Origins of Depression
b. Durkheim E: Anomie
c. Habermas J: The Theory of Communicative Action
d. Parsons T: The Social System
e. Sullivan HS: The Interpersonal Theory of Psychiatry

Question 137

The following are protective factors against depressive disorder in men, except

a. Employment
b. Excessive social support
c. Good parental care when young
d. Social competence
e. Stable marriage

Question 138

The early psychosis intervention team wants to develop a new community support programme to reduce the suicide risk amongst people with schizophrenia. Which of the following groups of patients is the most at risk of suicide?

a. Female schizophrenia patients
b. Nonpsychotic schizophrenia patients
c. Schizophrenia patients who have never been admitted in the past
d. Schizophrenia patients with delusional expectation
e. Schizophrenia patients with low expectation

Question 139

There is evidence that media reports of suicide can be associated with further suicides. The editor of a local newspaper would like to consult you on the appropriate way to report suicide. You would recommend all of the following, except

a. Encourage distressed people to seek help after reading the article
b. Reporting followed by advertisements for helplines
c. Straightforward factual reporting
d. Suppression in suicide reporting
e. Undramatic reporting

Extended matching items (EMIs)

Theme: Clinical assessment and neuropsychological processes

Options:

a. Sensory memory
b. Short-term memory
c. Explicit memory
d. Implicit memory

Lead in: Select the most appropriate answer for each of the following. Each option may be used once, more than once or not at all.

Question 140
This particular form of memory comprises largely procedural knowledge.

Question 141
Classical and operant learning involve this particular type of memory.

Question 142
This form of memory involves both the visual association cortex and the auditory association cortex.

Question 143
This form of memory involves both the temporal lobe and the occipital area.

Question 144
This particular form of memory requires a deliberate act of recollection and can be reported verbally.

Theme: Clinical assessment and neuropsychological processes

Options:

a. Anterograde amnesia
b. Retrograde amnesia
c. Post-traumatic amnesia
d. Psychogenic amnesia
e. False memory
f. Transient global amnesia
g. Amnestic syndrome
h. Amnesia involving episodic memory

Lead in: Select the most appropriate answer for each of the following. Each option may be used once, more than once or not at all.

Question 145
This refers to the memory loss from the time of the accident to the time that the patient can give a clear account of recent events.

Question 146
This particular form of amnesia is usually associated with indifference.

Question 147
This refers to the loss of memory for events that occurred prior to an event or condition.

Question 148
This particular form of memory is associated with confabulation, report of false events and false confessions.

Question 149
This particular form of memory loss is associated with abrupt onset of disorientation, loss of ability to encode recent memories and retrograde amnesia for variable duration.

Theme: Delusional types

Options:

a. Delusional jealousy
b. Delusion of infestation
c. Delusion of poverty
d. Delusion of pregnancy
e. Delusion of reference
f. Doppelganger
g. Erotomania
h. Nihilistic delusion
i. Somatic delusion

Lead in: Select the most appropriate answer for each of the following. Each option may be used once, more than once or not at all.

Question 150
John came into the emergency department demanding to see the nurse who treated him 2 weeks ago. He claimed that she was in love with him.

Question 151
Ross was sent into the emergency services following an attempt to burn herself in the backyard of her garden. She tells the doctors that she is dead and her intestines are rotting.

Question 152
Peter has been feeling that a double of himself exists somewhere.

Question 153
Mary has been avoiding picking up the phone calls and watching the television. She claims that the people on the television are speaking about her.

Question 154
A core trainee was asked to see Samuel who strongly believes that he is pregnant. He has been feeling this way since he learnt of the news that his wife was pregnant 6 months ago.

Question 155
Gillian has been to multiple dermatologists seeking help as she believes that she needs treatment for her skin condition. She believes that her skin is infested by parasites.

Theme: Suicide and risk factors

Options:

a. Schizophrenia
b. Affective psychosis
c. Neurosis
d. Alcoholism
e. Personality disorder

Lead in: Select the most appropriate answer for each of the following. Each option may be used once, more than once or not at all.

Question 156
The high risk factors for this condition are aggressiveness and impulsivity. Which condition is this?

Question 157
There is an estimated 15% mortality from suicide in this condition. Usually it tends to occur later in the course of the illness and especially in those who are depressed.

Question 158
In this condition, nearly 90% of the patients have a history of para-suicide and with a high proportion having threatened suicide in the preceding month.

Question 159
In this condition, there is 15% mortality from suicide. Men who are older, separated, widowed, living alone and not working are predisposed. Which condition is this?

Question 160
In this condition, there is 10% mortality from suicide. Those who commit suicide are usually young, male and unemployed and usually with chronic relapsing illness.

Theme: Prevention of depressive disorders and suicide

Options:

a. Primary prevention
b. Secondary prevention
c. Tertiary prevention

Lead in: Select the most appropriate answer for each of the following. Each option may be used once, more than once or not at all.

Question 161
It is advisable to have close monitoring of patients post discharge.

Question 162
It is advised that people with a strong family history of depression should space out their pregnancies to prevent poor parenting of the child.

Question 163
This refers to the early detection and treatment of psychiatric conditions.

Question 164
It is recommended that there is better community support and enhanced psychiatric outreach efforts. Which form of prevention is this?

Theme: Psychotherapy

Options:

a. Aversive conditioning
b. Chaining
c. Flooding
d. Habituation
e. Insight learning
f. Latent learning
g. Penalty
h. Premack's principle
i. Reciprocal inhibition
j. Shaping
k. Systematic desensitization
l. Token economy

Lead in: From the aforementioned list of behavioural techniques, select the option that best matches each of the following examples. Each option might be used once, more than once or not at all.

Question 165
The staff of a hostel for learning disability patients want to train their clients to clean up the tables after meals. They develop a successive reinforcing schedule to reward their clients. The clients will be rewarded successively over time for removing their utensils from the dining table into the kitchen. Then they need to wash and dry the utensils and put them back into the right drawers. (Choose one option.)

Question 166
A 2-year-old son of a woman is scared of dogs. His mother tries to reduce his fear by bringing him to see the dogs in the park. The fear-provoking situation is coupled and opposed by putting him on her lap and allowing him to drink his favourite juice. (Choose one option.)

Question 167
A 40-year-old woman staying in London develops fear of the tube (underground metro) and she sees a psychologist for psychotherapy. The psychologist has drafted a behavioural programme in which the patient is advised to start with travelling

between two tube stations with her husband and gradually increase this to more stations without her husband. At the end of the hierarchy, she will travel alone on the long journey from Heathrow terminal station to Cockfosters station along almost the entire length of the Piccadilly line. (Choose one option.)

Theme: Pharmacodynamics

Options:

a. $5\text{-}HT_{1A}$ agonist
b. $5\text{-}HT_{1A}$ partial agonist
c. $5\text{-}HT_{1A}$ antagonist
d. $5\text{-}HT_{2A}$ agonist
e. $5\text{-}HT_{2A}$ partial agonist
f. $5\text{-}HT_{2A}$ antagonist
g. $Alpha_2$ agonist
h. $Alpha_2$ partial agonist
i. $Alpha_2$ antagonist
j. D_2 agonist
k. D_2 partial agonist
l. GABA-A agonist
m. GABA-A antagonist
n. NMDA agonist
o. NMDA antagonist

Lead in: Select the most appropriate psychodynamic mechanisms for the following antidepressants. Each option might be used more than once or not at all.

Question 168
Aripiprazole (Choose three options.)

Question 169
Diazepam (Choose one option.)

Question 170
Lofexidine (Choose one option.)

Theme: Antipsychotics

Options:

a. 1
b. 2
c. 5
d. 15
e. 25
f. 35
g. 45
h. 55
i. 65
j. 75

Lead in: A 17-year-old was referred to the early psychosis team for his first episode of schizophrenia. You prescribe risperidone 1 mg nocte. His mother requests an answer from you on the following questions. Each option might be used once, more than once or not at all.

Question 171
His psychotic symptoms are not controlled. His mother wants to know the minimum effective dose (in mg) of risperidone in his case. (Choose one option.)

Question 172
His psychotic symptoms are under control. His mother wants to know duration of antipsychotic treatment (in months) in his case. (Choose one option.)

Question 173
After 18 months of treatment, the patient has decided to stop the medication. His mother wants to know the risk of relapse in percentage. (Choose one option.)

Theme: Ethics

Options:

a. Accountability
b. Autonomy
c. Beneficence
d. Categorical imperatives
e. Cultural relativism
f. Ethical dilemma
g. Ethical relativism
h. Justice
i. Nonmaleficence
j. Phronesis
k. Privacy
l. Utilitarianism

Lead in: Match the above ethical principles to the following descriptions. Each option may be used once, more than once or not at all.

Question 174
A core trainee knows that he has to be an honest doctor and knows how to apply honesty in balance with other considerations in situations when medical errors occur causing suffering to his patients. (Choose one option.)

Question 175
In a multicultural society, different ethnic groups of people are supposed to have different ethical standards for evaluating acts as right or wrong. (Choose one option.)

Question 176
A lay person in the animal ethics research committee says, 'We can judge the heart of a principal investigator by his treatment of animals'. (Choose one option.)

Theme: DSM-IV-TR

Options:

a. 1–10
b. 11–20
c. 21–30
d. 31–40
e. 41–50
f. 51–60
g. 61–70
h. 71–80
i. 81–90
j. 91–100

Lead in: Choose the appropriate range of Global Assessment Functioning (GAF) Scale score for the following clinical scenarios. Each option might be used once, more than once or not at all.

Question 177
A 20-year-old university student is referred to you for mild anxiety before an examination. She has good functioning in other areas and is involved in a wide range of university activities. (Choose one option.)

Question 178
A 30-year-old woman is referred to you for frequent shoplifting. She cannot control the impulse to steal and fulfil the diagnostic criteria for kleptomania. She was arrested earlier that resulted in serious impairment in social and occupational functioning. (Choose one option.)

Question 179
A 25-year-old man suffers from schizophrenia and stays in a secure setting because of recurrent episodes of violence. He is unkempt with persistent inability to maintain personal hygiene. (Choose one option.)

Theme: Neuropsychological tests

Options:

a. Clock Drawing Test
b. Cognitive Estimates Test
c. Digit Span
d. Goldstein's Object Sorting Test
e. Go–No Go Test
f. Mini Mental State Examination
g. National Adult Reading Test

h. Raven's Progressive Matrices
i. Rorschach Ink Blot Test
j. Rey–Osterrieth Complex Figure Test
k. Rivermead Behavioural Memory Test
l. Sach's Sentence Completion Test
m. Stroop Test
n. Wechsler Memory Scale
o. Wisconsin Card Sorting Test

Lead in: A 35-year-old woman presents with sexually transmitted disease and promiscuity. Men have taken advantage of her for sexual advancement. She appears to be apathetic and has difficulty to comprehend the risks associated with sexually transmitted diseases. She has a history of epilepsy and has been unemployed for many years. The nurses are concerned about her IQ level. Which of the aforementioned tests is recommended to assess the following? Each option might be used once, more than once or not at all.

Question 180
Her current performance IQ (Choose one option.)

Question 181
Her concrete thinking (Choose one option.)

Question 182
Her executive function (Choose one option.)

Theme: Freud's dream interpretation

Options:
a. Condensation
b. Displacement
c. Latent content
d. Manifest content
e. Symbolism

Lead in: Match the aforementioned Freudian terms to the following definitions. Each option may be used once, more than once or not at all.

Question 183
Secondary elaboration of acceptable images in a narrative manner and those images are often linked to day residue or events prior to sleep. (Choose one option.)

Question 184
The process where impulses are transferred to acceptable images. (Choose one option.)

Question 185
True meaning of the dream in expressing unconscious thoughts and wishes. (Choose one option.)

Theme: Sleep disorders

Options:

a. Circadian rhythm sleep disorders
b. Myoclonic jerks
c. Non-24-hour sleep-wake syndrome
d. Nonorganic insomnia
e. Nightmare
f. Night terror
g. Restless leg syndrome
h. Rhythmic movement disorder
i. Sleep apnoea
j. Somnambulism

Lead in: Match the aforementioned sleep disorders to the following clinical scenarios. Each option may be used once, more than once or not at all.

Question 186
A 25-year-old man with a history of epilepsy complains of sudden contractions of muscles on both sides of his body while falling asleep. (Choose one option.)

Question 187
A 28-year-old woman complains that she sleeps at 3 AM but wakes up at 10 AM. She has always been late for work, and she has been dismissed by three companies. (Choose one option.)

Question 188
You are working in the Child and Adolescent Mental Health Service. An anxious mother has brought her 10-year-old son to see you. He has body-rocking and head-banging movements at bedtime and naptimes. (Choose one option.)

Question 189
A 55-year-old man complains that it is impossible for him to sleep at normal times and his sleep-wake cycle is changing every day after he developed bilateral blindness as a result of cataracts. (Choose one option.)

Theme: The British history of insanity defence

Options:

a. First recorded psychiatric testimony
b. First right versus wrong test
c. Offspring of a delusion
d. The irresistible impulse test
e. Wild beast test

Lead in: Most of the laws in the Western countries originated in England. The British law was built on the principle of precedence. Identify which of the aforementioned descriptions best describes the following trials. Each option may be used once, more than once or not at all.

Question 190

Edward Oxford, who attempted to murder Queen Victoria, was 18 years old when the offence occurred in 1840. He described in his notebooks how he was to be the instrument of a plot of an imaginary secret society, and to this end, had purchased pistols and practised with them. Because of the medical evidence of mental illness, the defence succeeded and a verdict of 'guilty but insane' was issued. After the trial, Oxford was admitted to Bethlem Royal Hospital. (Choose one option.)

Question 191

Earl Ferrers lived with his wife at Stanton Harold in Leicestershire in the mid-1700s. He was an alcoholic, and his chronic drinking led to psychosis and rage. He also made false accusation against a man, Mr Johnson, who lived in his estate for robbery. He ordered Mr Johnson to come to his house and then shot him. Later, Mr Johnson died and Earl Ferrers was charged with murder. He was tried by his fellows in the Tower of London. A plea of insanity was refused and Earl Ferrers was found guilty and sentenced to hang. (Choose one option.)

Question 192

James Hadfield fired a pistol at King George III at the Theatre Royal during the playing of the national anthem on the evening of 15 May 1800. Hadfield was tried for treason and was defended by a prominent barrister. Later, Hadfield pleaded insanity. Three doctors testified that Hadfield had delusions which were the consequence of his earlier head injuries. Hadfield was detained in Bethlem Royal Hospital for the rest of his life. (Choose one option.)

Theme: Piaget's cognitive development

Options:

a. Accommodation
b. Animism
c. Artificialism
d. Assimilation
e. Centration
f. Circular reaction
g. Egocentrism
h. Failure of conservation
i. Finalism
j. Hypothetico-deductive thinking
k. Object permanence
l. Mastery of conservation
m. Reflective thinking
n. Seriation
o. Syncretic thought
p. Transductive reasoning
q. Sensorimotor stage
r. Preoperational stage
s. Concrete operation stage
t. Formal operational stage

Lead in: Identify which of the aforementioned terms and stages derived by Piaget best describes the following descriptions. Each option may be used once, more than once or not at all.

Question 193
Children see the world from their own standpoint but cannot appreciate that other people may see things differently. (Choose two options.)

Question 194
An infant can add new information into the existing schema. (Choose two options.)

Question 195
An adolescent can hold several possible explanations in mind for a phenomenon and think of possible outcomes. (Choose two options.)

MRCPSYCH PAPER A1 MOCK EXAMINATION 4: ANSWERS

GET THROUGH MRCPSYCH PAPER A1: MOCK EXAMINATION

Question 1 Answer: b, Thought withdrawal
Explanation: This refers to thought withdrawal. This is the delusion that one's thoughts are being removed from one's mind by an external agency.

Reference: Puri BK, Hall A, Ho R (2014). *Revision Notes in Psychiatry*. London: CRC Press, p. 7.

Question 2 Answer: b, The patient would have repeated regular fixed patterns of movement that are not goal directed.
Explanation: (b) is the correct answer. Stereotypies refer to repeated, regular, fixed patterns of movement, or even speech, which are not goal directed.

Reference: Puri BK, Hall A, Ho R (2014). *Revision Notes in Psychiatry*. London: CRC Press, p. 3.

Question 3 Answer: e, Allow the GP to strengthen the patient and help them to stabilize
Explanation: The key objective of supportive psychotherapy is to help strength defences and help the patient to enhance his or her adaptive capacity. It does help to maintain and improve self-esteem of the patient, but this is not done so by simply agreeing with them. It is helpful in improving symptoms, preventing relapses and also developing adaptive and reasonable behaviour. It also helps patients set goals and have a positive thinking.

Reference: Puri BK, Hall A, Ho R (2014). *Revision Notes in Psychiatry*. London: CRC Press, p. 331.

Question 4 Answer: a, Neuroleptic malignant syndrome
Explanation: The most likely clinical diagnosis would be neuroleptic malignant syndrome. Samuel has some of the signs and symptoms that are characteristic of the condition, and in addition, he was just initiated on a course of antipsychotics. Neuroleptic malignant syndrome is characterized by hyperthermia, fluctuating

level of consciousness, muscular rigidity, autonomic dysfunction such as tachycardia, labile blood pressure, pallor, sweating and urinary continence.

Reference: Puri BK, Hall A, Ho R (2014). *Revision Notes in Psychiatry*. London: CRC Press, p. 253.

Question 5 Answer: d, Confides readily
Explanation: All of the aforementioned are characteristic of paranoid personality disorder, with the exception that the individual usually does not confide readily due to chronic fears of betrayal. The common clinical features are as follows: grudges are usually held without justification; excessive sensitivity to setbacks; threats and hidden meanings are read into benign remarks; fidelity of spouse is unjustifiably doubted; attacks on character or reputation are perceived; confides reluctantly because of fears of betrayal and trustworthiness of others is doubted without due cause.

Reference: Puri BK, Hall A, Ho R (2014). *Revision Notes in Psychiatry*. London: CRC Press, p. 442.

Question 6 Answer: d, There are times when they desire for the presence of close friends.
Explanation: These individuals usually have no desire for or possession of any close friends or confiding relationships. The common clinical features include solitary lifestyle, indifference to praise and criticism, no interest in relationships, no interest in sexual experience, solitary activities and cold and detached emotions.

Reference: Puri BK, Hall A, Ho R (2014). *Revision Notes in Psychiatry*. London: CRC Press, p. 440.

Question 7 Answer: a, Substance abuse
Explanation: Bulimics are more prone to developing substance-related disorders. They are more likely to abuse substance (20%). Their lifetime rates of alcohol dependence are considered to be much higher as well. The presence of these factors also predicts poorer outcomes for bulimics: depression, personality disturbance, greater severity of symptoms, longer duration of symptoms, low self-esteem, substance abuse and childhood obesity.

Reference: Puri BK, Hall A, Ho R (2014). *Revision Notes in Psychiatry*. London: CRC Press, p. 584.

Question 8 Answer: e, The conditioned stimulus is paired with a second conditioned stimulus, which, on presentation, by itself elicits the original condition response.
Explanation: (e) is the correct definition of higher-order conditioning. (a) refers to delayed conditioning, (b) simultaneous conditioning, (c) trace conditioning and (d) backward conditioning.

Reference: Puri BK, Hall A, Ho R (2014). *Revision Notes in Psychiatry*. London: CRC Press, p. 25.

Question 9 Answer: d, Nihilistic delusion
Explanation: Nihilistic delusion or Cotard's syndrome is the belief that one is dead or the external world does not exist. It can also take the form of believing that parts of the body do not exist. Nihilistic delusions can be secondary to severe depression, schizophrenia or an organic disorder.

Reference and Further Reading: Puri BK, Hall AD (2002). *Revision Notes in Psychiatry*. London: Arnold, p. 382.

Question 10 Answer: c, Thought broadcasting
Explanation: Thought broadcasting is the delusion that one's thoughts are being broadcast out loud, for example via a radio or by an external voice, such that others can perceive them. Thought broadcasting is a type of thought alienation under the passivity phenomenon.

Reference and Further Reading: Puri BK, Hall AD (2002). *Revision Notes in Psychiatry*. London: Arnold, p. 153.

Question 11 Answer: d, Premack's principle
Explanation: Premack's principle states that more probable behaviours can be used to reinforce less probable behaviours. If high-probability behaviours (i.e. video games) are made contingent upon lower-probability behaviours (i.e. doing homework), the lower-probability behaviours are more likely to occur.

Reference and Further Reading: Mitchell WS, Stoffelmayr BE (1973). Application of the Premack principle to the behavioral control of extremely inactive schizophrenics. *Journal of Applied Behaviour Analysis*, 6: 419–423.

Question 12 Answer: c, Serotonergic and noradrenergic reuptake inhibitor
Explanation: Duloxetine belongs to the serotonergic and noradrenergic reuptake inhibitor class.

Reference: Puri BK, Hall A, Ho R (2014). *Revision Notes in Psychiatry*. London: CRC Press, p. 239.

Question 13 Answer: a, Amisulpride
Explanation: Amisulpride is the only antipsychotic amongst the options given that belongs to the class of a substituted benzamide.

Reference: Puri BK, Hall A, Ho R (2014). *Revision Notes in Psychiatry*. London: CRC Press, p. 238.

Question 14 Answer: b, Lithium
Explanation: The usage of lithium would result in the aforementioned clinical disorder. Long-term treatment with lithium may give rise to the following: thyroid function abnormalities such as goitre, hypothyroidism and memory impairments, nephrotoxicity, cardiovascular changes such as T-wave flattening on the ECG and also arrhythmias.

Reference: Puri BK, Hall A, Ho R (2014). *Revision Notes in Psychiatry.* London: CRC Press, p. 254.

Question 15 Answer: a, De Clerambault's syndrome
Explanation: De Clerambault's syndrome or erotomania is a condition in which a person holds the delusional belief that someone of a higher social status is in love with him or her. This condition is more common in women than in men.

Reference and Further Reading: Puri BK, Hall AD (2002). *Revision Notes in Psychiatry.* London: Arnold, p. 382.

Question 16 Answer: c, This process was developed in conjunction with both classical conditioning and operant conditioning.
Explanation: This process is known as extinction. Extinction has treatment implication in deconditioning anxiety responses from conditioned stimulus. Extinction applies to both biological and psychological conditioned responses. The conditioned responses usually disappear gradually and return by spontaneous recovery.

Reference and Further Reading: Puri BK, Treasaden I (eds) (2010). *Psychiatry: An Evidence-Based Text.* London: Hodder Arnold, p. 199.

Question 17 Answer: d, 4 days
Explanation: The duration for a manic episode is usually one week. In contrast, the duration for a hypomanic episode is only 4 days. Hypomanic episode has the same requirement of the number of symptoms as manic episode. The only difference is that patients should have no impairment in functioning.

Reference: Puri BK, Hall A, Ho R (2014). *Revision Notes in Psychiatry.* London: CRC Press, p. 378.

Question 18 Answer: a, Pervasive development disorder
Explanation: It has been well established and suggested that the lack of development of a theory of mind has been associated with disorders such as autism. In primate research, theory of mind refers to the abilities of primates to mentalize their fellows. In humans, the theory of mind refers to the ability of most normal people to comprehend the thought processes (such as attention, feelings, beliefs, false beliefs and knowledge) of others. Research into children would tend to suggest that at the age of 3 years, normal human children do not acknowledge false belief as they have difficulty in differentiating belief from world. Formulating a theory of mind appears not to be inevitable, but relies on cognitive changes that happen around the age of 4.

Reference: Puri BK, Hall A, Ho R (2014). *Revision Notes in Psychiatry*. London: CRC Press, p. 59.

Question 19 Answer: a, Bowlby
Explanation: Attachment theory was proposed by Bowlby in 1969. Attachment refers to the tendency of infants to remain close to certain people (attachment figures) with whom they share strong positive emotional ties. Monotropic attachment is when the attachment is to one individual, usually the mother. Polytropic attachment is less common. Attachment usually takes place from infant to mother. In contrast, neonatal–maternal bonding takes place in the opposite direction. Both processes can start immediately after birth.

Reference: Puri BK, Hall A, Ho R (2014). *Revision Notes in Psychiatry*. London: CRC Press, p. 63.

Question 20 Answer: e, Increased tubular secretion
Explanation: All of the aforementioned are pharmacokinetics parameters that are changed in the elderly, with the exception of (e). There would be an increment in the percentage of the total body fat, an increase in the gastric pH, a reduction in the renal clearance as well as a decrease in the serum protein binding. However, it is important to note that the rate of gastrointestinal absorption remains the same. There is no evidence currently that mentions that the rate or the extent of absorption of orally administered psychotropic medications is changed in the elderly. Reduction in clearance may increase the steady-state plasma drug concentration in old people. Hence, because of the lowered renal clearance, lithium doses in the elderly should be approximately 50% lower than in the young. All other psychotropic drugs are cleared by hepatic biotransformation, which is reduced with age. As a result, the half-life of psychotropic medication can be markedly prolonged, having residual effects for weeks after discontinuation.

Reference: Puri BK, Hall A, Ho R (2014). *Revision Notes in Psychiatry*. London: CRC Press, p. 685.

Question 21 Answer: d, Auditory
Explanation: Depression with psychotic features typically is associated with auditory hallucinations. The hallucinations are usually either second person or derogatory in nature. Previous studies (Spiker et al., 1985) have found a superior response when an antidepressant and an antipsychotic are used in combination in psychotic depression.

Reference: Puri BK, Hall A, Ho R (2014). *Revision Notes in Psychiatry*. London: CRC Press, p. 8.

Question 22 Answer: c, It occurs usually in the outer objective space.
Explanation: It is classified as a pseudohallucination and usually would arise from the subjective inner space of the mind. A pseudohallucination lacks the substantiality of normal perceptions. An eidetic image is a vivid and detailed reproduction of a previous perception.

Reference: Puri BK, Hall A, Ho R (2014). *Revision Notes in Psychiatry.* London: CRC Press, p. 8.

Question 23 Answer: c, Classical conditioning
Explanation: In post-traumatic stress disorder, the patient tries to avoid stimuli (e.g. army camp, firearms, the word, 'Iraq') associated with severe trauma by classical conditioning. This is not avoidance or escape conditioning because the aversive event (i.e. gun battle and resulting injury) will not occur in the UK. Escape conditioning, avoidance conditioning and punishments are known collectively as aversive conditioning.

Reference and Further Reading: Puri BK, Treasaden I (eds) (2010). *Psychiatry: An Evidence-Based Text.* London: Hodder Arnold, pp. 197–200.

Question 24 Answer: a, Habituation
Explanation: Habituation is the decrease in response to a stimulus after repeated exposure. This is an essential component in the treatment of OCD using exposure and response prevention. The aim of the exposure technique is to reduce the levels of anxiety associated with the eliciting stimuli through habituation.

Reference and Further Reading: Puri BK, Hall AD (2002). *Revision Notes in Psychiatry.* London: Arnold, p. 7.

Question 25 Answer: c, Delusional perception
Explanation: A delusional perception is a normal perception falsely interpreted by the patient and held as being significant to him. It is one of Schneider's first-rank symptoms.

Reference and Further Reading: Sims A (2003). *Symptoms of the Mind: An Introduction to Descriptive Psychopathology.* London: Saunders, p. 166.

Question 26 Answer: a, An example is when a young animal learns the characteristics of its parents.
Explanation: Psychological imprinting refers to learning occurring at a particular stage of life. The learning process is rapid and independent of the consequences of behaviour. Genetic imprinting is a different concept. When the expression of inheritance is altered, depending upon whether it was passed to the foetus through the egg or the sperm, the phenomenon is known as genetic imprinting. The term 'imprinting' refers to the fact that some genes are stamped with a 'memory' of the parent from whom they came. In the cells of an infant, it is possible to tell which chromosome copy came from the maternal chromosome and which was inherited from the paternal chromosome. This expression of the gene is called a 'parent-of-origin effect' and was first described by Helen Crouse in 1960.

References: Barlow-Stewart K (2007). Genetic imprinting, in *Genetic Fact Sheets* (6th edition). Sydney, AU: Centre for Genetics Education; Crouse HV (1960). The controlling element in sex chromosome behavior in Sciara. *Genetics*, 45: 1429–1443.

Question 27 Answer: d, Antihistaminergic
Explanation: Histamine H_1 and H_3 receptors have been specifically recognized as mediators of energy intake and expenditure, and histamine agonists have been shown to attenuate body weight gain in humans. On the other hand, the first-generation antipsychotics are known to be associated with antihistamine effects. Furthermore, the antihistamine properties of first-generation antipsychotics may sedate the patients and slow down the metabolism. This will contribute to the weight gain.

Reference: Masaki T, Yoshimatsu H (2010). Neuronal histamine and its receptors: Implication of the pharmacological treatment of obesity. *Current Medicinal Chemistry*, 17: 4587–4592.

Question 28 Answer: e, The mild or moderate cognitive impairment due to long-term use of alcohol would not improve with abstinence.
Explanation: All of the aforementioned are true and generally observed in individuals with alcoholic dementia with the exception of (e). Those who have abused alcohol chronically for some years commonly do suffer from mild-to-moderate cognitive impairment. However, these impairments do improve over a number of years of abstinence. Women who are keen to suffer physical complications of alcohol abuse earlier than men also develop cognitive impairment much earlier in their drinking histories. A CT or structural MRI scan of the brain in alcoholics commonly shows ventricular enlargement and sulcal widening, which does not correlate with the degree of cognitive impairment and would also resolve on quitting drinking.

Reference: Puri BK, Hall A, Ho R (2014). *Revision Notes in Psychiatry*. London: CRC Press, p. 518.

Question 29 Answer: c, Avoidant attachment
Explanation: The child seemed to be displaying what might be avoidant attachment. When a child has this form of attachment, he would be keeping a distance from his mother and may even sometimes ignore his mother. Avoidance attachment is usually caused by rejection by his mother and might lead to chronic problems such as poor social functioning later in life.

Reference: Puri BK, Hall A, Ho R (2014). *Revision Notes in Psychiatry*. London: CRC Press, p. 64.

Question 30 Answer: b, Disorganized schizophrenia
Explanation: The ICD-10 only includes the following subtypes for schizophrenia: paranoid, hebephrenic, catatonic, undifferentiated and residual.

Reference: Puri BK, Hall A, Ho R (2014). *Revision Notes in Psychiatry*. London: CRC Press, p. 353.

Question 31 Answer: c, Presence of suggestibility
Explanation: This means that one is easily influenced by others or circumstances. Suggestibility is usually present in the aforementioned disorders.

Reference: Puri BK, Hall A, Ho R (2014). *Revision Notes in Psychiatry.* London: CRC Press, p. 451.

Question 32 Answer: a, Assess attention
Explanation: Serial seven or serial three tests mainly assesses attention. If the patient cannot perform calculation, the interviewer can ask the patient to count the month starting from December in descending order or spell the word, 'WORLD' backwards.

Reference and Further Reading: Puri BK, Treasaden I (eds) (2010). *Psychiatry: An Evidence-Based Text.* London: Hodder Arnold, pp. 92, 179–194, 502–503, 515, 516, 786, 1101.

Question 33 Answer: d, 1 year
Explanation: The ICD-10 classification system states that the diagnosis of alcohol dependence would be made if there are three or more of the classical symptoms that have been present together at some time over the past 1 year.

Reference: Puri BK, Hall A, Ho R (2014). *Revision Notes in Psychiatry.* London: CRC Press, p. 508.

Question 34 Answer: d, 48 hours
Explanation: The onset of withdrawal fits usually occurs within 48 hours of quitting drinking. Oral medications such as lorazepam can be used as first-line treatment for delirium tremens or seizures.

Reference: Puri BK, Hall A, Ho R (2014). *Revision Notes in Psychiatry.* London: CRC Press, p. 516.

Question 35 Answer: c, Fregoli syndrome
Explanation: In Fregoli syndrome, the patient has a delusional belief that a familiar person has taken on different appearances. The patient often believes that he or she is being persecuted by the person in disguise. Primary causes include schizophrenia and organic disorder.

Reference and Further Reading: Puri BK, Hall AD (2002). *Revision Notes in Psychiatry.* London: Arnold, p. 382.

Question 36 Answer: c, Recognition
Explanation: Recognition is the ability to match a stimulus to stored material in memory. Recognition is easier than recall because the cue is the actual object or fact one is trying to recognize. There is often a sense of familiarity because one detects a match between the cue and what is in their memory. An example of recognition is multiple-choice tests, where the answer is present and there is a need to match the answer with what is known in memory.

Reference and Further Reading: Ciccarelli SK, Meyer GE (2006). *Psychology*. Upper Saddle River, NJ: Pearson Education, pp. 227–228; Puri BK, Treasaden I (eds) (2010). *Psychiatry: An Evidence-Based Text*. London: Hodder Arnold, p. 250.

Question 37 Answer: e, 75%

Explanation: If she stops taking the antidepressant, the chance of relapse is 75%. This 32-year-old woman should be reminded that fluoxetine is safe during pregnancy based on a large amount of clinical information on the effects associated with prenatal exposure to fluoxetine. Fluoxetine is not associated with a greater risk of miscarriage or major congenital malformation. Third-trimester use of fluoxetine has been linked with higher rates of perinatal complications (e.g. tachypnea, jitteriness, premature delivery) in some patients.

References: Hendrick V, Altshuler L (2002). Management of major depression during pregnancy. *Am J Psychiatry*, 159: 1667–1673; Cohen LS, Altshuler LL, Stowe ZN (1999). MGH Prospective Study: Depression in pregnancy in women who decrease or discontinue antidepressant medication, in *1999 Annual Meeting Syllabus and Proceedings Summary*. Washington, DC: American Psychiatric Association; Einarson A, Selby P, Koren G (2001). Abrupt discontinuation of psychotropic drugs during pregnancy: Fear of teratogenic risk and impact of counseling. *J Psychiatry Neurosci*, 26: 44–48.

Question 38 Answer: d, Histrionic personality disorder

Explanation: The most likely diagnosis is histrionic personality disorder. In this personality disorder, individuals usually crave to be the centre of attention. They value their own appearances and view certain interpersonal relationships as much closer compared to others. They are seductive in nature and might also have exaggerated expression of emotions.

Reference: Puri BK, Hall A, Ho R (2014). *Revision Notes in Psychiatry*. London: CRC Press, p. 451.

Question 39 Answer: c, Assimilation

Explanation: Assimilation is defined as incorporation of a new or novel information into existing thought patterns. Schemas are cognitive structures or patterns of behaviour or knowledge. Accommodation involves adjustment or modification of existing schemas to facilitate comprehension of new information.

Reference and Further Reading: Puri BK, Treasaden I (eds) (2010). *Psychiatry: An Evidence-Based Text*. London: Hodder Arnold, pp. 113–115.

Question 40 Answer: e, Other neurotic disorder F48

Explanation: Neurasthenia is defined as the persistent complaint of mental tiredness, even after minimal exertion. It is classified under other neurotic disorder F48, in the ICD-10 diagnostic criteria.

Reference: Puri BK, Hall A, Ho R (2014). *Revision Notes in Psychiatry.* London: CRC Press, p. 18.

Question 41 Answer: d, Checking with the patient whether he is able to tell the occupation or the identity of a doctor or an allied health-care staff
Explanation: Orientation is a common aspect covered by the MMSE (Folstein et al., 1975), the ACE-R (Mioshi et al., 2006) and also the MoCA (Nasreddine et al., 2005). Orientation to person would be the best assessment of orientation in an inpatient. It is usually affected much later, as compared to other domains of assessment.

Reference: Puri BK, Hall A, Ho R (2014). *Revision Notes in Psychiatry.* London: CRC Press, p. 689.

Question 42 Answer: c, BPRS
Explanation: For routine screening purposes, the CAGE questionnaire is usually used. Positive answers to two or more of the four questions are indicative of problem drinking. The Clinical Institute Withdrawal Assessment (CIWA) Scale is usually used to quantify the severity of alcohol withdrawal syndrome and monitor patients during detoxification. AUDIT and MAST are also appropriate questionnaires. BPRS is a rating scale that clinicians and researchers usually use to measure psychiatric symptoms such as depression, anxiety and also hallucinations and other psychotic psychopathology.

Reference: Puri BK, Hall A, Ho R (2014). *Revision Notes in Psychiatry.* London: CRC Press, pp. 521–523.

Question 43 Answer: b, Primary memory has been found to have a duration of approximately 7 seconds
Explanation: Short-term (primary or working) memory has a storage duration of 20 seconds, unless the information is rehearsed. Primacy and recency effects are collectively known as the serial position effect and account for the increased probability of correctly recalling information in the beginning and the end of a list of items. Chunking involves rearranging information into chunks such that there is an increased amount of information in each chunk, thereby increasing short-term memory capacity. There is a limited capacity of 7 ± 2 registers.

Reference and Further Reading: Puri BK, Treasaden I (eds) (2010). *Psychiatry: An Evidence-Based Text.* London: Hodder Arnold, pp. 247–249; Puri BK, Hall AD (2002). *Revision Notes in Psychiatry.* London: Arnold, pp. 17, 21.

Question 44 Answer: d, Somatic delusion
Explanation: Somatic delusion is based on false belief being held at absolute conviction in explaining disturbance in an organ. Nihilistic delusion is a delusion of nonexistence of either oneself or the entire world. Hypochondriasis refers to the misinterpretation of physical signs and symptoms unrealistically as indicative of serious disease.

Reference and Further Reading: Campbell RJ (1996). *Psychiatric Dictionary.* Oxford, UK: Oxford University Press.

Question 45 Answer: b, 1%–3%
Explanation: A study of prenatal exposures to sertraline, paroxetine and fluvoxamine found that the rates of major malformations and preterm labour were no higher than those of non-exposed subjects. The rate of major malformation is around 1%–3%.

Reference: Kulin NA, Pastuszak A, Sage SR, Schick-Boschetto B, Spivey G, Feldkamp M, Ormond K, Matsui D, Stein-Schechman AK, Cook L, Brochu J, Rieder M, Koren G (1998). Pregnancy outcome following maternal use of the new selective serotonin reuptake inhibitors: A prospective controlled multicenter study. *JAMA*, 279: 609–610.

Question 46 Answer: b, The remission rate was 20%.
Explanation: The remission rate was noted to be around 30%, instead of 20%. It is correct that one-third of participants reached a remission or virtual absence of symptoms during the initial phase of the study, with an additional 10%–15% experiencing some improvement. There were consistent findings across both standard and patient-rated depression rating scales. It was noted that one in three depressed patients who previously did not achieve remission using an antidepressant became symptom-free with the help of augmenting with another antidepressant. One in four achieved remission after switching to a different antidepressant. At level 3, 20% of participants became symptom-free after 9 weeks. Patients taking T3 complained of fewer side effects than those taking lithium.

Reference: Puri BK, Hall A, Ho R (2014). *Revision Notes in Psychiatry.* London: CRC Press, p. 392.

Question 47 Answer: a, Schizotypal personality disorder
Explanation: Schizotypal personality disorder is classified differently in the ICD-10. It is clustered under Schizophrenia, Schizotypal and delusional disorders are given a code of F21 Schizotypal personality disorder.

Reference: Puri BK, Hall A, Ho R (2014). *Revision Notes in Psychiatry.* London: CRC Press, p. 24.

Question 48 Answer: d, Lewy body dementia
Explanation: The aetiology given the clinical presentation and the scan results are suggestive of Lewy body dementia. Dementia with Lewy bodies is the third most common causes of dementia. Lewy bodies are usually found located in the cingulated gyrus, the cortex and the substantia nigra. They contain eosinophilic inclusion with high amyloid content but absence of tau pathology. The specialized scan refers to the DaTSCAN.

Reference: Puri BK, Hall A, Ho R (2014). *Revision Notes in Psychiatry.* London: CRC Press, p. 702.

Question 49 Answer: c, Onset is usually gradual and slow
Explanation: Onset is usually rapid, intense and unexpected. According to ICD-10 criteria, koro is not just restricted to men but also applies to women.

Reference and Further Reading: Puri BK, Treasaden I (eds) (2010). *Psychiatry: An Evidence-Based Text*. London: Hodder Arnold, pp. 309–318; World Health Organisation (1994). ICD-10 Classification of Mental and Behavioural Disorders. Edinburgh, UK: Churchill Livingstone.

Question 50 Answer: e, Taijinkyofusho
Explanation: This is a common culture-bound syndrome that occurs in Japan. The individual is afraid that he would make others uncomfortable through his inappropriate behaviour or self-presentation (such as offensive odour or physical blemish).

Reference: Puri BK, Hall A, Ho R (2014). *Revision Notes in Psychiatry*. London: CRC Press, p. 462.

Question 51 Answer: d, K-SADS
Explanation: Around 6.6% of adolescents have been diagnosed with depression at the age of 15 years; 60%–70% of depressive symptoms are associated with adverse life events. Symptoms are largely similar to an adult's presentation, with a minimum of 2 weeks of sadness, irritability, loss of interest and loss of pleasure. The diagnostic interview that is recommended would be the Kiddie-Sads-Present and Lifetime Version. It helps to provide information about current diagnosis as well as symptoms over the past one year.

Reference: Puri BK, Hall A, Ho R (2014). *Revision Notes in Psychiatry*. London: CRC Press, p. 648.

Question 52 Answer: c, Social role
Explanation: Social role is the behaviour expected of a person who is in a particular social position. The experiment demonstrated that social roles can be so powerful that the personal identities and personalities can get lost. Social identity is part of an individual's self-concept based on one's view of self in a particular social group. Social categorization is the assignment of people to groups based on common characteristics the new person has with the people in a particular category. Social norms are the acceptable behaviours, values and beliefs of a group. Social influence is the effect of words, actions or presence of others on a person's thoughts, feelings and behaviour.

Reference and Further Reading: Aronson E, Wilson TD, Akert RM (2007). *Social Psychology*. Upper Saddle River, NJ: Prentice Hall, pp. 274–275.

Question 53 Answer: c, Those in a couple relationship
Explanation: Induced psychosis is a delusional disorder shared by two people who are usually closely linked together emotionally. Usually, one of the individuals has

a genuine psychotic disorder, and his or her psychotic disorder is then transferred or induced in the other individual. The other individual may be dependent or less intelligent than the first person.

Reference: Puri BK, Hall A, Ho R (2014). *Revision Notes in Psychiatry.* London: CRC Press, p. 373.

Question 54 Answer: b, Convert the phone number into six items: 18-00-33-77-92-4
Explanation: Working memory holds 7±2 bits of information. The difficulty arises because there are eleven items or digits in this phone number. By chunking, the 11-item phone number is converted into smaller number of pieces of information. The working memory should be able to handle six items or six bits. Option (a) is not easy to remember because there are too many digits in each item.

Reference and Further Reading: Puri BK, Treasaden I (eds) (2010). *Psychiatry: An Evidence-Based Text.* London: Hodder Arnold, pp. 247-248, 504, 505, 507.

Question 55 Answer: c, occur in stage 1 of non-REM sleep
Explanation: Hypnagogic hallucinations are usually auditory and occur at the point of falling asleep. Hypnagogic hallucinations do not require antipsychotic medication.

Reference and Further Reading: Rechtschaffen A, Kales A (1968). A Manual of Standardized Terminology, Techniques and Scoring System for Sleep Stages of Human Subjects. Washington, DC: Public Health Service, U.S. Government Printing.

Question 56 Answer: d, The course organizer should emphasize the participants to store the information in their brain and advise them to reduce access to the information during the course.
Explanation: Option (a) is useful. The lecturer can either present information in small segments or use chunking to convert larger amounts into smaller number of pieces of information. Option (b) is useful. The lecturer should project information onto a screen; this will minimize the demand on working memory. Option (c) is useful and course organizers should rehearse key points often enough to keep them active in working memory. Option (d) is not useful. The course organizer should allow the participants to have access to the information whenever it is needed. Option (e) is useful. Information is temporarily stored in working memory for 15–30 seconds and needs to be transferred to long-term memory as soon as possible. The course organizer should also help the participants to retrieve the information to working memory whenever it is needed.

Reference and Further Reading: Puri BK, Treasaden I (eds) (2010). *Psychiatry: An Evidence-Based Text.* London: Hodder Arnold, pp. 247–248, 504, 505, 507.

Question 57 Answer: c, Fregoli syndrome
Explanation: In Fregoli syndrome, a patient perceives that a familiar person has assumed another bodily form. In reverse Fregoli syndrome, a patient believes that other people are suffering from Fregoli syndrome and misidentifying himself or herself. In Capgras syndrome, a familiar person is perceived as being replaced by identical doubles. There are two types of subjective double syndrome. In subjective double syndrome, a patient perceives that his or her own double is projected onto another person but cannot see himself or herself in the mirror.

Reference and Further Reading: Puri BK, Hall AD (2002). *Revision Notes in Psychiatry*. London: Arnold, p. 382.

Question 58 Answer: b, Brain fag
Explanation: This is considered to be a widespread low-grade stress syndrome that has been described in many parts of Africa. It is commonly encountered among students. Five symptom types have been described: head symptoms, eye symptoms, difficulties in grasping the meaning of the spoken or written words, poor reactivity and sleepiness on studying.

Reference: Puri BK, Hall A, Ho R (2014). *Revision Notes in Psychiatry*. London: CRC Press, p. 463.

Question 59 Answer: d, Phobias
Explanation: The common defence mechanism used in phobia includes displacement, projection and denial.

Reference: Puri BK, Hall A, Ho R (2014). *Revision Notes in Psychiatry*. London: CRC Press, p. 137.

Question 60 Answer: c, Denial
Explanation: Klein believed that the infant was capable of object relations. Klein believed and proposed the concept of paranoid-schizoid position, which developed as a result of the frustration during the first year of life with pleasurable objects such as the good breast. The paranoid-schizoid position, characterized by isolation and persecutory fears, developed as a result of the infant viewing the world as part objects, using the following defence mechanisms: introjection, projective identification and splitting.

Reference: Puri BK, Hall A, Ho R (2014). *Revision Notes in Psychiatry*. London: CRC Press, p. 135.

Question 61 Answer: a, Wechsler Adult Intelligence Scale
Explanation: The Wechsler Adult Intelligence Scale (WAIS-IV) was released in 2008. It allows for four index scores to be derived: the verbal comprehension index, the perceptual reasoning index, the working memory index and the

processing speed index. It is regarded as the most evidenced based and the gold standard in the assessment of intelligence. It is important to note that the Full Scale IQ follows a normal distribution with a mean of 100 and a standard deviation of 15.

Reference: Puri BK, Hall A, Ho R (2014). *Revision Notes in Psychiatry.* London: CRC Press, p. 91.

Question 62 Answer: b, In attribution theory, people tend to attribute their own behaviour to their personality traits.
Explanation: In attribution theory, people tend to attribute their own behaviour to situational factors and attribute other people's behaviour to dispositional factors. This is known as fundamental attribution error. A person's feelings can influence attribution. For example, in a happy marriage, the spouse tends to attribute positive events to an internal attribution and negative events to an external cause. In an unhappy marriage, the reverse is true.

Reference and Further Reading: Puri BK, Hall AD (2002). *Revision Notes in Psychiatry.* London: Arnold, p. 52.

Question 63 Answer: b, Depressive stupor
Explanation: The most likely clinical diagnosis is depressive stupor. The patient might be unresponsive, akinetic, mute and fully conscious. Following the episode, the patient can recall the events that have taken place. It is essential to note that there might be periods of excitement that might occur between episodes of stupor.

Reference: Puri BK, Hall A, Ho R (2014). *Revision Notes in Psychiatry.* London: CRC Press, p. 380.

Question 64 Answer: d, Self-awareness
Explanation: Déjà vu refers to how an individual feels that the current situation has been seen or previously experienced. Jamais vu refers to the illusion of failure to recognize a familiar situation.

Reference: Puri BK, Hall A, Ho R (2014). *Revision Notes in Psychiatry.* London: CRC Press, p. 9.

Question 65 Answer: b, Thought insertion
Explanation: James is experiencing what is known as thought insertion. This is a delusional ideation that an individual's thoughts are no longer one's own, but are inserted into the mind by some external agency.

Reference: Puri BK, Hall A, Ho R (2014). *Revision Notes in Psychiatry.* London: CRC Press, p. 6.

Question 66 Answer: e, When he studies, he usually feels sad. In the examination he often puts down the answer 'don't know' when answering MCQs as he also feels sad during the examination.
Explanation: The state-dependent effect should theoretically facilitate recall. His low mood during the examination may lead to low motivation. The patient has poor motivation to attempt the questions rather than memory deficit or forgetfulness. Option (a) refers to the decay or trace decay theory. Option (b) refers to displacement theory. Option (c) refers to cue-dependent forgetting, and option (d) refers to context-dependent forgetting.

Reference and Further Reading: Puri BK, Treasaden I (eds) (2010). *Psychiatry: An Evidence-Based Text.* London: Hodder Arnold, pp. 256–262.

Question 67 Answer: b, Peak age of onset is 20–29 years.
Explanation: All of the following statements are true, with the exception that the peak age of onset is 20–29 years. The peak age of onset should be 15–19 years. Based on the ECA study, it has been found that there are approximately 11 cases in 20,000 persons studied. The incidence is noted to be 10 times higher in females as compared to males. There is a higher prevalence in higher socioeconomic classes and Western Caucasians and a significant association with greater parental education.

Reference: Puri BK, Hall A, Ho R (2014). *Revision Notes in Psychiatry.* London: CRC Press, p. 575.

Question 68 Answer: d, Depersonalization
Explanation: Depersonalization is the experience of change in awareness of oneself, as though one is 'unreal'. Some associated characteristics include emotional numbing, changes in body/visual/auditory experiences and changes in the subjective experience of memory and loss of feelings of agency. It is associated with unpleasant emotion. Derealization is the feeling of unreality in objects of the outer perceptual field, whereas depersonalization applies to the person feeling that he/she is 'unreal'.

Reference and Further Reading: Sims A (2003). *Symptoms of the Mind: An Introduction to Descriptive Psychopathology.* London: Saunders, pp. 83, 95, 230–233.

Question 69 Answer: b, The DSM-IV-TR and ICD-10 do not require the presence of depressive episode in the past.
Explanation: The presence of past depressive episode is not required to fulfil the DSM-IV-TR and ICD-10 diagnostic criteria for bipolar disorder, manic episode. Only DSM-IV-TR classifies bipolar disorder into bipolar I and bipolar II disorder but not the ICD-10.

References and Further Reading: American Psychiatric Association (2000). *Diagnostic Criteria from DSM-IV-TR*. Washington, DC: American Psychiatric Association; World Health Organisation (1994). ICD-10 *Classification of Mental and Behavioural Disorders*. Edinburgh, UK: Churchill Livingstone; Puri BK, Treasaden I (eds) (2010). *Psychiatry: An Evidence-Based Text*. London: Hodder Arnold, pp. 624–634.

Question 70 Answer: e, Seasonal pattern
Explanation: Seasonal pattern is a special feature for DSM-IV-TR bipolar disorder with manic episode.

Reference and Further Reading: American Psychiatric Association (2000). *Diagnostic Criteria from DSM-IV-TR*. Washington, DC: American Psychiatric Association; Puri BK, Treasaden I (eds) (2010). *Psychiatry: An Evidence-Based Text*. London: Hodder Arnold, pp. 624–634.

Question 71 Answer: b, Brain serotonin systems have not been shown to be implicated in the modulation of appetite.
Explanation: Brain serotonin systems have been shown to be implicated in the modulation of appetite, mood, personality variables and neuroendocrine function. In fact, an increase in the intrasynaptic serotonin would cause a reduction in food consumption. A reduction in serotonin activity increases food consumption and promotes weight gain.

Reference: Puri BK, Hall A, Ho R (2014). *Revision Notes in Psychiatry*. London: CRC Press, p. 575.

Question 72 Answer: c, Procedural memory is affected later than verbal memory in Alzheimer's disease.
Explanation: Episodic memory (early loss of recent events) deficits are an early feature of Alzheimer's disease. Certain parts of the brain show volume reductions with age, especially the prefrontal cortex and hippocampus. Both are important for the functioning of episodic memory, which plays a critical role in remembering past events. Verbal memory depends on episodic memory and is affected earlier than semantic and procedural memories. In contrast to the steady declines in episodic memory across all decades of life, semantic memory (e.g. languages, objects, places, spatial relationships, social norms) is not only preserved, but also shows improvement until around the eighth decade of life. The preservation of a wide variety of semantic memory (i.e. knowledge about objects and their relationships) has been demonstrated for both healthy elderly adults and patients with Alzheimer's disease. Spatial awareness (e.g. remembering visuospatial information) is part of the semantic memory and affected later than procedural memory (e.g. bicycle riding) because procedural memory is affected by speed and reaction time. Elderly with or without dementia may perform these tasks more slowly owing to other factors such as arthritis and muscle weakness.

There is a difference between recall and recognition. Recall is affected earlier than recognition in aging. The dissociation between recall and recognition is why we often fail to recall the name of a movie we saw whereas we can easily recognize when the movie is presented to us.

Reference and Further Reading: Ober BA (2010) Memory, brain and aging: The good, the bad and the promising. *California Agriculture*, 64: 174–182.

Question 73 Answer: c, Palinopsia

Explanation: Palinopsia is a reoccurrence or prolongation of visual perception after the stimulus has been removed. Palinopsia is associated with mania, depression and substance dependence. LSD is a hallucinogen that causes this phenomenon.

Reference and Further Reading: Abert B, Ilsen PF (2010). Palinopsia. *Optometry*, 81: 394–404.

Question 74 Answer: e, Rapid cycling disorder is a separate entity in ICD-10.

Explanation: Rapid cycling disorder is not a separate entity or course specifier in ICD-10.

References and Further Reading: American Psychiatric Association (2000). *Diagnostic Criteria from DSM-IV-TR*. Washington, DC: American Psychiatric Association; World Health Organisation (1994). ICD-10 Classification of Mental and Behavioural Disorders. Edinburgh, UK: Churchill Livingstone; Puri BK, Treasaden I (eds) (2010). *Psychiatry: An Evidence-Based Text*. London: Hodder Arnold, pp. 611, 625, 628.

Question 75 Answer: c, Based on the DSM-IV-TR and ICD-10 criteria, intervening periods of normal mood should not be present.

Explanation: The DSM-IV-TR and ICD-10 criteria allow intervening periods of normal mood. DSM-IV-TR specifies that the duration of normal mood cannot be longer than 2 months.

References and Further Reading: American Psychiatric Association (2000). *Diagnostic Criteria from DSM-IV-TR*. Washington, DC: American Psychiatric Association; World Health Organisation (1994). ICD-10 Classification of Mental and Behavioural Disorders. Edinburgh: Churchill Livingstone; Puri BK, Treasaden I (eds) (2010). *Psychiatry: An Evidence-Based Text*. London: Hodder Arnold, pp. 610, 634.

Question 76 Answer: b, It is a condition that is most common in the lower social classes.

Explanation: Bipolar affective disorder is a condition that is most common in the upper social classes. The sex ratio has been shown to be the same. The point prevalence in Western countries is 0.4%–1.2% in the adult population. In the general population of Western countries, the lifetime risk of suffering from a bipolar disorder is 0.6%–1.1%. The average age of onset is around the mid-twenties. Being unmarried is associated with higher rates of bipolar disorder.

Reference: Puri BK, Hall A, Ho R (2014). *Revision Notes in Psychiatry*. London: CRC Press, p. 384.

Question 77 Answer: a, Delusional perception
Explanation: The psychopathology is delusional perception. It is important to bear in mind that a delusion is a false belief that is based on incorrect inference about external reality that is firmly sustained despite what almost everyone else believes and despite what constitutes incontrovertible and obvious proof or evidence to the contrary.

Reference: Puri BK, Hall A, Ho R (2014). *Revision Notes in Psychiatry*. London: CRC Press, p. 6.

Question 78 Answer: e, Memory retrieval procedure
Explanation: Option (a) involves participants learning a list of paired words (e.g. 'table' and 'shoe'). They are then presented with one of the words (e.g. 'table') and the participant must recall the word pair ('shoe').

Option (b) involves matching a stimulus to what is already stored in memory. An example would be a multiple-choice test.

Option (c) and (d) are recall techniques used to measure memory. In free recall, participants have to actively search their memory stores to retrieve information. An example would be examinations in the form of essays. There are little retrieval cues available, unlike recognition. Memory-span procedure is similar to serial recall. Participants are given a list of digits or letters and asked to immediately repeat the same digit span in the same order that was presented to them. This technique is called digit span, which is one of the subtests in the Wechsler Adult Intelligence Scale.

Option (e) is the correct answer; there is no such procedure.

Reference and Further Reading: Puri BK, Treasaden I (eds) (2010). *Psychiatry: An Evidence-Based Text*. London: Hodder Arnold, p. 250.

Question 79 Answer: b, Ambiguous figures
Explanation: These are examples of ambiguous figures. Rubin's vase is a common example of the figure-ground reversal. The Necker's cube illustrates depth reversal, and Boring's old/young woman illustrates object reversal.

Reference and Further Reading: Puri BK, Treasaden I (eds) (2010). *Psychiatry: An Evidence-Based Text*. London: Hodder Arnold, pp. 234–236.

Question 80 Answer: c, 3 years
Explanation: Based on the existing ICD-10 diagnostic criteria, the diagnosis is only made if there is the presence of abnormal development manifested before

the age of 3 years. This might include abnormal receptive or expressive language, abnormal selective or reciprocal social interaction and abnormal functional or symbolic play.

Reference: Puri BK, Hall A, Ho R (2014). *Revision Notes in Psychiatry*. London: CRC Press, p. 624.

Question 81 Answer: b, Standardized scores on tests of recognition memory are higher than standardized scores on tests of free recall.
Explanation: Standardized scores on tests of recognition are lower than standardized scores on tests of free recall in people with feigned amnesia. Furthermore, people with feigned amnesia have a forced-choice recognition test performance that is worse than chance.

References and Further Reading: Cercy SP, Schretlen DJ, Brandt J (1997). Simulated amnesia and the pseudo-memory phenonmena, in Rogers R (ed) *Clinical Assessment or Malingering and Deception*. New York: Guilford Press; Trimble M (2004). *Somatoform Disorders – A Medico-Legal Guide*. Cambridge, UK: Cambridge University Press; Puri BK, Treasaden I (eds) (2010). *Psychiatry: An Evidence-Based Text*. London: Hodder Arnold, pp. 93–95, 149, 252–254, 260, 557–559, 581, 667, 1160, 1165.

Question 82 Answer: c, False memory syndrome is a recognized diagnostic criterion in ICD-10.
Explanation: False memory syndrome describes a condition in which a person's identity and relationships are affected by memories that are factually incorrect but strongly believed. During clinical interview and psychotherapy, the interviewer or therapist should avoid leading questions which may suggest false memory. It is not a recognized diagnostic criterion in ICD-10.

Reference: McHugh PR (2008). *Try to Remember: Psychiatry's Clash over Meaning, Memory and Mind*. New York: Dana Press.

Question 83 Answer: a, Schemas persist even after evidence for the schema has been discredited.
Explanation: Schemas persist after evidence for the schema has been discredited because the old schema has been activated more times than the new, modified schema and would be reactivated when there are little cognitive resources or time to activate the new schema and suppress the old one. Automatic, low-effort thinking involves schemas as people make use of previous knowledge, stored as schemas, to quickly process a new situation. Thus, schemas help speed up mental processing. Schemas are used to resolve ambiguity when a situation can be interpreted in various ways. When people act on their schemas, their actions can affect the way they treat other people, changing how the person reacts to them and, as a result, supporting their schema. This cycle illustrates self-fulfilling prophecy.

Reference and Further Reading: Aronson E, Wilson TD, Akert RM (2007). *Social Psychology*. Upper Saddle River, NJ: Prentice Hall, pp. 58–72.

Question 84 Answer: c, B_2 antagonist
Explanation: B_2 antagonist is not associated with tremor but B_2 agonist does. Amphetamine, B_2 agonist and caffeine are associated with physiological tremor. Risperidone is associated with extrapyramidal side effects.

Reference and Further Reading: Ward N, Frith P, Lipsedge M (2001). *Medical Masterclass Neurology, Ophthalmology and Psychiatry*. London: Royal College of Physicians; Puri BK, Treasaden I (eds) (2010). *Psychiatry: An Evidence-Based Text*. London: Hodder Arnold, p. 523.

Question 85 Answer: a, Dual role transvestism
Explanation: This includes the wearing of clothes of the opposite sex for part of the time in order to enjoy temporary membership or experience of the opposite sex. This occurs without the desire for a more permanent sex change. There is usually no sexual excitement that is derived from the cross-dressing.

Reference: Puri BK, Hall A, Ho R (2014). *Revision Notes in Psychiatry*. London: CRC Press, p. 603.

Question 86 Answer: e, Stupor
Explanation: Schneider has identified the following to be first-rank symptoms: auditory hallucinations, delusions of passivity, somatic passivity and delusional perception. Auditory hallucinations include the following: repeating the thoughts out loud, in third person, or in the form of a running commentary. Delusions of passivity include thought insertion, withdrawal and broadcasting. They include made feelings, impulses and actions as well.

Reference: Puri BK, Hall A, Ho R (2014). *Revision Notes in Psychiatry*. London: CRC Press, p. 351.

Question 87 Answer: c, Transexualism
Explanation: This refers to the desire to live as a member of the opposite sex, with intense discomfort about one's anatomical sex and a wish to change bodily features into those of the preferred sex. In order to make this diagnosis, the symptoms must have persisted for 2 years and it should not be attributed to any other mental health disorder.

Reference: Puri BK, Hall A, Ho R (2014). *Revision Notes in Psychiatry*. London: CRC Press, p. 603.

Question 88 Answer: e, Aggression is associated with high levels of serotonin.
Explanation: Aggression is associated with low levels of serotonin and high levels of testosterone. Serotonin has an inhibiting effect on impulsive aggression.

According to the social learning theory, aggression is a learned response, acquired through observation, imitation and operant conditioning. Aggression can also be learnt through positive reinforcements.

Reference and Further Reading: Puri BK, Hall AD (2002). *Revision Notes in Psychiatry*. London: Arnold, p. 55; Puri BK, Treasaden I (eds) (2010). *Psychiatry: An Evidence-Based Text*. London: Hodder Arnold, pp. 293, 1130, 1173, 1175.

Question 89 Answer: d, Rapid cycling bipolar disorder
Explanation: This woman suffers from at least four episodes of mood disturbance in the previous year and she meets the criteria of rapid cycling disorder based on the DSM-IV-TR criteria. Ultra-rapid cycling bipolar disorder requires at least four episodes of mood disturbance per month.

Reference and Further Reading: American Psychiatric Association (2000). *Diagnostic Criteria from DSM-IV-TR*. Washington, DC: American Psychiatric Association; Puri BK, Treasaden I (eds) (2010). *Psychiatry: An Evidence-Based Text*. London: Hodder Arnold, pp. 611, 625, 628.

Question 90 Answer: a, Degenerative spinal disease
Explanation: Degenerative spinal disease is associated with back and leg pain. Option (b) is correct because fine distal tremor is occasionally seen as part of a peripheral neuropathy. Options (c) and (d) are associated with physiological tremor. Physiological tremor is a small-amplitude, higher-frequency tremor, enhanced by fear or anxiety. Option (e) is correct because tremor may be an early feature in 30% of Wilson's disease.

Reference and Further Reading: Ward N, Frith P, Lipsedge M (2001). *Medical Masterclass Neurology, Ophthalmology and Psychiatry*. London: Royal College of Physicians; Puri BK, Treasaden I (eds) (2010). *Psychiatry: An Evidence-Based Text*. London: Hodder Arnold, pp. 523, 548.

Question 91 Answer: d, Proximity
Explanation: The closer the objects or events are to one another, the more likely they are to be perceived as belonging together.

Reference and Further Reading: Puri BK, Treasaden I (eds) (2010). *Psychiatry: An Evidence-Based Text*. London: Hodder Arnold, pp. 229–232.

Question 92 Answer: a, Fregoli syndrome
Explanation: This is a very rare delusional disorder in which the patient believes so. Primary causes would include schizophrenia as well as other associated organic causes. In this condition, the patient believes that a familiar person who is often believed to be the patient's persecutor has taken on different appearances. It is

important to differentiate this from (c), which is also a rare condition, but the essential feature of that condition is that a person who is familiar to the patient is believed to have been replaced by a double.

Reference: Puri BK, Hall A, Ho R (2014). *Revision Notes in Psychiatry*. London: CRC Press, p. 373.

Question 93 Answer: d, Exhibitionism

Explanation: In this clinical diagnosis, it is defined as the recurrence or the persistent tendency to expose the genitalia to strangers or people of the opposite sex in public places. There is usually sexual excitement, and this is often followed by masturbation.

Reference: Puri BK, Hall A, Ho R (2014). *Revision Notes in Psychiatry*. London: CRC Press, p. 605.

Question 94 Answer: d, People's expectation of a person influences their behaviour towards that person, resulting in that person acting in line with the expectation.

Explanation: Self-fulfilling prophecy is the process whereby a person's expectations of another affects his/her behaviour towards that person, resulting in the person acting in line with the expectation and hence confirming the 'prophecy'. An example would be a teacher who thinks a certain student is academically gifted and might give the student more opportunities to answer challenging questions during class, resulting in the student performing better.

Reference and Further Reading: Aronson E, Wilson TD, Akert RM (2007). *Social Psychology*. Upper Saddle River, NJ: Prentice Hall, pp. 67–70, 440.

Question 95 Answer: a, Displacement

Explanation: This 24-year-old woman has displaced her anger from the psychiatrist to the health care assistant.

Reference and Further Reading: Puri BK, Hall AD (2002). *Revision Notes in Psychiatry*. London: Arnold, pp. 168–169.

Question 96 Answer: c, Dhat

Explanation: The four core symptoms of dhat syndrome include excessive loss of semen, specific sexual dysfunction, anxiety about present or future sexual function and multiple physical/psychological symptoms. Most of the empirical studies on dhat syndrome have emerged from Asia (India), whereas its concepts have been described historically in other cultures, including Britain, the USA and Australia.

Reference: Sumathipala A, Siribaddana SH, Bhugra D (2004). Culture-bound syndromes: The story of dhat syndrome. *The British Journal of Psychiatry*, 184: 200–209.

Question 97 Answer: d, La boufféedélirante
Explanation: Haiti was previously a French colony. In French psychiatric nomenclature, la boufféedélirante refers to acute delusional psychosis with a favourable outcome. This condition has no genetic link to schizophrenia.

Reference: Campbell RJ (1996). *Psychiatric Dictionary.* Oxford, UK: Oxford University Press.

Question 98 Answer: e, Familial pattern of essential tremor is common
Explanation: Essential tremor is defined as uncontrollable shaking of part of the body that lasts for at least a few seconds. It is a common movement disorder among old people that usually affects the arms and hands, but can affect the head, jaw, face, feet and tongue. It is inherited in autosomal dominant manner. Essential tremor attenuates with alcohol use and puts patients at risk for alcohol misuse. Early essential tremor is absent at rest but present during action.

Reference and Further Reading: Puri BK, Treasaden I (eds) (2010). *Psychiatry: An Evidence-Based Text.* London: Hodder Arnold, p. 523.

Question 99 Answer: b, Social phobia
Explanation: The clinical diagnosis would be social phobia. Based on the ICD-10 diagnostic criteria, social phobia is defined as anxiety that is restricted to or predominates in a particular social situation. The phobic situation is usually avoided whenever possible. There is marked fear of being the focus of attention and marked avoidance of being the focus of attention.

Reference: Puri BK, Hall A, Ho R (2014). *Revision Notes in Psychiatry.* London: CRC Press, p. 408.

Question 100 Answer: c, Mitgehen
Explanation: This is an example of mitgehen. There is usually excessive limb movement in response to even the slightest amount of applied pressure, even when the person is told to resist movement. In another example, the examiner wants to move the patient's arm upward and asks the patient to resist movement. However, even with a slight touch, the person continued to move his or her arm upwards and then return to the original position after the test.

Reference: Puri BK, Hall A, Ho R (2014). *Revision Notes in Psychiatry.* London: CRC Press, p. 2.

Question 101 Answer: b, Common fate
Explanation: Objects moving in the same direction (common fate) at the same speed are perceived together.

Reference and Further Reading: Puri BK, Treasaden I (eds) (2010). *Psychiatry: An Evidence-Based Text.* London: Hodder Arnold, pp. 229–232.

Question 102 Answer: a, Cortisol-releasing hormone
Explanation: Cortisol-releasing hormone is usually increased in patients suffering from anorexia nervosa because of the central activation of the hypothalamus–pituitary and adrenal axis.

Reference and Further Reading: Puri BK, Treasaden I (eds) (2010). *Psychiatry: An Evidence-Based Text London: Hodder Arnold*, pp. 687–703, 1063.

Question 103 Answer: a, Self-serving bias
Explanation: Self-serving bias refers to the tendency to attribute our successes to internal, dispositional factors and failures to external, situational factors. In-group bias is the positive feelings towards people belonging to one's in-group and negativity towards one's out-group. Actor/observer bias refers to the tendency to attribute other people's behaviour to internal, dispositional factors, and to use external, situational factors to explain our own. Hindsight bias is the tendency to see events as more predictable after the event has occurred. Fundamental attribution error is the tendency to overestimate the extent to which a person's behaviour is due to internal, dispositional factors and to underestimate the role of external, situational factors.

Reference and Further Reading: Aronson E, Wilson TD, Akert RM (2007). *Social Psychology*. Upper Saddle River, NJ: Prentice Hall, pp. 30, 109, 116–117, 120, 424–426.

Question 104 Answer: e, A doctor's native motive to provide morally correct care to his or her patients, and focus solely on the rightness and wrongness of the actions themselves, and not on the consequences of the actions
Explanation: The deontological theories emphasize on a doctor's motive to provide morally correct care to his or her patients. They focus solely on the rightness and wrongness of the doctor's actions and not on the consequences of the actions themselves.

Reference: Puri BK, Hall A, Ho R (2014). *Revision Notes in Psychiatry*. London: CRC Press, p. 146.

Question 105 Answer: d, Autonomy
Explanation: This is an example of autonomy. Autonomy refers to the obligation of the doctor to respect his or her patients' rights to make their own choices in accordance to their beliefs and wishes. Nonmaleficence refers to the obligation of a doctor to avoid harm to his or her patients. Beneficence refers to the commitment of a doctor to provide benefits to patients and balance benefits against risks when making such decisions.

Reference: Puri BK, Hall A, Ho R (2014). *Revision Notes in Psychiatry*. London: CRC Press, p. 146.

Question 106 Answer: c, Prima Facie Duty
Explanation: The ethical theory that is being referred to would be the 'Prima Facie Duty'. This refers to a duty that is always to be acted upon unless it conflicts on a particular occasion with an equal or stronger duty. For example, a psychiatrist would have to maintain his or her own patient's confidentiality (this is a Prima Facie Duty). However, if one day one of his patients mentions that he or she has a plan to harm others, then the psychiatrist would have to consider carefully the various ethical principles involved and decide whether it would be appropriate to breach confidentiality.

Reference: Puri BK, Hall A, Ho R (2014). *Revision Notes in Psychiatry*. London: CRC Press, p. 146.

Question 107 Answer: c, Capacity is a legal term
Explanation: Capacity is not a legal term but competence is. A person is deemed to be competent if he or she has the capacity to understand and act reasonably. Competence is a legal term and determined by the legal system.

Reference and Further Reading: Puri BK, Treasaden I (eds) (2010). *Psychiatry: An Evidence-Based Text*. London: Hodder Arnold, pp. 1226–1227.

Question 108 Answer: d, Wernicke's encephalopathy
Explanation: Hyperemesis gravidarum in the first trimester may cause thiamine deficiency and result in Wernicke's encephalopathy. Wernicke's encephalopathy is characterized by confusion, ataxia and ophthalmoplegia.

Reference and Further Reading: Puri BK, Treasaden I (eds) (2010). *Psychiatry: An Evidence-Based Text*. London: Hodder Arnold, pp. 531, 697, 716, 1028.

Question 109 Answer: a, Bizarre delusions
Explanation: The delusions involved in a delusional disorder are usually non-bizarre in nature. A delusion is defined as a false belief based on incorrect inference about external reality that is firmly sustained despite what everyone else believes and despite what constitute as incontrovertible and obvious proof or evidence to the contrary. The belief is usually also not accepted by members of one's culture.

Reference: Puri BK, Hall A, Ho R (2014). *Revision Notes in Psychiatry*. London: CRC Press, p. 6.

Question 110 Answer: e, More than 23
Explanation: A patient with bulimia nervosa may have normal or even high BMI. BMI = Weight/Height (in metres)^2 = 60/1.6^2 = 23.44.

Reference and Further Reading: Puri BK, Treasaden I (eds) (2010). *Psychiatry: An Evidence-Based Text*. London: Hodder Arnold, pp. 694–695, 1063.

Question 111 Answer: b, Interactions with a member of the out-group
Explanation: Option (b) is incorrect as interacting with only one member of an out-group would lead to no change in the stereotype. This is because the single out-group member would be seen as an exception to the stereotype. Exposure to multiple non-stereotypical members of the out-group would help to reduce prejudice.

Reference and Further Reading: Puri BK, Hall AD (2002). *Revision Notes in Psychiatry*. London: Arnold, pp. 54–55.

Question 112 Answer: d, No implicit consent
Explanation: Both explicit and implicit consent can be considered as valid consent. Implicit consent is used to describe situations where it is judged that the nature and risk of a procedure (e.g. blood taking) are such that a less formal or retrospective transfer of information about the intervention is considered sufficient. The use of explicit and implicit consent is also dependent upon the building up of rapport and trust between clinicians and patients.

Reference and Further Reading: Puri BK, Treasaden I (eds) (2010). *Psychiatry: An Evidence-Based Text*. London: Hodder Arnold, pp. 1224–1225.

Question 113 Answer: a, Admit own feelings and inform the patient that the staff are frightened of his aggression and anger
Explanation: Option (a) may confuse the patient and give the wrong impression to the patient that the staff are incompetent in handling his aggression and anger. Patients with antisocial personality disorder may see this as weakness of the team and manipulate the situation by escalating his aggression and anger. Psychiatrist in this situation should deliver a clear and correct message to inform the patient that physical violence is not acceptable and there are chemical and physical interventions to help him calm down.

Reference: Poole R, Higgo R (2006). *Psychiatric Interviewing and Assessment*. Cambridge, UK: Cambridge University Press.

Question 114 Answer: c, Holmes–Adie syndrome
Explanation: The triad of Holmes–Adie syndrome is classically described as unilateral pupillary dilatation, poor constriction to light and accommodation and depressed deep tendon reflexes. This syndrome commonly affects young women. The pupil may become small over time.

Reference: Ward N, Frith P, Lipsedge M (2001). *Medical Masterclass Neurology, Ophthalmology and Psychiatry*. London: Royal College of Physicians.

Question 115 Answer: c, Thought block
Explanation: Passivity phenomenon refers to a delusional belief that an external agency is controlling aspects of self that are normally entirely under one's own

control. Passivity phenomena include thought alienation (which includes thought insertion, thought withdrawal, and thought broadcasting. In addition, made impulses, made feelings, made actions and somatic passivity are also part of the passivity phenomenon.

Reference: Puri BK, Hall A, Ho R (2014). *Revision Notes in Psychiatry*. London: CRC Press, p. 7.

Question 116 Answer: b, Egoistic suicide
Explanation: This is commonly referred to as egoistic suicide. This usually results when individuals feel that they are being socially further distanced from social norms and restraints, such that meaning in life is being questioned.

Reference: Puri BK, Hall A, Ho R (2014). *Revision Notes in Psychiatry*. London: CRC Press, p. 118.

Question 117 Answer: e, The best clinical approach to mental state examination is in a conversational and informal manner.
Explanation: Option (e) is correct because unskilled interviewers often conduct the mental state examination in a rigid schema with a lot of technical questions. It will prevent the patient from opening up and volunteering new information. This also explains why option (d) is incorrect. Option (a) is incorrect because the psychiatrist should focus on possible psychopathology based on information obtained in history-taking. Option (b) is incorrect because probe questions about psychopathology are best framed with reference to activities and ideas that are familiar to the patient. Option (d) is incorrect because state interrogations are unreliable methods of judging the progress of treatment or changes in patient's mental health.

Reference and Further Reading: Poole R, Higgo R (2006). *Psychiatric Interviewing and Assessment*. Cambridge, UK: Cambridge University Press; Puri BK, Treasaden I (eds) (2010). *Psychiatry: An Evidence-Based Text*. London: Hodder Arnold, pp. 91–92.

Question 118 Answer: e, The doctor should not inject him with depot antipsychotics and respect his wish.
Explanation: This man has the capacity to make decisions and is able to communicate his preference. His wish should be respected and the doctor should not inject him with depot antipsychotics.

Reference and Further Reading: Puri BK, Treasaden I (eds) (2010). *Psychiatry: An Evidence-Based Text*. London: Hodder Arnold, pp. 1094, 1226–1227.

Question 119 Answer: e, Homelessness
Explanation: An acute anomie is caused by a sudden change or crisis that leaves the individual in an unfamiliar situation. The causes of an acute anomie would include

migration, bereavement, redundancy and losses. It does not include homelessness. Homelessness and long-term employment are causes of chronic anomie.

Reference: Puri BK, Hall A, Ho R (2014). *Revision Notes in Psychiatry*. London: CRC Press, p. 118.

Question 120 Answer: a, Amaurosis fugax
Explanation: Amaurosis fugax is defined as a transient monocular visual loss. Carotid artery stenosis causes transient ischemic attacks (TIAs). TIAs usually last less than 24 hours and the patient presents with unilateral motor weakness or sensory loss and amaurosis fugax in one eye.

Scotoma is defined as an area of reduced vision (e.g. central scotoma) and is commonly caused by demyelinating diseases such as multiple sclerosis or macular degeneration. Hemianopia is defined as loss of half of visual field of both eyes (either left side or right side). Damage to the right posterior portion of the brain usually causes a loss of the left half of visual fields in both eyes. Similarly, damage to the left posterior brain usually causes a loss of right half of visual fields in both eyes. Homonymous quadrantanopia is defined as loss of either outer upper or lower quadrant of visual field of one eye. For example, left superior homonymous quadrantanopia is caused by right temporal lobe lesion. Bitemporal hemianopia is defined as loss of outer half of visual fields in both eyes and is commonly caused by pituitary tumour.

Reference and Further Reading: Hoya K, Morikawa E, Tamura A, Saito I (2008). Common carotid artery stenosis and amaurosis fugax. *Journal of Stroke and Cerebrovascular Diseases*, 17: 1–4.

Question 121 Answer: d, Barton
Explanation: Barton (1959) first used the term to describe a syndrome which he considered to be caused by institutions in which individuals show marked apathy, inability to plan for the future, submissiveness, withdrawal and low self-esteem.

Reference: Puri BK, Hall A, Ho R (2014). *Revision Notes in Psychiatry*. London: CRC Press, p. 124.

Question 122 Answer: a, Zimeldine
Explanation: Zimeldine was one of the first SSRIs introduced. It was withdrawn later as it caused an increased incidence of hypersensitivity syndrome and also demyelinating disease.

Reference: Puri BK, Hall A, Ho R (2014). *Revision Notes in Psychiatry*. London: CRC Press, p. 237.

Question 123 Answer: e, Breeder's hypothesis
Explanation: All of the aforementioned are possible explanations for the existence of a relationship between social classes and a given psychiatric diagnosis with

the exception of Breeder's hypothesis. Downward social drift proposes that there might be increased prevalence of schizophrenia in the lower social classes as a result of social drift. Environmental stress theory proposes that the lower social class is associated with adverse life situations, material deprivation and lower self-esteem that manual job entails. Differential labelling implies that individuals of certain origin are more likely to be detained under mental health legislation and diagnosed as suffering from schizophrenia. Differential treatment theory proposes that there are likely to be differences in the type of psychiatric treatment received by those who are from different social classes.

Reference: Puri BK, Hall A, Ho R (2014). *Revision Notes in Psychiatry*. London: CRC Press, p. 116.

Question 124 Answer: c, A functional hallucination
Explanation: A functional hallucination is defined as the hallucination that occurs when a patient simultaneously receives a real stimulus in the same perceptual field as the hallucination.

Reference and Further Reading: Hunter MD, Woodruff PWR (2004). Characteristics of functional auditory hallucinations. *American Journal of Psychiatry*, 161: 923.

Question 125 Answer: b, Couvade syndrome
Explanation: Couvade syndrome refers to the abnormal obstetric symptoms the husband experiences during his wife's pregnancy.

Reference and Further Reading: Sims A (2003). *Symptoms of the Mind: An Introduction to Descriptive Psychopathology*. London: Saunders, pp. 288, 290.

Question 126 Answer: a, Internal attribution
Explanation: Sandra has made what is known as an internal attribution. Attribution in itself refers to the rules that people use to infer and assume the cause of particular observed behaviours. An internal attribution is made when the person feels that he or she is primarily responsible for their behaviour. An external attribution is made when the cause of a behaviour is assumed to be due to other factors that are external to the person. Primary or fundamental error refers to the bias towards dispositional causes rather than situational causes when asked about the underlying motivation for other's behaviour.

Reference: Puri BK, Hall A, Ho R (2014). *Revision Notes in Psychiatry*. London: CRC Press, p. 59.

Question 127 Answer: c, Self-Image
Explanation: This refers to self-image. It is important to have a general understanding of the rest of self-psychology. Self-concept usually refers to the set of attitudes that one has about himself or herself. Self-esteem refers to one's own evaluation of self-worth and the associated feelings of being accepted by others.

Self-perception states that an individual would infer what his or her attitude should be through observation of his or her own behaviour.

Reference: Puri BK, Hall A, Ho R (2014). *Revision Notes in Psychiatry*. London: CRC Press, p. 58.

Question 128 Answer: e, False memory
Explanation: The concept test here is false memory. The false memory syndrome is a condition in which an individual's identity and interpersonal relationships are centred around the memory of a traumatic experience, which in itself is false. However, the individual would still have a firm belief that the experience did actually take place. It is important to note that false confessions might not always have an underlying psychiatric cause.

Reference: Puri BK, Hall A, Ho R (2014). *Revision Notes in Psychiatry*. London: CRC Press, p. 104.

Question 129 Answer: e, Theta wave
Explanation: Theta wave has a frequency between 4 and 7.5 Hz. Increase in theta wave is found in organic psychosis, Alzheimer's disease and hypoxia.

Reference and Further Reading: Puri BK, Treasaden I (eds) (2010). *Psychiatry: An Evidence-Based Text*. London: Hodder Arnold, pp. 400–409, 536.

Question 130 Answer: d, Needing to avoid social rejection
Explanation: In particular for normative social influence, the individual might openly conform to the ideas of a group, but might have a varying opinion deep within his self. The underlying rationale for conforming is largely to avoid social rejection.

Reference: Puri BK, Hall A, Ho R (2014). *Revision Notes in Psychiatry*. London: CRC Press, p. 60.

Question 131 Answer: e, Selective retention
Explanation: When cognitive dissonance occurs, the individual feels uncomfortable, may experience increased arousal and is motivated to achieve cognitive consistency. This may occur usually by changing one or more of the cognitions involved in the dissonant relationship, changing the behaviour that is inconsistent with the cognition or adding new cognitions that are consonant with the pre-existing ones. Cognitive consistency can also be achieved when attitude and behaviour are inconsistent by altering attitude.

Reference: Puri BK, Hall A, Ho R (2014). *Revision Notes in Psychiatry*. London: CRC Press, p. 58.

Question 132 Answer: c, Huntington's disease
Explanation: The patient is likely to have Huntington's disease. This is a genetic disorder that affects 5 in 100,000 individuals in the UK. It is characterized by a

slowly progressive dementia and associated continuous involuntary movement. Genetic studies have found out that transmission is usually due to a fully penetrant single autosomal dominant mutation, which is located on chromosome 4, and this might affect 50% of the offspring.

Reference: Puri BK, Hall A, Ho R (2014). *Revision Notes in Psychiatry*. London: CRC Press, p. 706.

Question 133 Answer: d, Sleep paralysis
Explanation: Sleep paralysis is the inability to move during the period between sleep and wakefulness and vice versa. Somnambulism refers to sleep walking.

Reference and Further Reading: Sims A (2003). *Symptoms of the Mind: An Introduction to Descriptive Psychopathology*. London: Saunders, p. 58.

Question 134 Answer: b, Dysmegalopsia
Explanation: Dysmegalopsia is also known as the Alice in Wonderland effect. Illusory change in the size and shape (both reduction and increase in size) is perceived visually. In this example, the objects (i.e. the heads) appear to be enlarged. This phenomenon is specifically known as macropsia. When the object is perceived as smaller than it actually is, this is known as micropsia.

Reference and Further Reading: Campbell RJ (1996). *Psychiatric Dictionary*. Oxford, UK: Oxford University Press.

Question 135 Answer: c, Depression
Explanation: The glucocorticoid receptor hypothesis is associated with depression.

Reference and Further Reading: Puri BK, Treasaden I (eds) (2010). *Psychiatry: An Evidence-Based Text*. London: Hodder Arnold, pp. 391–392, 612.

Question 136 Answer: a, Brown and Harris: Social Origins of Depression
Explanation: Brown and Harris stated that women with three young children under the age of 14, unemployed and with no confiding relationship are more likely to develop depression.

Reference and Further Reading: Brown, G, Harris T (1978). *Social Origins of Depression. A Study of Psychiatric Disorder in Women*. London: Tavistock.

Question 137 Answer: b, Excessive social support
Explanation: Excessive social support reduces the sense of personal control and this may be as damaging as little support. Hence, excessive social support may cause depression.

Reference: Krause N (1987). Understanding the stress process: linking social support and locus of control beliefs. *Journal of Gerontology*, 42: 589–593.

Question 138 Answer: b, Nonpsychotic schizophrenia patients
Explanation: Among the five groups, nonpsychotic schizophrenia patients are at maximum risk of suicide. Other high-risk groups include young male schizophrenia patients, high level of education status, unemployed, those with high and non-delusional expectations of themselves and those who are relatively nonpsychotic.

Reference: Paykel ES, Jenkins R (1994). *Prevention in Psychiatry*. London: Gaskell.

Question 139 Answer: d, Suppression in suicide reporting
Explanation: Appropriate reporting may be an important element in education of the public about suicide, and suppression in suicide reporting is not an appropriate recommendation

Reference: Paykel ES, Jenkins R (1994). *Prevention in Psychiatry*. London: Gaskell.

Extended matching items (EMIs)

Theme: Clinical assessment and neuropsychological processes

Question 140 Answer: d, Implicit memory
Explanation: Implicit memory is automatically recalled without effort and is learned slowly through repetition. It is usually not readily amenable to verbal reporting. It comprises of procedural knowledge, that is knowing how.

Question 141 Answer: d, Implicit memory
Explanation: Both classical and operant learning involve the implicit memory.

Question 142 Answer: a, Sensory memory
Explanation: The anatomical correlate of the iconic memory is probably the visual association cortex, while that of the echoic memory is the auditory association cortex.

Question 143 Answer: b, Short-term memory
Explanation: The anatomical correlate of auditory verbal short-term memory is the left (dominant) parietal lobe, whilst that of visual verbal short-term memory is possibly the left temporo-occipital area. The anatomical correlate of nonverbal short-term memory is possibly the right (nondominant) temporal lobe.

Question 144 Answer: c, Explicit memory
Explanation: This particular form of memory requires a deliberate act of recollection and can be reported verbally. It includes declarative memory and episodic memory, which are stored separately, since it is possible to lose one type of memory while retaining the other.

Reference: Puri BK, Hall A, Ho R (2014). *Revision Notes in Psychiatry*. London: CRC Press, p. 103.

Theme: Clinical assessment and neuropsychological processes

Question 145 Answer: c, Post-traumatic amnesia

Explanation: Post-traumatic amnesia, once present, tends to remain unchanged. Post-traumatic amnesia is confounded by sedatives that are given during admission and prolonged sleep. It does not correlate with the duration of consciousness loss.

Question 146 Answer: d, Psychogenic amnesia

Explanation: Psychogenic amnesia is part of the dissociative disorder consisting of a sudden inability to recall important personal data. The amnesia may be localized or generalized. The amnesia may be selective or continuous. The clinical presentation is usually atypical and cannot be explained by ordinary forgetfulness. It is associated with indifference and has a highly unpredictable course.

Question 147 Answer: b, Retrograde amnesia

Explanation: Retrograde amnesia refers to the loss of memory for events that occurred prior to an event or a condition. Such an event is presumed to cause the memory disturbances in the first place. Retrograde memory related to public events is more likely to be subjected to a greater memory loss than personal events.

Question 148 Answer: e, False memory

Explanation: False memory involves confabulation, report of false events (such as childhood sexual abuse) and false confessions. The false-memory syndrome is a condition in which a person's identity and interpersonal relationships are centred around a particular traumatic event.

Question 149 Answer: f, Transient global amnesia

Explanation: In transient global amnesia, the person presents with an abrupt onset of disorientation, loss of ability to encode recent memories and retrograde amnesia for a variable duration. The patient has a remarkable degree of alertness and responsiveness. This episode usually lasts for a few hours and is never repeated. The pathophysiology is a result of transient ischemia.

Reference: Puri BK, Hall A, Ho R (2014). *Revision Notes in Psychiatry*. London: CRC Press, p. 104.

Theme: Delusional types

Question 150 Answer: g, Erotomania

Explanation: This is a delusion that another person, usually of a higher status, is deeply in love with the individual.

Question 151 Answer: h, Nihilistic delusion

Explanation: This refers to a delusion of death, disintegration of organs and nonexistence.

Question 152 Answer: f, Doppelganger
Explanation: This is a delusion that a double of a person or place exists somewhere else.

Question 153 Answer: e, Delusion of Reference:
Explanation: The theme is that events, objects or other people in one's immediate environment have a particular and unusual significance.

Question 154 Answer: d, Delusion of pregnancy
Explanation: This is also commonly known as couvade syndrome and it is a delusion that one is pregnant. It usually involves the husband of a pregnant wife.

Question 155 Answer: b, Delusion of infestation
Explanation: This is also known as Ekbom's syndrome and it is a delusion that one is infested by parasites.

Reference: Puri BK, Hall A, Ho R (2014). *Revision Notes in Psychiatry*. London: CRC Press, p. 7.

Theme: Suicide and risk factors

Question 156 Answer: e, Personality disorder
Explanation: The risk factors for suicide in those with personality disorder include lability of mood, aggressiveness, impulsivity, being isolated from peers and associated alcohol and substance misuse.

Question 157 Answer: d, Alcoholism
Explanation: There is an estimated 15% mortality from suicide if there is an underlying disorder such as alcoholism. It tends to occur later in the course of the illness, and those affected tend to be also depressed. Associated with completed suicide are poor physical health, poor work record, previous para-suicide and also a recent loss of a close relationship.

Question 158 Answer: c, Neurosis
Explanation: Nearly 90% have a history of para-suicide with a high proportion having threatened suicide in the preceding month. There is a tendency after a failed attempt to resort to more violent means. There is a high risk in depressive neurosis and panic disorder, but a lower risk of obsessive-compulsive disorder.

Question 159 Answer: b, Affective psychosis
Explanation: There is a 15% mortality from suicide in affective psychosis. Men who are older, separated, widowed or divorced, living alone and not working are predisposed. Women who are middle-aged, middle class, with a history of para-suicide and threats made in the last month are predisposed.

Question 160 Answer: a, Schizophrenia
Explanation: There is a 10% mortality from suicide. Schizophrenics who commit suicide tend to be young, male and unemployed and have chronic relapsing illness.

It should be noted that fewer schizophrenic patients give warning of their intention to commit suicide as compared to patients in other age groups. The suicide is usually after recent discharge, with good insight.

Reference: Puri BK, Hall A, Ho R (2014). *Revision Notes in Psychiatry*. London: CRC Press, p. 398.

Theme: Prevention of depressive disorders and suicide

Question 161 Answer: a, Primary prevention
Explanation: The aim of primary prevention is to reduce the incidence of the disorder. Hence, close monitoring during the post-discharge period is essential, especially so for young men with schizophrenia and high educational background who have regained insight. Depressed elderly with somatic complaints should also be monitored closely.

Question 162 Answer: a, Primary prevention
Explanation: The aim of primary prevention is to reduce the incidence of the disorder. It is advised that people with strong family history of depression should space out their pregnancies to avoid poor parenting of the child. In addition, other interventions in parent–child relationship with a special focus on depressed mothers to improve parenting would also be crucial towards reducing the incidence of the disorder. Events centered interventions that target life events would also reduce the incidence of depressive disorder.

Question 163 Answer: b, Secondary prevention
Explanation: In secondary prevention, the aim is early detection and treatment of hidden morbidity in order to prevent the progress of the disorder. For depressive disorder, early detection of depressive disorders by GPs or through public education and use of screening instruments and psychiatric outreach services can help with this.

Question 164 Answer: c, Tertiary prevention
Explanation: The aim of tertiary prevention is to reduce the disabilities arising as a consequence of the disorder.

Reference: Puri BK, Hall A, Ho R (2014). *Revision Notes in Psychiatry*. London: CRC Press, p. 400.

Theme: Psychotherapy

Question 165 Answer: j, Shaping
Explanation: This phenomenon is known as shaping.

Reference and Further Reading: Puri BK, Treasaden I (eds) (2010). *Psychiatry: An Evidence-Based Text*. London: Hodder Arnold, p. 204.

Question 166 Answer: i, Reciprocal inhibition
Explanation: Reciprocal inhibition is a concept developed by Joseph Wolpe. Opposing emotions cannot exist simultaneously.

Reference and Further Reading: Puri BK, Treasaden I (eds) (2010). *Psychiatry: An Evidence-Based Text*. London: Hodder Arnold, pp. 655, 990.

Question 167 Answer: k, Systematic desensitization
Explanation: Systemic desensitization was developed by Wolpe.

Reference and Further Reading: Puri BK, Treasaden I (eds) (2010). *Psychiatry: An Evidence-Based Text*. London: Hodder Arnold, p. 990.

This question has been modified from the 2008–2010 examination.

Theme: Pharmacodynamics

Question 168 Answer: b, 5-HT$_{1A}$ partial agonist, f, 5-HT$_{2A}$ antagonist, k, D$_2$ partial agonist
Explanation: Aripiprazole is a 5-HT$_{1A}$ partial agonist, 5-HT$_{2A}$ antagonist and D$_2$ partial agonist.

Reference and Further Reading: Puri BK, Treasaden I (eds) (2010). *Psychiatry: An Evidence-Based Text*. London: Hodder Arnold, pp. 425, 426, 604, 904.

Question 169 Answer: l, GABA-A agonist
Explanation: Diazepam is a GABA-A agonist.

Reference and Further Reading: Puri BK, Treasaden I (eds) (2010). *Psychiatry: An Evidence-Based Text*. London: Hodder Arnold, pp. 648, 873, 905.

Question 170 Answer: g, Alpha$_2$ agonist
Explanation: Lofexidine is an alpha$_2$ agonist.

Reference and Further Reading: Puri BK, Treasaden I (eds) (2010). *Psychiatry: An Evidence-Based Text*. London: Hodder Arnold, p. 1040.

This question has been modified from the 2008 examination.

Theme: Antipsychotics

Question 171 Answer: b, 2
Explanation: 2 mg is the minimum effective dose in this case.

Question 172 Answer: d, 15
Explanation: This patient needs to continue for 2–24 months.

Reference: Taylor D, Paton C, Kapur S (2009). *The Maudsley Prescribing Guidelines.* London: Informa Healthcare.

Question 173 Answer: j, 75
Explanation: This risk of relapse is around 75%.

Reference and Further Reading: Puri BK, Treasaden I (eds) (2010). *Psychiatry: An Evidence-Based Text.* London: Hodder Arnold, pp. 632, 601, 602.

This question has been modified from the 2008–2010 examination.

Theme: Ethics

Question 174 Answer: j, Phronesis
Explanation: Phronesis is defined as the action of a person in a particular situation based on ethical principle. Phronesis was proposed by Aristotle and it is one of the appeals to character. The other two appeals are good will and virtue. Phronesis is a prerequisite for virtue.

Question 175 Answer: g, Ethical relativism
Explanation: Ethical relativism prescribes the way different groups of people ought to behave. In contrast, cultural relativism describes how different groups of people actually hold different moral standards for evaluating acts as right or wrong in a society.

Question 176 Answer: d, Categorical imperatives
Explanation: Immanuel Kant (1724–1804) proposed the concept of categorical imperatives. According to this theory, human beings occupy a special place among all categories of organisms. The views or proposition of a human being towards the other animals (i.e. the imperatives) determine his or her actions or morality.

Theme: DSM-IV-TR

Question 177 Answer: i, 81–90
Explanation: Her score is between 81 and 90 because her symptoms are mild and she demonstrates good functioning in wide range of areas.

Question 178 Answer: e, 41–50
Explanation: Her score is between 41 and 50 because the kleptomania results in serious impairment in social and occupational functioning.

Question 179 Answer: a
Explanation: This man got the lowest GAF score because he cannot maintain personal hygiene.

Reference and Further Reading: American Psychiatric Association (2000). *Diagnostic Criteria from DSM-IV-TR*. Washington, DC: American Psychiatric Association; Puri BK, Treasaden I (eds) (2010). *Psychiatry: An Evidence-Based Text*. London: Hodder Arnold, pp. 493, 494.

Theme: Neuropsychological tests

Question 180 Answer: h, Raven's Progressive Matrices
Explanation: The Raven's Progressive Matrices assess her performance IQ. In each test item of the Raven Progressive Matrices test, one is asked to find the missing pattern in a series and this is a nonverbal test of intelligence.

Question 181 Answer: d, Goldstein's Object Sorting Test
Explanation: The Goldstein's Object Sorting Test assesses her concrete thinking.

Question 182 Answer: o, Wisconsin Card Sorting Test
Explanation: The Wisconsin Card Sorting Test assesses her executive function.

Reference and Further Reading: Puri BK, Treasaden I (eds) (2010). *Psychiatry: An Evidence-Based Text*. London: Hodder Arnold, pp. 96, 509, 536.

This question has been modified from the 2008–2010 examination.

Theme: Freud's dream interpretation

Question 183 Answer: d, Manifest content
Explanation: Manifest content is the secondary elaboration of acceptable images in a narrative manner and these images are often linked to day residue or events prior to sleep.

Question 184 Answer: a, Condensation
Explanation: Condensation is the process where impulses are transferred to acceptable images.

Question 185 Answer: c, Latent content
Explanation: Latent content refers to the true meaning of the dream in expressing unconscious thoughts and wishes.

Theme: Sleep disorders

Question 186 Answer: b, Myoclonic jerks
Explanation: Myoclonic jerks are caused by sudden muscle contractions. Myoclonic jerks are seen in people with neurological disorders such as Creutzfeldt–Jakob disease, Parkinson's disease and epilepsy.

Reference and Further Reading: Puri BK, Treasaden I (eds) (2010). *Psychiatry: An Evidence-Based Text.* London: Hodder Arnold, p. 523.

Question 187 Answer: a, Circadian rhythm sleep disorders
Explanation: She suffers from circadian rhythm sleep disorders because she cannot sleep and wake up at the time, which correspond to normal routine in the general population and result in decline in occupational function.

Reference and Further Reading: Puri BK, Treasaden I (eds) (2010). *Psychiatry: An Evidence-Based Text.* London: Hodder Arnold, pp. 142–143, 398; Puri BK, Treasaden I (eds) (2010). *Psychiatry: An Evidence-Based Text.* London: Hodder Arnold, pp. 541–552.

Question 188 Answer: h, Rhythmic movement disorder
Explanation: Rhythmic movement disorder (RMM) includes a group of stereotyped movements such as body rocking and head banging is usually seen in early childhood. When the movements occur, they usually last less than 15 minutes. The large muscles of the body, often in the head and neck, are usually involved. RMM occurs during the transition between sleep and wake states, at bedtime and naptimes, during arousals from sleep at night and sometimes during light sleep.

Question 189 Answer: c, Non-24-hour sleep-wake syndrome
Explanation: In non-24-hour sleep-wake syndrome, patients feel that a day is longer than 24 hours and there is 1- to 2-hour daily delay in sleep onset and wake times compared to other individuals in the society. This condition is common among blind people who cannot see light.

Theme: British history of insanity defence

Question 190 Answer: d, The irresistible impulse test
Explanation: The Edward Oxford trial (1840) is associated with the irresistible impulse test.

Question 191 Answer: a, First recorded psychiatric testimony
Explanation: The Earl Ferrers trial was the first recorded psychiatric testimony in the history of British law.

Question 192 Answer: c, Offspring of a delusion
Explanation: James Hadfield was known as the offspring of a delusion.

Reference: Bewley T (2008). *Madness to Mental Illness. A History of the Royal College of Psychiatrists.* London: Gaskell.

Theme: Piaget's cognitive development

Question 193 Answer: g, Egocentrism, r, Preoperational stage
Explanation: Egocentrism occurs in preoperational stage (2–7 years).

Question 194 Answer: d, Assimilation, q, Sensorimotor stage
Explanation: Assimilation occurs in sensorimotor stage (0–2 years).

Question 195 Answer: j, Hypothetico-deductive thinking, t, Formal operational stage
Explanation: Hypothetical–detective thinking occurs in formal operational stage (older than 11 years).

Reference and Further Reading: Puri BK, Treasaden I (eds) (2010). *Psychiatry: An Evidence-Based Text.* London: Hodder Arnold, pp. 113–115.

MRCPSYCH PAPER AI MOCK EXAMINATION 5: QUESTIONS

GET THROUGH MRCPSYCH PAPER AI: MOCK EXAMINATION

Total number of questions: 193 (133 MCQs, 60 EMIs)
Total time provided: 180 minutes

Question 1
A 70-year-old woman is referred by her general practitioner (GP) to you for psychiatric assessment. She mistakes her husband for her deceased father and later for her elder brother. She believes that she has never married. She also mistakes her daughter for her younger sister. The psychopathology being described is
a. De Clerambault's syndrome
b. Capgras syndrome
c. Fregoli syndrome
d. Intermetamorphosis syndrome
e. Othello syndrome

Question 2
The community mental health team visits a 40-year-old man who describes the experience of being able to hear conversations from the police station in the neighbouring town. The psychopathology being described is
a. Autoscopy
b. Doppelgänger
c. Extracampine hallucination
d. Hypnagogic hallucination
e. Hypnopompic hallucination

Question 3
When the condition response seems more prominent after multiple exposure to the original conditioned stimulus, it is typically known as
a. Generalization
b. Discrimination
c. Incubation
d. Stimulus preparedness
e. Extinction

Question 4
Based on your understanding of pharmacology, neuroleptic malignant syndrome is classified under which of the following particular type of side effect?
a. Idiosyncratic reaction to medication
b. Time-dependent side effect
c. Dose-dependent side effect
d. Toxicity side effect
e. Withdrawal side effect

Question 5
Which of the following statements regarding the neurodevelopment and the neurochemistry of attention deficit hyperactivity disorder (ADHD) is incorrect?
a. September is considered to be the peak month for births of children with ADHD and without comorbid learning disorders.
b. Early infection, inflammation, toxins and trauma would cause circulatory, metabolic and physical brain damage, which might lead to ADHD in adulthood.
c. Psychosocial adversity is not one of the key factors associated with ADHD in childhood.
d. A dysfunction in noradrenaline might lead to negative feedback to the locus coeruleus.
e. A dysfunction in noradrenaline might lead to a reduction of noradrenaline in the central nervous system (CNS).

Question 6
A 30-year-old man is suspected to be a malingerer who tries to avoid court hearing and admitted himself to an orthopaedic ward for sudden paralysis. You want to examine his gait. Which of the following features strongly suggest that this man is indeed a malingerer?
a. Bending forward and advancing with rapid shuffling gait
b. Gait improves with suggestion
c. Reeling clownish gait
d. Unable to commence gait during examination
e. Walking like a pigeon

Question 7
In this form of dysphasia, there are difficulties with comprehension. Which form of dysphasia would this be?
a. Receptive dysphasia
b. Expressive dysphasia
c. Conduction dysphasia
d. Global dysphasia
e. Paraphasia

Question 8
A 60-year-old male suffered from a stroke recently, and after treatment, he is left with some speech difficulties. He is able to comprehend and understand what

others are saying, but he is not able to formulate and say a sentence such that others would understand. Which form of dysphasia would this be?

a. Receptive dysphasia
b. Expressive dysphasia
c. Conduction dysphasia
d. Global dysphasia
e. Paraphasia

Question 9

A 25-year-old man with a history of cocaine misuse feels bugs on his skin. He scratches at the 'bugs' trying to remove them, gouging his skin and leaving scars. The psychopathology being described is

a. Formication
b. Functional hallucination
c. Gustatory hallucination
d. Reflex hallucination
e. Visceral hallucination

Question 10

The concept of systematic desensitization that is being used in the treatment of anxiety-related disorders are based on which of the following behavioural models?

a. Reciprocal inhibition
b. Habituation
c. Chaining
d. Shaping
e. Cueing

Question 11

A 30-year-old male has had a history of bipolar disorder and he has been on lithium monotherapy. He just returned from a trip to Singapore, where he did a lot of outdoor activities in the sun. He just also developed diarrhoea. Currently, he noticed that he has hand tremors. Which of the following side effect is he suffering from?

a. Idiosyncratic reaction
b. Time dependent
c. Dose dependent
d. Toxicity
e. Withdrawal

Question 12

Which of the following is not considered to be a core symptom of adult ADHD?

a. Hyperactivity
b. Impatient
c. Forgetfulness
d. Distractibility
e. Chronic procrastination

Question 13
A 50-year-old man has been diagnosed with acquired immunodeficiency syndrome (AIDS). He is concerned about getting other infections. Which opportunistic infection is the commonest life-threatening opportunistic infection seen in patients with AIDS?
a. Leishmaniasis
b. Pneumocystis carinii
c. *Streptococcus pneumoniae*
d. *Toxoplasma gondii*
e. Tuberculosis

Question 14
A 60-year-old man has just suffered from an acute stroke. Immediately after the stroke, he realized that he is unable to understand written materials. However, when his care-giver spells the words out loud, he can immediately recognize them. He is still able to write. Which of the following is the most appropriate diagnosis?
a. Alexia without agraphia
b. Alexia with agraphia
c. Apraxia
d. Acalculia
e. Anarithmetria

Question 15
Which of the following is the most characteristic and consistent abnormality in delirium?
a. Agitation
b. Disturbance in attention
c. Disorientation to place
d. Short- or long-term memory loss
e. Visual hallucination

Question 16
Which of the following is the most lethal combination of medications in causing serotonin syndrome?
a. Phenelzine and fluoxetine
b. Phenelzine and amitriptyline
c. Phenelzine and meperidine
d. Methylphenidate and MDMA
e. Moclobemide and paroxetine

Question 17
The local dual addictions services just introduced a new programme aimed at promoting cocaine abstinence. The new programme would last for 12 weeks, and for the initial 6 weeks, the participants would earn cash vouchers if their urine sample showed a 25% decrease in the amount of cocaine, and in the next 6 weeks, they would continue to earn cash vouchers if their urine sample was entirely

negative. This method of promoting cocaine abstinence is based on which of the following psychological theories?

a. Cueing
b. Chaining
c. Shaping
d. Gradual approximation
e. Variable reinforcement scheduling

Question 18

A 60-year-old man, Peter, is referred by his GP to you for auditory hallucinations before he falls asleep. Which of the following is the most common presentation of such psychopathology?

a. Hearing classical music
b. Hearing, 'Peter, Peter'
c. Hearing, 'You are useless'
d. Seeing flash lights
e. Seeing a view of wide area

Question 19

A 3-year-old boy has a fear of dogs. When he sees a dog around, he experiences marked tachycardia and increased arousal and then he feels an intense feeling of fear. His experience of fear would be best described by which one of the following theories?

a. James–Lange theory
b. Cannon–Bard theory
c. Cognitive labelling theory
d. Cognitive appraisal theory
e. Emotion-regulation theory

Question 20

A medical student is puzzled as to why there are so many different subtypes of schizophrenia. She wonders which one of the following terminologies best describes a form of schizophrenia that is characterized by the development of prominent negative symptoms, without much positive symptoms.

a. Paranoid schizophrenia
b. Hebephrenia schizophrenia
c. Simple schizophrenia
d. Post-schizophrenia depression
e. Residual schizophrenia

Question 21

The core trainee on examination of a patient noticed that the patient has been having difficulties with performing movements involving that of the face, lips, tongue and cheek. The patient is not able to pretend to blow out a match. What specific type of apraxia is this?

a. Ideational apraxia
b. Ideomotor apraxia

c. Orobuccal apraxia
d. Construction apraxia
e. None of the above

Question 22

When a 2-year-old child is separated from his mother, it will lead to all of the following emotions except

a. Protesting by crying
b. Searching behaviour
c. Marked apathy and misery
d. Detachment
e. Anger

Question 23

Which of the following is not included under 'Mental Retardation' International Classification of Diseases (ICD) classification system?

a. Mild mental retardation
b. Moderate mental retardation
c. Severe mental retardation
d. Profound mental retardation
e. Mental retardation not otherwise specified

Question 24

Which of the following symptoms is not a part of the Diagnostic and Statistical Manual of Mental Disorders (DSM)-IV-TR diagnostic criteria for melancholia?

a. Distinct quality of depressed mood
b. Depression regularly worse in the evening
c. Marked psychomotor agitation
d. Significant anorexia or weight loss
e. Excessive or inappropriate guilt

Question 25

A 25-year-old woman presents with anxiety. You order a thyroid function test. Her serum thyroid-stimulating hormone (TSH) level is 0.3 mU/L (normal range: 0.5–5 mU/L) and her total thyroxine is 90 mmol/L (normal range: 70–140 mmol/L). The patient does not have a non-thyroidal illness and is not on drug treatment that could suppress TSH. Physical examination shows no goitre. What is your next step?

a. Check serum free thyroxine (FT4) and free triiodothyronine (FT3).
b. Order isotope scan.
c. Refer for specialist management.
d. Recheck TSH in 1 week.
e. Start levothyroxine therapy.

Question 26

In order to make the diagnosis of post-schizophrenia depression, the schizophrenic illness must have occurred within which of the following duration of time?

a. Last 3 months
b. Last 6 months

c. Last 8 months
d. Last 12 months
e. Last 24 months

Question 27
A 60-year-old woman complained of depression and her GP started her on citalopram. After 2 weeks of treatment, she complains of lethargy, muscle weakness and nausea. The GP wants to know the most likely cause for her symptoms. Your answer is
a. Acute confusional state
b. Generalized anxiety disorder
c. Hyponatraemia
d. Serotonin syndrome
e. Somatization disorder

Question 28
You have been asked to interview a prisoner, as the prison officers have noticed abnormalities in his behaviour. It was noted that he would not eat his food unless they were packaged, and at times, he attempted to cover his head with his clothes. When the officers asked him the reasons for doing so, he told them he needed to do so as he believed that there were people around who could get to know what he was thinking. What psychopathology does this represent?
a. Passivity experience
b. Hallucinations
c. Delusional ideations
d. Thought broadcasting
e. Thought echo

Question 29
A 45-year-old man is recently diagnosed with Huntington's disease. He is very concerned about the diagnosis. He has read information from the Internet about Huntington's disease. Which of the following statements is false?
a. Patients with Huntington's disease may suffer from akinetic mutism at late stage.
b. Patients with Huntington's disease have a higher risk of committing suicide compared to the general population.
c. Patients with Huntington's disease will die in 5–10 years after the onset of visible symptoms.
d. Most patients with Huntington's disease die of pneumonia.
e. The longer length of trinucleotide repeats is associated with faster progression of symptoms.

Question 30
The core trainee was administering the Mini Mental State Examination for one of the patients. It was noted that the patient was unable to draw the interconnected double pentagon. What form of apraxia is this?
a. Ideational apraxia
b. Ideomotor apraxia

c. Orobuccal apraxia
d. Construction apraxia
e. Dressing apraxia

Question 31

An 11-month-old baby is shown his favourite toy. His mother then covers the toy with a cloth. The baby reaches out to remove the cloth and grasps the toy. According to Piaget, which concept best describes the aforementioned phenomenon?

a. Invisible displacement
b. Conservation
c. Problem solving
d. Circular reaction
e. Object permanence

Question 32

A 25-year-old man is referred by his GP for depression after the death of his father. Based on the DSM-IV-TR diagnostic criteria, which of the following symptoms favours the diagnosis of bereavement rather than major depressive disorder?

a. Auditory hallucination of hearing voices from his father
b. Guilt about delay in sending his father to the hospital
c. Marked psychomotor retardation
d. Thought of dying with his father
e. Worthlessness

Question 33

Based on Parsons's model, the role of doctors includes all of the following, with the exception of

a. Defining the underlying illness
b. Legitimizing the illness
c. Imposing an illness diagnosis
d. Offering help when needed
e. Imposing the appropriate cost

Question 34

The Camberwell Family Interview has been used to assess expressed emotions. Which combination of factors has been identified to be predictive of relapse?

a. Critical comments, hostility, emotional over-involvement
b. Critical comments, hostility, warmth
c. Critical comments, emotional over-involvement, warmth
d. Hostility, emotional over-involvement, warmth
e. Emotional over-involvement, warmth, positive remarks

Question 35

Based on the Holmes and Rahe Social Readjustment Scale, which of the following is associated with the highest life change value?

a. Marital separation
b. Marriage
c. Pregnancy
d. Birth of a child
e. Problems with boss

Question 36

All of the following statements accurately reflect the similarities between depression in the young and depression in the old, with the exception of

a. Sleep disturbances (such as early morning awakening, subjective poor sleep quality)
b. Poor appetite
c. Weight loss
d. Depressive pseudo-dementia
e. Reduction in interest

Question 37

A junior doctor is having her first night call. She sees a man walking alone in the hospital corridor at 3:00 AM. Based on her experience, there should be staff working in the hospital in the middle of the night. She deduced this man is either a medical or nursing staff. Which of the following types of processing is she most likely using in her deduction?

a. Bottom-up processing
b. Central processing
c. Control processing
d. Information processing
e. Top-down processing

Question 38

A core trainee was asked to review a newly admitted patient prior to the ward rounds. During physical examination, he noted that on attempting to move the patient's arm upwards, it stays in the same position thereafter. He is unable to ask the patient to relax his arm and this lasted for a total duration of 2 hours. This sign is commonly referred to as

a. Posturing
b. Stereotypies
c. Waxy flexibility
d. Tics
e. Parkinsonism

Question 39

A 25-year-old man drinks alcohol every morning before going to the office and he is often late to work due to slowness. He drinks again during lunchtime. After coming home, he usually needs to drink at least 8 units of alcohol before he sleeps because he has repeated thoughts that alcohol calms his nerves. His drinking habit has been the same for the past 5 years. A medical student wants to describe his behaviour. Which of the following description is incorrect?

a. Compulsion to drink
b. Lack of resistance to control drinking
c. Obsession with alcohol
d. Rationalization of the need to drink
e. Tolerance to the effects of alcohol

Question 40

The following are signs and symptoms indicative of an insult to the dominant parietal lobe, with the exception of

a. Gerstmann's syndrome
b. Astereognosis
c. Ideomotor apraxia
d. Impairment in two-point discrimination
e. Asomatognosia

Question 41

A 25-year-old man is referred by his GP for depression after the death of his father. He exhibits almost all symptoms of depression except worthlessness and active suicidal ideation. Based on the DSM-IV-TR criteria, what is the maximum duration of symptoms to meet the diagnostic criteria of uncomplicated bereavement rather than major depression?

a. 1 month
b. 2 months
c. 3 months
d. 4 months
e. 6 months

Question 42

A widely used toolkit for further research into life events and associated psychiatric disorder would be the Life Events and Difficulties Schedule (LEDS) proposed by Brown and Harries (1978). All of the following statements regarding LEDS are true, with the exception of

a. It is based on a semi-structured interview.
b. Forty areas are being probed during the interview.
c. Detailed narratives are obtained regarding events, including their circumstances.
d. It has a high level of reliability.
e. It has a high level of validity.

Question 43

Which one of the following toolkits would be most useful for evaluating damage to the brain?

a. Mini Mental State Examination
b. Halstead–Reitan Battery

c. Luria Neuropsychological Battery
d. Nebraska Neuropsychological Battery
e. Repeatable Battery for the Assessment of Neuropsychological Status

Question 44
Which of the following statements about Piaget's cognitive development theory is correct?
a. In the preoperational stage, rules are believed to be inviolable.
b. The preoperational stage is linked to circular reactions.
c. Piaget held that conservation was established in the preoperational stage.
d. Object permanence gets fully developed during the preoperational stage.
e. The preoperational stage is linked to conservation of fluid volume.

Question 45
A 30-year-old pregnant woman finds it difficult to not drink at all throughout pregnancy. She is currently 10-weeks pregnant. She wants to know the upper limits of units of alcohol she can take per week. Your answer is
a. Absolutely 0 units
b. 1–4 units
c. 3–6 units
d. 5–8 units
e. 7–10 units

Question 46
A 45-year-old female is here to seek help from the CAMHS psychiatrist. She shared that her son James has been too much for her to handle. He not only skips school for no reason, but has been getting himself into bad company and has been recently using drugs too. What diagnosis do you think the CAMHS consultant would label James with?
a. ADHD
b. Pervasive development disorder
c. Conduct disorder
d. Oppositional defiant disorder
e. School refusal

Question 47
Which of the following antidepressants exhibit alpha-receptor antagonism and serotonin receptor inhibition?
a. Amitriptyline
b. Duloxetine
c. Mirtazapine
d. Reboxetine
e. Venlafaxine

Question 48
A 25-year-old male has been referred by his GP to the mental health service. Over the past 3 months or so, he has been feeling increasingly troubled by his neighbours. He

believes that they are deliberately sending in radiation to harm him and his mother. In addition, he claims that he is able to hear his neighbours making demeaning remarks by the wall. At times, he is even more troubled as they seemed to be commenting on his every action. What form of psychopathology does he present with?

a. Extracampine hallucinations
b. Pseudo-hallucination
c. Thought interference
d. Passivity phenomenon
e. Running commentary

Question 49

A junior doctor is having her first night call. She sees a man walking alone in the hospital corridor at 3:00 AM. He wears a white coat and holds a stethoscope. She deduces that he must be a medical doctor. Which of the following types of processing is she most likely using in her deduction?

a. Bottom-up processing
b. Central processing
c. Control processing
d. Information processing
e. Top-down processing

Question 50

A 25-year-old male has been seen by the addiction services and he has since been abstinent from alcohol for the past 3 months. However, he is still bothered by recurrent auditory hallucinations. Which of the following is the most likely clinical diagnosis?

a. Alcohol withdrawal
b. Delirium tremens
c. Alcoholic hallucinosis
d. Delusional disorder
e. Schizophrenia

Question 51

A 42-year-old man is referred by his GP for depression, memory impairment, fidgety hands and flycatcher's tongue. His father committed suicide at the age of 47. His grandfather suffered from behavioural problems and died at the age of 50. Which of the following is the most likely diagnosis?

a. Cervical myelopathy
b. Huntington's disease
c. Malignant spinal disease
d. Parkinson's disease
e. Wilson's disease

Question 52

Which stage of Kohlberg theory of moral development is achieved at the conventional stage?

a. Universal ethical principle orientation
b. Social-order-maintaining orientation

c. Instrumental purpose orientation
d. Punishment and obedience orientation
e. Social-contract orientation

Question 53
A 21-year-old female medical student was brought in by the university counsellor as she was in shock and anger after being informed that she had failed in all subjects in her examinations and that she would need to repeat the first year. When you examined her, she was in a daze with purposeless overactivity. The counsellor would like to know when her symptoms would start to disappear. Based on the ICD-10 criteria, the answer is
a. 1 hour
b. 12 hours
c. 24 hours
d. 48 hours
e. 60 hours

Question 54
A 22-year-old university student has decided that he needs to see a psychiatrist as he has a fear of darkness since youth. However, he tells the psychiatrist that he is not overtly distressed when he is in the dark and he does not take measures to avoid being in darkness. Which one of the following statements is true?
a. He has a specific phobia, as the fear of darkness is out of proportion to the norm.
b. He has a specific phobia, as the fear of darkness cannot be reasoned or explained away.
c. He has a specific phobia, as the feelings of fear are way beyond his own voluntary control.
d. He has no specific phobia, as the fear of darkness is not included in the list of specific phobia.
e. He does not have specific phobia, as there is no avoidance behaviour in his case.

Question 55
A 30-year-old woman suffers from bipolar disorder and she has been treated with lithium. She is concerned about renal and thyroid dysfunction. She wants to change the mood stabilizer. Which of the following medications has the least prophylactic effect against future manic episodes?
a. Carbamazepine
b. Olanzapine
c. Risperidone
d. Sodium valproate
e. Topiramate

Question 56
A medical student is puzzled and confused about the signs and symptoms associated with mania and hypomania. Which of the following is not one of the classical signs and symptoms of someone with a diagnosis of mania?
a. Elevated energy level
b. Marked irritability, out of keeping with character

c. Elevated mood
d. Spending more than usual
e. Memory disturbances

Question 57
Which of the following metabolic causes is least likely to cause chorea?
a. Hypercalacaemia
b. Hyperglycaemia
c. Hyponatraemia
d. Hypoglycaemia
e. Hypomagnesaemia

Question 58
Nondominant temporal lobe damage could potentially lead to impaired performance on this particular test:
a. Object learning test
b. Synonym learning test
c. Paired associated learning test
d. Rey–Osterrieth Test
e. Benton Visual Retention Test

Question 59
With regards to the aetiology of schizophrenia, which of the following statements is true about the risk of developing schizophrenia among immigrants?
a. Social factors are less in importance in predisposing individuals towards schizophrenia as compared to biological factors.
b. Afro-Caribbean immigrants to the United Kingdom have a higher risk of schizophrenia.
c. Afro-Caribbean immigrants have the same risk as the population in their native countries.
d. First-generation immigrants are more likely to develop schizophrenia and hence efforts should be focused on them.
e. The higher rates of schizophrenia in urban areas is mainly due to migration.

Question 60
A mother is worried that her child will develop bipolar disorder. Which of the following genes has been found to be associated with an increased risk of developing bipolar disorder?
a. Tryptophan hydroxylase gene
b. Serotonin transporter gene
c. COMT gene
d. APOE3 gene
e. Presenilin-2

Question 61
This is a psychiatric disorder that is characterized by the following cluster of symptoms: cataplexy and excessive daytime sleepiness. The most likely clinical diagnosis would be
a. Narcolepsy
b. Circadian rhythm disorder
c. Primary hypersomnia
d. Secondary hypersomnia
e. Sleep terror

Question 62
Which particular subtypes of schizophrenia has been believed to have an increased rate of suicide?
a. Paranoid schizophrenia
b. Hebephrenic schizophrenia
c. Catatonic schizophrenia
d. Post-schizophrenia depression
e. Simple schizophrenia

Question 63
A 30-year-old woman suffers from depression and she is very concerned about gastrointestinal side effects. Which of the following antidepressants causes the most intense gastrointestinal side effects?
a. Citalopram
b. Mirtazapine
c. Paroxetine
d. Sertraline
e. Venlafaxine

Question 64
Which of the following statements about emotion is true?
a. According to the James–Lange theory, emotions have primacy over physiology.
b. Distress is a primary emotion.
c. According to the Cannon–Bard theory, the emotion-arousing stimulus is processed by the hypothalamus.
d. According to Lazarus, emotions can be without cognition.
e. Facial expression can affect emotional response.

Question 65
A patient who has a long-standing history of schizophrenia has been on continuous follow-up with the community psychiatric nurse. He has been concordance to treatment. However, lately he vocalizes that some of his symptoms seem to be coming back. He is complaining of having difficulties in thinking as he

believes that the every black car that passes by his house has an electronic device within to jam up his thoughts. What form of psychopathology is this?

a. Thought insertion
b. Thought withdrawal
c. Passivity phenomenon
d. Hallucinations
e. Delusional perception

Question 66

The triad of narcolepsy is classically defined as

a. Daytime sleep attacks, catalepsy, hypnogogic hallucination
b. Daytime sleep attacks, catalepsy, hypnopompic hallucination
c. Daytime sleep attacks, cataplexy, hypnogogic hallucination
d. Daytime sleep attacks, cataplexy, hypnopompic hallucination
e. Night-time sleep attacks, cataplexy, hypnopompic hallucination

Question 67

Which of the following statements regarding diagnostic criteria for panic disorder is false?

a. Based on the DSM-IV-TR, panic disorder is classified into panic disorder with agoraphobia and panic disorder without agoraphobia.
b. Based on the DSM-IV-TR, agoraphobia is classified into agoraphobia without history of panic disorder and panic disorder with agoraphobia.
c. Based on the ICD-10, agoraphobia is classified into agoraphobia without history of panic disorder and panic disorder with agoraphobia.
d. Based on the ICD-10, panic disorder is classified into panic disorder with agoraphobia and panic disorder without agoraphobia.
e. Based on the ICD-10 criteria further define severe panic disorder of having at least 4 panic attacks per week over a 4-week period.

Question 68

The following statements about the Mini Mental State Examination (MMSE) are true, with the exception of

a. It is a relatively brief test that could be routinely used to rapidly detect possible underlying dementia.
b. It could help to estimate the relative degree of severity of dementia.
c. It could help to follow up on dementia and progression over a period of time.
d. It cannot be used to differentiate between dementia and delirium.
e. It includes tests of short-term memory and immediate recall memory.

Question 69

Which one of the following dementia rating scales could be given to caregivers for an assessment of the cognitive functions of an individual?

a. Blessed Dementia Scale
b. Information-Memory-Concentration Test
c. Geriatric Mental State Schedule

d. Cambridge Neuropsychological Test Automated Battery
e. Gresham Ward Questionnaire

Question 70
There has been much media attention about how dangerous patients with schizophrenia could be. What is the actual estimated risk of violence amongst patients with schizophrenia?
a. 0.01
b. 0.05
c. 0.08
d. 0.10
e. 0.20

Question 71
A 50-year-old man, after brain injury to the nondominant parietal lobe, came to believe that he has seen himself on a number of occasions while travelling to different cities in his country. He is aware of himself both inside and outside his body. He feels that his office has been copied and exists in two different cities. Which of the following statements is false?
a. The knowledge of having a double is occasionally a delusion, or hallucination but more commonly is a variant of depersonalization.
b. This condition can occur in other people without psychiatric illness.
c. This condition consists of a delusion that a double of a person or place exists somewhere else.
d. This condition is known as reduplicative paramnesia.
e. This condition is a perceptual rather than ideational or cognitive disturbance.

Question 72
Which of the following is not one of Cannon's critiques of the James–Lange theory?
a. Physiological arousal is not sufficient.
b. Emotions can be independent of bodily responses.
c. Similar visceral changes can accompany different emotions.
d. Overt behaviour can lead to emotions without visceral changes.
e. Emotions can occur before somatic responses.

Question 73
Which of the following is the most common type of violence demonstrated by patients with schizophrenia?
a. Verbal aggression
b. Physical aggression towards objects
c. Physical aggression towards others
d. Self-directed violence
e. None of the above

Question 74
Restless leg syndrome is most commonly associated with
a. Calcium deficiency
b. Iron deficiency

c. Potassium deficiency
d. Sodium deficiency
e. Zinc deficiency

Question 75
Which of the following is an assessment scale that involves a structured interview with a relative?
a. Geriatric Mental State Schedule
b. Cambridge Examination for Mental Disorders
c. Crichton Geriatric Behavior Rating Scale
d. Stockton Geriatric Rating Scale
e. Clifton Assessment Schedule

Question 76
Which of the following statements about Amok is incorrect?
a. This is a condition that was initially described in Malays in the mid-sixteenth century.
b. It occurs only in Malays and there have not been reports of Amok from any other countries.
c. It consists of a period of withdrawal, followed by a sudden outburst of homicidal aggression in which the sufferer will attack anyone within reach.
d. The attack usually lasts for several hours until the sufferer is overwhelmed.
e. Following the attack, the person typically passes into a deep sleep or stupor for several days, and would have subsequent amnesia of the event.

Question 77
Which of the following statements regarding diagnostic criteria for post-traumatic stress disorder is true?
a. The DSM-IV-TR and the ICD-10 specify acute and chronic PTSD.
b. The DSM-IV-TR and ICD-10 specify PTSD with delayed onset.
c. The DSM-IV-TR specifies the minimum duration of disturbance of PTSD is more than 2 months.
d. If duration of symptoms is less than 4 months, it will be specified as acute PTSD.
e. The ICD-10, but not the DSM-IV-TR, specifies acute and chronic PTSD.

Question 78
You are a core trainee who has just started out your inpatient psychiatry posting. The consultant asked you to review a patient prior to the ward rounds. When speaking to the patient, you noticed that the patient appeared to keep repeating whatever word you have just mentioned. The phrase that correctly describes this form of psychopathology is
a. Approximate answer (Vorbeireden)
b. Cryptolalia
c. Echolalia
d. Perseveration
e. Neologism

Question 79

A 26-year-old man was exercising at the neighbourhood park at night. He was sweating profusely, and his heart was palpitating. The lights were out at one section of the park, and he became aware of how dark and quiet the surroundings were. The awareness of his surroundings made him feel scared. Which of the following theories best describes the aforementioned phenomenon?'

a. Cannon–Bard theory
b. Ekman–Paul theory
c. Plutchik theory
d. James–Lange theory
e. Schachter–Singer theory

Question 80

A 30-year-old woman attempts suicide after ingesting 25 50-mg tablets of amitriptyline prescribed by her GP. The patient looks alert. The Accident and Emergency Department consultant asks you to admit this patient to the psychiatric ward, as he thinks that the psychiatric risk is higher than the medical risk. You are concerned about her medical condition. Which part of the ECG would be most significant in assessing her cardiac risk?

a. Length of P wave
b. Length of QRS interval
c. Length of RR interval
d. T wave inversion
e. Pathological U wave

Question 81

A 50-year-old man presents with a 6-month history of forgetfulness and urinary incontinence. Physical examination shows gait disturbance. Which of the following conditions is the most likely?

a. Chronic subdural haematoma
b. Hypothyroidism
c. Normal-pressure hydrocephalus
d. Neurosyphilis
e. Vitamin B_{12} deficiency

Question 82

In clinical practice, it is often difficult to differentiate obsession from delusion. Which of the following strongly indicates that a patient suffers from obsessive-compulsive disorder (OCD) rather than delusional disorder?

a. Better occupational functioning.
b. No other psychotic phenomenon such as hallucinations.
c. The thought content is less bizarre.
d. The patient believes that the origin of thoughts is from his or her own mind.
e. The patient tries to resist his thoughts.

Question 83

A 44-year-old man suffers from depression. He had severe aortic regurgitation, and aortic valve replacement was performed after percutaneous coronary intervention. He takes warfarin 2 mg every morning. The prothrombin time (PT) is 24.5 seconds (normal range: 12.0–14.5 seconds) and the international normalized ratio (INR) is 3.60 (normal range: 2.50–3.50). Based on the National Institute of Clinical Excellence (NICE) guidelines, which of the following antidepressants would you recommend?

a. Citalopram
b. Fluoxetine
c. Fluvoxamine
d. Mirtazapine
e. Sertraine

Question 84

In Alzheimer's disease, the most common EEG pattern is

a. Loss of alpha activity and decrease in diffuse slow waves
b. Loss of alpha activity and increase in diffuse slow waves
c. Loss of delta activity and decrease in diffuse slow waves
d. Loss of delta activity and increase in diffuse slow waves
e. Loss of theta activity and decrease in fast activity

Question 85

Which one of the following statements about the culture-bound condition 'Dhat' is incorrect?

a. It is most prevalent in Nepal, Sri Lanka, Bangladesh and Pakistan.
b. This is a condition that strictly affects individuals of the Indian culture.
c. It includes vague somatic symptoms.
d. It includes sexual dysfunction.
e. Individuals usually attribute the passage of semen as a consequence of excessive indulgence in masturbation or intercourse.

Question 86

A recent immigrant from Inuit suddenly presents with a marked change of behaviour in public. From the information obtained, she went wild for no reason and started to roll around shouting obscenities. She is now referred to the psychiatrist for assessment. The culture-bound syndrome that the patient is likely to have is

a. Amok
b. Latah
c. Koro
d. Piblotoq
e. Frigophobia

Question 87

A 44-year-old man suffers from depression. He has a history of myocardial infarction and takes aspirin 100 mg every morning. Based on the NICE guidelines, which of the following antidepressants would you recommend?

a. Citalopram
b. Fluoxetine

c. Fluvoxamine
d. Mirtazapine
e. Sertraline

Question 88

A callus on a tree resembled a monkey, and villagers flocked to the tree to pay homage to the 'Monkey God'. Which of the following statements about the aforementioned phenomenon is true?

a. This phenomenon appears in villagers' vision after the exposure to the tree has ceased.
b. This phenomenon is a form of pseudo-hallucination.
c. This phenomenon is increased by attention.
d. This phenomenon is associated with delusion shared by villagers.
e. This phenomenon occurs the first time villagers look at the tree and does not persist.

Question 89

A 30-year-old woman has informed the psychologist that she is not coming for the psychotherapy session and intends to leave the world. The psychologist gives you a call and you have decided to contact the patient. Her colleagues mention that she has just swallowed a large amount of medication in the office and she is sent to the hospital. Later, you are informed that this patient is admitted to the Accident and Emergency Department. On admission, her arterial blood gas result is as follows: pH = 7.0 (normal: 7.35–7.45), HCO_3 = 20 (normal: 22–26) and CO_2 >40 (normal: 35–45). Her QTC interval is 600 ms. The consultant from the intensive care unit wants to consult you because they want to know which of the following agents is most likely to contribute to her clinical picture. Your answer is

a. Diazepam
b. Fluoxetine
c. Haloperidol
d. Imipramine
e. Risperidone

Question 90

A 60-year-old man with a history of depression complains of vertigo and tinnitus. The tinnitus has worsened his depression. Which of the following condition is the most likely?

a. Anxiety
b. Cervical spondylosis
c. Epilepsy
d. Postural hypotension
e. Meniere's disease

Question 91

A patient has requested to have a word with her psychiatrist regarding the therapy session that she has been undergoing. She has undergone four sessions and decided that she needs to stop the sessions. She claims that she is not comfortable with the therapist and finds the therapist to be harsh and critical, much like what her parents used to be like. Which one of the following best explains her negative experiences?

a. Transference
b. Countertransference
c. Therapeutic resistance
d. Acting out behaviour
e. Learned helplessness

Question 92

In terms of prevention of genetic conditions such as Down's syndrome, genetic screening at what number of weeks would show the presence of raised human chorionic gonadotropin, lowered alpha-fetoprotein and lowered unconjugated estriol?

a. 4 weeks
b. 6 weeks
c. 8 weeks
d. 12 weeks
e. 16 weeks

Question 93

Which one of the following is true with regards to the risk of inheriting bipolar disorder amongst first-degree relatives of patients with bipolar disorder?

a. 1%–2% increment
b. 2%–4% increment
c. 5%–10% increment
d. 15%–20% increment
e. More than 30% increment

Question 94

Which one of the following is not one of the phases of psychosexual development proposed by Freud?

a. Oral phase
b. Anal phase
c. Phallic phase
d. Stagnant phase
e. Genital phase

Question 95

A 28-year-old mother has been very concerned about Tom, her 4-year-old son. He has developmental delays and poor communication skills. He is unable to reciprocate and interact with others and occasionally does have stereotype mannerisms. Which of the following would be the most likely clinical diagnosis?

a. Learning disability
b. Autistic disorder
c. Hyperkinetic disorder
d. Separation anxiety disorder
e. Emotional disorders of childhood

Question 96

Elective mutism usually occurs amongst which of the following age groups?

a. 3–4 years old
b. 5–6 years old
c. 10–12 years old
d. 15–17 years old
e. 18–20 years old

Question 97

A 28-year-old female is at a welcoming cocktail party for new psychiatric trainees. While she is talking to a consultant, she suddenly hears that someone calls her name. Which of the following attention allows Lucy to recognize her name is called?

a. Automatic attention
b. Controlled attention
c. Divided (dual) attention
d. Focused (selective) attention
e. Sustained attention

Question 98

Which of the following statements regarding alcoholic hallucinosis is false?

a. Auditory hallucinations are more common than visual hallucinations.
b. The hallucinations may be fragmentary in the beginning.
c. The hallucinations are characteristically fragmented.
d. The hallucinations can lead to persecutory delusions.
e. The hallucinations respond favourably to antipsychotics.

Question 99

A 25-year-old man informs you that he took an antidepressant from a GP and developed priapism. Which of the following antidepressants is most likely to be associated with the aforementioned phenomenon?

a. Imipramine
b. Moclobemide
c. Paroxetine
d. Trazodone
e. Venlafaxine

Question 100

A teacher has requested Tom's parents to bring him to the CAMHS service. He has been extremely difficult and disruptive in class. He does not wait for his turns, is impulsive and is always on the go. He is also not performing well in his school work, as he is not able to concentrate well. Which one of the following would be the most likely clinical diagnosis?

a. Conduct disorder
b. Oppositional defiant disorder
c. Hyperkinetic disorder
d. Separation anxiety disorder
e. Normal behaviour of childhood

Question 101
Based on Freud's psychosexual developmental theory, which is the phase during which the sex drive remains relatively stable and latent?
a. Oral phase
b. Anal phase
c. Phallic phase
d. Latency phase
e. Genital phase

Question 102
A core trainee was asked during his weekly tutorial about the differences between ICD-10 and DSM-5 in the classification of personality disorder. Which one of the following personality disorders could be found on the DSM-5 and not on the ICD-10?
a. Paranoid personality disorder
b. Schizoid personality disorder
c. Histrionic personality disorder
d. Narcissistic personality disorder
e. Dependent personality disorder

Question 103
Based on the Holmes and Rahe Social Readjustment Rating Scale, which one of the following events has been considered to be the most stressful, which may precipitate a psychiatric illness?
a. Death of a close spouse
b. Death of a close family member
c. Poor martial relationship
d. Separation from children
e. Imprisonment

Question 104
A 60-year-old Irish man staying in the countryside of Ireland complains of seeing wide views of huge skyscrapers and great avenues in front of him and he feels like he is suddenly in New York City. He has history of epilepsy. The lesion is most likely to be found in which of the following neuroanatomical areas?
a. Cingulate gyrus
b. Frontal lobe
c. Occipital lobe
d. Parietal lobe
e. Temporal lobe

Question 105
All of the following are factors that might predispose one to acquire schizophrenia, with the exception of
a. Residing in the urban settings
b. Being of Afro-Caribbean ethnicity
c. High level of expressed emotions within the family
d. Winter excess of birth in schizophrenics
e. Being of high birth weight

Question 106
Carl Jung founded the psychoanalytic school of analytic psychology. He has proposed five different archetypes. Which one of the following correctly describes 'the masculine prototype within each person?'
a. Anima
b. Animus
c. Persona
d. Shadow
e. Self

Question 107
Which of the following statements about panic attacks is incorrect?
a. It usually involves recurrent unpredictable attacks of severe anxiety.
b. These attacks usually last only for a few minutes only.
c. There might be a sudden onset of palpitation, chest pain, choking, dizziness, depersonalization, and together with a secondary fear of dying, losing control or going mad.
d. It does not result in subsequent avoidance of similar situations.
e. It may be followed by persistent fear of another attack.

Question 108
A 70-year-old woman is referred to old-age psychiatric service. She reports several incidents when she suddenly saw several four-inch-high beings wearing hats parading in front of her. She tried to catch one, but could not. She has no past psychiatric history. Her only medical problem is macular degeneration. The patient is most likely to be suffering from
a. Behcet's syndrome
b. Charles Bonnet syndrome
c. Leber's syndrome
d. Horner's syndrome
e. Reiter's syndrome

Question 109
A 20-year-old woman seeks outpatient treatment for her binge eating and self-induced vomiting. Which of the following antidepressants is contraindicated?
a. Bupropion
b. Citalopram
c. Fluoxetine
d. Fluvoxamine
e. Sertraline

Question 110
The following are aetiological factors that might predispose a child to have conduct disorder, with the exception of
a. Conduct disorder is associated with the inheritance of antisocial traits from parents who have demonstrated criminal activities.
b. Biological factors include the presence of elevated plasma dopamine levels.

c. Psychological factors include the difficult temperament and a poor fit between temperament and emotional needs.
d. There has been an association with parental criminality.
e. There has been an association with repeated physical and sexual abuse.

Question 111

A 25-year-old woman is referred by her lawyer after a road traffic accident which occurred one month ago. Her lawyer wants you to certify that she suffers from post-traumatic stress disorder (PTSD). Which of the following clinical features is not a predisposing factor in PTSD?

a. Childhood trauma
b. Inadequate family support
c. Low premorbid intelligence
d. Lack of control of the accident
e. Recent stressful life events

Question 112

A 30-year-old woman developed depression 2 weeks after delivery. Which of the following is not a risk factor for her condition?

a. Ambivalence towards pregnancy prior to delivery
b. Age
c. Episiotomy during vaginal delivery
d. Lack of support from her husband
e. Obstetric complications

Question 113

Which of the following statements is false?

a. Acculturation is a cultural change.
b. Culture has a pathoplastic effect on psychopathology.
c. Personality is not shaped by culture.
d. The ethnic-minority patients may not perceive the practice of psychiatry as benign.
e. The nosological systems employed by psychiatry are largely anglocentric and eurocentric.

Question 114

Which one of the following co-morbidities is known to increase the incidences of mortality amongst women with anorexia nervosa?

a. Alcohol dependence
b. Depressive disorder
c. Anxiety disorder
d. Younger age of onset
e. Poor social support

Question 115

A 23-year-old male came for his routine outpatient appointment and tells the psychiatrist that he is no longer keen to continue on his selective serotonin reuptake inhibitor (SSRI) antidepressant, as it has affected the sexual side of his relationship. This is commonly due to the action of SSRI on which of the following receptors?

a. GABA receptors
b. Histamine receptors
c. 5-HT2A/2C receptors
d. Noradrenaline receptor
e. Adrenaline receptors

Question 116

A 50-year-old with a history of mitral valve replacement takes warfarin on a daily basis. Her GP has recently prescribed fluoxetine to treat her depression. The interaction between fluoxetine and warfarin will cause which of the following symptoms?

a. Bruising
b. Headache
c. Palpitation
d. Tremor
e. Vomiting

Question 117

A 45-year-old woman complains of seeing herself outside her body. Which of the following statements about this phenomenon is false?

a. The double image typically appears as semi-transparent.
b. The experience rarely lasts longer than a few seconds.
c. The mean age of onset of this phenomenon is 40.
d. The most common emotional reactions after seeing her double are sadness and bewilderment.
e. This phenomenon is more common in women.

Question 118

Which of the following is not a typical cause of olfactory hallucination?

a. Alcohol withdrawal syndrome
b. Amphetamine intoxication
c. Cocaine withdrawal
d. Migraine
e. Temporal lobe epilepsy

Question 119

A 25-year-old man suffering from schizophrenia committed suicide one day after discharge from the psychiatric hospital. He killed himself under the influence of command hallucinations. The hospital sentinel event committee found that the patient was discharged prematurely, psychosis was not fully treated and no proper suicide assessment was conducted. The sentinel event committee concluded that this could be a case of negligence. The following constitutes negligence in this case, except

a. Family members did not agree with the premature discharge and their opinions were not sought.
b. Other psychiatrists would have conducted a proper suicide assessment before discharge.
c. The premature discharge caused physical damage (i.e. death).
d. The premature discharge is one of the direct causes of suicide.
e. The psychiatrist-in-charge must act in the patient's best interests before discharge.

Question 120

The first textbook in psychiatry, *Medical Inquiries and Observations,* was authored by

a. Celsus
b. King George III
c. Philippe Pinel
d. Willhelm Griesinger
e. Benjamin Rush

Question 121

The terminology 'schizophrenia' was first invented by

a. Morel
b. Hecker
c. Emil Kraepelin
d. Bleuler
e. Langfeldt

Question 122

The individual who was responsible for coining the term catatonic was

a. Ewald Hecker
b. Karl Ludwig Kahlbaum
c. Paul Broca
d. Sir William Gall
e. Theodor Meynert

Question 123

The core principles of medical ethics include

a. Autonomy, nonmaleficence, beneficence, justice
b. Autonomy, nonmaleficence, beneficence, paternalism
c. Autonomy, nonmaleficence, beneficence, virtue
d. Autonomy, nonmaleficence, beneficence, deontology
e. Autonomy, nonmaleficence, beneficence, confidentiality

Question 124

A 35-year-old female has been visiting the emergency department at least three times each week. She has been telling the doctors that she has been feeling unwell and she would need more detailed investigations. She is willing to go for any surgery. The emergency doctors referred her to see the psychiatrist, to whom she eventually confessed that she has been lying and giving the doctors a soiled urine specimen many a times. What do you think is her most likely clinical diagnosis?

a. Malingering disorder
b. Factitious disorder
c. Munchausen syndrome
d. Conversion disorder
e. No specific mental health disorders

Question 125

Which of the following anticonvulsants is the least likely to cause visual side effects?

a. Carbamazepine
b. Gabapentin
c. Sodium valproate
d. Topiramate
e. Vigabatrin

Question 126

A core trainee has been asked to perform a suicide risk assessment for a patient who has just been admitted to the emergency department following an overdose on 60 tablets of lamotrigine. Which of the following questioning techniques should he not use when he performs the assessment?

a. Open-ended questions
b. Reflective listening
c. Summarizing
d. Silence
e. Suggestive probes

Question 127

Mood is often assessed during psychiatric interview. Which of the following statements about mood is incorrect?

a. Mood can change over a short period of time.
b. Mood has a complex and multi-faceted quality.
c. Mood is reactive to circumstances.
d. Mood refers to a static unidimensional emotion on a depression–mania spectrum with depression and mania at the extremes and euthymia in the middle.
e. Within normal experiences, happiness can include blissfulness, contentment and playfulness.

Question 128

Dementia praecox was a term coined by

a. Morel
b. Kahlbaum
c. Sommer
d. Emil Kraepelin
e. Bleuler

Question 129

You are able to assess a 20-year-old man who is aggressive and angry towards the staff at the Accident and Emergency Department. Which of the following measures is least useful?

a. Admit own feelings and inform the patient that the staff are frightened of his aggression and anger.
b. Encourage the patient to verbalize his aggression and anger.
c. Inform the patient that restraint or seclusion will be used if necessary.
d. Inform the patient that physical violence is not acceptable in the hospital setting.
e. Offer the option of using psychotropic medication to calm the patient.

Question 130

Plato and Aristotle were responsible for proposing the virtue theory. Which one of the following statements correctly describes what the theory encompasses?

a. The theory emphasizes that a doctor needs to be caring, compassionate, committed and conscientious in nature.
b. The theory emphasizes the importance of the doctor in provision of morally correct care to his or her patients.
c. The theory emphasizes the need to maximize the benefits for the greatest number and also minimize the risks involved.
d. The theory emphasizes that all parties involved should receive equal consideration.
e. The theory emphasizes that all parties involved should receive impartial consideration.

Question 131

A 38-year-old female mother reports to the CAMHS psychiatrist that she has been having problems with her son. She claims that James, her son, gets angry very easily and would argue with her frequently. He does not obey any of the house rules. Which one of the following would be the most likely clinical diagnosis?

a. Conduct disorder
b. Oppositional defiant disorder
c. Emotional disturbances in childhood
d. Bipolar disorder
e. Normal behaviour of childhood

Question 132

The emergency trainee is seeing a patient who has complaints of having vivid, unpleasant dreams and improved appetite after consuming a certain drug. Which one of the following drugs should the trainee suspect that the patient has consumed?

a. Cocaine
b. Benzodiazapine
c. Amphetamines
d. Opiate
e. Caffeine

Question 133
A 30-year-old woman suffers from first episode of bipolar disorder and her psychiatrist has started lithium. She wants to find out the onset of action of lithium. Your answer is

a. 5–10 hours
b. 18–24 hours
c. 2–3 days
d. 5–14 days
e. 21–28 days

Extended matching items (EMIs)

Theme: Psychosexual development

Options:

a. Oral phase
b. Anal phase
c. Phallic phase
d. Latency phase
e. Genital phase

Lead in: Select the most appropriate answer for each of the following. Each option may be used once, more than once or not at all.

Question 134
This phase occurs around 30–36 months of age.

Question 135
This is the phase in which boys pass through the Oedipal complex.

Question 136
This is the phase in which the sexual drive remains relatively latent.

Question 137
This is the phase in which successful resolution of conflicts would lead to a mature well-integrated adult identity.

Theme: Psychodynamic theory of defence mechanisms

Options:

a. Repression
b. Reaction formation
c. Isolation
d. Undoing
e. Projection
f. Projective identification
g. Identification
h. Introjection
i. Incorporation

j. Turning against the self
k. Rationalization
l. Sublimation
m. Regression

Lead in: Select the most appropriate answer for each of the following. Each option may be used once, more than once or not at all.

Question 138
This refers to how an impulse which is meant to express to another is turned against oneself.

Question 139
This refers to how sexual instincts are being used to motivate creative activities.

Question 140
This refers to how one returns to an earlier level of maturational functioning.

Question 141
This is a common defence mechanism seen in paranoid patients.

Question 142
This is a common defence mechanism seen in patients with OCD.

Theme: Competency and capacity

Options:

a. Competency
b. Capacity
c. Testamentary capacity
d. Capacity for informed consent
e. Advocacy
f. Appointeeship
g. Powers of attorney
h. Court of protection

Lead in: Select the most appropriate answer for each of the following. Each option may be used once, more than once or not at all.

Question 143
A person needs to have this in order to prove that he/she is of sound disposing mind to be able to make a will.

Question 144
A person is deemed to have this if he or she is able to weight the information in balance to arrive at a choice.

Question 145
This refers to a legal concept and construct and refers to the capacity to act and understand.

Question 146
This refers to a person who would speak on the patient's behalf, but has no legal status.

Question 147
This refers to someone who has been authorized by the department of social security to receive and administer benefits on the behalf of someone else.

Theme: Basic psychology

Options:

a. Acceptance
b. Multi-perspective internalization
c. Naivety
d. Redefinition and reflection
e. Resistance and naming

Question 148
A 20-year-old African-Caribbean man was born in the UK and his parents migrated to the UK 30 years ago. He was brought up and received education in the UK. From the aforementioned list of five stages of culture consciousness development, select the stage that best matches with each of the following examples. Each option might be used once, more than once or not at all.

He has no awareness of African-Caribbean and British cultural influences on his own self. The colour of skin, ethnicity and cultural identity play no role in his life. (Choose one option.)

Question 149
His cultural identity is defined by his friends and partner. (Choose one option.)

Question 150
He identifies himself as a 'black' man and understands the full meaning of his identity in society. He feels that it is more difficult for him to climb up the social ladder compared to white British. (Choose one option.)

Question 151
After repeated thoughts and analysis, he establishes a personal consciousness of cultural identity in his own right. (Choose one option.)

Question 152
He is able to see himself as having a 'black' identity and take pride in himself. (Choose one option.)

Theme: Psychopathology

Options:

a. Audible thoughts
b. Hearing voices arguing
c. Command hallucination
d. Écho de pensee
e. Elementary hallucination

f. Gediankenlautwerden
g. Running commentary
h. Second person hallucination
i. Third person hallucination

Lead in: Identify which of the aforementioned terms best describes the following clinical scenarios. Each option may be used once, more than once or not at all.

Question 153
'Look at what he's doing now, he's sitting in the library and reading a book. Now he's walking to the counter to borrow the book.' (Choose two options.)

Question 154
'You should take the knife from the kitchen and get the fish from the refrigerator. You should cut the fish and then smell the fish's head for 10 times.' (Choose two options.)

Question 155
Female voice: 'She will fail the exam. She is an idiot and cannot focus in her study.'

Male voice: 'Shut up, leave her alone. She will pass the exam. Susan, you should reject her and not listen.'

Female voice: 'Don't tell me to shut up. My prediction is always correct' (Choose two options.)

Theme: Abnormal experiences

Options:

a. Elementary hallucination
b. Extracampine hallucination
c. Functional hallucination
d. Haptic hallucination
e. Hygric hallucination
f. Hypnagogic hallucination
g. Hypnopompic hallucination
h. Kinaesthetic hallucination
i. Lilliputian hallucination
j. Reduplicative hallucination
k. Reflex hallucination

Lead in: Identify which of the aforementioned terms best describes the following clinical scenarios. Each option may be used once, more than once or not at all.

Question 156
A 30-year-old woman is admitted to the hospital after an attempt to stab herself. She feels that her abdomen is filled with a large amount of fluid and she needs to

release the fluid. Physical examination shows a soft, non-tender abdomen without any distension or presence of air-fluid level. (Choose one option.)

Question 157
A 25-year-old man with schizophrenia describes the sensation that somebody is touching his body in intimate areas. (Choose one option.)

Question 158
A 40-year-old man asks the orthopaedic surgeon to arrange for the amputation of a third lower limb that he feels he has developed. (Choose one option.)

Theme: Psychopathology

Options:
a. Complex visual hallucination
b. Dysmegalopsia
c. Illusion
d. Macropsia
e. Micropsia
f. Pareidolia
g. Peduncular hallucination
h. Pseudohallucination
i. Simple visual hallucination
j. Visual hyperaesthesia

Lead in: A 65-year-old woman is found to be disorientated in time and place. During your assessment, she gives a history of the following experiences. Identify which of the aforementioned psychopathological terms best describes the following clinical scenarios. Each option may be used once, more than once or not at all.

Question 159
She is terrified and shouts, 'White Lady, White Lady, Go away.' She perceives the curtain as a female ghost. (Choose one option.)

Question 160
She finds the colour in the ward appears to her to be brighter and more vivid than usual. (Choose one option.)

Question 161
She mentions that the bed and other furniture look smaller or larger than they should be. (Choose one option.)

Question 162
She feels that her body size is smaller than that of a foot tall compared with the size of the wardrobe. (Choose one option.)

Question 163
She sees the face of Jesus Christ in the callus of a tree outside the ward. (Choose one option.)

Question 164
She reports that she saw a colourfully dressed clown and children dancing in the ward last night. (Choose one option.)

Theme: Type of prevention

Options:

a. Primary prevention
b. Secondary prevention
c. Tertiary prevention

Lead in: Identify which of the aforementioned type of prevention best describes the following scenarios. Each option may be used once, more than once or not at all.

Question 165
An early psychosis programme involves efforts to reduce the prevalence of first episode of schizophrenia by reducing the duration of untreated psychosis. (Choose one option.)

Question 166
The Department of Health promotes an alcohol misuse treatment programme specifically targeting at women of childbearing age. This programme aims at reducing the number of new cases of foetal alcohol syndrome in the community. (Choose one option.)

Question 167
A rehabilitation programme is designed to reduce the severity and disability associated with head injury. (Choose one option.)

Theme: Prevention strategies in schizophrenia

Options:

a. Listen to loud stimulating music to drown out the auditory hallucinations not responding to antipsychotic treatment
b. Maintenance in antipsychotic treatment
c. Psychoeducation about schizophrenia
d. Reduction in perinatal trauma
e. Reduction in stress associated with migration
f. Successful treatment of middle ear disease in childhood
g. Teaching problem-solving skill

Lead in: The Department of Health have devised various strategies to prevent schizophrenia in the UK. Classify the aforementioned prevention strategies into the following type of prevention. Each option may be used once, more than once or not at all.

Question 168
Primary prevention (Choose three options.)

Question 169
Secondary prevention (Choose two options.)

Question 170
Tertiary prevention (Choose one option.)

Theme: Neurology

Options:

a. Classical migraine
b. Cluster headache
c. Costen's syndrome
d. Cranial arteritis
e. Orbital onset migraine
f. Occipital onset migraine
g. Post-herpetic neuralgia
h. Tension headache

Lead in: A 50-year-old woman with a history of depression complains of chronic pain in her face. Match the aforementioned lesions or neurological conditions to the following descriptions. Each option might be used once, more than once or not at all.

Question 171
The pain is centred around her right eye, right forehead and usually extends to involve the whole right head. She also sees zigzag lines and feels nauseated (Choose one option.)

Question 172
The pain starts around the right orbit and may extend across to the opposite eye and to the adjacent facial, frontal and temporal areas but the main pain remains in the right orbit. (Choose one option.)

Question 173
The pain starts as a tightness in the occipital area and extends forward around the temporal area or over the top of the head. The ultimate location of the headache is around her right eye. (Choose one option.)

Question 174
The pain has a quality like a tight band around her head, coming forwards to the forehead. (Choose one option.)

Options:

a. 3–5 years
b. 6–8 years
c. 9–11 years

d. 12–14 years
e. 15–17 years

Lead in: A young person's grandmother recently died of cancer. Identify which of the aforementioned age ranges best resembles the following grief reactions. Each option might be used once, more than once or not at all.

Question 175
He needs more information about his grandmother's death to gain sense of control. (Choose one option.)

Question 176
He is confused and asks repetitive questions about his grandmother. He struggles to understand the abstract concept of death. (Choose one option.)

Question 177
He understands death and talks openly about his grandmother. He has magical thinking that grandmother will come back. (Choose one option.)

Question 178
He exhibits similar grief reaction compared to other adults. (Choose one option.)

Theme: Clinical diagnosis (I)

Options:

a. Acute stress disorder
b. Adjustment disorder
c. Avoidant personality disorder
d. Asperger's syndrome
e. Bipolar disorder – manic episode
f. Catatonic schizophrenia
g. Depressive episode
h. Delirium tremens
i. Disorganized schizophrenia
j. Dysthymic disorder
k. Malignant catatonia
l. Manic stupor
m. Neuroleptic malignant syndrome
n. OCD
o. Obsessive-compulsive personality disorder
p. Paranoid schizophrenia
q. Postnatal psychosis
r. Post-traumatic stress disorder
s. Psychotic depression
t. Separation anxiety disorder
u. Social phobia

Lead in: Match the aforementioned diagnoses to the following clinical scenarios. Each option might be used once, more than once or not at all.

Question 179
A 30-year-old man is admitted to the psychiatric ward and he appears to be stiff. Prior to admission, he was standing in the Oxford Street for 3 hours. His wife described him as still as a 'statue'. When he was asked the purpose of standing in the Oxford Street, he replied, 'Satan sent me there and I was controlled by Satan'. He has been hearing multiple voices for the past 6 months. (Choose one option.)

Question 180
A 23-year-old British solider goes missing in action in Afghanistan and is found collapsed on a bridge. When the medics examine him, he has no wounds and there is no sign of recent crossfire. He is unconscious and appears to be rigid and dehydrated. His body temperature is 39°C, and his blood pressure is 150/90. (Choose one option.)

Theme: Clinical diagnosis (II)

Options:

a. Acute stress disorder
b. Adjustment disorder
c. Avoidant personality disorder
d. Asperger's syndrome
e. Bipolar disorder – manic episode
f. Catatonic schizophrenia
g. Depressive episode
h. Delirium tremens
i. Disorganized schizophrenia
j. Dysthymic disorder
k. Malignant catatonia
l. Manic stupor
m. Neuroleptic malignant syndrome
n. OCD
o. Obsessive-compulsive personality disorder
p. Paranoid schizophrenia
q. Postnatal psychosis
r. Post-traumatic stress disorder
s. Psychotic depression
t. Separation anxiety disorder
u. Social phobia

Lead in: Match the aforementioned diagnoses to the following clinical scenarios. Each option might be used once, more than once or not at all.

Question 181
A 30-year-old mother gave birth to her first baby 6 months ago. She has been coping well initially. She starts feeling down, loses weight, complains of tiredness, eats poorly, wakes up before dawn and expresses guilt in her poor care to the baby.

Her husband also notices that she worries constantly that accident will happen to her baby after she read the news on a baby who died of choking after breastfeeding. She begins checking her baby every 5 minutes. (Choose one option.)

Question 182
A 40-year-old unemployed man is admitted after he was arrested by police for dangerous driving. He drove in the opposite direction at 120 km/hr on the M5 southbound because he firmly believed that the paparazzi tried to harm him. He informs you that he wants to pursue a PhD degree at this moment. He has incurred £100,000 in food business, although he worked as a technician before. He also sent email to the Prime Minister to advise him on how to attract investments for the UK from overseas investors. He first consulted a psychiatrist 10 years ago and he developed psychiatric complications after taking an antidepressant. He firmly believes that he suffers from schizophrenia because he hears voices when nobody is around. (Choose one option.)

Question 183
A 50-year-old man is referred by a gastroenterologist. He firmly believes that his gut has rotted and he is already dead. The gastroenterologist is very concerned as he has ceased to eat or drink. (Choose one option.)

Theme: Defence mechanisms

Options:

a. Isolation
b. Intellectualization
c. Displacement
d. Splitting
e. Idealization
f. Sublimation
g. Repression
h. Undoing
i. Denial
j. Regression
k. Projection

Lead in: Match the aforementioned defence mechanisms to the following. Each option may be used once, more than once or not at all.

Question 184
A man is passed over for promotion at work. He does not get upset while at work but loses his temper at another driver on the way home. (Choose one option.)

Question 185
It is suggested to him that perhaps some of his anger is related to his relationship with his boss. He denies this saying that 'She's like a mother to me – always kind and supportive.' (Choose one option.)

Question 186
He suggests that his anger is due to his childhood and then begins to speak about all the books he has recently read on child rearing across different cultures. (Choose one option.)

Theme: Concepts of dynamic psychotherapy

Options:

a. Acting-out
b. Affirmation
c. Boundary violation
d. Counter-transference
e. Empathetic failure
f. Holding environment
g. Metaphor
h. Mirroring
i. Parallel process
j. Process interpretation
k. Resistance
l. Transference

Lead in: A 30-year-old man is seeing a core trainee for brief dynamic psychotherapy. You are supervising the core trainee. Identify which of the aforementioned terminology resembles the following clinical examples encountered by the core trainee. Each option might be used once, more than once or not at all.

Question 187
The patient is very forthcoming during the session but he only talks about superficialities. The core trainee tries to probe further but without success. (Choose one option.)

Question 188
The core trainee was on leave for one month. After his return, the patient is in a withdrawn state in a session and the core trainee feels that the patient is angry because of his leave. (Choose one option.)

Question 189
The core trainee reflects on his positive qualities when he was confronted with a challenge to self-esteem at work. (Choose one option.)

Theme: General adult psychiatry

Options:

a. Allport's theory
b. Cattell's theory
c. Eysenck's theory
d. Type A personality

Lead in: Identify which of the aforementioned resembles the following descriptions. Each option may be used once, more than once or not at all.

Question 190

Personality comprises of common traits and individual traits. (Choose one option.)

Question 191

Personality has four dimensions: introversion, extroversion, neuroticism and psychoticism. (Choose one option.)

Question 192

Personality has three sources of data: L-data, Q-data and T-data. (Choose one option.)

Question 193

Personality comprises of achievement strivings and impatience irritability. (Choose one option.)

MRCPSYCH PAPER AI MOCK EXAMINATION 5: ANSWERS

GET THROUGH MRCPSYCH PAPER AI: MOCK EXAMINATION

Question 1 Answer: d, Intermetamorphosis syndrome
Explanation: Intermetamorphosis syndrome is a misidentification syndrome and the patient develops the delusional conviction that various people have been transformed physically and psychologically into other people.

Reference and Further Reading: Campbell RJ (1996). *Psychiatric Dictionary*. Oxford, UK: Oxford University Press.

Question 2 Answer: c, Extracampine hallucination
Explanation: Extracampine hallucinations are hallucinations that occur beyond the limits of the sensory field. In this case, 'hearing' conversations from the neighbouring town is an auditory extracampine hallucination. Autoscopy is a visual hallucination of seeing a 'double' image of oneself viewed from within one's physical body. The Doppelgänger phenomenon is the subjective feeling of doubling, where the person feels like his exact 'double' is present both outside alongside and inside oneself.

Options (d) and (e) involve hallucinations that occur when one is falling asleep and waking up from sleep respectively.

Reference and Further Reading: Sims A (2003). *Symptoms of the Mind: An Introduction to Descriptive Psychopathology*. London: Saunders, pp. 105–106, 112, 217–220.

Question 3 Answer: c, Incubation
Explanation: Incubation refers to the increase in strength of the conditioned response, resulting from multiple repeated brief exposures to the conditioned stimulus. Generalization refers to the process whereby a CR has been established to a given stimulus; that response can also be evoked by other stimuli that are similar to the original CS. Discrimination is the differential recognition of and response to two or more similar stimuli.

Reference: Puri BK, Hall A, Ho R (2014). *Revision Notes in Psychiatry*. London: CRC Press, p. 26.

Question 4 Answer: a, Idiosyncratic reaction to medication
Explanation: Neuroleptic malignant syndrome has been classified as an idiosyncratic reaction to medication. Idiosyncratic reactions to mediations are adverse drug reactions that are not characteristic or predictable and that are associated with an individual human difference not present in members of the general population.

Reference: Puri BK, Hall A, Ho R (2014). *Revision Notes in Psychiatry*. London: CRC Press, p. 252.

Question 5 Answer: c, Psychosocial adversity is not one of the key factors associated with ADHD in childhood.
Explanation: Psychosocial adversity is one of the factors associated with ADHD in childhood. This might include factors such as maternal psychopathology, large family sizes, parental conflict and emotional deprivation.

Reference: Puri BK, Hall A, Ho R (2014). *Revision Notes in Psychiatry*. London: CRC Press, p. 631.

Question 6 Answer: d, Unable to commence gait during examination
Explanation: A malingerer is unable to commence gait during examination when he is being watched by the examiner. Option (a) refers to festinant gait found in Parkinson's disease. Option (b) is found in hysteria. Option (c) is found in Huntington's disease.

Reference and Further Reading: Puri BK, Treasaden I (eds) (2010) *Psychiatry: An Evidence-Based Text*. London: Hodder Arnold, pp. 682, 684.

Question 7 Answer: a, Receptive dysphasia
Explanation: This is an example of receptive dysphasia. This usually involves underlying damage to the Wernicke's area and this would thus result in a disruption of the ability to comprehend language, either written or even spoken. In addition, the individual might be unaware that his or her speech, though normal in rhythm and intonation, has abnormal content.

Reference: Puri BK, Hall A, Ho R (2014). *Revision Notes in Psychiatry*. London: CRC Press, p. 105.

Question 8 Answer: b, Expressive dysphasia
Explanation: This is an example of inherent damage to the Broca's area, thus resulting in the loss of the rhythm, intonation and grammatical aspects of speech. Comprehension is normal, and the individual is usually aware that his or her speech is difficult for others to follow.

Reference: Puri BK, Hall A, Ho R (2014). *Revision Notes in Psychiatry*. London: CRC Press, p. 105.

Question 9 Answer: a, Formication
Explanation: Formication is the sensation of insects crawling under the skin and is a form of haptic (tactile) hallucination. Haptic hallucinations are superficial sensations on or under the skin in the absence of a real stimulus. Option (e), visceral hallucination, on the other hand, is a deep sensation involving inner organs without any real stimuli.

Reference and Further Reading: Puri BK, Hall AD (2002). *Revision Notes in Psychiatry.* London: Arnold, p. 154.

Question 10 Answer: a, Reciprocal inhibition
Explanation: The concept of systematic desensitization is largely based on the concept of reciprocal inhibition. The theory of reciprocal inhibition states that relaxation would help to reduce the anxiety levels, and that the two states cannot coexist. This has been proven to be a useful technique to treat patients with a lot of anticipatory anxiety, for example, in specific phobias. Patients, with the guidance of their therapist, are encouraged to identify increasingly greater anxiety-provoking stimulus and then to form a hierarchy of anxiety situations. During treatment, they are gradually exposed to situations lower in the hierarchy, with each exposure being paired with appropriate relaxation exercises.

Reference: Puri BK, Hall A, Ho R (2014). *Revision Notes in Psychiatry.* London: CRC Press, p. 28.

Question 11 Answer: d, Toxicity
Explanation: He has developed what is commonly known as lithium toxicity. This usually occurs due to dehydration. It is important to note that the therapeutic index of lithium is low, and therefore regular plasma lithium level monitoring would be required. At lithium plasma levels of greater than 2mM, the following effects could occur: hyper-reflexes, toxic psychosis, convulsions, syncope, oliguria, circulatory failure, coma and death.

Reference: Puri BK, Hall A, Ho R (2014). *Revision Notes in Psychiatry.* London: CRC Press, p. 254.

Question 12 Answer: a, Hyperactivity
Explanation: Hyperactivity is not considered to be one of the core symptoms of adult ADHD. In adult ADHD, the symptoms of ADHD tend to focus on the inattentive symptoms. The symptoms of hyperactivity would have improved with time.

Reference: Puri BK, Hall A, Ho R (2014). *Revision Notes in Psychiatry.* London: CRC Press, p. 631.

Question 13 Answer: b, Pneumocystis carinii
Explanation: Pneumocystis carinii is the commonest life-threatening opportunistic infection seen in patients with AIDS.

Reference and Further Reading: Puri BK, Treasaden I (eds) (2010). *Psychiatry: An Evidence-Based Text.* London: Hodder Arnold, p. 789.

Question 14 Answer: a, Alexia without agraphia
Explanation: He has alexia without agraphia. The explanation for the clinical presentation is as follows: after the stroke, the patient starts off with right hemianopia and he cannot read in the right visual field. Then, the words have to be seen on the left side, and are projected to onto the right hemisphere. There is a lesion in the splenium that prevents the transfer of information from the right to the left. As a result, the patient is unable to comprehend any written materials, although he can write. As time goes by, he develops a strategy of identifying the individual letters in the right hemisphere. Saying each letter aloud enables him to access the pronunciation of words in the left hemisphere.

Reference: Puri BK, Hall A, Ho R (2014). *Revision Notes in Psychiatry.* London: CRC Press, p. 107.

Question 15 Answer: b, Disturbance in attention
Explanation: Disturbance in attention is the most characteristic and consistent abnormality in delirium.

Reference and Further Reading: Puri BK, Treasaden I (eds) (2010). *Psychiatry: An Evidence-Based Text.* London: Hodder Arnold, pp. 94, 503, 511–513.

Question 16 Answer: c, Phenelzine and meperidine
Explanation: All combinations will lead to serotonin syndrome but there are reports that the combination of phenelzine and meperidine has led to death on several occasions. Meperidine is a narcotic pain killer.

Reference and Further Reading: Sharav VH (2007). Serotonin syndrome: A mix of medicines that can be lethal. *The New York Times.* New York: The New York Times Company; Puri BK, Treasaden I (eds) (2010). *Psychiatry: An Evidence-Based Text.* London: Hodder Arnold, pp. 874–875.

Question 17 Answer: c, Shaping
Explanation: The underlying psychological theory is shaping. Shaping refers to the successive closer approximations to the intended behaviour (in this case, not using cocaine at all) which are reinforced gradually in order to achieve the intended behaviour. This is in contrast to chaining, which teaches aspects of a more complicated behaviour, and in the later stages, the individual learned behaviours are then connected to achieve the desired response.

Reference: Puri BK, Hall A, Ho R (2014). *Revision Notes in Psychiatry.* London: CRC Press, p. 29.

Question 18 Answer: b, hearing, 'Peter, Peter'
Explanation: This condition is hypnagogic hallucination. Hypnagogic hallucinations are false perceptions that occur when falling asleep. These can be auditory, visual or

tactile. These hallucinations usually occur suddenly and the person believes it wakes him or her up. Hearing one's name being called is the most common hypnagogic hallucination. These phenomena may be considered normal even though they are real hallucinations.

Reference and Further Reading: Sims A (2003). *Symptoms of the Mind: An Introduction to Descriptive Psychopathology*. London: Saunders, p. 112.

Question 19 Answer: a, James–Lange theory
Explanation: James–Lange theory would best explain what James has had experienced. Based on the theory, the experience of emotion is secondary to the somatic responses that an individual experiences. Thus, in the case of James, when he sees the dog, there will be an increased activity of his sympathetic nervous system and his feelings of anxiety and fear are due to the result of the increased sympathetic activity. This is in contrast to Cannon–Bard theory, which proposes that both somatic responses and the experience of the emotions would occur concurrently.

Reference: Puri BK, Hall A, Ho R (2014). *Revision Notes in Psychiatry*. London: CRC Press, p. 53.

Question 20 Answer: c, Simple schizophrenia
Explanation: In simple schizophrenia, there is an insidious onset of decline in functioning. Negative symptoms develop without preceding positive symptoms. Diagnosis usually requires changes in behaviours for over at least 1 year, with marked loss of interest and social withdrawal.

Reference: Puri BK, Hall A, Ho R (2014). *Revision Notes in Psychiatry*. London: CRC Press, p. 355.

Question 21 Answer: c, Orobuccal apraxia
Explanation: This is an example of orobuccal apraxia. The patient usually has difficulties in performing learned, skilled movements of the face, lips, tongue, check, larynx and pharynx on command. This might be due to a lesion involving the left inferior frontal lobe and insula.

Reference: Puri BK, Hall A, Ho R (2014). *Revision Notes in Psychiatry*. London: CRC Press, p. 109.

Question 22 Answer: e, Anger
Explanation: All of the aforementioned are correct, with the exception of anger. With separation, the child initially responds by protesting. This might include crying and searching behaviour. In the second stage, the child would be in despair. This presents itself as marked apathy and misery from a belief that the mother would not be returning. Finally, detachment occurs, in which the child grows to become emotionally distant from and indifferent to his mother.

Reference: Puri BK, Hall A, Ho R (2014). *Revision Notes in Psychiatry*. London: CRC Press, p. 64.

Question 23 Answer: e, Mental retardation not otherwise specified
Explanation: In the ICD-10 classification system, the following are included under mental retardation: F70 Mild Mental Retardation, F71 Moderate Mental Retardation, F72 Severe Mental Retardation, F73 Profound mental retardation, F78 Other mental retardation and F79 Unspecified mental retardation.

Reference: Puri BK, Hall A, Ho R (2014). *Revision Notes in Psychiatry*. London: CRC Press, p. 19.

Question 24 Answer: b, Depression regularly worse in the evening
Explanation: In melancholia, depression should be regularly worse in the morning but not in the evening. Patients can display marked psychomotor retardation or agitation. Core features of melancholia include loss of pleasure in almost all activities and lack of reactivity to usually pleasurable stimuli.

Reference and Further Reading: American Psychiatric Association (2000). *Diagnostic Criteria from DSM-IV-TR*. Washington, DC: American Psychiatric Association; Puri BK, Treasaden I (eds) (2010). *Psychiatry: An Evidence-Based Text*. London: Hodder Arnold, pp. 8, 613.

Question 25 Answer: a, Check serum free thyroxine (FT4) and free triiodothyronine (FT3)
Explanation: The next step is to check serum FT4 and FT3 to exclude overt hyperthyroidism if the serum TSH level is less than 0.4 mU/L. This woman is confirmed to suffer from subclinical hyperthyroidism if FT4 and FT3 are within the *Reference* range but TSH is suppressed.

Reference and Further Reading: Puri BK, Treasaden I (eds) (2010). *Psychiatry: An Evidence-Based Text*. London: Hodder Arnold, pp. 575–576, 681.

Question 26 Answer: d, Last 12 months
Explanation: In order for the diagnosis to be made, the schizophrenia must have occurred within the last 12 months, with some symptoms still being present. The depressive symptoms must fulfil at least the criteria for a depressive episode and must be present for at least 2 weeks.

Reference: Puri BK, Hall A, Ho R (2014). *Revision Notes in Psychiatry*. London: CRC Press, p. 355.

Question 27 Answer: c, Hyponatraemia
Explanation: Hyponatraemia is common in old people receiving SSRI treatment. They present with lethargy, muscle ache and nausea. More severe cases present with cardiac failure, confusion and seizure.

Reference and Further Reading: Puri BK, Treasaden I (eds) (2010). *Psychiatry: An Evidence-Based Text*. London: Hodder Arnold, pp. 1110, 1112.

Question 28 Answer: d, Thought broadcasting
Explanation: The psychopathology that the prisoner is experiencing is known as thought broadcasting. Thought broadcasting reefers to the delusion that one's thoughts are being broadcast out loud so that they could be perceived by others around.

Reference: Puri BK, Hall A, Ho R (2014). *Revision Notes in Psychiatry*. London: CRC Press, p. 7.

Question 29 Answer: c, Patients with Huntington's disease will die in 5–10 years after the onset of visible symptoms.
Explanation: Patients with Huntington's disease will die in 20 years after the onset of visible symptoms.

Reference and Further Reading: Puri BK, Treasaden I (eds) (2010). *Psychiatry: An Evidence-Based Text*. London: Hodder Arnold, pp. 546–547, 1101; Walker FO (2007). Huntington's disease. *Lancet*, 369: 219.

Question 30 Answer: d, Construction apraxia
Explanation: The concept tested is constructional apraxia. The patient usually would have difficulties with reproduction of simple geometric patterns and demonstrate inability to connect the separate parts together. This might be due to lesions involving the nondominant parietal lobe.

Reference: Puri BK, Hall A, Ho R (2014). *Revision Notes in Psychiatry*. London: CRC Press, p. 108.

Question 31 Answer: e, Object permanence
Explanation: Babies between the ages of 8 and 12 months develop the ability to find hidden objects. This ability is known as object permanence, the understanding that objects continue to exist even when they are out of sight. This is one of the most important developments during the sensorimotor stage as the baby displays goal-directed behaviour, which, according to Piaget, is the foundation of problem solving.

Reference and Further Reading: Puri BK, Treasaden I (eds) (2010). *Psychiatry: An Evidence-Based Text*. London: Hodder Arnold, pp. 113115.

Question 32 Answer: e, Worthlessness
Explanation: Based on the DSM-IV-TR diagnostic criteria, the presence of the following symptoms would suggest major depressive episode:

1. Guilt about things other than actions taken or not taken by the survivor at the time of the death

2. Thought of death other than the survivor feeling that he or she would be better off dead or should have died with the deceased person
3. Morbid preoccupation with worthlessness
4. Marked psychomotor retardation
5. Prolonged and marked functional impairment
6. Hallucinatory experiences other than thinking that he or she hears the voice of, or transiently sees the image of, the deceased person.

Reference and Further Reading: American Psychiatric Association (2000). *Diagnostic Criteria from DSM-IV-TR*. Washington, DC: American Psychiatric Association; Puri BK, Treasaden I (eds) (2010). *Psychiatry: An Evidence-Based Text*. London: Hodder Arnold, pp. 110, 111, 123, 881–887.

Question 33 Answer: e, Imposing the appropriate cost
Explanation: All of the aforementioned are correct, with the exception of imposing an appropriate cost. The role of the doctor includes defining the illness, legitimizing the illness, imposing an illness diagnosis if necessary and offering appropriate help. Doctors therefore control access to the sick role, and they and patients have reciprocal obligations and rights.

Reference: Puri BK, Hall A, Ho R (2014). *Revision Notes in Psychiatry*. London: CRC Press, p. 119.

Question 34 Answer: a, Critical comments, hostility, emotional over-involvement
Explanation: The Camberwell Family Interview includes five scales; Critical Comments, Hostility, Emotional over-involvement, Warmth and Positive remarks. The first three scales have been associated with high expressed emotions and are predictive of relapse.

Reference: Puri BK, Hall A, Ho R (2014). *Revision Notes in Psychiatry*. London: CRC Press, p. 121.

Question 35 Answer: a, Marital separation
Explanation: Death of spouse, divorce and marital separation are rated high on the life change value. Martial separation is associated with a life change value of 65, marriage with a life change value of 50, pregnancy with a value of 40, birth of a child with a value of 39 and problems with boss with a value of 23.

Reference: Puri BK, Hall A, Ho R (2014). *Revision Notes in Psychiatry*. London: CRC Press, p. 122.

Question 36 Answer: d, Depressive pseudo-dementia
Explanation: The biological symptoms such as sleep disturbance, poor appetite and weight loss are equally common in both the young and the old. The presence of mood symptoms in association with memory difficulties would be more prevalent in the old.

Reference: Puri BK, Hall A, Ho R (2014). *Revision Notes in Psychiatry*. London: CRC Press, p. 710.

Question 37 Answer: e, Top-down processing
Explanation: In top-down (conceptually driven) perceptual processing, perception is the end result of an indirect process that involves making inferences about the world based on the observer's knowledge and expectations. In suboptimal viewing condition, knowledge of the world and past experience allow the observer to make inferences about identity of the stimuli.

Reference and Further Reading: Puri BK, Treasaden I (eds) (2010). *Psychiatry: An Evidence-Based Text*. London: Hodder Arnold, pp. 229, 238, 243.

Question 38 Answer: c, Waxy flexibility
Explanation: The psychopathology that the patient has is waxy flexibility. There is a feeling of plastic resistance resembling the bending of a soft wax rod as the examiner moves part of the person's body, and that body part remains 'moulded' by the examiner in the new position.

Reference: Puri BK, Hall A, Ho R (2014). *Revision Notes in Psychiatry*. London: CRC Press, p. 3.

Question 39 Answer: c, Obsession with alcohol
Explanation: Based on the ICD-10 criteria, his repeated thoughts should be described as preoccupation with alcohol rather than obsession with alcohol.

Reference: World Health Organisation (1994). *ICD-10 Classification of Mental and Behavioural Disorders*. Edinburgh, UK: Churchill Livingstone.

Question 40 Answer: e, Asomatognosia
Explanation: Asomatognosia, which is the lack of awareness of the condition of all or part of the body, occurs usually when there is an inherent insult to the nondominant parietal lobe of the body. Other associated signs and symptoms that might occur due to an insult to the dominant parietal lobe include dysgraphesthesia and Wernicke's or Broca's aphasia.

Reference: Puri BK, Hall A, Ho R (2014). *Revision Notes in Psychiatry*. London: CRC Press, p. 114.

Question 41 Answer: b, 2 months
Explanation: In DSM-IV-TR, the category of uncomplicated bereavement is designated for virtually all symptoms of depression experienced during the first 2 months after the loss, with the exception of extreme feelings of worthlessness or active suicidal ideation. If the duration is longer than 2 months, the patient is considered to suffer from major depression and warrants antidepressant treatment.

Reference and Further Reading: American Psychiatric Association (2000). *Diagnostic Criteria from DSM-IV-TR*. Washington, DC: American Psychiatric Association; Puri BK, Treasaden I (eds) (2010). *Psychiatry: An Evidence-Based Text*. London: Hodder Arnold, pp. 110, 111, 123, 881–887.

Question 42 Answer: b, 40 areas are being probed during the interview
Explanation: The LEDS assessment tool looks into only 38 areas and not 40 areas. The LEEDS is a semi-structured interview schedule, with 38 areas being probed. It comprises detailed narratives collected about events, including their circumstances. It has high reliability and high validity.

Reference: Puri BK, Hall A, Ho R (2014). *Revision Notes in Psychiatry*. London: CRC Press, p. 122.

Question 43 Answer: b, Halstead–Reitan Battery
Explanation: The Halstead–Reitan Battery is a comprehensive test battery that could detect damage to the brain and whether the damage is lateralized, and if so, which hemisphere has been affected. It could also determine whether this is associated with an acute or a chronic disorder. It also determines whether the damage is focal in nature or more diffuse.

Reference: Puri BK, Hall A, Ho R (2014). *Revision Notes in Psychiatry*. London: CRC Press, p. 92.

Question 44 Answer: a, In the preoperational stage, rules are believed to be inviolable.
Explanation: The preoperational stage occurs between ages 2 and 7. At this stage, the child believes that rules are inviolable. This is known as authority morality. Circular reactions are repeated voluntary motor actions (e.g. imitation of familiar behaviours), which provide the child a means of adapting their first schemas. This occurs in the sensorimotor stage. Conservation is achieved in the concrete operational stage, and object permanence is fully developed by the age of 18 months, during the sensorimotor stage.

Reference and Further Reading: Puri BK, Hall AD (2002). *Revision Notes in Psychiatry*. London: Arnold, pp. 70–71.

Question 45 Answer: b, 1–4 units
Explanation: The Royal College of Obstetricians and Gynaecologists recommend that small amounts of alcohol during pregnancy (not more than one to two units, not more than once or twice a week) have not been shown to be harmful. Alcohol is measured in units. One unit of alcohol is the equivalent of a half a pint of lager or beer, a glass of wine or a single shot of a spirit (gin, vodka, rum).

Reference: Royal College of Obstetricians and Gynaecologists (1999). Alcohol Consumption and the Outcomes of Pregnancy (RCOG Statement 5). http://www.rcog.org.uk /womens-health/clinical-guidance/alcohol-and-pregnancy-information-you.

Question 46 Answer: c, Conduct disorder
Explanation: The clinical diagnosis in this case would be conduct disorder. Based on the ICD-10 classification system, there must be a repetitive and persistent pattern of behaviour in which either the rights of others or of age-appropriate societal norms are violated. Based on the ICD-10, these symptoms must have lasted for the past 6 weeks.

Reference: Puri BK, Hall A, Ho R (2014). *Revision Notes in Psychiatry*. London: CRC Press, p. 637.

Question 47 Answer: c, Mirtazapine
Explanation: Mirtazapine is a noradrenaline and specific serotonin antagonist.

Reference and Further Reading: Puri BK, Treasaden I (eds) (2010). *Psychiatry: An Evidence-Based Text*. London: Hodder Arnold, pp. 426, 661, 907, 1110–1111.

Question 48 Answer: e, Running commentary
Explanation: Samuel is experiencing auditory hallucinations (second person) as well as running commentary (he could hear them commenting about his actions). Running commentaries are classified as part of mood-incongruent complex auditory hallucinations. This might include voices discussing the person in third person as well as thoughts spoken out loud (thought echo).

Reference: Puri BK, Hall A, Ho R (2014). *Revision Notes in Psychiatry*. London: CRC Press, p. 7.

Question 49 Answer: a, Bottom-up processing
Explanation: In bottom-up (data-driven) perceptual processing, perception is a direct process and determined by the information presented to the sensory receptors of the observer. In suboptimal viewing condition, raw sensory information is analysed into basic features such as colour or movement. These features are then recombined at higher brain centres, where they are compared to stored images.

Reference and Further Reading: Puri BK, Treasaden I (eds) (2010). *Psychiatry: An Evidence-Based Text*. London: Hodder Arnold, pp. 229, 238, 243.

Question 50 Answer: c, Alcoholic hallucinosis
Explanation: This is a particular disorder that usually presents or recurs in those who are still drinking. This condition is characterized largely by auditory hallucinations in clear consciousness. They tend to show good prognosis and usually have a good response to antipsychotics.

Reference: Puri BK, Hall A, Ho R (2014). *Revision Notes in Psychiatry*. London: CRC Press, p. 518.

Question 51 Answer: b, Huntington's disease
Explanation: This man presents with chorea, and the most likely diagnosis is Huntington's disease in this age group supported by family history. Option (e)

is possible but unlikely to start at this age. Option (a) causes neuropathy or myelopathy. Option (c) causes back and leg pain.

Reference and Further Reading: Ward N, Frith P, Lipsedge M (2001). *Medical Masterclass Neurology, Ophthalmology and Psychiatry*. London: Royal College of Physicians; Puri BK, Treasaden I (eds) (2010). *Psychiatry: An Evidence-Based Text*. London: Hodder Arnold, pp. 523, 546–547, 1101.

Question 52 Answer: b, Social-order-maintaining orientation
Explanation: According to Kohlberg, at the pre-conventional level, morality is externally controlled by punishment and rewards. At the conventional level, societal laws cannot be disobeyed as they ensure societal order (i.e. social-order-maintaining orientation) and interpersonal cooperation (i.e. good-boy/good-girl orientation). At the post-conventional level, morality is defined in terms of abstract principles (i.e. social-contract and universal ethical principle orientations).

Reference and Further Reading: Berk LE (2006). *Child Development* (7th edition). Boston: Pearson, pp. 488–492; Puri BK, Treasaden I (eds) (2010). *Psychiatry: An Evidence-Based Text*. London: Hodder Arnold, pp. 118–119.

Question 53 Answer: d, 48 hours
Explanation: Based on the ICD-10 criteria for acute stress disorder. For transient stress which can be relieved, the symptoms begin to diminish after 8 hours.

Reference and Further Reading: World Health Organisation (1994). *ICD-10 Classification of Mental and Behavioural Disorders*. Edinburgh, UK: Churchill Livingstone; Puri BK, Treasaden I (eds) (2010). *Psychiatry: An Evidence-Based Text*. London: Hodder Arnold, p. 660.

Question 54 Answer: e, He does not have specific phobia, as there is no avoidance behaviour in his case.
Explanation: In this clinical situation, he does not have a specific phobia, as in order for the diagnosis to be made, the fear he experienced needs to be out of proportion to the norm, and cannot be reasons or explained away, and be beyond voluntary control and must have led to avoidance.

Reference: Puri BK, Hall A, Ho R (2014). *Revision Notes in Psychiatry*. London: CRC Press, p. 405.

Question 55 Answer: e, Topiramate
Explanation: Topiramate has the least prophylactic effects against future manic episodes.

Reference and Further Reading: Puri BK, Treasaden I (eds) (2010). *Psychiatry: An Evidence-Based Text*. London: Hodder Arnold, pp. 538, 699, 905, 910.

Question 56 Answer: e, Memory disturbances
Explanation: All of the aforementioned are classical clinical signs and symptoms of mania, with the exception of memory impairment. The core symptoms for mania include increased self-esteem, decreased need for sleep, being more talkative than usual, having flights of ideas, been easily distracted and having an increase in goal-directed activity or psychomotor agitation. There might also be excessive involvement in activities that have a high potential for painful and sexual consequences.

Reference: Puri BK, Hall A, Ho R (2014). *Revision Notes in Psychiatry*. London: CRC Press, p. 378.

Question 57 Answer: a, Hypercalcaemia
Explanation: Hypercalcaemia causes constipation, bone pain, nephrolithiasis and psychiatric symptoms. On the other hand, hypocalcaemia causes Trousseau sign (inflating the blood pressure cuff and maintaining the cuff pressure above systolic will cause carpal spasms) and Chvostek's sign (tapping of the inferior portion of the zygoma will produce facial spasms). Option (b) to (e) can present acutely with movement disorder and confusion.

Further Reading: Puri BK, Treasaden I (eds) (2010). *Psychiatry: An Evidence-Based Text*. London: Hodder Arnold, p. 523.

Question 58 Answer: d, Rey–Osterrieth Test
Explanation: The Rey–Osterrieth Test would be capable of picking up these deficits. In this visual memory test, the subject is presented with a complex design. The subject is asked to copy the design, and then, 40 minutes later, without previous notification that this will occur, the subject is asked to draw the same design again from memory. Nondominant temporal lobe damage could lead to impaired performance on this test, whereas domain temporal lobe damage tends not to (but is associated with verbal memory difficulties).

Reference: Puri BK, Hall A, Ho R (2014). *Revision Notes in Psychiatry*. London: CRC Press, p. 95.

Question 59 Answer: b, Afro-Caribbean immigrants to the United Kingdom have a higher risk of schizophrenia.
Explanation: The option (b) is true. This phenomenon is seen in the second generation of immigrants. The higher prevalence of schizophrenia in urban areas is a result of the interaction of genetic factors, migration, higher rates of social deprivation and social problems in the inner city.

Reference: Puri BK, Hall A, Ho R (2014). *Revision Notes in Psychiatry*. London: CRC Press, p. 358.

Question 60 Answer: a, Tryptophan hydroxylase gene
Explanation: The aforementioned gene has been implicated in the aetiology of predisposing individuals towards bipolar disorders.

Reference: Puri BK, Hall A, Ho R (2014). *Revision Notes in Psychiatry*. London: CRC Press, p. 263.

Question 61 Answer: a, Narcolepsy
Explanation: The core symptom would be excessive daytime sleepiness. There would also be other symptoms such as hypersomnia, sleep attacks, cataplexy, hypnagogic hallucinations and sleep paralysis.

Reference: Puri BK, Hall A, Ho R (2014). *Revision Notes in Psychiatry*. London: CRC Press, p. 616.

Question 62 Answer: d, Post-schizophrenia depression
Explanation: Post-schizophrenia depression has been associated with an increased risk of suicide. Post-schizophrenic depression is diagnosed when there is prolonged depressive symptom when the psychotic symptoms have subsided and depression then occurs within 12 months of the schizophrenic episode.

Reference: Puri BK, Hall A, Ho R (2014). *Revision Notes in Psychiatry*. London: CRC Press, p. 354.

Question 63 Answer: d, Sertraline
Explanation: Sertraline causes most intense gastrointestinal side effects.

Reference and Further Reading: Puri BK, Treasaden I (eds) (2010). *Psychiatry: An Evidence-Based Text*. London: Hodder Arnold, pp. 425–427, 603.

Question 64 Answer: e, Facial expression can affect emotional response.
Explanation: Option (e) is true. Laird tested the facial feedback hypothesis in his study on the effects of facial expression on the quality of emotional experience. It was found that participants rated cartoon slides as funnier when they had a 'smiling' expression, than while they were 'frowning'. They also described feeling angrier when 'frowning' and happier when 'smiling'.

According to the James–Lange theory, physiological changes occur before emotions. It is the interpretation of these physiological changes that give rise to the experience of emotions.

Distress is not a primary emotion. Ekman identified six primary emotions: happiness, surprise, anger, disgust, fear and sadness.

According to the Cannon–Bard theory, the thalamus processes the emotion-arousing stimulus and then sends the signals to the cortex, where emotion is consciously experienced, and to the hypothalamus, where physiological changes are activated.

According to Lazarus, some degree of cognitive processing is a prerequisite for an emotional response to a stimulus. He proposed that such cognitive appraisal does not have to involve conscious processing and can be fairly automatic.

Reference and Further Reading: Laird JD (1974). Self-attribution of emotion: the effects of facial expression on the quality of emotional experience. *Journal of Personality and Social Psychology*, 29: 475–485; Lazarus RS (1982).Thoughts on the relations between emotions and cognition. *American Physiologist*, 37: 1019–1024; Puri BK, Treasaden I (eds) (2010). *Psychiatry: An Evidence-Based Text*. London: Hodder Arnold, pp. 166–176.

Question 65 Answer: e, Delusional perception

Explanation: Delusional perception refers to the delusional theme that events, objects or other people in one's immediate environment have a particular and unusual significance.

Reference: Puri BK, Hall A, Ho R (2014). *Revision Notes in Psychiatry*. London: CRC Press, p. 6.

Question 66 Answer: c, Daytime sleep attacks, cataplexy, hypnogogic hallucination

Explanation: Narcolepsy refers to the daytime sleep attacks without warning. Cataplexy are episodes of partial (often face or jaw) or complete loss of muscle tone that result in the patient falling to the ground. Hypnogogic hallucinations are pre-sleep dreams associated with sleep-onset REM activity. Catalepsy refers to waxy flexibility and is found in catatonia.

Reference and Further Reading: Ward N, Frith P, Lipsedge M (2001). *Medical Masterclass Neurology, Ophthalmology and Psychiatry*. London: Royal College of Physicians; Puri BK, Treasaden I (eds) (2010). *Psychiatry: An Evidence-Based Text*. London: Hodder Arnold, pp. 845, 847–848, 851.

Question 67 Answer: d, Based on the ICD-10, panic disorder is classified into panic disorder with agoraphobia and panic disorder without agoraphobia.

Explanation: Only the DSM-IV-TR but not the ICD-10 classifies panic disorder into panic disorder with agoraphobia and panic disorder without agoraphobia.

Reference and Further Reading: American Psychiatric Association (2000). *Diagnostic Criteria from DSM-IV-TR*. Washington, DC: American Psychiatric Association; World Health Organisation (1994). ICD-10 Classification of Mental and Behavioural Disorders. Edinburgh, UK: Churchill Livingstone; Puri BK, Treasaden I (eds) (2010). *Psychiatry: An Evidence-Based Text*. London: Hodder Arnold, pp. 649–650.

Question 68 Answer: d, It cannot be used to differentiate between dementia and delirium.

Explanation: The MMSE could help to differentiate between dementia and delirium. The MMSE is a brief test that can be routinely used to rapidly detect possible dementia, to estimate the severity of cognitive impairment and to follow the course of cognitive changes over time. It can be used to differentiate between delirium and dementia.

Reference: Puri BK, Hall A, Ho R (2014). *Revision Notes in Psychiatry*. London: CRC Press, p. 98.

Question 69 Answer: a, Blessed Dementia Scale
Explanation: The Blessed Dementia Scale is a questionnaire that can be given to a care-giver or relative for administration. There are three sets of questions within the questionnaire. The first set of questions deals with activities of daily living. The second set of questions deals with further activities of daily living. The third set of questions assesses changes in personality, interest as well as drive.

Reference: Puri BK, Hall A, Ho R (2014). *Revision Notes in Psychiatry*. London: CRC Press, p. 99.

Question 70 Answer: b, 0.05
Explanation: The prevalence of recent aggressive behaviour among outpatients with schizophrenia has been estimated to be around 5%.

Reference: Puri BK, Hall A, Ho R (2014). *Revision Notes in Psychiatry*. London: CRC Press, p. 370.

Question 71 Answer: e, This condition is a perceptual rather than ideational or cognitive disturbance.
Explanation: This condition is Doppelganger. The Doppelgänger phenomenon is the subjective feeling of doubling, where the person feels like his exact 'double' is present both outside alongside and inside oneself. Statement (e) is false because Doppelganger is an ideational or cognitive rather than perceptual disturbance.

Reference and Further Reading: Sims A (2003). *Symptoms of the Mind: An Introduction to Descriptive Psychopathology*. London: Saunders, pp. 217–220, 221, 400.

Question 72 Answer: d, Overt behaviour can lead to emotions without visceral changes.
Explanation: Two studies by Valins and Laird suggested that overt behaviour could lead to emotions without visceral changes. These two studies support the James–Lange theory. According to the James–Lange theory, the experience of emotion is based on the interpretation of bodily changes by the cortex. It is argued that the James–Lange theory emphasizes skeletal changes rather than visceral changes.

References and Further Reading: Puri BK, Treasaden I (eds) (2010). *Psychiatry: An Evidence-Based Text*. London: Hodder Arnold, pp. 168–169; Puri BK, Hall AD. 2002: *Revision Notes in Psychiatry*. London: Arnold, p. 42; Valins S (1966). Cognitive effects of false heart-rate feedback. *Journal of Personality and Social Psychology*, 4: 400–408; Laird JD (1974). Self-attribution of emotion: The effects of facial expression on the quality of emotional experience. *Journal of Personality and Social Psychology*, 29: 475–485.

Question 73 Answer: a, Verbal aggression
Explanation: Amongst schizophrenic patients, the most common type of violence would be verbal aggression. It has a prevalence rate of around 45%.

Reference: Puri BK, Hall A, Ho R (2014). *Revision Notes in Psychiatry*. London: CRC Press, p. 370.

Question 74 Answer: b, Iron deficiency
Explanation: In restless leg syndrome, the patient has an irresistible urge to move his or her body to stop uncomfortable or odd sensation. One in five patients have iron deficiency but three in four patients may have increased iron stores. Nevertheless, restless leg syndrome is associated with iron deficiency but not other mineral or electrolyte deficiency.

Further Reading: Puri BK, Treasaden I (eds) (2010). *Psychiatry: An Evidence-Based Text*. London: Hodder Arnold, pp. 682, 850, 851.

Question 75 Answer: b, Cambridge Examination for Mental Disorders
Explanation: The CAMDEX involves a structured clinical interview with the patient to obtain necessary information about his current condition as well as past history. In addition, a series of neuropsychological tests are also done. A structured interview with a relative or other informant to obtain further information is also conducted. It also includes a range of objective cognitive tests that constitute a mini-neuropsychological battery, known as the CAMCOG (Cambridge Cognitive Examination).

Reference: Puri BK, Hall A, Ho R (2014). *Revision Notes in Psychiatry*. London: CRC Press, p. 99.

Question 76 Answer: b, It occurs only in Malays and there has not been reports of Amok from any other countries.
Explanation: Reports of Amok from other countries do exist, thus questioning its position as a culture bound syndrome.

Reference: Puri BK, Hall A, Ho R (2014). *Revision Notes in Psychiatry*. London: CRC Press, p. 461.

Question 77 Answer: b, The DSM-IV-TR and ICD-10 specify PTSD with delayed onset.
Explanation: The DSM-IV-TR and ICD-10 specify PTSD with delayed onset if onset of symptoms is at least 6 months after the stressor. Options (a) and (e) are incorrect because the DSM-IV-TR but not the ICD-10 specifies acute and chronic PTSD. Option (d) is incorrect because acute PTSD is defined as the duration of symptoms is less than 3 months by the DSM-IV-TR.

References and Further Reading: American Psychiatric Association (2000). *Diagnostic Criteria from DSM-IV-TR*. Washington, DC: American Psychiatric Association; World Health Organisation (1994). *ICD-10 Classification of Mental and Behavioural Disorders*. Edinburgh, UK: Churchill Livingstone; Puri BK, Treasaden I (eds) (2010). *Psychiatry: An Evidence-Based Text*. London: Hodder Arnold, pp. 643, 660.

Question 78 Answer: c, Echolalia
Explanation: The correct answer should be echolalia. Echolalia refers to the automatic imitation by the person of another person's speech. It can occur even when the person does not understand the speech form. Vorbeireden refers to approximate answers and usually occurs in Ganser syndrome. Cryptolia refers to speech that is in a language which no one could comprehend. Neologism refers to a new word that is being constructed by the person or an everyday word which is now being used in a special way by the person. Perseveration differs from the answer (echolalia), in that in perseveration, usually both speech and movement are affected. Mental operations are continued usually beyond the point at which they are considered relevant.

Reference: Puri BK, Hall A, Ho R (2014). *Revision Notes in Psychiatry*. London: CRC Press, p. 4.

Question 79 Answer: e, Schachter–Singer theory
Explanation: According to the Schachter–Singer theory, the experience of emotion is a function of physiological arousal and the cognitive appraisal of that arousal in light of situational cues. Schachter states that the type of physiological arousal is immaterial; it is the cognitive labelling of the particular emotion that influences its conscious experience. This theory is also called Schachter's cognitive labelling theory.

Reference and Further Reading: Puri BK, Treasaden I (eds) (2010). *Psychiatry: An Evidence-Based Text*. London: Hodder Arnold, pp. 171–175.

Question 80 Answer: b, Length of QRS interval
Explanation: Amitriptyline is associated with an increase in length of QRS interval.

Reference and Further Reading: Puri BK, Treasaden I (eds) (2010). *Psychiatry: An Evidence-Based Text*. London: Hodder Arnold, p. 907.

Question 81 Answer: c, Normal-pressure hydrocephalus
Explanation: The triad of normal-pressure hydrocephalus is classically defined as memory loss, urinary incontinence and gait disturbance. Subdural haematoma is associated with a history of head injury. Neurosyphilis causes general paresis and is now extremely rare.

Reference and Further Reading: Ward N, Frith P, Lipsedge M (2001). *Medical Masterclass Neurology, Ophthalmology and Psychiatry*. London: Royal College of Physicians; Puri BK, Treasaden I (eds) (2010). *Psychiatry: An Evidence-Based Text*. London: Hodder Arnold, p. 583.

Question 82 Answer: e, The patient tries to resist his thoughts
Explanation: Resistance is seen in people with obsessive-compulsive disorder but not delusional disorder.

Reference and Further Reading: Puri BK, Treasaden I (eds) (2010). *Psychiatry: An Evidence-Based Text*. London: Hodder Arnold, pp. 656–659.

Question 83 Answer: d, Mirtazapine
Explanation: According to the NICE guidelines, mirtazapine should be the antidepressant of choice if a patient takes heparin or warfarin on a daily basis.

Reference: NICE Clinical Guidelines 9, 2010. www.nice.org.uk.

Question 84 Answer: b, Loss of alpha activity and increase in diffuse slow waves
Explanation: In Alzheimer's disease, there is loss of high-frequency (e.g. alpha or beta) activity and increase in diffuse slow waves. There is an increase in low-frequency (delta and theta) activity.

Reference and Further Reading: Ward N, Frith P, Lipsedge M (2001). *Medical Masterclass Neurology, Ophthalmology and Psychiatry*. London: Royal College of Physicians; Puri BK, Treasaden I (eds) (2010). *Psychiatry: An Evidence-Based Text*. London: Hodder Arnold, pp. 405, 1103–1104.

Question 85 Answer: b, This is a condition that strictly affects individuals of the Indian culture.
Explanation: It was previously also prevalent in Europe before masturbation was prohibited by religion and emission was considered as sin.

Reference: Puri BK, Hall A, Ho R (2014). *Revision Notes in Psychiatry*. London: CRC Press, p. 462.

Question 86 Answer: d, Piblotoq
Explanation: This is a dissociative state seen amongst Eskimo women. The patient would tear off her clothing, scream, cry and run about wildly. It might result in suicidal or homicidal behaviour.

Reference: Puri BK, Hall A, Ho R (2014). *Revision Notes in Psychiatry*. London: CRC Press, p. 462.

Question 87 Answer: e, Sertraline
Explanation: According to the NICE guidelines, sertraline should be the antidepressant of choice if a patient has history of cardiac diseases.

Reference: NICE Clinical Guidelines 9, 2010. www.nice.org.uk.

Question 88 Answer: c, This phenomenon is increased by attention.
Explanation: This phenomenon is pareidolic illusion. Pareidolic illusion refers to the type of intense imagery ('Monkey God') that persists even when the person looks at a real object (callus of a tree) in the external environment. The image and percept occur together and the image is recognized as unreal. Pareidolic illusion is increased by attention as the image becomes more detailed.

Reference and Further Reading: Sims A (2003). *Symptoms of the Mind: An Introduction to Descriptive Psychopathology*. London: Saunders, pp. 96–97.

Question 89 Answer: d, Imipramine
Explanation: This patient presents with metabolic acidosis and prolonged QTc. This clinical picture is classically related to tricyclic antidepressant overdose. Hence, the best answer is (d).

Reference and Further Reading: Puri BK, Treasaden I (eds) (2010). *Psychiatry: An Evidence-Based Text*. London: Hodder Arnold, p. 907.

Question 90 Answer: e, Meniere's disease
Explanation: A history of tinnitus and deafness in the context of episodic vertigo points towards Meniere's disease. If ataxia and/or facial weakness is also present, it points towards a cerebello-pontine angle lesion, e.g. acoustic neuroma.

Reference and Further Reading: Ward N, Frith P, Lipsedge M (2001). *Medical Masterclass Neurology, Ophthalmology and Psychiatry*. London: Royal College of Physicians; Puri BK, Treasaden I (eds) (2010). *Psychiatry: An Evidence-Based Text*. London: Hodder Arnold, pp. 559, 646.

Question 91 Answer: a, Transference
Explanation: Transference is likely to be what is hindering the progress of the therapeutic relationship between the patient and the therapist. Transference is an unconscious process in which the patient transfers to the therapist feelings, emotions and attitudes that have been experienced previously. This in turn would have an effect on the way the new relationship has developed.
Reference:
Puri BK, Hall A, Ho R (2014). *Revision Notes in Psychiatry*. London: CRC Press, p. 132.

Question 92 Answer: e, 16 weeks
Explanation: These maternal serum markers have been known to be elevated at around 16 weeks of gestational age.

Reference: Puri BK, Hall A, Ho R (2014). *Revision Notes in Psychiatry*. London: CRC Press, p. 665.

Question 93 Answer: d, 15%–20% increment
Explanation: Previous studies have indicated that there is up to 18% incidence of inheriting bipolar disorder.

Reference: Puri BK, Hall A, Ho R (2014). *Revision Notes in Psychiatry*. London: CRC Press, p. 285.

Question 94 Answer: d, Stagnant phase
Explanation: The stages of psychosexual development proposed include oral, anal, phallic, latency and also the genital phase.

Reference: Puri BK, Hall A, Ho R (2014). *Revision Notes in Psychiatry*. London: CRC Press, p. 133.

Question 95 Answer: b, Autistic disorder
Explanation: Based on the current DSM-5 criteria, two main symptom clusters should exist. This should include persistent deficits in social communication, social interaction across contexts and the ability to maintain relationships; as well as restricted, repetitive patterns of behaviour, interests or activities.

Reference: Puri BK, Hall A, Ho R (2014). *Revision Notes in Psychiatry*. London: CRC Press, p. 625.

Question 96 Answer: b, 5–6 years
Explanation: The peak age of onset of the aforementioned disorder is usually between 5 and 6 years.

Reference: Puri BK, Hall A, Ho R (2014). *Revision Notes in Psychiatry*. London: CRC Press, p. 639.

Question 97 Answer: d, Focused (selective) attention
Explanation: Selective attention is the ability to attend to one type of information while ignoring other distracting information. The unattended information is still being processed simultaneously and the listener can rapidly switch channels if appropriate, which is why Lucy can recognize her name being called.

Reference and Further Reading: Puri BK, Treasaden I (eds) (2010). *Psychiatry: An Evidence-Based Text*. London: Hodder Arnold, pp. 179–186; Puri BK, Hall AD (2002). *Revision Notes in Psychiatry*. London: Arnold, p. 16.

Question 98 Answer: e, The hallucinations respond favourably to antipsychotics.
Explanation: The hallucinations respond poorly to antipsychotics. The hallucinations may lead to persecutory delusions and it is termed as substance-induced psychotic disorder with hallucinations in DSM-IV. Auditory hallucinations are more common than visual hallucinations. The auditory hallucinations are well-localized, derogatory and in second person. The voices are called phonemes, which are fragmented words or short sentences.

Reference and Further Reading: Campbell RJ (1996). *Psychiatric Dictionary*. Oxford, UK: Oxford University Press; Sims A (2003). *Symptoms of the Mind: An Introduction to Descriptive Psychopathology*. London: Saunders, p. 100.

Question 99 Answer: d, Trazodone
Explanation: Trazodone is associated with priapism at high doses. It can be used as a hypnotic between 25 and 150 mg/day without causing tolerance, dependence or rebound insomnia.

Reference and Further Reading: Puri BK, Treasaden I (eds) (2010). *Psychiatry: An Evidence-Based Text*. London: Hodder Arnold, pp. 744, 912.

Question 100 Answer: c, Hyperkinetic disorder
Explanation: The diagnostic criteria for hyperkinetic disorder state that there must be a persistent pattern of inattention, hyperactivity and impulsivity across two different settings and this must have resulted in significant functional impairments. The diagnostic criteria also state that the onset should be prior to the age of 7.

Reference: Puri BK, Hall A, Ho R (2014). *Revision Notes in Psychiatry*. London: CRC Press, p. 631.

Question 101 Answer: d, Latency phase
Explanation: The sexual drive remains relatively latent during the latency stage, which typically occurs around the age of 5–6 years.

Reference: Puri BK, Hall A, Ho R (2014). *Revision Notes in Psychiatry*. London: CRC Press, p. 133.

Question 102 Answer: d, Narcissistic personality disorder
Explanation: All of the aforementioned could be located on both the ICD-10 and DSM-5, with the exception of narcissistic personality disorder.

Reference: Puri BK, Hall A, Ho R (2014). *Revision Notes in Psychiatry*. London: CRC Press, p. 439.

Question 103 Answer: a, Death of a close spouse
Explanation: Death of a close spouse has been considered to be the most stressful event with 100 life change units.

Reference: Holmes TH, Rahe RH (1967). The social readjustment scale. *Journal of psychosomatic research*, 11: 213–218.

Question 104 Answer: e, Temporal lobe
Explanation: This man is hallucinating a panoramic view which involves seeing a wide area. This is a form of complex hallucination and is found in people with temporal lobe epilepsy.

Reference: Nožica T, Marković D, Maračić L, Franko A, Gregorović E, Radolović-Prenc L (2006). Temporal lobe epilepsy with panorama hallucination. *Journal of Hospital Pula*, 3(3): 75–77.

Question 105 Answer: e, Being of high birth wright
Explanation: All of the aforementioned are factors that are deemed responsible for someone to develop schizophrenia. Low birth weight and urban birth have been known to be risk factors for schizophrenia.

Reference: Puri BK, Hall A, Ho R (2014). *Revision Notes in Psychiatry*. London: CRC Press, p. 360.

Question 106 Answer: b, Animus
Explanation: Based on his theory, the animus correctly describes the masculine prototype that is present within every individual.

Reference: Puri BK, Hall A, Ho R (2014). *Revision Notes in Psychiatry*. London: CRC Press, p. 133.

Question 107 Answer: d, It does not result in the subsequent avoidance of similar situations.
Explanation: In order to fulfil the diagnostic criteria, the onset of the panic disorder usually would result in a hurried exit and a subsequent avoidance of similar situations.

Reference: Puri BK, Hall A, Ho R (2014). *Revision Notes in Psychiatry*. London: CRC Press, p. 413.

Question 108 Answer: b, Charles Bonnet syndrome
Explanation: Charles Bonnet syndrome is characterized by the presence of complex visual hallucinations occurring in persons with visual impairment and no demonstrable psychopathology. The hallucinations vary from elementary (geometric figures) to complex hallucinations (seeing human figures or animals) and are more vivid than the limits of their impaired vision. There is usually insight that the hallucinations are not 'real' and the percepts may be modified by voluntary control. The syndrome is also associated with some fears of developing a mental illness.

Reference and Further Reading: Sims A (2003). *Symptoms of the Mind: An Introduction to Descriptive Psychopathology*. London: Saunders, pp. 104–105.

Question 109 Answer: a, Bupropion
Explanation: Bupropion is contraindicated because of seizure risk in bulimia nervosa. Fluoxetine has the best evidence to reduce binge eating, purging and psychological problems of bulimia nervosa. Higher doses of fluoxetine are required to treat bulimia nervosa compared with severe depressive disorder.

Reference and Further Reading: Puri BK, Treasaden I (eds) (2010). *Psychiatry: An Evidence-Based Text*. London: Hodder Arnold, pp. 611, 907, 913.

Question 110 Answer: b, Biological factors include the presence of elevated plasma dopamine levels.
Explanation: Biological factors include the presence of low plasma dopamine levels instead of elevated levels. It is true that conduct disorder is associated with the inheritance of antisocial traits from parents who have demonstrated criminal activities. Previous research has demonstrated an association with parental criminality as well as with repeated physical and sexual abuse.

Reference: Puri BK, Hall A, Ho R (2014). *Revision Notes in Psychiatry*. London: CRC Press, p. 635.

Question 111 Answer: d, Lack of control of the accident
Explanation: The aforementioned options are predisposing factors for PTSD, except option (d).

Reference and Further Reading: Puri BK, Treasaden I (eds) (2010). *Psychiatry: An Evidence-Based Text*. London: Hodder Arnold, pp. 660–661.

Question 112 Answer: c, Episiotomy during vaginal delivery
Explanation: This woman suffers from postnatal depression. Episiotomy during vaginal delivery or vaginal delivery is not an established risk factor for postnatal depression. Old age is an aetiological factor for postnatal depression.

Reference and Further Reading: Puri BK, Treasaden I (eds) (2010). *Psychiatry: An Evidence-Based Text*. London: Hodder Arnold, pp. 635–636, 722–724.

Question 113 Answer: c, Personality is not shaped by culture.
Explanation: Option (c) is false. Personality is shaped by culture and associated values and norms. Culture has a great impact on child-rearing patterns and this will ultimately shape personality. The term 'personality disorder' is culturally biased.

Option (b) is true. Culture has a pathoplastic effect on psychopathology because culture can influence overall psychopathology as well as individual symptoms. The contents of delusions and hallucinations can be modified according to cultural and prevalent social norms. For example, mustard gas formed a key component of delusions immediately after the Second World War, and attacks by terrorists formed a key component of delusions after the Iraq War.

Option (d) is true. Both hallucinations and paranoid thoughts are said to be more common in ethnic-minority groups who may feel persecuted by the mainstream culture. Ethnic-minority patients may not wish to reveal their true mental state to psychiatrists who are from the mainstream culture.

Option (e) is true. The nosological systems employed by psychiatry are largely anglocentric (e.g. DSM-IV-TR) and eurocentric (e.g. ICD-10). The DSM-IV-TR and ICD-10 diagnostic criteria assume that the mental illnesses commonly found in European patients present in the similar way in the non-European patients.

Reference and Further Reading: Bhugra D, Bhui K (2001). *Cross-Cultural Psychiatry: A Practical Guide*. London: Arnold.

Question 114 Answer: a, Alcohol dependence
Explanation: The usage of alcohol in an individual with anorexia nervosa is known to increase the incidence of mortality.

Reference: Puri BK, Hall A, Ho R (2014). *Revision Notes in Psychiatry*. London: CRC Press, p. 581.

Question 115 Answer: c, 5-HT2A/2C receptors
Explanation: The stimulation of 5-HT2A/2C receptors by SSRI would lead to sexual side effects. This is also associated with circadian rhythm disturbances.

Reference: Puri BK, Hall A, Ho R (2014). *Revision Notes in Psychiatry*. London: CRC Press, p. 230.

Question 116 Answer: a, Bruising
Explanation: Fluoxetine inhibits the metabolism of warfarin and increases bleeding tendency. This will lead to bruising.

Reference and Further Reading: Puri BK, Treasaden I (eds) (2010). *Psychiatry: An Evidence-Based Text*. London: Hodder Arnold, pp. 698, 708, 724, 762.

Question 117 Answer: e, This phenomenon is more common in women.
Explanation: This phenomenon is autoscopy. Autoscopy is a visual hallucination of seeing an image of oneself viewed from within one's physical body. The double imitates the movement and facial expressions of the original, as if being a reflection in a mirror, and typically appears as semi-transparent. Associated auditory, kinaesthetic and emotional perceptions are frequent. The autoscopic episode usually lasts for a few seconds with the subject seeing his own face, mostly occurs when lying in bed and is often accompanied by distress, fear, anxiety and depression. Autoscopy is more common in men with M:F ratio = 2:1. It also occurs in organic disorders such as parietooccipital lesions, temporoparietal lobes, epilepsy, schizophrenia and substance misuse. Neurological and psychiatric disorder can occur in 60% of cases.

Reference and Further Reading: Sims A (2003). *Symptoms of the Mind: An Introduction to Descriptive Psychopathology*. London: Saunders, pp. 105–106.

Question 118 Answer: c, Cocaine withdrawal
Explanation: Cocaine intoxication typically causes olfactory hallucination. Cocaine withdrawal causes depression, insomnia, anorexia, fatigue, irritability, restlessness and craving. Olfactory hallucinations are associated with the sense of smell and strong emotional component. The smell may or may not be pleasant and has a unique significance to the person.

Reference and Further Reading: Sims A (2003). *Symptoms of the Mind: An Introduction to Descriptive Psychopathology*. London: Saunders, p. 107.

Question 119 Answer: a, Family members did not agree with the premature discharge and their opinions were not sought.
Explanation: Negligence causes direct damage. Negligence occurs when a doctor deviates from fiduciary duty and dereliction. Option (b) refers to dereliction which means that a doctor must exercise a reasonable degree of knowledge and skills exercised by other members of the profession in similar circumstances. For option (c), damages include both physical and psychological harm. Option (e) refers to fiduciary duty which means that a doctor must act in the patient's best interests.

Reference and Further Reading: Puri BK, Treasaden I (eds) (2010). *Psychiatry: An Evidence-Based Text*. London: Hodder Arnold, pp. 1221–1222.

Question 120 Answer: e, Benjamin Rush
Explanation: Benjamin Rush and Samuel Merrit published the first textbook in psychiatry in 1812.

Reference: Puri BK, Hall A, Ho R (2014). *Revision Notes in Psychiatry*. London: CRC Press, p. 139.

Question 121 Answer: d, Bleuler
Explanation: It was in 1911 that Bleuler introduced the term schizophrenia, applied it to Kraepelin's cases of dementia praecox and expanded the concept to include what today may be considered schizophrenia spectrum disorders. He considered the symptoms of ambivalence, autism, affective incongruity and disturbance of association of thought to be fundamental, with delusions and hallucinations assuming secondary status.

Reference: Puri BK, Hall A, Ho R (2014). *Revision Notes in Psychiatry*. London: CRC Press, p. 351.

Question 122 Answer: b, Karl Ludwig Kalbaum
Explanation: Karl Ludwig Kahlbaum was responsible for coining the term 'catatonia'.

Reference: Puri BK, Hall A, Ho R (2014). *Revision Notes in Psychiatry*. London: CRC Press, p. 140.

Question 123 Answer: a, Autonomy, nonmaleficence, beneficence, justice
Explanation: The four core ethical principles are autonomy, non-maleficence, beneficence and justice. Autonomy refers to the obligation of a doctor to respect his or her patients' rights to make their own choice in accordance with their beliefs and responsibilities. Non-maleficence refers to the obligation of a doctor to avoid harm to his or her patients. Beneficence refers to the fundamental commitment of a doctor to provide benefits to patients and to balance benefits against risk when making such a decision. Justice refers to fair distribution of medical services or resources.

Reference: Puri BK, Hall A, Ho R (2014). *Revision Notes in Psychiatry*. London: CRC Press, p. 146.

Question 124 Answer: c, Munchausen syndrome
Explanation: In such a disorder, the patient would intentionally produces physical or psychological symptoms but the patient is unconscious about his or her underlying motives. Most of the time, the patient would have some prior working experience in the healthcare setting. Common presenting signs would include bleeding, diarrhoea, hypoglycaemia, infection, impaired wound healing, vomiting and rashes.

Reference: Puri BK, Hall A, Ho R (2014). *Revision Notes in Psychiatry*. London: CRC Press, p. 471.

Question 125 Answer: c, Sodium valproate

Explanation: In general, new anticonvulsants are more likely to cause visual side effects than the older anticonvulsants. For example, carbamazepine causes visual hallucination but relatively rarely. Gabapentin causes visual-field defects, photophobia, bilateral or unilateral ptosis and ocular haemorrhage. Topiramate causes acute onset of decreased visual acuity and/or ocular pain. Vigabatrin causes concentric visual-field defects.

Reference and Further Reading: Puri BK, Treasaden I (eds) (2010). *Psychiatry: An Evidence-Based Text*. London: Hodder Arnold, pp. 532, 538.

Question 126 Answer: e, Suggestive probes

Explanation: Open-ended questioning, reflective listening, summarizing and allowing for silence would be appropriate. Suggestive probes would not be appropriate as they tend to mislead the patient, and in this case (suicide risk assessment), it would be of importance to gather a precise and accurate history.

Reference: Puri BK, Hall A, Ho R (2014). *Revision Notes in Psychiatry*. London: CRC Press, p. 332.

Question 127 Answer: d, Mood refers to a static unidimensional emotion on a depression-mania spectrum with depression and mania at the extremes and euthymia in the middle.

Explanation: Option (d) is incorrect because mood is a dynamic and multidimensional emotion which includes normal variation such as happiness and reactivity to environments.

Reference and Further Reading: Poole R, Higgo R (2006). *Psychiatric Interviewing and Assessment*. Cambridge, UK: Cambridge University Press; Puri BK, Treasaden I (eds) (2010) *Psychiatry: An Evidence-Based Text*. London: Hodder Arnold, pp. 985–986.

Question 128 Answer: d, Emil Kraepelin

Explanation: In 1896, it was Emil Kraepelin who grouped together catatonia, hebephrenia, and the deteriorating paranoid psychosis under the name of dementia praecox. Dementia praecox has a poorer prognosis compared with manic-depressive psychosis, which has a better prognosis.

Reference: Puri BK, Hall A, Ho R (2014). *Revision Notes in Psychiatry*. London: CRC Press, p. 351.

Question 129 Answer: a, Admit own feelings and inform the patient that the staff are frightened of his aggression and anger.

Explanation: Option (a) may confuse the patient and give the wrong impression to the patient that the staff are incompetent in handling his aggression and anger. Patients with antisocial personality disorder may see this as weakness of the team and manipulate the situation by escalating his aggression and anger. Psychiatrist in this situation should deliver a clear and correct message to inform the patient that physical violence is not acceptable and there are chemical and physical interventions to help him to calm down.

Reference: Poole R, Higgo R (2006). *Psychiatric Interviewing and Assessment*. Cambridge, UK: Cambridge University Press.

Question 130 Answer: a, The theory emphasized that a doctor needs to be caring, compassionate, committed and conscientious in nature.
Explanation: The virtue theory emphasizes on the key personality qualities that a doctor would need. Plato and Aristotle emphasized that a doctor needs to be caring, compassionate, committed and conscientious in nature.

Reference: Puri BK, Hall A, Ho R (2014). *Revision Notes in Psychiatry*. London: CRC Press, p. 146.

Question 131 Answer: b, Oppositional defiant behaviour
Explanation: The ICD-10 classification system states that there must be a repetitive and persistent pattern of behaviour in which either the basic rights of others or major age-appropriate social rules are being violated. The minimum duration of the symptoms should last at least 6 months. It is important to note that children with oppositional defiant disorder tend to have temper tantrums, be very angry and spiteful, initiate arguments with adults, defy rules and blame others for it. It is crucial to note that children with oppositional defiant disorder should not have more than two symptoms related to physical assault, damage of properties and running away from school or home.

Reference: Puri BK, Hall A, Ho R (2014). *Revision Notes in Psychiatry*. London: CRC Press, p. 637.

Question 132 Answer: c, Amphetamines
Explanation: Amphetamines could cause excessive release of dopamine and this would usually lead to a hyper-excitable state. This might lead to symptoms such as tachycardia, arrhythmia, hyperthermia and irritability.

Reference: Puri BK, Hall A, Ho R (2014). *Revision Notes in Psychiatry*. London: CRC Press, p. 542.

Question 133 Answer: d, 5–14 days
Explanation: Lithium remains a first-line treatment for bipolar disorder. It has equal effectiveness in mania to valproate, carbamazepine, risperidone, quetiapine and first-generation antipsychotics. Its onset of action is around 5–14 days. Its antimanic effects are proportional to a plasma level between 0.6 and 1.2 mEq/L. Lithium shows a superior effect to placebo in acute bipolar depression.

Reference and Further Reading: Puri BK, Treasaden I (eds) (2010). *Psychiatry: An Evidence-Based Text*. London: Hodder Arnold, pp. 613, 623, 630, 632, 633, 909–910.

Extended Matching Items (EMIs)

Theme: Psychosexual development

Question 134 Answer: b, Anal phase

Explanation: The anal phase occurs from around 15–18 months to around 30–36 months of age. Erotogenic pleasure is derived from stimulation of the anal mucosa, initially through faecal excretion and later also through faecal retention.

Question 135 Answer: c, Phallic phase

Explanation: This phase takes place from around 3 years of age to around the end of the fifth year. Boys pass through the Oedipal complex. Girls develop penis envy and pass through the Electra complex.

Question 136 Answer: d, Latency period

Explanation: This is a phase that occurs from 5–6 years to the onset of puberty. The sexual drive remains relatively latent during this period.

Question 137 Answer: e, Genital phase

Explanation: It should be noted that from the onset of puberty to young adulthood, a strong resurgence in the sexual drive takes place. Successful resolution of conflicts from this and previous psychosexual stages leads to a mature well-integrated adult identity.

Reference: Puri BK, Hall A, Ho R (2014). *Revision Notes in Psychiatry*. London: CRC Press, p. 133.

Theme: Psychodynamic theory of defence mechanisms

Question 138 Answer: j, Turning against the self

Explanation: Turning against the self refers to how an impulse which is meant to express to another is now turned against oneself.

Question 139 Answer: l, Sublimation

Explanation: Sublimation refers to the process that utilizes the force of a sexual instinct in drives, affects and memories in order to motivate creative activities having no apparent connection with sexuality.

Question 140 Answer: m, Regression

Explanation: Transition, at times of stress and threat, to moods of expression and functioning that are on a lower level of complexity, so that one returns to an earlier level of maturity and functioning.

Question 141 Answer: e, Projection

Explanation: In projection, unacceptable qualities, feelings and thoughts or wishes are projected onto another person or thing. This is very often seen in paranoid patients.

Question 142 Answer: d, Undoing
Explanation: This refers to an attempt that is made to negate or atone for forbidden thoughts, affects or memories. This defence mechanism is seen, for example, in the compulsion of magic in patients with obsessive-compulsive disorders.

Reference: Puri BK, Hall A, Ho R (2014). *Revision Notes in Psychiatry*. London: CRC Press, p. 136.

Theme: Competency and capacity

Question 143 Answer: c, Testamentary capacity
Explanation: To make a will, a person must be of sound disposing mind. This means that the person must understand to whom he or she is giving personal property, understand and recollect the extent of personal property and understand the nature and extent of the claims upon the person, both of those included and of those excluded from the will.

Question 144 Answer: d, Capacity for informed consent
Explanation: It is the responsibility of the doctor to judge whether a patient has the capacity to give a valid consent. The doctor has a duty to provide information in a language understandable by a lay person about a condition, the benefits and the risks of a proposed treatment and alternatives to a treatment. The high court has held that an adult has capacity to consent to a medical or surgical treatment if he or she can (a) understand and retain the information relevant to the decision in question, (b) believe in the information and (c) weigh the information in balance to arrive at a choice.

Question 145 Answer: a, Capacity
Explanation: Competence is a legal concept and refers to the capacity to act and understand. Competence is determined only by the legal system, such as the competence to adopt a child.

Question 146 Answer: e, Advocacy
Explanation: An advocate enters into a relationship with the patient, to speak on his or her behalf and to represent the patient's wishes to stand up for his or her rights. An advocate has no legal status: the patient should have an idea of personal p*Reference*: s so that the advocate truly represents the patient's wishes.

Question 147 Answer: f, Appointeeship
Explanation: An appointee is someone authorized by the Department of Social Security to receive and administer benefits on the behalf of someone else who is not able to administer money derived from social security and cannot be used to administer any other income or assets. If benefits accumulate, application may need to be made to the Public Trust Office or the Court of Protection to gain access to the accumulated capital.

Reference: Puri BK, Hall A, Ho R (2014). *Revision Notes in Psychiatry*. London: CRC Press, p. 148.

Question 148 Answer: c, Naivety
Explanation: This refers to naivety because colour of skin, ethnicity and cultural identity play no role in this person's life.

Question 149 Answer: a, Acceptance
Explanation: This can be passive or active acceptance. This may also create conflict within oneself.

Question 150 Answer: e, Resistance and naming
Explanation: Although the full meaning of one's own cultural identity in the broader society is understood, this understanding may lead to anger and frustration.

Question 151 Answer: d, Redefinition and reflection
Explanation: Redefinition and reflection refer to the establishment of cultural identity in a person's own right.

Question 152 Answer: b, Multi-perspective internalization
Explanation: Multi-perspective internalization is the final stage when a person can appreciate his or her own cultural identity with pride.

Reference and Further Reading: Bhugra D, Bhui K (2001). *Cross-cultural Psychiatry: a Practical Guide*. Arnold: London.

Theme: Abnormal experiences

Question 153 Answer: g, Running commentary, i, Third person hallucination
Explanation: Running commentary is an auditory hallucination consisting of voices commenting on the patient's behaviour.

Question 154 Answer: c, Command hallucination, h, Second person hallucination
Explanation: Command hallucination is an auditory hallucination in which the voices command the person to perform certain acts.

Question 155 Answer: b, Hearing voices arguing, i, Third person hallucination
Explanation: The third person auditory hallucinations involve two voices arguing.

Question 156 Answer: e, Hygric hallucination
Explanation: Hygric hallucination is a superficial hallucination in which the person feels the presence of fluid in his or her body.

Question 157 Answer: d, Haptic hallucination
Explanation: Haptic hallucinations are superficial sensations of touch on or under the skin.

Question 158 Answer: j, Reduplicative hallucination
Explanation: Reduplicative hallucination refers to the sensation of the presence of a duplication of a certain body part.

Reference and Further Reading: Puri BK, Hall AD (2002). *Revision Notes in Psychiatry.* London: Arnold, p. 154.

Question 159 Answer: c, Illusion
Explanation: Illusion. It is an involuntary false perception in which a transformation of a real object (i.e. curtain) takes place.

Question 160 Answer: j, Visual hyperaesthesia
Explanation: Visual hyperaesthesia refers to changes in sensory perception in which there is an increased intensity of visual stimuli.

Question 161 Answer: b, Dysmegalopsia
Explanation: Dysmegalopsia (also known as the Alice in Wonderland effect); illusory change in the size and shape (both reduction and increase in size).

Question 162 Answer: d, Macropsia
Explanation: Macropsia refers to visual sensation of objects being larger than their actual size.

Question 163 Answer: f, Pareidolia
Explanation: Pareidolia refers to the type of intense imagery (i.e. Jesus' face) that persists even when the person looks at a real object (callus of a tree) in the external environment.

Question 164 Answer: g, Peduncular hallucination
Explanation: Peduncular hallucination is a form of vivid and colourful visual hallucination.

Reference and Further Reading: Puri BK, Treasaden I (eds) (2010). *Psychiatry: An Evidence-Based Text.* London: Hodder Arnold, pp. 234–237.

Theme: Type of prevention

Question 165 Answer: b, Secondary prevention
Explanation: Secondary prevention is usually directed at people who show early signs of disorder and the goal is to shorten the duration of the disorder by early and prompt treatment.

Question 166 Answer: a, Primary prevention
Explanation: Primary prevention efforts are directed at people who are essentially normal, but believed to be 'at risk' from the development of a particular disorder.

Question 167 Answer: c, Tertiary prevention
Explanation: Tertiary prevention is designed to reduce the severity and disability associated with a particular disorder.

Reference: Paykel ES, Jenkins R (1994). *Prevention in Psychiatry*. London: Gaskell.

Theme: Prevention strategies in schizophrenia

Question 168 Answer: d, Reduction in perinatal trauma, e, Reduction in stress associated with migration, f, Successful treatment of middle ear disease in childhood

Explanation: Primary prevention targets at people before the onset of schizophrenia and it includes reduction of schizophrenia-like psychosis, prevention of perinatal trauma and targeting at adverse social factors (e.g. stress associated with migration). Successful treatment of middle ear disease in childhood may reduce the risk of temporal lobe epilepsy and schizophrenia-like psychosis.

Question 169 Answer: b, Maintenance in antipsychotic treatment, c, Psychoeducation about schizophrenia

Explanation: Secondary prevention targets at people who have developed schizophrenia. Secondary prevention strategies include drug treatment and social treatment (e.g. psychoeducation of schizophrenia).

Question 170 Answer: a, Listen to loud stimulating music to drown out the auditory hallucinations not responding to antipsychotic treatment

Explanation: Tertiary prevention is designed to reduce the severity and disability associated with schizophrenia such as auditory hallucination not responding to treatment.

Reference: Paykel ES, Jenkins R (1994). *Prevention in Psychiatry*. London: Gaskell.

Question 171 Answer: a, Classical migraine

Explanation: Classical migraine may be associated with visual phenomena (fortification spectra) and most patients feel nauseated. Additional features such as weakness, paresthesia, aphasia, diplopia and visual loss are often worrying but can all happen as part of migraine aura.

Question 172 Answer: e, Orbital onset migraine

Explanation: Orbital onset migraine starts in and around the orbit.

Question 173 Answer: f, Occipital onset migraine

Explanation: Occipital onset migraine starts in the occipital area.

Question 174 Answer: h, Tension headache

Explanation: Tension headache

Reference and Further Reading: Ward N, Frith P, Lipsedge M (2001). *Medical Masterclass Neurology, Ophthalmology and Psychiatry*. London: Royal College of Physicians; Puri BK, Treasaden I (eds) (2010). *Psychiatry: An Evidence-Based Text*. London: Hodder Arnold, pp. 519–520.

Question 175 Answer: c, 9–11 years
Explanation: Children aged 9–11 years need more information and facts to gain control. They also try to avoid negative emotions by preoccupying themselves with activities.

Question 176 Answer: a, 3–5 years
Explanation: Children aged 3–5 years are usually confused and ask repetitive Questions regarding the deceased. They may display inappropriate reactions and have difficulty to understand abstract concept of death.

Question 177 Answer: b, 6–8 years
Explanation: Children aged 6–8 years understand death. They do not have ego-strength to cope and may blame themselves for the death. They may have magical thinking.

Question 178 Answer: e, 15–17 years
Explanation: Adolescents aged 15–17 years have grief reactions most similar to adults.

Theme: Clinical diagnosis

Question 179 Answer: f, Catatonic schizophrenia
Explanation: This person suffers from catatonic schizophrenia. When he was in the catatonic state, he exhibited waxy flexibility. Hence, he was described as still as a 'statue'.

Reference and Further Reading: Puri BK, Treasaden I (eds) (2010). *Psychiatry: An Evidence-Based Text.* London: Hodder Arnold, pp. 579, 925.

Question 180 Answer: k, Malignant catatonia
Explanation: This solider suffers from malignant catatonia.

Question 181 Answer: g, Depressive episode
Explanation: This woman suffers from moderate-to-severe depressive episode. The childbirth is a distractor because this patient does not meet the diagnostic criteria for postnatal depression as the onset of depression is too late. Her checking behaviour is secondary to low mood and pessimism.

Reference and Further Reading: Puri BK, Treasaden I (eds)(2010). *Psychiatry: An Evidence-Based Text.* London: Hodder Arnold, pp. 614–624.

Question 182 Answer: e, Bipolar disorder – manic episode
Explanation: This man is in the manic phase as evidenced by grandiosity (pursuing a PhD degree, advising the Prime Minister), delusion of persecution as a result of grandiosity (probably he thought that he was a celebrity and chased by paparazzi), dangerous driving and foolhardy investment in the food business. The patient

firmly believes that he suffers from schizophrenia but this is a distractor as he may hear mood-congruent auditory hallucination. The antidepressant was stopped as a result of antidepressant-induced mania.

Reference and Further Reading: Puri BK, Treasaden I (eds) (2010). *Psychiatry: An Evidence-Based Text*. London: Hodder Arnold, pp. 624–634.

Question 183 Answer: s, Psychotic depression
Explanation: This 50-year-old man exhibits nihilistic delusion and it is considered to be a mood-congruent delusion in patients with severe depressive episode.

Theme: Defence mechanisms

Question 184 Answer: c, Displacement
Explanation: This is displacement. Negative emotions are transferred from their original object to a less threatening substitute.

Question 185 Answer: i, Denial
Explanation: This is denial. The external reality of an unwanted or unpleasant piece of information is denied.

Question 186 Answer: b, Intellectualization
Explanation: He avoids disturbing feelings by engaging in excessive abstract thinking. This is intellectualization.

Reference and Further Reading: Puri BK, Hall AD (2002). *Revision Notes in Psychiatry*. London: Arnold, p. 168–169.

Theme: Concepts of dynamic psychotherapy

Question 187 Answer: k, Resistance
Explanation: This man is exhibiting resistance and the trainee cannot probe further.

Reference and Further Reading: Puri BK, Treasaden I (eds) (2010). *Psychiatry: An Evidence-Based Text*. London: Hodder Arnold, pp. 948–949.

Question 188 Answer: j, Process interpretation
Explanation: The trainee has performed process interpretation and attributed client's anger to his leave.

Reference and Further Reading: Puri BK, Treasaden I (eds) (2010). *Psychiatry: An Evidence-Based Text*. London: Hodder Arnold, pp. 947–953.

Question 189 Answer: b, Affirmation
Explanation: This process is known as affirmation.

Theme: General adult psychiatry

Question 190 Answer: a, Allport's theory

Explanation: Common traits are basic modes of adjustment applicable to all members of a society (e.g. the level of aggression of each member of a society can be assessed by a scale of aggression). Individual traits are unique sets of personal dispositions and ways of organizing the world based on life experiences.

Question 191 Answer: c, Eysenck's theory

Explanation: This is Eysenck's theory.

Question 192 Answer: b, Cattell's theory

Explanation: L-data (L stands for life) refer to ratings made by the observers. Q-data (Q stands for questionnaires) refer to the scores on personality questionnaires. T-data (T stands for tests) refer to the objective tests that are specifically designed to measure personality.

Question 193 Answer: d, Type A personality

Explanation: Type A personality is associated with increased systolic blood pressure, heart rate, plasma adrenaline, noradrenaline levels and cortisol levels.

Reference and Further Reading: Puri BK, Treasaden I (eds) (2010). *Psychiatry: An Evidence-Based Text.* London: Hodder Arnold, pp. 278–284.

INDEX

D

E

O

P

Q

R

S

T

U

V

W

Z

Relationship Economics

The Social Capital Paradigm and it's Application to Business, Politics and Other Transactions

LINDON J. ROBISON
and
BRYAN K. RITCHIE

Routledge
Taylor & Francis Group
LONDON AND NEW YORK

First published in paperback 2024

First published 2010 by Gower Publishing

Published 2016 by Routledge
4 Park Square, Milton Park, Abingdon, Oxon OX14 4RN

and by Routledge
605 Third Avenue, New York, NY 10158

Routledge is an imprint of the Taylor & Francis Group, an informa business

Publisher's Note
The publisher has gone to great lengths to ensure the quality of this reprint but points out that some imperfections in the original copies may be apparent.

Gower Applied Business Research
Our programme provides leaders, practitioners, scholars and researchers with thought provoking, cutting edge books that combine conceptual insights, interdisciplinary rigour and practical relevance in key areas of business and management.

British Library Cataloguing in Publication Data
Robison, Lindon J.
Relationship economics : the social capital paradigm and
its application to business, politics and other transactions.
1. Social capital (Sociology) 2. Social capital
(Sociology)--Economic aspects. 3. Economics--Sociological aspects.
I. Title II. Ritchie, Bryan K.
306.3-dc22

Library of Congress Cataloging-in-Publication Data
Robison, Lindon J.
Relationship economics : the social capital paradigm and it's application to business, politics and other transactions / by Lindon J. Robison and Bryan K. Ritchie.
p. cm.
Includes index.
ISBN 978-0-566-09169-8 (hbk.)
1. Economics--Sociological aspects. 2. Social capital (Sociology) I. Ritchie, Bryan K. II. Title.
HM548.R63 2010
306.3--dc22
2009037461

ISBN 13: 978-0-566-09169-8 (hbk)
ISBN 13: 978-1-03-292374-1 (pbk)
ISBN 13: 978-1-315-60470-1 (ebk)

DOI: 10.4324/9781315604701

Contents

List of Figures

List of Tables

Reviews for *Relationship Economics*

"Social relationships shape who we are, what we value and how we make our way in the world, yet paradoxically the social sciences have often struggled to incorporate this reality into how we understand human behavior and inform policy priorities, focusing instead on individuals or institutions. Robison and Ritchie correct this imbalance by revisiting Adam Smith's notion of sympathy, using it to outline a fascinating new framework for restoring social relations to the center of our deliberations of business, politics and community life."

Michael Woolcock, World Bank

"Robison and Ritchie have written a tour de force that shows the importance of social capital (what they call relationships economics) in relation to power, culture, globalization, poverty, ethics, and politics. The book stimulates thought and research ideas regarding social capital's role in diverse realms from intimate relations to community development to high finance and national cultural differences and international politics. The frequent boxes with apt real-world examples make the book accessible to undergraduate students and academic researchers alike."

Jan Flora, Iowa State University

"Accessible and well-written, the book shows how the creation and maintenance of relationships allows achievement of individual and collective goals in a manner that is often efficient, equitable and productive. Mobilizing a large body of scholarly literature, introducing myriad useful concepts, and sharing findings from the authors' own ground-breaking research, the book demonstrates that in satisfying others' socio-emotional needs, we become better able to reach mutually beneficial ends. In so doing, Relationship Economics *presents a compelling alternative to the radically individualistic outlooks that have been the target of a growing chorus of social criticism."*

Steven J. Gold, Michigan State University

"With a convincing array of examples... They document how social capital can make major differences not only in individual transactions, but in success versus failure of both corporations and sovereign economies in developing countries. Furthermore, their arguments sound a word of alarm about declining social capital in developed counties that are increasingly reliant on impersonal electronic trading and big-box retailing, and increasingly lacking the ethics of work, thrift, and honesty. This book is essential reading for anyone interested in the role of social capital in economics or the potential failures of typical economic analysis."

Richard E. Just, University of Maryland

"This book makes clear the need to put community back into business and economics. It is rich with a wide-variety of examples and cases to help this essential task."

Gary Lynne, University of Nebraska-Lincoln

Preface

Few concepts have traveled across the social sciences as well as social capital theory. Political scientists, sociologists, economists, business scientists, and anthropologists to name a few have all made important applications of social capital, leading some to hope for increased cooperation and understanding among social science colleagues.

While the shared interest in social capital offers hope for increased collaboration, there are significant challenges that must be satisfied for this cooperation to occur. The main challenge is that different disciplines view new concepts and theories from their specific perspectives and traditions. Deep-seated biases work against the acceptance of new ideas and cross-fertilization can be as threatening as it can be liberating. To be successfully adopted and applied cooperatively across the social sciences, we need a new paradigm that demonstrates how each of the social sciences contributes to applications and understanding of social capital. This paradigm must include a definition of social capital consistent with both capital and social, and that leads to testable hypotheses and measureable outcomes. Finally, we need a paradigm that connects the contributions of the various social capital scholars into one whole—making them all synergistic.

This book does precisely that. It demonstrates the interdisciplinary nature of social capital theory. It defines social capital along the lines of Adam Smith as the sympathy between people, and defends it as being consistent both with capital and social. It then uses examples to demonstrate how social capital leads to both testable and measureable outcomes. It connects some important contributions from several of the social sciences into one paradigm and demonstrates the synergism that results. The outcome of combining different views has been to create a rigorous paradigm for social capital that clarifies when and where relationships matter in our social exchanges, especially our economic exchanges. From this theoretical foundation we are able to uncover insights into important social issues, including poverty, income distribution, globalization, and the political interaction between rulers and citizens, among others.

Like all books, but especially those with a multi-disciplinary focus, this work would not have been possible without a tremendous amount of input, both monetary and intellectual. In what was probably the most intensive effort to bring together scholars from different disciplines and perspectives, Dr. Kenneth Kory, former Dean of the College of Social Science at Michigan State University created the Social Capital Interest Group (SCIG), a multidisciplinary team of scholars with the charge of developing a definition of social capital that could be accepted by various disciplines. To this end, SCIG organized the first international conference on social capital in 1998, "Bridging Disciplines, Policies and Communities" with generous financial and other support from Dr. Lou Anna K. Simon, former Provost and current President of Michigan State University along with many other sponsors from the university and private foundations. More than 250 domestic and international scholars, graduate students, and practitioners attended the conference. In addition to seeking common definitions and perspectives, the conference discovered new applications for social capital in education, economic development, poverty reduction, immigration, and other fields.

Building on this initial effort, Marcelo E. Siles and others created the Michigan State University Social Capital Initiative. With support from Michigan State University's Provost Office, College of Social Science, College of Agricultural and Natural Resources, and the Michigan Agriculture Experiment Station, SCI promoted both research and teaching to extend the theory and application of social capital throughout multiple disciplines. This book is the culmination of much of the findings of these earlier research efforts and owes much of its insights to the fertile academic environment created by the SCIG and SCI.

Additional research for the book was funded by generous grants from the James Madison College at MSU, the Office of Research and Graduate Studies at MSU, and the Andrew W. Mellon Foundation.

In particular we recognize the important contributions of Marcelo E. Siles to this work. Many of his efforts, often with colleagues, are reported in this book and gratefully acknowledged. We are also grateful to a number of colleagues who read portions or all of the manuscript at various points of completion, and in particular A. Alan Schmid. It has also been a joy to work with Gower Publishing and its extremely capable editorial staff. We're grateful for the efforts of all of these people in reducing the errors of thought, writing, and reason in earlier versions. Any errors that remain are ours.

Finally, in addition to tremendous financial, intellectual, and editing support, we have been blessed by the emotional support of our families in ways that have enriched our lives and made our work on this project possible. To these people, especially Bonnie and Susan, we dedicate this work.

Lindon J. Robison and Bryan K. Ritchie
East Lansing, Michigan, USA

CHAPTER 1 *Introduction: Relationships Matter*

No man is an island entire of itself; every man is ... part of the main .... Any man's death diminishes me because I am involved in mankind; and therefore never send to know for whom the bell tolls; it tolls for thee ...

John Donne, Meditation XVII, Devotions upon Emergent Occasions, (1624).

Introduction

The poet John Donne claimed that we are all connected. We agree. And, because we are all connected, relationships matter—a lot. For the individual, relationships matter because they influence where we live, what we study, our economic and social well-being, how we earn our living, and with whom we interact. For the larger units of society, relationships matter because they influence the adoption of laws, economic activities, care of the environment, and with whom we write treaties and go to war. Because relationships matter—a lot—we need to pay more attention to how, why, where and when they do matter.

Trying to reach one's economic and social goals without paying attention to relationships is like trying to navigate blindfolded through a crowded lobby on the way to an important meeting. As we attempt to navigate without sight we bump into each other in ways that hinder our progress and irritate others. With help along the way, in the form of direction and encouragement from our friends, we can successfully cross the lobby.

This book aims to describe relationships and how to manage them in such a way to make it easier to achieve economic, political, and social objectives more efficiently, and with greater return and equity. We wrote this book because insufficient attention is paid to relationships and their importance in achieving almost all our social and economic objectives. Someone once quipped that fish were the last to discover water. Humans, it seems, sometimes appear to have not yet discovered that the waters we swim in are relationships. We are literally in a crowded room of relationships, and our ability to navigate depends on our ability to manage these relationships. The opportunities for successful isolationists are limited.

The focus of this book, simply stated, is to explain how relationships—an invisible resource—influence our ability to take care of friends and business. Our tool for explaining how relationships matter and how we can use them to care for friends and business is the Social Capital Paradigm. So let's begin at the beginning by exploring what John Donne

WINNING FRIENDS AND WINNING AT BUSINESS

The grandfather of people-skills books is *How to Win Friends and Influence People*. Written by Dale Carnegie, this relationship-focused book has sold over 16 million copies. In an editorial review for Amazon, Joan Price wrote that Carnegie's book is successful because "it teaches readers the underlying principles of dealing with people so that they *feel important and appreciated*."

Source: http://cc.msncache.com/cache.aspx?q=72893285550667&mkt=en-US&lang=en-US&w=dal9e3f3&FORM=CVRE3 (emphasis added).

may have meant when he wrote that we are all connected or, in the language of this book, that relationships matter.

How We Are Connected

The easiest way to observe that relationships matter is by simply examining our physical and economic connections. We do not make our own clothes, build our own homes, raise our own food, or perform our own healthcare services. We depend on others for these products and services and thousands of others that could be listed. These economic connections are made possible because of specialization and trade that improve our economic well-being compared to the lives we would lead if we tried to supply all our own economic needs.

In addition to economic needs we also have socio-emotional needs. These include the need to experience caring, the need for validation, and the need to be informed about each other, events affecting our lives, our surroundings, and the outcomes of our choices. Just as our economic needs require that we be economically connected, our socio-emotional needs require that we be socially connected. It would be just as difficult to satisfy our socio-emotional needs in isolation as it would be to satisfy our economic needs in isolation.

HAPPIER TOGETHER

Simple interactions such as exchanging chit-chat over coffee at the local diner, helping out at a churchyard bake sale, or raising a voice at a school board meeting are the kinds of pleasures money cannot buy, and a new study says they may be more important than money to people's happiness.

This study, a nationwide survey conducted by Harvard University and the Center on Philanthropy at Indiana University, examined "social capital"—the connections that bind people together and strengthen the places they live. Researchers found that areas where residents had high civil involvement were happier than those with more wealth but less community participation.

Source: Associated Press (2001).

Despite claims that socio-emotional needs and the socio-emotional goods (SEGs) that satisfy them are important, social scientists, especially economists, have given them far less attention than economic needs and economic goods. Indeed, when economists teach and research the various elements of our economic system, the analysis most often takes

place from the perspective of impersonal participants organizing to produce, finance, market, and consume economic goods and services in the most efficient manner. What is missing from most economic analysis is the recognition that economic agents have important socio-emotional needs that require SEGs to satisfy. Perhaps we ignore our socio-emotional needs and SEGs because of the difficulty we have when we attempt to identify them. Indeed, our efforts to measure our emotional health usually lead us to seek physical manifestations of our consumption of SEGs.

Consider the challenge we face when attempting to describe our SEGs and the value derived from our socio-emotional exchanges. We cannot observe directly what happens inside us where our emotions dwell when we are greeted in a caring manner or when our work is acknowledged as important by someone whose opinions we value. We cannot observe directly how the exchange of SEGs changes our relationships when gifts are exchanged or service is rendered. We cannot count the negative SEGs produced by our separation from family and friends who most often are the source of our experiences of caring and validation. We cannot write down precisely an equation to describe the need for SEGs. And there is no weight or volume measure associated with our need for information that captures our attention and energy even when knowing isn't important to our physical well-being or safety. Yet, we know that SEGs are important because they produce physical responses, including educational achievements.

SMALLER (AND MORE CONNECTED) IS BETTER

William Raspberry writes: "Bill Gates believes that one of the problems with America's high schools is that they are too big to allow for meaningful connections." Mr Gates, putting his money where his mouth is, donated $51.2 million to create 67 small high schools in New York City.

Prior to Mr Gates' announcement, the Commission on Children at Risk had just issued a report in which it argued that the loss of connectedness is devastating America's youth. The report listed symptoms associated with a loss of connectedness that included "major depression, suicide attempts, alcohol abuse, and a wide variety of physical ailments, including asthma, heart disease, irritable bowel syndrome, and ulcers."

The commissioners who wrote the report, many of whom are physicians and mental health professionals, say that human beings have an inborn need for connections: first with their parents and families, then with larger communities. They added that the weakening of the connections between children and their extended families and communities is producing a virtual epidemic of emotional and behavioral problems.

Source: Raspberry (2003).

Harlow's study of monkeys produced other important evidence of the connection between physical and emotional well-being.

THE INTERDEPENDENCE OF OUR SOCIO-EMOTIONAL AND ECONOMIC WELL-BEING

Harlow demonstrated that a monkey's emotional and physical well-being is connected. We intend to demonstrate that our economic and socio-emotional well-being is connected.

A (MONKEY'S) MOTHER'S LOVE

The important insight that our socio-emotional and physical well-being is connected was demonstrated by sick monkeys in a University of Wisconsin lab. The lab was operated by Harry Harlow who imported monkeys from India. Occasionally, the monkeys arrived with serious diseases, which often spread among the other monkeys in the lab. Harlow and his staff attempted to solve the disease problem by isolating sick monkeys, including newborn monkeys, from their mothers. The isolation dumbfounded the newborn monkeys, who would often sit rocking, staring into the air, and sucking their thumbs. Later, when the isolated monkeys matured and were brought together to breed, they backed away from each other and refused contact.

Then researchers found that the little monkeys were fanatically attached to cloth diapers that lined the cages to provide a little softness and warmth against the floor. Harlow wondered if the cloth was substituting for a mother's love. His idea that mother's love was essential for a healthy monkey was in opposition to the prevailing theory—that babies didn't love their mothers or need them, except for food. To prove his point, Harlow and his colleagues created cloth dolls with heads. If the head of the doll was changed, the baby monkeys screamed because they bonded to a particular face.

The critical test of the importance of love was when Harlow and his colleagues created a wire mother that held a baby bottle with food. The monkeys were then allowed to choose between the wire mothers with food versus the barren, cloth mothers. If the infant–mother relationship was based on food, then the bottle-holding surrogate would be chosen whenever she had the food advantage. However, the monkeys chose the cloth surrogate mothers:

> *The graphs that reported the time the monkeys spent with the wire surrogate mother versus the time they spent with the cloth surrogate mothers showed that by the age of six months, monkeys are spending about eighteen hours a day with the cloth mom. The graphs seem to have invisible writing running through them, saying that food is sustenance but a good hug is life itself.*

Source: Blum (2002: 159).

Indeed, the main point of this book is that our economic and socio-emotional well-being is interdependent because the flow of physical and SEGs and services travel together. And because our socio-emotional and economic transactions are interdependent, efforts to understand or describe them separately will likely lead to inaccurate representations of human activities. Indeed, to make the warning explicit and to place the theme of this book in plain view, we restate our basic claim: our physical, economic, and socio-emotional well-being depend on relationships.

THE FLOWER FUND

Consider an example of what may happen when we ignore the SEGs embedded in an economic good. In some departments at the university where we are employed, it is the custom to maintain a flower fund. Faculty and staff contribute to the fund. Then, when someone is in the hospital or their family experiences an important event such as a birth, a serious accident or a death, flowers are sent to the hospital or mortuary in the name

MAKE FRIENDS AND LIVE LONGER (AND HAPPIER)

Researchers monitored the health of nearly 7,000 Californians over 17 years. They found that those lacking social connections were two to three times more likely to die prematurely than their more socially connected counterparts. This was true regardless of age, gender and health practices.

A study of nearly 1,400 people with heart disease found that those with a spouse or confidant died at about one-third the rate as those who had no one in whom to confide. This was true regardless of the severity of the heart disease.

Researchers who exposed 276 healthy volunteers to a cold virus found that those with more diverse social networks were somehow more disease-resistant: Only 35 percent of those with six or more social relationships actually came down with a cold, as opposed to 62 percent of those with three social relationships or fewer. Again, differences in overall health or health habits could not "explain away" these findings.

Source: "Answers for Healthier Living" (1999).

of the department. A department staff member orders and pays for the flowers so that contributors to the fund are sometimes unaware of any particular disbursement.

The flower fund operates efficiently—much more efficiently than if an individual faculty or small groups of faculties had to collect funds and order flowers each time a flower-worthy event occurred. In addition, the system is more equitable because those willing to contribute to flowers would likely vary depending on the intended recipient. Indeed, one important benefit of the efficient flower fund collection and distribution system is that it ensures that even unpopular colleagues will be recognized in times of distress.

Still, something seems awry with the way the flower fund operates. In this example, the desire for efficiency has minimized transaction costs. But what makes the flower a valued gift *is* the high transaction costs that embed the flower with SEGs. High transaction costs reflect the personal involvement of those sending the flower. Absent these costs, the flower loses most of its value and becomes only a commodity.

The flower fund teaches that the relationship between people can change the value of the good they exchange. Identical flowers enjoyed under identical circumstances may provide identical sight and smell value and therefore claim an equal economic value. But the validation value of the flower to the recipient depends on who sent it and how difficult it was to do so. A flower sent by a jealous co-worker who may be taking advantage of an illness has a negative validation value. A flower from co-workers who feel an obligation to provide a flower may have a positive value but not as much as the flower from a person who surprises you with her caring. This unexpected flower provides the recipient with unexpected validation greater than that provided by the flower sent under obligation.

The flower fund also teaches that we reveal our relationships by the way we organize to give gifts and more generally in the way we participate in economic activities. The case of the faculty flower fund says something about the relationships among the faculty. Since donating to the fund is voluntary it says that good will in the department is sufficient to sustain the fund. It also says that it's okay for individuals to donate different amounts

depending on their circumstances, an expression that the effort is fair. We also learn that colleagues care about each other, but at a respectful distance.

Finally, the flower fund teaches that there will always be a sort of ambiguity in our exchanges with each other. For example, many motives may prompt donations to the flower fund. Some may donate out of genuine caring. Others may view their contributions as an insurance scheme to which they contribute, thereby ensuring themselves against the unhappy prospect of facing sickness or death unacknowledged. Others may have a combination of motives. So, in this book, we will always be fairly tentative in ascribing motives. But we will, with some energy, protest against the assumption that nearly all behavior is motivated by selfish preferences—an assumption that underlies so much of economic analysis. We address the details of this claim more fully in Chapter 4.

Our Ambivalence Toward Relationships

Asserting that relationships matter in almost everything we do sometimes causes a conflict between what we want to believe and what actually exists. Many economists believe that markets organize production and consumption activities in the most efficient way possible, given existing distributions of resources. Most formal economic models do not consider relationships. Many bankers want the public to believe that loan approval depends on objective financial criteria. Lending activity based on relationships can sometimes be illegal and, in a survey of Michigan bankers, most declared relationships did not influence their decision (Siles, 1992). Some medical-care providers want to project an image of caregivers whose service provision is independent of relationships between medical personnel and their patients. Employers—especially government employers—want the public to believe that the employment offers depend solely on the applicant's job skills. And current college admission procedures are being challenged because they consider an applicant's ethnic backgrounds (a special kind of relationship) as well as merit.

Allowing relationships to alter outcomes often makes us uncomfortable because our ethical senses are usually associated with arm's-length outcomes. To admit "it's who you know" that determines one's success violates our sense of fair play that emphasizes merit. Recognizing that relationships alter outcomes, we often take steps to reduce the influence of relationships.

For example, reviews of articles submitted to many professional journals are conducted anonymously. Unless relationships influenced reviews, anonymity in the review process would be unnecessary. Anonymity, however, appears to be justified since the evidence indicates that relationships *do* influence the outcomes of the review process (Blank, 1991).

The symbol of our courts, Lady Justice, wears a blindfold. She wears a blindfold because we believe that justice requires that her decisions not be influenced by her relationship with the individuals before the bar. Jury selection is based on the assumptions that relationships may alter verdicts and that only jurors with arm's-length relationships to the defendant are considered.

Civil rights laws preclude employment being denied when the basis of the discrimination is race. These laws recognize that race, a special kind of relationship, sometimes influences employment decisions. Finally, we often disparage such groups as

"old boys' (girls') clubs" because they convey privileges based on relationships that are not available to those outside the club. Then we pass laws limiting the acceptable traits over which discrimination can be practiced. Nepotism laws, imposing restrictions on close relatives being hired by government employers in the same agency, are designed to ensure that employment offers are based on merit, not relationships. These laws are necessary because of the tendency of some government employers to grant advantages to their relatives. We react strongly when it is revealed that public officials have offered favors on the basis of personal relationships.

NEPOTISM IN THE CITY

Critics of Warren Michigan Mayor Mark Steenbergh call him JFK—and that doesn't stand for John Fitzgerald Kennedy, they say. It stands for Jobs for Kinfolk. In his three years in office, Steenbergh has appointed at least nine relatives of Warren City Hall workers or politicians. Although the appointments do not technically violate the city's anti-nepotism law, they make many residents and businesspeople feel that the government is under the influence of a few families.

Source: Schabath and Martindale (1998).

While we discourage relationships that lead to nepotism, we often encourage other relationships because of desirable outcomes. Teachers who develop sympathetic relationships with their students achieve superior results compared to those who provide education at arm's length. Coaches often attribute their success to "team chemistry" among team members. Poor relationships in the home are highly correlated with children who struggle in almost every category of social activity. They have lower high school graduation rates, they are more likely to be involved in crime, they have higher truancy rates, and they suffer higher infant mortality rates. Sympathetic relationships in the workplace reduce enforcement costs and improve productivity compared to work places characterized by arm's-length relationships. Community investment programs often depend on relationships among community members. And, finally, psychologists have long known that human relationships are critical to an individual's socio-emotional health and positive outlook.

The combination of positive and negative outcomes associated with relationships leads to a general ambivalence. Sometimes we view relationships as harmful to certain groups and limit their influence, while at other times we encourage relationships believing them to be helpful. But most often we say that relationships are helpful for those who enjoy the benefits of membership in a group and a disadvantage for nonmembers who are denied benefits associated with group membership. Finally, we might also add that relationships that lead to the formation of certain groups may sometimes create conflicts between groups.

Instead of viewing relationships as good or bad, a more productive approach is to recognize that relationships are a resource. And, like other resources, relationships can be used for positive or negative outcomes. Thus, our task is to find out how relationships can be used for positive outcomes.

Evidence that Relationships Matter: Rethinking Self-Interest's Role as Sole Motive

Few would argue that economic agents often act selfishly. On the other hand, an increasing amount of evidence supports the view that what an agent considers as his or her self-interest is modified by relationships, social bonds, and values (Swedburg, 1991). As a result, economic agents may make choices based on how their actions affect others.

Everyday events support the view that relationships alter economic behavior. For example, realtors recognize that the sale price of a particular parcel of land depends on the relationship between the seller and buyer. Friends and family trade at different levels and terms than do strangers (Robison, Myers, and Siles 2002). Customer loyalty depends on the relationships between customers and employees (Hanson, Robison, and Siles, 1996).

Many people make significant efforts to return lost items even though they belong to a stranger. The reason for such actions may be based on a relationship to oneself that, to be positively maintained, requires actions consistent with an internalized set of values. This internalized relationship is sometimes referred to as one's conscience.

Many donate food, other material, time, and money to victims of natural disasters or misfortunes. Rarely do these donors seek recompense or earn public recognition. For many, the reward of seeing the well-being of another improved is reward enough. Other groups of people who fail to fit the selfish preferences caricature include those who vote even when the outcome is not in doubt, or individuals who buy life insurance for beneficiaries from whom no reciprocal action is expected. Other individuals frequently exchange gifts without any enforceable contract for a repayment in kind. The explanation for the gift-giving is most often that there exists a special relationship between the gift provider and the gift recipient (Webley and Lea, 1993).

It is frequently the case that preferential offers in business arrangements are made when a relationship exists. Granovetter's influential 1973 article emphasized that "weak ties" (relationships) were an important factor in finding a job. According to a US Bureau of Labor study in 1975, 63.4 percent of jobs are a result of informal contacts where the job-seekers exercise their own initiative in building on personal contacts. Gwilliam (1993) found that 89 percent of Michigan farmland leases were between friends or family. Moreover, farmland leases between related individuals tend to be oral and more successful than leases between unrelated lessees and lessors (Johnson et al., 1987). Nelton (1990) noted that family businesses account for 76 percent of Oregon's small companies. Finally, Calonius (1990) stated that 75 percent of US companies are family-owned or controlled. Even international giving appears to be relationship-based, because so many individuals care.

Finally, in the United States, about 61.2 million people, or 26.7 percent, volunteered through or for an organization at least once between September 2005 and September 2006, according to the Bureau of Labor Statistics of the US Department of Labor (2007).

Unless there can be found a taste for giving away one's money and time, billions of dollars worth of economic activity in the US economy is largely unaccounted for by the selfishness of preferences assumption which focuses on promoting one's selfish interests through two-way exchanges. Frank summarizes the conflict between the assumption of selfish preferences in economics and observed preferences:

GOVERNMENT VERSUS PRIVATE GIVING

Sometimes the U S government is criticized because its international giving, as a proportion of its income, is less than that of other developed countries. It turns out that this criticism is unjustified because individuals and other members of the private sector are so generous in their giving.

According to a report published by a Washington research organization, the United States is the single largest donor of foreign economic aid, but, unlike many other developed nations, Americans prefer to donate their money through the private sector Of the $122.8 billion of foreign aid provided by Americans in 2005, $95.5 billion, or 79 percent, came from private foundations, corporations, voluntary organizations, universities, religious organizations and individuals, says the annual *Index of Global Philanthropy*.

For example, US foundations gave more—in money, time, goods and expertise—than 11 of the 22 developed-country governments each gave in 2005, and donations from private voluntary organizations in the United States totaled more than those of each of the governments of Japan, the UK, Germany, and France.

More than half of all US assistance to developing countries, $61.7 billion, came in the form of private remittances by individuals living in the United States to their families abroad, the report says. According to the report, those remittances not only reduce poverty, but, in some cases, also increase countries' creditworthiness and underwrite their trade imbalances.

Source: Center for Global Prosperity (2007).

> *Economists, for their part, point with pride to the power of self-interest to explain and predict behavior, not only in the world of commerce but in networks of personal relationships as well. And yet, the plain fact is that many people do not fit the me-first caricature. They give anonymously to public television stations and private charities. They donate bone marrow to strangers with leukemia. They endure great trouble and expense to see justice done, even when it will not undo the original injury. At great risk to themselves, they pull people from burning buildings, and jump into icy rivers to rescue people who are about to drown. Soldiers throw their bodies atop live grenades to save their comrades. Seen through the lens of modern self-interest theory, such behavior is the human equivalent of planets traveling in square orbits.*
>
> Frank, 1988: ix.

In contrast to the evidence that relationships and values matter, one recent study confirms that economists practice what they teach about selfishness. In a study designed to test willingness to contribute to a social versus a private account, Maxwell and Ames (1981) found that economics students contributed an average of only 20 percent of their endowments to the public account—significantly less than the 49 percent average for all other subjects. Carter and Irons (1991) found that economists also behaved more selfishly in ultimatum bargaining games.

Perhaps supported by observations of their own behavior, some economists continue to reject the view that relationships matter. Hirshleifer's Presidential Address to the Western Economics Association reaffirmed his faith in selfish preferences:

> *... I am among those who remain skeptical about the significance of self-reported contributions to charity, or about behavior in hypothetical or small-stakes Prisoners' Dilemma experiments. My guess is that economists are not more selfish, but only more acceptant of human selfishness as a fact of life.*
>
> Hirshleifer, 1994: 1.

Despite the evidence that economic students are more selfish than other students, when they have developed a relationship with another or when their relationship to themselves (conscience) is involved, they behave similarly to others—and exhibit selfishness much less than 95 percent of the time.

Frank, Gilovich, and Regan (1993) wrote that economists reported spending as much time as others in volunteer activities, and were only marginally less likely than others to vote in presidential elections. And more important for our work, when they developed relationships with others, by promising to cooperate, before engaging in Prisoner's Dilemma games, they cooperated at nearly the same rate as others.

Furthermore, when it comes to matters of conscience like returning lost wallets, three professors at George Washington University dropped stamped, addressed envelopes containing $10 in cash in different classrooms. In the economics classrooms, 56 percent of the envelopes were returned with the money inside. It appears that in matters involving one's conscience, economics students aren't any more selfish than other students; they just claim to be (Bennett, 1995).

Evidence also supports the view that relationships matter in the aggregate as well as at the individual level. For example, sister cities develop special cultural and trade relationships. Most favored nation status provides some countries with special advantages not available to other nations, including cultural, language, geographic, or other features that bind them together. Countries thus bound together often establish special trading relationships that do not develop between countries which lack that particular bond. Finally, nations often act to restrict trade when unfavorable relationships exist. For example, national policies such as apartheid or human rights abuses within a country often lead to restricted trade with other countries even though the undesirable behavior is not imposed outside the country.

In response to such evidence, some economists concede that relationships matter, but not in important ways. Economists who support this view believe that we can continue business as usual with selfish preferences as the foundation for our models (Gardner, 1995).

Some important economic transactions may not be affected by relationships. For example, in perfectly competitive markets in which many anonymous buyers and sellers trade standardized goods, relationships may not be important. On the other hand, strong evidence suggests that, in transactions in which the buyer and seller are known to each other, relationships matter. Moreover, from our interpretation of the evidence we expect that as the contact between buyers and sellers becomes more personalized, the more

important will be the effect of the relationships on the transactions. We explore these ideas more in Chapter 15 on globalization.

Relationships and Social Capital

We recognize the importance of physical, human, and financial capital in the production of physical goods and services and spend a great deal of academic toil studying how they are formed and used to better our economic well-being. We propose that social capital—another form of capital that exists in relationships—is essential not only to our economic well-being, but also to our socio-emotional well–being, because it is the origin of SEGs. Therefore, we need to examine how this form of capital can be better employed to improve both our socio-emotional and economic well-being.

In some ways, the world has never been a better place in which to live. Poverty has fallen continuously throughout the last century, and wealth and luxury have been extended to more of the world's population than ever before. But our ability to take the final steps to alleviate poverty completely and create a more equal distribution of goods and services seems to elude us. We will argue in Chapter 2 that understanding and applying the concept of social capital might provide the missing key to our continued progress not only on this front, but also perhaps on many others.

Conclusion

In this book we assert that relationships matter—a lot. They matter precisely because the effective use of all other forms of capital depends in one way or another on relationships. Finally, we assert that the interdependence between social capital and other forms of capital needs to be better understood.

To understand the interdependence of various forms of capital requires that we recognize the interdependence of the social sciences. Each social science discipline provides an important insight about how relationships affect human exchanges made up of both physical and socio-emotional goods and services. Indeed, we claim that we need the combined views from each of the social sciences to complete our understanding of how relationships help us take care of friends and business.

Science may sometimes narrow our inquiry until we know more and more about less and less. In many cases our scientific progress requires such a restricted focus. Nevertheless, sometimes our progress requires that we combine our information into a composite whole to better inform our inquiry. This book may be viewed in that light—a composite of information from several social sciences that contributes to our understanding of human exchange and well-being and how relationships matter. Once we understand social capital better, we can organize and manage our relationships for our well-being—both economically and socially.

The extent to which the concept of social capital will be useful depends critically on our capacity to define and measure it. Indeed, one of the biggest problems of the social capital literature, as we show later in the book, is the inability of scholars and disciplines to agree on a definition and measure of social capital. Without a workable definition, the term "social capital" has come to mean many things, which vastly diminishes its

worth and usefulness as a concept. Once clearly defined, social capital can be applied to understand social, political, and economical outcomes through individual, community, and international relationships.

In the chapters that follow, we expand on the ideas we've presented in this introductory chapter. In Chapter 2 we define social capital and describe its capital-like qualities. Then, in Chapters 3 and 4 we explain why relationships and social capital are important and why selfish motivations are not always the best predictors of social or economic behavior.

In Chapters 5–10, we explain in detail the social capital paradigm which acknowledges the contributions of a broad range of social science perspectives and yet does so in a rigorously defined and measurable way. We begin in Chapter 5 with the end in mind by first giving the reader a view of the complete paradigm with all the interactions of the component parts. Then we define and clarify the components of the paradigm: SEGs (Chapter 6), attachment values (Chapter 7), institutions (Chapter 8), networks (Chapter 9), and power (Chapter 10).

Finally, Chapters 11–17 apply the social capital paradigm to empirical areas of interest. Chapters 11–13 focus on exchanges, distributions, and poverty. The last four chapters, 14–17, introduce topics in an effort to encourage research that examines the possibilities of the social capital paradigm. Each of these topics, we suggest, can be approached from the perspective of this paradigm.

The key question driving the empirical examples in Chapters 11–17 is: how do relationships matter? For example, to determine when using our relationships is ethical we must understand when caring behavior becomes corruption. Processes of globalization and localization can be understood as a trade-off between the efficiency of impersonal relationships versus emotionally satisfying personalized relationships. Poverty reduction can be explained by access to "right" relationships, or relationships with those who have resources and capacities to enrich us. The degree to which our relationships lead us to passive or active participation in politics determines to a significant extent our political structures. Social connections impact on the value of our products and the terms under which they are exchanged. And, finally, social capital-rich networks can be thought of in terms of the way in which relationships define externalities.

In none of these chapters are we able to explain fully ethics, globalization, networks, poverty, politics, and so forth. Nor do we try. Our goal is to point out that relationships impact every one of these areas. As modest as this objective is, we believe strongly that this is an important advancement in the understanding of the ongoing enterprise of human exchange and development.

CHAPTER 2 *Relationships and Social Capital*

There is a soul to an army as well as to the individual man, and no general can accomplish the full work of his army unless he commands the soul of his men, as well as their bodies and legs.

General William Tecumseh Sherman, (quoted in Hanson, 1999).

Introduction

In one of those rare alignments of science, the term "social capital" has emerged as a concept applied to relationships by nearly all the social sciences. Moreover, this common interest in social capital provides an important opportunity for cooperative research across the social sciences that focuses on the importance of relationships. Up until now, however, such cooperation has been slow to emerge, largely because agreement on the definition of social capital has been hard to come by. Like "risk" and "love", social capital has become a word that has meaning for most people but has no mutually agreed upon definition. So, if we are to understand how relationships influence our social transactions, social capital, while generally understood, must be precisely defined, and its definition must be consistent with the words "social" (having to do with relationships) and "capital" (having to do with an inventory of potential services).

The challenge is not trivial. Emery Castle notes that "[u]nless the social capital concept is used with some degree of precision and in a comparable manner, it will come to have little value as an analytical construct" (1998: 623). According to Castle and others, the problem with so many different definitions of social capital is that it has taken on so many meanings and is enlisted to fight so many battles that it risks becoming the ether that fills the universe.

Our objective in this chapter is to define social capital in such a way that cooperative research across the social sciences is not only possible, but encouraged. To be successful, a definition must satisfy important requirements. First, whatever is defined as social capital must remain true to the properties of capital while at the same time capturing the importance of social relationships. Second, our definition must take into consideration the capacity of social capital to produce both socio-emotional and economic goods.

Bridging Across Disciplines, Policies, and Communities

On April 20 through April 22, 1998, social scientists and applied problem-solvers from around the world and across disciplines gathered to define, discuss measures, and suggest

applications of "social capital." At the beginning of the conference, presenters were asked to respond to alternative definitions of social capital proposed by social capital scholars. Table 2.1 contains 12 definitions of social capital that had been published in leading journals at that time. Beside each definition is a Likert scale summarizing the conference attendees' support for each of the definitions. Not surprisingly, no single definition was generally supported.

Table 2.1 Agreement (disagreement) with alternative definitions of social capital

	Agree								Disagree
Scale Used	1	2	3	4	5	6	7	8	9	10

Summary of Alternative Definitions	**No. of Respondents**	**Mean of Responses**	**STD Error of the Mean**
1. Social capital is the expectations for action within a collectivity that affect the economic goals and goal-seeking behavior of its members, even if these expectations are not oriented toward the economic sphere.	$n = 55$	5.2	.30
2. Social capital is information, trust, and norms of reciprocity inhering in one's social networks.	$n = 55$	3.7	.31
3. Social capital is a variety of different entities having two characteristics in common: some aspect of social structure; and they facilitate certain actions of individuals who are within the structure.	$n = 55$	5.1	.33
4. Social capital is the sum of resources, actual or virtual, that accrues to an individual or a group by virtue of possessing a durable network of more or less institutionalized relationships of mutual acquaintance and recognition.	$n = 55$	3.8	.31
5. Social capital is friends, colleagues, and more general contacts through whom you receive opportunities to use other forms of capital. Also, social capital is relations within and between firms.	$n = 55$	4.1	.30
6. Social capital is naturally occurring social relationships among persons which promote or assist the acquisition of skills and traits valued in the marketplace. Social capital is also an asset which may be as significant as a financial bequest in accounting for the maintenance of inequality in our society.	$n = 54$	5.1	.31
7. Social capital is those features of social organizations, such as trust, norms, and networks, that can improve the efficiency of society by facilitating coordinated actions.	$n = 53$	4.0	.32
8. Social capital is the capacity of individuals to command scarce resources by virtue of their membership in networks or broader social structures.	$n = 55$	4.1	.29
9. Social capital is accumulated past experience in interpersonal relationships that constrain or stimulate persons' behavior toward other persons, or behavior in matters that affect other persons very directly, in the present.	$n = 55$	5.1	.31
10. Social capital is an argument in a person's preference function that incorporates the influence of past actions by peers and others in an individual's social network and control system.	$n = 52$	6.3	.27
11. Social capital is a moral resource including trust and other cultural mechanisms used to define and reinforce the boundaries of particular status groups.	$n = 52$	5.9	.32
12. Social capital is the potential benefit, advantages, and preferential treatment resulting from one person or group's sympathy and sense of obligation toward another person or group. Social capital also includes the potential benefits, advantages, and preferential treatment that originate from one person's sympathy and sense of obligation toward his or her idealized self.	$n = 52$	5.0	.36

Origins and Differences in the Definition of Social Capital

In 1916 Hanifan was the first to use the term "social capital" in academic circles. More recently, several scholars have contributed to the popularity of the term and concept (see Bourdieu, 1985; Coleman, 1990; Fukuyama, 1995a; Narayan, 2000; Portes, 1998; Putnam, 1993, 2000). Even before these scholars wrote about social capital, many social scientists were aware of the concept, even though they may have called it something else. Woolcock (1998) has identified several other names used by scholars for a concept similar to social capital including "intangible assets," "social energy," "social capability," "sociability," and "moral resources" to name a few (see also Durlauf, 1999). For many, social capital may be like old wine in a new bottle, an old concept dressed up in a new name. What is different now is that many social scientists and problem-solvers recognize their shared interest in social capital and are talking about it with each other.

Perhaps one reason why researchers have produced so many different definitions is because their definitions have not been limited to answering the question "What is social capital?" Past definitions have included answers to such questions as: "Where does social capital reside?," "How can social capital be used?," and "How can social capital be changed?"

Portes and Sensenbrenner defined social capital as: "The expectations for action within a collectivity that affect the economic goals and goal-seeking behavior of its members, even if these expectations are not oriented toward the economic sphere" (1993:1323). This definition appears to combine *what social capital is* (the expectations for action within a collectivity) with *what social capital can be used to achieve* (affect the economic goals and goal-seeking behavior of its members).

Coleman (1990) defined social capital as a variety of different entities having two characteristics in common: namely, some aspect of social structure and the ability to facilitate certain actions of individuals who are within the structure. These entities include obligations, expectations, trust, and information flows. This definition, like the one suggested by Portes and Sensenbrenner (1998), combines *what social capital is* (a variety of structures) with *what social capital can be used to achieve* (facilitate certain actions of individual members of the group where the group is defined by some aspect of social structure).

Narayan and Pritchett define social capital as "the quantity and quality of associational life and the related social norms" (1998: 872). Then they describe five processes in which social capital changes outcomes for the better by facilitating greater cooperation (what it does).

Burt (1992) defined social capital as friends, colleagues, and more general contacts through whom you receive opportunities to use other forms of capital. This definition combines a statement of *where social capital resides* (with friends, colleagues, and more general contacts) with *what it can be used to accomplish* (receive opportunities to use other forms of capital).

Portes (1995) provides another example of a definition that combines a statement of what social capital is with where it resides. He defined social capital as the capacity of individuals to command scarce resources by virtue of their membership in networks or broader social structures. This definition can be separated into a statement of *what social capital is* (the capacity of individuals to command scarce resources) with a statement of *where social capital resides* (networks or broader social structures).

Sometimes a definition of social capital combines statements about what gives rise to social capital with what social capital can be used to achieve. For example, Putnam defines social capital as features of social organizations such as trust, norms, and networks that can improve society's efficiency by facilitating coordinated actions (Putnam, Leonardi, and Nanetti, 1993). In this definition, the *basis for social capital* (trust and norms) can be separated from statements of *what social capital can do* (improve the efficiency of society by facilitating coordinated actions) and *where social capital resides* (networks).

Woolcock investigates social capital within the context of economic development policy. He suggests that bottom-up development depends on intra-community ties labeled "integration" and extra-community networks labeled "linkages." Top-down development involves state–society relations labeled "synergy," and institutional coherence, competence, and capacity are called "organizational integrity" (Woolcock, 1998). The latter is related to what others call "organizational capital." This conception involves a mixture of what capital is and where it resides.

How the content of ties and networks and other institutions is illuminated by the capital metaphor is not elaborated. All understandings which coordinate action in a particular way are not capital even if they are "productive" in the broad sense of the word. Social scientists do not need another word for all the institutions that further economic and social development, especially if that word implies characteristics of capital that not all institutions have.

Social Capital as Sympathy

Rather than focusing on social capital's applications, residence, or (dis)investment possibilities, the definition of social capital should be a statement of the form *A* equals (is) *B*. We propose an elegantly simple definition of social capital that takes the capital metaphor seriously and accounts for those social relationships that are most capital-like in character.

Our proposed definition is:

Social capital is a person's or group's sympathy for another person or group.

To equate sympathy to social capital requires that we define sympathy. According to *Webster's Ninth Collegiate Dictionary*, sympathy is an affinity, association, or relationship between persons or things wherein whatever affects one similarly affects the other. Therefore, social capital makes our welfare interdependent. A's well-being directly affects B's well-being. In addition, because the well-being of those who have social capital are internalized by those who provide social capital (sympathy), the providers of social capital often offer the objects of their social capital (sympathy) preferential terms of trade and favors. As a result, social capital really is capital because it has the capacity to produce a potential benefit, advantage, and preferential treatment for another person or group of persons beyond that expected in an anonymous exchange (arm's-length) relationship (Robison, Schmid, and Siles, 2002: 6).

The Nature of Sympathy

Our definition equates social capital to sympathy because sympathy is the essential resource required for interpersonal transactions and social power.[1] According to Sally, "If by social capital we mean those assets grounded in and valuable to social interaction, sympathy, again, is the essential personal process" (2000: 575). Cooley (1902) claims that sympathy is a requisite to social power and that, without it, man is a mere animal, not truly in contact with human life, and, because he is not in contact with human life, he can have no power over it.

Sally (2002: 3) cites several authors to make the point that sympathy leads to an enlarged self-interest that produces relationships in which self-interest is "undivided" (Merleau-Ponty, 1969), "merged" (Davis et al., 1996), or "overlapping" (Aron, Aron, and Smollan, 1992). Cooley writes:

> *He whom I imagine without antipathy becomes my brother. If we feel that we must give aid to another, it is because that other lives and strives in our imaginations, and so is a part of ourselves .... If I come to imagine a person suffering wrong, it is not 'altruism' that makes me wish to right that wrong, but simple human impulse.*
>
> Cooley, 1902: 115.

Regarding the ubiquity of sympathy, Sally summarizes:

> *[T]he urge to identify with another is embedded in our social natures, and insofar as we are impelled to succeed within a social structure, the motivation to sympathize will be heightened. We have the ability to read and predict (or, at least, to generate the belief that we read and predict) people's thoughts and feelings both because the basic consistency of the human constitution is such that similar situations and stimuli cause the same internal reactions ... and because our thoughts and feelings are linked with visible, comprehensible signs ... Finally, as we shall see further on, the belief that we can read the mind of another and have our own mind read may be self-fulfilling, especially within the interaction order. In sum, sympathy is integral to social interaction and person perception as sight is to visual perception.*
>
> Sally, 2000: 572.

Political philosophers have long recognized the importance of sympathy in economic and social transactions and have foreshadowed the concept of social capital. David Hume described the importance of sympathy in *A Treatise of Human Nature*:

> *The minds of all men are similar in their feelings and operation; nor can any one be actuated by any affection of which all others are not in some degree susceptible. As strings equally wound up, the motion of one communicates itself to the rest; so all the affections readily pass from one person to another, and beget corresponding movements in very creature.*
>
> Hume, 1978[1740]: 576.

---

1 This section draws heavily from Sally's encyclopedic review and applications of sympathy, which provide the basis for much of what follows, and many of the references to sympathy we cite appear in his works.

F.Y. Edgeworth was the first economist to postulate a specific utility function incorporating sympathy. He proposed that agents maximize their own utility plus the utility of another weighted by a coefficient of sympathy (see Collard, 1975). The coefficient of sympathy reflects the degree of "overlap" between the expanded self and the other. Sally (2000) used this linear utility function to analyze the famous Prisoner's Dilemma game when sympathy exists between players. Other extensions of the model in economics have been made by Becker (1974), Bruce and Waldman (1990), Montgomery (1991), Rotemberg (1994), and Robison and Hanson (1993).

Adam Smith defined sympathy as "our fellow-feeling with any passion whatever" that arises from "changing places in fancy with the sufferer"(1966a[1759]: 6) and suggested a basis for determining the coefficient of sympathy or what some now call the "social capital coefficient." Smith thought that sympathy decayed within the extended family as the blood ties thinned. He declared that we can sympathize more readily with friends than with acquaintances, and more easily than with strangers. Hume had a similar metric in mind when he expressed his view that "[w]e sympathize more with persons contiguous to us, than with persons remote from us: With our acquaintance, than with strangers: With our countrymen, than with foreigners" (Hume, 1978[1740]: 581).

Smith makes an important distinction between sympathy and altruism. Sympathy, not altruism, is ultimately dependent on the reciprocity of feelings and thoughts. "[N]othing pleases us more than to observe in the other men a fellow-feeling with all the emotions of our own breast; nor are we ever so much shocked as by the appearance of the contrary" (Smith, 1966a[1759]: 13).

We agree with Smith and Hume that sympathy has varying levels of intensity. Sympathetic feelings may include admiration, caring, concern, empathy, regard, respect, sense of obligation, or trust for another person or group. Inevitably, equating social capital to sympathetic relationships leads to a debate on whether sympathy or empathy is the correct word. We defend our choice as follows. We may see a hungry child and feel some sense of unease and even a desire to mitigate the child's suffering. But, even though there is a degree of empathetic feeling, we do not confuse ourselves with the child: there is still some distance separating us. However, empathetic relationships are the extreme form of sympathy that blurs the distinction between self and others.

The Capital Metaphor

We intend to defend the definition of social capital proposed in this chapter by demonstrating that it satisfies the essential requirements of capital and is social in nature. However, we must first define capital.

Capital is a *commodity* created to permit increased production of other goods and services in the future (Smithson, 1982: 111). Capital in this sense represents an accumulation of foregone consumption—an amount saved for later use.

Our definition of social capital can be made consistent with the definition of capital generally accepted by economists by substituting the word "sympathy" for the word "commodity." Just as economists increasingly believe that human intelligence is the core commodity that makes up human capital, we argue that sympathy is the core commodity

which makes up social capital, and which emphasizes motive as the foundation of social capital.[2]

Consider again the definition of social capital: a person's or a group's sympathy for another person or group that may produce a potential benefit, advantage, and preferential treatment for another person or group of persons beyond that expected in an exchange relationship. This definition separates what it is (sympathy) from what it does (provide potential benefit) and focuses on the transformative capacity of capital residing in human relationships.

For a long time, the meaning of capital was limited to human-made tangible objects such as buildings and equipment. However, as our list of goods has expanded, so have the kinds of capital we have identified as useful to their production. As a result, the capital metaphor has been extended to financial capital, human capital, organizational capital, intellectual capital, cultural capital, and social capital.[3]

Capital-like Properties of Social Capital

It is natural to ask what evidence we could provide, if asked to do so by those interested in capital, that proves social capital has the essential characteristics of capital. Or could we, if challenged to do so, compare social capital with other forms of capital and find that they possessed similar qualities? Table 2.2 compares social capital with other forms of capital.

An object must possess several properties to be identified as capital. First, capital produces services that have value and have the capacity to transform the function, meaning, and value of other objects. Second, capital maintains its identity even while providing services and transforming other objects. In other words, capital is durable. Third, capital depends on other forms of capital and expendables to do its work. Capital never works alone. Fourth, capital has a residence, a place where it exists and from where it provides its services. However, capital can be alienated and transferred between owners. And, fifth, capital is subject to physical and social institutions. To what extent does social capital, as defined earlier, possess these essential capital-like properties?

---

2 Motive is also the foundation of other types of capital, such as financial capital.

3 Human capital has many of the same properties as physical capital. Fundamentally, human capital emphasizes a surplus value and represents an investment in education and skills that resides in individuals. (Schultz. 1961; Becker, 1964/1993). Human capital is not destroyed by use and, when combined with other capital goods, it transforms inputs into outputs.

Organizational capital is described in terms of where it resides: "organizational relationships, particular members of organizations, the organization's repositories of information, or some combination of the above." Organizational capital can be combined and "embodied in workers in the form of attitudes and knowledge created through the socialization processes" (Tomer, 1999: 1049).

Cultural capital includes "language and linguistic style, values, definitions of basic knowledge and assumptions ...." (De Bruin, 1999: 169). Cultural capital can be combined with human capital: "Embodied cultural capital can be understood as the ability, talent, style, or even speech patterns of people in a group." These characteristics are acquired "through the socialization process and tend to be the marks that distinguish one group from another" (ibid.).

One important difference between social capital and some other forms of newly identified capital is that social capital resides in a social relationship. In contrast, human capital can reside in the individual alone. This is not to say that human capital creation is not collective. Even physical capital is, in large part, a collective phenomenon as Veblen (1908) emphasized. It is created in such institutionalized collectivities as corporation, universities, governments, and informal associations of people wherein knowledge and visions are formed and transferred (O'Hara, 1998).

Table 2.2 Common characteristics of capital and social capital

Characteristics of capital	**Characteristics of social capital**
Capital is durable.	*Social capital* is durable. Sympathetic relationships can last a lifetime and beyond.
Capital produces a flow of services that have value.	Social capital produces a flow of *socio-emotional goods* that have value because they satisfy socio-emotional needs.
Capital never works alone. Moreover, when it works on other objects it transforms their function, meaning, and value.	Social capital requires conveyances to produce and exchange socio-emotional goods. Socio-emotional goods sometimes become embedded in their conveyances. Embedding objects with socio-emotional goods transforms their function, value, and meaning. The change in the value and meaning of an object embedded with socio-emotional goods is the object's *attachment value.*
Capital has a residence and can be alienated: i.e., we can transfer capital from one owner to another.	Social capital resides in persons whose connections form *networks.* We can transfer social capital's residence. (A friend of my friend can become my friend.)
One form of capital can substitute for, and sometimes complement, other forms of capital. One's ability to exercise influence or power depends on one's capital.	Social capital can substitute for other forms of capital. (I will provide help for money or for friendship). One's ability to influence the actions of others depends in part on one's *power* that resides in one's social capital.
Physical and social laws regulate the creation and use of capital.	*Formal and informal institutions* (laws) regulate the creation and use of social capital.

CAPITAL IS DURABLE

Durability associated with physical capital refers to its ability to retain its identity after and during the process of providing services. A tractor, after delivering pulling services, is still recognized as a tractor with the potential to pull and provide transportation. A young cow, after producing offspring and milk, is still recognized as a cow with milk and offspring-producing potential. In contrast to durables are expendables that lose their identity during their provision of services. For example, seed and fuel are usually considered to be expendables because in the process of providing growing and energy services they lose their identity. Seeds become plants and fuel becomes energy, and neither expendable is recognized for what it was before it provided services.

Social capital possesses different degrees of durability. There may be weak sympathy capable of producing only a limited amount of services before disintegrating. A casual friend may be willing to provide free transportation a few times but then become unresponsive to requests later. Some strong forms of sympathy are durable almost to the point of being indestructible. These extremely durable forms of social capital are often associated with

family connections that remain unchanged even when repeated service extractions are made. (How many dinners and laundry services can children extract from their parents before further services are refused because their sympathy has been exhausted?)

Capital whose service potential is nearly indestructible are called *endurables*. Endurables are little affected by time or use. A fine-jeweled watch may keep time for generations. The service potential of land, for example, is almost unaffected by reasonable use. So it is with certain kinds of social capital. Social capital that resides in family members may be nearly indestructible, an endurable, while social capital invested in causal friends with whom you attend sporting events may be of limited durability and may need continual maintenance.

The durable nature of social capital leads to a particular approach to its examination. Possibilities for maintaining, investing (disinvesting), and earning a return on one's social capital depends on its durability. Levels of durability also influence the possibility of economies of scale (volume) once the initial investment is made. Finally, levels of durability influence relative values of services, suggesting that a relatively expensive, but durable, social capital might be compared to a cheaper, but more expendable, form of social capital

Decay (maintenance) refers to the manner in which the service capacity of capital is reduced or fostered. Physical capital's service potential decays mostly through use, the passage of time, and the absence of maintenance. Wear is a natural feature of nearly all forms of physical capital. Consider a barn that provides storage services. The service capacity of the barn is related to the physical dimension of the facility and the condition of the structure. In this instance, the barn's decay depends on the passage of time and the application of maintenance rather than use, since its decay is unrelated to the number of objects stored. In contrast, the increasing number and frequency of engine revolutions directly alters the potential of many mechanical durables whose decay depends on use. Finally, some durables' service capacity varies little with time or use, like paintings in a museum (if properly maintained), while other durables, such as paper cups, may have rapid decay functions.

Social capital, like physical capital, is subject to decay from use, the passage of time, and lack of maintenance. One might develop social capital that provides valuable services with a neighbor. But when the neighbor moves, the lack of maintenance in the form of face-to-face contacts, despite efforts to "stay in touch," eventually diminishes the strength of the ties and the potential to extract services. A friend who is never called on for help may feel ignored and become less friendly. In endurable relationships, such as might exist between family members, the passage of time and the absence of regular face-to-face contacts does very little to diminish the social capital service potential. Even so, sometimes the too-frequent request for services may exhaust one's social capital or potential to receive preferential treatment. In contrast, some social capital may require use to be sustained, even in the most durable of relationships.

CAPITAL HAS THE POTENTIAL TO PRODUCE FLOWS OF GOODS AND SERVICES

Capital produces a flow of services. Examples of physical capital and their potential to produce flows of goods and services include factories and utilities with their potential to produce heat; cars, buses, and planes with their potential to provide transportation services; surgical equipment with the potential to supply medical services; and housing

with its potential to provide shelter services. Obviously, capital is distinct from the services it produces. Unfortunately, some have confused social capital with what it does—the services it produces. For example, social capital is not civic-mindedness, networks, or participation, although social capital enhances and influences each of these things.

What social capital produces are *socio-emotional goods* (SEGs). And SEGs have value because of the socio-emotional needs they satisfy. The main point is that human sympathy is required to produce the SEGs that satisfy our most basic socio-emotional needs.

CAPITAL NEVER WORKS ALONE

Capital can never do its work alone. It must act on something and most often what it acts on is transformed. Transformation capacity is one of capital's essential catalytic characteristics. Capital must possess the capacity to transform inputs into outputs while maintaining its own identity. Capital goods, like factories and machines, transform raw material inputs into other forms, including both consumption goods and/or additional capital goods. Of course, a capital good's capacity to transform depends on the presence of other inputs. If social capital satisfies the fundamental requirements of the capital metaphor, it, too, must have the capacity to transform inputs into outputs with changed meaning, value, and function.

To be effective, social capital requires conveyances to deliver the SEGs it produces. In most cases, people deliver SEGs. In other cases, other conveyances are used when personal delivery of SEGs is not available. For example, physical distance may separate us from our friends—from personalized exchanges of SEGs. So, we find alternative conveyances. These may include personalized letters, electronic exchanges, photos, and gifts. On other occasions the workplace may provide a setting for sympathetic workmates to express validation for each other's efforts. A plaque at an awards ceremony may also be used as a physical conveyance of SEGs, even though there may be no physical separation between those exchanging SEGs.

Often, the conveyances used to exchange SEGs may become embedded with the SEGs they convey. As a result of this embedding of SEGs in the conveyances, the value, function, and meaning of the conveyance may be changed. For example, consider a family photo: its value and meaning to a family member in the photo differs from that for a stranger who may be only interested in the picture because of its attractive frame. Social capital has changed the value, function, and meaning of the photo for the family. The change in the value and meaning of an object used to convey SEGs is referred to here as its *attachment value*. It is important to remember that attachment value is distinct from social capital, just as a transformed input, such as a piece of wood transformed into furniture, is distinct from the capital used to produce the transformation (in this case, woodworking tools).

Included in capital's ability to transform objects is its ability to create the same or different kinds of capital. For example, metal presses are used to create metal products for final use, to create parts for still other metal presses or used to create new forms of capital such as a lathe. We recognize, however, that what is created is distinct from the original capital used in the creation process. Likewise, social capital can be used to strengthen existing levels of social capital or be used to create new forms of social capital. For example, suppose persons A and B and persons B and C share social capital. Then, because of their friendship with B, persons A and C develop social capital, although it is

unlikely, at least initially, to be the same kind of social capital that exists between persons A and B and persons B and C.

SOCIAL CAPITAL AND CAPITAL CREATION

Social capital, like other forms of physical capital, can also be used to create forms of capital different from itself. For example, earlier in American history, publicly elected officials approved the Morrill Act, which resulted in the creation of the Land Grant Universities. Those responsible for creating the Land Grant System were undoubtedly influenced in their action by sympathy for others, since the system was designed to provide an education to those less fortunate. However, what they created was something different from social capital—namely an institution with resources, rights, and responsibilities and the ability to grant preferential treatment to many individuals. In addition, over time and perhaps during its creation, Land Grant Universities acquired attachment value, which helps sustain the social capital that resides in networks, departments, and among individuals within these universities.

PHYSICAL AND SOCIAL LAWS GIVE ORDER AND MEANING TO THE CREATION AND USE OF CAPITAL

Physical laws define possible transformations and their outcomes for physical capital. For example, heat applied to metal will produce certain well-known physical transformations of the metal. In the same way, socially created laws often direct the use and creation of capital in that they may restrict pollution or the speed of vehicular traffic. Similarly, *institutions* (laws) give order and meaning to the creation and use of one's social capital. For example, some institutions prohibit the use of one's social capital to obtain employment in a government agency or influence the jury's verdict in a court trial. Formal institutions apply without regard to social capital. Informal institutions may vary, depending on the social capital that exists between transacting parties.

Capital can substitute or complement other forms of capital and goods. The economic way of thinking asks about complements and substitutes. Tractors provide pulling services in most developed countries, but animals may substitute for these services in many less developed agricultural settings. Barns and silos provide storage services, but trees and tents may substitute for these services in emergencies. Tractors and plows are complementary. Each one enhances the productivity of the other.

A person who has sympathy for you will not be opportunistic. In turn, commitment and obligation are substitutes for monitoring. Worker cooperatives can reduce monitoring costs if self-determination enables employees to identify with the corporation, which reduces motives to shirk (Lutz, 1997). We may receive a loan based on our social capital. But we could also earn credit (borrowing trustworthiness) and exchange it for a loan. Or we might resort to physical force and take the loan without permission. In most arrangements, different kinds of resources or power can be used to complete a transaction. Our point here is simply that social capital is an important resource whether it substitutes for other kinds of power or is used to complement them.

Reference has already been made to the complementarity and partial substitutability of capital goods, social capital, cultural capital, and organizational capital. Some further elaboration may be useful. In some cultures, parents teach their children to return lost

objects and always to tell the truth. Because of the parents' social capital with their children and the reinforcement from the community, the children may also adopt the values of returning lost objects and always telling the truth. Visitors to this culture might find this form of cultural capital particularly helpful in setting up a business and, if pressed, could even place a dollar value on the cultural capital to which they have access. For example, many firms will only recruit from certain graduate business schools because of the tradition of their graduates' ethical behavior.

It is useful to distinguish these learned and internalized behavioral norms from social capital. A person can return lost objects from a learned sense of commitment without any (or much) sympathy with the owner. Amartya Sen, the Nobel development economist distinguishes sympathy from commitment (Sen, 1982). The person enmeshed in cultural capital may not even consider alternative behavior and be little influenced by thoughts of what would happen if the norm were not implemented (see also Minkler, 1999). Behavior contrary to the norm would destroy the person's image of their ideal self. When cultural capital is widely shared, it increases the opportunities for reinforcement and the generality of benefits or what Fukuyama (1995) calls the "radius of spontaneous cooperation."

When groups of individuals form certain cultural norms accepted by the population, or cultural capital, these may sometimes substitute for personalized social capital. When a person has access to cultural capital that promotes honesty and the return of lost objects, the person may not need to depend on personalized forms of social capital to gain access to reliable information and lost objects. When these facilitating cultural norms are absent, individuals may need to depend on more personalized forms of social capital to achieve the same outcome.

The same honest behavior might also be produced by formal legal institutions and sanctions. Again, this might be valuable to those contemplating investment is a business. In addition, the nation-state is not the only source of governance. Organizations make rules which apply to their members/employees. Some organizational rules become learned habits, in which case the rules are often referred to as "business culture." Similarly, some rules are honored because of sanctions within the organization, including expulsion or jail terms.

Cultural capital and organizational capital may also provide the commonality essential for the development of social capital. Agreement on cultural values and norms suggests an absence of conflict between individuals in a relationship. These commonalities (shared kernels) are potentially most powerful for the creation of social capital when they are recognized outside the boundaries in which they were created. Beginning with an agreement on cultural norms and values, cultural capital may provide the opportunities to find other kernels of commonality and develop synergistic activities that increase both sympathy and individual and collective investments in social capital. Class, gender, and race constitute affinity groups or kernels of commonality, which can be used both for advantage and disadvantage (Egerton, 1997).

CAPITAL HAS A RESIDENCE AND CAN BE ALIENATED

Existing capital may be transferred from its creator to others by gift, inheritance, sale, or rental. One may inherit some forms of capital such as factories, land and buildings, and paintings. Indeed, most families have determined an inheritance plan to pass on capital to heirs upon the death of the capital's owners. Like physical capital, one may inherit

social capital created by one's family members or friends. For example, friends of my parents may become my friends because of the efforts of my parents. A baby is born into a particular social structure and, in particular, to a family, and may immediately own social capital. This capital is inherited because the parents identify the child as belonging to them. Despite many service withdrawals, the baby and, later, a small child mostly maintain their social capital. Only when the child grows to independence does the social capital supply show some signs of change and the child's responsibility to maintain and invest in its own social capital increase. A common example of such capital exists among Chinese diaspora families. One's last name is often enough to acquire a loan.

Physical capital goods can be rented or purchased from their original creators or subsequent owners. But, since existing social capital is a relationship, it cannot be transferred by its beneficiary without the consent of the benefactor(s). In that sense, it is misleading to speak of owning social capital. Nevertheless, implied in many social capital arrangements is the informal institution that "a friend of my friend is my friend too." Alienation is not essential to the definition of capital or we could not speak of human capital. Human capital is embodied in a person and cannot be alienated separately from that person. I can teach others my skill for a fee, but I cannot transfer it directly to another by ceasing to use it, as in the case of a factory.

Social capital is partly fungible because providing SEGs generally requires personalized social capital. A friend of a friend may give us access to physical goods and services on preferential terms to please our common friend. However, this same friend of a friend is likely unable to provide us SEGs because these require a personalized relationship that doesn't exist. Similarly, human capital is only partly fungible because we do not permit slavery or involuntary servitude.

Implications of the Capital-like Nature of Social Capital

If we are correct that social capital as sympathy can be thought of as a form of capital that is based on relationships there are a number of important implications that follow.

SOCIAL CAPITAL IS A RESOURCE

Dale Carnegie suggested that our successes will depend to a significant degree on our ability to build, manage, and maintain relationships. If we misuse, neglect, fail to maintain or fail to invest in our social capital resources, then the socio-emotional and economic benefits that could be derived from our social capital will be less than possible or optimal. Moreover, social capital is not only a resource that needs to be studied and understood if it is to be managed properly, but also a resource of such significance that, without it, other resources are likely to be misused.

Robert Putnam pointed out what many people perceived and believed was a problem: our collective social capital resource was declining—at least, we weren't bowling together as much as we once did. But how do we know? We must determine the extent of this resource and how it is distributed. Then we need to examine how the distribution of social capital affects the distribution of other resources. We also need to know how to preserve and invest in our social capital—even in hostile settings.

TEATIME AND ARTILLERY SHELLS

In nearly every interpersonal exchange, social capital appears to make a difference. Captain J.R. Wilton, an officer in the British Army, was having tea with his fellow soldiers in the mud near Armentières, France. It was August 1915 and World War I had become a trench-lined struggle for barren stretches of countryside. Wilton's teatime was suddenly disrupted when an artillery shell arced into the camp and exploded. The British soldiers quickly got into their trenches, readying their weapons and swearing at the Germans.

Then from across no-man's-land, writes Wilton in his diary, a German soldier appeared above his trenches. "We are very sorry about that," the soldier shouted. "We hope no one was hurt. It is not our fault. It is that damned Prussian artillery."

Enemy soldiers might seem like the last people on Earth who would cooperate with each other, but they did, suggesting that social capital is important even among enemies.

Source: Allman (1984: 30).

TERMS AND LEVELS OF TRADE DEPEND ON SOCIAL CAPITAL

We assert (indeed, it is the principal theme of our book) that most transactions include both economic and socio-emotional goods, both of which are valued. Moreover, the number of SEGs included in exchanges depends on the social capital of the transacting parties. If we describe exchanges only in terms of the economic goods exchanged, the terms and levels of trade will be difficult, if not impossible, to understand. We simply must consider the social capital of the transacting parties and the relative volume of SEGs exchanged to understand and predict the terms and levels of transactions. We may observe the physical terms of trade, such as the quantity and price of the exchange, but then recognize that these do not fully describe the nature of transactions because they do not account for the SEGs included in the transactions.

Put simply, terms and levels of trade depend on social capital. Indeed, it is difficult to exchange physical goods and services without also exchanging SEGs. Thus, an exchange of a physical good for money with a friend is not the same transaction as with a stranger, even if the physical goods and environment for the exchange are the same. All other things equal, people prefer to trade with those with whom a sympathetic relationship

CUSTOMERS AND CASEROS

In a recent trip to Sucre, Bolivia, a street vendor greeted Lindon with the word "*casero.*" The meaning of the word implies a special relationship created by repeated transactions. A *casero* is a special customer who receives preferential treatment. During a meat shortage, *caseros* of meat venders are still able to buy meat. During normal times these same *caseros* are sold the best meat cuts and from the fresher beef carcasses or other animals. Becoming a *casero* has its rewards, but it requires repeat purchases. (Mexican vendors use the word *machante* in the same way.) Indeed, many languages use verb forms that allow those conversing to distinguish between different kinds of customer relationships.

exists. Indeed, there are some exchanges of physical goods and services that are made solely for the intent of investing in one's social capital. In most cases, gifts are given for this precise motive—to invest in one's social capital.

INVESTMENTS IN SOCIAL CAPITAL AND OTHER CAPITAL FORMS ARE COMPLEMENTARY

Social capital is an essential complement (substitute) for other types of investments. Consider briefly how investments in social capital complement investments in human capital. Human capital is created by changes in the skills and capabilities of individuals that allow them to act in new ways. Human capital, like social capital, is not a physical substance, but rather is embodied in the skills and knowledge acquired by an individual. James Coleman, a social capital pioneer, observed that social capital was a significant factor in explaining investments in human capital by high-school sophomores. He found that social capital in the family and in the adult community surrounding the high school significantly reduced the percentage of students dropping out of high school and increased human capital formation (Coleman, 1988).

DIAMONDS OF TRUST

Wholesale diamond markets exhibit a property that is remarkable to an outsider. Among certain diamond merchants, there exists a high level of social capital. This social capital produces a trust that influences the way they conduct their exchanges. In the process of negotiating a sale, a merchant will hand over to another merchant a bag of stones for the latter to examine in private at his leisure, with no formal insurance that the latter will not substitute one or more inferior stones or a paste replica. The merchandise may be worth thousands, or hundreds of thousands, of dollars. Such free exchange of stones for inspection is important to the functioning of this market. In its absence, the market would operate in a much more cumbersome, much less efficient fashion. Among diamond traders, social capital facilitated investments in diamonds by reducing transaction costs.

Source: Coleman (1988: S98).

We routinely use social capital to motivate the substitution of one capital form for another. For example, whenever we ask a friend for a good or service as a favor, our social capital and provision of SEGs motivates our friend to act. For example, a friend may offer his or her human capital or other forms of capital to substitute for commercially provided capital. However, social capital motivates the substitution; it is not the substitution itself. Whenever a friend alerts us to an event, opportunity, or potential danger we are benefiting from social capital that motivates the substitution of one capital form for another that produces information and warning. When a work colleague helps us solve a complex problem without a *quid pro quo* agreement for reimbursement, social capital has motivated the substitution for our own lack of financial capital.

Whenever a transaction is secured because of a relationship, social capital is substituting for legal guarantees, another form of capital based on relationships.

SOCIAL CAPITAL REDEFINES EXTERNALITIES

Social Capital redefines externalities and provides a resource for managing them. An externality is a cost or benefit imposed on others without their consent. Examples of externalities abound. In a world in which relationships don't matter, the solution to negative externalities is to force the offending party to "internalize the externality." This approach to solving the problem of externalities is to impose costs on those who create negative externalities and to offer benefits to those who create desirable externalities. By penalizing (benefiting) those who create negative (positive) externalities, the externalities are experienced and internalized by those who create them. For example, laws limiting the rights of smokers have proliferated, especially since successful litigation against large tobacco companies has established the negative externality of smoking—namely, the harmful effects of second-hand smoke.

But laws and legal remedies are not the only solutions to the problems created by negative externalities. A story is told of a rude driver who cut in front of another driver, imposing a negative externality. At the next traffic lights the offended driver leaped from his car to confront the rude and reckless driver. As both drivers emerged from their cars, they were surprised to find that they were neighbors and friends, and what could have been an unpleasant exchange was quickly resolved with apologies and laughs. In this case, social capital internalized the externality voluntarily, which was more effective and did not harm either party to the externality. Laws that internalize externalities are costly to enforce and largely unsuccessful unless supported by most of the people.

The lesson from the drivers is the following: externalities are defined by relationships and social capital. Taking an action that harms the object of one's social capital imposes personal costs. Social capital, in effect, leads people to internalize externalities voluntarily. This both reduces negative externalities and encourages positive externalities that often take the form of investments in public goods.

Another solution to the problem of externalities is to organize group rewards. When success is defined by the team's efforts, team members become supportive of one another because their individual effort depends on the team's success. Furthermore, each member comes to evaluate and base his or her effort on its contribution to the team's success. While this is often successful, opportunities to practice this principle are limited. For one thing, an absence of social capital often sabotages this approach. For example, some may free-ride, arguing that, since the team is winning, they don't need to contribute. Or a selfish individual may mismanage resources intended for the group's success—a problem called the tragedy of the commons. Most successful group outcomes depend on social capital.

Investments in public or high exclusion-cost goods—resources used by the public and costly to limit their use to selected groups—require social capital. In effect, social capital provides an incentive to manage the resources for the group rather than exploit it for personal profit.

SOCIAL CAPITAL PROVIDES ALTERNATIVE MOTIVATIONS

Social capital provides insights about different motivations as well as introducing a new form of capital and a new class of goods that can find new solutions to solve old problems. Not every solution must begin by asking how we create a profit motive to solve

this problem. There are other ways to influence people's behavior that don't depend completely on personalized penalties or profits. Investment in goods that are shared in the community may be maintained just as well by providing social capital incentives as by providing profit incentives.

LESS LITTER AND MORE HAMBURGERS

A popular public good is the vista from our highways. An externality is created when travelers litter the highway. Trash and debris that litter the highways reduce travelers' enjoyment of litter-free roadsides, pollute drinking water, and cause death or harm to animals. Yet, the cost of maintaining a clean landscape is significant.

Interestingly enough, a solution for many miles of highways has been the "adopt a highway" program which depends on different groups and individuals adopting, or accepting the responsibility for, certain stretches of highway. These volunteers are not paid, and it is hard to explain their motive as profits. But suppose we tried.

Suppose, as we're driving down the highway, we see a sign that reads: "The next two miles of highway are maintained by Beth and Bill's Hamburger Buffet." "Ah hah," we exclaim. "Bill and Beth only maintain the highway to increase their hamburger sales!" Then, we reflect, why would we buy more hamburgers from someone who cleans the highway compared to someone who doesn't? The answer has nothing to do with hamburgers. It has to do with the social capital created by Bill and Beth in their highway activity.

MEANING AND VALUE DEPENDS ON ATTACHMENT VALUES AND SOCIAL CAPITAL

The meaning and value of objects depends on embedded SEGs as well as on objects' physical properties. A baseball is a round object covered with leather, which can be purchased for roughly $10—until it is hit by Barry Bonds or Sammy Sosa to break a home-run record. Then the monetary value of the round object covered with leather increases to over $1 million. But the embedded SEGs that alter the value of the baseball depend on the social capital of Bonds and Sosa. And should they lose their social capital—for example, if they were to be convicted of steroid use—one can imagine that the baseball would also lose its value.

PHELPS AND POT PICTURES

Michael Phelps won a record eight gold medals during the 2008 Beijing Olympics and, in the process, earned a large amount of social capital from admiring fans. Producers of major products such as Kellogg's, were eager to benefit commercially from Phelps´s social capital and so paid him significant sums of money to endorse (embed with SEGs) their products.

But what goes up often comes back down, and so it was with Phelps's social capital. A British tabloid newspaper published a picture of Phelps with a water pipe commonly used for smoking "pot." Phelps admitted that he had made a mistake and vowed, for the second time, not to repeat it. But the damage to his social capital was significant—so much so that Kellogg's was no longer interested in him endorsing its products.

Because SEGs embedded in objects account for such a significant portion of value, we need to study social capital to assess the value of objects that are attributed to SEGs and social capital and also learn how these values are produced. For example, wrapping gifts with a personal touch is one way of increasing the value of a physical good by embedding SEGs in it. Ultimately, it is not just the physical properties of a product or service that imbue it with value, but what its relationship is to us. Although a loved grandfather's watch may be worth only a few dollars (it probably doesn't even keep good time), it may be priceless to the grandchild for whom it is a reminder of a tender relationship.

SOCIAL CAPITAL SUSTAINS INSTITUTIONS

Institutions are rules for ordering and giving meaning to transactions. Without agreed rules, an ordered society is impossible. We can relate to each other only when we agree on what are the institutions.

However, institutions are obeyed and supported only when people are motivated to do so. For example, I may respect your property because I know you will call the police, or at least take legal action against me if I don't (the stick motivation). I may respect your property rights because there is some economic reward from doing so (the carrot motivation). Moreover, you may be a customer of mine, and I will lose your business if I don't respect your rights. Finally, I may respect your property rights because it's the right thing to do (and because it provides me ease of conscience), because I care about you (the hug motivation), and because I want to contribute to an orderly society (a distant hug motivation). We could summarize many (but not all) these motives by returning to Boulding's (1989) taxonomy of carrot, stick, and hug power.

The important point to make here is that rules that require the exercise of the carrot or stick in any significant degree cannot be long maintained. History has proven this point. Only when relationships are such that people respect each other's rights for reasons other than the carrot or the stick do we have sustained institutions that provide our exchanges with order and meaning.

SOCIAL CAPITAL PROVIDES A BRIDGE ACROSS THE SOCIAL SCIENCES

Finally, social capital provides a bridge across the social sciences that facilitates communication and cooperation. It also tends to collect into a single paradigm many of the insights that are often ignored when social analysis is performed by an isolated discipline. Defining social capital as sympathy allows for a multi-disciplinary application and testing of the concept.

Conclusion

Individuals or groups have social capital when they are the recipients of another person's or group's sympathetic feelings. Individuals or groups provide social capital to others when they have sympathetic feelings for them. Those who have social capital have access to resources from social capital providers on preferential terms compared to what might be expected in arm's-length relationships.

Social capital is, above all else, capital—a resource (motivation) to be managed to produce benefits. To maximize the advantages from one's social capital requires that it be understood, managed, and maintained. Once we recognize the importance of social capital we are inclined to revisit many of our allocations and services and ask if social capital resources are being properly managed. Can counselors provide SEGs without having social capital? Can musicians write music that provides SEGs without caring? Does it matter if we believe that the only way in which people can be motivated is by appealing to their selfishness?

Increases in social capital promote cooperative actions, alter terms and levels of trade, encourage exchanges, reduce free-riding, internalize externalities, and increase investments in public or high exclusion-cost goods among individuals and groups who possess social capital. It also leads to the creation of, and support for, formal and informal institutions and networks, and can substitute or complement other resources, often unleashing their potentials. It is frequently overlooked and mismanaged. Without understanding social capital it is difficult to understand other important concepts like institutions, networks, and SEGs.

CHAPTER

3 *Different Kinds of Social Capital*

Every man feels his own pleasures and his own pains more sensibly than those of other people ... After himself, the members of his own family, those who usually live in the same house with him, his parents, his children, his brothers and sisters, are naturally the objects of his warmest affection.

Adam Smith, The Wealth of Nations.

Introduction

Sympathetic relationships, or social capital, often have their origin in shared individual traits. Furthermore, different kinds of shared traits often lead to different kinds of relationships and different kinds of social capital.

We refer to shared traits that lead to the development of varying kinds of social capital as *kernels of commonality*. This chapter describes the role of kernels of commonality in the production of different kinds of social capital.

Shared Traits and Kernels of Commonality

Common to all sympathetic relationships are shared traits—kernels of commonality. Shared traits define areas of agreement that can lead to socio-emotional exchanges that develop relationships of sympathy or social capital. For example, if the shared kernel is membership in the same political party, then each person in the relationship can more easily develop sympathy for the other person because they agree with and validate the other's political views. In this sense, shared kernels of commonality are the catalysts that facilitate socio-emotional exchanges that produce social capital.

Shared traits or kernels can be broadly divided into two classes: those that are inherited and those that are earned by purposeful choices and sometimes by coincidental connections. The most important distinction between earned and inherited kernels is their exclusivity. Considered below are several examples of inherited and shared kernels of commonality.

INHERITED KERNELS OF COMMONALITY

Inherited kernels of commonality are determined by the conditions of one's birth rather than by one's purposeful choice or coincidental connections. Since inherited kernels

cannot be changed, social capital based on the conditions of one's birth is expected to be more permanent and less depreciable than kernels that are chosen and changed. As a result, we often find social capital based on inherited kernels being used as a form of insurance—you always have your family to fall back on.

Since one is born with one's inherited kernels, membership in the group defined by the inherited kernel is exclusive. A person either has or doesn't have the kernel. Societies organized around inherited kernels sometimes tend to be rigid and inflexible and display what Mancur Olsen (1984) calls sclerosis. Societies sometimes take actions to limit the exclusivity created by associations organized around inherited kernels of commonality by prohibiting actions that discriminate on the basis of inherited kernels. For example, it is unlawful for many employers to base hiring decisions on age, gender, or race. In other cases, associations based on inherited kernels are not illegal, but still exclusive.

INHERITED KERNELS OF COMMONALITY AND CAFETERIAS

Walk into any racially mixed high school cafeteria at lunchtime and you will instantly notice that in the sea of adolescent faces there is an identifiable group of black, Asian, Latino, or other ethnic students sitting together. Conversely, it could be pointed out that there are many groups of white students sitting together as well, though people rarely comment about that. The question on the tip of everyone's tongue is "Why are the ethnic groups sitting together?" Principals want to know, teachers want to know, white students want to know, and the ethnic students who aren't sitting at the table want to know. The answer is that they have organized around an inherited kernel of commonality.

Source: Olson (1984).

EARNED KERNELS OF COMMONALITY

In contrast to inherited kernels, earned kernels of commonality are not determined at birth and can be acquired. Societies organized around earned kernels tend to be more flexible than those organized around inherited kernels because they admit change. For example, people may voluntarily join an athletic team and the shared kernel, membership in the athletic team, may be the catalyst for the development of social capital. Other earned kernels may be shared interests in topics such as trout fishing, woodworking, or enthusiasm for a sports team.

Sometimes the earned kernels may be shared experiences such as having graduated from the same school, lived in the same town, known the same people, studied the same subject, or participated in the same war. Other earned kernels may be membership in the same club, validation by similar awards, or by equivalent positions in one's employment. And still other kernels may be shared religious convictions, compatible political views, and similar values on a range of topics, including the importance of family values, the environment, taxes, public education, prayer in public school, healthcare, abortion, homosexuality, social security, migration, and capital punishment, to name but a few. The lack of an important earned kernel may sometimes lead to exclusion.

JOB SECURITY AND EARNED KERNELS OF COMMONALITY

Sometimes the more productive employee is passed over by a mediocre employee because the lesser worker has won favor with their superiors by keeping them better informed, by joining their social activities, and by recognizing and becoming an integral part of the company's work culture. One worker was quoted as saying: "I was recently passed over on a promotion opportunity to replace my boss who is nearing retirement ... My performance ratings have been outstanding to exemplary for the last 10 years."

Management employees often have no idea they are about to lose their jobs or be passed over for promotion. They thought that their loyalty to the company, plus the good results of their work, would carry them upward, not outward. What they forgot is the importance of building personal alliances in their organization to achieve career success. Developing social capital around earned kernels appears to be an important factor in determining one's success on the job.

Source: http://www.officepolitics.com/advice/?p=59.

Earned kernels may be temporary or permanent. One's current political view is an earned kernel, and can change. The high school from which we graduated is also an earned kernel, but is permanent and will not change. As a result, permanent earned kernels produce social capital that is stable and permanent, like social capital based on inherited kernels.

A special class of earned kernels is based on compacts or covenants that create obligations to further the well-being of their members. The more durable is the compact, the more durable is the social capital that the compact produces. Examples of relationships based on covenants include married couples, religious orders, military units, and fraternities and sororities. Not all compact groups need to rely on formal covenant-making processes such as a marriage contract; they may instead rely on implicit compacts indicated by participation in the group. In some societies, covenant relationships take on many of the intense bonding characteristics associated with inherited kernels.

DIFFICULT DISTINCTIONS

Sometimes it is difficult to distinguish between earned kernels and inherited kernels. For example, we might consider a degree from an exclusive law school to be an earned kernel. But if admission to the school relies to no small degree on past contributions made by your ancestors to the school, then your degree may be both inherited and earned.

As another example, consider the cars we drive, which can be an example of both an earned and an inherited trait. A friend drives cars made by General Motors. Because his father always told him that GM cars were better than the others he has always bought GM cars. Is his driving a GM car an inherited or earned kernel? The correct answer is that it is both. To make this point in another context, Lindon once interviewed a young lady who was attending the University of Nebraska. He asked her what influenced her decision to attend this particular college. She responded that she wanted to attend Kansas State University, but when she expressed this preference to her family, her mother sternly responded, "We wear red here, not purple."

DISTRIBUTIONS OF SOCIAL CAPITAL

Each society distinguishes itself by the emphasis it places on inherited versus earned kernels that are either permanent or temporary. In some Nicaraguan communities, upper-class social capital is based on both inherited and earned traits related to one's current income and wealth (although the latter trait was facilitated by one's social capital). The upper class appears to discriminate against members of the lower and middle class by offering their own class preferential terms of trade and other benefits of public office. For example, membership of organizations such as Rotary and Lions clubs appears to be strictly an upper-class phenomenon—a shared trait that represents a combination of earned and inherited kernels of commonality.

One interesting display of earned social capital among the Nicaraguan poor occurs in a strictly defensive circumstance. It seems that when a member of the lower middle class dies, especially in the case of the lower middle class living in urban settings, solicitations are made among the neighbors to pay for the burial.

Other forces affecting the distribution of social capital include globalization, economic conditions that favor some and disadvantage others, communication facilities, education, dissemination of religious values, cultural norms, integrity of families, and the political environment that encourages or discourages participation.

Important Kernels and Strong Ties

We recognize that not all kernels produce social capital or feelings of sympathy. For example, most of us share earned kernels with drivers on the road between our work and our homes on most weekdays between 5:00 p.m. and 7:00 p.m. But this kernel of a shared driving experience does not lead to increased social capital. On the other hand, we may attend regular services of worship with people with whom we share important religious beliefs. With this latter group, we have more social capital than with our "road–warrior" companions. The following sections describe some of the reasons why some kernels are more important for building social capital than others.

THE NUMBER OF PEOPLE SHARING THE KERNEL

Large numbers of people sharing the same kernel may detract from the kernel's uniqueness and diminish its importance. For example, one kernel is citizenship. The number of people with US citizenship is so large that very few exchanges of SEGs are likely to occur because of this shared kernel. However, a group of US citizens living in a suburb of Lima, Peru, got together on the Fourth of July and celebrated Independence Day, even though they were relatively unknown to each other. The reason was the increased importance of their shared kernel of US citizenship on account of their isolation from the main group and their low numbers.

OPPOSITION FROM THOSE LACKING THE KERNEL

During the Vietnam War, two kernels of commonality were support for, and opposition, to the war. What made these two kernels important was the emotional distance between those holding one kernel and those holding the alternative kernel. During that era

these two kernels accounted for strong exchanges of socio-emotional goods (and socio-emotional bads) that increased the kernels' significance.

APPROVAL FROM SIGNIFICANT OTHERS

Veterans at the end of World War II were greeted upon their return with welcome ceremonies and parades. Later they were given assistance in their educational pursuits and given preferential medical assistance. Finally, service in the armed forces during World War II often provided individuals with preferential employment opportunities. Thus, the kernel of service in World War II was important and useful in many circumstances, partly because this shared trait had gained such widespread favor.

DURABILITY OF THE TRAIT

Relationships, like other forms of capital investments, require time and maturation. As a result, kernels become more effective when they have sufficient longevity to be meaningful. Inherited and permanent earned kernels, of course, exist forever and may be one reason why they are such an important source of social capital. On the other hand, kernels based on clothing fads appear to be unreliable—they can never be counted on to last.

MAINTENANCE COSTS OF THE KERNEL

We all have many friendships and acquaintances that are based on shared kernels that are no longer important. Unfortunately, we do not make the socio-emotional investments necessary to maintain our social capital in many of these relationships because the cost of doing so is high. We tend to emphasize relationships which are less costly to maintain and from which we are likely to earn the most return.

SHARED OUTCOMES

Kernels which lead to shared outcomes are generally important if the outcomes are important. For example, members of a sports team win or lose together. This shared kernel of team membership leads each to internalize the well-being of others and facilitates the exchange of SEGs.

CHEAP SOCIAL CAPITAL

There is nothing like a shared threat for building social capital. The possibility of sharing a bad outcome or facing a common enemy often produces increased social capital. When the kernel is a real or imagined threat to one's safety, economic survival, or social acceptance, the formation of social capital among the threatened most often leads to the exchange of SEGs during efforts to reduce the threat. Political despots use this knowledge of how to create social capital by creating threats to strengthen their regimes. Hitler blamed Germany's economic problems on the Jews. Rulers in Iran claim that the US is a threat to their way of life. The generals in Argentina blamed Great Britain for their lack of international power.

Social capital based on a threat or common enemy is referred to as *cheap social capital* because it requires so little to create. On the other hand, its survival depends on maintaining the threat. If the threat is removed, the social capital based on the shared threat also disappears unless other earned kernels have grown up to replace the threat-based kernel.

THE ENEMY OF MY ENEMY IS MY FRIEND

Sitting in a small, hot, and muggy room in Kuala Lumpur, Bryan had the opportunity to interview the leader of the political opposition coalition contesting elections in Malaysia. The notable thing about this opposition coalition was that it comprised Islamic Malays and Christian Chinese—two groups known not to cooperate well in the past. Bryan asked whether the cooperation between the two groups was based solely on their mutual distaste for the ruling regime. "Oh, no," the leader replied, "we have truly found common ground beyond our shared dissatisfaction with the ruling party." But when Bryan asked the Chinese representative of the coalition about his partner's stated goal to implement an Islamic state after assuming political power, he admitted that the coalition had not negotiated how power or political objectives would be shared if they indeed won power. In other words, it was their shared enmity to the ruling party that provided the glue for the coalition.

Different Degrees of Sympathy and Social Capital

Social capital exists in a continuum of sympathetic emotions. Weak sympathetic ties may be characterized by awareness. Stronger social capital ties may be characterized by support for, and agreement with, others on subjects ranging from politics to religion to business practices. Still stronger social capital ties reflect sacrifices for the well-being of one's objects of social capital—acting on one's social capital. Finally, at the strongest end of the social capital continuum is empathy in which one person hardly distinguishes his or her own well-being from another. Corresponding to this continuum of social capital is a wide variety of kernels of commonality with the varying qualities described above that facilitate the development of social capital.

Although social capital can be measured continuously, it is helpful to group social capital ties into discrete categories. The categories we assign to various social capital ties are *bonding, linking,* and *bridging* social capital. Although the labels bonding, linking, and bridging social capital are used elsewhere there is disagreement about their differences. In other words, the distinctions we make here are not universally accepted. We describe each below in turn.

BONDING SOCIAL CAPITAL

Bonding social capital exists among those with strong feelings of sympathy. It is often an intense permanent or long-term commitment that may be inherited or solemnized with a bond or pact. It is most often based on inherited kernels or permanent earned kernels and sustained with a long-term commitment and frequent personal contact. Bonding social capital can be characterized by intense feelings of caring, affection, and concern as might exist among family members, committed couples, long-time business partners, or members of an oppressed minority. In the extreme, bonding social capital becomes empathy in which one person's well-being becomes indistinguishable from that of another.

LINKING SOCIAL CAPITAL

Linking social capital exists in semi-socially close relationships and is most often based on temporary earned kernels and moderate-term commitments. It is similar to the links in a chain that are of the same size and strength, and share the same stress. Linking social capital can be characterized by feelings of respect, trust, and collegiality as might exist among colleagues, co-workers, members of the same team, club, or community, and people who perform similar tasks or share similar responsibilities. People with linking social capital often have sympathetic views about politics, religion, and how to rear children. They may also have business interests in which the outcomes are synergistic.

BRIDGING SOCIAL CAPITAL

Bridging social capital exists in asymmetric relationships. It can be thought of as a bridge that connects two different bodies of land that differ in size, resources, and populations. Bridging social capital can be characterized by asymmetric feelings of sympathy that might exist between a boss and an employee, a parent and a child, a teacher and a student, a famous person and a fan, a leader of a country and a citizen of the country, a political official and a constituent, and between people alive today and people from the past.

Bridging social capital may be based on inherited or earned kernels and can lead to exploitation. For example, many may feign an exchange of SEGs to receive some material benefits from their bridging social capital. Because of the potential for exploitation, bridging social capital is often unstable.

Combinations of Social Capital in the Community

Different combinations of the three types of social capital within communities result in different kinds of social interaction—a theme we explore in a political context in Chapter 16. One might imagine a community where there are strong social capital bonds between families, but weak social capital ties to the rest of the community and its leaders.

MISTRUST AND A BACKWARD SOCIETY

In his classic book, *The Moral Basis of a Backward Society*, E.C. Banfield concluded that the backward condition of Montegranesi in Southern Italy (the name is fictitious) could be attributed to adherence to the rule that one's objective was to maximize the short-run advantage of one's nuclear family and assume that all others will do likewise. This philosophy led the citizens of Montegranesi to suspect others and to discourage collective and even beneficent behavior. As a result, no-one in Montegranesi concerned themselves with public affairs and were suspicious of those that did. Informal organizations that often create SEGs largely failed to develop, laws were disregarded unless punishment for disobedience was likely, and in general no-one was willing to concern themselves with the good of the rest. The conclusion: mistrust kills collective and beneficent acts.

Source: Banfield (1958).

Other Social Capital Issues

SOCIAL CAPITAL AND SYMMETRY

The stability of one's investments in social capital with people of similar resources is related to the symmetry of relationships. If individuals in a social relationship provide each other with different levels of social capital, then the person who is the object of the greater social capital may exploit the relationship. This exploitation, however, usually leads to a reduction in the social capital of the exploiter that continues until symmetric levels of social capital exist in the relationship. An exception to the requirement for symmetric relationships may be bridging relationships in which unequal social and physical resources permit asymmetric relationships to persist. An example of a persistent asymmetric relationship is one that may exist between loving parents and a spoiled child who has little regard for the welfare of his or her parents (Becker, 1981).

One reason why asymmetric relationships may exist in bridging relationships is because people holding unequal levels of social and physical resources may often have unequal desires to invest in social capital. Those in resource-rich positions may be reluctant to increase the social capital they provide to those in resource-inferior positions because it may obligate them to provide resources on preferential terms. On the other hand, those in resource-inferior positions may desire increased social capital investments with the wealthy because, with increased social capital, their access to resources improves.

ASYMMETRY IN RELATIONSHIPS

In the movie (and novel) *Gone with the Wind,* Scarlett O'Hara is facing the loss of her estate, Tara, if she cannot pay $300 in taxes. She visits a possible benefactor, Rhett Butler, who is imprisoned by the Yankees. Rhett has expressed affection for Scarlett in the past, but Scarlett has not reciprocated. This asymmetry in their relationship is characteristic of bridging social capital. Rhett desires SEGs from the relationship; Scarlett is more interested in money and is willing to feign caring to obtain the goods she needs. The need for money motivates Scarlett to pretend symmetric levels of sympathy during her visit to which Rhett responds enthusiastically until he discovers Scarlett's sympathy is feigned.

BORROWED SOCIAL CAPITAL

An important characteristic of capital is its alienability—the ability to enjoy the benefits of capital without owning it. For example, taxi passengers enjoy the transportation benefits of taxis without owning them, and telephone users enjoy the benefits of communication services without owning the telephone lines and equipment required for communication.

Social capital satisfies the alienability requirement because the benefits of one's social capital can be transferred. Letters of referral and recommendation are often used to transfer the benefits of one's social capital to another. Many examples of alienable social capital exist.

ALIENABLE SOCIAL CAPITAL AND WEDDING RINGS

Lindon's father-in-law enjoyed a sympathetic relationship, social capital, with a wholesale jeweler in Salt Lake City, Utah. After Lindon received permission from his father-in-law to marry his daughter, Lindon learned about the jeweler and visited him, intending to purchase an engagement and wedding ring. When he first met the jeweler the relationship was formal. But when he told him that the ring was intended for Earl Baxter's daughter, the relationship immediately changed. Lindon was shown rings that were not on public display, and when he made a selection, the jeweler made a significant reduction in the price. Lindon enjoyed borrowed social capital.

LATENT SOCIAL CAPITAL

Social capital may exist in a latent form among people who share kernels of commonalities, but who have not discovered them in each other. Converting latent social capital into active social capital requires interactions in which the shared kernels are discovered. In other cases, social capital can be created in the process of growing earned kernels. For example, students from many diverse backgrounds may attend a university and, as a result of shared experiences, create an earned kernel, which becomes the basis for their social capital.

The Downside of Social Capital

Social capital has its disadvantages, costs, or downside, but so do all other forms of capital. For example, the downside of our transportation capital is pollution and the exhaustion of our natural resources. But we don't say that a car isn't capital because it emits unhealthy exhaust fumes. Nor should we say that social capital is not capital because it has its downside.

Consider some disadvantages of having social capital. On the one hand, having social capital provides access to resources on preferential terms. On the other hand, social capital comes with obligations which sometimes require support for norms and values that are not necessarily our own. This obligation to conform is sometimes referred to as peer pressure and may lead to mob rule. In some settings, social capital's tendency to promote conformity may discourage superior performances that distinguish between workers and performers, or it may cause a reduction in the importance of merit in favor of associations and allocations that are based on one's social capital (Portes and Landolt, 1996).

The most obvious downside of social capital accrues to those without it. Such individuals may possess skills and talents that are not employed for the benefit of a community simply because they lack social capital—for instance, the boss's nephew gets promoted over the more qualified plant manager, and inefficiency in the work place is accepted. Waldinger Aldrich, and Ward (1990) describe how an absence of what we call social capital excludes African-Americans and keeps West Indians employed at lower levels in the New York building contracting industry.

Wacquant argues that because persons living in poor areas lack social capital, government and business have withdrawn positive "state social capital" from declining

urban areas. The outcome for these neglected areas are losses of physical safety, legal protection, welfare, education, housing and healthcare as well as a reduction in residents' ability to sustain themselves. As Wacquant puts it:

> *These institutions have turned into instruments of surveillance, suspicion and exclusion rather than vehicles of social integration and trust-building. Together with the withdrawal of the wage-labor economy in the context of extreme racial segregation, their debilitation has accelerated the shrinking of the ghetto's indigenous organizational basis and helped concentrate in it the most dispossessed segments of the urban (sub)proletariat.*
>
> Wacquant, 1998: 25.

As important as may be the disadvantages that can be associated with social capital, the most significant disadvantages of social capital are associated with negative social capital. Completeness requires that we address the negative form of social capital—that is, feelings of antipathy. We define negative social capital as:

> *A person's or group's antipathy for another person or group. Antipathy may include feelings of disgust, lack of concern, hostility, disregard, disrespect, lack of responsibility, or mistrust for another person or group.*

Negative social capital frequently results from the absence of shared kernels or the presence of conflicting kernels that lead to disagreements and contests over economic outcomes, values, power, and information.

The consequences of negative social capital include a lack of sharing, unwillingness to provide aid or engage in mutually beneficial exchanges, acts of exclusion, fraud, discrimination, and malevolence—the willingness to bear a cost to harm others. In short, it is a willingness to bear the costs to hurt others. If sympathy derives added benefits from constructive efforts to aid a friend, antipathy receives satisfaction from hurting an enemy, even if one is made worse off in the effort. We first noticed the power of hostility in a survey designed to measure discounts and premiums in the sale of used cars (Robison and Schmid, 1989), and have since confirmed it in a number of other surveys. For example, in a study of minimum-sell prices for land, hostility added a premium of over 18 percent to the price that in effect precluded land exchanges between those with hostile relationships (Robison, Myers, and Siles, 2002).

Negative social capital is often accompanied by distrust (you are different therefore I can't trust you). Distrust increases transaction costs and economic cooperation, which in turn may produce low levels of economic activity and income, thereby increasing income and wealth inequality. In the extreme, negative social capital may lead to abuse, business and political acts that harm others, and war and terrorist acts that maim and kill.

Of course, negative social capital can be borrowed, just as social capital can be borrowed. The enemy of my friend is my enemy as we saw in the Malaysian example. Finally, if we wish to consider the human condition, we must admit that much of human misery and poverty created by war, abuse, exclusion, and neglect are motivated by various gradations of negative social capital. Worse, it has proven difficult to disinvest in negative social capital. Conflicts in Northern Ireland, the Balkans, and in Africa had their origins in negative social capital often created hundreds of years ago.

Conclusion

History is often a description of conflicts and cooperative efforts among groups of individuals who shared kernels of commonality that served as catalysts for social capital. Sometimes history is a record of conflicts between groups who lacked kernels of commonality or who held mutually exclusive kernels. The Civil War was organized around those who had the kernel, or support, for the "peculiar institution" and those who opposed it.

Strong emotional exchanges often occur when persons holding a particular kernel are opposed by groups lacking it. As described in the Chapter 1, social and economic exchanges are usually integrated so that social relations are reflected in economic ones and vice versus. For example, the essential kernels for Marx and Engels were ones that defined economic classes. Kernels that defined these groups were land and physical capital ownership versus non-ownership.

Using kernels of commonality to understand the differences between levels of sympathy helps us categorize social capital into bonding, linking, and bridging types. It also makes evident that social capital can be both negative and positive and does not necessarily have to be symmetric. These insights will be important as we explore the different ways in which social capital influences social interactions, including poverty alleviation, globalization, politics, institutions, ethics, and so on.

CHAPTER

4 Do Social Capital Motives Matter (Much)?

How selfish soever man may be supposed, there are evidently some principles in his nature, which interest him in the fortune of others, and render their happiness necessary to him, though he derives nothing from it, except the pleasure of seeing it.

Adam Smith, The Theory of Moral Sentiments (1759).

Introduction

The definition of social capital proposed in this book makes it clear why relationships matter; it is because our sympathy for others (their social capital) makes their well-being our own. In contrast, central to the neoclassical economic paradigm is the assumption that rational economic agents allocate resources to maximize their own consumption of physical goods and services which meet their wants and desires. This is referred to as the selfishness of preferences assumption (Quirk and Saposnik, 1968). Moreover, in most neoclassical economic models, the identity of participants in an economic exchange does not affect the outcome (Telser and Higenbotham, 1977). The literature supporting neoclassical economists' emphasis on selfish preferences is well known. Edgeworth, a famous nineteenth-century economist, wrote: "The first principle of Economics is that every agent is actuated only by self-interest" (quoted in Rescher, 1975: 13). Mueller (1986) added that only the assumption of egoism was essential to a descriptive and predictive science of human behavior. Tullock, convinced of the importance of self-interest, wrote: "The average human being is about 95 percent selfish in the narrow sense of the term" (quoted by Mansbridge, 1990: 12). Summarizing the focus on self-interest, Etzioni wrote: "The neoclassical paradigm, we have seen, attempts to show not merely that there is an element of pleasure (self-interest) in all seemingly altruistic behavior, but that self-interest can explain it all" (1991: 3).

Social capital theory agrees that selfish preference for physical goods and services is an important motive. However, social capital theory recognizes that individuals are also motivated by the need for socio-emotional goods (SEGs), which are the product of social capital-rich relationships. In these relationships we may value SEGs that express caring, validation, and information for ourselves and for those we care about. Finally, social capital theory asserts that SEGs are important and that the social capital that produces them is as important as other forms of capital. In this chapter we support the claim that relationships matter—a lot.

Social Capital and Self-interested Behavior

An important consideration and one of the strongest arguments for the study of social capital is that both physical goods and SEGs are interdependent: it is almost impossible to separate the two. Currently, mainstream economics largely ignores SEGs (and hence social capital). Economists might justify excluding SEGs (and social capital) from their analysis if its relative importance is small. But the evidence presented in this chapter suggests that SEGs are critical. Therefore, any analysis of transactions must account for their influence.

Introducing social capital and SEGs into economic analysis alters the way in which we think about selfishness. Assume for a minute that neoclassical assumptions of selfish behavior and selfish motives are independent of changes in the well-being of others. From this perspective, selfish behavior increases one's own income without regard for the consequences of one's choices on others except for their influence on one's own ability to earn income.

Self-interested behavior, in contrast, allows for changes in the welfare of others to influence one's own welfare because of social capital. Social capital internalizes the welfare of others so that changes in another's welfare alter one's own well-being, preferences, and motivations. Selfish behavior is focused on physical goods and services. Self-interested behavior recognizes that preferences exist for both SEGs and physical goods. Both selfish preferences and self-interested preferences are rational and consistent with the utility-maximizing behavior postulated in economics.

Perhaps an example will clarify the difference between selfish versus self-interested behavior. Are parents selfishly motivated to sacrifice for the education of their children even though they expect no financial rewards from doing so? Sensible parents would immediately recognize that such sacrifices are not selfish but self-interested because they receive SEGs from the success of their children to which they contribute. These SEGs may include validation that they are successful in their parenting role or they may be SEGs resulting from their children expressing appreciation for their parents' sacrifices.

Self-interested behavior can be summarized in five common motivations (Robison and Schmid, 1996). Note that four of the five motives involve social capital investments. They include:

1. *What's in it for me?* Selfish individuals increase their well-being by increasing their *own* income.
2. *I'm glad when you're glad.* Self-interested individuals increase their well-being by increasing the well-being of those they care about. In this case the rewards are socio-emotional rather than financial.
3. *It's not good to be alone.* Self-interested individuals recognize that sometimes we cannot significantly alter the well-being of those we care about. So, to increase the SEGs from the relationships, they attempt to increase the closeness they feel toward the objects of their social capital.
4. *Reach out and touch someone.* Selfish and self-interested individuals take deliberate acts to increase the sympathy that others have toward them. Although their allocations are motivated by the desire for increased social capital, the returns from the increased investment in social capital may be both SEGs and/or increased income.

5. *Who is the person in the mirror?* Selfish and self-interested persons increase their sense of well-being by increasing their self-respect. Individuals investing in this type of social capital do so by acting in ways that align their actual self with their ideal self. One might think of investments in one's self-respect as investments in social capital provided by one's ideal self. Again, the motive is based on one's desires for SEGs.

WHAT'S IN IT FOR ME?

The totally selfish person cares nothing for others and is completely opportunistic. For example, they might exploit legal opportunities by enforcing a contract provision after an unforeseen event creates a hardship on the other party. They might cheat on a business partner or employer. They will illegally use harmful pesticides or feed additives for higher profits if they sense a low probability of detection. Bottom line? These people take what they can.

SELFISH BUTCHERS

Two famous passages from Adam Smith's renowned books on how nations become wealthy have often been used to support the assumption of selfishness in economics. Smith argued that people are selfish in their market transactions:

> *It is not from the benevolence of the butcher, the brewer, or the baker, that we expect our dinner, but from their regard to their own interest. We address ourselves, not to their humanity but to their self-love, and never talk to them of our own necessities but of their advantages.*
>
> Smith, 1966b[1776].

Smith also wrote: "We are not ready to suspect any person of being defective in selfishness" (1966a[1759]).

I'M GLAD WHEN YOU'RE GLAD

Popular singer, Barry Manilow, crooned: "You see I feel sad when you're sad/I feel glad when you're glad."[1] These lyrics describe an important motivation of a self-interested person. Such individuals seek to improve the well-being of those they care about. Studies show that sellers offer price concessions to those with whom they feel sympathy and whose incomes are less than their own. Feelings of sympathy explain why we offer favors and gifts without expecting repayment, make contributions to our alma mater, and support welfare payments for dependent children. On an international and national basis, it may help explain "most favored nation" trading status, food stamps, and welfare relief programs.

Social capital, then, leads to funding support for neighborhood and community development projects. For example, we may vote for increased taxes for education when we have no children in the system because our neighbor's children are the objects of our social capital. Similarly, we may support community improvements because we care about

1 From Barry Manilow, "Can't Smile Without You," Arista, 1978.

the general well-being of members of our communities. While both ends have elements of selfish motivations, they are primarily driven by our concern for others—because they are the objects of our social capital.

Individuals who provide social capital for others adopt practices that regulatory efforts fail to achieve. There can never be enough police to catch the food processor who ignores diseased animals or the feedlot operator who uses a drug for too long. But when the food processor and feedlot operator care about their customers, even if only to maintain their buyers' trust, they adopt practices that regulatory efforts fail to achieve.

IT'S NOT GOOD TO BE ALONE

A newcomer in a town or school often wants to increase his or her sense of belonging and the SEGs they receive from others. Toward this goal they may join the local Rotary or farm organization, participate in parent–teacher organizations, or volunteer for services. Increasing one's sympathy for the community and its members increases the pleasure derived from goods valued only for their physical properties. A retiree gets more satisfaction from school taxes by becoming closer to others' children.

Schools and other organizations in rural communities often provide opportunities for voluntary work. When they participate in such activities, individuals often develop a deepened sense of belonging that increases support for local businesses and helps sustain institutions in rural communities.

TEAM PENNANTS AND WIN–LOSS RECORDS

Displaying team pennants attached to car windows seems to be a recent trend in the United States. These are particularly popular on game day in most university towns. However, it is noticeable that the percentage of cars displaying team pennants is highly correlated to the team's win–loss record. Apparently, we want to increase our closeness to winning teams by displaying their pennants (though it likely does little to contribute to the team's success or failure). But many fans have little desire to increase the social capital they provide to losing teams and hence fail to unfurl their team pennants.

REACH OUT AND TOUCH SOMEONE

In business, customer loyalty counts. Even when financial incentives encourage them to switch, a loyal customer may continue business with the same firm. Thus, firms benefit if consumers have brand and store loyalty. Businesses may seek to build customer loyalty and goodwill through contributions to local charities. In other words, businesses may seek to materially benefit from increases in their social capital.

For example, banks try to convince customers that they know their special circumstances and are therefore able to take their financial needs into account. AT&T suggests that it can deliver "your world." In the competition for the beverage market, beer and soft-drink producers have linked consumption to having fun with friends, while milk producers have focused on health with consequent less emotional impact and sales success. All these companies are attempting to create feelings of goodwill in the customer by appealing to things that the customer desires.

Another factor in improving customer goodwill is fairness. Research shows that customers react to notions of fairness in business practice (Kahneman, Knetsch, and Thaler, 1986). If customers perceive unfair price mark-ups in the context of temporary shortages, the higher prices may defeat all the goodwill built by the business through advertising and service. Profit-seeking business cannot ignore the effects of goodwill on returns to advertising and pricing policy.

Fairness also improves employee goodwill toward the business and affects its productivity. Fairness in promotion, firing, and relative wages within the firm builds goodwill and increases productivity. Until recently Japanese firms have better understood the importance of employee goodwill or social capital than US firms, and this may be part of our competitive problem. Many Japanese firms make commitments to lifetime employment and are more aware of how management salaries and perks, relative to those for plant workers, affect morale, monitoring costs, and productivity. In contrast, much has been made of the hefty salaries American CEOs make in relation to their workers. Perceptions of greedy, overpaid, and out-of-touch executives, coupled with bad customer service, are diminishing the loyalty some American consumers feel for certain producers.

Like manufacturers and service providers, farmers also benefit from society's nostalgia toward them, even if the warmth of these feelings has cooled somewhat. The "warm glow" which urban people have felt toward agriculture in the past substituted for, and complemented, raw political power. Nowadays the public is increasingly aware of how farming practices affect the environment and food safety. How agricultural production responds to these increasing concerns will affect the extent of society's care for those engaged in agriculture.

WHO IS THE PERSON IN THE MIRROR?

Psychologists observe the need for individuals to find conformity between their beliefs and actions. Acting in ways contrary to one's internalized set of values reduces self-respect or social capital associated with one's ideal self. Some people who are eligible for food stamps do not apply for them because participation in the scheme does not fit their self-image. Studies report individuals returning lost purses with cash inside even though it required a personal sacrifice to do so. Many return excess change when miscounted at the grocery store. Why? Because keeping it affects how we feel about ourselves.

How one feels about one's actions is sometimes referred to as one's conscience. Consider how conscience drove Abraham Lincoln.

MY FRIEND DOWN INSIDE OF ME

Facing re-election and the loss of popular support for the Civil War, Abraham Lincoln was in despair. Should he give into popular opinion and negotiate an end of the war? Or should he continue the course of preserving the Union and the elimination of slavery, even though the suffering measured in property and human life was immense? Being personally committed to preserving the Union and converted to the cause of freedom for all, he committed himself to continue the war. Lincoln said: "I desire to conduct the affairs of this administration, that if at the end, when I come to lay down the reins of power, I have lost every friend on earth, I shall have at least one friend left and that friend shall be down inside me."

Source: Bachelder (1995).

Do Social Capital Motives Matter?

Having introduced the different motives that may influence behavior, we are now confronted with the question: what is the relative importance of the five motives?[2] This also leads us to the question: can social capital and its influence be measured? Can we really tell the extent to which an agent's resource-allocation decisions are influenced by changes in the well-being of others with whom a relationship has been established? If relationships are unimportant, then an agent's resource-allocation decisions should be unaffected by changes in the well-being of others. Under these conditions, the traditional neoclassical model that emphasizes selfishness of preferences is acceptable. If, however, relationships are important, then modeling how an agent's choices affect the well-being of others should add insights to agents' economic behavior and improve the predictive ability of economic models.

SOCIAL CAPITAL AND PRISONERS OF WAR

To test for the relative importance of social capital, a survey was designed to elicit respondent allocation decisions that match the five motives described earlier. The survey was administered to a capstone course of senior-level students from the College of Agricultural and Natural Resources at Michigan State University. The students represented a cross-section of students at the college, and the course was designed for students to reflect generally on working with others in teams to solve problems. The survey was repeated multiple times to different groups of students with nearly identical results. Students were asked to assume the following:

> *Assume you are a member of the American task force sent to Bosnia. Unfortunately, you have been captured by one of the hostile groups in the region. Life as a prisoner of war is unpleasant, with life-sustaining but tasteless food and few other comforts. You have no way of knowing when or if you will be released. In the midst of this Spartan life, you receive a box of Hershey candy bars. Red Cross rule enforcement assures you that these candy bars cannot be taken from you. So you may do with them what you choose. Please indicate in the first line below how many of the candy bars you would eat and how many you would share with others described in questions 2 through 5.*

We measured the importance of selfish preferences—the motive described earlier as "What's in it for me?"—using the percentage of candy bars consumed by the subject, and labeled the result "Own consumption."

We measured the importance of investments in own social capital—the motive described as "Who is the person in the mirror?"—using the percentage of candy bars given away to keep a promise, and labeled the result "Promise keepers."

We measured the importance of investments in the well-being of people we care about—the motive described as "I'm glad when you're glad"—using the percentage of candy bars shared with a friend, and labeled the result "Sharing."

---

2 It is important to note that the five motivations we identify are not capable of capturing the myriad different configurations of motives that people might possess. They are, instead, points along a continuum that help identify key configurations of motivations and are useful for heuristic purposes.

We measured the importance of investments in the social capital that others provide—the motive described as "Reach out and touch someone"—using the percentage of candy bars given to the guards, and labeled the result "Goodwill,"

We measured the importance of investments in the social capital we provide others–the motive described as "It's not good to be alone"—using the percentage of candy bars shared with fellow prisoners to promote an escape effort, and labeled the result "Together."

The data were examined using an econometric model. Table 4.1 shows the estimated allocations and their statistical relevance.

Table 4.1 Prisoners of war: empirical results

	Own consumption α_1	**Promise keepers** α_2	**Sharing** α_3	**Goodwill** α_4	**Together** α_5
Coefficients	.33	.19	.25	.09	.14
t stat	13.67	10.97	18.61	5.79	11.02
$\overline{R^2}$	57%	49%	69%	11%	56%
DW	.92	1.45	1.08	1.43	1.71
$\overline{X_0}$	6.8	3.9	5.4	2.2	2.7
2-Tail Significance	.000	.000	.000	.000	.000

As the table shows, the percentage allocation of the candy bars equals the coefficients which together sum to 1 (.999). All the coefficients are significant at levels of less than 1 percent. The "Own consumption" coefficient, at .33, is the largest, as neoclassical economists might have predicted. However, the "Sharing" coefficient was 76 percent of the "Own consumption" coefficient and 25 percent of the total consumption. Next in significance was the "Promise keepers" coefficient (.19); the "Together" coefficient (.14) was next; and last came the "Goodwill" coefficient (.09).

The correlation matrix of these outcomes provides some interesting insights about the different motives (see Table 4.2). The most significant correlation was between "Own consumption" and "Promise keepers." The more an agent consumes, the less likely he or she is to keep promises. The next most significant correlation was between sharing with friends and supporting the camp escape effort. These two allocations represent two different social capital investment approaches: bonding and linking. It might be inferred that the survey respondents made the choices either to concentrate social capital investment in a friend or tended to more generally invest social capital in the group. Finally, selfish behavior can be manifested by either consuming or building goodwill with the guard. Efforts to build goodwill with the guard, however, are meaningful only if the agent believes that social capital investments are possible. Own consumption and investing in goodwill with the guard are two selfish activities that are negatively correlated and viewed as substitute activities.

Table 4.2 Prisoners of war: partial correlation coefficients

	Own consumption	Promise keepers	Sharing	Goodwill	Together
Own consumption	1	-.58	-.08	-.32	-.24
Promised keepers		1	-.38	.10	.35
Sharing			1	.12	-.36
Goodwill				1	-.06
Together					1

Conclusion

To test the proposition that relationships affect resource allocation, we extended the neoclassical model by introducing relationships using social capital coefficients to represent the motives described earlier in this chapter. The resulting model was then used to generate several hypotheses describing how relationships influence the way in which economic agents allocate their resources. Empirical results generated from survey data provided preliminary support for the hypothesis that relationships alter resource-allocation decisions. Rather than people being 95 percent selfish in their allocations, we found selfish motivations to be important about 33 percent of the time.

The implications of these findings are significant. They suggest, for example, that the use of potentially harmful pesticides will be reduced if those affected are related to, or have friendly relations with, the producer. Those without children will support tax increases for schools if they know the schoolchildren who will be attending. Companies will support community endeavors in an attempt to create emotional attachments with potential customers. People often value certain outcomes because of their benefits to others, thereby reducing monitoring costs and the amount of regulation necessary to constrain behavior.

Most importantly, our findings provide strong evidence that one cannot analyze resource-allocation decisions only in the narrow context of selfish motivations for the consumption of physical economic goods. Relationships do matter and must be included in the decision model.

Most of the world's economic policies are designed from the perspective that economic agents act independently and selfishly. Beginning with this assumption leads to the view that people can be motivated to alter activities that may impose costs on others only by threat of litigation or by income incentives. Social capital theory suggests that people may respond to other motives. Social capital or feelings of sympathy may lead people to act in socially desirable ways without any external threats or subsidies. Understanding this interdependence of social relationships and economic decision-making will help clarify economic behavior and lead to more enlightened policy decisions.

CHAPTER

5 An Introduction to the Social Capital Paradigm

It was six men of Indostan
To learning much inclined,
Who went to see the Elephant
(Though all of them were blind),
That each by observation
Might satisfy his mind.

The First approached the Elephant,
And happening to fall
Against his broad and sturdy side,
At once began to bawl:
"God bless me! But the Elephant
Is very like a wall!"

The Second, feeling of the tusk,
Cried, "Ho! What have we here
So very round and smooth and sharp? To me 'tis mighty clear
This wonder of an Elephant
Is very like a spear!"

The Third approached the animal,
And happening to take
The squirming trunk within his hands, Thus boldly up and spake:
"I see," quoth he, "the Elephant
Is very like a snake!"

The Fourth reached out an eager hand, And felt about the knee.
"What most this wondrous beast is like Is mighty plain," quoth he;
"'Tis clear enough the Elephant
Is very like a tree!"

The Fifth who chanced to touch the ear,
Said: "E'en the blindest man
Can tell what this resembles most;
Deny the fact who can,
This marvel of an Elephant
Is very like a fan!"

The Sixth no sooner had begun
About the beast to grope,
Than, seizing on the swinging tail
That fell within his scope,
"I see," quoth he, "the Elephant
Is very like a rope!"

And so these men of Indostan
Disputed loud and long,
Each in his own opinion
Exceeding stiff and strong,
Though each was partly in the right, And all were in the wrong!

So oft in theologic wars,
The disputants, I ween,
Rail on in utter ignorance
Of what each other mean,
And prate about an Elephant
Not one of them has seen!

John Godfrey Saxe, "The Blind Men and the Elephant" (1873).

Introduction

We began in Chapter 1 by declaring that "relationships matter!" Any number of social scientists would respond: "Of course relationships matter. Relationships are what I study!" The problem, we would answer, is that while each of the social sciences studies an aspect of relationships, much could be gained by pooling their combined insights into a single paradigm. One problem facing the social sciences is the one facing the six blind men of Indostan described above. Each of our disciplines examines an aspect of relationships, but still needs the insights of others to accurately describe them. The solution to our problem is to combine important insights from all, or at least several, of the social sciences to form a more complete and correct answer to the question: "Why do relationships matter?" In short, we need a social capital paradigm.

For our purposes, a scientific paradigm is a set of practices that define a scientific discipline during a particular period of time. Thomas Kuhn (1996) described a paradigm as *what* is to be observed and scrutinized, and the kind of *questions* that are supposed to be asked, and probed for answers in relation to these factors: *how* these questions are to be structured and *how* the results of scientific investigations should be interpreted.

According to Kuhn, the concept of paradigm was inappropriate for the social sciences because social scientists are never in agreement on theories or concepts (1996: x). We hope to remedy Kuhn's perceptions by proposing a social capital paradigm for the social sciences that answers the following questions: what is social capital? What does social capital produce? How are the goods produced by social capital conveyed? Where does social capital live? How are investments and uses of social capital organized or regulated? And what is the distribution of social capital?

Relationships and the Social Capital Paradigm

From our first consciousness in this life, human beings recognize the need for relationships. Nurture, protection, and sustenance come from another. Nor does it change as we mature. Thomas Hobbes, a well-known English philosopher, argued that humans created social contracts to collectively provide what was once provided to the individual by his or her mother. In fact, without such contracts, Hobbes suggested that life was solitary, poor, nasty, brutish, and short (Hobbes, 1651).

Most of us know this intuitively. So much so that we might at this point sigh and ask ourselves, "Why read any further?" But, despite knowing intuitively the importance of relationships, we are still hard-pressed, over 300 years after Hobbes's death, to understand exactly why, where, when, and how much relationships matter. In fact, it is only lately that many of our leading social sciences have even begun a formal study of social capital and its influence on relationships in human exchange, politics, and society. The study of relationships and social capital, to this point, has been hampered by fragmented approaches, limited communication, rival definitions, confusing specifications, and ambiguous measurements.

Our aim in this chapter is to satisfy Kuhn's requirement for a scientific paradigm. We intend to assemble a social capital paradigm that includes important insights on the subject from across the social sciences. We seek to combine into a single paradigm the various views of social scientists pertaining to the motivations and outcomes of human exchanges. Through this effort we intend to highlight the complementary contributions of each of the social sciences and to eliminate the sometimes sharp differences in their explanations of the same event. To apply the introductory metaphor, we hope to help the men from Indostan to pool their knowledge for a better description of the elephant.

Although social capital can be influential in a number of realms, we begin with its role in facilitating the exchange of economic goods and services. Our interest in the motivation and outcomes of economic exchanges draws from the foundations of the economic science.

Adam Smith, in *The Wealth of Nations*, noted that specialization allowed pin workers to increase pin production from one pin per day working alone to 4,800 pins per worker when ten workers worked together and each one performed only part of the pin production process (Smith, 1966b[1776]). However, specializing in pin production required that pin workers traded with others to obtain what they gave up producing to make pins. Thus, at the core of human well-being is the ability to obtain in exchanges what one does not produce.

Each of the social sciences has contributions to make to our understanding of the motivations and outcomes of human exchanges. Of course, our synthesis about the motivations and outcomes of human exchanges will be imperfect because we, as authors of this work, represent only two different disciplines. However, we have consulted widely and, to the best of our abilities, have incorporated and connected important views of professionals across the social sciences. Undoubtedly, some social scientists will conclude that their contributions are not fully or accurately represented. This is only to be expected, and we invite those who hold such an opinion to expand on, and improve, our work. Nevertheless, we expect each social science to be able to see their views represented in the paradigm that follows—an eclectic effort to portray the complex process of human exchange that includes both physical and socio-emotional goods (SEGs).

The economics discipline has made significant strides in understanding exchange systems that have contributed to economic growth and development. Economists may rightly claim that their efforts have led directly to dramatic wealth creation and poverty reduction and, indirectly, to rising life expectancy, educational attainment, and technological progress in many parts of the world. Yet, in many other parts of the world, economic models simply fail to explain the failures to overcome poverty and the absence of growth—two important outcomes of the exchange process (see Easterly, 2006; Rodrik, 1999). In too many cases, economic progress is derailed simply because the underlying assumption of the neoclassical model—that relationships among agents have no effect on exchanges—is not true, leading us to a fundamental premise for this work (reflecting more broadly the views of most of the other social sciences): relationships alter the terms and levels of exchange of goods and services transactions.

Toward the end of the twentieth century, academics began to suggest that perhaps we did not fully understand all the variables that might be operating within this complex equation of growth and development. Instead of thinking of just physical capital as a key input to development, they argued, we should also be thinking of human, intellectual, and social capital. These new ideas proliferated rapidly across intellectual disciplines and boundaries. But, although the resulting ideas and theories held great promise for additional progress, by and large the promise has not yet been fulfilled, partly because many who might make use of these concepts are not yet convinced that they exist, while in other cases the definitions and usages have been stretched so far as to make them mutually unintelligible and collectively inapplicable.

Social capital holds great promise for advancing our understanding of social interactions, which include economics but also extend to politics and society in general. Yet, in its current form, the social capital paradigm is fragmented. Sociologists emphasize networks, economists the nature of the exchange relationship, psychologists the concepts of SEGs, anthropologists the influence of attachment values, and political scientists the power structures within relationships. We propose a new social capital paradigm—definitions, rules, measurements, and expected causal relationships—that takes all these perspectives seriously.

Challenging the Selfishness of Preferences Assumption

The assumption that selfishness of preferences is the motivating force behind economic profit and can explain the totality of our human interactions leads to a perverse view of people—namely that no matter what the good deed, if we dig deep enough we will find people's selfish core that really explains their motivation. On this point Schmid writes:

> *A person may make an apparent gift or join a club or neighborhood association strictly for a calculated future business gain. But people also do these things because they hold social capital for others. The motive can make a difference in the flow of goods that would not be expected from greed alone.*
>
> Schmid, 2002: 747.

The origin of the emphasis on selfishness can be traced to the conflict between the historical school of economics led by the German economist Gustav von Schmoller and the Austrian school led by Carl Menger:

> *Menger believed human wants to be largely determined by physiological needs. The content of an individual's needs was considered an objective fact, independent of volition, about which the individual might easily be ignorant or mistaken.*
>
> White, 2007.

Menger also believed that real progress in economics depended on the contributions of both historical and theoretical economics. Despite his effort, the synthesis failed, and economics moved away from the study of social bonds and networks, the focus of the historical school. Afterwards, neoclassical economic theory, which evolved from Menger's work, increasingly described economic agents as connected to each other through monetary exchanges (see Swedburg, 1991).

While some in society lament increasing selfishness, some important economists are not alarmed. Instead, they believe that Adam Smith's "invisible hand" manages humankind's selfish motivations and promotes society's best interest. Well-respected economist Kenneth Arrow wrote:

> *There is by now a long and fairly imposing line of economists from Adam Smith to the present who have sought to show that a decentralized economy motivated by self-interest [selfishness]. would be compatible with a coherent disposition of economic resources that could be regarded, in a well-defined sense, as superior to a large class of possible alternative dispositions.*
>
> Arrow and Hahn, 1971: vi.

The danger derived from assuming selfishness is that we treat each other as though the assumption were true and, in the process, mismanage our social capital resources. In addition, always assuming selfishness may lead us to confuse what is irrational and rational behavior. Indeed, economists sometimes accuse sociologists of accepting the assumption that humans act irrationally. Sociologists often agree. At least they agree that human behavior is shaped by values, environment, and customs that often lead them away from profit or wealth-maximizing behavior. And this behavior, when viewed through the lens of selfish preferences, does seem irrational. However, when the alternative assumptions of the social capital paradigm are introduced, what was once considered irrational behavior is seen as completely rational.

The assumption that people are selfish is a logical and consistent argument to make if people's utility functions depend only on physical goods and services that they personally consume. If, indeed, people only depended on physical goods and services that are purchased with money, then economists should be given their dues and people could be allowed to maximize their income and the goods that they can purchase with their income.

On the other hand, consider the alternative assumption that people's well-being depends not only on physical goods and services, but also on SEGs. If this assumption is true, then we must be concerned not only with when and how we produce our own

income, but also with how and when we produce SEGs for increasing our social capital and own consumption. It is this concern with the production of SEGs that leads us to focus on the relationships from which they are derived. So, is it irrational to donate one's goods to charity and to help a neighbor in distress if, in the process, one produces SEGs that are valued, in some cases, more than the income that might be earned through other selfish activities? Why, for example, would one ever help a friend complete a household project? Unless there was some additional benefit in taking this action, the so-called "rational" act of maximizing one's own income would dictate other choices. We must, therefore, distinguish between selfish behavior focused on producing one's own income and enlightened self-interest in which we recognize the importance of SEGs, as well as our own income, as a source of well-being.

We can no longer build business and public policy solely on the assumption that people don't need to care for each other as long as markets organize their selfishness. Total selfishness may lead to mischief and missed opportunities for cooperation and exchange. Social capital reflecting caring, goodwill, and loyalty can contribute to the success of a variety of efforts, including formation of business partnerships, support for local schools, and community promotion of new jobs, reduction of environmental hazards, and the creation of development projects. The result is often increasing returns to inputs in ways that create positive-sum payoffs for all involved.

Social capital also provides a new approach for reducing the persistent problem of poverty that is not obvious if one assumes that individuals are 95 percent selfish. Economists generally express their concern that efforts to assist the poor using the resources of the rich will reduce the well-being of both groups by disrupting the consequences of their choices. It will hurt the working wealthy because they have less motivation to produce because they receive less pay. It will hurt the poor because they will produce less because, if they get it free, why would they work? Furthermore, some economists find some support for these expected consequences from the experiences of socialized economies that have in effect reduced output and efficiency through their efforts to redistribute incomes.

But these dire consequences expected from efforts to redistribute income all assume that economic agents are selfishly motivated. But this is not the case in social capital-rich societies where each pursues the interest of his neighbor as well as his own. Increased social capital motivates members of society to work hard for those they care about, even if it doesn't increase their own profit. Yes, there is a problem in the world with the distribution of resources, and believing that we are all selfishly motivated has not led us to a solution. Perhaps it is time to consider alternative assumptions provided by social capital. We should do so because the need for a solution to poverty is great.

In his classic work, *Three Faces of Power* (1989), Kenneth Boulding described how we influence the behavior of others through our use of the carrot (economic rewards), the stick (physical threats and punishment), and the hug (SEGs). The historical divide between economic approaches has been between the use of the carrot and the stick. A focus on the carrot in capitalism has sometimes led to exploitive labor, degradation of the environment, graft and corruption, and inequality. On the other hand, relying on the power of the "stick" in controlled economies has produced a similar set of bad outcomes. These include degradation of the environment, loss of human freedoms, suppression of dissent, inequality, graft and corruption. Social capital theory offers a third road, the "hug" approach that recognizes the importance of SEGs as carrots or the loss of SEGs as a stick.

AN OVERVIEW OF WORLD POVERTY

Stark inequality reigns. In the United States, 1 percent of the population holds roughly 40 percent of the nation's household wealth, up from about 19 percent in 1976 (Lardner, 2000). In 1960 the ten wealthiest nations were 30 times as rich as the ten poorest nations, measured on a per capita basis. Today the wealthiest nations are 72 times as rich as the ten poorest nations (Gergen, 1999). In 2000/2001 "[t]he average income in the richest 20 countries is 37 times the average in the poorest 20—a gap that has doubled in the past 40 years" (World Bank, 2001: 3).

The plight of the world's poor is a desperate struggle for survival. Of the world's 6 billion people, 2.8 billion live on less than $2 a day and 1.2 billion live on less than $1 a day. In poor countries, 50 percent of all children under five are malnourished. In many Third World countries, 20–30 percent of the population is homeless (ibid.). According to United Nations estimates, roughly 1.5 billion people are deprived of decent health care, resulting in millions of deaths from malaria, yellow fever, typhoid, and other diseases. Two billion people lack access to pure water and, as a result, suffer the effects of toxic poisons and parasites.

Even if what we've argued to this point is true, it is of little value if it cannot be applied widely and does not provide with us new insights and solutions for particularly intractable problems. We've alluded to the possibility that social capital can help us better understand how to create sustainable growth and development while also addressing difficult problems like poverty reduction. But social capital has also proven useful in a broad array of empirical applications and explanations, including educational achievements (Coleman, 1990), conspicuous consumption (Frank, 1999), healthcare (Miringoff and Miringoff, 1999), crime reduction (Sampson, Raudenbush, and Earls, 1997), investment in human capital (Coleman, 1988), investment in high exclusion-cost goods (Bromley, 1992), customer retention (Buchanan and Gilles, 1990), advertising (Tye, 1998), community development (Flora and Flora, 2003), management (Baker, 2000), economic growth (Knack and Keefer, 1997), trade (Fafchamps and Minten, 1998), discrimination (Ayres and Siegelman, 1995), and poverty reduction (Narayan, 2000). Some of these contributions of social capital will be discussed in later chapters of this book.

Components of the Social Capital Paradigm

Creating new paradigms is always a somewhat uncomfortable process. Old ideas are necessarily abandoned, new concepts must be defined, and resulting insights, ramifications, and understandings defended. We do not claim to be the definitive work on any of the individual components of the social capital paradigm, but instead propose an eclectic approach (describing the major components of the elephant)—something we believe has yet to be done.

We identify the components of the social capital paradigm and their interactions that form the core of the social capital paradigm. Each is connected to, and dependent on, social capital. The components of the paradigm besides social capital are: SEGs, attachment values, institutions, networks, and power. Yet, none of these components in isolation

makes social capital influential in shaping human exchange. All the components interact to shape the nature and application of the other components in an endogenous cycle.

We introduce the connections between components of the social capital paradigm in Table 5.1. Each cell in the table connects two components of the social capital paradigm and describes their interdependence. The sections that follow provide additional detail about each particular pair of connections.

Table 5.1 The social capital paradigm connections

	Socio-emotional goods (SEGs)	**Attachment value goods (AVGs)**	**Networks**	**Institutions**	**Power**
Social capital	1. Social capital can produce SEGs. When people exchange SEGs, their social capital increases.	2. AVGs may preserve people's social capital by serving to remind them of past flows of SEGs.	3. Social capital lives in networks. Different kinds of social capital reside in different kinds of network.	4. Institutions provide rules for maintaining and investing in social capital.	5. Social capital is an important source of power. Social capital theory describes how to use power without destroying social capital.
Socio-emotional goods (SEGs)		6. When SEGs become embedded in objects, the meaning and value of the objects change—i.e., the objects acquire attachment value.	7. Networks connected by social capital must be maintained by exchanging SEGs.	8. Institutions, particularly informal ones, describe how to create and exchange SEGs.	9. SEGs satisfy an important need. Those who supply SEGS have power.
Attachment values			10. AVGs facilitate the creation and maintenance of networks, especially when contact is limited.	11. Institutions must acquire attachment value to be voluntarily sustained.	12. AVGs are often used to enhance the power of their owners.
Networks				13. Institutions live in organized networks. Institutions plus networks are required by organizations.	14. Social capital networks describe the distribution of social capital-based power.
Institutions					15. Institutions reflect the power, purposes, and source of power of their creators.

SOCIAL CAPITAL AND SEGS

The production of SEGS requires social capital (Robison, Schmid, and Barry, 2002). SEGs that express caring must come from someone who, we believe, really cares about us. SEGs of validation must come from someone whom we trust has the capacity and integrity to honestly evaluate our qualities.

Obviously, different kinds of social capital produce different kinds of SEGs. Given the connections between social capital and SEGs, it follows that different transactions involve exchanges of SEGs. For example, bonding social capital will be required to exchange SEGs of caring and strong feelings of attachment.

On the other hand, transactions involving mostly physical goods and services may only require awareness or even recognition of shared traits that may only require weak ties or linking social capital. The relationships between kinds of social capital and the kinds of SEGs produced and exchanged are illustrated in Figure 5.1.

SOCIAL CAPITAL AND HIGH ATTACHMENT VALUE GOODS (AVGS)

When social capital-produced SEGs become embedded in objects, the value and the meaning of the object is changed. This change in value and meaning is referred to the object's attachment value. AVGs may be efficiently used to attract persons with similar traits. Bringing people together who have attachment values for the same object provides opportunities for building social capital because they have shared kernels. For example, people may join a club because they have an attachment value for a sport, a cause, or a

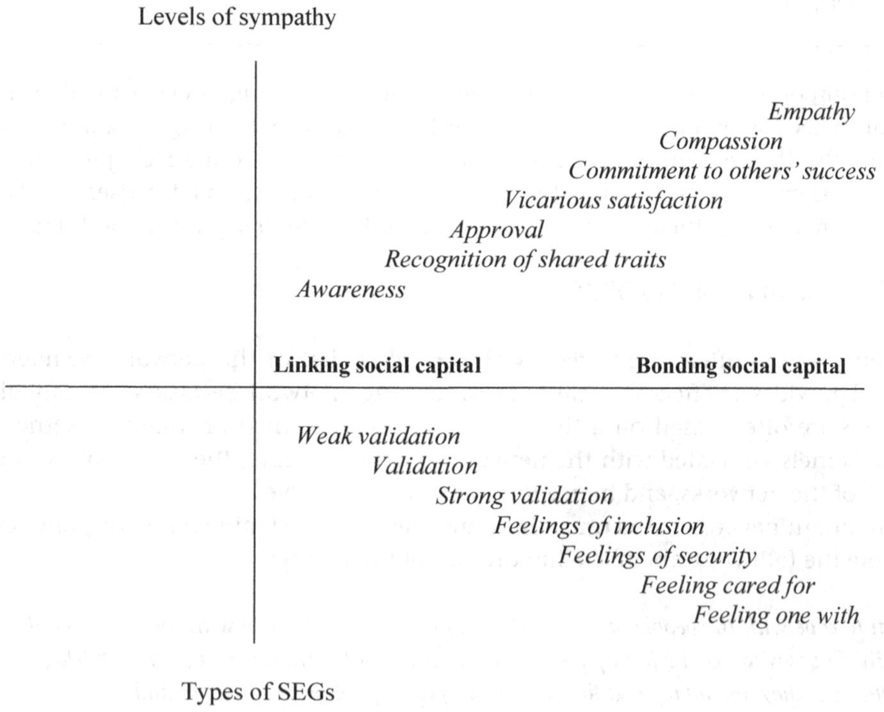

Figure 5.1 Connections between different types of social capital and SEGs

public program emphasized by the club and its members. Once in the club they find others with shared traits or kernels, which become the basis for building social capital with those they might never have met were it not for the shared membership in the club.

Another important connection between attachment values and social capital is the use of famous people or people with attractive features to create attachment value for products. For example, Michael Jordan, for a time, had large amounts of social capital, especially among Chicago Bulls sports fans. "Be like Mike" was the theme of advertisements and also a movie. Attachment values and social capital also have a negative side. For example, suppose a sports team has a poor season. Its poor performance may lead to a loss of its attachment value. One way to preserve the unit's attachment value is to focus the blame on an individual—say, the coach. Then everyone can express their frustration with the coach rather than lose attachment value for the team.

BOOS FOR BOBBY

The Michigan State football team was completing one of its worst seasons in history. Not only was it losing games, but it was losing by large margins. The fans were hurt. After being defeated by Wisconsin, the fans started chanting, "Fire Bobby," referring to Bobby Williams, the MSU football team's coach. A fan-behavior psychologist analyzed: "The chanting was a self-defense mechanism ... it was a way for fans to protect themselves from another bruising football defeat for Michigan State University and the team they identify with." From the perspective of the social capital paradigm, it was a way of preserving attachment value for the school and the team by sacrificing social capital with the coach, Bobby Williams.

Source: Rook (2002).

Another important way of building attachment value using social capital is to personify an object by giving it the name of, and in some ways treating it as, a person. For example, the White Mountains in New Hampshire are named after US presidents. Money almost always carries the caricature of a famous person. When advertisers market products, they may name them after famous people or have their signatures on them.

SOCIAL CAPITAL AND NETWORKS

Durable networks are often connected by the social capital of the network members. Social capital provides an effective means of maintaining a network because social capital-rich networks are often based on a foundation of shared, earned or inherited kernels. The type of kernels associated with the networks often determines the permeability and adaptability of the networks, and hence their capacity to survive.

One important network based on an inherited kernel is the family network. James Q. Wilson wrote the following about the importance of the family:

> *We learn to cope with the people of this world because we learn to cope with the members of our family. Those who flee the family flee the world; bereft of the [family's] affection, tutelage, and challenges, they are unprepared for the [world's] tests, judgments, and demands.*
>
> Wilson, 1993: 163.

Because of the advantages described earlier, family networks appear to be very successful in business.

FAMILY TIES AND PROFIT

The backbone of the American economy continues to be the family business. More than 75 percent of companies in the United States are family-owned or controlled. One-third of the Fortune 500 companies are family firms. Family businesses generate 60 percent of the GNP. Family businesses employ more than 40 million people. Selling the firm ends the dynasty. Going public means relinquishing cherished privacy. When it works right, nothing succeeds like a family firm. The roots run deep, embedded in family values. Unfortunately, the advantages of a family network for legitimate business also apply equally to illegal family businesses.

Source: Calonius (1990).

SOCIAL CAPITAL AND INSTITUTIONS

Institutions are the rules that give order and meaning to transactions. Informal institutions often describe the conditions under which SEGs are exchanged between people with high levels of social capital. Formal institutions usually order the exchange of physical goods and services between people whose social capital is limited to linking social capital. Both formal and informal institutions can lead to investments in social capital because transactions that occur according to agreed rules are more likely to produce mutually positive results than those that occur without agreed rules.

The adoption or rejection of institutions may also facilitate investments or disinvestments in social capital. In the first case, the voluntary adoption of an institution signals agreement. It also creates a shared kernel—the institution which all agree to support. Conversely, failure to agree on an institution signals divisions and may lead to disinvestment in social capital as people come to realize their lack of a shared kernel and divide into smaller groups to oppose each other's interests.

OLD EUROPE

The decision to invade Iraq without the support of the United Nations Security Council deeply divided former allies—in particular, France and the United States. Donald Rumsfeld, then US Secretary of Defense, may have given voice to US frustration with the French when he referred to them as "Old Europe" and announced the US intention to seek support from "New Europe." The disinvestment in social capital between the two countries may have been symbolized in the United States by some people renaming French fries and French toast freedom fries and freedom toast. More significantly, the breach may have been responsible for the cancellation of a $1.5 billion contract between Whitney and Pratt (a mostly US firm) and Europe's Air Bus (Watson, 2003).

From the perspective of the social capital paradigm, the unwillingness of "Old Europe" (particularly France and Germany) and the United States to agree on institutions regarding military action in Iraq resulted in a significant loss of social capital between the peoples of the United States and Old Europe.

Since the adoption of an institution generally requires compromises, it is hard to imagine how institutions could be created or sustained without social capital—unless the parties supporting the institutions have social capital that allows people to internalize each others' well-being, compromises leading to the creation, adoption, and support of an institution might well be impossible to achieve.

SOCIAL CAPITAL AND POWER

Social capital is a source of power—an influence on the behavior of others. Of course there are many kinds of power that one can use to influence others, but social capital power is unique because it doesn't depend to the same extent as other forms of power on financial and physical resources. This is because when individuals share social capital they will modify their behavior on the basis of what they perceive as the well-being of others.

What happens to one's social capital power when interpersonal transactions are separated by an impersonal object, such as a computer, an ATM, a car, or the like? Some believe that road rage results from drivers separated from each other by steel and glass that act as a barrier to the role of social capital in resolving disputes. Likewise, it is easier to kill using a bomb or a missile that eliminates the necessity of encountering the victim face-to-face. Similarly, what are the consequences of separating students from their instructors by a television screen or by time such as occurs when listening to a recorded lecture or watching the Olympics delayed and on tape? The quick answer is that the possible exchange of SEGs and social capital-based power has been reduced. On the other hand, if technology increases the flow of SEGs by creating exchanges that otherwise would not occur, then we can claim that one's social capital power has been increased.

Interactions Between the Components of the Social Capital Paradigm

SEGS AND AVGS

SEGs require a means of conveyance. These conveyances may include a place, a time, a community, a ceremony, music, flowers, gifts, other physical objects, or a host of other goods. It is likely that some of these conveyances will become associated with, or embedded with, the SEGs they convey. When this association occurs, we create attachment values. Thus, objects with SEGs embedded in them become a means of storing and recalling SEGs.

On the other hand, objects may be acquired in the belief that they have attachment value to others who are expected to provide SEGs. Purchases of expensive cars, clothes, vacations, and similar goods are often intended to communicate one's social standing, which is expected to be reciprocated with SEGs. Alternatively, conspicuous consumption[1] may be motivated by the desire to demonstrate one's connectedness to particular causes, parties, or individuals and to experience their success vicariously. Similarly, we might

1 The term "conspicuous consumption" was originated by Thorsten Veblen (1899). He used the phrase to describe the ostentatious squandering of resources by the wealthy classes.

engage in conspicuous consumption to signal membership and shared traits. However, we might also engage in conspicuous consumption to demonstrate our differences with others, especially those who can't afford to drive the expensive car, wear the expensive clothing, or take expensive vacations.

SEGS AND NETWORKS

Social capital-rich networks are sustained by the exchange of SEGs. Of course, different kinds of network may support different kinds of resource flow, but to maintain social capital within a network, network members must exchange SEGs.

The flow of SEGs may well be influenced by network size. We only have so much social energy to expend on maintaining personalized social capital. Thus, as the size of a network increases, the average level of social capital invested in network members must at some point decrease or shift from bonding to linking.

As the social capital changes in the network and also as the structure of the network itself changes, so do the direction and intensity of the flows of SEGs. For example, hierarchal networks are more likely to exchange SEGs of validation and information than of caring. On the other hand, dense and horizontal networks are likely to exchange SEGs associated with caring and belonging.

SEGS AND INSTITUTIONS

Institutions expedite the exchange of SEGs, AVGs, and economically valued goods (EVGs) and services. For example, an institution in which prices are the same regardless of the relationships between buyers and sellers reduces transaction costs. But, in many parts of world, an informal price systems exist that require a significant amount of haggling until an agreed on price is reached; these systems involve more of a personalized exchange that may include the exchange of SEGs.

Formal institutions permit fewer SEGs to be exchanged because their conditions are supposed to apply to all, independent of relationships. As we discuss in Chapter 8, formal institutions are often established to meet the demands of increasingly complex and numerous transactions involving large numbers of people. For example, as families provide less and less care to their elderly parents and grandparents, society must create formal institutions to take on this service. While these new institutions are an efficient way of providing the physical component of elderly care, because they shift the direct care of aged parents from children to others, they change the intensity and flow of SEGs. Interestingly, however, as some formal institutions reduce the level of SEGs in exchanges, other institutions may emerge to increase the exchange of SEGs. Now, even large corporations, such as Wal-Mart, advertise both the economic and socio-emotional components of products available for consumption.

SEGS AND POWER

The potential to supply SEGs is a powerful force for motivating behavior, as is the potential to supply socio-emotional "bads". Law-enforcement officials frequently use shaming, a socio-emotional "bad", to influence the behavior of others, partly because it requires fewer financial and physical resources to employ than other negative enforcement sticks.

AVGS AND NETWORKS

Social capital-rich networks are often organized around a shared kernel. The kernel may be earned or inherited, a characteristic of the network that most often determines its permeability and adaptability. Of course there are other kernels that are not used as the basis for organizing networks simply because they fail to acquire attachment value. The reasons that determine the importance of kernels as the basis of social capital are the same reasons why some objects and not others acquire attachment value and then become useful for the organization of networks.

Objects with attachment value play an important role in the organization of networks. Advertising the kernels of the network allows people to join the network in the knowledge that they will find opportunities for exchanging SEGs and investments in social capital because they have similar attachment values.

AVGS AND INSTITUTIONS

As has already been discussed, institutions require attachment value to be voluntarily sustained and supported. However, important institutions can *create* attachment value. For example, consider the institutions that create fan clubs, service organizations, alumni support groups, or clubs of Corvette owners. Providing an institution around which people can share their attachment values with others may increase that attachment value. Some institutions establish and identify the quality of goods being traded. Inspection laws establish quality standards with the consequence that the attachment value of goods which have passed inspection increases. For example, some institutions specify the requirements for products to be represented as organically produced. People who have an attachment value for a particular agricultural production method then have an opportunity to express their attachment value for the goods and also, increase their attachment to them in the purchasing process.

AVGS AND POWER

AVGs have a long history of being associated with power. Such objects include the Roman eagle, the Nazi swastika, the Christian cross, the star of David, the crescent of Islam, national and state flags, symbols of political parties, team mascots, family photos, and patriotic songs. All these objects have something in common—namely, the power to trigger experiences involving SEGs that then influence the behavior of others.

Creating attachment value for products influences consumer behavior. Creating attachment value for religious symbols influences religious observances. Creating attachment value for military regiment symbols has often produced solidarity and increased sacrifice. Attachment value is power.

NETWORKS AND INSTITUTIONS

Institutions live in networks. Networks plus institutions, sustained by attachment values, produce an organization. One of the first institutions required by organizations is the one that establishes membership requirements. Sometimes one organization organizes institutions for other organizations. Some organizations are intersections of multiple

membership requirements. We create networks because of the advantages of working together and the necessity of interpersonal transactions to meet socio-emotional needs.

Organized networks exist because the actions we take affect others, often without their consent, creating an externality. Externalities can prove destructive when people linked through externalities cannot formulate institutions to regulate their flows in mutually acceptable ways. Unregulated flows include criminal activities, wars, sabotage, character and physical assassination, and the like. However, the high cost of unregulated flows that produce externalities may lead to the creation of institutions, at least among sub-networks. Indeed, institutions exist among criminals and inmates (honor among thieves), and international rules of war regulate the treatment of prisoners of war, non-combatants, and the like. Of course, these rules are sometimes violated, but their existence is a testimonial to the need for institutions to regulate externalities, even among enemies.

The maintenance of institutions depends on the maintenance of the linkages that connect people in the network. If individuals leave the network, the influence of the institutions has diminished. If individuals join the network, the influence of the institutions has increased (Hirschman, 1970). The point is that, if linkages are based on bridging social capital that depends on mutually beneficial flows of economic goods, the linkages will break down once the advantages to any one member disappear. But the network may be sustained, even when the institutions are unacceptable to some, if the linkages also include the social capital (loyalty) of the members.

NETWORKS AND POWER

Networks are a source of power. Moreover, the power of individuals in a network may be related to the structure of the network and their location in the network. For example, a person (broker) or organization that fills a structural hole—a gap between or within networks—has significant power because of his/her or its ability to regulate the flows of SEGs within the network. Power is more evenly distributed among members of networks with dense connections.

Networks adopt certain institutions and values that are sustained by network members and nonmembers alike. When an individual considers violating one of the network's institutions, the potential loss of network members' social capital acts as a restraint, exerting power or influence over his or her behavior. Economic theory has focused on the individuals and only considers networks of market participants. At least some scientists now recognize that networks matter–even in economics as illustrated below.

TRIBAL NETWORKS AND ECONOMIC POWER

Bill Powell of *Newsweek* writes:

For the past 45 years, economists have sought to make a "science" of their field, trying to convince the world that a nation—any nation—need only adopt a set of responsible policies to ensure a reasonably vibrant economy ... Now comes Kotkin arguing that ethnicity and culture, not just monetary policy and balanced budgets, can be critical in determining economic success. What Kotkin claims is that the history of modern capitalism has been shaped by global tribes [networks], dispersed groups held together by a common culture.

Kotkin's critics argue that he's never met a tribe he didn't like and he therefore ignored many tribes that are not economically successful. What Kotkin and his critics do agree on is that like-minded people who work together, work hard, and respect authority tend to be successful as a group.

Source: Powell, 1993: 47.

INSTITUTIONS AND POWER

Institutions convey rights and responsibilities, and distribute rewards and punishments (carrots and sticks). Obviously, particular institutions may increase or diminish people's power. Considerable effort is exerted to alter or use institutions to gain power. Attempts to replace formal institutions with informal ones constitute corruption, whereas replacing informal institutions with formal ones creates bureaucratic power.

BUCKS IN A BRIEFCASE

A Kenyan government minister found what appeared to be a forgotten briefcase. On opening the case, the minister found a large sum of money stuffed inside and realized that this was not a forgotten briefcase, but a bribe left by one of the wealthiest men in Kenya. Insulted by the man's gesture, the minister called security, returned the briefcase to the man, and had him removed from the building.

In Kenya this is a wonderful sign—for years, government officials have put the well-being of the nation aside in exchange for money from wealthy men, such as the one thrown out of the building. Now the people of Kenya hope that their long days of government corruption are over and that neighboring countries have the proof they need to believe that Kenya truly is reforming its government.

Source: Lacey (2003: A6).

Conclusion

The social capital paradigm is a synthesis of concepts of interest to various social science disciplines. The concept of capital is an idea developed best in economics, as is the concept of production from various capital inputs. Economics is also interested in exchange theory and has much to contribute when it comes to explaining exchanges involving two types of goods—physical and socio-emotional.

The concept of socio-emotional needs and SEGs is closely related to theories developed in psychology. Maslow's work, for instance, emphasizes important socio-emotional needs and how our self-interest may lead us to exchange physical goods for socio-emotional ones.

Anthropologists are interested in how the meaning and value of objects change when they become embedded with SEGs and what are the conditions under which embedding of SEGs in objects can occur.

Political scientists and economists are interested in institutions, the rules for ordering exchanges, both formal and informal, and what role social capital plays in the formation and maintenance of institutions. They are also interested in how institutions and networks facilitate the accumulation and use of power.

Sociologists emphasize that social capital resides in networks (and organizations), and their interest focuses on how the network influences individuals both inside and outside the network.

Finally, all social scientists might find something of interest in the general study of power, since it can originate from the exercise of social capital as well as other forms of capital.

Bringing all these ideas together creates exciting new insights to help explain human exchange. Our focus in this chapter on the interdependencies between pairs of elements of the social capital paradigm is arbitrary, somewhat like trying to isolate two elements of a baked cake. Like a cake that combines all of its elements, most transactions involve more than two elements of the paradigm. The next task, which we tackle in the following five chapters, is to expand our understanding of both the individual components of the paradigm, as well as how they interact with all of the other component parts *simultaneously* to produce the effects of social capital on human exchange.

CHAPTER

6 The Social Capital Paradigm: The Role of Socio-emotional Goods

What literature needs most to tell and investigate today are humanity's basic fears: the fear of being left outside, and the fear of counting for nothing, and the feelings of worthlessness that come with such fears ...

Orhan Pamuk, "My Father's Suitcase," Nobel Lecture, December 7, 2006.

Introduction

Socio-emotional goods (SEGs) are human expressions that validate, express caring, or provide personalized information. SEGs have value because they satisfy universal socio-emotional needs for self-awareness, self-regard, and information. As a result, the terms and levels of exchange of physical goods and service can be altered by including SEGs in the exchange. The economic implications of including SEGs in exchanges are significant. It means that trading patterns of physical goods and services will not necessarily follow patterns that maximize physical efficiency or profits (Kahneman, Knetsch, and Thaler, 1990).

Regarding exchanges of SEGs and physical goods and services, Elster observes:

... the claim is not that the emotions [SEGs] fully determine choice, or that there is no tradeoff between emotional rewards and other rewards. Rather, it is that the tradeoff itself is modified by one of the rewards that is being traded off against the other.

Elster, 1998: 73.

The importance of SEGs is evidenced by industries in which SEGs are one of the major outcomes of production. For example, Hochschild described industry efforts to produce SEGs for airline passengers as "emotional labor" (Hochschild, 1983).

Early economists recognized the importance of SEGs or what Becker (1974) called social income. Nassau Senior, an early classical economist, wrote that the desire for distinction "is a feeling which if we consider its universality, and its constancy, that it affects all men and at all times, that it comes with us from the cradle and never leaves us till we go into the grave, may be pronounced to be the most powerful of all human passions" (quoted by Marshall, 1962: 87).

An example of an important exchange of money for SEGs is Ted Turner's donation of $1 billion to the United Nations.

TED TURNER AND FEELING GOOD

Can SEGs explain what was behind Ted Turner's $1 billion pledge to the UN? In a candid interview, the media magnate weighs greed versus ambition. Turner observes that Scrooge was very rich, but he was much happier when he started giving money away (Stossel, 1997). Apparently, Warren Buffett agrees with Turner's assessment. He partnered with the Gates Foundation to give billions of his money back to society. Mr Buffett explained that he opted to give his money to the Gates Foundation because he liked and admired Bill and Melinda (Loomis, 2006).

"SMILE AT YOUR CUSTOMER! IT'S YOUR JOB"

The term "emotional labor" is a form of work that requires the management of one's feelings to create a publicly observable facial and bodily display. Emotional work may include face-to-face or voice-to-voice contact with the public designed to produce an emotional state in another person. For example, a waitress at a restaurant is expected to do emotional work, such as smiling and expressing positive emotions toward clients. In the process of supplying SEGs, workers modify their own emotions and expressions to provide the displays consistent with the demands of their employment.

Source: http://en.wikipedia.org/wiki/Emotional_labor.

So why aren't SEGs included more transparently in the theory of economic exchange? Gary Becker explained that, as the theory of consumer demand was formalized in economics, the importance of SEGs in economics decreased. He described the decline of interest in social income or what we call SEGs:

> *As greater rigor permeated the theory of consumer demand, variables like distinction, a good name, or benevolence were pushed further and further out of sight. Each individual or family generally is assumed to have a utility function that depends directly on the goods and services it consumes.*
>
> Becker, 1974: 1065.

Despite its neglect in much of economics, a strong argument can be made for re-emphasizing the importance of SEGs. The argument for including SEGs in exchange theory is that almost any personalized exchange of physical goods and services also includes an exchange of SEGs. For example, a businessperson may conduct a financial transaction at a bank and, in the process, earn financial rewards. But if the bank staff also provides friendly service that validates the businessperson's self-regard, then the bank has provided its customer both financial services and SEGs. The value of both goods determines the customer's satisfaction with the bank-centered transaction. Banks generally recognize that they can increase their customers' loyalty by providing them both financial services and SEGs (Hanson, Robison, and Siles, 1996).

Physicians are expected to have acquired technical competence. However, their ability to provide SEGs, described as their "bedside manner," is increasingly recognized as essential to their success with patients. Furthermore, a lack of ability to communicate, a means of providing patients with SEGs, increases the likelihood of patients complaining to authorities.

COMMUNICATION AND COMPLAINTS

Physicians with the lowest patient communication scores on a national clinical skills exam are more likely to have a patient complain to regulatory authorities than physicians with high scores, according to study findings published in the September 5, 2007 issue of the *Journal of the American Medical Association*. Lower patient–physician communication scores were associated with a higher rate of retained complaints, especially for scores in the bottom quartile. Scoring two standard deviations below the mean was associated with a 38 percent increase in the complaint rate.

Source: Tamblyn, Abrahamowicz, and Dauphinee (2007).

Three Categories of SEGs

SEGs can be subdivided into at least three categories: those that validate; those that communicate information; and those that express caring. We consider each in turn.

SEGS THAT VALIDATE

Here, validation means to confirm the value of someone or something associated with the person. Validation often involves comparing a person to a standard. Sometimes the validation standard is another person. These relative comparisons lead us to "keep up with the Joneses" and engage in "conspicuous consumption" (Veblen, 1908). It may also lead us to choose a "pond" in which we are relatively important, rather than the absolute greatest (Frank, 1987).

Validation leads to self-awareness and self-regard both of which are considered essential for human socio-emotional and physical well-being (Whetten and Cameron, 1995). Carl Rogers (1961) suggested that we all have a basic need for self-regard, which he found in his clinical cases to be more powerful than physiological needs. Homans writes: "All of the evidence suggests that for many men social approval is a valuable reward, and that it is difficult to satiate them with it" (1971: 457). Hayakawa (1962) has asserted that the first law of life is not self-preservation, but self-image preservation. Maslow noted that: "We tend to be afraid of any knowledge that would cause us to despise ourselves or to make us feel inferior, weak, worthless, evil, shameful" (1962: 57) Harris observed that self-knowledge is mostly gained in social settings that depend on feedback from others.[1]

Another validation standard is one's ideal self. One's image of an ideal self may be formed by observing the traits of people we admire, from ethical teachings, or from

1 As cited in Whetten and Cameron (1995: 56–58). This entire paragraph benefits from the excellent summary provided by Whetten and Cameron on the subject of self-awareness.

personalizing religious values. This ideal self and the standard it sets for validation is what Etzioni (1988) calls the moral dimension. He characterized the conflict between our physical self and our ideal self with the example: "I want to go to the movie, but I ought to go visit my sick uncle in the hospital." Sometimes the standard of our ideal self is referred to as our conscience.

Sometimes we purposefully create resources or conditions in which validation can be acquired. For example, we may create competitive activities in which we seek validation by excelling over others. Then we validate ourselves or are devalued by others, depending on whether we win or lose. These competitive activities in economic spheres make economic outcomes more important than their monetary value because they provide SEGs as well as physical goods and services. Indeed, we may engage in many strenuous activities and commit considerable resources to activities such as races, contests, and games even when there is no physical or financial reward. In ancient Greece athletes competed for a wreath. Today we compete for plaques, certificates, and employee-of-the-month parking places.

A person's capacity to validate others depends in turn on the status and social capital of the person providing validation. If the evaluator is not viewed as having the credentials required to provide validation, his or his efforts to validate convey few, if any, SEGs. The importance of validation has been demonstrated in worker surveys in which worker satisfaction has been shown to depend more on one's validation than on one's salary after certain levels of physical well-being have been achieved (Herzberg, 1987).

Whether the need for validation leads to competition or cooperation with others may often depend on social capital. When persons A and B lack social capital they derive no vicarious satisfaction from each other's success, in which case validation may lead them to compete and to attempt to exceed each other's achievement. However, competition succeeds when it devalues its opponent (beats the competition) and, in the process, can often destroy social capital if any existed beforehand. As a result, the potential loss of social capital often serves as a deterrent to personalized competitive games.

On the other hand, the presence of social capital means that persons A and B internalize each other's well-being, leading them to make efforts to improve each other's well-being as well as their own. Thus, social capital often leads persons A and B to form teams or establish agreements in which they can pursue their goals cooperatively.

SEGS THAT INFORM

The human mind craves information. Information has meaning when it establishes how objects and persons are connected. Thus, information that describes shared kernels is valued because it establishes the basis for building one's social capital and generating SEGs. Indeed, when two people meet for the first time, much of their initial conversation constitutes an information search to identify shared kernels.

The kind of information that is shared between individuals depends on their level of social capital. Those with bonding social capital may discuss things of a more intimate nature than those with weak linking ties. Indeed, those with weak linking ties will most likely share information in that area of work or recreation in which they are connected. Conversations with strangers often focus on the weather. Only with our close friends do we risk personal information about our disappointments and triumphs.

Sharing information is an essential activity for establishing the necessary basis for transactions. For example, significant talk and information-sharing must precede important transactions.

TALK AND TRUST

Persuasion is information that is designed to establish trust. Persuasion that establishes trust is, of course, necessary for doing business. Chatter in the stock market is an example of information exchanges in the economy designed to establish trust. Portfolio managers talk full-time in order to decide whether to buy or sell. Stockbrokers talk to clients and to each other. To some degree, economic institutions resemble religious ceremonies or social gatherings. They need to be read in terms of human intentions and beliefs. An economy that depends on speech is one that can be listened to and read, like a text.

Source: McCloskey and Klamer (1995).

SEGS THAT PROVIDE EXPERIENCES OF CARING

To be the object of caring is an essential human need. Although this need is especially strong for babies, it does in fact persist throughout life. It is the inherent need for caring that leads humans to spend great amounts of time and energy investing in social capital. The important insight into the need for caring (love) was discovered quite by accident in a University of Wisconsin lab in which the behavior of monkeys was being studied. As we pointed out in Chapter 1, these monkeys valued the love of a mother over other goods, including physical nourishment. Is our health also dependent on expressions of caring as was the health of the monkeys?

THE SURPRISING BENEFITS OF HUGS, HANDSHAKES, AND HEART-TO-HEARTS

You kiss your husband and children goodbye in the morning. You exchange pleasantries with neighbors, greet the gas-station attendant. You call your mother once a week for a chat. These connections to other people—your family, friends, even casual acquaintances––tend to make you feel better, more plugged into life. But they do much more than that, researchers are finding. These links also serve a vital role in safeguarding your health. "They're like a web protecting you from life's stresses," says Thomas Vogt, M.D., M.P.H., program director of epidemiology and disease prevention at Kaiser Permanente Center for Health Research.

Researchers have discovered that women with breast cancer who met weekly in support groups lived twice as long as those who didn't go to meetings. More recently it's been found that heart-disease patients without a spouse or close friend are three times more likely to die after a heart attack than those involved in a caring relationship.

Kukula, 1996: 40.

Sometimes we express our caring by offering gifts and sacrificing our own well-being for the benefit of others. Sometimes we express our caring by foregoing opportunities to exploit the weaknesses of others. Caring is an intangible good that cannot be purchased directly. In some cases, sycophants gain the favor of the wealthy by pretending to supply caring and social capital as illustrated by the very young bride marrying the very old millionaire. In other cases, advertisers and others may seek to manipulate behavior by pretending to offer SEGs. But all these efforts are likely to enjoy limited success because counterfeits for caring are easily recognized.

SEGs and Social Capital Investments

A fundamental social capital paradigm hypothesis is: *social capital investments require the exchange of SEGs*. Thus, transactions that provide validation, expressions of caring, or personalized information not only create consumption goods, but also result in social capital investments. In other words, the social capital available to A is provided by B. So if A hopes to increase her social capital provided by B , she invests in her relationship with B—often by giving B SEGs or, in some cases, other forms of goods.

This fundamental hypothesis is critically important for the advancement of social capital theory as a program. We may find convincing evidence that social capital facilitates a number of positive outcomes, but unless we can invest in it, we are helpless to exploit it for beneficial purposes. On the other hand, if it is subject to investment, then it is a resource to be managed and worthy of our careful study. So we must become interested in the question: "How can we invest in social capital?"

SEGS WITHOUT SOCIAL CAPITAL

In relationships characterized by social capital, SEGs are produced by acts of cooperation, gift-giving, information-sharing, exchange of supportive information, and sharing of resources. In arm's-length or hostile relationships, people attempt to earn SEGs through conspicuous consumption, exclusion, and competitive acts designed to establish rank and to control and reallocate resources (Veblen, 1899). While these acts may produce some SEGs for winners provided by other winners similar to themselves and on the same team, they inevitably produce socio-emotional bads for the losers, who may respond with feelings of increased antipathy and resolve to disadvantage the winner in some future contest. The essence of conspicuous consumption and other ranking activities is to reduce the social capital of transacting parties by demonstrating their absence of shared kernels.[2]

SEGS AND SURPLUS

A corollary to our social capital investment hypothesis is that exchanges of physical goods and services at levels consistent with the expectations of transacting parties do

2 We, of course, recognize that conspicuous consumption may be motivated by other desires, such as to demonstrate one's connectedness to particular causes, parties, or individuals. Wearing the sports jacket of a particular athletic team is an example of conspicuous consumption that is designed to demonstrate support for an association with a particular group.

not produce SEGs or investments in social capital. Transactions that produce SEGs and investments in social capital have a common element. They are perceived as providing value beyond that expected in arm's-length transactions. For example, person A may stop at a roadside fruit stand and buy some of the fruit offered for sale by person B. If the conditions of the sale equal A's expectations of what should be expected in an arm's-length's transaction, no social capital is created. On the other hand, if vendor B engages in a personal conversation that expresses an interest in person A's background or well-being (validation and caring), suggests interesting places to visit and quality dining places (information), and even possibly offers a discount or provides more product than expected for the given price (an economic surplus), then B has earned some social capital from person A.

The processes used to create SEGs (bads) that lead to investments (disinvestments) in social capital vary in intensity and durability. The intensity of the social capital investment depends on the intensity of the human relation experience and is related to communication. Intense communications are face-to-face and occur on a regular basis. Less intense communications occur periodically through a medium such as the phone, mail, e-mail, and messages passed through a third party. The intensity of communication may also depend on the relationship between those communicating. Face-to-face communication between strangers is likely less intense and open than face-to-face communication between a husband and wife, a priest and a penitent, and a parent and child. Finally, the intensity of social relations may be a function of the purpose for the communication. When the purpose of the communication is to enhance one's economic position, validate or be validated, to exchange information, or to express caring, the intensity of the communication is different.

One fundamental reason why social capital investments have such value is that humans have great difficulty producing their own SEGs. They can create many other goods for their own consumption, but not SEGs. These are created mostly in exchange with others. Moreover, since nearly all personalized transactions involve some level of SEGs, we have important incentives to invest in social capital so that our exchanges may result in the consumption of SEGs rather than socio-emotional bads that result from transactions with people with whom one has negative social capital.

If our hypothesis is true that investments in social capital require exchanges of SEGs, what can be done to facilitate their exchange and what can produce surpluses and increase investments in social capital? First, we need to recognize the conditions that favor the creation of SEGs and investment in social capital. Second, we need to identify transactions likely to create SEGs and investments in social capital.

Conditions Favorable for the Exchange of SEGs and Investment in Social Capital

THE PRESENCE OF SHARED KERNELS

One important condition that facilitates the exchange of SEGs and social capital investments is shared kernels. One important shared kernel is a shared threat. Community members facing a flood or other disaster not only have a shared kernel, but their efforts to meet the threat also benefit each other. When transacting partners share kernels such

as shared values, experiences, resources, training, interests, or other aspects associated with one's identity, they validate each other. For example, two people may meet away from home and find out they both graduated from the same high school, share the same religious beliefs, have similar marital experiences, are near the same age, enjoy the same entertainment or food, are committed to similar political positions, or are members of the same ethnic group. Such shared qualities identified in others not only validate their importance in one's own self, but also create SEGs and the possibility of investing in social capital.

ECONOMIC PRESSURES TO COOPERATE

Another condition favorable for the exchange of SEGs and social capital investments is economic pressures to cooperate. These pressures may take many forms. One might be capital constraints that require people to pool their resources or cooperate in other ways to obtain necessary capital. In the process of such cooperation, SEGs are likely to be created. Another pressure that often leads to the creation of SEGs is team outcomes in which success depends on the achievement of the group. And if the outcome is viewed as creating a surplus for the individual actors, then this surplus may very well result in social capital investments among the participants.

In some developing countries, markets fail for a variety of reasons. As a result, social capital must be used to create the SEGs necessary for completing essential transactions. Ironically, market failures often require reliance on social capital which creates SEGs and increases social capital among transacting parties. In other words, when institutions cannot complete markets, or simply do not exist, relationships are needed to effect transactions.

PRE-EXISTING LEVELS OF SOCIAL CAPITAL

If person A perceives she has social capital with person B and B acts, then A is more likely to interpret B's action positively, and the action is more likely to create SEGs and surplus than if the parties shared no social capital. Without social capital, A examines B's actions differently than she would if a pre-existing level of social capital were present. Furthermore, pre-existing levels of social capital provide a sort of economy in the production of social capital compared to transactions with a stranger. It is not at all clear that the principle of diminishing marginal returns apply to investments in social capital: each new investment may indeed generate more social capital than previous investments. A second advantage of pre-existing levels of social capital is that objects associated with A's and B's relationship may acquire attachment value and serve to reinforce and enhance future social capital investments.

HIGH LEVELS OF EXTERNALITIES

When people belong to a group in which their actions have the potential to create externalities, the need for social capital to internalize these externalities often leads to exchanges of SEGs and investments in social capital.

Neighbors who repeatedly interact are likely to exchange SEGs and invest in social capital because they want to improve the quality of neighborhood life. If social capital

CAR POOLING WITH YOUR PALS

A popular Carpool Etiquette website advises: "Nothing can disrupt a happy carpool faster than chronically late riders." Of course, creating offensive smells, talking too much, failing to respect other's interest in music, and asking your car pooling pals to wait while you grocery shop are all externalities that can destroy social capital in a carpool. On the other hand, agreeing to rules that limit or internalize these externalities has its own reward. The Carpool Etiquette site summarizes: "Most carpoolers agree that the good company of their fellow carpoolers is a benefit that they really enjoy and hadn't anticipated."

Source: http://www.carpool.ca/carpool_etiquette.asp.

fails to develop among neighbors, they are likely to move. When people have frequent and sustained interactions, they are likely to invest in social capital because investments in social capital make it possible to internalize any externalities that might be created.

Transactions Likely to Create SEGs and Investments in Social Capital

Returning to our fundamental assumption—the exchange of SEGs is required for social capital investments—we consider the following. A transaction intended to produce only economic benefits for the transacting parties is unlikely to produce SEGs. The difference between flattery and sincere praise is that the goal of flattery is economic advantage, not the expression of true caring necessary to provide SEGs.

So one of the difficult requirements for those who produce SEGs is that their efforts must be perceived as genuinely motivated by their desire to improve the well-being of their exchange partner. In other words, they must be perceived as motivated by concern for the other person's well-being. Someone who does not care and has no interest in validating the worth of another is unlikely to offer an expression that can lead to the creation of social capital. Of course, we may disguise our intentions, but concealing our pecuniary interests under a mask of social capital is difficult to do.

In what follows, we consider some social transactions likely to facilitate the creation and exchange of SEGs that lead to investments in social capital.

GIVING GIFTS

Physical goods are useful for conveying SEGs. However, it must be obvious that the terms of exchange of physical goods are intended to create a surplus for the recipient. Gifts do this best of all, but not all gifts do it equally well. The gifts most likely to convey SEGs are those that are most personalized and least likely to be exchanged for economic gain. For example, a gift from the corporation delivered according to some formula does not have the same SEGs attached as a gift from a husband to his wife, remembering their special day. Similarly, flowers from the company fail to convey SEGs of caring and support in the same way as flowers sent by individual members of the company. We would consider a person gauche if they gave a co-worker a gift of money. But if that money were converted into a gift voucher, the gift would effectively convey SEGs. Wrapping gifts may accomplish

the same objective because it demonstrates that the gift is more than a physical object—it includes embedded SEGs.

GIFT-GIVING

Gift-giving has often puzzled economists, especially because efficient gifts—like cash or giving exactly what a person asks for—seem crass or inappropriate. It has been shown in a formal game-theoretic model that gifts serve as "signals" of a person's intentions about future investment in a relationship.

Source: Camerer (1988).

RESOLVING CONFLICT

Much of what appears to be investment in social capital is, in reality, a search for agreements about the distribution of economic goods and SEGs, and finding facts. Conflicts reduce the rate of return on one's social capital and, if serious, can prevent future social capital investments.

Traditional methods of resolving conflicts rely on the exercise of power and will be discussed in more detail in Chapter 10. To be forced to accept a resolution to a conflict through the exercise of "stick" power is the strongest form of social capital disinvestment possible.

Conflicts may convey an absence of shared kernels. For example, if I promote a particular public policy which you oppose, then we may challenge each other's ethics. Conflicts may also convey disagreement over relative values. We may agree that supporting the elimination of the caste system in India is important, but disagree over whether our commitment to this issue should come before our commitment to the American Cancer Society. Often, our social capital influences these priorities.

Whatever the conflict, the process of resolving it is one of best methods for building social capital and SEGs. It communicates a commitment to the creation of social capital and that investment in social capital trumps the particular conflict. Investing in conflict resolution is a real investment that requires an extension of trust sufficient to explore and reveal differences, and to demonstrate a certain willingness to be flexible for the sake of the relationship.

SHARING RESPONSIBILITY

Sharing responsibility is a way of validating each other's ability to contribute and be responsible. Sharing responsibility is also a way of expressing confidence in the relationship. It communicates a message that I have confidence that you will manage the resources in such a way to minimize negative externalities and maximize positive externalities. Sharing responsibilities also puts in place a procedure for reducing future conflicts. It acknowledges that each person has different responsibilities and suggests willingness for each to recognize the sovereignty of the other over their individual area of responsibility.

IDENTIFYING AND CREATING SHARED KERNELS

Earlier we noted that shared kernels create an environment favorable to the creation of SEGs and investment in social capital. Thus, transactions designed to identify and create shared kernels will likely lead to the creation of SEGs and social capital investment.

SEGs are often exchanged when individuals identify shared kernels. Initial conversations between strangers often begin by exploring areas where shared kernels might exist. This search looks for joint acquaintances, shared experiences such as having visited the same place, attended the same school, or read the same book. It might also look for shared political, cultural, and religious views. Sometimes this search for shared kernels is facilitated by creating opportunities to visually identify shared traits. One's gender, age, and dress often communicate one's kernels. Or merely attending a group meeting where members share certain traits might allow one to identify with others with traits similar to one's own—e.g., attending a church service while on vacation or traveling. Identifying a shared kernel is a means of validating one's own kernel and that of others.

CREATING AND IDENTIFYING SHARED OBJECTIVES

Sometimes sympathetic relationships are created by creating or identifying shared objectives. For example, individuals may participate in a team with a shared objective to win. Their shared team experience becomes a shared kernel that leads to relationships of sympathy and social capital. Sometimes this method of building social capital is referred to as team-building. Teams may be organized around athletic contests, community investments, political objectives, support for schools, opposition to externalities, and others.

CREATING MUTUALLY AGREED-ON INSTITUTIONS

Institutions give meaning and order to transactions. Without institutions, chaos reigns and reduces the likelihood that social transactions will lead to the creation of SEGs. Institutions increase the likelihood that parties to the transaction will agree on the terms and conditions of the exchange and thereby reduce conflict. They also define what should be considered a surplus in a transaction. Put simply, institutions clarify when surpluses are being exchanged with the intention to create SEGs and invest in social capital.

Each new relationship requires that the parties agree on the informal institutions that will order their exchanges. An ability to create and sustain these informal institutions communicates shared values, norms and desires to maintain the relationship. These institutions can lead to synergistic activities in which one's success depends on the success of another and therefore are more likely to lead to the creation of SEGs. On the other hand, institutional arrangements can also create activities in which the success of one party requires the failure of another and the creation of socio-emotional bads.

CREATING MARKETS

One of the ironies of the social capital paradigm is that it provides a powerful defense of market institutions. Physical goods and services exchanged voluntarily in a market setting frequently have SEGs attached to them, so that the market exchanges often

result in increased social capital. While neoclassical economists may recommend market systems organized by selfish preferences because of their efficiency and ability to organize productive activities, social capital theory justifies and supports voluntary market systems because of their ability to create social capital by facilitating exchanges of SEGs.

ESTABLISHING METHODS FOR VALIDATING MEMBERS

All successful organizations establish methods for validating their members. Sometimes these efforts are recognized by material rewards, such as pay increases, improved office space, or access to reserved parking or the executive dining room. Sometimes they are validated by SEGs that may include a personal message of recognition.

It is a strange phenomenon that validating goods that cost so little to provide and yet yield such valuable SEGs are so infrequently purchased. The cost of SEGs is often very small—at least when measured in units of physical goods. They are often nothing more than a greeting, a thank-you note, a congratulation note, or a note of shared sympathy. Furthermore, organizations and groups that function well are those that regularly, and almost without being reminded to do so, exchange SEGs directly. Some practical examples of SEGs provided in a business setting include recognition of employees of the month, newsletters that communicate events in the lives of members of the business (weddings, deaths, graduations, births), company celebrations of holidays and retirements, getting acquainted events, company picnics, golf outings, and the like.

CREATING CLIMATES IN WHICH SEGS CAN BE CREATED AND EXCHANGED SUBCONSCIOUSLY

Is there a contradiction between individual or collective investment in social capital that implies calculation and the emotive non-calculating response of an individual for another? Person A can consciously try to get closer to person B and acquire social capital. If A is aware of it and calculates her response, we have the usual process of exchange. But, if B is unaware of A's intent (or A is not really consciously trying to create social capital), there are elements of emotion, and the dynamic is partly unconscious. Social scientists, labor mediators, and politicians may consciously create an environment in which the emotive elements are directed in a certain way even if the participants are partly or wholly non-calculating in their response. While the source of sympathy may be emotive and non-calculating, it can lead to calculation of how to be of most use to the recipient of one's sympathy.

Conclusion

Investment (disinvestment) opportunities refer to one's ability to create new capital (or destroy existing capital). Investment (disinvestment) opportunities associated with physical capital are generally recognized. Inputs of cement and steel are combined with services from other capital forms to make a building. Inputs of steel, human labor, and electrical energy are all employed in the production of machines. Social capital is produced in a similar way to a machine: by combining inputs and services from other forms of capital. Social capital is created through acts of service, gift-giving, mutually beneficial

interactions, and discovering and creating shared kernels of commonalities. Identifying and creating kernels of commonality such as lifestyles, beliefs, and values, which often distinguish "us" from "them," are likely to facilitate the creation of SEGs among us (while destroying it between us and them).

A key observation is that the value of an exchange can be increased by including SEGs. However, because SEGs depend on social capital, those with social capital are more likely to exchange goods than those lacking social capital, all other things being equal. Second, because trades are facilitated by one's social capital, patterns of trade often reflect investments in social capital. As a result, production of physical processes influenced by investments in social capital may not always be organized in the most physically efficient manner. Perhaps the boss may need to spend some resources building goodwill with her employees before building the business. And, finally, SEGs may substitute for money and physical goods in an exchange. As a result, the monetary price of an object in an exchange may not reflect the object's full value. Furthermore, altering the proportion of SEGs included in an exchange will alter the terms of trade measured in monetary units.

CHAPTER 7

The Social Capital Paradigm: The Role of Attachment Values

Man's only true happiness is to live in hope of something to be won by him, reverence something to be worshipped by him, and love something to be cherished by him, forever.

John Ruskin (1819–1900).

Introduction

Capital requires that the goods and services it helps produce be conveyed to their intended use and sometimes stored until needed. Of course, capital may sometimes be its own means of conveyance and storage. For example, a car is also the conveyer of transportation services. In other instances, capital must employ other conveyances and storage devices to deliver and store their goods and services. For example, a power generator employs electric lines to convey electricity to end users and may employ batteries to store the electricity it has produced until it is used. When a conveyance becomes embedded with the goods and services produced by capital, its value changes. For example, a fully charged battery has a value beyond its physical characteristics.

Social capital produces SEGs and services. These are conveyed by objects and people. When the conveyances of SEGs become embedded with, and provide storage for, SEGs, the value and meaning of the conveyances change (like the battery charged with electrical energy). This change in the value and meaning of conveyances as a result of embedded SEGs is called *attachment value*, and the goods whose value is mostly determined by their attachment value are called attachment value goods (AVGs).[1]

Physical objects that convey SEGs may include pets, photos, places, gifts, flags, and souvenirs of past events, such as dried flowers from a first date. Non-physical conveyances of SEGs include music, poems, traditions, institutions, and words of admiration, respect and love.

AVGs acquire their attachment value when they become embedded with SEGs produced in social capital-rich exchanges. Imagine receiving a door prize at a local department store. The prize may be valued for its physical properties, but it is not likely to convey SEGs because people, not local department stores, provide social capital. On the other hand, imagine receiving the same object as a gift from a close friend or family member. The gift now conveys SEGs and is valued not only for its physical properties, but

1 The term "attachment value" was suggested by Professor Jan Bokemeier.

also for the SEGs it conveys each time the recipient experiences the gift. The point is that social capital and the creation of SEGs precede the creation of attachment value.

Since AVGs depend on the creation of SEGs derived from social capital, changes in social capital can change the meaning and value of AVGs for better or for worse. For example, a divorce most often reflects a loss in social capital and, consequently, a loss in attachment value for objects once owned jointly. These AVGs sometimes get sold at "fire sale" prices at the time of the separation because they have lost their attachment value. Similarly, the attachment value of memorabilia associated with sports teams and famous people often change with the teams' win/loss records and the successes or failures of the famous people. In the latter case, perceived moral failures, such as drug use and involvement in sex scandals, have a particularly negative effect.

Famous entertainment and sports stars claim large amounts of social capital from their fans, and this gives them the ability to create attachment values for products they endorse. Product promoters pay them large amounts of money for using their social capital to create attachment values, but, once the celebrity falls from grace, they often lose their social capital and hence their value to the promoters.

Sometimes significant distance exists between an object with attachment value and the individual or individuals who created the SEGs that produced the attachment value. For example, no one now alive personally exchanged SEGs with George Washington. Yet Mount Vernon, his home, and the Washington monument constructed to honor him have attachment value. Many people own objects with attachment value that once belonged to deceased individuals. Sometimes the individuals responsible for creating attachment value may be diffuse. For example, Memorial Day has attachment value even though we may not have any particular soldier in mind when we celebrate it. And places like one's hometown have attachment value created by multiple exchanges of SEGs.

Attachment values live in our memories and change over time. AVGs invoke the memories that reproduce the SEGs embedded in them. For example, visiting one's hometown, looking at a photo of one's family, watching a sunset, singing the national anthem, and watching sports teams representing one's alma mater may all remind us of past associations and re-create socio-emotional experiences. The connections between attachment value objects and memories are illustrated in the movie *Cast Away*.

TOM HANKS AND A DYSFUNCTIONAL WATCH

In the movie *Cast Away* the main character, Chuck Noland, played by Tom Hanks, is stranded on a deserted island. One high attachment value object on the island is a pocket watch, a gift he was given by his fiancé. In the movie, the watch's value is unrelated to its physical quality of keeping time (because it no longer works); it has attachment value because it reminds Noland of a valued relationship and the SEGs exchanged with his fiancé.*

* *Cast Away* is a 2000 film by Twentieth Century Fox about a FedEx employee who is stranded on a deserted island after his plane goes down over the South Pacific.

AVGs differ from objects lacking attachment value, even though the physical properties are nearly identical. For example, consider the baseball hit by Barry Bonds that broke the annual home-run record. Because this ball was associated with the famous player, it now has attachment value that distinguishes it form other baseballs with nearly identical

physical properties. Objects with attachment value may re-create emotions. Identical objects lacking attachment value can only generate physical goods and services.

For an object that conveys SEGs to have attachment value, one requirement is that it has some permanence so that it can be used repeatedly as a conveyance. For example, a bowl of ice cream that is consumed may be valued for its physical properties but not for its attachment value because it lacks permanence. We will only eat it once. Of course, the ice cream's flavor or the business that sold the ice cream may acquire attachment value, but only because they will be encountered repeatedly.

Value Added and the Creation of Attachment Value

Much work is still needed to identify and understand how specific conveyances acquire attachment values. Nevertheless, we can identify several possibilities, a few of which are discussed below.

ASSOCIATE THE OBJECT WITH INDIVIDUALS WITH SOCIAL CAPITAL

The first possibility is through an object's association with an individual or individuals with high levels of social capital. A respected family member may give a personalized object to another family member, and the object acquires attachment value because of the social capital between the giver and receiver of the object. Flowers to a friend, a letter to an admirer, or recognition from an expert fall into this category. MasterCard has used this approach successfully in its advertising campaign associating the use of their credit card with "priceless" experiences with friends and family.

MASTER CARD AND PRICELESS EXPERIENCES

Ruth Ann Marshall, the president of MasterCard North America is sitting in her Purchase, New York office, referring to snapshots of sentimental real-life moments that she believes hold value beyond money.

There's the image of baby boomer siblings surprising their parents with a 60th wedding anniversary party, a father playing catch with his young son in the backyard before departing for their first big-league ball game, and a mother window-shopping with her daughter for a wedding dress. Then when Marshall is asked to assess the value of her company's unlikely vault to credit card dominance, she smiles and, without missing a beat, offers a simple one-word answer: "Priceless."

MasterCard's "Priceless" advertising campaign adopted the view that living the good life was not the accumulation of material things, but the sharing of meaningful moments with loved ones and close friends. In the language of the social capital paradigm, the company recognized that the SEGs conveyed by physical objects have attachment value. Consistent with this view, MasterCard advertises that its credit card can be used to purchase the objects that convey SEGs. The success of its advertising program attests to the fact that the company has found a way of connecting with its customers.

Source: Flanagan (2003).

Indeed, many products are produced with explicit associations between the product and famous individuals. Thus, team jackets, autographed sports gear, and cereal boxes carrying pictures of famous people and athletes are all designed to increase attachment values and earn a profit.

HOOPS AND INCREASED ATTACHMENT VALUES

After the 2007 Florida Gator basketball team's victory that concluded a back-to-back championship season, merchandisers were finding ways to cash in on the team's increased social capital. Nowadays, screen printers and spirit shops begin printing immediately following the game. A limited number of locker-room T-shirts and hats are produced for the team before the victory for the team's celebration. The rest of the apparel sold to the general public is printed after the game. Merchants recognize that SEGs created by winning sports teams create attachment values for a large number of products associated with the winning team.

PROVIDE THE OBJECT WITH PUBLIC APPROVAL

A second way in which an object can acquire attachment value is through gaining public approval. Popular causes with high public support, institutions, or organizations may all acquire attachment value because support for them produces approval. Thus, a nation's flag or a successful team's pennant may have attachment value because so many approve of what the AVG represents.

ACQUIRE THE OBJECT IN SOCIAL CAPITAL-RICH SETTINGS

Another important way of increasing the attachment value of an object is to acquire the object in social capital-rich settings. Bonnie Wise created attachment value for plastic containers by selling them in social capital-rich settings where SEGs became embedded in her plastic products.

PLASTIC CONTAINERS FILLED WITH ATTACHMENT VALUES

At the end of World War II, Bonnie Wise was a divorced single mother from Detroit. By 1954 she had become a marketing genius. Her secret? Tupperware. She figured out how to sell more covered plastic containers to more people worldwide than any Wharton School graduate ever dreamed possible. To do it, she defied all the established rules of business—focusing not on product, but on people. She feminized retail. She built a multi-million-dollar company by promising self-esteem and human interaction in an isolated, postwar suburban world. She also invented a sales vehicle that would forever change American business: the Tupperware party. Tupperware was withdrawn from stores and sold in homes only. Tupperware parties were a 1950s version of the longtime desire of women to meet in groups. Quilting circles and book and investment clubs today are all part of this tradition.

Source: Adapted from Spake (1999).

CREATE AN ASSOCIATION BETWEEN THE OBJECT AND THE POTENTIAL BUYER

One marketing ploy assumes that, once a customer has had an association with a product, the product will gain attachment value. Consequently, marketers are sometimes willing to offer products initially at reduced prices or below cost, and sometimes offer free gifts in an attempt to create an association with their products that will eventually lead to the creation of attachment values.

ATTACHMENT VALUES AND TOUCH

Ohio State University researchers have demonstrated that a sense of ownership can occur by simply touching an object, even for a very short time—30 seconds or less. Participants in the study were shown an inexpensive coffee mug, and were allowed to hold it either for ten seconds or 30 seconds. They were then allowed to bid for it. On average, people who held the mug for longer bid more for it. People who held the mug for 30 seconds bid more than the retail price four out of seven times (Wolf, Arkes, and Muhanna, 2008).

James Wolf, the study leader, observed: "By simply touching the mug and feeling it in their hands, many people begin to feel like the mug is, in fact, their mug. Once they begin to feel it is theirs, they are willing to go to greater lengths to keep it" (Thompson, 2009).

CREATE A SENSE OF OWNERSHIP

Kahneman, Thaler and others demonstrated that one way in which we create attachment value is by granting ownership of an object. They called the changed value of the object resulting from ownership an "endowment effect" (see, for example, Thaler, 1980). In a series of carefully constructed experiments, Kahneman, Knetsch, and Thaler (1986) demonstrated that the value of objects such as coffee mugs, pens, and binoculars increased for individuals once they were given ownership. The endowment effect—what we call attachment value—produces a difference between willingness to pay and willingness to sell. Kahneman and his colleagues associated the increased value with loss aversion. However, they observed that not all objects demonstrate the endowment effect. Specifically, those objects with perfect substitutes, such as coins or other units of money, did not. The effect on ownership in the creation of attachment value was underscored by former Harvard President Larry Summers who noted: "In the history of the world, no one has ever washed a rented car" (quoted in Friedman, 2003).

Endowment effects are consistent with what we call attachment values. SEGs may become embedded in an object through ownership. Indeed, when one owns an object, one's self-awareness and self-regard is more likely to be associated with it. However, SEGs may become embedded in an object even without the ownership of the object being transferred. For example, the Grand Canyon may gain attachment value as a result of a positive experience, involving an exchange of SEGs, with a friend at that location. Or it may gain attachment value because it is admired by people who have social capital. This sense of appreciation for an object that occurs without ownership has sometimes been referred to as "existence values." Krutilla writes: "When the existence of a grand scenic wonder or a unique and fragile ecosystem is involved, its preservation and continued

availability are a significant part of the real income of many individuals ... to whom the loss of species or the disfigurement of a scenic area cause acute distress and a sense of genuine relative impoverishment" (1967: 779). In all such cases, a sense of responsibility, if not ownership, can lead to the creation of attachment value.

Limitations on the Sale of AVGs

Social capital facilitates the creation of SEGs that become embedded in objects. The implication of this principle is important. People who share social capital are likely to have attachment values for the same objects. Those who do not share social capital are unlikely to value the objects for their attachment value, only for their physical properties and usefulness.

To illustrate, auctions frequently sell AVGs to strangers for a fraction of the value they once held for their owners who valued them for their embedded SEGs. These might include family heirlooms like a grandmother's rocking chair, a grandfather's tools, or a collection of old photos full of memories. Such objects may be of great worth to family members, but, because the circle of people sharing the attachment value for the objects being sold is very small, the sale price at auction is unlikely to reflect the value they place on them.

Conversely there are some objects, such as works of art or items of historical interest, which have high attachment value for large groups of people. In these instances, markets exist in which their owners can sell the objects at a price that reflects their attachment value.

The difference between an object's arm's-length price (a price absent of attachment value) and the price that includes the object's attachment value is often significant. This difference often creates difficulties when insurance companies attempt to settle claims in which the owners want to be compensated for the object's attachment value. It may also create problems when market value is used as the basis for payment for land taken under eminent domain. In these cases, owners would never have sold their land voluntarily for the market value because they are not compensated for the loss of attachment value—and, as a result, they are disadvantaged by the sale.[2]

A further difficulty is that those who exchange AVGs for money are sometimes seen by the person responsible for embedding the object with SEG as lacking social capital.

MARY TODD LINCOLN: HOW COULD YOU?

Mary Todd Lincoln, wife of Abraham Lincoln, was generally excoriated when she sold her husband's personal effects to raise money to pay her debts (Baker, 1987). The implication was that Mary Todd Lincoln wasn't really a devoted wife, otherwise how could she sell items (such as his shirts) that were associated with him?

Selling AVGs leads to the suspicion that no social capital in fact existed between the seller of the goods and those responsible for creating the attachment value—hence the

2 See Benedict (2009) for a modern illustration of how eminent domain cost one home owner her attachment values.

common sentiment that AVGs should not be traded for money. As a result, AVGs tend to be donated to charities or museums or exchanged as gifts between people with shared social capital rather than sold in the marketplace.

Sometimes we buy goods with little physical value but willingly pay high prices that exceed the physical utility of the object in order to embed the object with SEGs. Indeed, the purchase of a gift that has little or no physical utility except to convey SEGs is more likely to acquire attachment value than a gift whose value is mostly physical. For example, a vacuum cleaner purchased for an anniversary is unlikely to acquire attachment value or convey SEGs. An expensive ring with little physical utility, on the other hand, is likely to acquire attachment value because it was given with that intention.

Attachment Values and Culture

Attachment values are, in many cases, culture-specific. An object may acquire attachment value in one culture, but not in others. Animals have a particular capacity to acquire attachment values that, in some cases, are culture-specific. For example, in Western cultures, dogs, cats, and horses have acquired attachment value whereas in other parts of the world some breeds of these animals may be valued for food. The Chinese eat dog meat and the French eat horse meat. Making news on December 16, 1998 was the discovery that several hundred coats made in China were being recalled. The reason? The fur used was from dogs and cats. What is the difference between dog and cat fur and, say, fox and rabbit fur? The difference is that dogs and cats, and even horses, have attachment value as pets.

CARTOON CHARACTERS AND ATTACHMENT VALUE

Beef is a dietary staple in Western culture. This would be unlikely if beef cattle had acquired attachment value. So there are no favorite beef cattle cartoon characters. Animals that someday might be bound for the butcher's shop and found in hamburger buns are unlikely to acquire personalities on children's TV programs.

TV Guide compiled a list of the 50 most popular cartoon characters. Beef and poultry characters need not apply. A pig did make it, but barely. Porky Pig ranked 47 out of 50.

Source: http://archives.cnn.com/2002/SHOWBIZ/TV/07/30/cartoon.characters.list.

Attachment values depend on shared values often reflected in our culture. However, our cultures may sometimes be in conflict, and lead some to value an object for its attachment value while others disdain it for its negative attachment value. A conflict over the Confederate battle flag illustrates the case of divergent attachment values.

Attachment values sometimes get in the way of change. For example, some people have a high attachment value for doing things the old way with old products. This often retards the adoption of new technology. Even though new practices and techniques may offer significant advantages, they are not adopted because they have not acquired attachment value.

THE CONFEDERATE FLAG AND FEELINGS

"The Confederate battle flag, called the 'Southern Cross' or the cross of St. Andrew, has been described variously as a proud emblem of Southern heritage and as a shameful reminder of slavery and segregation" (Bruner, n.d.). Depending on one's point of view the flag has positive or negative attachment value. The difference in attachment values has created a conflict over whether the Confederate battle flag should or should not fly over selected state capitals, or worn on students' T-shirts, and whether it should be waved at football games.

Attachment Values and Words

We have noted already that conveyances for SEGs may often be important physical symbols such as flags, family photos, flowers, ceremonies, and costumes. However, there are other intangible conveyances of SEGs that may acquire attachment value, such as sounds, sights, songs, and, important for this discussion, words. Recognizing that words can convey SEGs, promoters of products and causes carefully select words embedded with SEGs to represent them. For example, words and phrases like "pro-choice" and "pro-life" that represent alternative positions on the ethics of abortion are carefully chosen to convey positive SEGs. Pollsters have also long recognized that responses to surveys that ask the same question can vary, depending on the words used in the surveys.

Advertisers recognize the importance of using words embedded with SEGs to increase the demand for their products (Tye, 1998). Words like "new," "improved," "sure," "gain," "certain outcomes," "investment," and "guaranteed results" have all been used as what some call "power words."

Just as there are words that are embedded with SEGs, there are many words embedded with socio-emotional bads. Words embedded with negative SEGs include "risk," "uncertainty," "death," "loss," "gamble," "chance," and "lottery." Finally, there is some evidence that combining a socio-emotional good with a socio-emotional bad deepens the socio-emotional bad. For example, the words "certain loss" have more socio-emotional bads embedded in them than the word "loss."

SAVE AND DIE: POWER WORDS WITH ATTACHMENT VALUE

Tversky and Kahneman discovered what we refer to as attachment values to words. (Kahneman was later recognized for his work with the Nobel Prize. Tversky would also have been recognized had he still been alive.) They recognized that words "die" and "saved" are powerful words with negative and positive emotions embedded in them. When these words are varied in surveys, the SEGs embedded in the survey are varied, even though the factual content of the survey has not changed.

Tversky and Kahneman proposed the following scenario to two groups.

Imagine that the United States is preparing for the outbreak of an unusual Asian disease, which is expected to kill 600 people. Two alternative programs to combat the disease have been proposed. Assume that the exact scientific estimate of the consequences of the programs are as follows:

> *[Program A:] If program A is adopted, 200 people will be saved.*
>
> *[Program B:] If program B is adopted, there is a 1/3 probability that 600 people will be saved, and a 2/3 probability that no people will be saved.*
>
> Seventy-two percent of group one preferred option A and 28 percent preferred option B.
>
> *[Program C:] If program C is adopted, 400 people will die.*
>
> *[Program D:] If program D is adopted, there is a 1/3 probability that nobody will die and a 2/3 probability that 600 people will die."*
>
> Twenty-two percent of group two preferred option C and 78 percent preferred option D.
>
> The difficulty with the responses, according to Tversky and Kahneman, was that programs A and C and programs B and D were identical except for the use of the words "saved" and "die".
>
> *Source:* Tversky and Kahneman (1981: S260).

To experience firsthand attachment values associated with words, consider the alternatives posed by a newsletter published by a leading investment firm: "If you were on a diet, would you choose an ice cream that is '90 percent fat-free' or one that is '10 percent fat?' Most people surveyed preferred the '90 percent fat-free' ice cream because 'fat-free' sounds more appealing" ("The Psychology of Investing," 2003). Why? Although the two choices are equivalent, "90 percent fat-free" evokes appealing images of slender and fit physiques and popular individuals—the words, laden with attachment value, produce SEGs. The reverse is true for "10 percent fat."

One puzzle concerning words with attachment value is yet to be resolved. If words of praise, respect, and love are so inexpensive to produce and so valuable to their recipients, why are they so scarce?

Symbols, Logos, Icons, and Attachment Values

Once we become aware of objects with attachment values, we find them to be ubiquitous. Nearly every school has a mascot which has attachment value for school's students and alumni. But why are they important? They are important because they provide an important means for creating and maintaining social capital among students, alumni, teachers and staff. It is hard to imagine any important organization that does not have AVGs to increase and maintain social capital among its members.

The symbol for Lions Club members is the lion. For Rotary Club members it is the wheel with spokes. For many Christian churches it is the cross. For Muslims the symbol is the crescent; for Jews, the star of David. In the past, families or clans created coats of arms, which developed high attachment value within their families.

Most advertised products are associated with a symbol of some kind. For one bread company, the symbol is a Roman soldier. For one cereal maker, it is a Quaker. Car manufacturers also adopt shapes or symbols to identify and gain attachment value for their products. Food scientists expend considerable effort in identifying shapes and color combinations likely to create attachment values for their products. The image of Betty Crocker is intended to connect a person to his or her mother, and the list goes on.

Non-physical objects for which attachment values are essential are institutions. If laws and customs are to be willingly obeyed, they must enjoy attachment value. Otherwise, other forms of motivation would be required to enforce the laws which are costly to maintain. For example, some US states have enacted laws that require bikers to wear helmets. Because, for some, this requirement has negative attachment value, the law is frequently disobeyed and enforcement is difficult.

When objects are associated with someone we dislike or with a cause of which we disapprove, negative attachment values are created. Examples of objects with negative attachment values for some are the centuries-old statues of Buddha destroyed by the Afghanistan Taliban., The personal property of individuals or groups who are disliked frequently acquires negative attachment values. Examples include the personal property of divorced couples, symbols of the Nazi party, and personal injury lawyers' advertisements.

Businesses take advantage of social capital and attachment value to increase the demand for, and the value of, their products. Our demand for physical goods and services is probably fairly limited, and if producers were limited to supplying our physical needs, the markets might soon be saturated. If goods and services are embedded with SEGs, demand for goods can stimulated to a greater level than might be suggested by only our physical needs. For example, fashion designers create the impression that their line of clothing has attachment value capable of creating exchanges of SEGs. In other cases, products are sold as if their purchase will produce SEGs.

One way in which producers have created a demand for AVGs has been through the commercialization of holidays. The attachment value acquired by holidays helps those who celebrate them experience SEGs. Each holiday now comes with the expectation of receiving AVGs embedded with SEGs. No doubt, the commercialization of holidays has been a boon for business. In many cases, advertising campaigns are adopted specifically because of their potential to create the expectation of receiving AVGs—the expensive good that will confirm you are loved.

Some professions, especially military and police organizations, have uniforms and emblems with high attachment value to inspire loyalty and service among those who wear them. Rituals such as funeral services and wedding marches become embedded with SEGs, and become powerful experiences as a result. When organizations that we depend on fail, we often find scapegoats with negative attachment value to blame, so that we can continue our association with the organization. For example, in the US, when our chosen political party fails to deliver policies we desire, we more often blame the opposing party's opposition than turn away from our party. In organizations that mostly provide SEGs for us in return for our contributions of physical goods and services, such as churches and sports teams, corruption, loss of goodwill or poor performance can hinder their ability to provide us with SEGs, which is their only offering in exchanges.

Conclusion

There are economic goods and socio-emotional goods, and goods that are combinations of economic goods and socio-emotional goods. Demand for goods on the basis of our physical needs is small and quickly satiated. However, our demand for SEGs and for SEGs embedded in objects may be unlimited. Thus, in the developed economies much of the value of goods is associated with AVGs.

This important aspect of our economy and our well-being is best understood in the context of the social capital paradigm that connects social capital with the creation of SEGs and their being embedded in objects. While the creation and exchange of AVGs can be distinct from the creation and exchange of physical goods, both are important to the understanding of human exchange.

CHAPTER 8

The Social Capital Paradigm: The Role of Institutions

Men may die, but the fabrics of free institutions remains unshaken.

Chester A. Arthur, first inaugural speech (1881).

Introduction

Imagine participating in an athletic contest. Everything is there, the opposing team, the cheering crowds, the coaches, even proud parents. But then you realize one thing is missing—the rules! Or perhaps there are some rules, but your team and the opposing team disagree on what they are, when they are to be applied, or who is responsible for their enforcement. The result? Chaos!

For the same reason we need rules to organize an athletic event, we need rules to organize how we invest in and use our social capital. Sets of laws or customs that are man-made and deal with human interactions and relationships are called institutions.[1] Natural laws, such as the conservation of energy, are self-enforcing and are ignored at one's peril. Man-made laws, such as speed limits and noise ordinances, require human effort to enforce and are sometimes violated.

This chapter introduces the concept of institutions and explains how institutions organize our lives, including the ways in which we invest in social capital, how we extract and convey socio-emotional goods (SEGs), and how we create attachment values.

Here we consider three types of institution: those that *describe* human interactions and relationships, those that *define* human interactions and relationships, and those that *connect* causes and consequences of human interactions and relationships. Institutions that describe human interactions and relationships use words that provide details about people and their interactions with each other. Institutions that describe may take the form: "A has the property B." An example of an institution that describes is: "Men and women have the right to life, liberty, and the pursuit of happiness."

1 Alternative definitions of institutions include: "A way of thought or action of some prevalence and permanence which is embedded in the habits of a group or the customs of a people" (Hamilton, 1932); "Settled habits of thought common to the generality of men" (Veblen, 1908); "Rules of the game" (North, 1990); and "Sets of ordered relationships among people that define their rights and opportunities and their exposure to the rights of others, their privileges and responsibilities" (Commons, 1931).

Institutions that define do so by equating words or groups of words using connectors like "is" and "equals." These institutions may take the form: "A is B" or "A equals B." Defining institutions can be very useful, especially when we wish to know more about A, using information we already know about B. An example of an institution that defines and is the subject of much debate declares: "Marriage *is* the union of one man and one woman." Ethical behavior is defined by special institutions that declare action, "*legal* or *illegal, ethical* or *unethical, socially acceptable* or *socially unacceptable*."

Institutions that define or describe provide the foundations for institutions that connect actions and their consequences, which generally take the form: "if A then B" or "because of A, then B." For example, *if* you park in an unauthorized parking place, *then* your car may be towed away. *If* you dress causally for a formal event, *then* you will meet with disapproving glances.

Professions and careers have been devoted to the study of institutions, producing a wealth of information. This means that our single chapter on the subject of institutions must be very focused and will therefore concentrate on the connections between social capital and formal and informal institutions.

Briefly, formal institutions are expected to apply to people and their interactions with others without regard to their social capital investments. These are written in legislation, judicial rulings, and administrative action. Informal institutions vary, depending on the social capital between exchange partners, and are learned and internalized in people's way of thinking and acting. Our claim is that most institutions are directly or indirectly social capital-dependent. We support this claim and explore its implications after first describing what institutions do.

What Institutions Do

Institutions make possible ordered and meaningful exchanges between people. They also define property rights and responsibilities, freedoms and exposure, duties and privileges. They also describe membership requirements in organizations, establish procedures for resolving disputes and for establishing new institutions, and allow the preferences of different people to be manifest and alter outcomes. Institutions represent the collective response of identifiable groups of people to their surroundings and to the actions of others. Institutions are pervasive and are located in, but are distinct from, organizations. Without institutions, chaos reigns. While it is impossible to identify all that institutions do, we identify five of their major roles.

INSTITUTIONS MANAGE INFORMATION FLOWS

First, and perhaps most important, institutions manage and organize information flows. Interpersonal exchanges require the flow of information. Whether that information is accurate, credible, complete, or timely is another matter altogether. But without information, nothing happens.

Thus, many institutions are designed to either facilitate or impede the flow of information. For example, tobacco products marketed in the United States must now carry a label stating that consumption of the product is dangerous to one's health. Food products must describe their nutritional values. Public weather services are expected to

warn citizens of difficult weather conditions. On the other hand, some institutions limit the flow of information, such as those that forbid the exchange of secret information. A less dramatic example of institutions that limit the flow of information are those that preclude unauthorized access to information that has proprietary value, such as food-industry recipes, realtors' multiple listing information, and marketers' lists of contacts.

INSTITUTIONS ORGANIZE MARKETS

Markets are organized by institutions that govern the exchange of economic goods and services in a myriad ways. Market institutions perform the following services.

- They limit or encourage competition. Strong anti-trust and patent laws in the United States encourage competition. On the other hand, milk marketing associations in agriculture limit competition among their members by specifying quotas. Similarly, the NCAA limits competition for recruiting college athletes by imposing scholarship quotas. Even laws that require truth in advertising limit competition.
- They allocate, specify, and enforce property rights. Examples of institutions that establish property rights among individuals include licensing and title requirements, the liability of owners, and the responsibilities of tenants.
- They specify terms, standards, and other conditions of exchange. To illustrate, the US Department of Agriculture (USDA) places a stamp of approval on meat that is of a certain quality and stored under proper conditions. Without the USDA's stamp of approval, meat cannot be marketed commercially. In like fashion, inspections of gas station pumps ensure that the right amount of gas is being dispensed.
- They influence the distribution of resources. To illustrate, Israeli kibbutz communities have adopted institutions that emphasize communal ownership and one's responsibility to the community. Other institutions describe how goods and services are to be distributed through some kind of hierarchal arrangement, such as the primary distribution of stock benefits to holders of preferred issues and secondary distribution to holders of common issues. Some institutions specify *quid pro quo* exchanges or exchanges of like goods separated by time. Others threaten penalties, promise benefits, or offer goodwill to effect a change in the distribution of goods. Some specify how goods can be used and what exchanges are and are not permissible.
- They identify who can and who cannot participate in the market. The performance of labor markets is influenced by the rules of collective bargaining. Other institutions describe who is considered an acceptable credit risk and who is not. Other institutions may describe what standards must be observed for goods to be sold in an open market. Still other institutions may describe one's liability for products sold in the market.

INSTITUTIONS ORDER SOCIAL INTERACTIONS

Institutions manage our social interaction in the following ways:

- They distinguish between members and nonmembers of networks. For example, immigration laws distinguish between legal or illegal residents of our country. They also identify who and who cannot be joined in marriage.

STATES AND MARRIAGE LAWS: CHANGE IS COMING

As of November 2003, 37 states had institutions that prohibited the civil marriage of gays and lesbians, choosing instead to define marriage as a contract between a man and woman. This institution, however, is coming under increasing pressure for change. In what some argue was a momentous decision, the conservative-leaning supreme court in Massachusetts ruled that the state could not withhold the protection, benefits, and obligations of civil marriage to gays and lesbians. Chief Justice Margaret Marshall's majority opinion limited the role of the state to define the institution of marriage by declaring "[the state's] obligation is to define the liberty of all, not to mandate our own moral code."

Those opposing the ruling argued that marriage should include a "favorable setting for procreation and child-rearing," clearly indicating that, for them, marriage included family. However, for the court, marriage was not about begetting children, but "the exclusive and permanent commitment of the marriage partners to one another." Certainly this new definition of marriage is far from solidified and will most likely usher in a new round of litigation. Nor are those that oppose the ruling likely to go quietly. Governor at the time, Mitt Romney, declared that the ruling was purposively vague so as to allow the state time to propose alternatives, such as civil unions, that would provide for many of the same benefits and rights without actually extending the institution of marriage to gays and lesbians.

Source: Various articles in *The New York Times*, November 19 and 20 (2003).

- They describe consequences, both positive and negative, for those who impose benefits or costs on others without their consent (externalities). For example, the threat of legal action and fines is an institution that assigns costs to those who speed on the highway. Speeding endangers the lives of other drivers. Since these travelers have not agreed to have their safety compromised, those who drive recklessly create an externality. Lawmakers purposefully create institutions that limit negative externalities and encourage positive externalities.
- They influence the distribution of SEGs. Most professional organizations have awards or certificates guided by institutions that recognize individuals who have satisfied certain requirements. Validation symbols associated with these honors might be the size of one's workspace, one's salary and other benefits, or a wood, metal, or script plaque.
- They provide meanings associated with socio-emotional exchanges. For example, institutions describe the meaning and obligations of the marriage contract. Others describe the significance of certain gifts.
- They specify how to express caring and respect. A generally accepted US institution that expresses caring indicates that sending flowers is a proper means for expressing caring and respect. Another accepted form of caring and respect is expressed by a hug. These are obviously highly context-specific and might differ by nationality, culture, ethnicity, and time, whether it is rubbing noses in the Aleutian Islands, "waying" in Thailand, or kissing cheeks in France.
- They distinguish between personal and public areas of responsibility. For example, in some countries constitutions define the responsibility of the people for their government and the government's responsibilities to the people.

- They describe the processes to be followed when creating organizations. In this case, institutions describe the responsibilities, benefits, and characteristics of members versus non-members and what processes must be followed to become a member.

INSTITUTIONS DISTRIBUTE POWER

Institutions make important contributions by describing who has what power. They distribute power in the following ways:

- They delineate legal systems and enforcement. They determine the rights of the accused, how due process will work, and what are acceptable forms of punishment; they establish formal and informal ties to organized politics, and wherein lies the burden of proof.
- They create procedures that distribute power. Examples include voting laws, corporate board composition and their decision-making power, electoral systems, and a government structure that includes powers and checks and balances.
- They specify the rights and responsibilities of states and citizens. This is usually accomplished through constitutions, and ranges along a continuum from authoritarian dictator to democracies. The Bill of Rights established specific rights for US citizens. It also established the duties of the various branches of government. An important feature of the US Constitution is that rights not specifically granted to the government belongs to the citizens.

INSTITUTIONS REFLECT VALUES

Finally, institutions reflect values. Inevitably, not everyone will agree with the values reflected by their institutions, because institutions cannot benefit all people equally. Nevertheless, institutions reflect the values of those creating the institutions by the way in which they impose benefits and costs.

Before the Revolutionary War established the American colonies' independence from Great Britain there was a conflict about who had the right, described by an institution, to levy taxes. The colonists demanded an institution that exempted them from paying taxes to Great Britain unless they had a voice in the process that determined the tax. This reflected a shared value that men and women were endowed with certain rights by their Creator that gave them power over the distribution of their property.

TAXES AND TRAITORS

The English parliament claimed that, because the colonists were subjects of the king and had benefited from the protection provided by English soldiers from the French and Indians, it had a right to levy taxes without their consent. Though the amount of the tax was minimal, the dispute escalated into the Revolutionary War, which was fought over a conflict in institutions that established the rights of individuals not to be taxed without representation—a value so deeply held that the colonists were willing to fight and die for this institution.

Interestingly enough, institutions also reflect values through their definitions. For example, in the eyes of the English government, those who threw the tea into the ocean at Boston

harbor equaled common criminals, but, in the eyes of the colonists, they equaled patriots. The difference in values between the English and the colonists was reflected in their defining institutions.

INSTITUTIONS CONNECT ACTIONS AND OUTCOMES

One of the essential functions of institutions is to connect actions and outcomes across space, time, and classes of individuals. Of course, these connections will be differentiated by the values of the individuals creating and enforcing the connection. In some countries, some institutions prescribe the death penalty for certain crimes. In other countries, the death penalty is proscribed even for the same crime that carries the death penalty elsewhere. One unique consequence for gambling in Indonesia that came under criticism in the United States was caning—a public flogging of a guilty person.

PAIN OR SHAME?

> *The Indonesian province of Aceh has held its first public caning under the region's special Islamic laws.*
>
> *Fifteen people were caned for gambling offences outside a mosque in the town of Bireuen on Friday ... The province has a higher proportion of Muslims than other areas of Indonesia, and many Acehnese practice a stricter version of Islam.*
>
> *The 15 men were flogged with a rattan cane on a specially-constructed stage in front of the Grand Mosque following midday prayers on Friday.*

This unique connection between causes and consequences is required by Sharia law, special Islamic laws, put into place in Aceh province in 2001 as part of a deal on autonomy offered to Muslims (who make up a high proportion of the province's population) by the Jakarta government.

> *According to a BBC reporter in Bireuen, Maskur Abdullah, crowds of people, including children, watched the proceedings—cheering and booing as the culprits were brought onto the stage to receive their punishments ...*
>
> *On Thursday Bireuen's district chief Mustafa Geulanggang explained why the authorities had decided to implement caning as a punishment.*
>
> *"It's not about pain," he told the BBC. "The aim is to shame people and deter them from doing the same criminal acts in the future."*

Source: BBC News Channel (2005).

Formal and Informal Domains of Institutions

All institutions, especially those that connect actions and their consequences, have a domain. An institution's domain defines for whom, where, when, and how the institutions are to be applied.

Geographic domains define in which area certain institutions apply. Some institutions apply only in the United States and are clearly distinguished from those that apply in the European Union. On the other hand, when exchanges involve persons living in the United States and the European Union, there are institutions whose domain includes them both.

But even within the same geographic area, institutions are differentiated by personal domains. In other words, even for individuals living in the same geographic area there are different institutions that order their behavior. For example, some institutions apply differently to people of different ages, genders, marital status, mental capacity, and a host of other distinctions.

Some institutions have their domains distinguished by their hierarchy within a set of rules. Hierarchy is important when two laws exist simultaneously that cannot both be obeyed. For example, in the United States federal law supersedes state laws. States are not allowed to pass laws that conflict with federal statutes. Similarly, communities cannot pass laws that conflict with either state or federal law. In addition, sometimes family institutions and institutions established by peers of family members collide. Issues of conflict between parents and children may include appropriate dress codes, curfews, and dating behavior.

Some institutions have their domains distinguished by the types and kinds of goods being exchanged. For example, institutions that apply to the exchange of SEGs are often distinct from those that apply to the exchange of primarily economically valued goods (EVGs).

Sometimes an institution's domain differs depending on the time. Some institutions apply during rush hour. Others apply differently depending on weather conditions. Some institutions apply during a time of war or hostility.

An institution's domain may also differ depending on the means used to enforce it. Enforcement incentives may range from threats to offers of rewards, including the granting or required payments of physical goods and services. In other cases, rewards and penalties used to enforce institutions may include SEGs and EVGs.

Finally, the domain of some institutions may be distinguished by the social capital that exists between exchange partners. An institution that applies to the exchange between two people *independent* of their social capital was defined earlier as a formal institution. An institution that applies to the exchange between two people and varies depending on their social capital was defined earlier as an informal institution. Because social capital differentiates the domains of formal and informal institutions, we now direct our attention to the connections between social capital and formal and informal institutions.

The Domains of Formal and Informal Institutions

The domain of formal and informal institutions can be distinguished by the ways they order the exchanges of different types of goods. It may be argued that exchanges of EVGs

should be the domain of formal institutions. The argument in favor of formal institutions ordering the exchange of these goods is that when informal institutions manage their exchange, they sometimes produce corruption, preferential treatment, and inefficiency. As Adam Smith foresaw, limited and personal economic networks limit trade and hence the capacity to generate wealth.

It may also be argued that exchanges of SEGs should be the domain of informal institutions. Indeed, it may be that SEGs can only be exchanged between individuals if they have social capital because of the way in which SEGs are produced. One can hardly imagine receiving SEGs of caring from someone who lacks sympathy, or validation from someone lacking credentials, or information from the uninformed. This is because socio-emotional transactions will vary in content depending on the relationships between those transacting. Therefore, a strictly formal institution that didn't allow for these differences would be ineffective.

Considerable conflict centers on when, how, and where to apply formal versus informal institutions. When formal institutions are employed in ordering exchanges of attachment-valued goods (AVGs) or SEGs, sometimes silly results emerge. Since words are embedded with SEGs, considerable care should be applied in how we restrict their use.

THE OLDER PERSON AND THE WATER

The Older Person and the Water is the politically correct title of Ernest Hemingway's book, *The Old Man and the Sea,* according to Dianne Ravitch, a former education official in President George H.W. Bush's administration and a consultant to the Clinton administration. Ravitch has exposed a list of 500 words banned by publishers. The publishers deny that they are censoring books; they are only applying what they call applied rules of sensitivity. "Old" is ageist, "man" is sexist, and sea can't be used in case a student lives inland and doesn't grasp the concept of a large body of water. Ravitch claims that publishers aim to avoid controversy and, in the process, dumb down the books.

From the perspective of the social capital paradigm, words may enjoy high attachment value when they are embedded with SEGs. However, they may also be embedded with socio-emotional bads. The desire to limit the use of words embedded with socio-emotional bads has prompted publishers to adopt formal institutions to restrict their use. The difficulty is that whether words convey SEGs or socio-emotional bads will depend on one's social capital. As a result, any formal institutions designed to restrict the use of some words to please one group is likely to offend another and is likely to suffer from a lack of attachment value.

Source: CNN.com (2003).

Another difference in the domains of formal versus informal institutions lies in their scope—the number of people directed by the institution. When many people are involved in a transaction, such as stock market trades, retail purchases, and the use of credit cards, formal institutions reign for two logical reasons. First, when large numbers of people are involved in a transaction, it is unlikely that much social capital exists between them (they likely don't know the others with whom they are transacting), making it impossible to discriminate on the basis of social capital differences. Second, the transaction costs would

be enormous. Imagine Wal-Mart offering different prices to their customers depending on their relationship to the Wal-Mart employees or stock holders.

On the other hand, exchanges between small groups of friends and family can be expected to differ from their exchanges with strangers. This is because failing to differentiate terms and level of exchange between friends and family versus strangers would limit the exchange of SEGs and AVGs. Examples of informal institutions are the ways in which households celebrate birthdays and other special events, accepted practices for grieving, how people care for children and the aged, accepted practices of giving and receiving gifts, and ways in which people care for one another in times of distress.

The domains of formal and informal institutions also differ in the means used to enforce them. Both formal and informal institutions use rewards and penalties to encourage compliance. Yet the kinds of rewards and penalties and the monitoring costs differ significantly between formal and informal institutions.

Monitoring costs of formal institutions—the constitution, tax laws, civil codes—can be supported as long as most people agree to observe them voluntarily. But if the formal institution does not enjoy widespread support by the people—that is, unless it has attachment value—then it will almost certainly be abandoned and replaced by an informal one. Because formal institutions are costly to maintain unless they are generally accepted, they are always at risk of being replaced by informal institutions. In other words, formal sanctions that are applied independent of relationships are costly to apply and can only be supported if those violating the institutions are few. This means that the greater incentive to comply with formal institutions must come from the approval or disapproval of others who share attachment value for the institution. Consequently, formal institutions must be legitimized by their acquiring attachment values if they are to be maintained at a reasonable cost. Consider institutions that establish our taxes.

PAYING TAXES

Some people take advantage of high monitoring costs of formal institutions and cheat on their taxes. But, in developed societies with successful tax codes, most pay their taxes because they believe it is the right thing to do, not because they fear they will be found out if they cheat—in other words, even tax codes have attachment value for large numbers of people.

Yet this willingness to comply, at least in the United States, may be declining. The Associated Press reported "The number of Americans who believe it's OK to cheat 'a little here and there' on their taxes has risen 50 percent in the past four years." Moreover, the number who claimed that it was OK to "cheat as much as possible" rose from 3 percent to 5 percent.

Source: Associated Press (2003).

The enforcement of informal institutions also requires rewards and penalties. However, these usually involve gains or losses of SEGS and social capital. Furthermore, these rewards or penalties may vary between individuals. Shame, for example, works to encourage compliance among those that share social capital, as shown in the following example of teenage vandals in New Hampshire.

SHAMING AND SOCIO-EMOTIONAL BADS

George Will writes:

> *A New Hampshire state legislator says of teenage vandals, "These little turkeys have got total contempt for us, and it's time to do something." His legislation would authorize public, bare-bottom spanking, a combination of corporal punishment and shaming–degrading to lower the offender's social status. (Will, 1996)*

From the perspective of the social capital paradigm, shaming imposes social-emotional bads on offenders by placing them in conditions likely to result in the loss of their social capital. Of course, such efforts may backfire and result in an increase in sympathy.

Other efforts to enforce institutions by shaming include publishing in newspapers or on billboards or broadcasting the names of drug users, drunk drivers, or men who solicit prostitutes or are delinquent in child support. Of course, none of these methods surpasses the shame of wearing the large "A" Hester wore for committing adultery in Nathaniel Hawthorne's book, *The Scarlet Letter.*

The Need for Both Formal and Informal Institutions

We need both formal and informal institutions to promote our social, as well as our economic, well-being. Each type of institution has a domain in which it performs best. Informal institutions are appealing because they can facilitate the exchange of both SEGs and EVGs on preferential terms. Furthermore, the added value from exchanges of SEGs and EVGs among friends is often higher than the value added from the exchange of only EVGs between strangers. Thus, not surprisingly, trades between friends will often be preferred to trades among strangers.

Finally, we need informal institutions because human exchange is so complicated that it simply cannot be prescribed by only formal institutions. To make this point, labor unions, to emphasize their views, may institute a "work to rule" plan that requires work be done according to the formal institutions, with almost always disastrous results.

Formal institutions are preferred in many cases because the exchange of SEGs creates something like a barter system in which each exchange is individualized. There is simply no way that the myriad transactions that occur in today's global markets could be organized by informal institutions and still be efficiently completed.

To understand how we all rely on both formal and informal institutions, consider the plight of the poor. Unless the poor accept formal institutions they will be excluded from the advantages of the formal economy, including health care, educational services, and police protection. On the other hand, it is often informal institutions, such as family support during times of crisis, which allow them to survive.

Informal and formal institutions are both needed to manage conflict. Conflict often accompanies the creation of formal institutions because they impose highly visible costs and distribute highly visible benefits. Indeed, some people may gain power by promising to adopt or enforce an institution, such as immigration laws, that benefit certain groups at the expense of others. Social capital is essential to limit conflicts associated with the creation and maintenance of formal institutions. Without a minimum level of social

capital, people are unwilling to work together under existing institutions in place, even though they do not reflect every individual's point of view. Indeed, one of the essential measures of a government's attachment value is its ability to create and maintain formal institutions without insurrection or resorting to violence. Indeed, those who disagree with formal institutions, yet support their maintenance, are sometimes referred to as the "loyal opposition." Democracies are *prima facie* evidence of a country's widespread social capital; coercive governments are testaments to its absence.

Finally, much of the difference between informal and formal institutions has been focused on the efficiency that results from their applications. The claim is that informal institutions do not always organize economic transactions in ways that maximize economic efficiency (e.g., the boss hires his sister's son even though he is not a good worker). On the other hand, economic efficiency may be increased through informal institutions that require the boss to hire his sister's son because he will be loyal, while some other employees may be opportunistic. And, then again, efficiency measures arbitrarily define what inputs and outputs are included in the efficiency measure and generally exclude SEGs from the measure. So, who is to say what exchanges would be most efficient if the measures were to account for SEGs and AVGs?

The Emergence of Formal and Informal Institutions

Not only are new formal and informal institutions being constantly created, but there is also a constant migration between them—formal institutions becoming informal ones, and informal institutions becoming formal ones. Finally, continuous efforts are made to replace one formal institution with another through the legislative process and sometimes through civic actions of the people such as occurred during the civil rights protests.

There is a long history of informal institutions eventually becoming common law or formal institutions. These replacements occur over time as attachment values for the informal institutions increase in importance and scope. Of the numerous reasons why institutions emerge, change, or migrate, three appear especially important:

- when there are conflicts that require coordination or collective actions;
- when there are inefficiencies and changing needs; and
- when there are shifts in relative power.

Below we consider each of these three reasons explaining the emergence of institutions.

RESOLVING CONFLICTS

In our highly interdependent world, our actions invariably create costs and benefits for others, and often without their permission—i.e., they create externalities. To prevent externalities from creating hostilities and even armed conflicts, we create institutions that impose rights and responsibilities on each other. These rules constrain and manage the creation and operation of externalities. For example, one person's loud music is someone else's noise and, to resolve their conflict and to manage the externality created by playing loud music, institutions may set maximum decibel levels and specify hours during which music can be played. In short, institutions are created to reconcile different preferences

of different people so as to avoid the discomfort of noise even if it means limiting the thrilling throb of loud music.

Other forms of potential collective dilemmas addressed by institutions include the following:

- We create institutions to capture the benefits lost from uncoordinated acts. For example, we all benefit from mail delivery services provided by the US Post Office. But, without the institutions created by the federal government to collect, distribute, and pay for mail services, it would not exist.
- We create institutions to manage resources owned in common with others. Communities frequently share common resources, such as parks, water supplies, and streets. Without institutions that establish remuneration and enforcement, these assets are often plundered. For example, grazing areas were once unrestricted, resulting in overgrazing. Institutions now manage these resources.

IMPROVING EFFICIENCY OR MEETING CHANGING NEEDS

Douglas North, the Nobel Prize Laureate, observed that we create institutions when we need to reduce transaction costs and improve efficiency (North, 1990). Consider the situations that can be improved by the adoption of institutions.

- We create institutions to reduce the transaction costs associated with the exchange of goods and services. For example, lemon laws reduce the risk of buying and make it easier to purchase a used car.
- We create institutions to define responsibilities. Each formal organization has the duties of its members and officers specified by institutions. Liability for the safety and performance of products are specified by institutions.
- We create institutions when a significant number of people are dissatisfied with the status quo, including existing institutions. The lack of support may be caused by perceived inequities in existing institutions, a view that the intended outcomes of particular institution are not being realized, or problems stemming from the absence of institutions. Often this change happens in an evolutionary way. But sometimes people may change or create institutions through political institutions, such as representative democracy, or through litigation. Where these paths to change or creation are not available, change may come through rebellion or revolution.
- We create institutions when we learn new information about causes and consequences. For example, pesticide application laws before Rachel Carson's *Silent Spring* were generally lax. Then, when information detailing the effect of certain pesticides on birds was made known, there was a general response to a widely shared kernel that values wildlife. When more information about the harmful effects of tobacco was made public, laws regulating where smoking could occur were revised or created. Sometimes new technology creates new cause-and-effect relationships that require new institutions. For example, wireless communication systems have required new institutions to manage and internalize their externalities.
- We create institutions when our values change. As values change, we can expect institutions to change. Of course, when the values of some people change and the values of others do not, there will be conflicts between those whose values do not

change (conservatives) and those who find their values have changed (liberals). One change in values that occurred during World War II was connected to women working outside of the home. When male labor was in short supply because of the requirements of war, women increasingly began to work outside their homes, performing duties which had previously been reserved for men.

SHIFTING RELATIVE POWER BALANCES

Sometimes people in power will tend to form or change institutions to benefit themselves (Knight, 1992). Such people are said to have structural power. When power shifts, new groups of people dismantle or alter existing institutions in favor of changed or new ones that now benefit them. For example:

- As the population in the United States ages, power and influence is shifting to older Americans. In response, institutions are being created or adopted to address their unique concerns.
- As the proportion of America's farm population declined, economic institutions supporting them changed and began to focus more on urban business owners and workers.
- When political elites are removed from office through election or other means, new leaders often change the rules by which the country operates its domestic and international affairs. Hence, foreign countries watch elections in the United States with every bit as much (if not more) anxiety and hope as do Americans.

Conclusion

Institutions are critical to our social and economic well-being. They help manage information, organize markets, reflect values, and distribute power and a host of other essential functions that allow people to exchange EVGs, AVGs, and SEGs. To perform these functions, we need both formal and informal institutions.

To benefit the most from informal and formal institutions, we must distinguish between their domains. Confusion over their respective domains can lead to undesirable outcomes. For example, the substitution of an informal institution for a formal one may lead to charges of corruption, as we will discuss in Chapter 14 on ethics.

Formal institutions are needed to achieve economic advantages of specialization and trade in large networks. Informal institutions, by comparison, are needed to exchange SEGs between individuals with social capital. So, in practice, we live with a combination of formal and informal institutions because most of our exchanges involve both EVGs and SEGs.

Institutions change for a variety of reasons including changing values, new information, efforts to redistribute power, and opportunities for improved efficiencies. Informal institutions may be replaced with formal ones when networks lack social capital or when large numbers of individuals are disadvantaged by the informal institution. Equally, formal institutions may be replaced with informal ones where socially unacceptable outcomes are produced by the formal ones. For example, some formal institutions create hardships and inefficiencies that can be avoided with the adoption of informal institutions. If a

medical emergency requires immediate hospitalization, traffic laws may be ignored with no penalty. Yet, although this substitution is considered acceptable, other cases might be considered corruption.

To be maintained, formal and informal institutions must be communicated. Because formal institutions often have to be communicated to large numbers of people, they are written down, sometimes described and debated in formal public gatherings, and made available on demand. Informal institutions, on the other hand, are rarely written down, communicated openly, or accepted or changed through formal procedures. Instead, they are usually communicated orally or by example. Part of the reason for this is because a portion of what is transferred through informal institutions is SEGs, and these goods are difficult to transfer through impersonal means.

Finally, the main point of this chapter is that, to be maintained in the long run, both formal and informal institutions depend directly or indirectly on social capital. It may be argued that not all formal institutions require social capital, even indirectly, because they are sustained by habit and feedback accumulated over extended time periods. However, it is likely that habits and feedback were at one time social capital-dependent even though they may not be currently linked to any particular individual or group of individuals.

CHAPTER 9

The Social Capital Paradigm: The Role of Networks

An empowered organization [network] is one in which individuals have the knowledge, skill, desire, and opportunity to personally succeed in a way that leads to collective organizational success.

Stephen R. Covey (1992: 212).

Introduction

Capital, because it is durable, must have a home—a place where its service potential resides. The service potential of physical capital may live in a warehouse, a factory, or in a machine. Financial capital may live in a bank's vault, financial statements, mortgages, in a plastic card in one's wallet, or in government-printed paper or coined metals—and, ultimately, in the minds and hearts of people who respond to financial symbols in a particular way.

Social capital, like other forms of capital, must also have a home—where its service potential resides. Social capital lives in people and combinations of people organized into networks. Networks form when people share any number of traits that connect them to each other. For example, one network may include all people in one's telephone directory, fellow members of a local church, children attending the same school, and so forth. In this chapter we are interested in a particular kind of network—networks of people whose members are connected directly or indirectly by social capital. Social capital-rich networks convey important benefits (and costs) to network members. Consider a few of the outcomes as social capital increases within networks:

- Network members reduce those activities that impose negative externalities on other members of the network.
- Network members increase their investments in public or high exclusion-cost goods that produce positive externalities for members of the network.
- Network members are more likely to share information and access to resources and information owned by network members.
- Transaction costs between network members, including the costs of gathering information, reaching an agreement, and enforcing commitments, decrease. As a result, network members specialize and trade more, leading to increased productivity.

- Productivity of network members and their average income increase, while their disparity of income decreases.
- Increases in the number of network members (up to some optimal size) produce the same effect as increases in social capital within an established network.
- Social capital between network members and nonmembers may decrease and produce undesirable consequences. These undesirable consequences are generally the opposite of those consequences produced among network members who experience an increase in social capital.

In the remainder of this chapter we explore the structure of networks and how different network structures influence how networks function. We then go on to describe the shared traits, or kernels of commonality, around which networks are organized, and follow up with a discussion of network maintenance requirements. Finally, we discuss what kinds of institutions are required for networks to function effectively; what kinds of goods, including socio-emotional goods (SEGs), are exchanged within networks; and how network structure affects the effectiveness of networks.

Network Structure

A social network consists of individuals (nodes) and connections (branches) between individuals. We are interested in those networks in which individuals are connected by social capital. In these networks, the connections are supported by the exchange of SEGs, in addition to other types of goods. The structure of networks describes the distribution of social capital resources within the network. The more social capital connections that an individual has within a network, the greater is that person's social capital.

Networks, of course, can have a variety of structures—in some sense, as varied as snowflakes. Athletic teams and an orchestra can illustrate this variety of different network structures.

DENSITY OF NETWORKS AND TEAMS

Athletic teams are networks. Yet, their patterns of exchange differ by sports. Consider a basketball team. All members of the team on the floor at the same time are interacting (transacting) with each other. Each team member can be expected to pass the ball and receive passes and assistance from all other members of the team. Because each team member is connected to every other member of the team, we describe this kind of network as "dense."

An American football team is a network that is less dense. All the action, at least on offense, centers on the quarterback. He gives directions to the rest of the team, receives the snap from the center, hands it off to a running back or passes to a tight end. Tackles and guards protect the quarterback from the members of the opposing team's defense, but never touch the ball. The quarterback is the key player in this semi-dense network, giving instructions to the offensive line as well as to the backs and receivers. Information exchanged between other offensive players usually passes through the quarterback.

Other kinds of teams have their own network structure and density. Tennis teams are a collection of individual players. They perform separately from the other team members, although they may practice together. A similar structure exists for debate teams and chess teams. Soccer teams are denser than tennis teams, but probably less dense than basketball teams simply because they have more people on the field at any one time. While we may not be active members of a sports team, chances are we belong to a network whose density varies like those of the teams described (Drucker, 1992).

An orchestra represents another kind of network with both dense and less dense sub-networks. Within the orchestra network, there are embedded smaller or sub-networks such as orchestra members playing the same instrument or those in the brass section. Other orchestra sub-networks include those who perform administrative services. The sub-networks may perform separately sometimes and jointly at other times. For example, the percussion section may hold separate practices, but they actively participate with the other sub-networks when the orchestra performs.

As you might imagine, there are many different kinds of network. Considered below are some characterizations of networks that emphasize social capital, including the "dense network," the "key-player network," the "hierarchal network," the "asymmetric network," and the "sabatoged network."

THE DENSE NETWORK

In a perfectly dense network, all members have social capital with and exchange SEGs with every other member. A dense network suggests that members share a kernel strong enough to maintain ties even in the face of conflict and differences. Using the athletic team analogy, a dense network is best represented by a basketball team in which all players interact with each other. Completely dense networks facilitate trade among all members. Investments in high exclusion-cost goods are likely since the entire community is connected. As Adam Smith would have predicted, dense ties among all members of a network encourages specialization. Furthermore, a dense network is likely to eliminate special trading advantages and is the type of network most likely to achieve a fairly equal distribution of incomes. As the density of a network increases, so do the number of possible transactions.[1]

THE KEY-PLAYER NETWORK

The key-player network is a semi-dense network in which many, but not all, members of the network are connected. Key players are essential in less dense networks because they facilitate the formation of social capital connections between network members. In business, brokers connect buyers and sellers. The orchestra director connects members of the orchestra. Lois Weisberg apparently connects nearly everyone within her reach.

1 Certainly this number is bounded by physical laws. That is, one person can only conduct so many transactions with others. The point is that as networks become increasingly dense, the theoretically possible transactions rise dramatically.

THE LOIS WEISBERG CONNECTIONS

Lois Weisberg is a grandmother who lives in a big house in Chicago and very well may run the world. Lois is one of those individuals who knows everyone. The *New Yorker Magazine* explained that:

> *In the course of [Lois's] seventy-three years she has hung out with actors and musicians and doctors and lawyers and politicians and activists and environmentalists, and once, on a whim, she opened a secondhand-jewelry store named for her granddaughter Becky Fyffe, and every step of the way Lois has made friends and recruited people, and a great many of those people have stayed with her to this day.*
>
> Gladwin, 1999: 32.

Cindy Mitchell first met Lois 23 years ago, when she bundled up her baby and ran outside into one of those frigid Chicago winter mornings because some people from the Chicago Park District were about to cart away a beautiful sculpture of Carl von Linné from the park across the street. Lois happened to be driving by at the time, and, seeing all the commotion, she slammed on her brakes, charged out of her car—all five feet of her—and began asking Cindy rapid-fire questions: "Who are you? What's going on here? Why do you care?" By the next morning, Lois had not only persuaded two *Chicago Tribune* reporters to interview Cindy and turn the whole incident into a *cause célèbre*, but had also recruited Cindy into a network she'd just started called "Friends of the Parks." Then, when she found out that Cindy was a young mother at home, who was too new in town to have many friends, she told her, "I've found a friend for you. Her name is Helen, and she has a little boy your kid's age, and you will meet her next week and the two of you will be best friends." That's exactly what happened, and, what's more, Cindy went on to spend ten years as president of "Friends of the Park." "Almost everything that I do today and eighty to ninety per cent of my friends came about because of her, because of that one little chance meeting," Cindy says. "That's a scary thing. Try to imagine what would have happened if she had come by five minutes earlier."

Source: Adapted from Gladwin (1999: 32).

THE HIERARCHAL NETWORK

Another kind of less dense network is the hierarchal network. A hierarchal structure reflects bridging social capital such as might exist between a supervisor and an employee. In this network, person 1 supervises, and has a relationship with, person 2. Person 2 supervises, and has a relationship with, person 3, etc.

The US military and many corporate organizations employ hierarchal networks. The officers supervise and direct noncommissioned officers. The two types of officer live in separate housing and attend separate clubs, but, during duty, they work with each other, with orders and directions coming from the top down. The noncommissioned officers supervise and direct the enlisted men to satisfy the orders they receive from their officers. And if the enlisted soldiers want to connect with the officers, they will most likely "go through" the noncommissioned officers to reach the top.

ASYMMETRIC NETWORKS

Related to the hierarchal network is the asymmetric network, characterized again by bridging social capital. In asymmetric networks, persons A and B may be the object of each other's social capital, but not to the same degree. The famous performer may provide some social capital for her fans, but not the same kind of social capital that the fans provide for the performer. Parents and children may provide each other with social capital, but the social capital that parents provide for teenagers in the middle of their self-discovery is not likely to be the same kind that teenagers provide for their parents. Nevertheless, they are part of the network which is most evident at mealtimes.

THE SABOTAGED NETWORK

For completeness, consider a network which is not only asymmetric, but where one member has antipathy toward another member. As a result, exchanges that might otherwise be productive are sabotaged by another party. For example, competitors who share the same production network often sabotage their competitor's dealings with a mutual supplier or customer. Sabotage might also occur in the form of competitors poaching each other's skilled labor. In most cases, such relationships cause market failures and much less desirable outcomes than if the parties had been able to cooperate.

Other Network Structure Considerations

There are several other issues besides the structure of connections in networks,. These include the strength of ties between network members, the types of kernel around which the network is organized, whether the direction of influence is from the individual or from the network, and the network's focus.

STRENGTH OF TIES

Regardless of the network structure or density, an important characteristic of networks is the strength of social capital ties—i.e. the intensity of sympathy—between network members, which depends primarily on the exchange of SEGs. If network members exchange SEGs frequently and in a variety of settings, their social capital ties will be strong.

The strength of ties between network members will also be influenced by the size of the network. Individuals have a limited supply of social energy that can be used to invest (disinvest) in social capital. As the number of members in a network increases, the social interaction between any two members at some point is likely to decrease. As a result, the strength of ties is likely to decrease as the size of the network increases. However, weak ties can be extremely valuable, as Mark Granovetter has demonstrated.

NETWORK FOCUS

Network focus is related to a network's orientation. Is the network focused inward or outward? In inward-focused networks, the attention is on encouraging transactions

THE IMPORTANCE OF WEAK TIES

Granovetter's most famous work, "The Strength of Weak Ties" (1973) is considered to be one of the most influential sociology papers ever written. In marketing or politics, weak ties (such as casual relationships) enable individuals to reach populations and audiences that are not accessible to them via their strong ties (such as family relationships). Granovetter explains how some phenomena, such as riots, getting a new job, and creating fads, depend more on connecting with people outside of one's circle of strong ties.

between network members. In outward-focused networks, members are encouraged to transact with people outside their network. Most networks encourage activities both within and between networks that strengthen both within and without network ties. Examples of networks with both an inward and outward focus include families, some religious sects with strong missionary efforts, ethnic groups, fraternities and sororities, and literary and art clubs.

NETWORK MEMBERSHIP REQUIREMENTS AND NETWORK PERMEABILITY

Members of a network must share a similar trait. For example, membership requirements for an athletic team may be related to some form of physical dexterity, and those for a business network may be some form of business experience. Membership requirements for an academic network may be related to academic training and achievements. Yet another network membership requirement may be the approval of existing network members—reflecting one's social capital in the network. In general, traits around which networks are organized are either inherited or earned.

Inherited traits include one's gender, genealogy, ethnic background, age, or physical characteristics. The permeability of networks whose membership requirements are inherited depends on the number of individuals possessing the trait. For example, some networks may restrict their membership to males or females. But since nearly half of the population possesses this inherited trait, networks that require this trait are still permeable. However, additional membership criteria based on inherited or earned traits may be added, which can create impermeability. To illustrate, a network limited to women of a certain age with considerable financial resources is a network with limited permeability.

The danger of networks with impermeable membership requirements is their exclusivity and isolation. Such networks tend to ignore new trends and are unresponsive to demographic changes that may warrant changes in membership requirements. Furthermore, exclusive networks often produce SEGs by emphasizing the differences between themselves and people in other networks—an attitude that may breed contention.

Most networks have membership requirements associated with at least some earned traits that may include one's training, interests, skills, political or religious beliefs, travel experience, or interests. Networks whose membership requirements are based on earned traits are often more flexible and adaptive than networks based on inherited traits because one need not be born with a specific trait to join. Conversely, some earned traits may be so restrictive that the boundaries of the network are difficult to penetrate. For example, the

network of past US presidents is based on an earned trait, but the difficulty of acquiring the trait makes it impermeable.

NETWORK MAINTENANCE

Social capital, like other forms of capital, must be maintained, usually through new social capital investments and the exchange of SEGs. For major corporations, such as United Airlines, network maintenance is a major concern and may require network managers to readjust the institutions to changing economic or social conditions if the networks are to survive.

UNITED AIRLINES' LONG BANKRUPTCY

For more than two years beginning in 2002, United Airlines was bankrupt. In an effort to reconstruct itself, it laid off thousands of workers, reworked airport services, reduced wages for baggage handlers and pilots, and restructured its in-flight services. However, United Airlines knew that these efforts were not enough to insure survival. The company needed to regain (maintain) its social capital with its customers. Toward this end, and in an attempt to take care of its business, United Airlines wrote an apologetic letter about its changing service and decline in service quality to each of its frequent flyer customers.

Table 9.1 summarizes the discussion so far by characterizing networks according to the kernels around which they are organized, the density of their connections, their maintenance costs, and their focus. As an example the 'Service clubs' row is completed based on a characterization of the Rotary Club.

Formal versus Informal Institutions and Networks

A properly functioning network must be directed by institutions that facilitate efficient exchanges among its members. Otherwise, opportunity to benefit from the skills, insights and efforts of others is limited. An absence of sufficient institutions to facilitate exchanges leaves the network vulnerable to conflicts over the allocation of material and intangible benefits.

Sustainable formal institutions require attachment values created by network members. Attachment value for the network's formal institutions can be created in a number of ways. However, attachment values begin with the exchange of SEGs, which requires social capital. Attachment to the network's formal institutions may be aided by creating attachment values to network symbols that may include the network's goals, its flag, familiar songs, celebrations, and physical objects associated with the network.

Another important requirement to sustain a network's formal institutions is the "fair" distribution of benefits and responsibilities among all members of the network. Whenever a significant number of a network's members view the distributions of benefits and responsibilities as unfair, the network's formal institutions are at risk.

Networks also depend on informal institutions to facilitate the exchange of SEGs. One of the main differences between formal and informal institutions is their radius of

Table 9.1 Characterizations of networks

Examples of networks	Kernels around which networks are organized		Density	Maintenance costs	Focus	
	Inherited	Earned			Internal	External
Families	X		H	L	X	
Religious groups		X	Varies	L/M	X	X
Ethnic groups	X		H	L	X	X
Service clubs (e.g. Rotary Club)*		X	M/H	M	X	X
People with shared interests		X	Varies	H	X	
Geographic communities	X		L	M/H	X	
Gangs		X	M/H	L/M	X	X
Work groups/ unions		X	M	H	X	X
Athletic teams		X	Varies	M	X	X
Political parties		X	Varies	H	X	X
Economic clubs		X	L/M	H	X	
Literary/cultural groups	X		M	L	X	X
Electronic groups		X	Varies	H	X	
States/nations	X		H	L	X	X

Key: L = Low; M = Medium; H = High.

* Cell contents are assumed for illustration purposes only.

application. The radius of formal institutions is usually far-reaching compared to the more local radius of most informal institutions. Social capital-rich networks usually support informal institutions. In contrast, formal institutions with more far-reaching radiuses depend more on attachment values. However, formal and informal institutions are closely connected. Formal institutions must be legitimized by informal institutions if they are to be maintained without force or threat; and if informal institutions exist and are in conflict with the formal ones, then punitive measures may be required to maintain the formal ones.

Successful networks maintain a proper balance of formal and informal institutions. However, there always exists a danger of losing this proper balance, of developing an excess of either formal or informal institutions. A network culture of excessive formal institutions precludes opportunities to form social capital and exchange SEGs. In these

rule-bound networks, transactions can only be motivated with carrots and sticks. Moreover, formal institution maintenance costs will be high. In these less than healthy networks, ties are likely thin and weak.

On the other hand, a network with excessive informal institutions based on social capital may facilitate the exchange of SEGs, but fail to meet the necessary economic and physical goals required to survive. Then, when the network is unsuccessful in its economic mission, people often become participants in zero-sum games to protect themselves that eventually end up destroying social capital. Much of the conflict between labor and management can be characterized as a conflict between excessive informal institutions that exist among workers or managers and efforts to impose formal rules without attachment values to support their acceptance.

Economically competitive and socially viable networks adopt a proper balance between formal and informal institutions. They recognize that economically viable networks work for more than carrots or to avoid sticks: their socio-emotional needs require other kinds of reward for their efforts. On the other hand, economic competitiveness requires formal institutions that facilitate specialization and trade. Maintaining the balance in networks between economic and socio-economic rewards, formal and informal institutions, social capital and arm's-length relationships, and economic goods and goods with high attachment values requires economically skilled and socially sensitive managers and leaders.

The universal challenge of maintaining the proper balance between formal and informal institutions is illustrated by a *maquiladora* located in Mexico's Yucatan.

PRODUCTIVITY AND THE GODFATHER

Maquiladora X is a highly successful business network that produces dental equipment and braces. Its president is an affable and skilled executive who appreciates the advantages of social capital. As a result, he knows the names of most of his employees. Moreover, he regularly eats with his employees at mealtime and attends, and sometimes organizes, social events for his workers. On special occasions he presents employees with special gifts and recognizes outstanding services. Finally, he has helped instill a sense of purpose among his employees, which is to set an example of high-quality production for other Mexican firms.

Maquiladora X has realized some important tangible benefits from its president's enlightened social capital management approach. While employee turnover rate for similar *maquiladoras* often exceeds 100 percent per year, the annual turnover rate in *Maquiladora* X is minimal—never more than 10 percent. Moreover, many of *Maquiladora* X's employees return after they leave, when circumstances permit. A second tangible benefit of *Maquiladora* X's social capital is that its employees are committed to producing a high-quality product. In effect, *Maquiladora* X employees receive both SEGs and economically valued goods (EVGs) for their services. In return, they support the formal institutions and economic goals of the network.

However, the social capital that exists between employees at *Maquiladora* X and its president has a cost. The president related to Lindon that some employees expect preferential treatment because of their social capital. On occasion he has been approached to be the godfather of an employee's child. The question he raised—one that can be raised by most leaders of networks—is the following. How can the network benefit from social capital and still avoid having its formal institutions replaced with informal ones?

In far too many cases, social capital leads to the replacement of formal institutions with informal ones. As a consequence, benefits and responsibilities then become distributed according to relationships. Once this happens, networks become corrupt, are no longer competitive and can no longer be sustained. Recent headlines involving insider trading in the stock market (e.g., Martha Stewart) and too cozy a relationships between auditors and company officials (e.g., Enron and Tyco), have highlighted the harmful consequences when formal institutions in business networks are replaced by informal ones.

Determining the proper balance between informal and formal institutions depends on the mission and type of network. A family network or a social unit may safely adopt more informal institutions than a business or a governmental network can. This is because of the relative importance of producing SEGs versus economically valued goods (EVGs). Determining the benefits and costs of alternative levels of formal and informal institutions is what makes leadership of networks an art rather than a precise science.

What Networks Do

One way of characterizing networks is by what they do. If a network is to be connected by social capital, then its members must have their socio-emotional needs met within the network. Other networks may be connected by their members' requirement to meet their economic needs.

Economic needs include the need for goods and services that provide the means for survival and physical enjoyment. In developed economies, economic needs are met by exchanging labor, effort, and other physical resources that produce income used to buy food, shelter, transportation services, entertainment, and other goods that provide physical satisfaction.

Socio-emotional needs, described in Chapter 6, can be divided into three categories: the need for experiences of caring and socialization; the need for validation and identity; and the need for information.

Humans are social beings whose emotional and physical health requires social interactions and a sense of belonging. One form of punishment is to deny people in confinement access to social interaction. A sense that one is cared for by others promotes trust and reciprocal feelings of caring.

Second, humans need to believe that they matter. This need is satisfied through various means of validation which are established in social interactions and must generally be interpersonally valued. Informal institutions usually determine the manner in which SEGs of validation are exchanged. Sometimes the need for validation is satisfied by the work we do, the awards we earn, the positions we hold, our physical appearance, the status symbols we own, the people with whom we associate, and the service we have performed.

Finally, humans have a need for information that helps them understand their environment. Sometimes this information connects consequences with their causes and is required for informed decision-making. Chaos exists when an ordered connection between actions and outcomes is lacking or not understood, so we seek information and understanding about consequences and their causes to rescue order from chaos. Finally, we seek comparative information—e.g., A is like or is the same as B. This kind of information allows us to transfer lessons learned in one setting to a different one.

Most networks strive to meet both economic and socio-emotional needs, although they vary widely in their emphasis on any one particular need. For example, the local Rotary Club meets socially over lunch. After lunch a guest speaker is invited to address the Club's informational need. Another purpose of the Rotary Club is to provide services to people and causes distinct from the club. These efforts are often organized at the weekly meetings and are usually performed on weekends. The Club's service projects provide a validation service for its members without which the Club would likely cease to exist. Finally, during some social, information-sharing, and service/validation activities, members sometimes arrange business deals. Thus, the local Rotary Club or a local business roundtable helps its members meet their economic needs, their need to matter, their need for caring, and their need for information.

It may be helpful to classify networks according to the needs they emphasize though their transactions. Most networks facilitate transactions that include the exchange of both SEGs and physical goods and services. Table 9.2 creates a classification of networks based on the network's purpose, the social capital location, and the relative importance of the needs served.

Table 9.2 The purpose of networks and their social capital locations

Where Social Capital Resides	**Purpose**			
	Economic	**Social or caring**	**Validation**	**Information**
Families	7	10	10	4
Religious groups	1	10	10	10
Ethnic groups	7	5	5	5
Service clubs	3	8	9	3
Person(s)	8			
Geographic communities	7	5	3	6
Gangs	7	8	10	3
Work groups/unions	10	3	3	10
Athletic teams	Varies	1	1	1
Political parties	7	1	7	10
Economic clubs	10	1	1	10
Literary/cultural groups	1	1	9	7
Electronic groups	Varies	Varies	Varies	Varies
States/nations	10	1	5	8

Key: 1 = Low to 10 = High

Note: Cell numbers are assumed for illustration purposes only.

But what happens when the flow of goods is between people via an impersonal object, such as a computer, ATM, a car, or the like? The quick answer, as we pointed out in Chapter 5, is that the possible exchange of SEGs has been reduced. Furthermore, because much of what we do is motivated by the flow of SEGs, the reduced flow of SEGs will likely have a negative impact unless there are supplemental SEGs supplied through other links. Supporting these conclusions is a study by two economics professors at Michigan State University.

TEACHERS OR TV MONITORS?

Two Michigan State University economics professors wanted to know if students in traditional face-to-face classes did as well as students in virtual classes. So they compared their exam grades. They found that exam grades for students in traditional face-to-face classes were significantly higher than for students in virtual courses of Principles of Microeconomics. Marketing sophomore Parag Humbad was enrolled in the virtual course. He observed: "the hardest part about virtual classes is pretty much trying to get the motivation to watch the lectures by yourself." From the perspective of the social capital paradigm, one receives SEGs from attending classes with other students and professors that are lacking in virtual settings. The reward of SEGs has an influence on how students prepare for the class.

Source: Frye (2002: 2).

Network Dynamics

Networks are dynamic because the relative importance of members' needs changes over time, and the ability of networks to satisfy needs must also change if the network is to survive. As a result, networks must routinely reassess their mission and performance to remain viable.

To illustrate the dynamic nature of a network, consider the family. New members of the family depend completely on inherited social capital to meet their economic and socio-emotional needs. When children start school, however, their dependence on the family for complete need satisfaction is reduced as some of their social needs may be increasingly met by school friends. Then, as they grow older, their information is increasingly supplied by people outside the home through numerous communication channels. Finally, children may join athletic or cultural groups that provide validation, some of which was previously produced at home. So, as the ages of family members increase, the relative importance of the needs supplied by the family diminishes.

FORMING NETWORKS

Networks are efficient vehicles for organizing individuals with shared traits. By advertising the traits of its members, networks will attract individuals with those traits. Those traits held in common then become the basis for the development of social capital. Bringing individuals with shared traits together in a network where they can meet and develop social capital with others possessing the same trait is much more efficient than individuals

conducting independent searches for people with similar traits. Thus, one important function of a network is to efficiently collect people with similar interests and traits.

Being a member in one network may lead an individual to discover other shared kernels with people in their own and other networks. This may lead them to join other networks. Undiscovered shared kernels, once discovered, can be used to convert latent social capital into actual social capital. For example, the network organized around the shared kernel of military service has often led its members to discover other shared kernels around which other networks are formed. For example, a group of individuals may form a network around their shared politics and then observe a sub-network forming around shared religious views.

RELIGION AND POLITICS

A new survey showing the religious affiliations of Michigan's 148 lawmakers has rekindled the heated debate of religion's role in government. The survey did not intend to spark controversy but rather wanted to show that "legislators are not ogres or fierce fellows for the most part, but rather good people who earnestly try to be people of faith." Religious beliefs can come into play when voting but so can legislators' ethnic backgrounds, hometowns, and other issues connected to particular networks. Often legislators will form a variety of networks based on a variety of different unifying constructs. On one bill a legislator may vote with his or her ethnic compatriots, while on another he or she may vote with those holding similar religious views.

Source: Adapted from Swarup (1995: 2A).

NETWORK STAGES OF DEVELOPMENT

Networks may pass through well-recognized stages of development. In stage one, members recognize in each other an opportunity for synergistic exchanges (forming). At this point, members of the network ask and answer several questions. What are our shared kernels? Do we face synergetic opportunities? Do we face a common enemy?

In stage two, members of networks experience conflicts because their actions produce externalities on other members of the network. In this stage (storming), conflicts have to be resolved by answering important questions. Who is going to lead? How are benefits and costs shared? What values does our network reflect? What are the institutions that define membership? What are the penalties for violating agreements? Do we have important shared kernels? These and many other questions are confronted in the storming stage of networks.

Management texts, such as Whetton's and Cameron's *Developing Management Skills*, refer to optimal levels of conflict, saying that with too little conflict there are no new approaches examined while too much conflict may defeat any effort to reach a consensus (Whetten and Cameron, 1995: 418). In the same book, methods for resolving conflict are also discussed including: forcing (the stick); accommodating (giving in); avoiding the conflict (neglecting interests of both parties); compromising (each gets half a loaf); and collaborating (find the best solutions).

Stage three of successful networks produces resolutions that allow the network to continue. Synergism is discovered. A network structure is defined. Values are defined.

Dealing with these and other issues produces agreement and conformity in the network, which allows it to go forward.

The final stage of the successful network is the performance stage. In this stage members perform. They work synergistically together. They exchange SEGs and build social capital. They create attachment values for their institutions. They earn new kernels. Finally, they act in each other's and the network's interest.

PRESSURES TO CHANGE

As a result of pressures from inside and outside of the network, network structures are constantly changing. To illustrate, a collection of students may initially form a network because of a common interest in a subject matter which leads them to register for the same class. Then, as a consequence of group projects and synergistic group studies, class members may develop social capital for each other that may lead them to exchange SEGs.

Another group may form around a common interest in an activity that meets a socio-emotional need. For example, one such group may organize to play bridge. However, this group may invest in social capital and, as a result, form an investment club. Now their group not only meets their needs for sociability, but also provides a useful economic activity (investing) that may further their economic interests (earning returns on their investments). Most service clubs, such as the Rotary Club or Kiwanis, organize not only to meet members' social needs, but also to provide service to their communities. These clubs would be unlikely to prosper if their only purpose was to advance members' social needs.

The Productivity and Distributional Consequences of Networks

The enduring insight of Adam Smith is that specialization and division of labor increase productivity. Letting our imagination run, we might ask what production levels could be achieved by thousands of workers cooperating together.

In Adam Smith's day, the size of the network was restricted to the number of workers in the same neighborhood—those who could travel back and forth on foot or horseback between their homes and work in a day. But what about modern-day networks in which fiber-optical cables connect workers around the world? Is social capital important in these worldwide networks?

A related point that we make with our examples is that if specialization and trade produce increased productivity, then one's share in that productivity should be related to one's contacts. In the case of the perfectly dense network, each of the network members enjoys the same number of contacts and the distribution of benefits can be expected to be equal. Asymmetric, key-player, or hierarchal networks have unequal distributions of contacts—and likely unequal distributions of rewards. Thus, can development ever occur in an isolated African village, despite advances in technology that should be their ally?

As social capital and density increases within a network, productivity will increase and differences in income will decrease among network members, although differences in productivity and income between network members and nonmembers may increase. Thus, one of the causes of poverty must be linked to exclusion of the poor from productive

networks. Consider the trend with single-parent families, whose networks may be assumed to be roughly half the size of a two-parent network.

THE REDUCED NETWORKS OF SINGLE-PARENT FAMILIES

One network is established by the marriage of a man and a woman. This network can lead to an expanded network that includes the two extended families to which the marriage partners belong. This expanded network provides both SEGs and EVGs. When the family consists of a single parent (most often a single female) the network is disadvantaged because its scope is limited to the socio-emotional and economic support of the single parent's network. The evidence is that households headed by a single female with own children are economically and socio-emotionally disadvantaged compared with households headed by a married couple with own children.

The *Economic Report to the President of the United States* describes the socio-emotional and economic disadvantages of children raised in a single-parent family. Children under age six who live apart from their fathers are about five times as likely to be poor as children with both parents at home. Girls without a father in their life are two and a half times as likely to get pregnant and 53 percent more likely to commit suicide. Boys without a father in their life are 63 percent more likely to run away and 37 percent more likely to abuse drugs. Children without father involvement are twice as likely to drop out of high school, roughly twice as likely to abuse alcohol or drugs, twice as likely to end up in jail, and nearly four times as likely to need help for emotional or behavioral problems than those with father involvement.

Source: Council of Economic Advisors (2000).

Networks and Power

Power is an important characteristic of networks. Power exercised in a network is the ability to influence the actions of others. Each member of a network has some power or is influenced by the power that others possess. An individual's power in the network depends on their resources including their social capital, number of connections, and position in the network. The distributions of power and social capital within a network are interdependent. As a result, we can learn a great deal about a network by observing how power is exercised within it.

Free-market economies, in which traders are generally allowed to choose their products and trading partners, have usually been promoted because they are efficient. However, it may be that the main advantage of a free-market economy is that it provides opportunities for synergistic exchanges that produce social capital and sympathetic relationships. For example, lenders and borrowers who successfully conduct business often produce good relationships in the process, as do salespeople and buying agents. These amicable feelings can then be used later on for customer retention and for negotiating preferential loan treatment. All the exchanges that have led to increased social capital also have the effect of increasing one's power.

Social capital-based relationships pursue a different kind of power because they value relationships and the SEGs they produce. In a sympathetic relationship, the well-being

of parties involved in the social interaction is internalized. Thus, it is unlikely that either party will engage in an activity that harms the other. Methods used in sympathetic relationships include mutually beneficial exchanges, exchanges of gifts, validating acts such as compliments and expressions of approval, expressions of caring, and personalized information that advantages its recipient.

Conclusion

The social capital paradigm is incomplete without a consideration of networks. Networks resolve one of the important conflicts that exist between some of the social sciences. Is the direction of influence from the individual to the group or vice versa? Does the individual control the network (micro-influence) or does the network control the individual (macro-influence)? Is social capital a micro- or macro-concept?

The social capital paradigm rationalizes the conflict between those who believe that social capital is a micro-concept and those who believe that it is a macro-concept by introducing networks. In one sense, social capital is a micro-concept because it is supplied and owned by individuals. On the other hand, it is a macro-concept because it resides in networks whose performance (team score) influences the behavior and rewards of individuals in the network. When a network is connected by social capital, each individual's well-being is internalized by members of the network to whom he or she is connected. As a result, there is a group sense of well-being. Finally, a network may demonstrate both micro- and macro-influences in that it discourages opportunistic behavior as this would either disadvantage all other members or damage the individual's social capital with resource-rich members.

We conclude with a point of clarification. Networks are not social capital. Social capital lives in people. However, people connected to each other in networks represent a significant resource. Networks can facilitate the development of social capital between their members when they adopt practices which facilitate the exchange of EVGs and SEGs and create AVGs that help to convey SEGs. Finally, networks that encourage members to interact in a wide variety of activities, including social and work activities, will facilitate the development of social capital because they allow cooperation and exchange over a wide range of settings and opportunities.

CHAPTER 10 The Social Capital Paradigm: The Role of Power

We shall continue to operate on the Italian donkey at both ends, with a carrot and with a stick ...

Winston Churchill, press conference, May 25, 1943.

Introduction

This chapter examines the use of negative and positive power to influence the behavior of others. To introduce the concept of negative and positive power, imagine a driver seated in a cart pulled by a donkey. The driver may motivate the donkey by hitting it with a stick or by holding a carrot on a string attached to a pole just out of the donkey's reach. The stick reflects a negative form of power—stick power. To avoid the stick, the donkey moves forward. On the other hand, the carrot represents positive power because the donkey, in an effort to reach the carrot, pulls the cart forward. In the one case, stick power motivates the donkey to avoid a "bad." In the other case, carrot power motivates the donkey to reach for a "good." And the power of most interest to us is the power inherent in social capital to increase the likelihood of transactions and to alter the terms and level of trade. This power arises because of social capital's ability to provide socio-emotional goods (SEGs) that are valued by others.

Social capital alters the likelihood and terms and level of trades by exercising two types of power. The first is negative power in which the likelihood and terms and level of trade are influenced by threatening the loss of social capital and access to SEGs. The second is positive power in which the likelihood and level of trade are influenced by offering to increase one's social capital and access to SEGs.

Like the driver who could employ positive or negative power to motivate the donkey, people can use their social and other capital to influence others by threatening them with negative (stick) outcomes or offering them positive (carrot) outcomes. Two kinds of carrots or goods that motivate are SEGs that convey acceptance, caring, and encouragement and mostly economically valued goods (EVGs) that can be used to acquire physical goods and services that produce satisfaction or pleasure. Two kinds of negative (stick) goods are socio-emotional bads that convey shame, antipathy, or exclusion and economic bads such as the loss of financial resources and the deprivation of physical goods that

financial losses imply. We next explore these different kinds of power and compare their effectiveness and the conditions under which they are most likely to be used.

Kinds of Power

NEGATIVE (STICK) POWER

The unique feature of stick power is its ability to force agents to choose between two (or more) bad outcomes. A criminal uses stick power when he points a gun at his victim and demands "Give me your wallet or your life," forcing his victim to choose between two bad outcomes. Nations use stick power when they threaten another nation with military action, embargos, or confiscations of their assets unless they agree to the demands of the threatening nation. Legal entities, such as local governments, use stick power to motivate people to obey the law when they threaten individuals with the loss of privileges such as drivers' licenses or incarceration, or with fines and lengthy litigation. Interrogators have used stick power to extract confessions through physical torture that can only be avoided by disclosing information. Stick power is used by extra-legal entities, such as crime syndicates, which threaten to destroy an individual's business or to harm their friends and family unless they pay protection money.

One problem with transactions that employ stick power is that they are never completed. Those who use stick power always want their subjects to choose between two (or more) bads, leaving them worse off than before they were required to choose. As a result, those who must choose between stick-imposed outcomes are never satisfied with the transaction, and most often view it as incomplete. The person using the stick may obtain his or her desired outcome in the short run, but the result will likely be contested in the future when the balance of stick power is changed. Thus, sticks must be constantly employed to maintain the original advantage gained in the stick-motivated transaction.

The other problem with stick power is that one can never be sure one has enough sticks to require the agent to choose between carefully selected options. Nearly all those subject to stick power have sticks of their own, and there are so many different kinds of sticks and opportunities to use them that one is almost always vulnerable to efforts to resist or to avenge earlier losses, whether real or imagined. Even powerful nations like the United States are not immune from damage caused by a relatively weak group intent on using stick power, including those groups who desire to commit acts of terrorism.

In many cases, stick power ignores existing institutions. For example, thieves ignore the institutions that guarantee property rights. Murderers ignore the right to life and liberty. Those who drive recklessly ignore traffic institutions designed to protect motorists. The willingness of those who use stick power to ignore institutions reflects their absence of attachment values for the institutions they ignore. This in turn suggests an absence of social capital for those who embed the institutions with attachment value.

Sometimes stick power is used simply because the individual lacks carrot power. In Victor Hugo's *Les Miserables*, for example, Jean Valjean has no food for his family and, because he is unable to meet his family's need for bread, he robs a bakery. He uses his stick power to achieve his ends even though it violates an institution. In other cases, people use sticks because of their antipathy toward others. Feelings of antipathy are satisfied when the well-being of the object of the antipathy is diminished.

Social capital can be used as a stick by providing negative forms of SEGs. These may include threats of shaming, a withdrawal of affection, devaluation, and exclusions. The essential difference between economic sticks and socio-emotional sticks is that the latter requires social capital. It is difficult, if not impossible, to shame someone who doesn't have social capital.

POSITIVE (CARROT) POWER

Carrot power is often associated with an offer of financial rewards, but it could just as easily be associated with socio-emotional rewards.

People with financial resources can use them in exchange for actions or goods they desire, giving them a form of power. In addition, ownership gives the power to withhold resources from others. Parents who offer financial rewards to their children if they earn good grades employ economic carrot power. Customers who make purchases at the grocery store or gas station employ carrot power. Businesses that offer financial returns to those who invest in their businesses employ carrot power.

Those who employ carrots differ from those who employ sticks because they offer choices that are supposed to leave those who accept them better off than before. Another important difference between carrot and stick transactions is that "none of the above" is always an option for those choosing between offers of carrots.

Socio-emotional carrots, like economic carrots, provide their owners with the opportunity to motivate others by offering rewards or desirable outcomes. Financial carrots provide power through the potential of financial rewards. Socio-emotional carrots provide power through the offer of SEGs conveyed through individuals or through high attachment value goods embedded with SEGs. Of course, one can only offer a socio-emotional carrot if one has social capital.

EMPLOYEE COMPENSATION AND TURNOVER RATES

Employers are anxious to influence their employees. In most cases, they use sticks on poorly performing employees and threaten to fire them or cut their pay if their performance does not improve. But what about their best employees—the ones they want to keep? They want them to remain for at least two reasons. When productive employees leave, company performance often suffers. The second reason why businesses fear losing productive employees is that the process of finding, hiring, and training new employees is expensive.

Common estimates of turnover costs range from $10,000 to $40,000 per person, depending on the position; while retention actually increases revenues. The *Harvard Business Review* reports that a 5 percent increase in retention results in a 10 percent decrease in costs and productivity increases ranging from 25 to 65 percent!

Many companies and organizations believe that economic carrots are the primary means available for them to retain productive employees. Consequently, employers attempt to "buy" employee satisfaction with increased pay and benefits. In today's competitive business environment this approach can only be taken so far. Fortunately, there is a much less expensive way to create greater employee satisfaction—using socio-emotional carrots. It is virtually cost-

free and it increases productivity, which significantly improves the "bottom line." Workers need respect as well as income.

In surveying 206 medium to large companies in 1998 William M. Mercer, Inc. found that in organizations with high employee turnover unsatisfactory compensation was the most common reason given for dissatisfaction. However, in companies with very low employee turnover, 40 percent of the respondents attributed their motivation to stay to perceived emotional factors (work satisfaction, good relationships with managers and other employees) against 21 percent who cited financial factors (satisfaction with compensation and benefits) as their motivation.

Source: Campbell (n.d.).

Social Capital and the Use of Power

One's power is manifest in transactions. However, the kind of power likely to be employed in different kinds of transactions varies, depending on the kind of social capital that exists between the transacting parties. The essence of the influence of social capital on exchange can be described as follows. Person *i*'s sympathy (social capital) for person *j* is represented by k_{ij}. In other words, k_{ij} is person *j*'s social capital provided by person *i*. Person *j*'s social capital is the power to influence person *i*'s behavior—by providing person *i* with SEGs in a transaction. (We can please those who have internalized our well-being.) The different kinds of relationships that may exist between two exchange partners are described in Table 10.1. Also described in Table 10.1 are the roles that relationships—social capital—have on the likelihood and terms of trade.

The results of Table 10.1 can also be described graphically. We begin by assuming that buyer *i* and seller *j* are considering the exchange of an economic good. The market price for the good is P_{market} which is available to both the buyer and the seller. The only reason buyer *i* and seller *j* would transact with each other rather than in the arm's-length market with a stranger is because the combined values of SEGs and EVGs exceeds the value of EVGs they would receive in an arm's-length market. However, the combined value of SEGs and EVGs available to buyer *i* and seller *j* depends on their relative social capital.

Consider the intersection of the horizontal and vertical axes in Figure 10.1. The vertical axis represents the price at which the good is exchanged. Prices below the horizontal axis represent prices below the market price. Prices above the horizontal axis represent prices above the market price. The horizontal axis represents buyer *i*'s (seller *j*'s) social capital k_{ji} (k_{ij}). Values on the horizontal axis to the right of the vertical axis represent positive levels of social capital. Values on the horizontal axis to the left of the vertical axis represent negative levels of social capital. It is assumed that positive (negative) SEGs are associated with positive (negative) levels of social capital. It is also assumed that SEGs increase (decrease) with increases (decreases) in social capital.

The positive sloping line in Figure 10.1 represents the buyer's maximum bid prices that depend on the market price P_{market} and the SEGs he or she receives from his or her social capital k_{ji}. The negative sloping line in Figure 10.1 represents the seller's minimum sell prices that depend on the market price P_{market} and the SEGs he or she receives from his or her social capital k_{ij}. In other words k_{ji} (k_{ij})>0 implies the buyer's (seller's) maximum bid (minimum sell) price will be above (below) the market price.

Table 10.1 The relative amounts of social capital power and economic power inherent in alternative social capital relationships described graphically in Figures 10.1 and 10.2

		Seller *j*'s social capital power k_{ij} provided by buyer *i*		
		$k_{ij} < 0$	$k_{ij} = 0$	$k_{ij} > 0$
Buyer *i*'s social capital power k_{ji} provided by seller *j*	$k_{ji} > 0$	(NW) The buyer's positive social capital increases the likelihood that a transaction will be completed. But the seller's negative social capital offsets the buyer's positive social capital, making the likelihood of a transaction possible. If a transaction occurs, the transaction price will be below the arm's-length price.	(NC) The buyer's positive social capital increases the likelihood that a transaction will be completed. The likelihood of a transaction is moderate. The transaction price will be below the arm's-length price.	(NE) Both the buyer's and seller's positive social capital increase the likelihood that a transaction will be completed. The likelihood of a transaction is high. The transaction price may be above or below the arm's-length price.
	$k_{ji} = 0$	(CW) The seller's negative social capital reduces the likelihood of completing a transaction. Only if the economic incentives of the buyer and seller are strong enough to overcome the seller's negative social capital will a transaction be completed. As a result, the likelihood of completing a transaction is very small. If a transaction does occur, the price will be below the arm's-length market price.	(Central) Both buyer and seller exercise economic power. A transaction is completed only if the buyer's maximum arm's-length bid price exceeds the seller's minimum arm's-length sell price. If a transaction is completed, the transaction price will be the arm's-length market price.	(CE) The seller's positive social capital increases the likelihood a transaction will be completed. The likelihood of a transaction is moderate. The transaction price will be above the arm's-length price.
	$k_{ji} < 0$	(SW) Both the buyer's and seller's negative social capital decrease the likelihood that a transaction will be completed. The likelihood of a transaction is only possible if the buyer and seller have strong economic incentives. In most cases, the likelihood of the buyer and seller completing a transaction is close to zero. If in the unlikely event a transaction is completed, the transaction price will depend on the buyer's and seller's relative economic power.	(SC) The buyer's negative social capital reduces the likelihood that a transaction will be completed. Only if the economic incentives of the buyer and seller are strong enough to overcome the buyer's negative social capital will a transaction be completed. As a result, the likelihood of completing a transaction is very small. If a transaction does occur, the price will be above the arm's-length market price.	(SE) The buyer's negative social capital reduces the likelihood that a transaction will be completed. But the seller's positive social capital offsets the buyer's negative social capital, making the likelihood of a transaction possible. The likelihood of a transaction is moderate. If a transaction occurs, the transaction price will be above the arm's-length price.

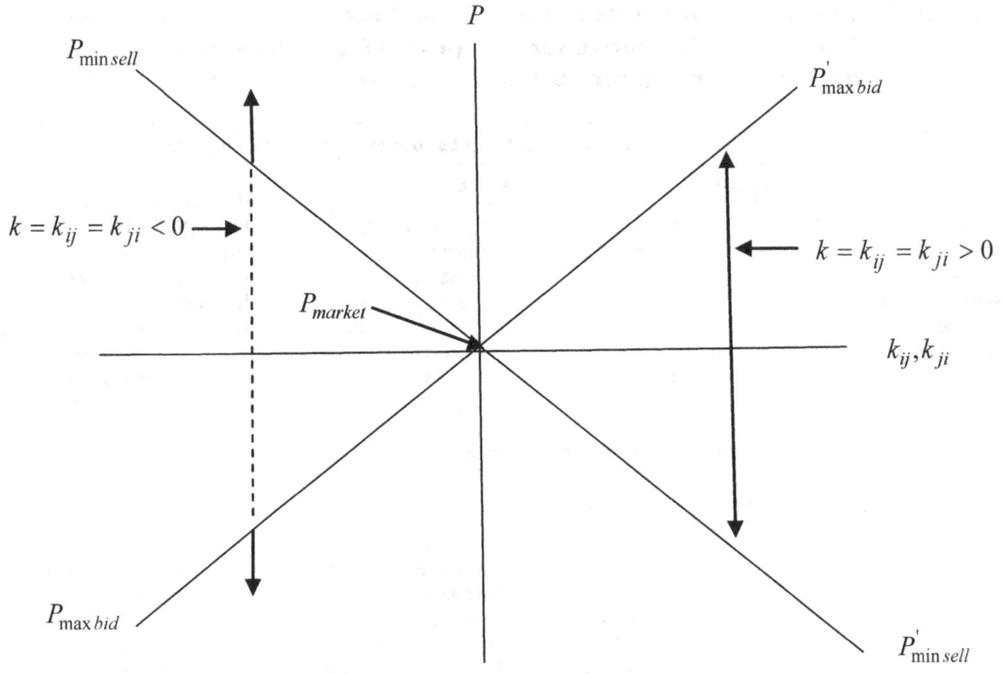

Figure 10.1 Acceptable exchange prices that depend on the social capital of the buyers and sellers

A transaction between buyer *i* and seller *j* can occur only when buyer *i*'s maximum bid price is equal to or exceeds seller *j*'s minimum sell price. In Figure 10.1 prices acceptable to the seller are on or above the line $P'_{\min sell}P_{\min sell}$. Prices acceptable to the buyer in Figure 10.1 are on or below the line $P'_{\max bid}P_{\max bid}$. When the social capital of the buyer and seller are equal and positive, e.g., $(k_{ij} = k_{ji} = k) > 0$ mutually acceptable prices are represented by the solid two-headed arrow that connects lines $P'_{\min sell}P_{\min sell}$ and $P'_{\max bid}P_{\max bid}$ in the NE and SE quadrants of Figure 10.1.

There are no mutually acceptable prices for equal levels of social capital in the NW or SW quadrants of Figure 10.1, e.g., where $(k_{ij} = k_{ji} = k) < 0$. There are, of course, other mutually acceptable prices where the buyer's and the seller's social capital are not equal. For example, in Figure 10.2, above market price P^* is acceptable for buyers and sellers when the seller's positive social capital is equal to or greater than $k^*_{ij} > 0$ and the buyer's negative social capital is equal to or greater than $k^*_{ji} < 0$. In this case, an exchange is possible even when the buyer's social capital is negative as long as the seller's social capital is sufficiently positive to offset the effect of the buyer's negative social capital.

Alternatively, below market price P^{**} is acceptable for buyers and sellers when the buyer's positive social capital is equal to or greater than $k^*_{ji} > 0$ and the seller's negative social capital is equal to or greater than $k^*_{ij} < 0$. In this case, an exchange is possible even when the seller's social capital is negative as long as the buyer's social capital is sufficiently positive to offset the effect of the seller's negative social capital.

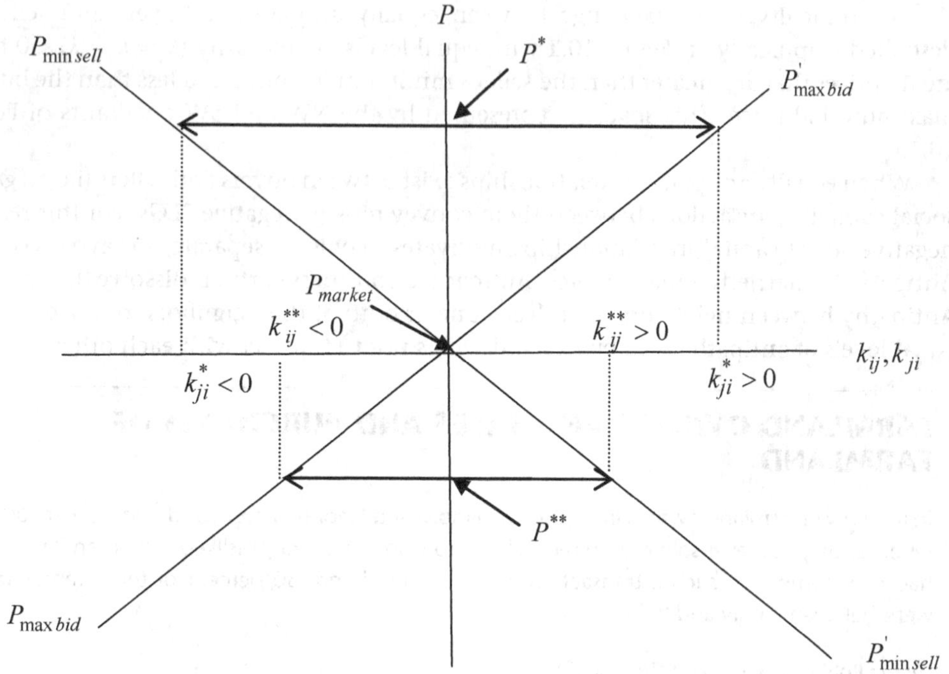

Figure 10.2 Acceptable exchange prices that depend on the social capital of the buyers and sellers

Power to Transact and Social Capital

In what follows, Table 10.1 and Figures 10.1 and 10.2 are combined to describe the power to transact in alternative relationships. The discussion is organized around cells in Table 10.1 and social capital levels k_{ij} and k_{ji} described in Figures 10.1 and 10.2. We first consider relationships in which the buyer and the seller provide each other equal levels of social capital. These are considered the norm simply because unequal levels of social capital admit exploitation that can only be sustained when resources are unequally distributed. However, for completeness, we do consider unequal social capital relationships because they may exist under the unequal resource distribution just described.

EQUALLY ANTIPATHETIC RELATIONSHIPS

Equally antipathetic relationships were described in the SW cell of Table 10.1 $(k_{ij} = k_{ji}) < 0$. In equally antipathetic relationships, persons *i* and *j* are unlikely to complete a transaction because socio-emotional bads exchanged are likely to offset the benefits they may receive from exchanging economic goods and services. This does not mean that exchanges between equally antipathetic persons can never occur; it's just that they are highly unlikely. When exchanges do occur, the potential for gain from exchanging economic goods and socio-emotional bads creates what some refer to as "strange bedfellows." The more usual outcome will be an absence of transactions. Simply put, negative social capital neutralizes the potential power that people can exercise through their financial and physical power.

The difficulty of an exchange between equally antipathetic buyers and sellers is described graphically. In Figure 10.1 with equal levels of antipathy $(k_{ij} = k_{ji} = k) < 0$ there are no prices that are greater than the seller's minimum sell price and less than the buyer's maximum bid price. This space is represented by the NW and SW quadrants of Figure 10.1.

When equally antipathetic relationships exist between buyers and sellers (i.e. negative social capital), transactions between them convey mostly negative SEGs. For this reason, negative social capital in relationships motivates people to separate—to avoid contact. Antipathetic married couples divorce. Antipathetic business partners dissolve the business. Antipathy between neighbors often leads one or both of the neighbors to move. Finally, equal levels of antipathy lead buyers and sellers not to transact with each other.

FARMLAND OWNERS AND SALES AND PURCHASES OF FARMLAND

In a survey of farmland owners in Michigan, Illinois, and Nebraska, farmland owners were asked whether they had ever sold or purchased land from someone they disliked. Less than 2 percent had ever completed such a transaction. On the other hand, 50 percent of their transactions were between family and friends.

Source: Robison, Myers, and Siles (2002).

Unfortunately, an absence of transactions sometimes leads to increased antipathy and attempts to use stick power to achieve what could not be obtained with carrot power. If stick power is fairly evenly distributed, at least in the minds of the combatants, we experience wars and other mutual acts of hostility. If stick power is unevenly distributed, the agents with the smaller sticks, who know they cannot prevail in a forced battle, may resort to terrorist acts, concealed crimes, hostage-taking and various other hostile acts that avoid direct confrontation with a superior force. Usually, the agent with the greater sticks gains the greater advantages and inflicts the most serious harm. As a result, transactions between agents with negative social capital increase inequalities.

Because antipathetic transactions that use sticks are never complete, we cannot, nor do we attempt to, model antipathy and the use of stick power. The note that follows derives from a piece written years ago after the bombing in Yemen, but its message is the same today. Antipathy and the use of stick power leave transactions incomplete and beyond the scope of the social capital paradigm; worse still, the attempt to resolve conflicts in the region continues.

STICKS, BOMBS, AND BLOODSHED

The Middle East is the birthplace of three religions and civilizations almost too numerous to count, but as it shuddered under escalating waves of violence last week, the Middle East was reminded why it has also been the grim graveyard of hope and aspiration. The blood from Israelis and Palestinians alike conjured nothing so much as hands strangling a peace, a peace that, just weeks ago, seemed near at hand. And now on the cusp of war, Israelis and Palestinians

will see if there is a way, somehow, to reverse the sickening spiral of violence—or not. For Israelis and Palestinians alike, it was a day that crystallized the mutual hatred that had survived—and even thrived—through seven years of US-led peacemaking ... The level of mistrust (it's hatred) is so great that it will take generations to repair the damage done by these events. Palestinians and Jewish Israelis are losing hope for negotiations. It appears that the only power in Palestine and Israel is the power derived from sticks.

Source: Adapted from Omestad, Derfner, and Toameh (2000).

EQUALLY NEUTRAL RELATIONSHIPS

Equally neutral relationships were described in the central cell of Table 10.1 ($k_{ij} = k_{ji} = 0$). In equally neutral or arm's-length relationships, persons *i* and *j* are likely to employ financial and economic carrots to influence each other because of the absence of social capital. When well-functioning markets for the good considered for exchange are available, the buyer has no incentive to pay more than the market price, and the seller has no incentive to accept less than the market price. Therefore, if an exchange is to occur in the absence of social capital, it will be at the market price P_{market}, and the likelihood of an exchange depends completely on the opportunities for mutually beneficial exchange of economic goods.

Neutral relationships between transacting parties known to each other in the exchange, however, are rarely stable. After even one exchange, the relationship will likely become mutually sympathetic or antipathetic.

TIPS FOR FRIENDS

In a survey of restaurant tipping behavior, researchers found the usual: tips for waiters who were friends and family were significantly higher than for tips for waiters who were strangers or known and not liked. Strangers received the average or industry normal tip of roughly 15 percent. Waiters who were known and disliked received less than the industry norm. What was interesting was that during repeat customer visits, tips for waiters who were previously considered strangers and provided satisfactory service during the previous visit found that their tips increased from $2.99 to $3.40—not all that different from the tips offered to waiters who were friends. This result suggests that relationships are dynamic, and positive economic exchanges can often lead to increased levels of social capital.

Source: Robison, unpublished survey (1998).

EQUALLY POSITIVE SOCIAL CAPITAL-RICH RELATIONSHIPS

Equally positive social capital relationships are described in the NE cell of Table 10.1 ($k = k_{ij} = k_{ji} > 0$). In social capital-rich relationships, persons *i* and *j* hold equal levels of social capital for each other, which enables them to exchange both economic and socio-emotional carrots. Because of their social capital, exchanges can include high attachment value goods, EVGs, and SEGs. Indeed, either one of the exchange partners might not require economic benefits from the exchange provided they are compensated with

SEGs. The most likely exchanges to occur are those between individuals in a mutually social capital-rich relationship because there are so many opportunities to benefit from exchanges. For example, if ($k = k_{ij} = k_{ji} > 0$), then all prices represented by the solid two-headed line in the NE and SE quadrants of Figure 10.1 are acceptable. What determines the final exchange price often depends on the relative wealth of the transacting parties, as a survey of faculty and graduate students at MSU shows.

SOCIAL CAPITAL AND USED CARS

Graduate students and faculty members of the Department of Agricultural Economics at Michigan State University were surveyed to determine their minimum sell price for a used car, with a market value of $3,000, which they were assumed to own. The potential buyers were friends, strangers, and antipathetic neighbors who were alternatively less wealthy, equally wealthy, or wealthier than the seller.

Controlling for differences in relationships, graduate students added a premium of $151 to their minimum sell price when they were less wealthy than the potential buyer, and they deducted $137 from their minimum sell price when they were wealthier than the potential seller. In contrast, the faculty members were hardly affected by differences in relative wealth. They offered neither a significant discount to less wealthier potential buyers nor added a significant premium to the price offered wealthier potential buyers. However, both graduate students and the faculty responded significantly and predictably to antipathy and sympathy in the prices they offered potential buyers.

Source: Robison and Schmid (1991).

ASYMMETRIC RELATIONSHIPS OF NEUTRALITY AND ANTIPATHY

Asymmetric relationships of antipathy and neutrality were described in the CW and SC cells of Table 10.1 ($k_{ij} < 0$ and $k_{ji} = 0$; $k_{ij} = 0$ and $k_{ji} < 0$). In asymmetric relationships of neutrality and antipathy, the likelihood of transactions is small. If the buyer (seller) has neutral feeling toward the seller (buyer) she/he has no incentive to offer a bid (sell) price above (below) the market price which would be required for the antipathetic exchange partner to agree to terms. Since person *i* (*j*) has antipathy toward *j* (*i*), he or she has no incentive to employ economic carrots that will leave *i* (*j*) in an improved condition unless he or she will also receive significant economic gains in the process.

On the other hand, if a transaction occurs, and the results are satisfactory for both parties, the relationship could easily move to mutually neutral or mutually sympathetic. When the antipathetic party holds significant economic and other forms of power, exploitation of the weaker party becomes the norm. In Figure 10.1, the quadrants in which there are no acceptable prices are the NW and SW quadrants above and below the horizontal axis and below the lines representing minimum sell prices and above the line representing maximum bid prices.

Special relationships between Rockefeller's Standard Oil and the railroads allowed them to exploit competitors who were attempting to operate under the mistaken assumption that transactions were between neutral parties. Instead, they were treated as though they were they were the objects of antipathy.

STICKS AND OIL

John D. Rockefeller began as a humble oil business book-keeper in Cleveland, Ohio and, in just seven years, rose to control a tenth of the entire US oil business. Rockefeller would secretly buy up or create new oil-related companies such as engineering and pipeline firms which would continue to give the appearance of being independent operators. However, Rockefeller and his close colleagues secretly controlled the firms and gave Standard Oil, Rockefeller's main oil company, hidden rebates.

Another way in which Rockefeller exercised his financial power was by buying up competing oil companies, again secretly. Officials from recently purchased companies could then be used very effectively to spy on, and give advanced warning of deals being hatched by, his real competitors. Almost certainly the most lucrative secret deals done by Rockefeller and his partners were with the railroads. These "in harmony" deals meant those refineries and oil traders not "in harmony" with Standard Oil would find that the railroads would refuse to move their oil at whatever price.

Rockefeller's secret railroad rebates on the transportation of his oil disadvantaged his competitors and allowed Standard Oil to sell at prices below what competitors could offer. Allan Nevins, who wrote the official biography of the Rockefeller empire, wrote of a railroad contract signed on October 17, 1877 that the contracts were ethically indefensible.

Source: Nevins (1953).

ASYMMETRIC RELATIONSHIPS OF NEUTRALITY AND SYMPATHY

Asymmetric relationships of neutrality and sympathy are described in the CE and NC cells of Table 10.1 ($k_{ij} > 0$ and $k_{ji} = 0$; $k_{ij} = 0$ and $k_{ji} > 0$). In asymmetric relationships of neutrality and sympathy, neutral person *i* is likely to employ carrots and pretend to offer SEGs and social capital in order to extract favorable terms of trade from sympathetic person *j*. The attempts are likely to be only partially successful, and person *i* is most likely to obtain economic goods and services with his or her carrot purchases. Person *j* is likely to sense that he or she is not the object of person *i*'s social capital, making the relationship unstable. There is a possibility of exploitation in this type of relationship, but it is less likely than in the case of Becker's "rotten kid" (see below) because of the absence of antipathy. However, exchanges of economic carrots are likely to provide each person with benefits, and the exchange price will always favor the party in the transaction who holds social capital.

ASYMMETRIC RELATIONSHIPS OF ANTIPATHY AND SYMPATHY

Asymmetric relationships of antipathy and sympathy are described in the SE and NW cells of Table 10.1 ($k_{ij} > 0$ and $k_{ji} < 0$; $k_{ij} < 0$ and $k_{ji} > 0$). In asymmetric relationships of antipathy and sympathy, antipathetic person *i* will take advantage of sympathetic person *j*'s sympathy to do him or her harm. This is the relationship of the "rotten kid" with his or her parents described by Gary Becker (1991). The social capital provided to the child by the parents and the antipathy of the child toward the parents leads to exploitation of the parents. Of all relationships, this is the most unstable and the most unlikely to persist over time. The likelihood of exchanges still exists, though, and is greater than the

likelihood of a transaction because person *j* need not receive any economic goods to be motivated to exchange

Externalities and Power

Stick power implies an imposed choice that leaves one agent worse off than before. However, people may impose costs and benefits on others without making others choose if they have the power to create externalities. However, externalities have at least one effect similar to stick-imposed outcomes: if the externality alters the well-being of others, the transaction is often viewed by those affected as incomplete.

Suppose person *i* imposes an externality on person *j* without his or her agreement. Since person *j*'s well-being is changed, *j* is likely to respond and attempt to restore his or her well-being at least to its original state. Positive externalities are likely to create social capital and improve the likelihood of future transactions. Negative externalities are likely to reduce social capital and possibly create antipathy that, in some cases, may lead to the use of stick power.

While economic and physical externalities are usually easily described and observed, we can just as easily imagine socio-emotional externalities. For example, if two suitors pursue a young lady, her choice of one in preference to the other will create a socio-emotional externality—and possible economic externalities as well. Two teams competing for the same prize create socio-emotional externalities in the form of validation or the loss of it, depending on which team wins.

The power to create externalities is also the power to create conflict and unresolved transactions. The team that loses resolves to win next year. The suitor who is rejected resolves to find another love. Our approaches to resolving conflicts depend as much on the nature of the conflict as on the relationships of those involved in the conflict. If the conflict is over SEGs, the solution is to build social capital or reduce hostility. If the conflict is over economic goods, the solution is re-establish the terms of the agreement. On the other hand, improving the SEGs included in the exchange can sometimes facilitate economic exchanges. If the conflict is over incorrect information, the resolution is to find better information. Of course, the interpretation of information is not independent of social capital.

Conclusion

An important element of the social capital paradigm is power. This chapter has focused on the importance of power and the different kinds of power that can be used to influence others. It is important to distinguish between positive, or carrot, power and negative, or stick, power. Positive power exercises an influence over people by offering them opportunities to choose between options that improve their well-being or to do nothing at all. Negative power, on the other hand, offers only the choice between two or more bads. The ability to exercise carrot power can be enhanced when an agent in a transaction has social capital because then the agent can include the exchange of SEGs in the transaction in order to influence the actions of others. Those without social capital are limited to the exchange of physical goods. An agent's economic sticks or carrot power,

in turn, depend on the physical and financial resources that he or she is able to bring to the exchange. John D. Rockefeller had a vast resource of economic carrots, and he used them as both sticks and carrots to influence other people.

The key point is that social capital is a form of power that can be used to influence the behavior of others. Positive social capital enhances forms of power that depend on physical carrots while reducing the probability that stick power will be used at all. At the same time, negative social capital, or its absence, deters the effectiveness of carrot power and makes the employment of stick power more likely.

CHAPTER 11 The Social Capital Exchange Theory

A business that makes nothing but money is a poor kind of business.

Henry Ford, interview, 1919.

Introduction

People exchange socio-emotional goods (SEGs) directly through verbal and nonverbal exchanges that convey approval, affection, or direction. When the exchange of SEGs becomes associated with an object, the object may become embedded with SEGs and have its value and meaning changed. The changed value or meaning of a good attributed to embedded SEGs is the object's attachment value. When attachment value is a significant portion of an object's total value, the object is referred to as an attachment value good (AVG). Activities involving AVGs often trigger the release of SEGs. As a result, AVGs are an indirect source of SEGs.

SEGS, AVGS, AND THE BROWN FAMILY REUNION

The Roger and Ethel Brown Family Reunion is held each year in the small Southern Utah community where Roger and Ethel raised their family. Roger's and Ethel's children, now grown up and with families of their own, look forward to the annual reunion because it gives them the opportunity to enjoy each others' company and to remember their shared history. Activities at the reunion include remembering and retelling important family events, visiting friends, sharing old photos, participating in a talent show, enjoying a picnic up the "creek," listening to grandmother tell stories of her ancestors, and decorating the graves of deceased family members. Roger's and Ethel's grandchildren are forming memories of their own, swimming with their cousins, riding off-road vehicles in the nearby mountains, and playing sports.

Many members of the Brown family travel long distances and at some expense to attend the reunion. They all leave the reunion feeling that the effort to attend and be with each other was a good investment of time, money, and effort. If you were to ask those who attended the reunion what made it worthwhile, they would certainly not mention SEGs or AVGs. Instead, they would probably say something like "We just enjoy being together, and seeing familiar places and things brings back so many emotions and memories."

But SEGs and AVGs are exchanged in more settings than family reunions. They tend to be part of nearly every interpersonal exchange. And being intangible doesn't diminish their importance. Indeed, the message of this chapter is that SEGs are included in most interpersonal exchanges, either directly or indirectly. And when they are included in exchanges, they alter the terms and level of trade.

To understand the role of SEGs in the exchange of EVGs and AVGs, this chapter reviews and revises some basic economic lessons of exchange. We conclude that if both the buyer and the seller receive SEGs in the exchange of an EVG, as might occur when the trade is between friends or family, the likelihood of trade is increased. On the other hand, if both the buyer and seller sacrifice SEGs in the exchange, as might occur when the trade includes an AVG, the likelihood of trade decreases. However, we will find that the effect on the terms of trade caused by including SEGs directly or indirectly in an exchange is indeterminate.

The Social Capital Exchange Theorem

The influence of SEGs on the terms and levels of trade are summarized in the Social Capital Exchange Theorem that follows.

> *If a buyer and seller include SEGs in their exchange of an economic good, the likelihood of them finding a mutually agreed price and exchanging increases, compared to the likelihood of the same exchange without the inclusion of SEGs.*
>
> *If a buyer and seller include SEGs in their exchange of multiple units of economic goods, the number of goods traded increases, compared to the same exchange without the inclusion of SEGs.*

The Social Capital Exchange Theorem is illustrated graphically in Figure 11.1. The vertical axis represents the observed price P paid in an arm's-length exchange. The horizontal axis represents unobserved units of SEGs exchanged between the buyer and the seller. For example, at point OE on the horizontal axis, the buyer provides the seller and the seller provides the buyer with OE units of SEGs.

The curved line $P'_{buyer}\ P_{buyer}$ represents combinations of alternative prices P and SEGs that are valued equally by the buyer. Where the curved line $P_{buyer}P'_{buyer}$ crosses the vertical axis identifies the buyer's maximum bid price for the good without SEGs included in the exchange.

The curved line $P_{seller}P'_{seller}$ represents combinations of alternative prices P and SEGs that are valued equally by the seller. Where the curved line $P_{seller}P'_{seller}$ crosses the horizontal axis identifies the level of SEGs at which the seller would offer the good as a gift or at a zero price. Where the curved line $P_{seller}P'_{seller}$ crosses the vertical axis identifies the seller's minimum sell price for the good without SEGs included in the exchange.

For the buyer and seller represented in Figure 11.1, there is no arm's-length price at which the buyer and the seller are willing to exchange. Only when at least OE units of SEGs are included in the exchange is there a mutually acceptable exchange price P. When OE units of SEGs are included in the exchange, the seller and buyer are willing to exchange the economic good for price $P_{exchange}$. As more than OE units of SEGs are included

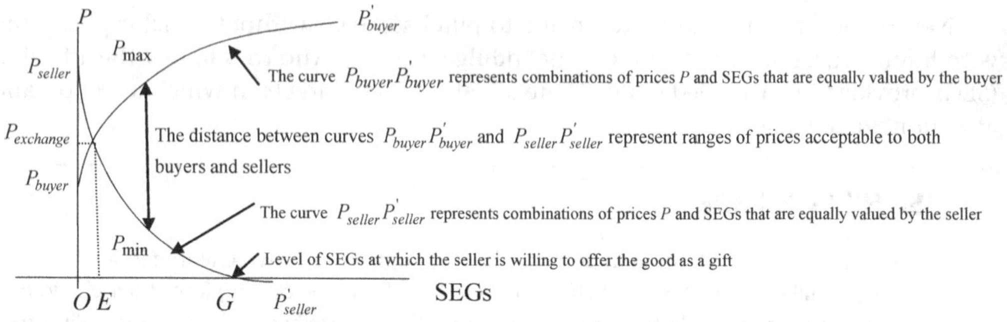

Figure 11.1 A seller's minimum sell price and a buyer's maximum bid price when SEGs are included in the exchange of an EVG

in the exchange, more than one market price is acceptable to both the buyer and seller. This range of acceptable prices is found between curved lines $P_{buyer}P'_{buyer}$ and $P_{seller}P'_{seller}$ and is indicated by the double-headed arrow.

The difference between curved line $P_{buyer}P'_{buyer}$ and $P_{seller}P'_{seller}$ represents a surplus—a gain to be divided between the buyer and the seller beyond what would be required to motivate an exchange. Thus, we infer that as the level of SEGs included in an exchange and the range of acceptable prices increase, so does the likelihood of an exchange, because there is much to be gained from the exchange. However, since the buyer is willing to pay more than $P_{exchange}$ and the seller is willing to accept less than $P_{exchange}$, the price at which the exchange actually occurs is indeterminate.

GUTTERS AND GIFTS

A local service club dedicates a service project each year to cleaning the rain gutters for several local and elderly widows. Some beneficiaries of the service project offered to pay for the effort. In the past, club members have always refused the payment, because the SEGs sacrificed by accepting the payment were valued more than the offered payment. In relation to Figure 11.1, what was offered was a price *P* and SEGs combination below the curved line $P_{seller}P'_{seller}$ and also less than the value of SEGs earned when the service was provided as a gift.

Are SEGs for Sale?

An interesting question arises from the discussion of Figure 11.1. If including SEGs in exchanges increase the likelihood of exchanges and, in addition, creates surplus benefits from the trade, why don't we produce and trade more SEGs? Are they too costly to produce? Can they only be exchanged when there is a certain kind of relationship between buyer and seller?

There are several answers to these questions. The main answer is that artificial SEGs are hard to pass off as real (Etzioni, 1988). Flattery and feigned affection are not all that difficult to distinguish from sincere expressions of validation and caring. This implies that SEGs are mostly, and perhaps only effectively, exchanged by those with social capital who have a sincere sympathy and respect for their exchange partner.

Nevertheless attempts are often made to purchase SEGs without social capital—and with limited success. One example is the indulgent parent who tries to buy the affection (SEGs provided by) a spoiled child. There are also other markets in which affection and attention are purchased.

> **A "SON" FOR HIRE**
>
> Mark Ritthaler rents himself out as a "son" to elderly people whose own children ignore them. Elderly people still need the love and affection that they should be getting from their children. Although he may not provide the love and affection that a family should, Mark is willing to provide a variety of services. He telephones his "parent" every morning and night. He takes his "parent" to the doctor, to the store, and to other places the "parent" needs to visit. He does odd jobs around the house. The loneliness is out there. Sometimes it runs in the family. The most interesting question is: can SEGs of love and affection be purchased by the elderly? Or, perhaps, does Mark Ritthaler *really* care about the well-being of his clients?
>
> *Source:* Greene (1996).

Markets and the Influence of SEGs included in Exchanges

Figure 11.2 portrays an arm's-length market in which the seller's (buyer's) willingness to supply (purchase) goods is represented by solid lines that increase (decrease) with prices. The market equilibrium where supply equals demand occurs at price P_{market} and quantity Q_{market}.

Now, suppose that the seller receives not only a dollar price for each unit of her good sold, but also a quantity of SEGs. This added benefit for the seller shifts her supply curve to the right in Figure 11.2 and is represented by a dotted line that increases with price. Under these new conditions, the seller would be willing to offer the same amount of

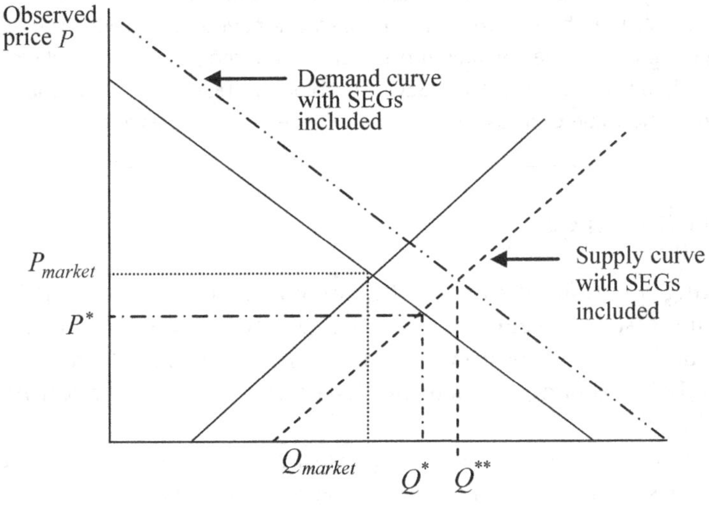

Figure 11.2 The effect of including SEGs with exchanges in markets that trade multiple units of a single good

goods at a lower price or increase the number of goods offered at the previous price. The new equilibrium price is reduced from P_{market} to P^* and the new equilibrium quantity is increased from Q_{market} to Q^*.

But suppose that the seller provides not only economic goods but also SEGs to the buyer. Under these conditions, the demand curve shifts to the right and is represented by the dashed line that decreases with price. The result of shifting the demand curve to the right is to increase still further the amount of the equilibrium goods exchanged from Q^* to Q^{**} and to increase the equilibrium exchange price above P^*. Whether the new equilibrium price is above or below the original market price P_{market} is indeterminate.

Exchanges of High Attachment Value Goods (AVGs)

A different set of consequences occur when people exchange SEGs along with AVGs. The deciding factor determining the effect of AVGs on the terms and likelihood of trade is whether the seller and/or buyer share significant attachment value for the good.

The seller's minimum sell price for an AVG good in an arm's-length sale is twofold. The first part is the present value of future income lost when the good is sold and is represented as π_{seller}. The second part represents the attachment value AV_{seller} which the seller would sacrifice when the good is sold. Thus the seller's minimum selling price equals $P_{seller} = \pi_{seller} + AV_{seller}$. Clearly, increasing the seller's attachment value increases the seller's minimum selling price.

The influence of attachment values on the likelihood of exchange and the terms of trade is described graphically in Figure 11.3. The curved solid lines $P_{buyer}P'_{buyer}$ and $P_{seller}P'_{seller}$ and the horizontal and vertical axes are the same as those represented in Figure 11.1. The dotted curved line represents combinations of SEGs and prices that are equally valued by the seller after the attachment value of the good for the seller increases. As a result of an increase in attachment value, the curve $P_{seller}P'_{seller}$ shifts up, increasing the exchange price from $P_{exchange}$ to $P^*_{exchange}$. The amount of SEGs required to reach an exchange price which both the seller and buyer can accept increases from OE to OE^*. Finally, the range of mutually acceptable prices for each level of SEGs exchanged and the area of surplus that motivates a trade are reduced.

Unless the buyer's attachment value for the good also increases, the seller's increased attachment value may well preclude the possibility of an exchange. If, however, the good's attachment value has increased for the buyer as well as for the seller, a sale may still be possible, albeit at a higher exchange price.

ATTACHMENT VALUES AND "ANTIQUES ROAD SHOW"

It is PBS television, and the program is *Antiques Road Show*. The camera zooms in on Zina, an elderly lady with what appears to be a nondescript painting. The *Road Show* expert quizzes Zina: "How much did you pay for the painting?"

She answers, "Less than five dollars at a yard sale."

Now the focus is on Zina's facial expression as the expert declares: "This painting is by the famous artist ... and at auction is worth a minimum of $25,000."

Zina squeals with delight, and the camera moves on to another antique owner.

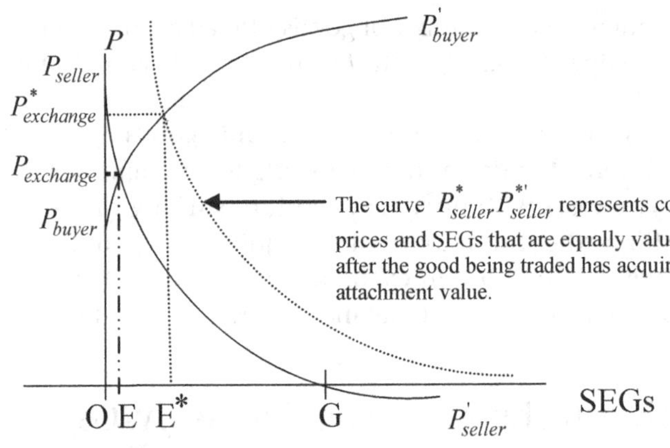

Figure 11.3 A demonstration that as the seller's attachment value for a good increases, the seller's minimum sell price for the good and the amount of SEGs required to reach an acceptable exchange price increase

Neither Zina nor the yard sale seller had any significant attachment value for the painting. But there were art aficionados who had a great deal of attachment value for the painting. The *Road Show* appraiser made Zina aware of these people and, in the process, increased the economic value, if not the attachment value, of the painting for Zina whose new arm's-length exchange price is now much closer to $25,000.

Are AVGs for Sale?

The previous discussion of attachment values raises an important question. If embedding economic goods with attachment value increases their value, why isn't more effort made to do so? The short answer is that considerable efforts are already being made to create attachment value for many goods. These may often take the form of creating attachment value for a brand or hiring famous people with widespread social capital to endorse products. But there are limitations on the commercialization of goods by increasing their attachment values.

There is a general consensus that some AVGs can't or shouldn't be sold for money. For example, communities generally prohibit prostitution because human physical relationships, most people believe, should reflect attachment value and not be treated as simply another economic good. Equally, we applaud the voluntary donation of body parts from one person to another, but are appalled when we find examples of them being sold. We have similar feelings about adoption: we do not believe that babies should be sold or purchased. In sum, there are many objects whose attachment value is diminished or lost if sold for money.

We have now described the effects of including SEGs and attachment values in exchanges. In what follows, we present evidence that SEGs and attachment values are included in exchanges and that their influence on the terms and level of trade are consistent with the Social Capital Exchange Theorem.

Evidence that Social Capital and SEGs Alter the Terms of Trade

We start by defining terms of trade as the agreement between buyers and sellers that determines the quantity, quality, risk, price, information content, timing, and location of goods and services traded. In various settings we recognize that relationships alter the terms and level of trade and that sometimes we make adjustments to preclude their influence.

Realtors and appraisers recognize that the terms of land sales between family members and friends who enjoy social capital are different from those without social capital. As a result, when land sales are recorded, a distinction is made between those sales between family members and arm's-length sales made between unrelated individuals (Gilliland, 1985).

We have long recognized the importance of social capital on hiring decisions. The practice of granting preferential employment opportunities to friends and family when the business is privately owned is generally accepted. But when one is making hiring decisions in behalf of others, employment decisions are not expected to be decided on the basis of relationships, but rather on the candidate's qualifications. Indeed, in recognition of the tendency of some government employers to grant employment advantages to their relatives, nepotism laws restrict them from hiring their close relatives. Civil rights laws preclude the denial of employment on the grounds of race/ethnicity in recognition of the fact that race/ethnicity often changes the relationship between employers and potential employees.

We recognize the value of SEGs on employee performance, and so companies routinely award high-performing employees not only with increased salaries, but also with AVGs, including plaques, certificates, impressive titles, a bigger office, or an allocated parking place. Universities, hospitals, and other public institutions exchange SEGs for monetary donations. These SEGs and attachment values are often conveyed by naming rooms, buildings, scholarships, and endowed faculty chairs after the donors, or at least by displaying plaques that recognize donors by name.

Waiters realize that their tips are tied not only to the quality of their service, but also to the level of SEGs they provide to their customers. So, successful waiters provide friendly as well as prompt service, and customers respond with higher than average tips.

Graduate students in the Department of Agricultural Economics at Michigan State University would sell a used car valued at $3,000 for $420 less than its market value if the buyer were a friend in need. However, these same graduate students would require $697 above the market price if the buyer were an unpleasant wealthy neighbor (Robison and Schmid, 1989).

A survey of 103 Michigan bankers serving communities of less than 10,000 found that good business and social relationships increased the probability of loan approval in some cases by 60 percent (Siles, Robison, and Hanson, 1994). Survey respondents reported that their willingness to bear risk depended on the consequences of their risk decision on significant others (Hanson and Robison, 2007). Finally, relationships have always been significant factors in customer retention (Hanson, Robison, and Siles, 1996).

GETTING TO KNOW YOU AND GIVING

Dawes, McTavish, and Shaklee found that when participants in public-good experiments were allowed to talk to each other, they cooperated 72 percent of the time. In contrast, when the participants were required to make their decisions anonymously, they cooperated only 31 percent of the time (Dawes, McTavish, and Shaklee, 1977: 5).

Frey and Bohnet reported that other-regarding behavior increased from 12 per to 78 percent when discussions were allowed before the Prisoner's Dilemma games were played. Similarly, other-regarding behavior increased from 26 percent to 48 percent when discussion was allowed before Dictator games were played. Frey and Bohnet concluded from their studies that:

> *When individuals communicate with each other, situations of conflict are mitigated because the extent of other-regarding behavior increases. The persons involved tend to act less egotistically and take the interest of the other discussants more into account. In a Prisoner's Dilemma situation, individuals are prepared to contribute to the common good by acting more cooperatively, that is they behave less like free-riders.*
>
> Frey and Bohnet, 2001: 104.

We infer from these experiments that personal contact allowed for the exchange of SEGs and also facilitated cooperative exchanges.

Social Capital, SEGs, and the Terms of Trade of Farmland

Robison, Myers, and Siles (2002) surveyed 1,500 farm owner-operators located in Illinois, Michigan, and Nebraska to determine the influence of relationships on minimum-sell prices for farmland.[1] Many respondents reported experience with selling farmland, and many of those experiences involved relatives, friends, and neighbors as buyers. In Illinois, 82 per cent of respondents reported a previous sale of farmland, while in both Michigan and Nebraska the percentage was 89 percent.[2]

The Robison, Myers, and Siles study provided an important example of how to measure the influence of social capital. Although we cannot measure social capital or sympathy directly, we can measure its influence when we have a standard against which to measure. Measuring the influence of social capital is similar to measuring the influence of risk. When we measure the influence of risk, we compare it to choices made without

1 Respondents were selected by random sampling across the geographic distribution of farmland in each state. The survey method followed Dillman's total design method, including a pre-survey postcard describing the survey and its purpose to respondents, mailing the survey, following the survey mailing with a postcard encouraging the respondents to mail in their questionnaires, and a second mailing of questionnaires to non-respondents. A total of 604 usable questionnaires were returned, representing a 40 percent response rate. The response rates by state were 39 percent for Illinois, 49 percent for Michigan, and 33 percent for Nebraska.

2 The average respondent was 57 years old, supported 1.96 dependants, and belonged to 1.31 organizations, including parent–teacher organizations or school boards, church organizations, service clubs, local government organizations, or environmental organizations. The highest level of educational achievement for over half of those surveyed (54 percent) was a high-school diploma. Almost 25 percent of those surveyed had completed a college degree or graduate degree. After-tax household income was less than $30,000 for 43 percent of those surveyed, while over 8 percent of the respondents earned an after-tax household income of $70,000 or more.

risk. When we measure the influence of social capital on exchanges, we compare then to exchanges between strangers.

So Robison, Myers, and Siles began their study by establishing a benchmark "arm's-length" land price not influenced by social capital. The questionnaire began by describing a plot of farmland for sale. The respondents were then asked to establish a reference price by estimating the values they believed a professional appraiser and a tax assessor would place on the parcel of land. Next, they were asked to state the minimum sell price they would accept from a complete stranger who intended to farm the land and whose agent would arrange and guarantee that the terms of the sale were fulfilled. Table 11.1 reports means and standard deviations for answers to these three valuation questions. On average, farmland was valued higher in Illinois than in either Michigan or Nebraska. In addition, the average minimum sell price to a stranger was higher than the average professional appraiser's valuation, which was higher than the average tax assessor's valuation in all three states. These outcomes were as expected.

Table 11.1 Mean land valuations by respondents

Type of Valuation	Illinois	Michigan	Nebraska	Total
Professional appraiser	$2,595 (64.68)	$1,367 (79.71)	$1,036 (58.38)	$1,677 (49.12)
Tax assessor	$1,984 (67.91)	$1,088 (62.03)	$818 (36.35)	$1,296 (39.88)
Sale to a stranger	$2,793 (79.09)	$1,414 (78.31)	$1,086 (60.71)	$1,786 (53.08)

Note: Standard errors are in parentheses.

Then the survey asked respondents to assume that a complete stranger had offered them the price they wrote down earlier—their minimum sell price to a stranger—but that the respondent had not yet accepted the offer. Then another individual, with whom the respondent has a personal relationship or social capital, asks to buy the land parcel. The respondent was asked to consider four different buyers with different levels of social capital:

- a friendly relative
- a friendly neighbor
- an influential person in the community
- an unfriendly neighbor.

In each case, the respondent was asked to provide the minimum sell price they would accept from each of these buyers, bearing in mind the minimum sell price they had already been offered by a stranger. The average minimum sell prices reported by respondents for each type of social capital relationship are given in Table 11.2. On average, respondents would accept the lowest price from a friendly relative at a 6.8 percent discount off the minimum sell price acceptable from a complete stranger. To a friendly neighbor they would offer a 5.6 percent discount. Both the influential person and the unfriendly neighbor would

be offered minimum sell prices above the arm's-length price, with average premiums of 5.1 percent and 18.4 percent respectively. Clearly, both the "influential person" and the unfriendly neighbor have negative social capital relationships with the respondents, on average, but the unfriendly neighbor has by far the most negative relationship. These results, displayed graphically in Figure 11.4, are qualitatively similar on a state-by-state basis (see Tables 11.2 and 11.3).

Table 11.2 Mean selling prices by relationship

Type of Relationship	Illinois	Michigan	Nebraska	Total
Stranger	$2,793 (79.09)	$1,414 (78.31)	$1,086 (60.71)	$1,786 (53.08)
Friendly relative	$2,603 (74.26)	$1,315 (78.11)	$993 (58.08)	$1,665 (51.14)
Friendly neighbor	$2,645 (177.40)	$1,334 (78.31)	$1,011 (75.05)	$1,686 (65.87)
Influential person	$2,826 (82.78)	$1,542 (95.06)	$1,167 (82.88)	$1,877 (75.01)
Unfriendly neighbor	$3,174 (105.45)	$1,783 (139.56)	$1,315 (90.38)	$2,115 (79.53)

Note: Standard errors are in parentheses.

Table 11.3 Paired t-tests for differences in mean selling prices by relationship

Base Relationship	Friendly relative	Friendly neighbor	Influential person	Unfriendly neighbor
Stranger	$124.57 (11.70)	$99.94 (11.95)	–$79.20 (–3.97)	–$323.79 (–5.05)
Friendly relative		–$23.67 (–3.12)	–$202.46 (–9.34)	–$445.47 (–6.84)
Friendly neighbor			–$179.03 (–8.98)	–$423.07 (–6.54)
Influential person				–$241.26 (–3.78)

Notes: Differences computed as the row price minus the column price, so numbers represent discounts (premiums, if negative) of the column relationship from the row relationship. Numbers in parentheses are t-statistics.

Finally, Robison, Myers, and Siles found that when they asked the 1,500 Midwestern farmers for their minimum sell price, a significant number responded that they would not sell for any price. In some cases, this land had been in the family for generations and had acquired significant attachment value which precluded its sale.

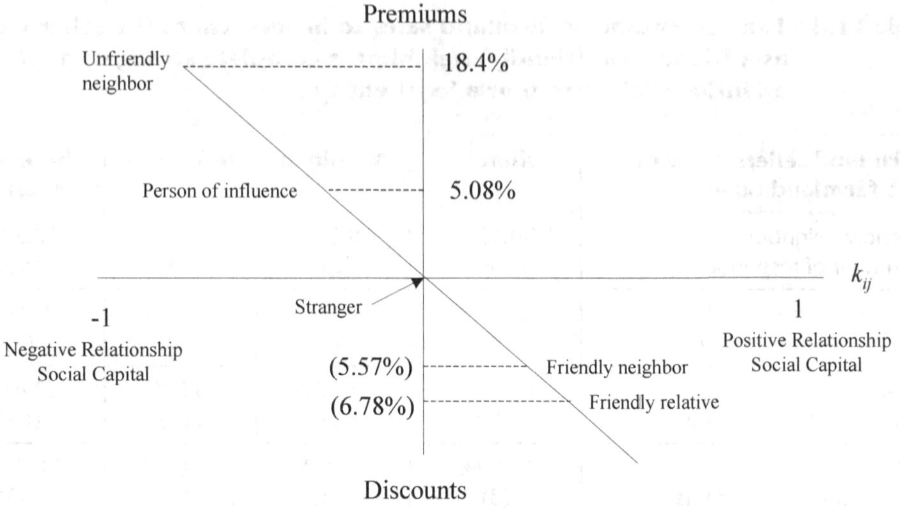

Figure 11.4 Premiums (discounts) that depend on the buyer's social capital with the seller

Evidence that Social Capital and SEGs Alter the Likelihood and Level of Trades and the Selection of Exchange Partners

Perry and Robison (2001) also found impressive evidence that social capital and the exchange of SEGs increased the likelihood of trade. They found that the very best land in Linn County, Oregon is most likely to be traded among family members. Furthermore, they found that a stranger buying an 80-acre parcel of Class II non-irrigated farmland through a realtor was projected to pay more than 20 percent more for the land than a neighbor.

Land sellers reported in Table 11.4 that 52 percent of their land sales were to relatives and friends, 38 percent to strangers, and less than 2 percent to someone they didn't like. Land buyers reported in Table 11.5 that 67 percent of their land purchases were from family and friends, 17 percent from strangers, and 2 percent from people they didn't like.

Obviously, the likelihood of land sales between family and friends is higher partly because they are more likely to exchange SEGs as well as land and partly because social capital reduces transaction costs. Typically, transaction costs are divided into information collection costs, costs of establishing mutually agreed and enforceable terms of trade, and costs of monitoring and enforcing agreements.

Social capital has an important role in each of these areas. First, social capital provides an incentive to share information that will benefit one's social capital network even when the person sharing the information expects no direct economic benefit. Thus, friends may share information about sales, entertainment, reliable places for repairs and medical care. Those engaged in business may share information about suppliers, product quality and price information, and marketing opportunities. The incentives for sharing information may be that they share vicariously in the improved well-being of their friends who benefit from the information or that sharing information improves their

Table 11.4 The percentage of farmland sales to buyers whom the seller viewed as a friendly (unfriendly) neighbor, a complete stranger, a relative, an influential person, or a legal entity

Farmland sellers' view of the farmland buyer	Illinois	Michigan	Nebraska	Three-state Average
Friendly neighbor (Number of respondents)	30.19% (16)	29.23% (19)	39.13% (18)	32.32% (53)
Unfriendly neighbor (Number of respondents)	0.00% (0)	0.00% (0)	6.52% (3)	1.83% (3)
Stranger (Number of respondents)	43.40% (23)	43.08% (28)	26.09% (12)	38.41% (63)
Relative (Number of respondents)	15.09% (8)	20.00% (13)	26.09% (12)	20.12% (33)
Influential person (Number of respondents)	1.89% (1)	3.08% (2)	2.17% (1)	2.44% (4)
Legal entity (Number of respondents)	9.43% (5)	4.62% (3)	0.00% (0)	4.88% (8)
Percent	100.00%	100.00%	100.00%	100.00%
Total	53	65	46	164

Table 11.5 The percentage of farmland purchases from sellers whom the buyer viewed as a friendly (unfriendly), a neighbor, a complete stranger, a relative, an influential person, or a legal entity

Farmland buyer's view of the farmland seller	Illinois	Michigan	Nebraska	Three-state Average
Friendly neighbor (Number of respondents)	32.93% (54)	45.30% (106)	34.78% (56)	38.64% (216)
Unfriendly neighbor (Number of respondents)	3.05% (5)	1.28% (3)	2.48% (4)	2.15% (12)
Stranger (Number of respondents)	18.90% (31)	15.81% (37)	17.39% (28)	17.17% (96)
Relative (Number of respondents)	29.27% (48)	27.78% (65)	29.20% (47)	28.62% (160)
Influential person (Number of respondents)	1.83% (3)	2.14% (5)	3.11% (5)	2.33% (13)
Legal entity (Number of respondents)	14.02% (23)	7.69% (18)	13.04% (21)	11.09% (62)
Percent	100.00%	100.00%	100.00%	100.00%
Total	164	234	161	559

social capital and increases their potential to extract favors and preferential treatment from their friends in the future.

Information shared in social capital-rich networks has an important advantage of being viewed as reliable. Agents whose motive is to benefit members in their group are more trusted than agents who have a private economic interest in the information. For example, suppose that you receive professional medical advice recommending an action that benefits the healthcare provider. How much do you trust the advice? If, over time, the healthcare provider has demonstrated a commitment to an ideal self who puts the well-being of patients above private returns, then the advice is to be trusted. Alternatively, consider a mechanic whose recommendation will influence your repair bills and his or her earnings. Do you trust the advice? If there are only a few and expensive means to check the validity of the advice, then your only recourse may be to appeal to social capital or to social capital with an honest ideal self.

Finally, when there is social capital between trading partners, it is easier not only to find acceptable terms of trade, but also to complete the necessary documentation to establish the evidence of the agreement. In many important transactions among social capital-rich partners, agreements are concluded verbally. Part of the reason why so little formal documentation to the transaction is required is that breaking the agreement would result in the loss of highly valued social capital.

The importance of social capital's ability to reduce transaction costs has important implications. In some markets, especially in less developed countries, transaction costs are very high. As a result, opportunities for mutually beneficial trade between strangers are limited. Thus, in high transaction-cost economies, we expect to find that trades between family and friends comprise a higher percentage of total trades than in low transaction-cost economies.

Conclusion

This chapter provided several examples of what we have called the Social Capital Exchange Theorem—namely that incorporating social capital and SEGs into an exchange increases the likelihood and level of exchange, and alters the terms of trade.

One detailed study of how social capital alters the level and terms of trade focused on the exchange of farmland. Farmland exchange is just one of many interesting valuation and exchange problems. Social capital is also likely to have significant effects in many other market exchanges and valuation problems, especially when the buyer and seller are known to each other and the sale involves interpersonal interactions.

So what does the Social Capital Exchange Theorem mean in practice? In the first instance, it means that relationships matter. It means that in many cases established patterns of trade are strengthened because of the relationships between trading partners. Second, it challenges that part of economic theory that is developed on the assumption that relationships don't alter the level and terms of trade. Third, the theorem calls us to take seriously the importance of SEGs and AVGs. We should pay more attention to the creation of value that depends on embedding objects with attachment value. And, finally, the theorem should alert us to the dangers of allowing relationships to alter the terms and level of trade when fairness should prohibit their influence.

The chapters that follow build on the results of this chapter. Since social capital alters the terms and level of trade, and the terms and level of trade influence income distributions, it follows that the distribution of social capital should be linked to the distributions of social capital and poverty. The connections between social capital, income distributions, and poverty will be the focus of Chapters 12 and 13.

CHAPTER 12 *Social Capital and the Distribution of Income**

The worst form of inequality is to try to make unequal things equal.

Aristotle (384–322BC).

It is better that some should be unhappy than that none should be happy, which would be the case in a general state of equality.

Samuel Johnson (From Life of Johnson, Volume 3: 1776–1780).

Introduction

The theme of this chapter and an important reason why relationships matter is because they alter the distribution of household income. Previous chapters demonstrated that increases in social capital between trading partners alter the terms of trade and increase the level of trade. However, such increases in social capital must also alter the distribution of benefits from economic production and exchange, which in turn alters the distribution of household incomes. Therefore, distributions of social capital and household income are related.

Another theme of this chapter has to do with what "economists know for sure"—that specialization increases productivity. (Remember Adam Smith and the pins—in which specialization increased pin production from one pin a day per worker to 4,800 pins a day per worker?) However, economic agents can only specialize in production if they can trade what they produce for what they need but don't produce. And because increases in social capital make it easier to both specialize and trade, then increases in social capital also improve one's productivity. Thus, the distribution of social capital in an economy has important income distribution consequences.

Some Important Economic Concepts

To demonstrate the connections between social capital and income distributions, we begin by establishing some fundamental economic concepts that describe the motivations and choices of decision-makers. In economic parlance we say that decision-makers allocate

* This chapter draws heavily from Robison and Siles, 1999.

their resources in such a way that it maximizes their utility or satisfaction. If goods that provide satisfaction to Jack or Ilene can be purchased for money, then Jack and Ilene will allocate their resources so their incomes are maximized. The reason they maximize their incomes is clear. The greater Jack's and Ilene's incomes, the more satisfying goods they can purchase. So they selfishly seek to maximize their own incomes.

In this book we have challenged the assumption that Jack and Ilene will act only in their selfish interests. We claim that they have other motives besides maximizing their own incomes. Recall that in Chapter 4 we described five motives that drive decision-makers. The first motive, to increase one's own consumption (to maximize one's income)—an assumption which dominates neoclassical economic theory—in our investigations accounts for roughly 33 percent of one's allocations. The second most important motive, to share one's income with friends and family, accounted for roughly 25 percent. Other motives were less important and, to simplify our presentation, are ignored in what follows. So consider how these two motives—to increase one's own consumption and to share one's resources with a friend—alter the outcomes predicted by the neoclassical model that focuses on maximizing one's own income.

Suppose that Ilene and Jack have neighboring businesses—Jack runs a bakery and Ilene runs a coffee shop. In an arm's-length relationship they operate their businesses independently of each other and seek to maximize their own profits. But they recognize that by cooperating they could both benefit. So Ilene and Jack agree to advertise for each other—Jack promotes Ilene's coffee shop and Ilene's promotes Jack's pastries, and both their profits increase. This outcome, predicted in the standard economic model (the famous Coase theorem), argues that if a profit is to be made, two strangers will negotiate to a profit-maximizing solution regardless of their relative resources, and hence there is no need for social capital to achieve economic efficiency, although it says nothing about achieving economic equality.

Now suppose that Jane, Jack's sister, recognizing an excellent business opportunity, decides to open up her own coffee shop nearby and, because of her social capital with Jack, exchanges socio-emotional goods (SEGs) and in return not only gets exclusive advertising rights in Jack's bakery, but also is able to purchase pastries at a reduced price compared to the price that Ilene pays—thereby gaining a competitive advantage. As a result, the Coase theorem results no longer apply precisely. Jack's and Jane's arrangement may not in fact maximize Jack's income or even their joint income, and certainly not the combined incomes of Jack, Ilene, and Jane.

But all is not lost for Ilene. She has in fact social capital from her loyal customers, and even though they can purchase coffee and pastries less expensively from Jane, many of them continue to frequent Ilene's place. So, in the end, over a cup of hot chocolate with pastries, Jack, Ilene, and Jane conclude that social capital alters the terms and level of trade and the distributions of their incomes.

Now here is the main point. Jane's income increased because of her social capital provided by Jack. Ilene's income was negatively affected by Jane's social capital. One could also imagine that, because of their social capital, Jack and Jane make decisions in such a way as to maximize the sum of their income rather than their individual incomes—and that they are also interested in reducing the disparity between their incomes. This result is the basis for the assertion in this chapter that increases in social capital in a social capital-rich network increase the average income of people within the network—but not for those outside of the network.

Now consider a related result. Suppose that Jack is required to invest in a resource, but is able to capture only a fraction of the proceeds from this investment. We call these investments externalities because some of their consequences are external to the decision-maker. From society's point of view, selfish decision-makers usually underinvest in externalities that provide positive consequences because they don't get to keep all the benefits. Or they overinvest if the externalities are negative because they aren't required to absorb the full cost. Social capital dramatically changes Jack's calculations of benefits by helping him internalize the externalities, leading him to allocate resources in a way that better meets society's interests. Thus, when the externalities of our investments are experienced by someone whom we care about, we internalize the externality—and we behave more as though we will experience the externality ourselves.

Furthermore, our willingness to create positive externalities and avoid negative externalities has much to do with reducing household income inequality. If, because of our collective social capital, the wealthy pay more taxes that will be used to make investments with positive externalities, such as roads, public safety, schools, public parks, and healthcare, the benefits of which are equally accessible to all, then differences in our well-being will be moderated by our social capital.

Social Capital, Internalizing Externalities, and Reducing the Disparity of Incomes

Consider an economy consisting of two economic agents *i* (Ilene) and *j* (Jack) who actively engage each other in production and marketing activities. Assume that Ilene earns more income than Jack. Also assume in this hypothetical two-person economy that Ilene is engaged in economic activities that produce externalities which benefit Jack. Then, as Jack's social capital provided by Ilene increases, Ilene increasingly internalizes the consequences of her actions that benefit Jack with the following effect on the distribution of income.

Theorem 12.1 If agent j's (Jack's) social capital available from agent i (Ilene), k_{ij}*, increases, then the combined incomes of agents i and j will increase, and the difference in their incomes will decrease.*

The importance of the connection between changes in social capital and changes in the level and disparity of incomes can be shown using four different externality models. The four externality models include: (1) the high exclusion-cost goods model; (2) the joint production model; (3) the common property resource model; and (4) the ubiquitous externality model.

HIGH EXCLUSION-COST GOODS (HEGS) MODEL

A high exclusion-cost good is one that allows agents to extract services from a resource independent of their contributions to the creation or maintenance of the resource. An HEG exists because of the cost of "fences" that deny access to the good to those who have not paid for its production. Examples of HEGs include: street lights, radio programs, dams providing downstream flood protection, extensive parks with many points of entry, water sanitation

plants, and neighborhood police protection. The income distribution conclusion described earlier implies that investments in HEGs by Ilene will increase as Ilene's social capital for Jack increases. Then, because of Ilene's increased investment in HEGs, the combined incomes of Ilene and Jack will increase and the difference in their incomes will decrease.

A simple example may help clarify how investments in HEGs may reduce the disparity of income. If a wealthy community member provides social capital for her neighbors, she might be inclined to donate enough money to the community to build a park. Her investment reduces her own wealth and increases the services available to community members—improving their well-being while not reducing their income. At the same time, the added value of the park improves everyone's quality of life while simultaneously raising property values.

JOINT PRODUCTION MODEL

A joint production model is one in which production depends on inputs supplied by more than one economic agent. Economic agents often engage in the production of both individual and jointly produced goods. For example, many vegetable farmers produce their crops individually, but join with other producers to transport, store, and market their produce. Theorem 12.1 implies that the production of jointly produced goods will increase as Jack's social capital increases. Because of the increased production of jointly produced goods, the combined incomes of Ilene and Jack will increase and the difference in their incomes will decrease.

ME VERSUS MY TEAM

To empirically test the role of social capital in joint production activities, the following test was conducted. Senior-level students in the College of Agricultural and Natural Resources at Michigan State University enrolled in a capstone team-building course were required to allocate their time between preparing for exams and team efforts to prepare case studies. Their grades were based on the combined total of individual points earned on their exams, and points earned on their case studies.

A survey asked students to indicate the portion of their time they would allocate to the joint project, a case study, knowing in advance the portion of time their partners allocated to the joint project. If students acted selfishly, they would select a time allocation that would maximize their total points independent of the effect of their efforts on their team members.

Students taking the survey were asked to consider three possible team members: a friend, a stranger, and an obnoxious cheat. Their social capital toward their hypothetical team-mates was estimated on the basis of the minimum selling price they would accept from their team-mates for a used computer they were selling with a market value of $600.

The survey results found that increases in social capital significantly increased an individual's participation in the joint project that benefited his or her partner, sometimes at the individual's own expense. Furthermore, the difference in own versus partner's expected grade was also a significant predictor of time dedicated to the joint project.

Source: Robison and Hanson (1995).

COMMON PROPERTY RESOURCES

A common property resource is a resource from which several agents have the right to extract goods and services. The marginal cost of extracting goods and services from a common property resource depends on the total goods and services extracted. In other words, as Ilene extracts goods and services from a common property resource, Jack's costs of extracting goods and services increases.

Examples of common property resources include wildlife populations, public lands used for grazing, fishing waters, public parks, and publicly owned roads. The income distribution conclusion implies that Ilene's service extraction and exploitation of the common property resource will decrease as Jack's social capital increases. Because of Ilene's decreased use of the common property resource, the resource will not be overexploited, the combined incomes of Ilene and Jack will increase, and the difference in their incomes will decrease.

THE TRAGEDY AND THE TRIUMPH

The "tragedy" of the commons is when commonly held resources are "overused" as unregulated individuals seek to maximize their individual gains from the resource. However, the more important story is how common property resources can be properly managed—a triumph, rather than a tragedy, of the commons.

Turner reports four conditions associated with successful management of common property resources. Below, we associate Turner's conditions with elements of the social capital theorem (shown in parenthesis):

1. The resource is managed by a well-defined social group bound together by kinship, place of residence, or investments of time, labor or capital (social capital and networks).
2. The managing group has the ability to exclude others outside of their group from using the resource (power).
3. There is a set of rules that limit the seasonality, extent or ways in which the resource is extracted by individuals (institutions).
4. The group has the capacity to monitor use and enforce rules.

Source: Turner (2007).

THE UBIQUITOUS EXTERNALITY MODEL

Production often involves the use of inputs that have incompatible uses. In other words, some inputs when used by Ilene to increase her profit are no longer available for use by Jack to increase his profits. For example, suppose Ilene raises pigs. Her pig operation requires such inputs as land, buildings, feed, and a place to put waste. However, the water, air, and land used to handle Ilene's pig's waste may be desired by Jack for other purposes. Theorem 12.1 implies that Ilene's use of resources that might be used for other purposes by Jack will decrease as Jack's social capital provided by Ilene increases. Because of Ilene's decreased use of resources with incompatible uses, the use of the resource is optimized,

allowing the combined incomes of Ilene and Jack to increase and the difference in their incomes to decrease, even though Ilene's income might decrease.

Social Capital, Externalities, and Voluntary Income Transfers

So far, the linkages between social capital, externalities, and the income distribution of Ilene and Jack have been described using production models. In many business arrangements, this linkage between voluntary economic actions and income distribution consequences may be accurate. However, in almost all economies there exist income redistribution possibilities besides voluntarily altering production arrangements. One means of redistribution is by income transfer. Voluntary transfers and involuntary transfers influence an agent's externality production in different ways. Theorems 12.2 and 12.3 below offer an important conclusion regarding income transfers, social capital, and externality production. Theorem 12.2 describes the limits of imposing involuntary income redistribution measures. Theorem 12.3 describes voluntary income redistribution measures in response to increases in social capital.

> *Theorem 12.2 If agent j, because of his or her superior income position relative to agent j, is forced to transfer income to agent j, then agent i will reduce (increase) his or her production of positive (negative) externalities.*[1]

> *Theorem 12.3 If the income transfers are voluntary, and agent i chooses an amount of his or her income to transfer to agent j that maximizes i's utility, then transfers to agent j will increase with increases in agent j's social capital from i.*

The conclusions about income transfers, social capital, and externality production described in Theorems 12.2 and 12.3 have some important implications. Externally imposed transfers intended to reduce income disparities may have their effects canceled by agents' voluntary production and investment responses. These offsetting income distribution effects should serve as warnings to social planners who believe that income inequities can be eliminated by involuntary transfers. On the other hand, awareness of social capital and its usefulness may offer policy-makers an important new approach for reducing income disparities, which we explore in more detail in Chapter 13 where we discuss social capital and poverty reduction. The new approach is to design programs that increase the social capital of the economically disadvantaged.

---

1 The conclusion that externally imposed income transfers will be offset to some degree by individual production decisions with external consequences is strengthened if the externally imposed income transfers reduce social capital. For example, those forced to contribute to the welfare of a particular group may come to dislike the group, which reduces the likelihood of voluntary efforts to redistribute income.

It is important to note the limitation of Theorem 12.2. It has not been demonstrated that these results can be applied to an *n* person economy. It may be that persons are willing to contribute to the well-being of others if they know that others are contributing as well. Thus, an externally imposed tax might have the effect of encouraging more general support for income transfers. The main point here is that social capital needs to be included in any effort to examine the likely consequences of income transfer policies.

Social Capital and Gains from Specialization and Trade

Specialization leads to increased productivity for at least two reasons. First, one's ability to perform a task is often improved through repetition. Second, labor specialization allows one to participate in economic activities for which one is best suited and for which the appropriate raw materials exist, etc. But labor specialization cannot occur without opportunities to trade for what one needs, but doesn't produce. Thus, trading and labor specialization are linked in any economic system. And because family networks are most likely to enjoy high levels of social capital, we are most likely to trade with our family and friends, which improves the likelihood of both specialization and trading.

TAKING CARE OF FAMILY

A family-owned business may be defined as any business in which two or more family members are involved and the majority of ownership or control lies within a family. In a summary of the importance of family owned businesses, Hilburt-Davis and Green report:

- *One-third of all Fortune 500 companies are family businesses and comprise 78 percent of the jobs.*
- *Two-thirds of all the companies traded on the New York Stock Exchange are family businesses.*
- *80 percent of the world's businesses are owned by families.*

Family businesses have good track records.

- *More than 30 percent of all family firms survive to the second generation.*
- *One-third of the S&P 500 companies are family firms and, according to Business Week and The Journal of Finance, they outperform the nonfamily firms.*

Hilburt-Davis and Green, 2009.

Recognizing that social capital opportunities influence trading opportunities, we next consider how changes in social capital may change the kinds of goods produced and the distribution of income. To begin, suppose in a world of N countries (firms or households) that each country produces one unique product that can be traded with the other ($N - 1$) countries for amounts of their uniquely produced good. Next, suppose that barrier-free trading opportunities exist among all N countries allowing for the possibility of $T_0 = N(N - 1)/2$ number of trades to occur.[2] As a result, each country would benefit from the productive skill of the other $N - 1$ countries and enjoy the opportunity to consume some of their exports. In addition, they might combine imported products to create new products. Indeed, each country could create ($N - 1$) new products by combining

2 To understand where this formula comes from, consider that all N countries can trade with the other $N - 1$ countries or all N countries trade $N(N - 1)$ times. But since two countries are involved in each trade, the number of unique trades must be divided by 2.

its uniquely produced good with the uniquely produced good obtained from each of the other countries so that T_0 new goods could be produced from unfettered trade. More complicated goods would require that goods from more than two countries be combined.

Next, suppose that the world of countries is divided into two groups of equal size, each with $\frac{N}{2}$ members. Assume also that near-perfect social capital exists within each group, but that antipathy exists between the two groups. Because of antipathy, it is assumed that trading happens only. In a world divided into two groups (one division), the number of unique trades available to each country is [(N / 2)-1], meaning that the trading opportunities within each group are reduced to

$$T_1 = \frac{\frac{N}{2}\left(\frac{N}{2}-1\right)}{2},$$

and world trading opportunities are reduced to $2T_1$ within each group. Furthermore, the ratio of all possible trades after one division, compared to no divisions, is equal to $2T_1 / T_0$ and when N is large reduces to:

$$\underset{N\to\infty}{Limit}\frac{2T_1}{T_0} = \frac{\frac{1}{2}-\frac{1}{N}}{1-\frac{1}{N}} = \frac{1}{2} \tag{12.1}$$

The implication of equation (12.1) is that, with one division, the number of possible trades and unique goods that could be produced is reduced by half.

However, the effect on a division on the production of more complicated goods with more unique inputs is even more impressive. One division of N countries into two equal groups reduces by 75 percent the total number of different goods that could be produced by combining three unique inputs, and also reduces by 87 percent the total number of different goods that could be produced combining four unique inputs. Other ratios of unique goods produced before and after divisions, depending on the number of inputs required, are described in Table 12.1.

It may be that not all of the N countries in our model produce unique products. If this were the case, the reduction in the total number of different goods produced as a result of dividing the N countries into groups of equal size would be less dramatic than the results described in Table 12.1. Nevertheless there is an important lesson to be learned—namely that a loss in social capital that leads to divisions and trade barriers between previously unified groups decreases dramatically the production of processed or complicated goods. In the absence of specialization and trade, which is enhanced by social capital-rich networks, economic activity becomes focused on goods that do not require inputs from other countries. Traditionally, these have been agriculture and resource extraction, both being activities that can be pursued with limited trading requirements. As a result, it is most often the poorest countries which have the highest percentage of their populations engaged in agriculture.

Finally, as the productivity of labor increases with increases in the membership of the social capital-rich trading group, the average income of the group can be expected to

Table 12.1 Percentage of goods produced after division(s) compared to the original number of goods produced before division(s)

Number of groups after division(s)	Number of unique inputs required per good produced								
	(2)	(3)	(4)	(5)	(6)	(7)	(8)	(9)	(10)
	Percentages								
1	100	100	100	100	100	100	100	100	100
2	50	25	13	6	3	2	1	0	0
3	33	11	4	1	0	0	0	0	0
4	25	6	2	0	0	0	0	0	0
5	20	4	1	0	0	0	0	0	0
6	17	3	0	0	0	0	0	0	0
7	14	2	0	0	0	0	0	0	0
8	13	2	0	0	0	0	0	0	0

rise. In addition, as membership in the social capital-rich group increases, externalities are internalized for an increasing number of economic agents and the results of Theorem 12.1 apply. These results suggest that, for the externality models already discussed, average income will increase with an increase in the membership of the group, and the disparity of income will decrease. The results of this section are summarized in Theorem 12.4.

Theorem 12.4 Increases in social capital within a social capital-rich trading group increases specialization and trade, increases the internalization of externalities, and increases the average income of group members.

Opportunities for trade within the group grow at an increasing rate as the size of the group increases. On the other hand, as the size of the group increases, the demand for bonding activities may also increase at an accelerating rate. In addition, the cost of maintaining social capital as the group size increases may effectively limit the size of the group unless efficient means of investing in social capital are introduced.

INCREASING DIVISIONS AMONG FORMERLY UNITED NATIONS

The discussion about group size has emphasized the advantages of trade. What makes the discussion relevant is an important empirical fact. In 1945, the year in which the United Nations was founded, the world was organized into 51 countries. This number increased to 100 in 1960. By 1994, the number of countries had increased to 192. Since 1994, the number of countries has continued to increase (Bradshaw and Wallace, 1996). If increasing the number

of countries results in trade restrictions between those who were formerly members of the same country, then we can expect less labor specialization and reduced income for each group member. In contrast, the European Union has grown from an initial membership of 6 countries to 27 countries.

A Graphical Connection between Distributions of Social Capital and Household Incomes

Our earlier discussion focused on social capital and specialization and trade between countries. We now consider the implications of alternative social capital distributions on income distributions within countries and for smaller units of government.

LEVEL AND DISPARITY OF INCOME FOR POPULATIONS CONSISTING OF TWO GROUPS OF VARYING SIZE

Suppose that there exists an economy of N households, all perfect and symmetrically endowed with social capital so that each values each other's income the same as their own. Assume also that each household's earnings depend on the size of the network in which it is located. Thus one's income depends on the size of the network. Now if everyone belonged to the same network, they would have both the highest possible income and a zero disparity between their incomes.

Next, suppose that a dispute arises that divides the N households into two groups of equal size. Assume also that the division destroys the social capital between the two groups, but, within the two groups, social capital remains perfect and symmetrically distributed. Under this new arrangement, one might argue that incomes remain equal within groups since perfect and symmetrical social capital exists. Furthermore, suppose that because the two groups are of equal size, the average income of the two groups is equal. Then, income must be evenly distributed for all N households, just as it was before the division. However, what is different is that the opportunities for specialization and trade have been reduced, as Table 12.1 described. Within the two groups, externalities are internalized to a lesser degree than they were when there was only one group. As a result, the average level of income has been reduced.

Suppose that the averages and the disparity of income measures associated with the household income distributions were plotted. The two distributions represented by their averages and disparity measures would be represented as two points on the vertical scale that measures the averages of household income for zero variations in household income. In Figure 12.1 the point representing the income distribution before the division is described as "maximum average income", and the point representing the income distribution after the division is described as "reduced average income" after one division. The two distributions are distinguished only by the difference in their averages, providing one example of how a decrease in social capital changes the average, but may leave the disparity in income unchanged.

Next, consider the distribution of incomes if the population consists of N members divided into two groups of size n and $N-n$. As before, assume that perfect and symmetrically distributed social capital exists within groups while hostility exists between the two groups. As a result, each member of the group earns the same income determined by the

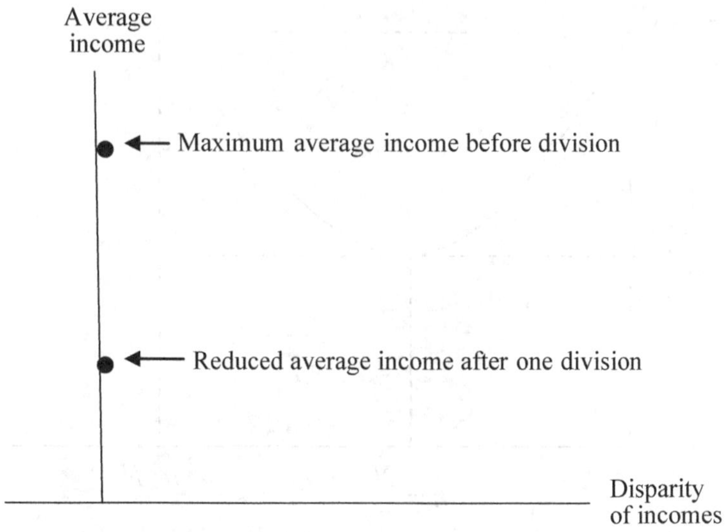

Figure 12.1 The distribution of income before and after a division

size of the group. So, for a particular value of n, the average income of the population $\overline{\pi}$ is defined as the weighted income earned by members of the two groups:

$$\overline{\pi} = \frac{n\pi(n)}{N} + \frac{(N-n)\pi(N-n)}{N}$$

where $\pi(n)$ and $\pi(N-n)$ are the incomes earned by members of the two group with membership equal to n and $N-n$ respectively. Average income $\overline{\pi}$ is graphed in Figure 12.2 as n increases from zero to N. As membership in the first group, n, grows from zero to N, membership in the second group, $(N-n)$, decreases from N to zero. As group sizes change, average income decreases from its maximum average income of $\overline{\pi} = \pi(N)$ to a minimum average income level of $\overline{\pi} = \pi\left(\frac{N}{2}\right)$, thereafter increasing to its previous maximum, $\overline{\pi} = \pi(N)$.

The reason why average income decreases as n grows to $N/2$ is because members of the larger group are joining the smaller group. As a result, they are exchanging a higher income for a lower income. Moreover, all members of the larger group suffer a loss in income whereas all members of the smaller group earn a higher income. Nevertheless, for $n<N/2$ the number of persons suffering a reduction in income is greater than the number of persons enjoying an increase in income. As n increases past $N/2$ in size, the average income increases to its original value obtained when $n = N$. Thus, the average income produces a "U"-shape pattern as n increases. The "U" pattern of average income in response to changes in n is described in Figure 12.2.

The effect of an increase in n on the disparity of income is more complicated than the effect of an increase in n on average incomes. Maintaining our assumption that the average income depends on the size of one's group, then the disparity of income is zero for $n = 0$, $n = N$, and $n = N/2$. In the first two cases, all N members of the population belong to one or other of the two groups. For the third case, all N members of the population

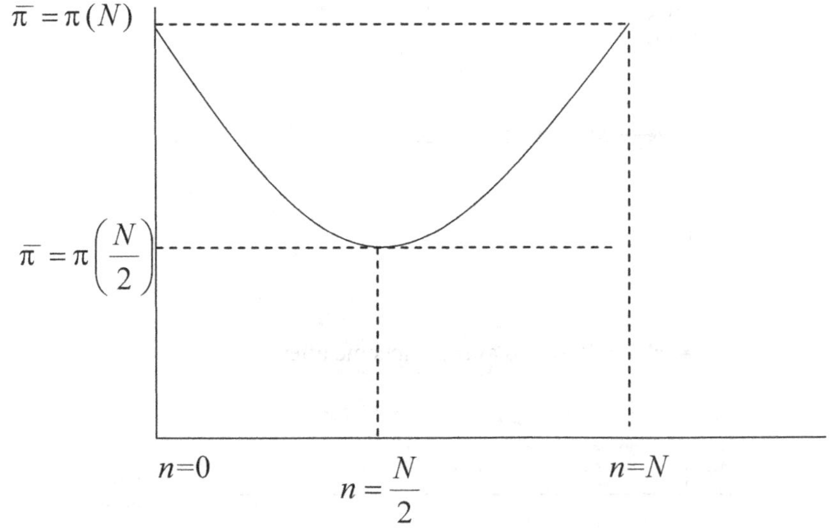

Figure 12.2 The effect on average income of changing group sizes

belong to groups of equal size and therefore earn equal incomes. Thus, the disparity of income first increases and then decreases toward zero as n approaches $N/2$. Then, as n increases beyond $N/2$, the pattern is repeated. The relationship between income disparity and increases in n is described in Figure 12.3.

Finally, income distributions measures in terms of their averages and disparity of income for increases in n are described in Figure 12.4 by combining Figures 12.2 and 12.3. Note that the disparity of income first increases and then decreases with increasing averages of income.

LEVEL AND DISPARITY OF INCOMES FOR A POPULATION CONSISTING OF TWO DIFFERENT KINDS OF GROUPS: AN APPLICATION

The social unit most likely to experience near-perfect social capital and the unit most likely to internalize externalities is the family or household. Supporting evidence for this conclusion is the dominance of family businesses. However, not all households enjoy the same level of social capital.

According to the US Bureau of the Census, median income for married-couple families with children younger than 18 years of age was $22,568 in 1980 and $40,693 in 1989. In contrast, median income for households headed by a single female with children younger than 18 was $8,002 in 1980 and $12,485 in 1989. The evidence is that households headed by a single female with children are economically disadvantaged compared with households headed by a married couple with children.

If social capital available in single-parent households with children is less than that available in two-parent and other households, then current trends should be of some interest. In 1970, single-parent families with children represented 11 percent of all families with children. By 1980, 19.5 percent of families with children were headed by a single parent, and by 1990 the percentage had reached 24 percent (Robison and Siles, 1999: 64).

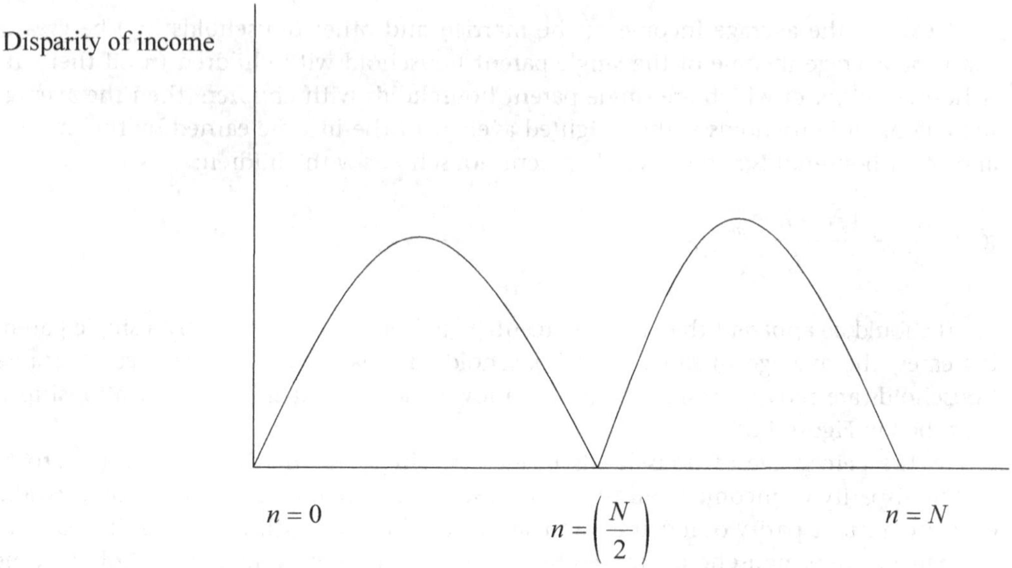

Figure 12.3 The effect of group size on disparity of income

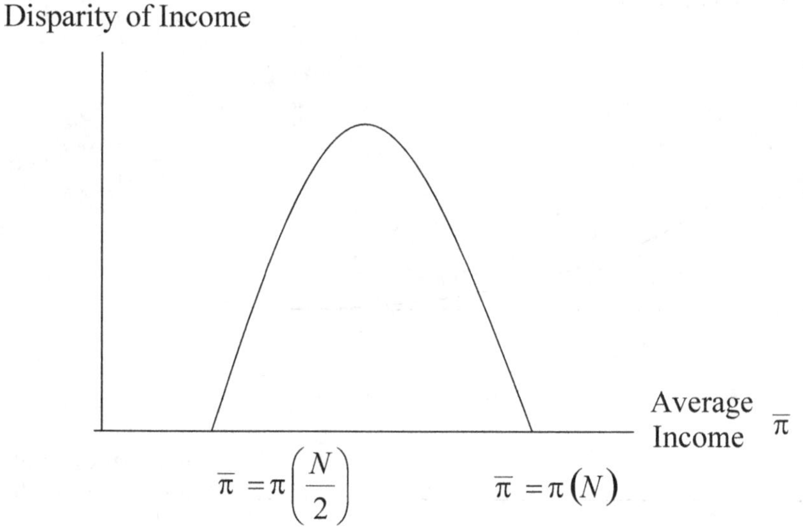

Figure 12.4 The result of changes in group size on average income and disparity of income

The effects on the level and disparity of household income associated with increases in households headed by a single parent with children can be described as follows. Suppose there exists an economy with households that all enjoy perfect and symmetric social capital within the household. Also assume that the households enjoy a social capital resource with individuals outside the household unit that depends on whether one or two parents are present, as well as on the size of the household and the age of the household members.

Next, let the average income of the married and other households (π_m) be greater than the average income of the single-parent household with children (π_s).If there are N households, n of which are single-parent households with children, then the average income of all households is the weighted average of the income earned by the married and other households and the single-parent households with children:

$$\bar{\pi} = \frac{n\pi_s}{N} + \frac{(N-n)\pi_m}{N}$$

It should be apparent that as the percentage of households headed by a single parent increases, the average income of all households decreases. This result occurs because households are moving from a higher to a lower earning category. This relationship is described in Figure 12.5.

As the percentage of households headed by single parents increases from zero to N, the disparity of income would first increase from zero and, after some point, would decrease until disparity of income was again zero. The relationship between increases in the percentage of households headed by a single parent and average household income and the disparity of household income was that described in Figure 12.4.

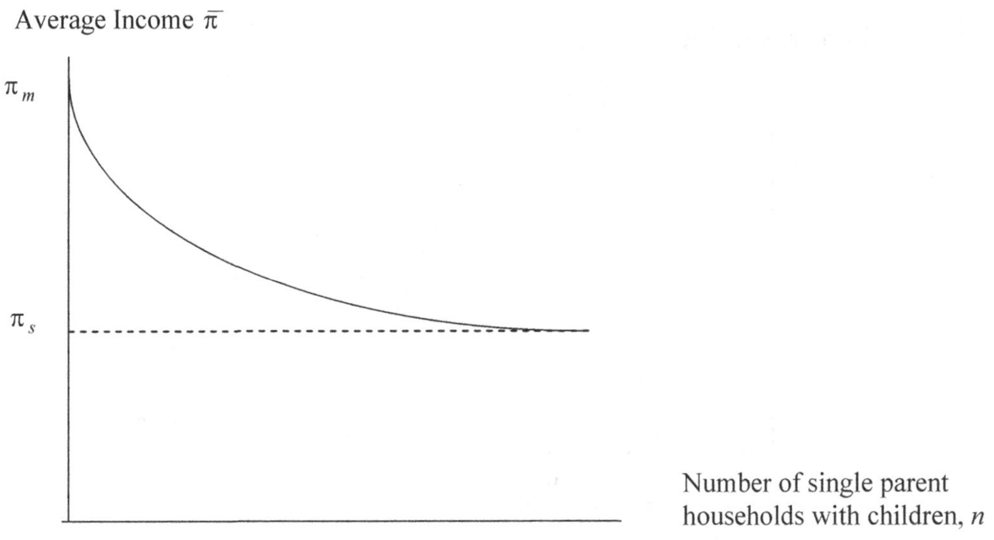

Figure 12.5 The inverse relationship between the percentage of households headed by a single parent with children and average household income μ

INCOME DISTRIBUTIONS AND SINGLE-PARENT HOUSEHOLDS

Robison and Siles empirically tested the relationship between changes in social capital indicator variables and changes in the distribution of household incomes using US census data for 1980 and 1990. Social capital indicator variables used to measure changes in social capital included measures of family integrity, including the percentages of households

headed by a single female with children, education achievement variables, crime rates, and labor force participation.

Income inequality among US households measured using coefficients of variation increased between 1980 and 1990 in all 50 states. The four factors used as social capital indicator variables were generally statistically significant, and supported the conclusion that changes in social capital have a significant effect on the disparity and level of household income.

Source: Robison and Siles (1999).

Conclusion

In this chapter we have argued that changes in social capital alter the terms and level of trade and therefore alter household income. The density and richness of one's social capital networks determines, to a large extent, the terms of trade one receives in exchange for one's goods and services. The result is that social capital influences one's average income.

We deduced the effects of changes in social capital on income distributions using two different approaches. The first approach used production models to show how social capital internalized externalities and increased the level and reduced the disparity of incomes. The second approach emphasized how social capital organized trade among social capital-rich groups. Moreover, since group size determined opportunities for trade and labor specialization and the extent to which externalities were internalized, income per group member was assumed to increase with group size.

CHAPTER 13 The Social Capital Paradigm and Poverty Reduction

Give a beggar a dime and he'll bless you. Give him a dollar and he'll curse you for withholding the rest of your fortune. Poverty is a bag with a hole at the bottom.

Anzia Yezierska, author (c. 1880–1970).

Introduction

Relationships create social capital, which alters the distributions of income and, by so doing, influences who lives in poverty. Indeed, the evidence is that the distribution of social capital is directly linked to the distribution of income. The distribution of social capital alters the distribution of income because, other things being equal, we are more likely to trade with friends and family than with strangers or those estranged from us. The reason for this is because when we trade with friends and family, we receive socio-emotional goods (SEGs) in addition to economically valued goods (EVGs). Thus, changes in social capital that alter the terms and levels of trade must also change the distribution of income—and the number and percentage of people living in poverty. A related point is that one's opportunities for economic and social advancement depend on resources inherent in one's networks. Furthermore, the poor are, and remain poor because their networks lack resources—that is, they have few, if any, wealthy friends and family. Since networks require some form of social capital, poverty alleviation programs, to be successful, will need to facilitate the formation of bridging social capital—and, in some cases, linking social capital—between the networks of the poor and those of the prosperous and powerful.

The social capital paradigm predicts that as social capital within a network increases, income disparities within the network decrease and the average level of income increases. This was one of the themes of Chapter 12. Three premises support these conclusions. First, an increase in social capital internalizes the external consequences of each agent's choices on the income of others. This leads the agent to choices that are more likely to benefit others and reduce income inequality. Second, as social capital internalizes externalities, members of the social capital-rich network are more willing to invest in high exclusion-cost goods which benefit their neighbors as well as themselves and which are not allocated on the basis of their income. Third, as social capital increases the benefits and likelihood of trades within one's social capital rich network, opportunities for specialization and benefits from trade will increase, raising average household income. However, and returning to the main point, one's future is a lot brighter in a wealthy

network than in a poor one. And if you don't believe it, interview the illegal immigrants in the United States, who sacrifice nearly all they have to change networks. But the wealth of the networks that immigrants want to access may have less to do with natural capital (nonrenewable resources), land, produced or built capital than with social capital or what a recent study called "intangible wealth."

THE ADVANTAGES OF BELONGING TO A RESOURCE-RICH NETWORK

According to a recent World Bank study, a Mexican migrant to the United States is five times more productive than one who stays home. Why? The answer is not the obvious one. It's because the average American has access to over $418,000 in intangible wealth while the stay-at-home Mexican's intangible wealth is just $34,000. No wonder Mexican migrants want to cross the border and join the US network.

Two years ago the World Bank set out to assess the relative contributions of various kinds of capital to economic development. It wanted to know: where is the wealth of nations? What it found was that, after adding up all the traditional forms of capital, the sum of machinery, equipment, and structure, and urban land, what was left to account for a country's economic development and income was intangible wealth. This intangible wealth included trust among people in a society, an efficient judicial system, clear property rights, and effective government. All this intangible wealth also boosts the labor productivity, results in higher total wealth, and constitutes the largest share of wealth in virtually all countries.

Wealthy nations have it. Poor ones don't. Organization for Economic Cooperation and Development (OECD) countries have $354,000 per capita in intangible wealth or capital. For low-income countries, the average is $7,216 per person.

Source: Bailey (2007: A9).

Our experiences with poverty reduction programs have often yielded less than expected results. It has been as though some other forces besides those included in standard economic models have altered the expected outcomes. We believe that one ingredient, unaccounted for in development models, has been social capital. Of course, we recognize that many forms of capital are necessary for poverty reduction, but the lesson of the last several decades and recent World Bank findings confirm that the productivity of physical, financial, human, and natural forms of capital is heavily influenced by social capital. The effect of ignoring social capital in development models can be compared to ignoring the gravitational pull of a planet and then attempting to predict the path of other planets.

POVERTY AND THE PLANETS

The movements of the planets are influenced by the location and mass of other celestial bodies. In the past, when the movements of a planet have been unpredictable, it has been because of the influence of an unobserved celestial body. For example, the planet Uranus was discovered in 1781 by William Herschel (Hamilton, 1995–2009). Later, it was observed that the orbital

path of Uranus varied from the one predicted, and this led scientists to discover the planet Neptune. Neptune, as scientists discovered, was exerting an unobserved effect on Uranus. We believe that development policies and theories of poverty reduction have often been less successful than expected because they have ignored the influence of a previously unobserved (measured) capital—namely, social capital.

Low levels of social capital hinder the acquisition of adequate levels of physical goods and services. Low levels of social capital also cause socio-emotional suffering among the poor. Listen to their voices.

FROM VOICES OF THE POOR

From a discussion group, Esmeraldas, Ecuador:

Some receive us, others don't. It's awful ... They are abusive ... They treat one almost like a dog ... The municipality only serves the high-society ones. (World Bank, 2001: 100)

Poor woman, Latvia:

Poverty is humiliation, the sense of being dependent on them, and of being forced to accept rudeness, insults, and indifference when we seek help. (World Bank, 2001: 3)

South Africa 1998

In our culture women tend to feel small. Men have always been the leaders; their voices are final. (Narayan, 2000: 180)

Understanding the Causes of Development (and Poverty)

To understand the role of social capital in poverty reduction, it is necessary to understand the traditional model for development. The traditional model emphasizes that development depends on our opportunities to specialize and trade. When tasks are divided and people specialize, they not only bring improved skills to each stage of production, but they also often bring resources and information to the process that are essential for efficiency.

When individuals specialize, they give up producing some goods and services essential for their well-being. To obtain these goods and services that they no longer produce, they trade with each other and, in the process, become dependent on the production of others. However, specialization requires institutions to organize the coordination of tasks and the distribution of products. As specialization and trade have become global, countries have become even more interdependent in terms of their economic well-being. Thus, the economic conditions in one country may affect the well-being of those that trade with them. Countries that do not trust others or fail to recognize the advantages of specialization and trade often adopt policies of self-sufficiency. Past experience tells us, however, that such policies rarely succeed. History and experience have supported Adam Smith. Specialization and trade are necessary for economic progress. President Mugabe

of Zimbabwe who has pursued an opposite economic formula has led his country to economic collapse.

CRONYISM, CORRUPTION, AND COLLAPSE

As reported by the Heritage Foundation in its *2009 Index of Economic Freedom,* Zimbabwe has transformed itself from the "breadbasket of Africa" into a starving, destitute tyranny. Virtually all areas of economic freedom score poorly. The government maintains a high average tariff rate, as well as non-tariff barriers embedded in its labyrinthine customs service. National expenditures are also high. State influence in most areas of the economy is stifling, and expropriation is common as the political executive pushes forward with its resource-redistribution-by-angry-mob economic plan. Political interference has wrecked the once-prosperous financial market, and the state has made a point of not welcoming foreign investment. Inflation is crippling, and the government directly subsidizes a wide array of goods.

Source: Heritage Foundation (2009).

If trades were restricted to barters, opportunities to trade would be severely limited. Only those who could find someone producing what they wanted and, in turn, desired what they produced could trade. So, money was invented to facilitate exchanges and as a store of value. Instead of limiting one's opportunities for trade to those who produce a desired item, money makes it possible to trade with nearly everyone who produces something of value. In effect, money allows us to acquire what we desire in two exchanges. We exchange what we produce for money, and then exchange money for what we desire that is produced by others. The traditional view emphasizes the importance of markets in which goods can be evaluated in terms of money and where formal institutions permit strangers to trade.

If trades were restricted to money on hand, opportunities to trade would also be limited because one's income and expenses are rarely perfectly synchronized. So credit was invented. Instead of limiting purchases to the availability of money on hand, credit is exchanged for loan funds to purchase goods and services, which are paid for in the future. The development of an economy and the possibility of personally prospering is linked to the availability of credit.

Finally, the traditional view emphasizes that efficient specialization and welfare-improving trades require that participants be motivated by opportunities for personal gain, most often measured in terms of physical goods and services, and access to power and position.

The Traditional Model and Policy Prescriptions

The traditional view of development has often led to rather predictable policy prescriptions. One of the most important economic policy approaches derived from the traditional view of development has been to encourage specialization and trade. One way to encourage specialization and trade is to reduce the cost of performing trades. Often this has been accomplished by limiting regulations that restrict trade and reducing tariffs, and import and export taxes.

A second policy approach has been to reward efforts to improve communications between suppliers and consumers. High taxes and generous welfare policies and other restrictions on trade are often opposed because they may distort market signals between suppliers and consumers that motivate trade, specialization, and risk-taking.

A third policy approach arising from the traditional model has been to encourage monetary and fiscal measures designed to stabilize currencies. The purpose of this policy approach is to provide a stable medium of exchange and to reduce the risk of investing.

Finally, some policy objectives are directed toward the development of institutions designed to secure property rights and ensure enforcement of agreements between trading partners. Some recent writings in this area argue that the poor may be disadvantaged because their property is not secure. For example, Hernando de Soto argues that many of the poor own housing capital, but they lack clear title to their properties. As a result, their housing capital cannot be used as collateral to obtain credit, which would permit them to purchase other forms of capital. Another way of describing de Soto's argument is to say that the poor are not protected by the formal institutions guarding property rights, and therefore their real estate capital cannot be leveraged to obtain other forms of capital (de Soto, 2000: 276).[1]

So what do leaders of developing countries think of the standard economic prescriptions included in what has been called the "Washington consensus"?

CONSENSUS AGAINST THE WASHINGTON CONSENSUS

Evo Morales is the sixth Latin American leader in seven years to take office after campaigning against the market-oriented economic policies that the United States has urged on its neighbors for two decades. Across the region, leaders rally against "savage capitalism." The market reforms, the so-called Washington Consensus, urged tight government budgets, privatized government services, deregulation and open markets. Latin American countries were often required to adopt market-friendly policies that often resulted in painful cuts in social programs or popular subsidies in order to obtain loan funds supplied by the International Monetary Fund, the World Bank, and the United States.

While the policies well may have contributed to stemming runaway inflation, the gains from the program have been uneven. In 2005, after more than a decade of belt-tightening punctuated by severe financial crises in Mexico, Brazil and Argentina, there were 128 million Latin Americans living on less than $2 a day. That was 3 million more than in 1990.

Source: Adapted from Lynch (2006).

The traditional approach has been credited for achieving many successes. Indeed, in most cases, it has proven to be a more successful economic system than alternatives,

1 The main tenet of de Soto's books is that people in developing countries lack such an integrated formal property system, leading to only informal ownership of land and goods. He argues that the fruition of economic success of American and Japanese capitalism relied on a clear system of property rights which was created during the times of the "frontier" in America and in pre-World War I feudal Japan. The lack of such an integrated system of property rights in today's developing nations makes it impossible for the poor to leverage their now informal ownerships into capital (as collateral for credit), which de Soto claims would form the basis for entrepreneurship. Hence farmers in much of the developing world remain trapped in subsistence agriculture. As such, he argues that this informal ownership should be made formal—e.g., by giving squatters in shanty towns land titles to the land they now live on.

including state-controlled economies. However, despite its successes, persistent poverty remains, even in developed countries. Critics of the traditional approach cite several reasons for its lack of success in eliminating poverty.

First, gains from specialization and trade benefit those with productive skills and resources. The wealthy are far more likely than the poor to be able to pay to acquire such skills and resources. Also, these skills and resources are often inherited rather than earned or determined in a market. When workers lack resources, including credit and skills that are in demand, they are excluded from the benefits of specialization and trade. Globalization and restructuring of trading patterns within an economy favor those who are mobile and well-trained. The poor, who are often neither, are often left behind as changes in the economy stimulate demand for new skills. Second, sometimes opportunities to participate in new production networks are structured to favor certain groups with inherited traits, such as ethnic or religious groups or the young. These discriminations and others often disadvantage the poor. Finally, changing economic opportunities that are created through the globalization of markets and restructuring within economies may provide incentives for some to redistribute their investments in social capital. This redistribution may have further consequences for the poor.

All exchanges take place in an institutional setting. The institutions or rules that describe the conditions for exchange also allocate benefits and costs, and are often controlled by an elite few and operated for their benefit and the benefit of their friends. Few are the connections between the poor and the powerful and, as a result, the rules rarely work in favor of the poor. We've all heard the saying: "Those with the money make the rules." Jack Knight (1992) formalized this argument by showing how those with power were the ones who created and modified institutions to distribute resources toward themselves.

Attempting to achieve economic development without, at the same time, developing a country's social capital, or what the World Bank refers to as "intangible wealth," is unlikely to meet with success. As Peter Bauer wrote:

> *If all conditions for development other than capital are present, capital will soon be generated ... If, however, the conditions for development are not present, then aid ... will be necessarily unproductive and therefore ineffective. Thus, if the mainsprings of development are present, material progress will occur even without foreign aid. If they are absent, it will not occur even with aid.*
>
> Bauer, 1972 quoted in Bailey, 2007: A7.

Social Capital, Development, and Poverty

We generally agree with the traditional model's list of requirements for economic development. Specialization does increase productivity. Trade is required for specialization to occur. Institutions are needed for orderly exchanges and the assurance of property rights. Stable currencies and credit are required to reduce transaction costs and to even out cash flows. But these are not enough, because underlying these requirements is the need for social capital.

People won't trade with, or provide credit to, others they don't like or trust. Institutions, especially those like property rights, require attachment value to exist. Finally, there is nothing in the traditional model that specifically addresses the issue of poverty. Poverty is a relative term, referring to the conditions of those who have a lot less than the average person. Even if specialization and trading occur with stable currencies and accessible credit under the umbrella of supportable institutions, what is there in the traditional model that would lead to a reduction in poverty? In what follows, we argue that social capital is essential for economic development, and is required for the reduction of poverty.

An absence of socially connected networks may prevent the productions of high-value and multiple-input products. High value-added products require inputs from a large number of participants (Ritchie, 2005a). Divisions created by antipathy or an absence of social capital prevent an economy from producing high-value products. In countries with many different ethnic, religious, and cultural divides, production is often limited to agricultural products and extraction of natural resources because these activities require fewer, smaller, and less dense networks than, say, data-processing firms that supply data-processing services whose workers process data in India, transmit their processed data around the world, whose financial accounts are managed in New York City, and whose company headquarters are in Connecticut. The dependence of poor countries on agriculture and extraction is described in Tables 13.1 and 13.2.

AN ABSENCE OF BRIDGING SOCIAL CAPITAL DISCONNECTS THE POOR FROM THOSE WHOSE POSITION AND RESOURCES COULD HELP THEM ESCAPE FROM POVERTY

One characteristic of the poor is their lack of social capital and shared kernels with the well-off (the poor usually lack wealthy friends). Too often, the poor and the rich attend

Table 13.1 Poor countries and agriculture

	% of population working in the agricultural sector (1990)	Per capita gross national product (1994) (US$)
Nepal	94	200
Rwanda	92	80
Burundi	92	160
Burkina Faso	92	300
Malawi	87	170
Mali	86	250
Ethiopia	86	100
Uganda	85	190
Guinea-Bisau	85	240
Tanzania	84	140

Source: World Bank, 1996.

Table 13.2 Rich countries and agriculture

	% of population working in the agricultural sector (1990)	Per capita gross national product (1994) (US$)
Netherlands	5	22,010
France	5	23,420
Israel	4	14,530
United Kingdom	3	18,340
Canada	3	19,510
Belgium	3	22,870
United States	3	25,880
Kuwait	2	19,420
Hong Kong	1	21,650
Singapore	0	22,500

Source: World Bank, 1996.

separate schools, live in separate locations, take their meals isolated from each other, worship at different times and places, marry within their own class, and obtain their medical services at different places. The poor are reminded by their frequent separation from the rest of society that they are different.

People often found in fewer and poorly endowed networks include members of households headed by a single parent (usually a mother) who has never been married, rural households without property, and other minority groups who are not socially integrated because of their unique customs or inherited kernels.

Our premise is that poverty is partly related to an individual's lack of social capital in resource-rich networks. This absence of social capital, we hypothesize, limits the poor's access to physical, human, and financial capital. In addition, a lack of social capital often creates unfavorable terms of trade compared to those who enjoy social capital.

Poor countries tend to be poor in a similar way: they all have resources concentrated in the hands of a few, while the disconnected masses suffer in poverty. Thus, a persistent common factor among poor countries is a low average level of income and a high disparity of income (Deininger and Squire, 1996). This common relationship between the average level of household income and dispersion of incomes not only holds between countries, but also appears to be true among households living in developed countries, such as the United States and Europe. When income disparity measures are regressed against per capita GNP for countries, we find the same relationship between low incomes and high levels of dispersion that can be observed to exist with US state-level data.[2]

2 When GDP is the dependent variable, the regression produces a coefficient of –1.41, significant at the .003 level.

AN ABSENCE OF DENSE SOCIAL CAPITAL CONNECTIONS AND FORMAL INSTITUTIONS WITH ATTACHMENT VALUES OFTEN LEADS TO CORRUPTION AND CIVIL WAR, STIFLING SPECIALIZATION AND TRADE

Corruption occurs when formal institutions that formalize the terms of trade are replaced by informal institutions that provide benefits on the basis of relationships. Corruption is most likely to occur when a lack of social capital fails to embed SEGs, necessary for the creation of attachment value, in formal institutions.

Corruption has the effect of increasing income inequality because it concentrates benefits among those with the power to replace formal institutions with informal ones. Indeed, corruption is made possible when a broad cross-section of society, who should have an interest in maintaining formal institutions, is disconnected.

BRIBES AND ROADBLOCKS

Corruption takes a toll on economic performance, undermines employment opportunities, and clouds prospects for poverty reduction. ... In West Africa, bribes in the transport industry are crippling. [For example,]...a transport trip in Benin encountered 25 roadblocks over 753 kilometers—roadblocks staffed by state agents who demanded bribes that added up to 87 percent of the cost of the trip.

World Bank, 2001: 102.

Other evidence of institutions without attachment value is crime. Criminal acts may require less social capital than corruption because they are often individual acts that disregard the property rights of others. These punish not only the victims but also the population at large because they discourage others from outside the country to invest and trade with the countries' businesses. As crime increases trade is discouraged and so are divisions of labor and specialization essential for economic progress. Worse, the poor suffer from crime the most.

CRIME AND NO PUNISHMENT

In Johannesburg, South Africa, rates of theft and violent crime are among the highest in the world. Wealthy residents can afford sophisticated alarms, security guards, and other forms of private policing to protect their property and persons. Poor people are stuck in poorly built homes, sometimes without even simple locks, and are vulnerable to theft, assault, murder, and other violent crimes.

World Bank, 2001: 103.

An absence of dense social capital connections leads to underinvestments in high exclusion-cost goods (HECs) whose benefits could serve to reduce income inequality.

Countries rich in social capital allocate resources to public goods or HECs whose benefits are distributed without regard to one's income. Such public goods include schools, roads, water and sanitation systems, crime prevention, and national defense.

In social capital-poor countries, with significant inequalities and poverty, there are fewer HECs produced, and many are replaced with private goods whose benefits do depend on

one's income. In effect, in social capital-poor countries, private goods replace public goods. For example, the wealthy hire private guards who substitute for inadequate public protection services. Bottled water substitutes for an unsafe public water system. Private schools and tutors substitute for ineffective public schools. Land Rovers substitute for adequate roads. Littered highways and polluted streams substitute for a public sanitation service.

In social capital-rich countries, most agree that all children should have the right to adequate schooling, safety, and healthcare, and are willing to allocate public resources to achieve these goals. These kinds of resource allocations have the effect of reducing income inequality and raising the level of incomes. Moreover, in social capital-rich countries civic organizations often arise to support public investments and organizations designed to reduce inequality.

CLUBS AND SOCIAL CAPITAL

Competitiveness debates have contrasted countries that have industrial policies, like Japan, with more *laissez-faire* countries like the United States. But Frank Fukuyama has noted that the pivotal difference is the level of a people's trust. High-trust societies are interlaced with voluntary organizations—Rotary clubs, bible study groups, civic organizations—and thus have social capital, which makes for the growth of large corporations in highly technical fields. Low-trust societies—France, Italy, Mexico, China—tend toward small, family-owned businesses dealing in basic goods. Social capital is not necessary for growth, but its absence tempts governments to intervene in the economy and imperil competitiveness.

Source: Fukuyama (1995b).

The Social Capital Paradigm and Poverty Reduction

The social capital paradigm recognizes that we value and exchange SEGs as well as EVGs. Indeed, it argues that exchanges almost always include some SEGs. Furthermore, since SEGs are most likely to be exchanged in social capital-rich relationships, terms and levels of trade in physical goods and services will favor and encourage specialization and trade among those with social capital. Thus, the productivity of one's physical and other resources will be influenced by one's social capital. We hypothesize that the poor, both individuals and nations, who often lack social capital in resource-rich networks, must often trade on disadvantageous terms. Furthermore, they often lack information about opportunities for advancement because they lack bridging connections to social capital-rich networks.

The traditional model predicts that, in the absence of transaction costs, production will occur in an optimal manner, given the existing institutions and distribution of resources. In contrast, the social capital paradigm suggests that resource allocations will be influenced by social capital and that the production of physical assets may not occur in an optimal manner even for the given distribution of resources and rights. (For example, hiring unqualified relatives may be motivated by the need to preserve one's social capital rather than to achieve economic efficiency.) Further, the social capital paradigm emphasizes that the distribution of resources need not be a given, and changes

in the distribution of resources are largely driven by changes in the distribution of social capital.

The social capital paradigm also connects the distribution of social capital and the distribution of income. The connection is straightforward. The distribution of social capital alters the terms and levels of trade, and the terms and levels of trade influence the distribution of income. Therefore, the distribution of social capital must be reflected in the distribution of household income. From this deduction emerges another conclusion—namely, that the distribution of household income can be altered by changing the distribution of social capital. In addition, the connection between distribution of social capital and income also predicts that societies of disconnected people who lack social capital will be disadvantaged economically because their lack of social capital will discourage trade and specialization.

It is well recognized that underinvestment in HECs, such as roads, public health, and safety, contributes to the persistence of poverty. The traditional model suggests that people must be motivated by self-interest to invest in HECs. However, the social capital paradigm expands the definition of outcomes that could be considered to be in one's self-interest. For example, an individual may find it in his or her interest to invest in public goods if it benefits those who are the objects of his or her social capital. A person may also invest in public goods if he or she receives SEGs from the investment. Or, he or she may invest in HECs if the place that would benefit from his or her support has attachment value.

One means of increasing the willingness of people to invest in public goods provided in their communities is to increase their attachment to a place or to their community. As community members come to view themselves as connected, and linking social capital develops among them, their willingness to invest in goods for the community increases. Another important strategy for poor countries is to develop bridging social capital with the world's rich and famous.

STARS AND SACRIFICES FOR THE POOR

Bono, who has been nominated for the Nobel Peace Prize, said it is "wholly unacceptable" for children to die for lack of cheap immunizations.

"I'm going to spend the rest of my life on this, I'm going to make that kind of extreme poverty history," Bono told reporters.

"I'm in," Brad Pitt responded.

Bono and Pitt were joined by Jack Valenti, the former top lobbyist for the film industry, and actor Djimon Hounsou, a native of the West African nation of Benin, where AIDS is a problem and over a third of the population is below the poverty line. Hounsou's film credits include "Beauty Shop," "Constantine," "Gladiator" and "Amistad."

The credit he wants the public to know about right now, however, is a one minute commercial for "ONE: The Campaign to Make Poverty History" ...

> *Others appearing in the ads include musicians Mos Def and Jewel; actors Brad Pitt, Penelope Cruz, Jamie Foxx, Tom Hanks and Al Pacino; and evangelist Pat Robertson and the Rev. Frank Griswold, the presiding bishop of the Episcopal Church in the United States.*
>
> Grace, 2005.
>
> If bridging social capital is an important resource for those living in poverty, the sacrifices of the stars is a good start.

The social capital paradigm also has trading implications. As we mentioned above, in the traditional model, money and credit permit all trades to be reduced to two steps. One trades goods and services for money and then uses the money obtained in the exchange to obtain other objects. In the social capital paradigm, social capital and SEGs may play the role of money and credit. Sometimes, among both the poor and the wealthy, an exchange of SEGs and investments in social capital can make otherwise unprofitable trades happen. For example, imagine person *A* offering person *B* a favor (e.g., car repair) with only the expectation that at some point *B* will so something for *A*. Their expectations or trust function like credit. Or, imagine how much easier it is to obtain assistance from a friend to complete a repair using one's social capital than to work out a financial agreement when there is no established market to value the assistance. In these cases, social capital is like credit and money; it can be used in a multitude of exchanges. Furthermore, because it is durable, it can be stored until such time that it is needed, even though some maintenance is required.

The traditional model equates well-being in terms of access to physical and financial resources and sometimes recognizes the value of these in obtaining high-status goods. The social capital paradigm suggests that SEGs are also important for well-being, and these are very difficult to self-produce. So, for most people, SEGs can only be obtained through exchanges in social settings. This recognition adds support to the traditional model's emphasis that we are truly interdependent—that we are "all part of the main."

Finally, the traditional model recognizes that, in some cases, markets fail to develop and these failures impede economic development. The social capital paradigm suggests that market failures may often be related to an absence of social capital and are sometimes related to hostile relationships that create unfavorable conditions for trade by creating negative attachment values. Indeed, the evidence is that few trades occur between hostile groups.

The social capital paradigm predicts that, in the absence of formal institutions and a generally connected society, social capital substitutes for other forms of capital. In such cases, one's social capital not only provides SEGs, but is also the resource that facilitates trades and economic survival. Of course, social capital used for mostly economic purposes is not as efficient as money, but it can be used as a partial substitute. The goal is, and should be, to move from social capital-dependent economies to economies that rely on formal institutions supported with attachment values. Indeed, as the number of people in trading networks expands beyond the number capable of maintaining personalized social capital (as all formal and developed economies must), formal institutions must be adopted and supported. However, this last step in economic development must be

preceded by the development of social capital that leads the members of the economic community to create attachment value for their formal institutions.

Even though the social capital of the poor may be concentrated and reside in resource-poor networks, it still represents a significant resource that can be used extensively. For example, in some communities, the poor use their social capital to cover the costs of funerals. In other cases, the poor exchange their social capital to cover emergency medical expenses or survival rations during economic crises. In effect, social capital of the poor is the difference between surviving or not. The poor "pay" in future service and respect.

Because the social capital of the poor is often geographically concentrated, they are often reluctant to move, even to take advantage of new economic opportunities, because it would cost them the advantages of their network. This immobility may be a significant impediment to their economic development, because globalization and other market adjustments often require relocation and participation in new networks, both of which are difficult for them.

In summary, the social capital paradigm enhances the traditional model and adds new insights about the causes of poverty. It suggests that the poor's lack of social capital in resource-rich networks may create unfavorable terms and levels of trade, and limit their ability to take advantage of new economic opportunities. Further, in the absence of social capital, owners of EVGs are unlikely to share them with the poor. Finally, the social capital paradigm also suggests that, without linking social capital, communities are likely to underinvest in HECs—an outcome whose negative consequences fall disproportionately on the poor. Moreover, there is evidence that the distribution of social capital alters the terms and levels of trade, which in turn influence the distribution of income.

What is the Evidence that Social Capital Can be Used to Reduce Poverty?

Fortunately, many "best" development practices already effectively use social capital (see Smith, 2001). Many of these have common elements. These practices expand the networks of the poor; they increase the poor's access to resources on favorable terms; they increase attachment values to place; they create linking and bridging social capital between people from different backgrounds; they increase investments in HECs or public goods; and they alter institutions to benefit the poor.

Some examples of how social capital has been used, or studies that connect social capital to the conditions of the poor, include the following:

- One of the earliest social capital studies demonstrated that educational achievements were related to the social capital environment of the students (Coleman, 1990).
- High-trust countries enjoy significant economic advantages (including economies of scale) compared to low-trust societies (Fukuyama, 1995).
- Communities with high levels of civil society and association prosper relative to communities with low levels of civic engagement (Putnam, Leonardi, and Nanetti, 1993).
- Household income disparity appears to decrease with increases in variables associated with increasing levels of social capital (Robison and Siles, 1999).

- Opportunities to purchase high-quality land depend on one's social capital (Perry and Robison, 2001).
- National economic growth is positively related to trust (Knack and Keefer, 1997).
- As trading contacts increase, so does one's income (Fafchamps and Minten, 1998). Empowering communities to choose and administer their own development projects has led to more successful investment outcomes and increased social capital in the community (Robison, Siles, and Owens, 2002).
- Too numerous to cite are the examples of destruction and poverty resulting from hostility or negative social capital, which disrupt and increase the cost of trades and reduce the opportunities for specialization. Acts of hostility that increase poverty include: war, crime, corruption, threats, discrimination, acts of terrorism, and destruction of the environment.
- Successful *maquiladoras* in Mexico's Yucatan depend on social capital (Biles, Robison, and Siles, 2002).
- Resource-conserving practices in the Alti-Plano were associated with social capital (Swinton, 2000).
- Maintenance of an irrigation system and equitable sharing of water in Nepal improved with the development of social capital (Uphoff, 2000).
- Savings and investment clubs have been successfully organized in the Philippines using social capital (Adams and Fitchett, 1992).
- Technology adoption depends on social ties (Isham, 1999).
- Sometimes, development requires that we first stop the destruction of lives and property. Betty Williams and Mairead Corrigan created the Peace People Organization, a movement of Catholics and Protestants dedicated to ending sectarian fighting in Northern Ireland. For their work they were awarded the 1976 Nobel Peace Prize (*Columbia Electronic Encyclopedia*).

The Social Capital Paradigm and Policy Recommendations

Having identified the lack of social capital in resource-rich networks as a significant cause of poverty, the prescriptions that follow suggest ways of increasing the social capital resources of the poor.

PROVIDE PUBLIC EDUCATION

Whenever possible, interactions between different economic classes of society should be encouraged, because these are required to build social capital. One of the most important opportunities for interactions across diverse groups is participation in public education.

PROVIDE ADULT EDUCATION

In some countries, poverty persists among certain groups because they cannot speak the generally accepted language. People in a language-confined group most often communicate and associate with others who share the restricted language kernel. Therefore, we suggest adult education courses designed for those who lack language, literacy, and other skills (Coleman, 1988).

FOCUS ON ENGAGEMENT

Most countries support research facilities that produce useful results. However, many of these important results are never employed by those who could benefit from them, because those who need the information are not capable of accessing or applying it. A delivery system for carrying basic information to the poor about hygiene, personal care, and the dangers of harmful substances is desperately needed in many places. Therefore, we recommend that certain people within communities be trained and empowered to provide information and training to their fellow community members.

BUILD ATTACHMENT VALUES INTO TECHNOLOGY TRANSFERS

Related to outreach efforts are new technologies. New technologies often lack attachment values and replace old technologies that have acquired attachment values. When delivered by people known to the potential users, attachment values are more likely to be positive than when delivered by strangers, or worse, by people not respected by members of the community. Therefore, we recommend that efforts be made to increase the attachment values of new technology.

ACTIVATE LATENT SOCIAL CAPITAL IN COMMUNITIES

There are many positive poverty reduction efforts that can be undertaken by an organized community that recognizes the collective value of its assets. When communities are connected, these social capital-rich networks can organize markets, improve water and sanitation systems, prevent crime, lobby government for improved services, create savings and investment funds, and increase investments in schools. But, too often, the poor are not organized because their social capital is latent—not developed.

Therefore, we recommend that communities convert their latent social capital to realized social capital by applying for direct support, and that this support be conditioned on the formation of local networks with widespread participation. We also recommend that the community networks be empowered by giving them the responsibility for administering supported projects, selecting contractors, supervising construction, and managing the completed projects. We also suggest that public funds intended for communities be placed under the direction of local community leadership with the stipulation that they demonstrate community consensus in the use of the funds.[3]

DEVELOP LEADERSHIP

The development of local social capital-rich networks requires local leaders who have social capital with their communities, which means that having leaders in communities must often precede the development of latent social capital. Therefore, we recommend that universities cooperate in the creation of leadership programs, with interns participating in community social capital-building programs. Aid to support these leadership programs should be provided by international donors and state and national governments.

3 Marcelo Siles suggested the term "latent social capital."

INTENSIFY THE USE OF EXISTING NETWORKS

Poverty reduction is all about gaining access to new resources and more fully employing existing resources. Many of the recommendations so far have suggested means for building social capital. Sometimes, however, there are opportunities to better use existing social capital resources. Therefore, we suggest that efforts to build social capital at the local level begin with efforts to identify existing community networks and then to use these networks for other purposes. Such efforts to assist communities to more fully utilize and expand their social capital could be assisted by community members trained in leadership skills, individuals from international support groups, such as the Peace Corps, and others.

USE SOCIAL CAPITAL INDIRECTLY

In some cases, we simply must admit that some poor communities have few means of acquiring social capital from the wealthy and the powerful within their countries or the agencies from which they need assistance. In such circumstances, it is important to recognize that social capital is fungible and can therefore facilitate indirect access to needed social capital resources. For example, a poor community may need the support of a government official but lack the social capital necessary to gain that support. However, the community may have social capital with international donors or other government agencies that have influence with that government official, and these social capital-rich relationships can be used in an indirectly to obtain the needed support. Therefore, we recommend that poor communities be encouraged to use their social capital indirectly.

MAINTAIN SOCIAL CAPITAL THROUGH EMPLOYMENT

Sometimes, especially in areas of high unemployment, the poor lack basic services as well as food, clothing, shelter, and medical attention. In these cases, public assistance is essential for their survival. However, when these goods and services, or EVGs, are delivered in ways implying that the poor are undeserving or inferior because they cannot provide for themselves, serious discomfort is created because the support is accompanied by negative SEGs. And, because the EVGs are desperately needed, the poor accept assistance even though they lose some sense of dignity in the process. However, the poor and unemployed almost always have some useful skills that they could offer to their communities and others, and if these could be employed in exchange for public assistance, the process need not be accompanied by negative SEGs.

During the Great Depression, the US government organized people to produce publicly provided goods, including roads, bridges, and libraries, and to write histories and produce paintings to be displayed in public buildings. Such projects gave people the advantage of being paid while at the same time receiving positive SEGs through the knowledge that they were providing services in exchange for receiving support.

Therefore, we recommend the establishment of a system of exchange in which those with a need for public assistance be provided with opportunities to give their services to the community or to others in need, in exchange for goods provided by the community.

WORKS IN PROGRESS

The Works Progress Administration (renamed during 1939 as the Work Projects Administration; WPA) was the largest and most comprehensive "New Deal" agency, employing millions of people and affecting almost every locality in the United States, especially rural and western mountain populations. It was created by ... presidential order, and funded by Congress ...

Headed by Harry Hopkins, the WPA provided jobs and income to the unemployed during the Great Depression in the United States. The program built many public buildings, projects and roads, and operated large arts, drama, media and literacy projects. It fed children, redistributed food, clothing and housing. Expenditures from 1935 to 1939 totaled nearly $7 billion.

http://en.wikipedia.org/wiki/Works_Progress_Administration.

PUBLICIZE HOSTILITY

Although we have recommended investing in the social capital of the poor as a means of escape from poverty, a careful investigation of the main cause of poverty reveals that poverty is not just caused by an absence of social capital, but also by the presence of hostility or negative social capital. Therefore, we recommend that the negative consequences of hostility be publicized and made known to those of goodwill. The consequences of hostility are most egregious when they are practiced by those employed in public service. To eliminate these consequences, those who practice discrimination and mistreatment of the poor should be eliminated from public service. A free press is essential for publicizing acts of hostility.

BUILD ATTACHMENT VALUES TO PLACE

Embedding SEGs in objects creates attachment values. One of the problems of developing countries and neighborhoods is that places of residence often lack attachment value. One consequence of this lack of attachment value is that those most able to contribute to the well-being of their country and community depart and take their potential contributions with them, leaving behind those who are immobile and uncommitted to their place of residence. Another consequence of lack of attachment value to countries and communities is the degradation of the environment and the squandering of natural capital, often by outside organizations, which further reduces attachment values.

Therefore, we recommend significant efforts be made to create attachment values for communities and countries. This can only be done by providing people with a sense of ownership and control over the conditions and events that occur in their place of residence. Enforceable property rights leads to investment by individuals, which in turn bolsters economies and increases attachment values. A sense of influence on local events could be encouraged by open forums, increased voter enrollments, and neighborhood organizations.

LAWLESSNESS AND THE LOSS OF INSTITUTIONAL ATTACHMENT VALUE

Numb with rage and humiliation, a 16-year-old Punjabi girl, Najma, sits with her mother on the bed where she was recently raped—an act of intimidation committed by agents of a feudal land baron seeking to drive the family off their tiny plot of land. As in many rapes involving either tribal custom or wealthy landowner, local police dismissed the case.

The outcome of such dysfunctional legal systems? Rashid Rehman, a human rights lawyer, observes that: "When people are powerless, they are easily manipulated."

Writes Don Belt, "It was a similar lawlessness that drove the people of Afghanistan into the arms of the Taliban in the mid-1990s." Must this also be the fate of today's Pakistan?

Source: Belt (2007).

EMPOWER LOCAL NETWORKS

Distributions of household income, information, and access to social services and property rights reflect existing distributions of social capital and configuration of networks. Poverty reduction requires that the social capital distributions and network configurations be changed to allow the poor access to the financial, physical, and human resources needed to improve their lives. But if the provision of these resources by aid donors reinforces and maintains existing networks that exclude and sometimes disadvantage the poor, then the benefits of the aid will be reduced. Therefore, we recommend that communities create public settings in which community members determine their most pressing needs and then organize to obtain the resources needed to achieve their goals. The quality of community life is linked to interlocking networks that create attachment values for place and support for its institutions.

UTILIZE THE ADVANTAGES OF FAMILY NETWORKS

One important network required for the alleviation of poverty is the firm. Many firms in developing countries limit their employment to members of their families and extended families. Family firms have advantages over other firms under several conditions and are likely to organize when transaction costs are high, when quality control of goods and services is difficult, when there are significant complementarities inherent in the firm that would be lost if the transactions were undertaken outside of the firm, when there are substantial SEGs that would be sacrificed by outsourcing the work, and when markets do not exist for goods and services required by the firm. Family firms often have significant social capital resources that are essential for success. Their difficulty is that they sometimes lack the human, physical, and financial resources required to successfully organize and manage a firm.

Therefore, we prescribe that the access of family organizations to credit and professional support be increased. The requirements would be that they have a network of participants, that they have a successful plan for their firm, and that they cannot obtain the needed resources elsewhere.

STRENGTHEN THE SOCIAL CAPITAL OF HOUSEHOLDS

Networks of households headed by a single mother and, to a lesser extent, those headed by a single parent generally tend to participate in networks with limited resources, simply because they have so few resources to invest in building their connections to other networks. Therefore, we recommend that youth be encouraged in a variety of religious, civic, and household settings to postpone child-bearing until after marriage and that marriage be used to build an expanded network for the new couple. Informal institutions that require costly marriage celebrations and that discourage formal marriages should be altered. Finally, significant effort must be made to provide training and opportunities to these single-parent households on terms they can access. For example, child support may be provided for single parents to improve their human and social capital.

STRENGTHEN MARKETS TO BUILD SOCIAL CAPITAL

An important opportunity for expanding one's network is participation in markets in which one's exchange partners are often strangers. Participation in an exchange in which both partners benefit is an important earned kernel that has the potential to create social capital. Therefore, we suggest that public funds be invested to create and support formal market settings. These may include investments to support the exchange of information, the establishment of grades and standards, and inspection services to promote the safety of consumers.

SUPPORT FORMAL INSTITUTIONS

Social capital formation occurs mostly from the bottom up, not from the top down. Since informal institutions are derived from personalized social capital, they must support and therefore precede effective formal institutions. Formal institutions that reflect racism and discrimination based on inherited kernels should be vigorously opposed. Opposition to institutions that tend to disadvantage the poor requires organized networks whose members share the kernel of the goal of equality.

Therefore, we recommend that poverty reduction strategies be focused on building social capital in households, then in communities, and then in larger networks. However, this does not mean that macro-policies of poverty alleviation should be ignored, although it does mean that, to be effective, macro-policies must be accepted and supported at the local and household level. Unless the poor accept formal institutions they will be excluded from the formal economy. However, they will only accept formal institutions if they have a voice in their creation—and in order for them to have a voice, those in power must cooperate.

Conclusion

Terms and levels of trade often favor those in resource-rich social capital networks. Therefore, the distribution of income and wealth and other forms of capital will reflect the distribution of one's social capital. In addition, institutions that establish property rights, impose costs, and allocate benefits also reflect the existing distribution of social

capital. As a result, those who have social capital in resource-rich networks have an important resource.

Because social capital and the production of SEGs alter the terms and levels of trade, there is no guarantee that existing production practices and existing distributions of social capital and other resources will reduce poverty by "trickling down" benefits to those who lack resources and whose social capital is invested in resource-poor networks. We must abandon the incomplete paradigm of development that declares that the problems of the poor will eventually be solved if the rest of the economy becomes wealthy enough. Development and equity should be viewed as compatible and complementary goals.

So, the question that emerges is: how do we increase the social capital and network connections of the poor? The challenges are twofold. First, how do the poor increase their linking social capital in their own neighborhoods and communities? And, second, how do the poor increase bridging social capital which will connect them to resources beyond those that are available locally? We anticipate that, the second will be the most difficult of the two challenges. Indeed, in some cases, expanded linking networks may need to acquire the political and social leverage that allows them to make progress without the benefit of bridging social capital.

One way for the poor to acquire needed social capital is by having a voice that counts. They must gain access to the media to communicate their conditions and register their needs. There is a latent potential for social capital and goodwill that often only needs to be activated. Those interested in the well-being of the poor need to recognize that when resources destined for the poor are channeled through established networks from which the poor are excluded, the needed resources are sometimes diverted and this often has the consequence of strengthening existing distributions of power and social capital.

Finally, we conclude by re-emphasizing that the conditions of the poor can be improved by improving their social capital and including them in resource-rich networks. We believe that significant progress can be made to reduce poverty by first recognizing the role of social capital in creating conditions of poverty and then by employing social capital effectively to reduce poverty and create development. Only the creation of social capital can reduce the intense hatreds, malevolence and negative social capital among religious, ethnic, and other groups that lead to civil war and terrorist acts which destroy physical capital faster than investments can create it.

CHAPTER 14 *Social Capital and Ethics*

I have argued that, while we expect individuals to act by and large in their self interest, there are circumstances in which we say such behavior is unethical. So too for countries.

Joseph Stiglitz (2005: 6).

Introduction

People with social capital often exchange goods and services at favorable terms and levels of trade not available to those lacking social capital. This chapter explores the question: when is it ethical to allow social capital to give to some access to resources at favorable terms and levels and to deny others the same opportunities? In short, when is it ethical to use one's social capital to take care of friends and business?

The easy answer is: it depends! It depends first on generally held moral values. It depends on the kinds of social capital being employed. It depends on the effects of using one's social capital on those lacking social capital. It depends on whose resources are being influenced by social capital to aid friends and business.

The difficulty in knowing when is it ethical to employ one's social capital in support of friends and business may tempt us to ignore social capital altogether. But this would be a mistake. Social capital matters nearly all the time, and refusing to recognize its role in resource allocations is akin to looking for one's lost wallet under the streetlight rather than in the dark alley where it was lost. Social capital does alter the terms and level of resource allocations, and this fact should not be ignored if we really want to advance our understanding of interpersonal transactions and ethical behavior.

The answer to the question of when it is ethical to allow social capital to alter terms and level of trade involves concepts of right and wrong behavior. However, we cannot begin to establish ethical rules that distinguish between right and wrong behavior unless we first establish a foundation of moral values from which ethical rules can be derived. So we discuss next, the origins and difficulty of agreeing on a set of moral values from which our ethical rules can be derived. Then we will apply our understanding of moral values to establish ethical rules regarding the proper use of one's social capital. We will find that in establishing ethical rules for the use of one's social capital, it will be important to distinguish between using one's social capital to alter the allocation of socio-emotional goods (SEGs) and high attachment value goods (AVGs) versus mostly economically valued goods (EVGs).

The organization of this chapter recognizes how philosophers organize their study of ethics. They study meta-ethics, where ethical principles originate; normative ethics, the

moral standards that regulate right and wrong conduct; and, finally, applied ethics, the examination of specific and often controversial ethical questions such as environmental concerns, abortion, and capital punishment using meta-ethics and normative ethics to resolve them (Fieser, 2006).

The Difficulty of Establishing a Moral Foundation for Ethical Rules

Moral values precede the establishment of ethical rules. But from where do these moral values originate? Sometimes, moral values are established by the common voice of the people. In other cases, men and women invoke religious codes and traditions as the moral basis from which they can ratify or justify ethical rules. Finally, people sometimes claim divine communication as the basis for moral values. The origin of moral values is a vast subject and well beyond the scope of this chapter. For our purposes, it is important to recognize that, regardless of their origins, moral values are required before an agreed set of ethical rules can exist.

Understanding that ethical rules are based on moral values helps us understand why ethical rules are so difficult to formulate. They are difficult to formulate because (1) moral values on which they are based change over time; (2) individuals hold conflicting moral values that limit the scope or networks of people who can agree on a set of ethical rules; (3) while equitable distributions are usually considered ethical, equitable is not always the same as being equal; and (4) even if ethical rights and wrongs can be identified, it is difficult to establish who has the moral responsibilities or resources to guarantee ethical outcomes.

CHANGING MORAL VALUES

A normative ethical rule is a prescribed guide for conduct or action consistent with a set of moral values. A moral value accepted by all major religions is some form of the golden rule: "Do unto others as you would have them do unto you." A moral code that guides the medical profession is: "Do no harm." In the United States an important moral value—one that was accepted by the voice of the people—is included in the Declaration of Independence: "We hold these truths to be self-evident, that all men are created equal, that they are endowed by their Creator with certain unalienable rights, that among these are Life, Liberty and the pursuit of Happiness." From this statement of moral values are derived societal laws and the rights of citizens. Yet moral values can change over time. What it means to be "created equal" has changed as women's suffrage and civil rights movements have altered our concept of equality.

LIMITED SCOPE OF MORAL VALUES

Scope has to do with the domain. In our case, scope defines the population of people who accept a particular moral value from which ethical rules are derived and applied. We sometimes have difficulty defining ethical codes because the scope of norms and moral values on which they are based are not universally accepted. Thus, what is ethical in one domain may not be accepted as ethical in another. The limited scope of moral values

suggests the possibility of conflict and disagreement over answers to questions about ethical behavior.

One question created by the limited domain of moral values is: do we have the ethical right to impose our moral values on others? For example, does the US have a right or responsibility to impose its ethical rules in countries that do not share its moral values—such as India which has a moral value that recognizes different castes? Do countries such as Iran and Saudi Arabia have the right to impose their interpretations of Islamic laws on their citizens? On their neighbors? Or on visitors to their countries? In an increasingly globalized world, do we need an ethical rule that guarantees workers of the world equal rights so that workers in China have the same protections as workers in California or Connecticut? As our world becomes globally connected and cultural interactions increase, we face increasing conflicts over the domain of moral values and ethical rules derived from those moral values.

WHAT IS ETHICAL AND EQUITABLE IS NOT ALWAYS EQUAL

One moral value is that humans are of equal worth and that normative ethical codes should reflect this equity. Unfortunately, even if there is an agreement about the moral imperative of equality, there is surely no agreement about the ethical rules that should be derived from this moral value. At the heart of the dilemma is the conundrum that an equitable allocation of resources rarely leads to equality of access. For example, equal access to a building requires different methods of egress for a person capable of walking compared to someone confined to a wheelchair. We have different grades and types of education facilities because we have different interests and aptitudes. Requiring everyone to take the same classes and to ignore differences could be considered unfair by many.

Suggesting that ethical treatment and equal treatment are not synonymous leaves us asking: what is the basis for ethical or equitable distribution of resources? Should everyone's needs be equally satisfied? And if needs provide the basis for equitable distribution of resources, then who decides which needs are the most important and who determines when they are equitably satisfied?

WHO WILL PAY?

Beyond identifying rights to resources and opportunities, we must also specify whose responsibility it is to assure that those rights are guarded. For example, if education is a right that is required for the pursuit of happiness, who has the responsibility to provide it? Should a parent's income or nationality be allowed to determine a child's opportunities for an education? Government policies of most developed countries respond to the notion that a child born in poor circumstances still has certain claims, even if her parents cannot provide them. These include, among others, healthcare, access to education, and freedom from slavery. But all ethical rules for allocating resources soon face economic reality. For example, should California residents be forced to provide education for the children of undocumented Mexican migrant workers? A majority of California voters didn't believe it was their responsibility. So whose responsibility is it?

HEY, HEY, WE WON'T PAY!

When California voters were asked their opinions about a proposed law giving illegal immigrants reduced tuition to state colleges and universities, 72 percent of those polled opposed the new law. Clearly, California voters do not believe that illegal immigrants possess equal rights to educational benefits compared to permanent (and legal) California residents.

Consistent with the preferences of California voters, in one of his final decisions on legislation as governor, Gray Davis vetoed SB 328, which would have allowed low-income illegal immigrants to have their fees waived at California Community Colleges. The dilemma facing Governor Davis was the ethical right to an education versus the ethical responsibility to pay for it.

Source: Weintraub (2003).

Establishing Ethical Rules for the Use of Social Capital

It may be tempting to admit that the formation of ethical rules is an impossible task, given the complications just described in establishing a generally agreed on set of moral values. But an ordered society requires ethical rules. And, besides, we may be more in agreement on fundamental moral values more than we thought.

SYMPATHY AND SHARED ETHICAL RULES

Imagine that you are with a group of people from your community, and will be given a sum of money on condition that you share it with an anonymous member of the group. You make an offer to share the cash, but neither you nor the other player will get a penny unless she accepts your offer. There is only one round of the game, and confidentiality is maintained. What do you think is a fair offer? In a world of only selfishness, the first player should offer as little as possible and the second player should accept it because something is better than nothing. However, when university students play the game, the most common offer is 50 percent, and the average is 40 percent. Furthermore, offers below 20 percent are almost always rejected—out of pure spite, because no one gains. Anthropologists fanned out across the world to play the game in a variety of cultures.

One conclusion that can be drawn from this study is that we generally agree on the moral requirement for fairness, which provides some hope that we agree more than we might have imagined about what is fair.

Source: Mace (2000: 248–249)

So, with the encouraging results of the study just described, we suggest some ethical rules for allowing social capital to alter the allocation of resources.

ALLOW SOCIAL CAPITAL TO INFLUENCE THE EXCHANGE OF SEGS

Allow social capital to alter the level and terms of exchange in accordance with informal institutions when significant amounts of SEGS are included in the exchange and the

scope of those included in the exchange is small. Informal institutions are rules that depend on the relationships between parties to an exchange. Thus, allowing social capital to influence exchanges is equivalent to adopting informal institutions. The strongest argument for our first rule is that formal institutions tend to limit our ability to exchange SEGs.

Suppose there was a formal institution, perhaps involving criminal sanctions for violators, that required husbands to give flowers embedded with SEGs on the first of each month to their wives in exchange for social capital? Would the wives recognize the SEGs embedded in the flowers? Perhaps, but many of the wives might wonder if the flowers were really intended for building social capital or for avoiding legal sanctions. The futility of using formal institutions to organize exchanges of SEGs, as often occurs during dating, is illustrated by the example that follows.

INTIMATE RELATIONSHIPS AND FORMAL INSTITUTIONS

Leonard Pitts Jr, a columnist for the *Miami Herald* writes:

> *It followed as naturally as broken promises follow elections, the inevitable by-product of Kobe Bryant's arrest last summer on charges of raping a 19-year-old hotel worker. She says he forced himself on her, he says the sex was consensual. A jury will decide. But a Los Angeles-based sex therapist says there's a way to avoid the next case of he-said, she-said altogether, a formal [intimate relationship] agreement.*

Then in a mocking tone, Pitts takes the position of the fly on the wall, observing a couple in a passionate moment with the man exclaiming:

> *[Before we exchange SEGs] you will need to sign this contract. Read it over and initial here and here. Oh, and you'll need to have it notarized.*

Source: Pitts Jr (2004).

Another way of justifying the need for social capital and informal institutions to allocate SEGs is to review the difficulty faced when we attempt to purchase them in formal institutional settings. While many service industries train their employees to provide courteous and respectful services, efforts to do so without genuine social capital are usually recognized as fraudulent. Amitai Etzioni observed that although there are benefits from acting in a way so that others believe you have altruism [social capital] for them, it involves high transaction costs to be a completely successful faker (Etzioni, 1988: 58).

ALLOW SOCIAL CAPITAL TO INFLUENCE THE EXCHANGE OF AVGS

The proposed rule that allows social capital to influence the exchange of SEGs within a small scope can also be applied to the exchange of AVGs. Arguments in support of this rule are similar to those used to allow social capital to alter the terms and level of trade involving SEGs.

AVGs, by definition, are mostly valued because they convey SEGs. Sometimes, we refer to AVGs as having sentimental value. Because AVGs are intended to convey SEGs, their exchange possibilities will depend on the social capital of the people involved in the exchange. If they share the social capital that embedded the objects with SEGs, then they are also likely to share attachment value for the good. If these could only be exchanged under formal institutional arrangements, their exchange value would likely be lost. The inadequacy of formal institutions to organize exchanges of AVGs is often made evident during insurance settlements.

BROKEN WATER PIPES AND A SOGGY AND SOILED BLANKET

Jan and Scott Baker left their Michigan home shortly before Christmas to spend the holidays with their daughter, son-in-law and new grandson. They had a wonderful time until their neighbors called, opening the conversation with: "We're sorry to have to call but …"

As it turned out, the Bakers' furnace had failed, and extremely cold temperatures had frozen and burst their water pipes. Their neighbors were alerted to the problem when a miniature ice pond formed in the Bakers' back yard.

So Jan and Scott returned home to a mess. Their basement was completely flooded, and other parts of the house were damaged as well. The costs of replacing the floors, repairing the pipes, and replacing damaged furniture were easily settled with the insurance company—since these items were insured at replacement cost. But then there was Jan's blanket, a beautiful hand-sewn gift from her grandmother. Growing up, she had treasured her blanket and had always imagined passing it on to her daughter. Now it was ruined. Her formal agreement with the insurance company required that they replace the soiled blanket with a new one which they agreed to do—but this was small compensation for her real loss.

In other cases, exchanges may involve objects with a high economic value which swamps the attachment value of the object. For example, a farmer may value his land partly because of his attachment to the land. But if the land is valued for development and he is required to the sell the land to the highest bidder, then those who valued the land mostly for its attachment value could not afford it. If social capital and informal institutions were not allowed to influence the terms and levels of exchange of AVGs, then only those AVGs with relatively low economic value would continue to serve as conveyors of SEGs. AVGs with very high economic value would be used for other economic purposes, and, while this may improve economic efficiency, it would not improve the overall well-being that accounts for both socio-emotional and economic values of the good.

ALLOW FORMAL INSTITUTIONS TO ORDER THE EXCHANGE OF SEGS WHEN THE SCOPE OF EXCHANGE IS LARGE

One of the requirements for allowing informal institutions to order exchanges was that the scope of those directly influenced by the exchange was small. The fact is that SEGs and AVGs may be, and often are, exchanged under conditions that influence a large number of people. Under these circumstances, the exchanges of even AVGs and SEGs should be ordered by formal institutions.

Consider the case for requiring AVGs to be sold when the conditions of the sale are determined by a formal institution. Such a case might include eminent domain—condemning an individual's home so that a public highway can be built raises an ethical question. If the home's attachment value is greater than its economic value, then shouldn't the public be required to pay the owner for the combined economic and attachment value of the property? And, if so, how would the property's attachment value be determined?

To illustrate the point, the Iowa constitution requires the payment of just compensation when private property is acquired for public use. However, just compensation is interpreted as fair market value determined by a willing buyer and willing seller who have an arm's-length relationship—a value determined by a formal institution (Iowa Department of Transportation, 2009). In other words, there is no provision in the Iowa constitution that allows for compensating individuals for their attachment value associated with condemned properties. In this case, the social capital rules seem to apply ethically and consistently with the moral value of equality.

Another example seems to be consistent with the application of the rule. Suppose that a famous person intentionally creates attachment value for objects for strictly economic gain. Then, because the scope of the object's attachment value is widespread, formal institutions require that we all pay the same price for our McDonald hamburgers and Nike footwear.

LIMIT THE INFLUENCE OF SOCIAL CAPITAL WHEN THE SCOPE OF EXTERNALITIES IS LARGE

Sometimes the scope of those involved in the exchange of SEGs and AVGs is made large through the creation of extensive externalities, justifying the application of formal institutions.

In social capital-rich networks, the production and distribution of SEGS and AVGs are likely limited, and externalities are internalized by the social capital of network members when the network is small. In such settings, members of the network are sensitive to how their actions will affect others in their social capital-rich network and voluntarily limit the production of negative externalities. On the other hand, when the activities of some create externalities for those well outside their social capital-rich network, formal institutions will be required to ensure ethical exchanges.

The framers of the US constitution recognized the difference between the domains of private and secular activities, and put in place safeguards to protect private and personal activities from being organized by formal institutions. Secular activities resulting in significant externalities were considered the proper domain of formal institutions. But those involving mostly AVGs and SEGs were left to the informal institutions—unless they produced significant levels of externalities for people outside the network. So, in the constitution we read that the federal government will make no laws that interfere with individual practices involving mostly: an establishment of religion; free exercise of speech and of the press; and the right of people to peaceably assemble, or to petition the government for a redress of grievances.

On the other hand, the distinction between activities—even protected ones—that create significant externalities and those that do not, sometimes become blurred. A case in point is the custom of wearing Muslim headscarves. For a majority of French legislators,

this activity, when practiced in a public educational setting, creates negative externalities and therefore should be subject to formal institutions.

EDUCATION VERSUS MUSLIM HEADSCARVES

The French National Assembly voted by an overwhelming majority, 494 to 36, to ban Muslim headscarves and other religious symbols from public schools. While the law has broad public support, it is certain to deepen resentment among France's large Muslim population.

Supporters of the new law claimed that wearing religious symbols in school constituted an interference of religion in the secular activities of the school. For example, the law includes a lengthy preamble demanding that public schools guarantee total equality including "coeducation in all of its teachings, particularly in sports and physical education."

France has been widely condemned in the Arab and Muslim world for the planned ban. Thousands of angry protesters from Beirut to Baghdad have held street demonstrations. In contrast, 65-year-old Telly Naar, who came to France from Morocco 40 years ago, agrees with the law. "Everyone should be able to practice religion at home. If one wants to wear the head scarf outside, fine, but not inside a school that is secular."

The issue of headscarves is a clear example of the conflict between the domain of religion and its informal institutions and secular society directed by formal institutions.

Source: Sciolino (2004); Ganley (2004).

STRICTLY LIMIT THE INFLUENCE OF SOCIAL CAPITAL FOR THOSE ACTING IN THE PUBLIC'S INTEREST

The scope of those who act in the public interest can be large. As a result, formal institutions are required to ensure that the interests of all people, including those lacking social capital, are protected. People employed by the public are guilty of nepotism if they grant special favors to family members. And a *quid pro quo* campaign contribution in return for votes would certainly be considered unethical. We would also consider it to be unethical if a congressman, senator, or the president of the United States tried to gain financially from his or her widespread social capital while in office. The reason? He or she is expected to be in the public service, not pursuing private gain. We impose similar expectations on public employees in general. Federal, state, and even local employees are paid to protect the public's interest and rise above social capital interests when allocating the public's resources.

In contrast, we generally allow people to benefit financially from their widely held social capital when they are privately employed—as long as some formal institutions regulate the means by which they convert their social capital into financial capital. Famous people whose social capital is broadly based, such as popular entertainers, high-profile sports figures, and public officials have opportunities to profit from their social capital by creating attachment value through their endorsements of products and causes. When a commercial item acquires attachment value, it earns increased profits for its

producers. Restaurant waiters attempt to do the same thing as superstars—but with only one table of patrons at a time.

ALLOW SOCIAL CAPITAL AND INFORMAL INSTITUTIONS TO MANAGE EXCHANGES NOT COVERED BY FORMAL INSTITUTIONS

Seldom, if ever, do formal institutions include enough details to prescribe all behaviors associated with a transaction. If they tried to do so, the imposed transaction costs would be high and limit the possibilities of exchanging mostly EVGs. As a result, it is generally recognized that even formal institutions depend on the adoption of informal institutions for their implementation.

However, when informal institutions pervert the intended outcome of the formal institution, then the substitution of an informal institution for a formal one creates corruption. For example, in the case of the Enron scandal, formal institutions about the use of the corporation's funds were violated, replaced by an informal institution and designed to benefit a few at the expense of the many. Moreover, the fraudulent efforts were abetted by the social capital that existed between Andrew Fastow and his wife Lea who at one time worked at Enron. Corruption cases generally have a similar pattern—informal institutions perverting the intent of formal institutions.

ALLOW SOCIAL CAPITAL TO INFLUENCE EXCHANGES WHEN FORMAL INSTITUTIONS CONFLICT WITH DEEPLY HELD MORAL VALUES

The legitimacy of formal institutions resides in their consistency with generally accepted moral values. One of the ethical challenges is when to obey formal institutions when they lack the legitimacy of a moral foundation. For example, the Bible contains an account of a Hebrew exile in Babylon, Daniel, who prayed to his God three times daily, despite King Darius's decree which forbade it. Because he disobeyed a formal institution, he was cast into a den of lions from which he was miraculously saved (Daniel 6:1–23). But an interesting question arises: should Daniel have used his social capital with King Darius to gain permission to pray openly to his own God? Daniel's violation of the formal institutions is applauded by most, mainly because the formal institution lacked moral authority, especially from the perspective of a liberal democratic polity.

The bigger question, then, is how do formal institutions gain attachment values from their connection to moral principles? The observations of a Marxist economist who visited the United States provide one possible answer.

RELIGIOUS TEACHINGS AND INSTITUTIONAL ATTACHMENT VALUES

After spending some time visiting the United States, a Marxist economist from China was asked by a Harvard colleague what he had learned that was most surprising to him. His response was: "I had no idea how critical religion is to the functioning of democracy and capitalism." He continued:

> *You don't see it because you grew up in this society. But to me it is one of the most unique things I have seen here. In this country most of you go to a church or a synagogue. These*

are institutions that people respect. When you are there, from your youngest years, you are taught that you should voluntarily obey the law. You are taught that you should respect other people's property, and not steal. You are taught to be honest, even when it's not comfortable. Religions teach that you should voluntarily pay your taxes—even though the probability that the government will catch tax cheaters is low. People believe that even if the police don't catch them if they break a law, God will surely catch them—and so they obey. Democracy works because people voluntarily obey the law.

Capitalism works because Americans have been taught in their churches that they should keep their promises and not tell lies. An advanced economy cannot function if people cannot expect that when they sign contracts, the other people will voluntarily uphold their obligations. In America, if you borrow money you repay it, without the lender having to hire thugs to force you to repay. If you order products from a company, they can ship them and trust that you will voluntarily send them a check. Capitalism works because most people voluntarily keep their promises. In many countries, banks cannot lend money to small businesses because there is no trust, and taking people who do not repay money to court is ineffective.

My friend then invited me to look around the world at those countries where, in his words, "America had naively snapped its fingers and demanded, 'We want democracy here, and we want it now!'" Unless there was already a strong religious foundation in those countries, he asserted, democracy has failed miserably. There are religions in every country, of course. But he made clear that democracy-enabling religions are those that support the sanctity of life, the equality of people, the importance of respecting others' property, and the importance of personal honesty. Those religions also had to be strong enough that they held power over the behavior of a large majority of the population. People had to believe that God would punish them even if the police and court system did not.

Source: Unpublished essay by Professor Clayton Christensen, shared with the author February 13, 2004.

ALLOW SOCIAL CAPITAL TO INFLUENCE EXCHANGES INVOLVING OWNERS OF PRIVATELY OWNED PROPERTIES WHEN ACHIEVING ECONOMIC EFFICIENCY REQUIRES IT

This rule—to allow social capital to alter the terms and level of exchanges between owners of privately owned properties—recognizes one of the fundamental consequences of social capital: that, in many circumstances, the level and equity of outcomes is improved by social capital—for those with social capital. There is clear evidence that family businesses and cooperatives among friends can often outperform arm's-length agreements.

When the scope is large, economists generally recognize that the employment of certain classes of goods is best organized with formal institutions. However, when the scope is small, social capital can often better achieve the public good that formal laws attempt to organize, but with fewer transaction costs.

Applications of Ethical Rules

In the previous section, a set of rules was proposed that described the conditions under which one could ethically allow social capital to influence the terms and level of trade. At the core of our suggested ethical rules was the appropriate domain of formal and informal institutions.

Corruption, the unethical use of one's social capital, involves the substitution of informal institutions based on personal ties (social capital) for formal institutions which are expected to be applied without regard to relationships. Unprecedented levels of corruption in which social capital has altered the terms and level of asset exchanges are evident in the economic meltdowns that have occurred in places like Russia, Asia, and Latin America. Furthermore, the problem of corruption is not confined to developing countries. In the United States the recent discovery of corruption among financial brokers has shaken the foundation of the country's financial markets and imposed huge financial and emotional costs on people disadvantaged by those in positions of influence who replaced formal institutions with informal ones because their social capital allowed it. A scandal in Malaysia illustrates how social capital can be used to benefit some and impose significant costs on others by replacing formal institutions with informal ones.

PERSONAL TIES AND CORRUPTION IN MALAYSIA

Tajudin Ramli, a close personal friend of Malaysia's Prime Minister, Mahathir Mohammad was selected in the early 1990s as Malaysian Airline Systems (MAS) CEO. But after an auspicious start and rapid growth, the airline ran into trouble, losing money and piling up debt. Many pinned the airline's woes on Mr Ramli's inept management. Others accused him of skimming profits and running the airline into the ground. Despite the obvious role Mr Ramli played in MAS's decline, the government agreed to buy out Mr Ramli's 29 percent share for seven ringgit per share—a 117 percent premium over the market price of 3.68 ringgit per share. No professional evaluation of the airline was ever done. In the words of outspoken UMNO maverick, Shahrir Abdul Samad, "We have to save the airline but need we save Tajudin too?"

Source: Shome (2002: 194).

One response to the misuse of social capital has been the introduction of ethics courses in university curriculum. Twenty-five years ago, few, if any, of the major business education curricula included a course on ethics. Today it's the odd program that does not. A related response to corruption and the misuse of social capital has been calls for increased transparency and reliance on formal institutions to govern resource allocation and distribution. However, the ethical question involving the proper use of one's social capital involves more than decreased reliance on one's social capital and increased use of formal institutions and transparency. Social capital is valuable because it can be used to good effect, and both formal and informal institutions have their place. The real questions are: when should we use our social capital and what are the proper domains of formal and informal institutions? For example, should we offer preferred treatment to friends and relatives not available to everyone? Should a teacher give an unearned passing grade to a nice student or an athlete? Should we ask for favors from an employer, teacher, or police officer who is a relative or friend of the family?

Another vexing issue related to the proper use of one's social capital is when a significant group views the formal institutions as unethical. In these circumstances, informal institutions replace formal ones—but few would view this process as corruption. Surely Rosa Parks didn't believe she acted unethically when she ignored the formal institutions that dictated proper seating on public buses.

Regarding the proper use of one's social capital, we know from earlier discussions that sometimes social capital must be present for the efficient allocation of certain kinds of resource. Indeed, internalizing the consequences of creating externalities, essential to the efficient management of externalities, is often only achieved when social capital is present. Nor do we always find it unethical to treat people differently depending on their social capital and, in some cases, our laws expressly demand it. For example, some laws recognize the special relationship between parents and their children and specify that parents have responsibilities to their own children different from their responsibilities to the children of other parents. If parents fail to provide for their children's essential needs, they can be punished by society.

Furthermore, the exchange of SEGs and AVGs must be based on relationships. Without social capital, couples are unlikely to successfully express caring for each other. If people in authority are not highly regarded, their ability to validate others is limited. During events with high socio-emotional content, SEGs are best provided by close friends and family who have social capital. In many cases, exchanges of physical gifts are motivated because the gift-giver expects SEGs in return, and, without this expectation, there would be no exchange. And all of these, for the most part, are considered to be ethical. Indeed, if these goods were required to be distributed according to formal institutions, the exchange of SEGs and AVGs would be impeded. So we ask: what is the appropriate use of social capital by the potential recipient, and what is the appropriate delivery and benefit for the potential giver? As we said before, it all depends!

Conclusion

The social capital paradigm helps frame the debate about the ethical allocation and use of resources. It does so by introducing the concept of social capital that lies at the heart of so much behavior that is considered unethical. It also helps frame the debate by clarifying the proper domains of formal and informal institutions and by distinguishing between EVGs versus SEGs and AVGs. When social capital is a significant factor in the creation of the good's value, social capital and informal institutions will likely have a significant role in ordering and providing meaning for exchanges. Finally, this chapter has pointed out that, even in the case of formal institutions, social capital plays a critical role in the creation of the attachment value necessary for their support.

One theme this chapter has adopted is that shared attachment values for ethical rules are essential to resolving ethical dilemmas. Perhaps this is why "correcting" ethical failures is so difficult. Responsibility for inculcating ethical values has traditionally been the responsibility of family, parents, religion, and community. It is a slow process, occurring over many years. If these same institutions and organizations are no longer disseminating and teaching shared values, do we believe that values can be taught and reinforced by formal, public institutions in a much shorter timeframe? For example, will

business school courses on ethics impart shared attachment values to ethical rules when attachment to these same rules does not extend broadly throughout society?

One question that emerges is: are moral values across large populations consistent enough to form formal institutions with high attachment value? Where there are conflicting moral values, conflicts in formal institutions based on these moral values cannot be far behind. For example, the definition of the formal institution of marriage as a union between a man and a woman was recently put to the vote in California. Institutional conflicts over abortion, affirmative action, gun control, and the right to consume harmful products such as tobacco show no signs of resolution—mostly because of conflicts over the moral values on which these institutions' attachment values are based.

Our point is that when attachment to such rules is not widely shared, they will have limited effect in shaping the actions of social actors. Ultimately, these values cannot be transferred in a three-month business school course. Although formal public institutions might reinforce values, they are less effective at transferring the values in the first place. Values are best transferred through informal institutions associated with family, religion, and community. Social capital thus plays an important role in the transmission of values and hence in the formation of workable ethical rules—a role that can be either positive or negative.

At this point, we inject a concern. A society that underinvests in social capital will also face decreased attachment value for its formal institutions. In this regard Harvard professor Robert Putnam describes a looming ethical crisis. Putnam claims that we are underinvesting in social capital and therefore threatening our ability to maintain cooperation and attachment value for institutions on which civil society depends.

BOWLING ALONE WITH LESS

A recent survey found that Valley residents don't volunteer, don't join clubs, don't know their neighbors, don't trust each other, and otherwise neglect the basic needs of democracy—the same woes that are plaguing America as a whole. The result: a nation of strangers who are increasingly unhappy, alienated, crime-ridden, and ever sicker (Herfmann, 2001).

The survey was an outgrowth of Robert Putnam's book, *Bowling Alone: Collapse and Revival of the American Community*, which cited bowling leagues as a symbol of civic connectedness. Putnam's research found that membership in all group activities has steadily fallen since the 1960s. That means that America's stockpile of "social capital," or trust and cooperation among citizens, has plummeted. The chief culprits include TV, sprawl, the rise of two-earner families, and increased ethnic diversity. In some sense, the survey uncovered the social capital equivalent of the digital divide: Americans lacking access to financial and human capital also lack access to social connectedness.

Putnam connects the depletion of social capital to a host of social ills: declining education standards, rising crime and use of illicit drugs, urban poverty and joblessness, economic stagnation, declining physical health, and ineffective government. Anxiety about stagnating incomes and the erosion of "the American dream" indicate that changes in the workplace have led to a breakdown in the sense of security provided by being a member of this society (Putnam, 2000).

CHAPTER 15 Social Capital and Globalization

There is just one global market today, and the only way you can grow is by tapping the global stock and bond markets for investment and selling into the global trading system what your factories produce. And the most fundamental truth about globalization is this: No one is in charge, you moron!

Thomas L. Friedman (1999: 109).

Introduction

Do far-away relationships matter? Do they matter in the global marketplace where country borders, continents, religions, race, and language separate trading partners and firms and clients? In this chapter we suggest that relationships and social capital matter even in the global marketplace. Social capital, it seems, has much to say about who produces and who buys what and where, as well as on the future of globalization.

Although there has been increasing interest and public discussion focused on globalization, the term "globalization" does not enjoy a precise, widely agreed-upon definition. We agree with the World Bank definition that globalization is everything related to international issues—cultural, political and global economic integration with its increasing "freedom and ability of individuals and firms to initiate voluntary economic transactions with the residents of other countries."[1]

In what follows, we review the technological changes that have facilitated global exchanges. Then we use the social capital paradigm to explain much of what globalization is all about—and why some believe globalization is a great good and others strongly oppose its influence. Finally, we use our understanding of social capital to evaluate the future of globalization.

How Things Have Changed

While globalization is not new (Columbus was looking for global trading opportunities), it is increasingly important because never before in the world's history has the interconnectedness of the world been so seamless and easy. Technology has made it nearly as easy to travel to Katmandu as to Indiana, to talk to a Chinese business partner

1 Cited at: http:// www.newworldencyclopedia.org/entry/globalization.html.

as to call Grandma, to ship products to Budapest as to mail a letter. Shipping and travel to the farthest reaches of the planet can be done "overnight," while communication is done at the speed of light over fiber-optic cables and satellites.

HOW THINGS HAVE CHANGED

Guglielmo Marconi, an Italian inventor, proved the feasibility of radio communication by sending and receiving radio signals in 1895. Charles Lindbergh crossed the Atlantic by air on May 20, 1927. Also in 1927, Beaver County Utah resident Philo Farnsworth transmitted a television image comprising 60 horizontal lines. The Trans-Atlantic telephone cable, inaugurated September 25, 1956, provided 30 telephone circuits to connect the United States, Great Britain, and Canada. Satellite communications began with the launch of Sputnik I in 1957. On 22 April, 1977, General Telephone and Electronics sent the first live telephone traffic through fiber optics. The first transatlantic telephone cable to use optical fiber went into operation in 1988. Before these inventions, the speed of travel, communication, and shipping was as fast as a railroad, a horse, or a ship with a strong motor or a good wind.

Source: http://en.wikipedia.org/wiki/Optical_fiber.

Peter Singer highlights the close connection between new technology and globalization:

> *Technology changes everything—that was Marx's claim, and if it was a dangerous half-truth, it was still an illuminating one. As technology has overcome distance, economic globalization has followed. In London supermarkets, fresh vegetables flown in from Kenya are offered for sale alongside those from nearby Kent. Planes bring illegal immigrants seeking to better their own lives in a country they have long admired. In the wrong hands, the same planes become lethal weapons that bring down tall buildings.*
>
> *Instant digital communication spreads the nature of international trade from actual goods to skilled services. At the end of a day's trading, a bank based in New York may have its accounts balanced by clerks living in India. The increasing degree to which there is a single world economy is reflected in the development of new forms of global governance, the most controversial of which has been the World Trade Organization (WTO), but the WTO did not create the global economy. (Singer, 2009: B7)*

Finally, globalization means, as Thomas Friedman has written, that the global electronic herd reigns. And don't expect the global herd to offer preferential terms of trade to its friends—it has none.

THE ELECTRONIC HERD HAS NO SOCIAL CAPITAL

Malaysia's Prime Minister, Mahathir Mohamad, denounced the evils of globalization, after Malaysia's stocks and currency were ravaged by global traders. Thomas L. Friedman responded:

> *The global market today is an electronic herd of anonymous stock, bond and currency traders, sitting behind computer screens. The members of this herd live everywhere there is*

a trading floor, everywhere there is a Bloomberg machine, everywhere that someone with a computer screen and modem can buy and sell Malaysian ringgit, stocks and bonds ... The electronic herd cuts no one any slack. It does not recognize anyone's unique circumstances. The herd only recognizes its own rules. But the rules of the herd are pretty consistent. The herd feeds in 180 countries, so it doesn't have time to look at you in detail. It makes snap judgments about whether you are living by its rules, and it rewards those countries that are transparent about what they are doing. The herd hates surprises.

Friedman, 1999:110.

Globalization Viewed Through the Lens of the Social Capital Paradigm

The social capital paradigm has much to say about globalization—who benefits, who doesn't, whether it is good, whether it is bad, and what its future is.

GLOBAL SOCIAL CAPITAL

As advances in travel and communication facilitate our global connections with other people and different resources, we find greater opportunities to benefit from skills quite different from our own at places farther and farther from our homes. As people have taken advantage of opportunities to benefit from global comparative advantages, local markets have been transformed into global ones, and exchanges between neighbors have been replaced with exchanges between trading partners separated by greater geographic and social distances.

According to the Social Capital Exchange Theorem, when people are connected at greater social and geographic distances from each other, the global market will value social capital goods less and economic goods more. It also means that the surplus which stabilizes exchanges between friends is reduced and, increasingly, exchanges are dictated by the global electronic herd.

Still, relationships between leaders of countries do matter. Globalization requires social capital between leaders of countries and even between peoples of countries since we won't trade with groups of people and governments for whom we have negative social capital. Perhaps this is why democracies trade with each other far more than with states with other types of governments. Similarly, we won't trade with countries in which there is little internal social capital, since, without, it these countries are less able to enforce institutions, particularly property rights.

OIL AND BAD BLOOD

All ready strained relationships between the United States and Venezuela were made less friendly when Venezuela sent packing a US embassy official accused of spying. In return, Washington expelled a Venezuelan official. This unhappy exchange was then followed by Hugo Chavez threatening to sell off all of Venezuela-owned Citgo Petroleum Corp.'s refineries and divert US oil exports to other countries.

"I could easily order the closing of the refineries that we have in the United States," Chavez said Saturday in a speech to supporters. "I could easily sell the oil that we sell to the

United States to other countries in the world ... (to) real friends and allies like China, India or Europe."

Associated Press, 2006.

GLOBALIZATION AND INSTITUTIONS

As economic power shifts from the local market to the global one, informal institutions that once managed credit at the corner store are replaced by credit sources with worldwide offices governed by formal institutions necessary to manage peoples, companies, and governments on different continents.

Globalization needed not only new communication and travel technologies for its rapid increase, but also new global institutions that could be trusted to organize world markets and relationships. Sometimes, the impetus behind the organization of these worldwide formal institutions has been multinational corporations (MNCs). These have created shared goals and allegiances among the populations of virtually every country that has led to a rising commitment to the same institutional standards.

Sometimes, global institutions have spread because of countries' and companies' reliance on resources controlled by international organizations such as the World Bank, the United Nations, and the International Monetary Fund. More recently, consumer pressure for companies to produce goods that connect to (are compatible with) other goods produced by other companies has moved us to shared standards and institutions. In still other cases, consumers have demanded that global institutions ensure product safety.

Globalization shifts the balance between informal and formal institutions. Local markets characterized by the exchange of goods between people who share social capital often rely on informal institutions to order their exchanges, to manage externalities, to define and resolve disputes over property rights, and to determine how resources should be allocated. For example, a bee farmer and an alfalfa farmer who share a border between their farms might rely on informal agreements to manage the externalities—both positive and negative—that might arise between them. But as the ownership of the farms transitions to large multinational agribusinesses, the ability to rely on informal arrangements gives way to formal contracts and oversight.

But formal institutions have their own challenges. When the focus of institutions shifts solely to profit and begins to ignore the SEGs typically found in more intimate and often informal institutions, it's possible that formal oversight will not be sufficient to regulate the institutions and keep them in check, as is evidenced with the financial debacle of AIG.

TOO BIG TO FAIL?

AIG, the world's largest insurance company, announced that it has lost US$ 61.7 billion. Put simply, AIG is financially insolvent.

Over the last decade, AIG has transformed itself from an insurance company that wrote individual policies for individual homes, autos, and life, to guaranteeing sophisticated financial instruments that aggregated loans for millions of homes, autos, and lives. The result was a

financial institution that was attached to virtually every other financial institution. When the recent housing crisis caused millions of loans to go belly-up, AIG found itself in a very difficult financial position. But so did all of many AIG's business partners. In the end, the government was forced to intervene and buy up a large majority of AIG's shares to keep the giant insurance company from imploding and taking many others with them in the vortex their destruction would have created.

The formal institutions that manage the global market are not value-free. When the IMF and World Bank intervene to assist troubled national economies, they impose a set of fiscal values on the recipient country. Local values associated with welfare, credit, political relationships, and business practices are suppressed or replaced with different values. Similar trends are evident with world religions and cultures that find their informal institutions threatened by new global, formal ones. The response is sometimes violent as people resist the encroachment of these new values and trends.

THE PRODUCTION OF SEGS AND AVGS VERSUS EVGS

As global markets have found faster and less expensive ways of producing goods of higher quality at lower prices, and as the physical and social distance between producers and consumers has widened, local exchanges that included socio-emotional goods (SEGs) and attachment value goods (AVGs) have been substituted for exchanges with strangers at lower prices. Expressed more accurately perhaps, SEGs have been wrung out of more and more exchanges. Trading at lower prices has often trumped trading locally with friends.

WAL-MART INVADES MEXICO

The largest corporation in America is now the largest employer in Mexico. Wal-Mart has invaded Mexico. Accounting for over 2 percent of Mexican GDP and 30 percent of all food sales, Wal-Mart now dominates Mexico's retail trade. Mexicans, however, are ambivalent about the changes associated with Wal-Mart's rise. On the one hand, consumers have benefited by rising competition and falling prices. Growing foreign investment and more jobs are also positives. At the same time, however, the American culture of pizza, hamburgers, and massive, but disconnected, retailers has replaced more local and traditional foods and retail channels. So far, consumers seem satisfied. As a chief NAFTA negotiator noted, "it's a total convergence."

Source: Weiner (2003).

In the past, social capital and the production of SEGs and AVGs have softened the hard hand of impersonal markets. Recall that the Social Capital Exchange Theorem claimed that when buyers and sellers include SEGs in their exchanges, the likelihood of them finding a mutually agreed price and concluding the exchange increased. The implication is that bank customers would still trade with their friends at the local bank even if the rates changed against them. Maria in Malaga, Spain, still purchased her fruits from the local *frutería* and her meat from the local *carnecería* even when they didn't offer the lowest prices. But in the wake of globalization, buyers and sellers are increasingly unknown to each other and that has left the market to search for "cheap," which often translates to a

search for the lowest-cost workers. As a result, the location where the work is performed has become less stable than before.

SKILLS, MULTINATIONAL FIRMS, AND ELECTRONICS

Southeast Asia has become the largest producer of hard disk drives in the world over the last 20 years. This dominant position has translated into jobs and growing wage earnings for workers in Singapore, Malaysia, and Thailand. But as wages have grown, companies have moved their low-end, labor-intensive manufacturing to China. However, this isn't the end of it. As wages in Malaysia and Thailand approach those in Singapore, firms have moved their high-skill jobs to Singapore to take advantage of a pool of highly skilled workers. Malaysian and Thai workers are left in a structural vice; they are neither price-competitive with China nor skill-competitive with Singapore.

Source: Ritchie (2005b).

AVGS AND GLOBALIZATION

Globalization makes it difficult to trade AVGs whose value is generated locally and valued only among local networks. However, this is not to say that sellers and buyers must share attachment value in order to trade AVGs. As long as buyers have attachment value for a product, and the attachment value is widespread, then sellers will be more than ready to supply the AVGs and reap the financial reward. For example, after 9/11, the American flag, with its high attachment value, was in great demand. Chinese producers supplied much of this demand, despite the fact that few, if any, of them had attachment value for it.

Global markets might also supply AVGs whose global attachment value is expected, rather than already established. For example, a certain brand of clothes may be expected to earn SEGs for those who wear them. Thus, prospective owners are willing to pay extra to obtain them. Also, any good for which a large number of people share attachment value can be traded in global markets.

We characterize the likelihood of EVGs replacing AVGs by using a two-dimensional graph. In Figure 15.1 the vertical and horizontal axes measure the social distance, $d_{i,j}$ ($d_{j,i}$) between agents *i* and *j*. Let social distance increase as differences between trading partners increase. These may include differences in nationality, ethnic background, first language, religion, social capital connections, attachment value, and cultural capital. As social distance increases and social capital decreases, the likelihood of exchanging SEGs and AVGs decrease, unless the demand for AVGs is extensive.

Figure 15.1 is characterized by zones. In zone 1—the zone with high levels of bonding and bridging social capital—transactions often include grants and gifts and exchanges of SEGs and AVGs. Zone 2—the zone with high levels of linking social capital—facilitates the exchange of both AVGs and EVGs Finally in zone 3, the connections between people are mostly shared attachment values to the institutions which organize their exchanges, their transactions are motivated by profit, and EVG exchanges dominate. In this zone, loyalty is replaced by the drive for reduced cost and higher profits, and this best characterizes global transactions.

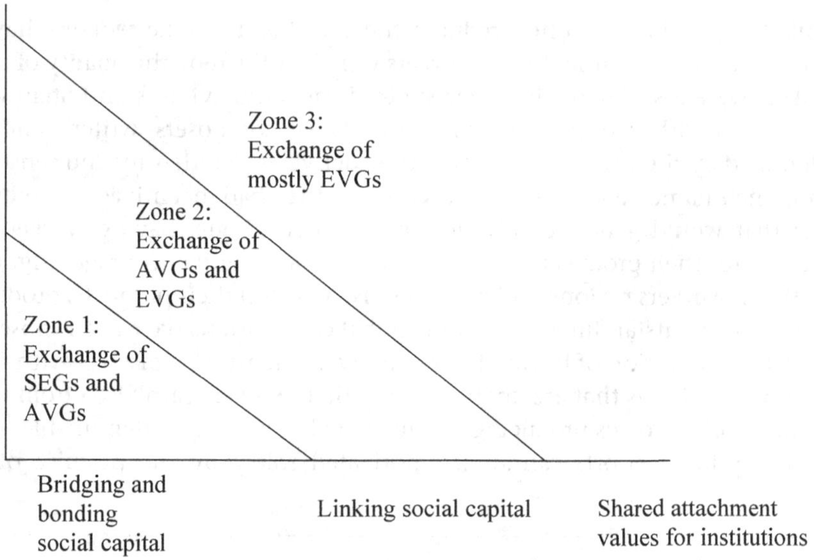

Figure 15.1 Social distance between trading partners

A significant proportion of goods and services sold in the world have attachment value. However, only those whose attachment value has become globalized are suitable for exchange in global markets. Music, movies, fashions, foods, and entertainment all have their values connected to their global attachment value. Much of world listens to music and movies produced in the United States. A significant part of the world's religious and political leaders wish this weren't the case and resist efforts to globalize attachment values.

For example, older generations in Europe are worried that their youth's attraction to McDonalds will spell the end of attachment value to their own cuisine, and they don't like the prospect.

ASSAULT ON MCDONALDS

McDonalds is now among the most recognized trademarks in the world. But not all the world loves the golden arches equally. In fact, many in Europe see McDonalds as standing for everything American and are doing whatever they can to discourage further expansion of the hamburger chain. They start by calling names, and they make:

> *... persuasive public arguments that involve taking a bad word and putting a "Mc" in front of it. Signs denouncing "McGreed," "McPollution," and corporate "McDomination" are staples of left-wing protests everywhere. And, of course, here [in the US] we're all accustomed to the complaints of welfare-state warriors who denounce so-called "McJobs," presumably because they think "job" is a bad word too.*
>
> *[But] [i]t's more than name-calling. In the last year, franchises in Switzerland, England, Belgium, China, the United States, and—surprise!—France have faced protests, boycotts, ransacking, and even bombings. In the last five years, more than 50 countries have hosted such assaults on the Golden Arches.*

Goldberg, 2005.

Similarly, globalization often reduces the attachment value workers have for the goods they produce. In earlier times, workers were identified by the quality of their work. Shoemakers were associated with their shoes. Stradivarius violins and Steinway pianos were associated with very best craftsmanship. Great composers, writers, and artists all were identified by their work from which they derived their identity and sense of worth. By having their names associated with their work, they had incentives to produce quality products that would generate SEGs for them. Interestingly, having workers associate themselves with their products creates attachment value, and encourages higher product quality. When workers no longer identify themselves with their products, product quality suffers. The most outstandingly successful global corporations have been those that have perpetuated the tradition of having their employees identify themselves with the quality of their products. Firms that are unable to help their workers earn SEGS from their work, even if that work involves producing for the global market, are often unable to compete because exceptional efforts cannot be motivated solely by the promise of financial rewards.

BUY THE UNION LABEL

One effort to increase the connection between workers and their products is the union label:

> *The union label shows that labor and management have signed a binding contract, with each side guaranteeing their best—their best work, their best compensation and their best benefits. It's a "win-win" arrangement for everyone—labor, management, consumers and the community, where the economy benefits from the paychecks and taxes of well-paid workers.*

The question remains however, is the union label a marketing tool or an attempt to create a sense of pride in the workers for the quality of their product? Whatever the answer, the implied plea is clear: look for the Union Label whenever and wherever you can!

Source: http://www.unionlabel.org.

Finally, there are important AVGs with broadly shared attachment values that can be traded in the global marketplace and at a profit. Nike shoes endorsed by David Beckham or Allen Iverson, while not universally in demand, have enough shared attachment to command a premium price among shoes. Flowers are enough of a universal gift that their cultivation and sales have become a worldwide phenomenon, with orchids grown in Thailand shipped to Peoria, Illinois, to be worn at school proms. As the global popularity of the flowers rises, so do their price and, ironically, their value as a gift embedded with SEGs.

NETWORKS AND GLOBALIZATION

Local markets can be characterized by distributions of social capital that reside in networks. In these markets participants exchange SEGs, AVGs, and EVGs by relying on combinations of formal and informal institutions that order and give meaning to

exchanges. Globalization occurs when local markets are combined into larger networks and markets that extend beyond national borders, reducing the social capital between buyers and sellers in the network.

The globalization of markets doesn't necessarily eliminate local markets and local networks; however, it does place them under considerable pressure to offer levels and terms of trade comparable with those offered in the global economy and global networks where mostly EVGs are exchanged. Local markets may insulate themselves, to some degree, from the effects of global markets by employing their social capital. By taking advantage of their social capital they often can trade at levels and terms distinct from those offered in the global markets. Or local markets may insulate themselves by offering AVGs and SEGs not provided in global markets.

An illustration of local markets insulating themselves from global markets is provided by some German brewers. When Germany joined the common market, it could no longer protect its brewers from foreign competition, as it had previously, by prohibiting any ingredients other than yeast, water, and barley. But they maintained sales by appealing to a German identity in its traditional ingredients.

As local market participants trade more with global partners and increasingly have their local transactions ordered by formal institutions, they may participate less in their local networks, sacrificing SEGs and AVGs and investments in locally distributed social capital. So it might be the case that, as we have less reason to exchange economic goods with our neighbors and more reasons to trade with Wal-Mart, we may soon notice fewer volunteers willing to manage the local little league team or fewer people interested in joining local bowling leagues.

MARKET POWER AND GLOBALIZATION

Another corollary of the Social Capital Exchange Theorem is that as globalization increases the scope of markets, formal institutions will become more important and informal ones less so as social capital between exchange partners decreases. Moreover, as globalization replaces informal institutions with formal ones, power that once resided in local networks may be lost. Such was the experience of the local tribes in Borneo who found themselves powerless to protest the consequences of globalization.

INDONESIAN RAIN FORESTS

The jungle forests on the island of Borneo are home to the local Asli and Iban tribes. These forests, however, are much more than the raw materials from which these peoples build their homes. They are a source of food, home to the gods, and key to happiness and well-being. But when logging companies found they could cheaply and quickly harvest the forests to meet the growing world demand for plywood, the native tribes could do little to stem the tide. Since the plywood companies ascribed nothing more than economic value to the wood, within a few short decades most of the hardwood stands of timber were felled, with little promise that regeneration would be effective. In the end, the formal institutions managed by central governments in Malaysia and Indonesia completely supplanted the indigenous and local informal institutions used to manage life in the forests for generations.

Source: Poffenberger (1997).

Globalization: Good or Bad?

So, is globalization good or bad? In no other debate are the lines for and against so ambiguous. At the World Trade Organization meetings in Seattle in the late 1990s, blue-collar workers and farmers sided with business executives and idealistic students to oppose increasing free trade. On the other side, academics, idealistic students, business executives, and the majority of middle-class consumers favored even more global interaction. Whose position is correct? Consider both the advantages and disadvantages of globalization.

On the positive side, globalization has made the world's inhabitants more aware of each other's plight. Fortunately, this increased awareness has often produced an increase of global social capital and a reallocation in favor of the world's poor. An illustration of this global sympathy has been the global efforts to protect young women from the brutal circumcision practices of many African and Middle East nations; vaccinate millions of children for polio, smallpox, and other fatal diseases; and provide HIV drugs to those infected with AIDs around the world. Volunteer organizations like the Peace Corp and Médécins sans Frontières work to improve social and physical infrastructure, and extend and preserve lives through health and dental care. Churches and civic groups provide food and direct assistance to the needy worldwide.

Globalization has also provided new and more efficient channels for the transfer of technology. Infrastructure technologies for water delivery, waste management, telecommunications, and transportation are common in all but the very poorest of countries and, in many cases, have leapfrogged the more developed countries. Cell phone technology is far more advanced in Thailand than in the US. For example, consumers can purchase Subscriber Identify Mobile (SIM) cards with prepaid minutes that can be inserted into any compatible handset, making usage of the system easy, flexible, and inexpensive. With SIM cards, telephone users can call around the world.

Made possible by new technologies, globalization has had an unambiguously positive impact on aggregate world wealth. As well-known economist Dani Rodrik noted, openness to trade and investment is now viewed as "the most potent catalyst for economic growth known to humanity" (quoted in Hughes and MacDonald, 2004: 110). By extending the size of the market to a global community we increase opportunities for specialization and trade that should, if Adam Smith was right, lead to more efficient use of resources. Technological advances are shared around the world, and consumers benefit from lower prices and improved products (World Bank, 2002). Moreover, many argue that growing interaction and interdependence reduces the threat of global conflict (Bueno de Mesquita et al., 1999).

However, the benefits of globalization have been uneven. Countries do not participate in the global economy equally. One reason for this is that, to participate in the global economy, one must be willing to accept global institutions. Herein lies one of globalization's problems. Many countries not only lack attachment value for global institutions, but also lack attachment value for even local formal institutions. Corrupt governments and countries with fractured social capital reduce attachment to formal institutions and are consequently excluded from participation in the global economy. Furthermore, because of this exclusion, countries which lack transparent and enforced formal institutions suffer economic hardship.

Those countries that are increasingly marginalized in the world economy are home to over 2 billion people. Most of these countries are in Africa and have experienced

declining per capita incomes, rising poverty, falling participation in the world economy, and rampant disease. Others are concerned with losing local jobs, cultural identity, and traditional ways of life.

FOREIGN INVESTMENT AND CORRUPTION

Chad and Bangladesh were considered the most corrupt countries in the world by Transparency International's 2005 *Corruption Perceptions Index*. In addition, *The Human Poverty Index* reports that Chad is the fifth poorest country in the world, with 80 percent of the population living below the poverty line. The GDP (PPP) per capita was estimated as US$1,500 in 2005. The effects on foreign investment of years of civil war are still felt today, as investors who left Chad between 1979 and 1982, have only begun to regain confidence in the country's future since 2000 when major foreign direct-investment projects in the oil sector began, boosting the country's economic prospects

Source: UNDP, 2009.

Limits to Globalization

Much has written about the power of the global markets and the forces behind globalization. However, many local markets continue to exist, and there is considerable resistance to the sweep of global markets. This conflict between local and global markets is reflected in the title of Thomas Friedman's popular book, *The Lexus* (an EVG) *versus the Olive Tree* (an AVG). The outcome of this conflict, however, is anything but clear. There are, to be sure, some signs that natural limits to globalization exist. We assess a few of these below.

IMMOBILE RESOURCES

Some things simply cannot be shipped overseas. We still have national institutions and attachment value for things that are home-made. Furthermore, there are few, if any, truly global institutions. Although we have some international agencies, such as the United Nations, the IMF, and the World Bank, none of these has truly global powers that supersede the rights of nations. Ultimately, nations still exercise a monopoly on the use of force within their borders; no force outside the nation has legitimacy within it. Consequently, war is still the only means by which one state can force another to do its will. It is also true that the global economy cannot survive without functioning and strong national economies to provide necessary services and institutions, especially those that manage and regulate finances and trade. No other entities are capable of producing the public goods that are essential for globalization. Most of the institutions that order and give meaning to exchanges are national, state, or local laws.

Finally, there are often natural limitations on mobility of resources. Most businesses are simply not able to move their operations to take advantage of location-specific assets, such as low-wage labor. It would be impossible to move McDonalds in North Dakota to the island of Negros in the Philippines to take advantage of lower wage rates. Nor could

the dairy cows in Wisconsin be moved to the Congo without drastically diminishing output.

A LACK OF ATTACHMENT VALUES FOR FORMAL INSTITUTIONS

Sometimes, those left behind by the global market may act to interfere with its operation and reinstitute local ways of doing business. They interfere with the formal institutions because these lack attachment value—and they resent them. For many of these people, often the poorest members of society, globalization is another word for exploitation. Consider the case of Bolivia.

BAD BLOOD IN BOLIVIA

> *The many Indian protesters who choked the streets and highways of this Andean nation … may be poor and speak broken or accented Spanish, but they have a powerful message.*
>
> *It is this: no to the export of gas and other natural resources; no to free trade with the United States; no to globalization in any form other than solidarity among the downtrodden peoples of the developing world.*

Part of their resentment results from their ancestors' earlier experience with globalization centuries ago with the age of exploration and the arrival of European colonizers:

> *"Globalization is just another name for submission and domination," [said] Nicanor Apaza, 46, an unemployed miner …*
>
> *"After 21 years, the economic model in place has not solved the problems of poverty and social exclusion," said Carlos Toranzo of the Latin American Institute for Research.*

Source: Rohter (2003).

LOCAL ATTACHMENT VALUES

An important implication of the Social Capital Exchange Theorum is that locally created and valued AVGs are unlikely to trade in global markets. Indeed, one could say that they are unlikely to trade outside the local market in which their attachment value exists. Thus, the size of the market in which AVGs are traded will depend on the network of those who share the attachment value. The reason for the limitation on the size of the market is the following. If the economic value of an asset is roughly equivalent in two markets, but, in one market, the object has attachment value, those who lack the attachment value for an object are unlikely to pay more for the object than its economic value. Second, when people trade without social capital, they are unable to pay for AVGs using their social capital. Thus, locally supported and created AVGs will of necessity trade in local markets.

SACRED WATERS AND PARCHED PLAINS

Lake Titicaca is a beautiful blue lake that sits on the Bolivian Altiplano. For the indigenous population who comprise over 60 percent of the Bolivian population, the waters of Lake Titicaca

are sacred and not for sale. In the language of social capital, they are embedded with SEGs and have acquired high attachment value. The high altitude makes the land near the lake relatively unproductive, permitting only limited cultivation and grazing. Yet the industrious Bolivians who live there have figured out how to eke out an existence.

On the other side of the Bolivian Altiplano are the parched plains of Chile, lacking only water to become productive. The Chileans would like to purchase water from Lake Titicaca, and, given that Bolivia is the one of the poorest nations in South America, it might reasonably be assumed that a mutually beneficial exchange could be arranged. But not so: sacred waters are not for sale, and especially not for sale to Chileans who, the Bolivians claim, illegally control their access to the Pacific Ocean.

An example of an AVG that currently cannot be traded in a global market are the waters of Lake Titicaca, located in the Altiplano of Bolivia.

CHEAP SOCIAL CAPITAL AND HARD TIMES

History has taught us that globalization is often limited by the formation of "cheap" social capital and "hard" times. During protracted economic downturns, those adversely affected often appeal to their local and national leaders to take care of their own first. Surviving locally appears to trump prospering globally.

END TAX BREAKS AND SAVE JOBS

It was an emotionally charged moment when President Barack Obama addressed a joint session of the US Congress for the first time during his administration. It was also a charged moment because of failing economies in the US and around the world. Congress and the public waited to hear how he proposed to help solve the problem. President Obama suggested several strategies for addressing the economic crisis, including keeping jobs at home: "We will restore a sense of fairness and balance to our tax code by finally ending the tax breaks for corporations that ship our jobs overseas." His proposal to keep jobs at home brought most members of Congress to their feet to cheer. The response from overseas was predictable: "Policies of protectionism will only hinder the revival of the world economy," said Suresh Senapaty, executive director and chief financial officer of the Indian company, Wipro Ltd.

Source: Joshi (2009).

The easiest form of social capital to form is cheap social capital—social capital that unites people around what they perceive to be is a shared threat. Unfortunately, hard times offer rich opportunities to blame someone—almost anyone different from ourselves—for

XENOPHOBIA IN SOUTH AFRICA

Last month, during two weeks in May, 2008, a series of attacks took place all over South Africa. In a clash between the poorest of the poor, gangs of local black South Africans descended on informal settlements and shanty towns, armed with clubs, machetes and

torches, and attacked immigrants from Mozambique, Malawi and Zimbabawe. Locals accused these immigrants of taking jobs away from them, among other grievances. Over the course of those two weeks, over 60 foreigners were killed, several hundred injured, and many thousands of immigrants are now displaced, or are returning to their home countries. Dealing with the aftermath of the attacks has become a large problem for South Africa—prosecuting attackers, accommodating refugees, dealing with a labor shortage, political damage control, seeking to address root causes, and some soul-searching are all taking place.

Taylor, 2008.

the current conditions. And immigrants, one of the faces of globalization, may be under increasing threat.

Conclusion

Technology has facilitated global communication and exchange. The wealth-creating opportunities created by specialization and trade have provided the incentive for globalization, and the formation of global institutions has provided the framework for conducting global exchanges. Yet, in so many ways, social capital will determine who buys and sells in the global markets and how the benefits of globalization will be distributed.

At the heart of the debate about whether globalization is good or bad is the unevenness of the distribution of its benefits, which often depends on the transparency of its local institutions and local social capital. A painful lesson for many is that the electronic herd which organizes so many of the global transactions has no friends.

Another key component of the globalization debate is the possibility of producing and exchanging SEGs and AVGs, given the global market's preference for trading EVGs. Nevertheless, some goods have global attachment value and can be traded globally, and, in some cases, these may threaten and sometimes replace attachment values for locally produced goods.

Of course, the future of globalization depends on finding an appropriate balance between economic efficiency and the exchange of EVGs and the softer side of markets that value SEGs and EVGs and, unlike the electronic herd, has, and values, friends. Certainly, too much social capital and too few formal institutions can slow development and growth. On the other hand, a worldwide economy, focused on exchanges of mostly EVGs, leaves us socio-emotionally empty.

The challenge is to find the proper balance between the soft glove of social capital and the hard hand of global capitalism. Companies must remain profitable to survive. If the soft glove of social capital requires preferential treatment that leaves companies and corporations unprofitable, they will cease to exist. On the other hand, the hard hand of market capitalism and survival of the economically fittest destroys local attachment values and creates significant income inequality. Is it worth it? Are there general principles for establishing the balance between the soft glove of social capital and hard hand of free-market capitalism? And if there are general rules for establishing this balance, could we agree to adopt them?

CHAPTER 16 *Social Capital and the Distribution of Political Power*

Politics is all about who gets what, when, and how.

Harold Lasswell.

Politics, n. Strife of interests masquerading as a contest of principles.

Ambrose Bierce, *The Devil's Dictionary* (1911).

Introduction

Politics is the contest for, and the management of, political power. Political power is the capacity to influence who gets what, when, and how through the administration of public resources and the creation of political institutions. This chapter describes how social capital can alter the distribution and exercise of political power.

The kinds, distribution, and exercise of political power in any society are shaped by kinds and distributions of social capital in several important ways. First, the social capital that rulers have for the civil society determines the benefits (goods and services), if any, the government provides for the people. Next, social capital shared among the civil society determines the capacity of the civil society to collectively organize and act. If civil society enjoys social capital, the members of that society can more easily generate the power to check or limit the power of their rulers, either by election, constitution, or, in extreme cases, by revolution. Finally, social capital that the civil society has for the rulers provides the resources and capacity (legitimacy) for the rulers to exercise their political power.

When social capital is high among and between the rulers and the civil society, governments are more likely to be democratic. Democracies tend to provide more public, or high exclusion cost (HEC) goods for their people (Baum and Lake, 2003), are built upon checks and balances among ruling elites enforced by the civil society, and derive legitimacy from the civil society through elections and constitutions. When social capital is low among and between the rulers and the civil society, governments are more likely to be autocratic. Autocracies provide fewer public goods and derive their legitimacy from creating fear through repressive measures.

Certainly with any large society, rulers cannot develop social capital with every citizen. Instead, those in power attempt to create attachment value for the institutions (including symbols) that represent power. When attachment values for these institutions fall below certain levels *and* social capital among the ruled rises beyond certain levels, revolution, coup, or other violent overthrow is likely. Examples abound that illustrate how societies revolt or implode when their rulers cannot claim social capital from the ruled and their institutions lack attachment value.

Revolutions which disempowered their rulers, like those in the US at the end of the eighteenth century, France at the turn of the eighteenth century, Russia in 1917, China in 1949, Vietnam between 1950 and 1970, and Iran in the mid-1970s, are examples of what happens when the civil society loses attachment value for political institutions and social capital for their rulers. In contrast, where attachment values for political institutions remain high *and* social capital among the civil society for those in power is high, political transition through peaceful mechanisms, such as democratic vote, is more likely.

A framework for the analysis of social capital's influence on political systems is summarized in Figure 16.1. The distribution of political power reflected in alternative political regimes depend on the kinds and level of social capital among and between the political regimes (the rulers) and civil society (the ruled). The kinds and distributions of social capital and political power will in turn influence the flows of goods from the political regimes to civil society and the source and kind of political legitimacy supplied to the political regimes by civil society. These flows of goods and legitimacy and centers of social capital are described in Figure 16.1.

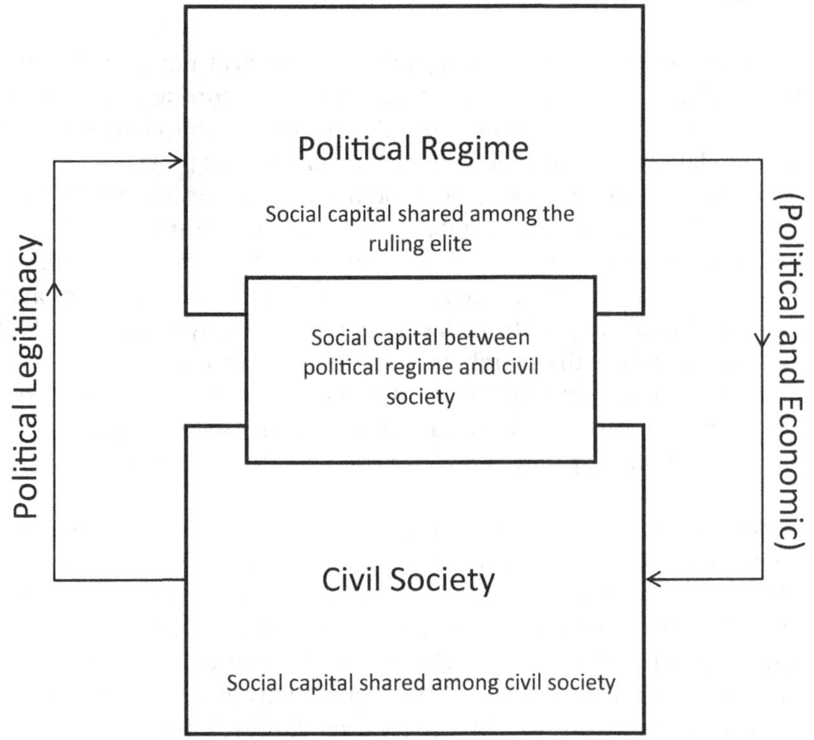

Figure 16.1 Politics and social capital

In the remainder of this chapter we describe in more detail how social capital influences social, economic, and political exchanges among groups of rulers and civil society. We then apply these insights to several different political systems.[1] As will become clear, social capital among and between the civil society and the ruling elite are important determinants of the distribution of political power and economic and other outcomes in the political system.

Social Capital Among the Ruling Elite

Social capital among ruling elites can be understood as shared attachment to political institutions, especially those that define transitions of power. In political systems where elites do not have attachment value for political institutions, transitions of power are forced and often bloody. Those in power do all they can to remain in power, including replacing formal institutions with informal ones if necessary. In such systems, conflict and competition between those in power and those seeking political power is high, often resulting in civil war, coups, and revolutions.

In political systems where elites—both those that rule and those that wish to rule—agree on a set of formal institutions that govern an orderly transfer of power, ruling elites can better concentrate on governing rather than staying in power. Institutions that create an orderly transfer of power also define the conditions upon which power can be reacquired. If both those who rule and those who wish to rule have attachment value for those institutions, the requirements for acquiring power are codified. Inter-elite conflict is more muted in these societies. Competition focuses on the opportunity for transition, not on the elimination of other groups. As a result, violent political contestation is rare.

Sometimes, bonding social capital ties between the rulers of different countries have been used to create foundations of legitimacy. The creation of bonding social capital has often been attempted through familial or marriage ties. History has shown, however, that blood relations have rarely dampened intrigue for power. Nor can social capital bonds found in relationships such as marriage extend easily to a large political community.

Social Capital Between Ruling Elites and Civil Society

The social capital that ruling elites have for the civil society is reflected by the amount of HECs government provides for the people. Goods are purely HECs if they meet two criteria: first, one person's consumption of the good does not hinder another's consumption (nonrival); and, second, no one can be kept from consuming the good (exclusion). Given this definition, pure HECs are rare. But even those goods that have some exclusionary and nonrival qualities can be usefully thought of as HECs. Such goods include roads, clean air, education, drinkable water, power, and other infrastructure. Perhaps the most well known of these goods is national security. The reason why HECs are such an important reflection of the social capital that the rulers have for the ruled is that they are intended to benefit the civil society rather than buy the allegiance of a focused privileged group of

1 We chose the political systems we did purely for illustrative purposes, and do not suggest that this is an exhaustive treatment of all possible variations of political systems.

beneficiaries. When ruling elites allow institutions that encourage participation by civil society in political processes, particularly economic policy, HECs are far more likely.

Political legitimacy is based on the right that the civil society gives to the rulers to rule. If we assume that political leaders desire most of all to stay in power, then the ruling elite must either obtain social capital from the civil society and attachment to institutions or rule through fear. One way in which rulers have attempted to develop their social capital with the civil society is through buying it.[2] Many rulers generate social capital by providing goods—e.g., roads, schools, ports, and so forth. On other occasions, rulers have attempted to develop their social capital with the civil society by claiming an external mandate, such as divine selection and sanction. This approach was taken by the early Asian emperors in China, Japan, and Korea, but also by Rome, and Islamic and other theological governments.

History, however, has shown that the social capital, legitimacy, and attachment to institutions that the civil society has provided the ruling elites are highly correlated with the country's economic prosperity. And a country's economic prosperity is tied to its ability to specialize and trade. To the extent that political regimes foster trade, economies flourish and rulers earn legitimacy.

Finally, legitimacy for the rulers and attachment to a country's institutions are often associated with attachment to symbols of the nation. This "nationalism," or devotion to, and pride in, the cultures or interests of a particular state, is often tenuous if the citizens of the country do not widely share the same cultures or interests. As Benedict Anderson (1989) recognized, nationalism is often equivalent to "imagined communities." Only when people exiled from their homelands met in foreign locales did they recognize the components of their shared nationalism.

Relationships associated with social capital create networks of exchanges that solidify and unify the perception and valuation of culture, rights, and mores. Rather than being purely imagined, shared attachment *defines* more universal meanings of nationalism. Indeed, without social capital, a shared culture, and attachment to symbols of the nation, nations frequently disintegrate into smaller, usually communal, components. With social capital, however, the civil society, even with disparate cultures and histories, can create national unity, as in Malaysia.

HOW DOES MALAYSIA DIFFER FROM KOSOVO?

Sixty percent of Malaysians are Malay, 35 percent are Chinese, 9 percent are Indians, and the rest are something else. But, except for a short outbreak of relatively small-scale violence in 1969, the country has enjoyed ethnic harmony. Part of the reason for this harmony has been the formation of institutions designed to redistribute wealth from the well-off Chinese to their less fortunate Malay neighbors. To make redistribution palatable, the government energetically fosters economic growth. Ironically, the policies that have forced Chinese companies to redistribute wealth have also encouraged the formation of social capital among the civil society by encouraging the various ethnic groups to work together to solve the country's problem. Thus, although the various ethnic groups differ by religion, history, and skin color, frictions are resolved politically rather than militarily.

2 Important insights into the concept of side payments and their influence on political outcomes can be found in Waldner, 1999.

WHEN RULERS AND RULED HAVE LINKING SOCIAL CAPITAL

Linking social capital, often found in democratic regimes, not only fosters the distribution of political power among the people, but also encourages the distribution of property rights among the civil society. The ability to acquire and maintain private property means that the state must assume a regulatory, rather than a stewardship, role over economic resources that devolve to the owners of the property. With linking social capital, individuals own property, SEGs, and rights to other goods and services. Furthermore, their institutions allow and encourage participation in the political system. To the extent that the state owns or maintains goods, it does so as a fiduciary stewardship for the people.

Linking social capital between the civil society and the ruling elite elevates the nation above ethnic, family, clan, and other differences. The rights preserved by the direct participation of the people against the state creates patriotism, a higher form of nationalism characterized not by mere devotion to the state, but by a love for what the political relationship between the state and people produces. When the products of a participatory regime are challenged, as happened in the US on September 11, 2001, patriotism naturally increases and can be manipulated for various purposes. As people participate in the government, either directly in policy formation and implementation or through elected representatives, social capital for the nation's rulers increases.

WHEN RULERS AND THE RULED HAVE BRIDGING SOCIAL CAPITAL

Bridging social capital between the ruling elites and selected groups in the civil society is characteristic of paternalistic regimes. In these cases, bridging social capital leads to allocations of resources based on considerations of political support: governments allocate goods and rights in proportion to the support they receive from particular groups. Favored groups get new schools, repaired roads, more business investment, and greater liberty at the expense of less favored groups. In these systems, the civil society is not engaged in the political system. Who gets what is determined by the ruling elites, who act in their own interest and in the interests of the objects of their bridging social capital.

When the relationship between the rulers and ruled is characterized by bridging social capital, legitimacy is based almost entirely on the spoils of government. To keep different groups within civil society connected is possible, but requires a balanced distribution of resources. Even if groups remain part of a single nation-state, however, each group may perceive its nationalism differently from others. Nor is it necessary for the subgroups to intermingle or assimilate to maintain their national cohesion as long as the groups are all benefited by the state. However, if the distribution of benefits among the different groups is perceived as unfair and unequal, the cohesion in the state will be damaged, and the state will deteriorate.

WHEN RULERS AND RULED HAVE BONDING SOCIAL CAPITAL

Finally, although bonding social capital can be found within family and inherited power structures, it does not extend to relationships between the ruling elite and the civil society in any regime now in existence. This, however, does not mean it has never existed. This bonding relationship between and among the rulers and the civil society has been the

goal of many societies. Muslims, Jews, and Christians are all familiar with the story of Enoch, whose city implemented a system of government in which the people were "of one heart and one mind." The bonding social capital behind this "oneness" facilitated an allocation based on consecration rather than on stewardship. Consecration meant that all things were had in common among the people. Because Enoch's people were one, there was no need for the allocation of goods for political purposes. And their at-one-ment ensured that all goods were allocated on the basis of need, resulting in there being "no poor among them."

WHEN RULERS AND RULED HAVE NO SOCIAL CAPITAL

When the ruling elites have no social capital for the civil society, ruling elites become predatory and work to transfer resources from society to themselves. This reallocation from the civil society to government includes intangible goods, such as rights, as well as tangible ones.

Without social capital, rulers rule without legitimacy. Autocratic rulers must therefore rely on fear as the primary motivator for citizen compliance, which sows the seeds of discontent and revolution. Even if the revolution is not violent, when citizens have the opportunity they will abandon the ruling class, as happened in East Timor.

INDONESIA AND EAST TIMOR

Unlike the rest of Indonesia, which was colonized by the Dutch, the eastern portion of the island of Timor was colonized by the Portuguese. When the Dutch conceded independence to a new Indonesia in 1949, East Timor was not included. In 1975 Indonesia's invasion of East Timor interrupted East Timor's processes of decolonization and independence from Portugal. But because of the force imposed on the East Timorese people, they never considered the Indonesian government as legitimate—the East Timorese never gave the Indonesian rulers legitimization. In 1999 this lack of legitimacy led the East Timorese, to vote in a referendum to become independent from Indonesia. Almost 30 years of Indonesia's rule of force had created no attachment value among the East Timorese people for Indonesian institutions—social or political. When the opportunity for independence was granted, the people took it.

When the rulers exploit and discourage participation in government by the civil society, loyalty devolves to sub-state units, like ethno-linguistic groupings, religions, clans, and families. Bonding social capital among subgroups, which directs loyalties to units other than the state, is the most likely outcome,. In her interesting book, *World on Fire* (2004), Amy Chua documents how revolutions have all had something in common. A small minority controlled most of the wealth, which often led to a loss of social capital with the masses.

When there is little or no social capital between and among the ruling and ruled, states become increasingly anarchic. Somalia, for example, has no legitimate single government, a tremendously fragmented civil society, and little, if any, social capital between groups in power and individuals in society.

SOMALIA AND PIRATES

Pirates are making a comeback. No, not the kind with eye patches and parrots, but a new breed of buccaneer who sail the waters of Eastern Africa looking for large oil tankers to hi-jack. Once commandeered, the pirates take the vessels to Eyl, a boomtown city that is a haven for pirates.

The problem is that Somalia's 14 provisional governments in the last 17 years have been unable to create any legitimacy among the civil society. Each has been highly corrupt and unable or unwilling to provide either economic goods or protection to society. Consequently there is no political legitimacy for the central government. Instead, political legitimacy has become fragmented among a large number of local warlords, each of whom control a portion of the country and are highly competitive. Safe harborage for pirates in Eyl is simply a matter of paying off the local warlord, who in turn has created a city that caters to the pirates' every need. How long Somalia can remain a country under these anarchic political conditions remains to be seen.

Social Capital Among the Civil Society

As linking social capital among the civil society increases, political institutions emerge that rely on the power of the people to limit state power, leading ultimately to constitutional government. As Tocqueville observed of late nineteenth-century America, "the social state ... is eminently democratic. It has ... a high degree of equality. Even the seeds of aristocracy were never planted" (1966: 50). High levels of social interaction among the colonists created linking social capital, which allowed the people to create a constitution that limited state powers. Although institutions within the government check and balance one another, the people were the great and last check through their power to choose and dismiss their leaders.

The civil society's ability to create its own laws and select its rulers fostered much higher levels of attachment value for institutions than would have been the case if laws and rulers had been imposed by an unelected ruler. Representative democracy depends on a system of relationships in which the ruler and the civil society are esteemed equally. In fact, today's rulers were yesterday's civil society, and, within broad limits, yesterday's civil society can become tomorrow's rulers. "Life, liberty, and the pursuit of happiness" depends on each individual being able to defend these rights from the ruling elite and the institutions that form the state. On the other hand, the state is the only defense against rapacious neighbors. To have property rights is to be able to call upon the state for the protection of one's right to property. And any state that cannot monopolize violence cannot create or protect rights to property.

Although a full explanation of why early America had such high levels of linking social capital among its citizens and between the citizens and government is complex and beyond the scope of this chapter, an analysis by two economic historians, Engermann and Sokoloff (2002), suggests that economic conditions of small, "yeoman" farmer-owned plots in the northern states demanded high interaction, competition, and institutions to mitigate conflicts. We can take this analysis further and suggest that this constant interaction and assimilation created sympathies for various groups that translated into

improved transactions, shared attachment to new institutions, and improved collective action.

In the southern states, plantation agriculture promoted few, large landholders and myriad slaves and poor landless farmers. The resulting relationships were more asymmetrical, less prone to assimilation, and had, we assume, less sympathy with, and thus shared less attachment to, political institutions, which may explain why the South was willing to leave the Union and was unwilling to grant the necessary power to a central government to effectively wage the Civil War.

Social capital among the civil society strongly influences the ability of rulers to impose their will. Less social capital among the civil society makes it easier for rulers to fragment the population, play the fears of one group off against another, and impose their rule and will. As groups in society connect and build sympathy one for another, it is easier to act collectively. Indeed, in his important analysis Robert Putnam showed how Northern Italy with its dense civic connections was able to organize economically more efficiently than groups in Southern Italy, which lacked such connections (Putnam, Leonardi, and Nanetti, 1993). The ability of groups to organize effectively increases their ability both to demand services and goods from government and to circumscribe the activities of that government.

These same mechanisms can also work for smaller groups. In some cases, although a majority of the population has social capital for existing political institutions, it's possible for smaller, elite classes not currently in power to use shared social capital to come together to limit the power of the ruling elite. For example, North and Weingast (1989) showed that when merchant and banking groups organized effectively, they were able to limit the power of the king. On the other hand, when groups do not share social capital, organization is much more difficult. This can be seen in the case of slaves from many different tribes thrown together in the same working conditions in South America in the sixteenth century.

SOUTH AMERICAN MINE MANAGEMENT

In 1570 there were close to 30,000 slaves working in Brazil for the Portuguese rulers. By the turn of the century this number had risen to over 4 million. But although slaves outnumbered their masters, sometimes by thousands to one, the slaves were unable to act collectively to overcome their masters. While the slaves certainly lacked guns and technology to oppose the Portuguese, they also lacked the linking social capital required to act collectively to move against the invading colonists. Part of the problem was that many of the slaves were imported from Africa. When these slaves were mixed with the local Indians, an inability to communicate and intermingle meant that social capital was almost non-existent, further exacerbating their difficulties in acting collectively.

Political Systems and Social Capital

Emerging in the mid-seventeenth century, nation-states are a relatively recent social invention. States created identifiable borders, and those living within the borders were managed by a particular political system that reflected a particular distribution of political power. These political systems vary in the protection, rights, and goods they offer citizens

and the responsibilities they demand in return. In what follows, we offer a simplified description of the relationships between rulers and the civil society and their connections to social capital distributions, rights, and responsibilities, and economic systems for specific political systems described in Table 16.1. The political systems we have chosen to describe illustrate our argument that social capital alters the distribution and exercise of political power.

Table 16.1 State types and social capital

	Types of governments			
	Despotic autocracy	**Monarchical autocracy**	**Pseudo-democracy**	**Liberal democracy**
State-to-society relationship	Predatory	Paternalistic	Developmental	Regulatory
Social capital between the ruled and rulers	Little if any	Bridging/ Bonding	Bridging	Linking
Rights of civil society	Few if any	Limited	Limited	Constitutionally specified
Responsibilities	Few if any	Limited	Moderate	Extensive
Economic system	Government-controlled or barter	Combined trade and import substitution	Export-oriented trade	Open trade*

*Although most developed liberal democracies tend to protect agricultural industries.

DESPOTIC AUTOCRACY

Autocratic despots most often come to power through force, usually through a violent and bloody contest between rival elite factions. Their legitimacy is often based on "cheap social capital"; the shared kernel is a dislike or hatred the ruled have for some particular group, usually an outside enemy. To the extent that citizens participate in the transition of power, it is usually as part of the army or rebel forces contesting on behalf of a particular political aspirant. The choice of which side to support usually devolves to a combined calculation of promised benefits, promised retributions, and likelihood of victory.

Political winners in despotic systems usually lack any significant social capital with the civil society beyond the closest core of advisors and cronies. As a result, acquiring and maintaining power in a despotic system requires asymmetric power, which in turn requires that the social capital in the civil society is kept low to prevent collective action against the rulers (see Figure 16.2). Extending rights to, or requiring participation from, the civil society exposes the despotic system to forces that might contest for power. Predatory regimes thus eradicate all participation except from a very narrow and elite subgroup of society.

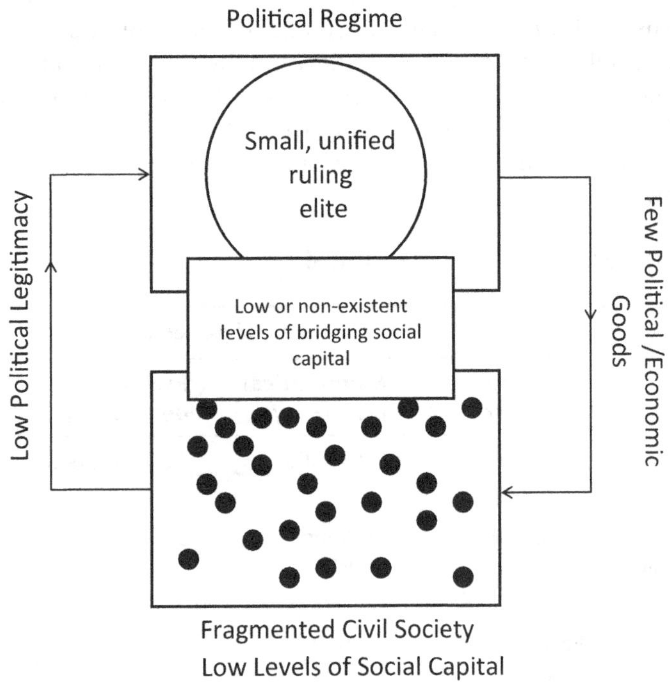

Figure 16.2 Social capital and despotic regimes

Autocratic rulers fragment the civil society through rule-by-fear. Group gatherings, places of social connections, and mass communications must be limited and/or tightly controlled. Cafes, newspapers, the Internet, religious meetings, and so forth must all be managed to ensure that collective action is limited. Since there is little, if any, legitimacy for the ruling elite, any ability to organize will almost certainly result in the removal of the government. This process leads inexorably to civil conflict, as in Angola.

ANGOLA'S LONG CIVIL WAR

Most of Angola's oil resource wealth has been siphoned off to support the government's long civil war against rebel forces. During the conflict, the government has done little for the population. Living conditions are abysmal. Over 1million people were displaced from their homes and almost another 4 million required outside assistance to survive. Funds lost to corruption far exceed the amount spent on the needs of the people. "Government forces routinely resorted to arbitrary arrests and detentions; restricted freedom of expression, assembly, association, and movement; committed extrajudicial killings; 'disappeared' people; and engaged in torture and rape." Experts are now predicting that the loss of legitimacy in Angola following the end of the civil war will not lead to more war, but to complete anarchy and lawlessness.

Source: Ganesan and Vines (2004).

Since the aim of despotic system governance is plunder, there is little need for HECs, other than the military, and hence no reason to foster participation or citizen rights. Citizens are allowed to provide for themselves as long as it does not encroach on the

government's ability to generate revenue, usually through a small number of very large natural-resource extraction companies (Ross, 2001). The government cannot allow constitutional limitations or other institutional checks and balances on the state's power to enforce its legitimacy. Those who oppose the government's views in any way must be eliminated; either they must be incarcerated as political prisoners, exiled, or killed.

The relationship between civil society and despotic rulers can best be characterized as predatory. The state seeks to extract the wealth of society for a small group of elites while minimizing the government costs of that extraction. This lack of inclusiveness leads to a loss of both attachment value for the government and social capital for those governing, which, together, make legitimacy extremely tenuous. States controlled by despotic rulers usually do not respond to the needs of the people. Rulers use figurative and literal sticks to keep people in line. In economies controlled by despotic rulers, economic transactions are limited, markets suffer, and some are reduced to subsistence exchange. Property rights and other institutions with the capacity to generate trust, risk-taking, and creativity are lacking, making it virtually impossible to expand or utilize the market (see de Soto, 2000). Without market institutions, specialization and trade are difficult except in extra-legal settings, such as black markets. People must provide for all of their needs, which is difficult under the best of circumstances.

AUTOCRATIC MONARCHY

Although it is possible to have a despotic monarch who has taken the throne by coup, we classify such regimes as despotic autocracies. For our purposes, autocratic monarchies are those political systems in which a royal descendent assumes the throne peacefully through inheritance and maintains the executive power over the country. Whereas the despotic ruler engenders virtually no social capital from the general population, bridging and/or asymmetric social capital, often in significant quantities, can exist in monarchical societies, both for the monarch and as attachment to the nation's social, political, and economic institutions. The social capital that the ruler has for the civil society is manifest primarily in the form of protection. Social capital, largely fragmented, among the citizens resembles that in despotic regimes (see Figure 16.3).

Monarchies have few formal institutions of power to which the civil society can become attached beyond the position of the king or queen. This poses a problem, however: what ensures that subjects remain subjects and do not become revolutionaries? The answer is the aristocratic class. Aristocrats are those royal family members who will never enjoy the opportunity to rule as the monarch, but on whom the monarch depends to maintain power. Although this group can be considered part of the monarchy in terms of power-sharing, there also exists a confrontation over power that must be purchased, usually through marriages, but also through side-payments such as land and money.

In England the aristocracy comprised the dukes and princes who exercised more direct control on the people and then answered, in turn, to the king or queen. In Thailand it was the Sakdina elite who managed the people for the king. Within the aristocratic class, linking social capital ensures that they act as a group vis-à-vis the monarch. Most goods produced beyond subsistence agriculture are produced for this group (or purchased through trade). As in despotic societies, the masses either need to be largely self-sufficient or provided for by the king, which in turn minimizes wealth creation. As with other

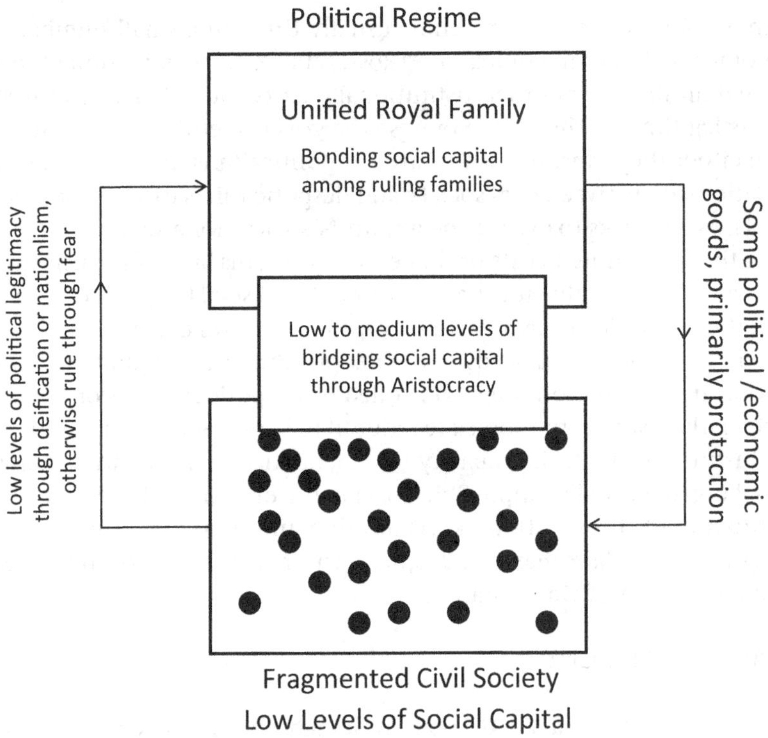

Figure 16.3 Social capital and monarchical regimes

forms of non-participatory rule, the monarch creates institutions that minimize civil society and the opportunity for groups to combine to form social capital.

Sometimes, as in pre-modern Japan, China, Thailand, and other countries, rulers claimed divine genealogies, elevating their "chosen" citizens in relation to other countries. Hierarchical and asymmetrical relationships between divinely chosen rulers and elevated subjects were mirrored in families, religious organizations, business, and other social settings. These relationships were often paternalistic, with a wise king, priest, business leader, or father making decisions for those under his stewardship. Aristocracies were related to the deified king, but had not been similarly chosen, placing them at odds both with the monarchy and the people. Interestingly, in many cases, including the French Revolution, the aristocracy is complicit in the overthrow of a monarch by the people. However, they often discover that the people are ungrateful for their help (or lack of obstruction) and find themselves suffering the same fate as the rulers.

Paternalistic monarchical relationships were certainly maintained through force and fear. But they were also maintained through the dissemination of benefits, which led to love and respect. Those in power were expected not only to demand the subservience of their subjects, but also to husband and manage resources for them. Legitimacy could be built through providing protection, food, employment, education, arts, and so forth. In exchange for the rights to these "goods," citizens were expected to respond to the king's demands to serve in the military, build roads and other infrastructure, and perhaps even pay taxes. Even so, when a monarchy has access to rich natural resource deposits, it may "buy off" both the rights and responsibilities of its citizens. For example, in the Middle

East, several monarchical states have tried to use oil wealth to purchase social capital and legitimacy from their citizens. In Saudi Arabia and Kuwait the royal families give a yearly stipend to every citizen. But no responsibility for taxation on the part of the individual citizen means that there is also no right to representation or other rights. Whereas early American colonists urged each other toward independence from Britain with the cry of "no taxation without representation," the Saudi government's motto might be "no representation without taxation."

The development of bonding social capital was often promoted within and between royal families. Common practice among monarchies was to wed a son or a daughter to a contending monarchy to reduce the possibilities of hostilities between them and, in many cases, combine the kingdoms over time. Thus, monarchies can also be, and often are, familial by nature. Nevertheless, the royal family rarely married commoners, making it difficult to develop bonding or linking social capital with the general population although, as mentioned earlier, bridging social capital was possible, especially if the population viewed the rulers as descended from deity. This lack of bonding social capital was evident in the case of Marie Antoinette.

AUSTRIA AND FRANCE IN THE EIGHTEENTH CENTURY

Marie Antoinette was the daughter of the Emperor and Empress of the Holy Roman Empire. Raised in Vienna, she was married to the heir to the throne of France. Her brother was the Emperor of Austria. But while the social capital that developed between Austria and France was evident among the nobles in France, especially when Marie's husband, Louis XVI, was crowned king, the same social capital clearly did not extend to the peasants. When Austria, led by Marie's brother, declared war on France, Marie's devotions were divided. In the end she sided with her brother and chose to pass military secrets to the Austrian army. On October 1793 the peasants beheaded Marie for passing information to the enemy.

Source: Lucidcafe.com (n.d.).

Economically, monarchies are typically not as predatory as other autocratic regimes. Longer-term perspectives and objectives mean that some form of HECs is desirable. While patron–client relationships are possible, *rentier* relationships are more common, especially when kingdoms are rich in natural resources. In these cases, government creates the HECs necessary to extract natural resource wealth, either within the kingdom's own borders or in its colonies, but does little to expand HECs not essential to this enterprise.

England and other European colonies, for example, created modern port facilities in Singapore, India, and Malaysia to facilitate the trade of the East India Company. Yet, they did very little to foster education, legal systems, and water and sewer systems in the interior of their colonies. Likewise, the gleaming highways and oil transportation systems in Saudi Arabia are conspicuous next to the antiquated or non-existing education, legal, and social systems. To the extent that monarchies created external trading networks among colonies, the people in the home country grew wealthy through new specialization, as happened in Britain in the nineteenth and early twentieth centuries. But the wealth did not trickle down to the colonies, and was based primarily on extraction. As we emphasized above, when the poor do not share social capital among themselves and also lack connections

to those with power, they are unable to change the rules of the game in ways that benefit them.

PSEUDO-DEMOCRACY

Samuel Huntington (1991) argued that the short history of nation-states has been marked by "waves" of democratization. Nevertheless, others have noted that the waves of democratizations have resulted in regimes that are not truly democratic. Specifically, many states that seem, to be democratic on the surface limit the rights and responsibilities of their citizens, making them only "pseudo"–democratic (Diamond, 1999).

With respect to rights, these governments allow citizen participation in selecting the government, but they skew the playing field in favor of the ruling party. Opposition parties are denied funding. Opposition leaders that get too powerful are jailed on trumped-up charges. The ruling party has access to the coffers of the state for its own re-election, either spending state resources directly on its campaign or offering pork-barrel projects in return for votes. In other words, the state has elections, but for various reasons they are not free or fair.

In contrast to the monarchical state, legitimacy is maintained not through genealogical claims, but often by economic development. The primary deliverable of the state is economic growth. States are capable of extracting taxes from their citizens and abrogating certain liberal rights, but must deliver year-on-year economic growth in return. The focus of the state is therefore developmental.

Like most monarchies, pseudo-democracies assume a paternalistic form and are almost universally characterized by patron–client relationships in which powerful political actors team up with powerful economic actors to create and implement political and economic policies favorable to both sides. Economic cronies provide income, and political patrons provide protection, licenses, and favorable access to financing and land. As with the *rentier* states, HECs emerge that facilitate the business and governance of the patron–client relationship. But other HECs, such as education, infrastructure, legal institutions, and so forth can be undersupplied. The result is large amounts of asymmetric social capital between the rulers and the civil society. Regular citizens form attachments to the regime, but only so long as the government delivers on economic growth.

LEE'S SINGAPORE

Singapore is notorious for its paternalistic social oversight. A well-known joke is that Singapore is a "fine" country—that is, one that fines its citizens for all kinds of behaviors that are accepted in other places. Where else can one be fined for chewing gum? But Singapore's government involvement reaches far deeper than appropriate substances on which to masticate. For example, government shapes reproductive trends by encouraging sterilization for uneducated parents while providing incentives for well-educated parents to have more children. Such oversight and control cannot be checked by citizen political involvement because the People's Action Party has effectively marginalized all contending political parties. Citizen participation, to the extent it is tolerated, is relegated to the economic sphere.

Pseudo-democracies often promote democratization to realize economic gains by creating institutional channels through which broader groups can participate in the

economy. Thus, although Singapore works to control many aspects of its citizens' lives, it also provides opportunities for them to participate in economic policy-making and implementation, as well as in skills development (see Ritchie, 2009). Dense linkages among the population and with the government create opportunities for trade and export, which in turn facilitates specialization and development.

SINGAPORE AND SKILLS TRAINING

Political participation in Singapore is limited outside the ruling party. Nevertheless, the government has established institutions that promote the involvement of the private sector in economic activities. For example, labor, business, and academia all play an important role in education and training. Participation creates "buy-in," which helps to make Singapore's training programs some of the best in the world. But, just as important, the process of involving many different actors in the process means that high levels of social capital are developed between the various groups and the government, which adds to the government's overall legitimacy.

Source: Ritchie (2001).

To the extent that pseudo-democracies limit interactions among the civil society, trade and specialization suffer. Broad participation ensures that policy payoffs are distributed as widely as possible. But economic participation may sometimes lead to more political checks and balances than is preferred by the ruling elite (see Doner, Ritchie, and Slater, 2005). The combination of relationships is seen in Figure 16.4.

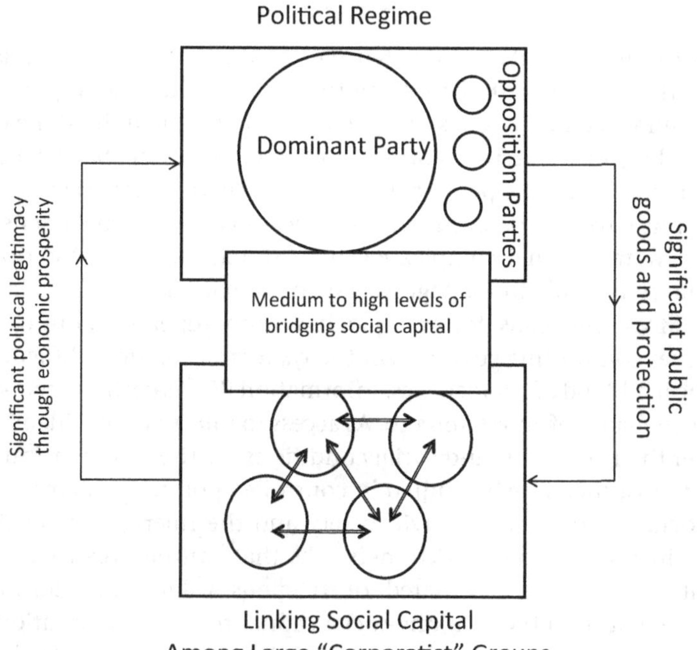

Figure 16.4 Social capital and pseudo-democratic regimes

LIBERAL DEMOCRACY

Liberal democracies are the rarest form of government, but also the most legitimate. Social capital is almost exclusively linking, characterized by relationships between equals. The state is not predatory, paternalistic, or developmental, but regulatory. The civil society's power over the state and rights, such as free speech, the freedom to exercise one's choice of religion, the freedom to choose associations, the right to bear arms, and legal protection, is constitutionally assured.

NEGATIVE AND POSITIVE RIGHTS—BRITAIN AND THE US

Different types of constitution can be identified by whether they provide negative or positive rights.

Negative rights mean that constitutions define exactly what the state can do. Everything else is reserved for the people. For example, Great Britain's constitution does not give the state the right to abrogate freedom of speech; therefore, the people retain that right. Positive rights mean that the constitution specifies what rights the people have. For example, the US constitution has a bill of rights specifying that the people have the freedom of speech.

While negative rights constitutions are exhaustive in the rights they provide their citizens, these rights are often ambiguous. Positive rights constitutions are specific, but often limited. To resolve these tensions, the US constitution provides both kinds of rights. It delineates positive rights in the Bill of Rights, but then reserves all other unspecified rights not given to the state for the people.

But with extensive rights come extensive responsibilities. All aspects of society are determined either directly or indirectly by the people. Thus, the responsibilities to vote, run for office, understand the issues, serve in the military, and uphold the laws are high. In fact, so demanding are the responsibilities of liberal democracy that a colleague of Bryan's recently commented that the political electoral system in Indonesia was so complex and demanding of its citizens that even most Americans could not make sense of it.

It may be, however, that complex electoral systems are only the tip of the iceberg. Perhaps far more difficult to manage is the complexity and overwhelming amount of information. Most Americans, for example, have only superficial, or no, insight into the important issues confronting government today. Yet information, difficult as it may be to manage, is the life-blood of democracies. Information flow is partly a socio-emotional good that promotes equality of access and use. As access to information widens, individuals can use it to better their economic and social conditions. Without it, political participation is impossible. It must therefore be limited in controlled political systems.

For democracies to work, the civil society and the rulers must coexist with linking social capital in the same networks—networks that can be organized around political parties, location of residency, shared or religious values. In addition, functioning democracies benefit from their linking social capital through the creation of attachment to the institutions of the political system, which is a powerful force for legitimacy.

The social capital which rulers have for the civil society is manifest in the form of institutions that facilitate economic well-being, social interaction and conflict

management, and military security. The social capital which the civil society has for the rulers can be seen in the legitimacy given to the rulers and the willingness of the people to operate within the institutional system, especially during transitions of power. Finally, high levels of social capital among the people facilitates interaction between interest groups, an ability to collectively act to check the power of the rulers, and the ability to work through conflict among competing interests (see Figure 16.5).

Liberal democracies encourage the will of the majority without suppressing or tyrannizing the minority. Although such sensitivities often lead to considerable social conflict over issues such as abortion, gay marriage, levels of taxation, and so forth, constitutional provisions work to resolve the conflicts through the participation of the citizenry, which lends credibility and legitimacy to the outcomes. Liberty is ensured as the majority "internalizes" the needs of the minority, which mirror their own minority views in other issues. Close and frequent contact ensures the visibility of the minority's issues.

In liberal democracies, deep networks and cross-cutting memberships distribute political power, making it harder for groups to exercise economic dominance over others. Linking social capital works best to create free-market interactions of the kind that support market institutions. When markets do not work to distribute wealth evenly, as in the US in the early 1900s, political power was sufficiently distributed to allow the formation of political institutions, such as antitrust legislation, to reallocate wealth and keep economic dynasties from continuing. When linking social capital diminishes between the ruled and rulers, the institutions necessary to maintain an equal distribution of economic information and political power also decline in number and strength, leading to a rise in income inequality.

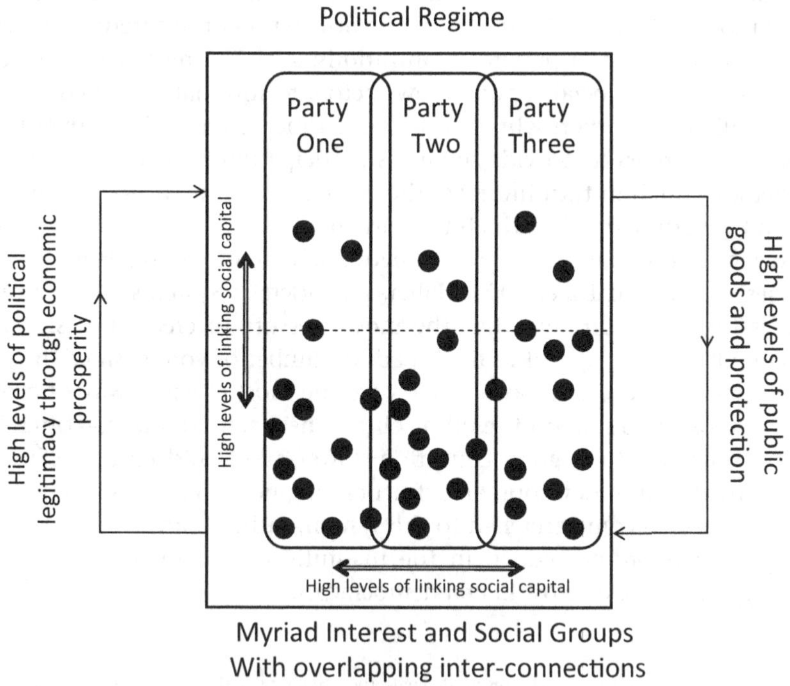

Figure 16.5 Social capital and constitutional democracy

All of this suggests that linking social capital creates the foundation of institutions upon which capitalism can provide the broadest benefits, including economic goods for most people. But if linking social capital diminishes, the ability of the people to control the distribution of the market also erodes, leading to income inequality.

If linking social capital declines among the people in a liberal democracy, then political power becomes easier to concentrate. Concentrated political power is translated into more wealth for those with political power, which exacerbates the cycle. Since rights are really only privileges that can be revoked at any time if those in power have not internalized the well-being of those not in power,[3] asymmetric relationships of power threaten participatory institutions.

If participatory institutions are extinguished, social capital among the people is lowered still further. Without the social capital needed to support liberal democracy, "stick" power predominates, and the majority often tyrannizes the minority. The "rights" we hold as inviolate in the Western liberal democracies depend on the ability of the people to check the power of the state. Thus, and ironically, although capitalism has created a foundation upon which linking social capital can thrive, which in turn has played a central role in the birth of representative democracy, if it gets too unequal in its distributive effects, it is also democracy's potential executioner.

The most robust and effective liberal capitalist societies are built on high levels of symmetric linking social capital. Equality of relationships fosters entrepreneurial behavior, trade, and its attendant specialization. Big firms do not dominate the economy, but coexist in a synergistic environment with entrepreneurial startups (see Baumol, Litan, and Schramm, 2007).

Symmetric linking social capital is fostered through broad political participation, which tends to mitigate the problems of free-riders—people who consume without contributing to the provision of the good. New research is showing that the extent to which HECs are provided by government or private organizations, such as unions, depends on levels of political participation. Social capital allows actors to internalize the costs of providing goods that will benefit others while, at the same time, reducing incentives to "free-ride" on the efforts of others to provide them. As participation rises, the need to manage by force decreases, which in turn increases the citizens' attachment to the initiatives, laws, policies, and government with which they are involved.

Democracies, therefore, do a much better job of providing HECs than do non-democracies (Baum and Lake, 2003). Liberal democratic systems of government boast the broadest participation, and thus the most pressure to create HECs. Political elites must create policies that appeal to the broadest number of voters, since the people have the power to remove those in power. HECs are the most efficient way of providing side payments to those who support the ruling elites. These side payments—often in the form of advanced infrastructure, good education, lower taxes, and basic welfare—stimulate economic growth and development, further augmenting government's legitimacy. Over time, citizens become attached to the system, rather than to any particular leader. Legitimacy is therefore embedded in the institutions that maintain the system—the constitution in the case of most liberal democracies.

3 Even liberal democracies have at times responded with force to abrogate rights previously enjoyed by their citizens. Further force is then used to force those who do not share attachment to the democracy's institutions to conform. Consider, for example, the Civil War period and the 1930s depression in the United States.

Conclusion

In this chapter we have proposed that social capital is necessary for state legitimacy. Ironically, the very way in which states are constructed has a significant impact on the ability of rulers to solicit and build social capital with their citizens.

Fundamentally, the civil society's rights and responsibilities are connected. In those regimes where citizens are given a large responsibility to participate, rights are more numerous and economic equality is higher. When participation falls, inequality grows and government legitimacy declines.

Without social capital in the civil society, those in power will always rule over those without power, often capriciously, unless they have internalized the well-being of their citizens, in which case they will include them in the processes of government. Social capital in the form of attachment for state institutions encourages participation in working to provide HECs, which in turn facilitates economic growth and political legitimacy in a virtuous cycle. When citizens are uninvolved, the state is less likely to internalize their well-being and will most often resort to either controlling the economy for its own ends (in a best-case scenario) or predating on the masses. If the masses do not share social capital, they lack the means to collectively act to check the government. As Robert Putnam observed in *Bowling Alone* (2000), a lack of social institutions that bind us together will act to reduce levels of social capital, which appear to be critical to the operation of democratic institutions.

Whether citizens are involved in government processes also determines the level and intensity of attachment to the nation itself. Without attachment to legitimate state institutions, group loyalty devolves to the clan, family, or gang. When the state is threatened, either from internal or external sources, no one comes to its defense. On the other hand, cross-cultural participation builds social capital that transcends individual groups and creates attachment to broader, national institutions and values. The resulting legitimacy reveals itself in heightened patriotism, which is stoked when the nation or its institutions comes under attack or duress.

Finally, the social capital created by different political regimes determines the allocation of resources. Where high levels of social capital are shared among the population and between the masses and government, income distribution is likely to be more equal. When participation falls, distribution becomes less equal. Ultimately, when those in power do not internalize the well-being of the less powerful, income distributions reflect the power structure. Highly symmetric linking social capital shapes highly participative political institutions that facilitate trade, both within and between nations. More trade leads to specialization, which generates productivity and wealth.

All of this leads us to conclude that for political regimes to be legitimate, they must reflect shared values. This is not that dissimilar from Tocqueville's insight over 100 years ago. But—and here's the rub—liberty does not allow us to force our values on one another. Without shared values, solutions to social problems cannot be found. Society cannot, therefore, be improved. The paradox, then, is that liberal democracy depends on shared values, but it can in no way create or force these values on its citizens. Values can only be created and shared in non-political institutions. The liberal democratic state, therefore, is dependent on the family, schools, and other social institutions to create the social capital necessary for its survival.

CHAPTER 17

Social Capital and Culture

If we learn anything from the history of economic development it is that culture makes all the difference ... what counts is work, thrift, honesty, patience, tenacity.

David Landes, (in Harrison and Huntington, 2000: 2).

Introduction

David Landes expounded that culture is an important determinant of much of what happens in our societies. On the point that culture matters, there is much agreement. There is much less agreement about what is culture, and on how to measure its influence and test hypotheses about its formation. And, for some, it is vague enough to ignore. Indeed, "most modern economics is exceedingly formal and rigorous and has thus little use for 'culture'" (Mokyr, 1999: 6). It could be said that scholars in political science, sociology, and other social sciences often feel the same way.

Despite disagreements over the definition of culture, many would agree that culture includes habits, shared attitudes, values, ways of thinking, and the expectations of others held by members of an organization or group. But where does culture come from? How did particular habits, shared attitudes, values, ways of thinking, and the expectations of others become adopted? And how are they maintained? Or changed?[1]

We suggest that the social capital paradigm has much to contribute to the debate on culture and answers the question of where culture comes from, how it is maintained, and how it is changed. Our main point is that certain aspects of culture are adopted and maintained because they acquire attachment values which in turn are acquired as they become embedded with socio-emotional goods (SEGs). Producing SEGs that become embedded in cultural objects requires relationships. Relationships produce SEGs that become embedded in actions that become habits, in thoughts that become attitudes, in choices that become values, in views that become a way of thinking, and in observations that become expectations of others. All of this leads us to define culture as habits, shared attitudes, values, ways of thinking, and the expectation of others that have acquired attachment value for a group or organization.

1 We recognize the long history and variety of approaches to the study of culture. The field of culture is vast. In contrast, our efforts to discuss culture in this chapter are very narrow in order to make the point that what many accept as aspects of culture, habits, values, ways of thinking, and expectations are influenced by, and in turn influence, social capital, exchanges of socio-emotional goods, the formation of attachment values, and the creation and maintenance of institutions.

In what follows, we promote the theme that culture can best be explained and understood through the lens of the social capital paradigm. Stated more clearly, our aim in this chapter is to understand how culture shapes, and is shaped by, relationships and social capital.

The Importance of Culture

Max Weber used culture to explain successful economic growth in America in the nineteenth century. The cultural variables that mattered most to Weber were the beliefs, values, and habits fostered by religion. Since Protestants believed that what they acquired on earth was a sign of God's favor toward them, economic growth and development became an indication of personal righteousness. Put simply, Protestants were focused on this world at least as much as the next. The work ethic, for Protestants, reflected this perception. In comparison, Catholics, Weber hypothesized, were taught that the next world was all that mattered. Since what one accomplished in this life had little bearing on what would happen in the next, there was little reason to focus on it (Weber, 1958). From the perspective of the social capital paradigm, habits, values, ways of thinking, and expectations of others that promoted economic growth acquired attachment values and became part of the culture for Protestants. But this was less so for Catholics.

Building on the idea that culture influenced economic and social interaction, David Landes, a well-respected historian, argued that Western European countries were able to effect an industrial revolution because of their shared cultural traits. He observed that all successful industrialized countries shared a similar commitment to work, thrift, honesty, patience, and tenacity. Until countries could figure out how to develop these traits, they would remain in poverty (Landes, 1998). And yet, even having recognized what kinds of traits would be beneficial, it is unclear how societies might embed these with SEGs to develop the cultural values needed for economic development, short of abandoning their original culture that was supposedly holding them down in one of the many possible "poverty traps."

The problem with these arguments that connect cultures to economic and social outcomes is often their scope. There appears to be a tendency to generalize culture by countries and ethnic origins. If the Protestant work ethic was essential to economic success, can we conclude that economically successful Chinese businesspeople are also Protestants? What about successful Japanese, Koreans, Chileans, or Israelis? Clearly, each of these cultures also boasts a strong work ethic. Some have suggested that the work ethic is "Confucian," "Samurai," formed from necessity, European-derived, or Jewish. But each of these explanations focuses on the deterministic characteristics of philosophy, history, structural (natural) conditions, and religion. But can't we also think of groups of these peoples that are not wealthy? Not all Chinese, Japanese, Israelis, Koreans, or members of any other ethnic, religious, or racial group are all equally well-off. Many Americans continue to live in poverty.

How, then, should we think about culture's impact on exchange and economic development? For the most part, culture is developed and shared in relationships, the most important of which are local rather than national or international. We adopt reluctantly the culture of those we don't care about or who we sense have little social capital for us. One couplet expresses the role of sharing culture and social capital: "I don't

care how much you know until I know how much you care." So culture is important, but it cannot exist in a social capital vacuum.

Relationships, Culture, and Trade

In contrast to the argument that ethnicity or religion is the key variable that determines the outcomes of exchanges, the social capital paradigm emphasizes the importance of relationships. Supporting this focus, Janet Landa (1991) identified relationships existing among culturally similar groups as the key variable that affects trade among various ethnic groups. She created a concept called "Ethnically Homogeneous Middleman Groups (EHMG). These EHMGs greased the skids of trade through their relationships. It's certainly true that relationships were formed on the foundation of shared kernels that include shared religion, language, symbols, and other cultural traits. But it is equally true that relationships, based on whatever was their shared kernel, were essential for embedding certain habits, values, ways of thinking and expectations with SEGs that created a trading culture.

ETHNIC CHINESE DIASPORA

Until only very recently, the Chinese population living on the mainland was very poor by world standards. However, in other Asian countries, the Chinese diaspora was very wealthy, often accounting for the bulk of economic activity in these countries: Thailand, 60–70 percent; Malaysia, 60 percent; Indonesia, 95 percent; and the Philippines, 60 percent. Although anthropologists might argue that many of people who moved out of China during the revolution of 1911 belonged to the entrepreneurial market class, the evidence supports the conclusion that the majority were laborers and just as often very uneducated. It makes more sense, then, to conclude that it has been the relationships within and across the Chinese diaspora that has facilitated risk-taking, innovation, financing, markets, and ultimately business growth.

Source: World Bank (2007).

But which came first—relationships or culture? If we were to say to a poor underdeveloped country that wanted to create more wealth in its society that culture and social capital were the keys, which would need to come first? Our answer is: once we have both chickens and eggs, speculating on which came first doesn't really add much. Take advantage of both. We have social capital that creates attachment value for habits, values, shared attitudes, and expectations of others which in turn lead us to form relationships with those with a similar culture and who adopt similar institutions. Shared culture can be used to form relationships that facilitate exchanges.

History can teach us much about how relationships have produced culture. The Spanish conquest of Latin America not only changed forever the relationships among Native Americans, but also introduced new relationships between them and the Spaniards. In addition, the conquest by Spain and, later, Portugal imposed new institutions on the Native Americas, to which they were obligated to conform while continually striving to maintain their previous relationships, culture, and institutions.

At the same time, the local customs and beliefs of the peoples of Latin America have also influenced the Catholic Church and, earlier, the Spanish government. The differences in the Catholic Church are observable from one Latin American country to another. Local traditions, deities, and beliefs shape the structure and operation of the Church, if not formally then certainly informally.

In modern times the globalization of culture includes one society adopting another society's cultural tastes for food, fashion, language, music, entertainment, technologies, and communication methods. One example, mentioned earlier, is the global taste for McDonald's hamburgers. At the same time, the English language and McDonald's foods are also influenced by the local cultures in which they are making inroads. Teriyaki burgers in Tokyo and new "ethnic" words in the English language being used back in the United States and other English-speaking countries are evidence of the bi-directional flow of cultural influences.

The Nature and Amount of Social Capital

We believe that the evidence suggests that culture and social capital are interdependent. Culture influences the nature of relationships, and relationships influence culture. How and to what extent people feel sympathy for others is clearly shaped by particular beliefs, values, ways of thinking, and expectations. But certainly the reverse is also true.

BONDING SOCIAL CAPITAL CULTURE

Societies high in bonding social capital have attachment to family over rational legal bureaucracies. This means that organizations based on family relationships will probably thrive. In these cultures, there is heightened respect for the aged and young, and externalities are internalized within the family. Since bonding social capital internalizes externalities within the family, extra-familial externalities may or may not be internalized. Thus family contracts (the mafia come to mind) are guarded above the laws of the land and ignore the external consequences of their choices on communities.

Examples of visible cultural outcomes might be that people choose to spend holidays with family rather than at office parties. If, because of one's beliefs, values, or habits, one chooses to invest social capital in a narrowly defined ethnic group, family, or clan (e.g., radical Muslims), informal institutions take precedent over formal ones. Family (clan, ethnicity) rules trump those of the state or wider community.

> **FEMALE CIRCUMCISION IN ENGLAND**
>
> Muslim families living in the UK have been hiring doctors from within their religion to perform female circumcision on their daughters despite the fact that the formal laws of the UK prohibit the practice. This is a case of bonding social capital shared among those with similar values within families, religions, and ethnicities that trumps the formal institutions and rules of the UK.

Second, intense bonding relationships increase the amount of SEGs enjoyed within certain groups. However, at the same time, a lack of bridging and linking social

capital reduces the amount of EVGs that are produced, since the coordination behind specialization and trade is difficult to attain. Timur Kuran (2004) argues that one of the possible reasons why Muslim economies have not produced the results that many Muslims had hoped for is because of a lack of connections between Muslim economies and richer Western economies. At the same time, it may be that resource endowments also shape the preferences people have for certain types of social capital. For example, where resources, such as oil, are plentiful, people may have few reasons to develop bridging or linking social capital. Without such relationships, it is harder to benefit from the technological upgrading and innovation that come from trade and specialization (see Ross, 1999).

LINKING SOCIAL CAPITAL CULTURE

Other predictions might also be possible. Using what we learned in earlier chapters, those societies with large amounts of linking social capital will have more support for formal institutions than for informal institutions. A value or kernel that cuts across families and tribes, and creates linking social capital, will strengthen formal institutions. This will encourage the ability to make and keep contracts, which is certainly a key component of establishing and maintaining property rights—another key variable to economic success (see de Soto, 2000). Thus, linking social capital societies are very efficient at producing economic goods.

If these same societies lack bonding social capital, they probably create fewer SEGs. People live in more individual settings, spend resources acquiring physical economic goods, and have few deep and ongoing relationships. Traditional institutions may diminish in importance and informal institutions wither as linking social capital replaces bonding social capital within the family. Some may argue that this is what is happening to developed Western countries. Young people quit investing in bonding social capital either by choice (leaving families) or have it thrust upon them (through divorce, etc.). People mourn the demise of the family, marriage, loyalty among friends, and even the reduction of close relationships in their everyday life. On the other hand, in such societies, there is more freedom to choose without the constraints of family, and, many are economically better-off.

BRIDGING SOCIAL CAPITAL CULTURE

Societies in which bridging social capital predominates are hierarchical. Perhaps the best example would be a military structure. If there were little or no other types of social capital, society would be based on asymmetric relationships between ruled and ruler. As we showed in Chapter 16, this is certainly the case in dictatorships around the world. Such societies would produce little in the way of either SEGs or EVGs. Without bonding social capital, SEGs would be difficult to produce. The lack of more equal linking social capital would make it difficult to create the relationships necessary for specialization and trade. Few would have the courage to disagree with a military superior or other authority figure regardless of the type of ruler. As a result, innovation stagnates, and progress is difficult.

COMBINATION CULTURE

Cultures that have a combination of types of social capital are probably more likely to support both formal and informal institutions. Loyalties and sympathies would cut across a wide range of groups and interests. This is likely what Tocqueville saw when he visited America and was impressed with the uniqueness of the economic and political systems. His observation that Americans were involved in many different civic groups and interests, which was the foundation for the country's uniqueness, may have been the result of an equal balance of all kinds of social capital (Tocqueville, 1966). Indeed, 150 years later, Robert Putnam (2000) observed that the number and types of groups with which Americans associate has fallen dramatically. Perhaps this is not an indication of an overall drop in the amount of social capital, but an indication of an imbalance in various types of social capital.

THE CONNECTIONS OF VIETNAM VERSUS NORTH KOREA

Compare Vietnam's and North Korea's distribution of social capital and their economic development. Both are communist countries and both have a history of antagonism toward Western countries and their economic systems. However, Vietnam has recently decided to do what is necessary to create relationships with the West. It is now deliberately developing linking social capital with Western nations, particularly with old enemies like the United States. The result is the creation of myriad economic and social relationships between Vietnam and the West. These relationships are creating tremendous economic growth and expansion in Vietnam.

In North Korea the distribution and kinds of social capital are very different as has been the country's economic development. North Korea has a dearth of social or economic linkages with Western economies. Instead, its culture is insular and self-focused, and views the outside world as enemies to be avoided rather than as friends and potential trading partners. The isolation has been so deep that there has been little recognition, even inside North Korea, of its economic plight. Decisions to de-link from the international economy have diminished North Korea's linking and bridging social capital with most countries, which in turn has shaped its cultural evolution.

In general, families, clans, ethnic groups, and other groups who share inherited kernels and bonding social capital share more cultural traits than other groups. But it may also be that anything that draws us closer together causes us to adopt more similar values and traits. The 9/11 crisis made many Americans feel more patriotic and connected to each other in the cause of freedom and liberty. This led them to voluntarily put aside their differences and emphasize their similarities—again, real or imagined. All this resulted in a period of time during which Americans came together more than they had in the recent past. We hear about similar phenomena during World War II and other major crises. One question is: for what purpose did people come together? For war or for social justice?

CULTURE AS A SOURCE OF RELATIONSHIPS

Relationships are easier to form with those who we share a cultural bond. Certainly, we are more likely to create relationships with those who are of the same religion, ethnicity,

race, and so forth. Go to the lunch room of any racially integrated high school in America and you are likely to find racially segmented groups eating lunch together: Hispanics, Caucasians, Blacks, and other races are more likely to congregate than integrate. But, if you push still further, you often find religious groupings and maybe even political ones.

But not all cultural bonds are equally strong, nor are they similar across different cultures. In Latin America the Catholic Church is exceptionally strong culturally—much more so than in Europe or the US (Htun, 2003). In Europe, which is much more secular than Latin America, church is not a strong organizing force, yet ethnicity is. Minorities from Africa, Turkey, and the Middle East provide both targets for discrimination, as well as networks underlying EHMG groupings that facilitate trade in particular goods and services.

Interestingly, our strongest cultural force for relationships might actually exist only when we meet others of similar cultural backgrounds *outside* the normal areas of that culture. Recall Benedict Anderson's suggestion that our strongest cultural linkages based on nationalism would occur only in exile (Anderson, 1989). Think of Chinatowns and other ethnic enclaves around the world. The most successful ethnic Chinese business networks have long been located outside China. Chinese businessmen in Thailand, Singapore, Indonesia, the Philippines, Malaysia, and a host of other countries and cities provide the lion's share of economic trading and other activity in these countries. Is it being Chinese that matters? Yes, but only to the extent that this helps form relationships that are beneficial economically. For example, Chinese business people in Thailand can go to other Chinese business people for capital, distribution, and technology which they could otherwise not obtain. Shared ethnicity and familial bonds ensure that loans will be repaid, shipments will be received, and innovations will be paid for and protected.

These cultural ties also create a pathway for relationships to provide SEGs and AVGs. Concentrations of culturally similar peoples facilitate intellectual exchange, religious worship, and access to familiar music, food, entertainment, and social structures. Certain fashions, music, ways of talking, and so forth identify people as belonging to certain cultures. Acceptance into particular groups requires more than knowledge of these things, but rather the ability to utilize, manipulate, share, and transmit them.

Institutions, and Social Capital and Culture

In previous chapters we explained how social capital influences the acceptance of formal and informal institutions. From a cultural perspective, economists, sociologists, and political scientists often talk of a society's ability to embrace or nurture the rule of law. Weber (1958) suggested that the difference between successfully developing countries and more backward countries was the degree to which a rational–legal bureaucratic structure existed and how well it functioned. But left unanswered is the question of why some countries could accomplish such a task whereas others could not.

Part of the answer may lie with levels of social capital and attachment values for the formal institutions that underlie the rational–legal infrastructure that is thought to be so important. Where attitudes and expectations are that laws and institutions will either not be enforced, will be ineffective, or will be quickly changed, there is little, if any, attachment to these institutions. When people lack attachment to institutions, the

institutions are almost guaranteed to fail. At the same time, when institutions are failing there is little to inspire confidence in them, further weakening the institution.

CONSTITUTIONS IN THAILAND

Since the overthrow of the absolute monarchy in Thailand in 1932, the country has experienced numerous coups that have led to changes in government. But although the leadership changes, the society underneath remains relatively stable, leading many to downplay the importance of the coups. However, with many of the changes in government, there has been a new constitution created. The problem is that with so many new constitutions being written, there is very little incentive to learn, apply, protect, and enforce the tenets of the existing constitution: the rapid changes make most people ambivalent at best.

When people have no attachment value for the constitution, people and their personalities remain larger than the institutions. In fact, instead of attachment value for their constitution, it becomes the social capital of individual leaders that controls the people, making it easier for demagoguery and other forms of "personality" leadership which, over the long run, damage the growth of liberal democracy.

However, positive, as well as negative, cycles exist between social capital, culture and institutions. Cultural expectations to revere the constitution, learn and apply it, and monitor and enforce it influence people to live by the constitution and expect others to do the same, which further enhances and strengthens the institution. Over time, the cultural expectation is to be governed by institutions—primarily the constitution—rather than individuals, who are primarily agents to protect, interpret, and enforce the constitution.

Conclusion

When pressed, most social scientists admit that culture matters to all kinds of social outcomes, including politics and economics. The problem has been the various ways in which culture has been understood and measured. Our emphasis in this chapter has been the interdependence of social capital and culture, and their combined influence on economic and political outcomes. Deeply held cultural values in society can dictate the ways in which individuals invest in social capital. For example, if society holds little regard for marriage or family institutions, more investment is likely to be made in linking social capital than in bonding social capital. Or, if the primary good is tradition and loyalty, emphasis will be placed on developing bonding social capital within one's family, clan, or ethnic identity.

At the same time, the investments we make in social capital can influence our cultural values. When bonding social capital is the focus, respect for families and the informal institutions necessary for their formation, operation, and so forth may well dominate the formal institutions of the state. Warlord or mafia families and clans might govern in such societies, and the state is likely to be very weak. Where linking social capital dominates, formal institutions that govern a society of equals are more likely. State-instituted laws

and rules will dominate the more informal institutions created in groups and bodies in society below the state. Clearly there is great deal of research still needed to examine the nexus of social capital and culture

Epilogue

This book began by declaring that relationships matter. Relationships matter because we have socio-emotional needs that are satisfied by intangible, socio-emotional goods produced in relationships. Our socio-emotional needs include the need for validation, for experiences that express caring, and for personalized information that are produced in sympathetic relationships. We may survive on physical goods, such as guns and butter, but to thrive and prosper requires a combination of both physical and socio-emotional goods.

Academic isolation has sometimes kept us from benefiting from the collective social science insights necessary for our understanding the role and importance of relationships. We believe that this lack of integration is especially noticeable in the analysis of interpersonal exchanges which include far more than the transfer of goods and services, the value of which depends primarily on their physical properties. An important component of such exchanges is also the transmission of socio-emotional goods and high attachment value goods—goods with high emotional content.

We can therefore say, with great certainty, that relationships alter the terms and level of trade. And because relationships alter the terms and level of trade, they alter the distribution of income. It's hard to overstate the significance of these insights. Understanding the full range of influences shaping human exchange offers opportunities for humanity to address longstanding and persistent problems, such as poverty, income inequality, and economic stagnation and underdevelopment.

To understand completely how relationships matter, we need a new kind of economic theory, a theory of relationship economics. And at the core of this new approach must be a new form of capital—call it social capital—which is generated in relationships of sympathy. Social capital—which is similar in its capital like-qualities to man-made capital, natural capital, human capital, financial capital, and cultural capital, to name but a few—is ubiquitous. It is difficult to find an exchange in which social capital has not, in some way, altered the terms or level of trade.

This new approach to economics, relationships economics, and this new form of capital, social capital, does not exist in a vacuum. A framework of rules or institutions organizes the use of, and investment or disinvestment in, social capital. Institutions also organize exchanges of goods and services, including those whose value is mostly physical, those with high attachment value, and the intangible socio-emotional ones. Yet no one rule or institution fits or organizes all exchanges. Informal institutions tend to organize exchanges of most socio-emotional goods. Formal institutions work well for organizing exchanges of goods whose value is primarily tied to the good's physical properties and for those goods whose high attachment value is widely shared.

Just as there are many kinds of institutions, there are as many different kinds and qualities of social capital, perhaps figuratively as many as the sands of the sea. And each of the different kinds of social capital—categorized for convenience as (strong) bonding, (weak) linking, and (asymmetric) bridging—has a different influence on exchanges, and

works best in distinct circumstances. Thus, different kinds of exchanges require different kinds of social capital.

But regardless of the kinds of exchanges or social capital, those who observe actual exchanges can not help but admit that relationships matter—a lot. Various examples in this book have shown that social capital influences who buys agricultural farm land (over 50 percent of the time it is friends and family of the land seller), who rents land (mostly friends and family of the landlord), who gets loans (those with social and business relationships with the lender have an edge), what rules we respect (those with attachment value), who we select for business partners (for small business, mostly family), who is hired to add attachment value to goods (those we admire most in the public arena, such as famous sports figures), and who are most likely to be poor (those who lack relationships with people who have resources).

Recognizing that relationships matter nearly all the time and everywhere will help us discover why we select the places we live, how we choose our professions, where we attend school, and how we form our religious and political beliefs. More generally, this book has shown how relationships, expressed as social capital, can influence ethics, globalization, the distribution of political power, and culture.

These are lofty claims for the importance of social capital! Or perhaps we are just reminding ourselves of important truths we've long understood intuitively. When Lindon was growing up, his father farmed a small parcel of land with the help of his distant cousin. The two men settled their business on a ditch bank with a brief discussion and a handshake. It was clear that the importance of their relationship with each other and with the community was far more important than any pecuniary advantage that might accrue from unfair or predatory business practices. But increasing specialization and business size have eliminated many of these "ditch-bank" business deals, if not in our farming communities, then at least on Wall Street where the results are not always what we had hoped they would be.

So, in the end, we return to where we started. Relationships matter. And the word seems to be getting out, even in places we might not expect. In Iran prominent political clerics worry about whether the loss of social capital with the people resulting from election irregularities and suppression will reduce the political legitimacy of the ruling regime (CNN.com/world, 2009). Maybe just as surprising, the Nobel committee selected Elinor Ostrom, a pioneer in social capital studies (Ostrom and Ahn, 2003), for her work emphasizing alternative methods for solving the problems of managing the commons. Clearly, more people are beginning to realize that relationships do indeed matter. Hopefully, we all now know a bit more about when, where, and how.

References

Adams, D.W. and D.A. Fitchett (1992). *Informal Finance in Low-Income Countries*. Boulder, CO: Westview Press.

Ajzen, I. and H. Fisbein (1972). "Attitudes and Normative Beliefs as Factors Influencing Behavior Intentions." *Journal of Personality and Social Psychology* 21: 1–9.

Allman, W.F. (1984). "Nice Guys Finish First." *Science* (October): 25–31.

Ambrose, S.E. (1992). Bank of Brothers: E Company, 506th Regiment, 101st Airborne from Normandy to Hitler's Eagle's Nest. New York: Touchstone.

Anders, J. (2007). "United States Is Largest Donor of Foreign Aid, Report Says: Americans Favor Private Giving, People-to-People Contacts." United States Information Service, US Department of State, May 24. At: http://usinfo.state.gov/xarchives/display.html?p=washfile-english&y=2007&m=May&x=20070524165115zjsredna0.2997553.

Anderson, B. (1989). *Imagined Communities*. London: Verso.

Anderson, E. (1990). "The Ethical Limitations of the Market." *Economics and Philosophy* (October): 179–205.

"Answers for Healthier Living" (1999). *Mayo Clinic Healthquest*, April, p. 1.

Aron, A.E.N. and D. Smollan (1992). "Inclusion of the Other in the Self-Scale and the Structure of Interpersonal Closeness." *Journal of Personality and Social Psychology* 63: 241–253.

Arrow, K.J. (1999). "Observations on Social Capital." In P. Dasgupta and I. Serageldin (eds), *Social Capital: A Multifaceted Perspective*. Washington, DC: World Bank, pp. 3–5.

Arrow, K.J. and F. Hahn (1971). *General Competitive Analysis*. San Francisco: Holden-Day.

Associated Press (2001). "Study: Civic Work, Happiness Linked." March 1. At:. www.cfsv.org/communitysurvey.

Associated Press (2003). "More Americans Say Cheating on Taxes is All Right." Washington, October 30.

Associated Press (2006). "Hugo Chavez Threatens US on Oil." FoxNews.com, February 7.

Axelrod, R. (1984). *The Evolution of Cooperation*. New York: Basic Books.

Axelrod, R. and D. Dion (1988). "The Further Evolution of Cooperation." *Science* (December): 1385–1390.

Ayres, I. and P. Siegelman (1995). "Race and Gender Discrimination in Bargaining for a New Car." *The American Economic Review* (June): 304–319.

Bailey, R. (2007). "The Secrets of Intangible Wealth." *The Wall Street Journal, Online*. September 29, p. A9.

Bachelder, L. (1965). *Abahmam Lincoln: Wisdom and Wit*. New York: Peter Pauper Press.

Baker, J.H. (1987). *Mary Todd Lincoln: A Biography*. New York: Norton.

Baker, W. (2000). *Achieving Success Through Social Capital: Tapping the Hidden Resources in Your Personal and Business Networks*. San Francisco, CA: Jossey-Bass.

Banfield, E.C. (1958). *The Moral Basis of a Backward Society*. Glencoe, IL: The Free Press, Research Center in Economic Development and Cultural Change, The University of Chicago.

Barber, B. (1996). *Jihad vs. McWorld: How Globalism and Tribalism are Reshaping the World*. New York: Random House.

Baron, J. and M. Hannon (1994). "The Impact of Economics on Contemporary Sociology." *Journal of Economic Literature* 32: 1111–1146.

Bauer, P.T. (1972). *Dissent on Development: Studies and Debates in Development Economics*. Cambridge, MA: Harvard University Press.

Baum, M.A. and D.A. Lake (2003). "The Political Economy of Growth: Democracy and Human Capital." *American Journal of Political Science* 47 (April): 333–347.

Baumol, W.J., R.E. Litan, and C.J. Schramm (2007). *Good Capitalism, Bad Capitalism and the Economics of Growth and Prosperity*. New Haven, CT: Yale University Press.

BBC News Channel (2005), "Aceh Gamblers Caned in Public." June 24. At: http://news.bbc.co.uk/2/hi/asia-pacific/4618595.stm.

Becker, G.S. (1974). "A Theory of Social Interactions." *Journal of Political Economy* 82: 1063–1093.

Becker, G.S. (1981). *A Treatise on the Family*. Cambridge, MA: Harvard University Press.

Becker, G.S. (1993[1963]). *Human Capital*. Chicago: University of Chicago Press.

Belt, D. (2007). "Struggle for the Soul of Pakistan." *National Geographic* 212 (September): 32–59. Available at: http://ngm.nationalgeographic.com/2007/09/pakistan/don-belt-text/7.

Benedict, J. (2009). *Little Pink House: A True Story of Defiance and Courage*. New York: Grand Central Publishing.

Bennett, A. (1995). "Economics Students Aren't Selfish, They're Just Not Entirely Honest." *Wall Street Journal*, January 18.

Biles, J.J., L.J. Robison, and M.E. Siles (2002). "Export-oriented Industrialization, the State, and Social Capital: A Case Study of Maquiladora Production in Yucatan, Mexico." *Papers and Proceedings of the Applied Geography Conference* 25: 157–165.

Blank, R.M. (1991). "The Effects of Double-Blind versus Single-Blind Reviewing: Experimental Evidence." *American Economic Review* 81: 1041–1067.

Blum, D. (2002). *Love at Goon Park: Harry Harlow and the Science of Affection*. Cambridge, MA: Perseus Publishing.

Boulding, K.E. (1989). *Three Faces of Power*. Newbury Park, CA: Sage Publications.

Bourdieu, P. (1985). "The Forms of Capital." In J.G. Richardson (ed.), *Handbook of Theory and Research for the Sociology of Education*. New York: Greenwood Press, pp. 241–258.

Bradshaw, Y.W. and M. Wallace (1996). *Global Inequalities*. Thousand Oaks, CA, Pine Forge Press.

Bromley, D.W. (ed.) (1992). *Making the Commons Work: Theory, Practice, and Policy*. San Francisco, CA: ICS Press.

Bruce, N. and M. Waldman (1990). "The Rotten-Kid Theorem Meets the Samaritan's Dilemma." *Quarterly Journal of Economics* 105: 155–165.

Brunner, B. (n.d.). "Confederate Flag Controversy." At: http://www.infoplease.com/spot/confederate1.html.

Buchanan, R. and C. Gilles (1990). "Value Managed Relationship: The Key to Customer Retention and Profitability." *European Management Journal* 8: 523–526.

Bueno de Mesquita, B., J.D. Morrow, R.M. Siverson, and A. Smith (1999). "An Institutional Explanation of the Democratic Peace." *American Political Science Review* 93(4): 791–807.

Burt, G. (1992). *Structural Holes*. Cambridge, MA: Harvard University Press.

Calonius, E. (1990). "Blood and Money." *Newsweek*, Special Edition: *The 21st Century Family*. Winter/Spring, p. 82.

Camerer, C. (1988). "Gifts as Economic Signals and Social Symbols." *American Journal of Sociology* 94, Supplement: S180–S214.

Campbell, J. (n.d.). "Increasing Employee Satisfaction and Reducing Turnover." At: http://www.selfgrowth.com/articles/Campbell.html.

Carnegie, D. (1981). *How to Win Friends and Influence People.* New York: Simon & Schuster.

Carter, J and M. Irons (1991). "Are Economists Different, and If So, Why?" *Journal of Economic Perspectives* 5(2) (Spring): 171–177.

Castle, E.N. (1998). "A Conceptual Framework for the Study of Rural Places," *American Journal of Agricultural Economics* 80: 621–631.

Center for Global Prosperity (2007). "Press Release: Hudson Institute Launches Second Annual Index of Global Philanthropy." May 21. At: http://www.global-prosperity.org.

Chua, A. (2004). *World on Fire: How Exporting Free Market Democracy Breeds Ethnic Hatred and Global Instability*. New York: Anchor Books.

CNN.com (2003). "Police Bar 'Old,' 'Blind.'" May 28. At: http://edition.cnn.com/2003/EDUCATION/05/28/life.language.reut.

Coleman, J. (1988). "Social Capital in the Creation of Human Capital." *American Journal of Sociology* 94: S95–S120.

Coleman, J. (1990). *Foundations of Social Theory*. Cambridge, MA: Belknap Press/Harvard University Press.

Collard, D. (1975). "Edgeworth's Propositions on Altruism." *Economic Journal* 85: 355–360.

The Columbia Electronic Encyclopedia (2007). 6th edn. Columbia University Press. Copyright ©2007.

Commons, J. (1931). "Institutional Economics." *American Economic Review* 21: 648–657.

Cooley, C.H. (1902). *Human Nature and the Social Order*. New York: Charles Scribner's Sons.

Cordes, S.J.A., R.C. Bishop, G.D. Lynne, L.J. Robison, V.D. Ryan, and R. Shaffer (2003). "Social Capital, Attachment Value, and Rural Development: A Conceptual Framework and Application of Contingent Valuation." *American Journal of Agricultural Economics* 85: 1201–1207.

CNN.com/world (2009). "Iran Blocks Opposition Party Newspaper." July 1. At: http://edition.cnn.com/2009/WORLD/meast/07/01/iran.election.karrubi/index.html.

Council of Economic Advisors (2000). *Economic Report of the President*. Submitted to Congress 2000. Washington, DC: US Printing Office.

Covey, S.R. (1992). *Principle-Centered Leadership*. New York: Simon & Schuster.

Davis, M.H., L. Conklin, A. Smith, and C. Luce (1996). "Effect of Perspective Taking on the Cognitive Representation of Persons: A Merging of Self and Other." *Journal of Personality and Social Psychology* 70: 713–726.

Dawes, R.M., J. McTavish, and H. Shaklee (1977). "Behavior Communication and Assumptions About Other People's Behavior in a Commons Dilemma Situation." *Journal of Personality and Social Psychology* 35: 1–11.

De Bruin, A. (1999)."Cultural Capital." In P. O'Hara (ed.), *Encyclopedia of Political Economy*. London: Routledge.

Deininger, K. and L. Squire (1996). "A New Data Set Measuring Income Inequality." *The World Bank Economic Review* 10(3): 565–591.

de Soto, H. (2000). *The Mystery of Capital: Why Capitalism Triumphs in the West and Fails Everywhere Else*. New York: Basic Books.

Diamond, L. (1999). *Developing Democracy: Toward Consolidation.* Baltimore, MD: John Hopkins University Press.

Doner, R.F., B.K. Ritchie, and D. Slater (2005). "Systemic Vulnerability and the Origins of Developmental States." *International Organization* 59(2) (Spring): 327–361.

Donne, J. (1839). *The Works of John Donne*. Vol. III. Ed. Henry Alford. London: John W. Parker, pp. 574–575.

Drucker, P. (1992). "There's More Than One Kind of Team." *The Wall Street Journal*, February 11.

Durlauf, S. (1999). "The Case 'Against' Social Capital." *Focus* 20: 1–5.

Easterly, W. (2006). *The White Man's Burden: Why the West's Efforts to Aid the Rest Have Done So Much Ill and So Little Good.* New York: The Penguin Press.

Easterly, W. and R. Levine (1997). "Africa's Growth Tragedy: Policies and Ethnic Divisions." *Quarterly Journal of Economics* 62: 1203–1250.

Egerton, M. (1997). "Occupational Inheritance: The Role of Cultural Capital and Gender." *Work, Employment and Gender* 11: 263–282.

Elster, J. (1998). "Emotions and Economic Theory." *Journal of Economic Literature* 36 (March): 47–74.

Engerman, S.L. and K.L. Sokoloff (2002). "Factor Endowments, Inequality, and Paths of Development Among New World Economics." NBER Working Paper No. 9259, October.

Etzioni, A. (1988). *The Moral Dimension: Toward a New Economics*, New York: The Free Press.

Etzioni, A. (1991). "Socio-Economics: A Budding Challenge." In A. Etzioni and P. Lawrence (eds), *Socio-Economics: Toward a New Synthesis.* New York: M.E. Sharpe, Inc..

Fafchamps, M. and B. Minten (1998). "Returns to Social Capital Among Traders." IFPRI-MSSD Discussion Paper No. 23. Washington, DC: IFPRI.

Fieser, J. (2006). "Ethics." *The Internet Encyclopedia of Philosophy.* At: http://www.utm.edu/research/iep/e/ethics.htm.

Flanagan, L. (2003). "Masterful." *Continental In Flight Magazine* (November): 43–46.

Flora, C.B. and J.L. Flora (2003). "Social Capital." In D.L. Brown and L. Swanson (eds), *Challenges for Rural America in the 21st Century.* Philadelphia: Pennsylvania State University Press.

Fox, J.A., J.F. Shogren, D.J. Hayes, and J.B. Kliebenstein (1998). "CVM-X: Calibrating Contingent Values with Experimental Auction Markets." *American Journal of Agricultural Economics* 80: 455–465.

Frank, R.H. (1987). *Choosing the Right Pond: Human Behavior and the Quest for Status.* New York: Oxford University Press.

Frank, R.H. (1988). *Passions within Reason: The Strategic Role of the Emotions.* New York, W.W. Norton.

Frank, R.H. (1999). *Luxury Fever: Why Money Fails to Satisfy in an Era of Excess.* New York: The Free Press.

Frank, R.H., T. Gilovich, and D.T. Regan (1993). "Does Studying Economics Inhibit Cooperation?" *Economic Perspectives* 7: 159–172.

Frey, B.S. and I. Bohnet (2001). "Identification in Democratic Society." In B.S. Frey (ed.), *Inspiring Economics: Human Motivation in Political Economy.* Northampton, MA: Edward Elgar Press, pp. 103–117.

Friedman, T.L. (1999). *The Lexus and the Olive Tree.* New York: Anchor Books.

Friedman, T.L. (2003). "Starting From Scratch." *New York Times.* August 27.

Frye, M. (2002). "Teachers or TV Monitors? " *The State News*, February 26, p. 3.

Fukuyama, F. (1995a). "Social Capital and the Global Economy." *Foreign Affairs* 74 (September/October): 89–103.

Fukuyama, F. (1995b). *Trust: The Social Virtues and the Creation of Prosperity.* New York: The Free Press.

Ganesan, A. and A. Vines (2004). "Engine of War: Resources, Greed, and the Predatory State." *World Report*, Human Rights Watch. At: http://www.hrw.org/wr2k4/14.htm.

Ganley, E. (2004). "France Bans Religious Attire in Schools." *The Cincinnati Post, Online Edition.* February 10. Available at: http://www.encyclopedia.com/doc/1P1-91033704.html.

Gardner, B.D. (1995). "Discussion on Social Capital." *Journal of Agricultural and Applied Economics* 27 (July): 81–85.

Gergen, D. (1999). "To Have and Have Less." *US News & World Report* 127 (July 26): 64.

Gilliland, C.E. (1985). "How to Investigate Rural Land's Market Value." *Farm Land Realtor* 37: 19–21.

Gladwin, M. (1999). "Six Degrees of Lois Weisberg." The New Yorker (January 11): 52–63.

Goldberg, J. (2005). "The Spectre of McDonalds." National Review Online. April 15. At: http://www.nationalreview.com/flashback/goldberg200504151023.asp.

Grace, F. (2005). "Bono's War on Poverty and Aids: Musicians, Actors, Clergy Unite in Campaign to Raise Awareness." CBSNews. April 7. At: http://www.cbsnews.com/stories/2005/04/07/entertainment/main686158.shtml.

Granovetter, M. (1973). "The Strength of Weak Ties." *American Journal of Sociology* 78: 1360–1380.

Greene, B. (1996). "Can a Mother Rent a Solution to Loneliness?" *The National Forum*, Tribune Media Services: 26.

Gwilliam, K.R. (1993). "Farmland Leasing and Contract Choice in Michigan: The Influence of Social Distance." PhD dissertation, Michigan State University.

Hamilton, C.J. (1995–2009). "Uranus." *Views of the Solar System.*

Hamilton, W.H. (1932). "Property According to Locke." *Yale Law Journal* 4: 964–980.

Hanifan, L.J. (1916). "The Rural School Community Center." *Annals of the American Academy of Political and Social Science* 67:130–138.

Hanson, S.D. and L.J. Robison (2007). "Impacts of Social Capital on Investment Behavior under Risk." Department of Agricultural Economics Working Paper (September).

Hanson, S.D., L.J. Robison, and M.E. Siles (1996). "Impacts of Relationships on Customer Retention in the Banking Industry." *Agribusiness: An International Journal* 12 (January/February): 27–36.

Hanson, V.D. (1999). *The Soul of Battle: From Ancient Times to the Present Day, How Three Great Liberators Vanquished Tyranny*. New York: The Free Press.

Harrison, L.E. and S. Huntington (2000). *Culture Matters: How Values Shape Human Progress.* New York: Basic Books.

Hayakawa, S.I. (1962). *The Use and Misuse of Language*. New York: Fawcett World Library, Crest, Gold Medal, and Premier Books.

Heilbroner, R.L. (1980). "The Wonderful World of Adam Smith." In R.L. Heilbroner (ed.), *The Worldly Philosophers*. New York: Simon & Schuster.

Herfmann, W. (2002). "Bowling with Immigrants ... " *The Arizona Republic* (March 1).

Heritage Foundation (2009). "Zimbabwe." *2009 Index of Economic Freedom.* At: http://www.heritage.org/Index/Country/Zimbabwe.

Herzberg, F.I. (1987). "One More Time: How Do You Motivate Employees?" *Harvard Business Review* 65 (September/October): 109–120.

Hicken, A. and B.K. Ritchie (2002). "The Origin of Credibility Enhancing Institutions in Southeast Asia." Paper delivered at the annual meeting of the American Political Science Association, Boston Copley Place Marriott, August 28–September 1.

Hilburt-Davis, J. and J. Green (2009). "Family Businesses Have Traits to Survive." *Providence Business News*. February 23. At: http://www.pbn.com/detail/40521.html.

Hirshleifer, J. (1994). "The Dark Side of the Force." *Economic Inquiry* 32: 1–10.

Hirshman, A. (1970). *Exit, Voice, and Loyalty.* Cambridge, MA: Harvard University Press.

Hobbes, T. (1651). *Leviathan, or the Matter, Forme, and Power of a Commonwealth, Ecclesiasticall and Civil.* London.

Hochschild, A.R. (1983). *The Managed Heart: Commercialization of Human Feeling*. Berkeley: University of California Press.

Homans, G.C. (1971). "Fundamental Processes of Social Exchange." In E.P. Hollander and R. Hunt (eds), *Current Perspectives in Social Psychology*. New York: Oxford University Press, pp. 450–462.

Htun, M. (2003). *Sex and the State: Abortion, Divorce, and the Family under Latin American Dictatorships and Democracies*. New York: Cambridge University Press.

Hughes, J.E. and S.B. MacDonald (2004). *Carnival on Wall Street*. New York: Wiley.

Hume, D. (1978[1740]). *A Treatise of Human Nature*. Oxford: Oxford University Press.

Huntington, S.P. (1991). *The Third Wave*. Norman: University of Oklahoma Press.

Iowa Department of Transportation (2009). "Highways and Your Land." September. At: http://www.iowadot.gov/rightofway/acquisition/highwaysandyourland.pdf.

Isham, J. (1999). "The Effect of Social Capital on Technology Adoption: Evidence from Rural Tanzania." Paper presented at the annual meeting of the American Economic Association, New York.

Johnson, B., L. Janssen, M. Lundeen, and J.D. Aiken (1987). "Agricultural Land Leasing and Rental Market Characteristics: A Case Study of South Dakota and Nebraska." Mimeo, 156 pages.

Joshi, M. (2009). "No Tax Breaks for Firms Offshoring Jobs: Obama." TopNews.in. February 26. At: http://www.topnews.in/no-tax-breaks-firms-offshoring-jobs-obama-2131462.

Kahneman, D., J.L. Knetsch, and R. Thaler (1986). "Fairness As a Constraint on Profit Seeking: Entitlements in the Market." *American Economic Review* 76: 728–741.

Kahneman, D., J.L. Knetsch, and R. Thaler (1990). "Experimental Tests of the Endowment Erffect and the Coase Theorem." *Journal of Political Economy* 98: 1325–1348.

Keane, W. (1999). "Why We Wrap Presents." Associated Press. December 13. At: http://www.applesforhealth.com/whywrap1.html.

Kirby, R. (1999). "It's Important Not to Give Gifts Bad Wrap." *The Salt Lake Tribune*, December 16.

Knack, S. and P. Keefer (1997). "Does Social Capital Have An Economic Payoff? A Cross-Country Investigation." *Quarterly Journal of Economics* 112: 1252–1348.

Knight, J. (1992). *Institutions and Social Conflict*. Cambridge: Cambridge University Press.

Krutilla, J.V. (1967). "Conservation Reconsidered." *American Economic Review* 57 (September): 777–786.

Kuhn, T.S. (1996). *The Structure of Scientific Revolutions*. 3rd edn. Chicago and London: University of Chicago Press.

Kukula, K.C. (1996). "Reach Out: The Surprising Benefits of Hugs, Handshakes and Heart-to-Hearts." *Woman's Day* (February 1): 40.

Kuran, T. (2004). *Islam and Mammon: The Economic Predicaments of Islamism*. Princeton, NJ: Princeton University Press.

Lacey, M. (2003). "A Sign of the New Kenya: A Briefcase Filled with Cash is Spurned." *New York Times* (March 29): A6.

Landa, J. (1991). "Culture and Entrepreneurship in LDCs: Ethnic Trading Networks as Economic Organization." In B. Berger (ed.), *The Culture of Entrepreneurship*. San Francisco, CA: ICS Press.

Landes, D. (1998). *The Wealth and Poverty of Nations: Why Some Countries Are So Rich and Others So Poor*. New York: W.W. Norton.

Lardner, J. (2000). "The Rich Get Richer." *U.S. News & World Report* 128 (February 21): 39–43.

Lin, N. (2001). "Building a Network Theory of Social Capital." In N. Lin, K. Cook, and R.S. Burt (eds), *Social Capital: Theory and Research*. New York: Aldine de Gruyter, pp. 3–30.

Loomis, C.J. (2006). "A Conversation with Warren Buffett." *Fortune*, June 25.

Lucidcafe.com (n.d.). "Marie Antoinette: Queen of France, 1755–1793." Lucidcafé: Library at: http://www2.lucidcafe.com/lucidcafe/library/95nov/antoinette.html.

Lutz, M. (1997). "The Mondragon Co-operative Complex: An Application of Kantian Ethics to Social Economics." *International Journal of Social Economics* 24: 1404–1421.

Lynch, D.J. (2006). "Anger over Free-Market Reforms Fuels Leftward Swing in Latin America." *USA Today* (February 9): 1B, 2B.

Mace, R. (2000), "Fair Game." *Nature* 406 (July 20): 248–249.

Mansbridge, J.J. (1990). *Beyond Self-Interest.* Chicago: University of Chicago Press.

Marc, L. (2003). "A Sign of a New Kenya: A Briefcase Filled with Cash is Spurned." *The New York Times* (March 29): A6.

Marshall, A. (1962). *Principles of Economics.* 8th edn. London: Macmillan.

Maslow, A.H. (1962). *Toward a Psychology of Being.* Princeton, NJ: D. Von Nostrand Company.

Matthew A.B. and D.A. Lake (2003). "The Political Economy of Growth: Democracy and Human Capital." *American Journal of Political Science* 47 (April): 333–347.

Maxwell, G. and R. Ames (1981). "Economists' Free Ride, Does Anyone Else? Experiments on the Provision of Public Goods, IV." *Journal of Public Economics* 15 (June): 295–310.

McCloskey, D. and A. Klamer (1995). "One Quarter of GDP is Persuasion." *American Economic Association Papers and Proceedings* 85: 191–195.

McKendrick, D., R.F. Doner, and S. Haggard (2000). *From Silicon Valley to Singapore: The Competitive Advantage of Location in the Hard Disk Drive Industry.* Stanford, CA: Stanford University Press.

Merleau-Ponty, M. (1969). "The Primacy of Perception and its Philosophical Consequences." In A.L. Fisher (ed.), *The Essential Writings.* New York: Harcourt, Brace.

Minkler, L. (1999). "The Problem with Utility." *Review of Social Economy* 57: 4–24.

Miringoff, M. and M.L. Miringoff (1999). *The Social Health of the Nation: How America is Really Doing.* New York: Oxford University Press.

Mokyr, J. (1991). "Eurocentricity Triumphant." *The American Historical Review* 104: 1241–1246.

Montgomery, J.D. (1991). "Social Networks and Labor-Market Outcomes: Toward an Economic Analysis." *American Economic Review* 81: 1408–1418.

Mueller, D.C. (1986). *Rational Egoism versus Adaptive Egoism as Fundamental Postulate for a Descriptive Theory of Human Behavior.* Melbourne: Centre of Policy Studies, Monash University.

Narayan, D. (2000). *Voices of the Poor: Can Anyone Hear Us?* Oxford: Oxford University Press for the World Bank.

Narayan, D. and Pritchett, L. (1999). "Cents and Sociability: Household Income and Social Capital in Rural Tanzania." *Economic Development and Cultural Change* 47: 871–897.

Nelton, S. (1990). "We Could Use a Few Good Numbers." *Nation's Business*, April: 53.

Nevins, A. (1953). Study in Power: John D. Rockefeller, Industrialist and Philanthropist. 2 vols. New York: Charles Scribner's Sons.

North, D.C. (1990) "Institutions, Institutional Change and Economic Performance." Cambridge: Cambridge University Press.

North, D.C. and Weingast, B. (1989). "Constitutions and Commitment: The Evolution of Institutions

Governing Public Choice in Seventeenth-Century England." *Journal of Economic History* 49(4): 803–832.

O'Hara, P.A. (1998). "Capital and Inequality in Today's World." In Doug Brown (ed.), *Thorstein Veblen in the Twenty-First Century.* Cheltenham: Edward Elgar.

Olson, M. (1984).*The Rise and Decline of Nations: Economic Growth, Stagflation, and Social Rigidities.* New Haven, CT: Yale University Press.

Omestad, T., L. Derfner, and K.A. Toameh (2000). "The Brink of War." *U.S. News and World Report* (October 23): 24–31.

Ostrom, E, and T.K. Ahn (2003). *Foundations of Social Capital*. London: Edward Elgar.

Perry, G.M. and L.J. Robison (2001). "Evaluating the Influence of Personal Relationships on Land Sale Prices: A Case Study in Oregon." *Land Economics* 77: 385–398.

Pitts, L. Jr (2004). "Pre-sexual Agreement, To Put It Kindly, Dubious Idea." Aberdeennews.com, posted Wednesday January 14. Available at: http://209.157.64.200/focus/f-news/1058468/posts.

Poffenberger, M. (1997). "Rethinking Indonesian Forest Policy: Beyond the Timber Barons." *Asian Survey* 37(5) (May): 453–469.

Portes, A. (1995). "Economic Sociology and the Sociology of Immigration: A Conceptual Overview." In A. Portes (ed.), *The Economic Sociology of Immigration: Essays on Networks, Ethnicity, and Entrepreneurship*. New York: Russell Sage Foundation.

Portes, A. (1998). "Social Capital: Its Origin and Applications in Modern Sociology." *Annual Review of Sociology* 22: 1–24.

Portes, A. and P. Landolt (1996). "The Downside of Social Capital." *The American Prospect* 26 (May/June): 18–24, 94.

Portes, A. and J. Sensenbrenner (1993). "Embeddedness and Immigration: Notes on the Social Determinants of Economic Action." *American Journal of Sociology* 98: 1320–1350.

Powell, B. (1993). "Tribal Networks and Economic Power." *Newsweek* (May 24): 47.

Putnam, R.D. (2000). *Bowling Alone: Collapse and Revival of the American Community*. New York: Simon & Schuster.

Putnam, R.D., R. Leonardi, and R. Nanetti (1993). *Making Democracy Work: Civic Traditions in Modern Italy*. Princeton, NJ: Princeton University Press.

Quirk, J. and R. Saposnik (1968). *Introduction to General Equilibrium Theory and Welfare Economics*. New York: McGraw-Hill.

Raspberry, W. (2003). "Environmentally Challenged." Washingtonpost.com. September 22, p. A23.

Rescher, N. (1975). *Unselfishness: The Role of the Vicarious Affect in Moral Philosophy and Social Theory*. Pittsburgh, PA: University of Pittsburgh Press.

Ritchie, B.K. (2001). "Innovation Systems, Collective Dilemmas, and the Formation of Technical Intellectual Capital in Malaysia, Singapore, and Thailand." *International Journal of Business and Society*. 2(2) (July): 21–48.

Ritchie, B.K. (2005a). "Is Economic Development Probable? Labor and Skills Formation in a Coordinated Liberal Economy." Working Paper. August 29. Prepared for the "Varieties of Capitalism in Asia: the State, Corporate Governance, and Social Policy," Korea University. September 9–10 2005.

Ritchie, B.K. (2005b). "Progress Through Setback or Mired in Mediocrity? Crisis and Institutional Change in Southeast Asia." *Journal of East Asian Studies*. 5(2) (June): 273–314.

Ritchie, B.K. (2008). "Economic Upgrading in a State-Coordinated, Liberal Market Economy." *Asia Pacific Jounral of Management* 26: 435–457.

Robison, L.J. and J.L. Flora (2003). "The Social Capital Paradigm: Bridging Across Disciplines." *American Journal of Agricultural Economics* 85:1187–1193.

Robison, L.J. and S.D. Hanson (1993). "Social Capital and Catastrophic Risk Responses." In *Quantifying Long-Run Agricultural Risks and Evaluating Farmer Responses to Risk*, Proceedings of a Seminar sponsored by S-232, Jekyll Island, GA, March 24–26, pp. 34–61.

Robison, L.J. and S.D. Hanson (1995). "Social Capital and Economic Cooperation." Journal of Agricultural and Applied Economics 27: 43–58.

Robison, L.J. and A.A. Schmid (1989). "Interpersonal Relationships and Preferences: Evidences and Implications." In R. Frantz and H. Singh (eds), *Handbook of Behavioral Economics*. Vol. 2. Greenwich, CT: JAI Press, pp. 347–358.

Robison, L.J. and A.A. Schmid (1996). "Can Agriculture Prosper Without Increased Social Capital?" In H.W. Ayer (ed.), *The Best of Choices, 1986–1996*. Ames, IA: American Agricultural Economics Association, pp. 160–162.

Robison, L.J. and M.E. Siles (1999). "Social Capital and Household Income Distributions in the United States: 1980, 1990." *Journal of Socio-Economics* 28: 43–93.

Robison, L.J., J. Lindon, and A.A. Schmid (1991). "Interpersonal Relationships and Preferences: Evidence and Implications." In R. Frantz et al. (eds), *Handbook of Behavioral Economics*. Vol. 2B. Greenwich, CT: JAI Press, pp. 347–358.

Robison, L.J., R.J. Myers, and M.E. Siles (2002). "Social Capital and the Terms of Trade for Farmland." *Review of Agricultural Economics* 24(Spring/Summer): 44–58.

Robison, L.J., A.A. Schmid, and P.J. Barry (2002). "The Role of Social Capital in the Industrialization of the Food System." *Agricultural and Resource Economics Review* 31(1) (April): 15–24.

Robison, L.J., A.A. Schmid, and M.E. Siles (2002). "Is Social Capital Really Capital?" *Review of SocialEconomy* 60: 1–21.

Robison, L.J., M.E. Siles, and J. Owens (2002). "A Performance Evaluation of the Nicaraguan Social Investment Funds." Department of Agricultural Economics Staff Paper No. 02-00. East Lansing: Michigan State University.

Rodrik, D. (1998). "Where Did All the Growth Go? External Shocks, Social Conflicts, and Growth Collapses." NBER Working Paper 6350. Cambridge, MA: National Bureau of Economic Research.

Rodrik, D. (1999). *The New Global Economy and Developing Countries: Making Openness Work*. Washington DC: Overseas Development Council.

Rogers, C.R. (1961). *On Becoming A Person*. Boston, MA: Houghton-Mifflin Co..

Rohter, L. (2003). "Bolivia's Poor Proclaim Abiding distrust of Globalization." *New York Times* (October 17). Available at: http://www.nytimes.com/2003/10/17/world/bolivia-s-poor-proclaim-abiding-distrust-of-globalization.html.

Rook, C. (2002). "Boos for Bobby." *Lansing State Journal*, October 30.

Ross, M.L. (1999). "The Political Economy of the Resource Curse." *World Politics* 51 (January): 297–322.

Ross, M.L. (2001). "Does Oil Hinder Democracy?" *World Politics* 53: 325–361.

Rotemberg, J.J. (1994). "Human Relations in the Workplace." *Journal of Political Economy* 102: 684–717.

Sally, D. (2000). "A General Theory of Sympathy, Mind-Reading, and Social Interaction, with an Application to the Prisoner's Dilemma." *Social Science Information* 39: 567–634.

Sally, D. (2001). "On Sympathy and Games." *Journal of Economic Behavior and Organization* 44: 1–30.

Sally, D. (2002). "Two Economic Applications of Sympathy." *Journal of Law, Economics, and Organization* 18: 455–487.

Sampson, R.J., S.W. Raudenbush, and F. Earls (1997). "Neighborhoods and Violent Crime: A Multilevel Study of Collective Efficacy." *Science* 277 (August 15): 918–924.

Schabath, G. and M. Martindale (1998). "Suburban Residents Rebel Against Nepotism." *The Detroit News* (October 11).

Schmid, A.A. (2002). "Using Motive to Distinguish Social Capital from its Outputs." *Journal of Economic Issues* 36: 747–68.

Schultz, T. (1961). "Investment in Human Capital." *The American Economic Review* LI: 1–17.

Sciolino, E. (2004). "French Assembly Votes to Ban Religious Symbols in Schools." *The New York Times*, February 11.

Sen, A. (1982). "Rational Fools: A Critique of the Behavioral Foundations of Economic Theory." Chapter 1 in *Choice, Welfare and Measurement*, Cambridge, MA: MIT Press.

Shome, A.S.K. (2002). *Malay Political Leadership*. London: Routledge/Curzon.

Siles, M.E. (1992). "The Role of Social Capital in Michigan Credit Markets." PhD dissertation, Michigan State University.

Siles, M.E. and L.J. Robison (1998). "Data Book: Supplement to Social Capital and Household Income Distributions in the United States: 1980, 1990." Department of Agricultural Economics, Report No. 595/S, Julian Samora Research Institute Research Report No. 18/S (October).

Siles, M.E., L.J. Robison, and S.D. Hanson (1994). "Does Friendly Service Retain Customers?" *Bank Marketing* (January): 47–49.

Singer, P. (2009), "The Chronicle of Higher Education," *The Chronicle Review* (March 13): B7.

Smith, A. (1966a[1759]). *The Theory of Moral Sentiments*. Reprints of Economic Classics. NewYork: Augustus M. Kelley.

Smith, A. (1966b[1776]). *The Wealth of Nations*. Chicago: Henry Regnery Co.

Smith, L. (2001). "Development of Rural Villages and Social Capital." Published by CHOICE Humanitarian for the Conference "Social Capital and Poverty Reduction in Latin America and the Caribbean: Toward a New Paradigm" held in Santiago de Chile, September 24–26.

Smithson, C.W. (1982). "Capital, a Factor of Production." In D. Greenwald (ed.), *Encyclopedia of Economics*. New York: McGraw-Hill, pp. 111–112.

Solow, R.M. (1999). "Notes on Social Capital and Economic Performance." In P. Dasgupta and I. Serageldin (eds), *Social Capital: A Multifaceted Perspective*, Washington, DC: The World Bank, pp. 6–12.

Spake, A. (1999). "Brownie Wise Had One Word for You: Plastics." *US News & World Report*, October 18 p. 82.

Stiglitz, J. (2005). "Ethics, Economic Advice, and Economic Policy." Initiative for Policy Dialogue. October 24. Available at: http://www.policyinnovations.org/ideas/policy_library/data/01216.

Stossel, J. (1997). "Ted Turner: Tender-Hearted Tycoon?" *USA Weekend* (November 28–30): 4.

Swarup, V. (1995). "Officials Debate if Religious Affiliation Plays Role in Government." *State News* (September 25): 2A.

Swedberg, R.M. (1991). "The Battle of the Methods: Toward a Paradigm Shift?" In A. Etzioni and P.R. Lawrence (eds), *Socio-Economics: Toward a New Synthesis*. New York: M.E. Sharpe, Inc., pp. 13–34.

Swinton, S.M. (2000). "More Social Capital, Less Erosion: Evidence from Peru's Altiplano." Selected paper for presentation at the American Agricultural Economics Association meeting, Tampa, Florida, July 30–August 2.

Tamblyn, R., M. Abrahamowicz, and D. Dauphinee (2007). "Physician Scores on a National Clinical Skills Examination as Predictors of Complaints to Medical Regulatory Authorities." *Journal of the American Medical Association* 298: 993–1001.

Tatum, B.D. (1999). *Why Are the Black Kids Sitting Together in the Cafeteria? Eating Alone?* New York: Basic Books.

Taylor, A. (2008). "Xenophobia in South Africa," The Big Picture supported by the Boston Globe. June 27. At: http://www.boston.com/bigpicture/2008/06/xenophobia_in_south_africa.html.

Telser, L. and H.N. Higinbotham (1977). "Organized Futures Markets: Costs and Benefits." *Journal of Political Economy* 85: 969–1000.

Terrell, K. and S. Hammel (1999). "Call of the Riled: Taking Action Against the Boors of the Wireless World." *U.S. News & World Report* (June 14): 62–64.

Tetens, K. (2002). "Online Learning Has Drawbacks, Researchers Find." University Relations, News Release, Michigan State University, February 25.

Thaler, R. (1980). "Towards a Positive Theory of Consumer Choice." *Journal of Economic Behavior and Organization* 1: 39–60.

"The Psychology of Investing" (2003). *Participant: Quarterly News and Performance from TIAA-CREF* (August 3).

Thompson, A. (2009). "Study: You Touch It, You Buy It." Livescience.com. January 16. At: http://www.livescience.com/culture/090116-touch-buy.html.

Tocqueville, A. de (1966). *Democracy in America.* Ed. J.P. Mayer, trans. George Lawrence. New York: Harper Collins.

Tomer, J. (1999). "Social and Organizational Capital." In P. O'Hara (ed.), *Encyclopedia of Political Economy*. London: Routledge, pp. 1049–51.

Transparency International (2005). *Corruption Perceptions Index 2005.* At: http://www.transparency.org/policy_research/surveys_indices/cpi/2005.

Turner, M. (2007). "Ecological Complexity and the Management of Common Property Resources." *Tenure Brief*, Land Tendure Center, University of Wisconsis-Madison, No. 5, August, pp. 1–7.

Tversky, A. and D. Kahneman (1981). "The Framing of Decisions and the Psychology of Choice." *Science* 211 (January 30): 453–458.

Tye, L. (1998). *The Father of Spin: Edward L. Bernays and the Birth of Public Relations*. New York: Crown Publishers.

UNDP (2009). *Human Poverty Index*. Available at: http://hdr.undp.org/en/humandev/hdi.

Uphoff, N. (2000). "Understanding Social Capital: Learning from the Analysis and Experience of Participation." In P. Dasgupta and I. Serageldin (eds), *Social Capital: A Multifaceted Perspective.* Washington, DC: The World Bank, pp. 215–249.

US Department of Labor, Bureau of Labor Statistics (1975). *Jobseeking Methods Used by American Workers*. Bulletin No. 1886. Washington, DC: Government Printing Office.

US Department of Labor, Bureau of Labor Statistics (2007). USDL 07-0019, Washington DC, January 10.

Veblen, T. (1908). "On the Nature of Capital, Intangible Assets, and the Pecuniary Magnate." *Quarterly Journal of Economics* 22: 104–136.

Veblen, T. (1899). *The Theory of the Leisure Class*. Available from The Project Gutenberg at: http://www.gutenberg.org.

Wacquant, L.J.D. (1998). "Negative Social Capital: State Breakdown and Social Destitution in America's Urban Core." *Netherlands Journal of Housing and the Built Environment* 13: 25–39.

Waldinger, R., H. Aldrich, and R. Ward (1990). "Opportunities, Group Characteristics, and Strategies." In R. Waldinger et al. (eds), *Ethnic Entrepreneurs.* Newbury park, CA: Sage Publications, pp. 13–48.

Waldner, D. (1999). *State Building and Late Development.* Ithaca, NY: Cornell University Press.

Watson, R. (2003). "Rumsfeld Seeks to Isolate 'Old Europe' Opponents." *The Times* (January 24).

Weber, M. (1958). *The Protestant Ethic and the Spirit of Capitalism.* New York: Scribner's Press.

Webley, P. and S.E.G. Lea (1993). "The Partial Unacceptability of Money in Repayment for Neighboring Help." *Human Relations* 46: 65–76.

Weiner, T. (2003). "Wal-Mart Invades, and Mexico Gladly Surrenders." *The New York Times*. December 6. Available at: http://www.nytimes.com/2003/12/06/world/wal-mart-invades-and-mexico-gladly-surrenders.html.

Weintraub, D. (1995). "Gray Vetoes Illegal Immigrant Tuition Bill." *Sacramento Bee* (October 3).

Whetten, D.A. and K.S. Cameron (1995). *Developing Management Skills*. 3rd edn. New York: Harper Collins, College Publishers.

White, L.H. (2007). "The Methodology of the Austrian School Economists: Carl Menger." At: http://www.mises.org/mofase/ch2.asp.

Whitman, D. with M. Loftus (1996). "I'm OK, You're Not." *US News and World Report* (December 16): 25–32.

Will, G. (1996). "Time to Review Corporal Punishment." *Lansing State Journal* (February 6).

Wilson, J.Q. (1993). *The Moral Sense*. New York: Free Press Paperback.

Wolf, J. R., H.R. Arkes, and W.A. Muhanna (2008). "The Power of Touch: An Examination of the Effect of Duration of Physical Contact on the Valuation of Objects." *Judgment and Decision Making Society for Judgment and Decision Making* 3(6): 476–482.

Woolcock, M. (1998). "Social Capital and Economic Development: Towards a Theoretical Synthesis and Policy Framework." *Theory and Society* 27: 151–208.

World Bank (1996). *World Development Indicators 1996*. Washington, DC: World Bank.

World Bank (2001). *World Development Report, 2000/2001: Attacking Poverty*. Oxford: Oxford University Press.

World Bank (2002). "Globalization, Growth, and Poverty: Building an Inclusive World Economy." Washington, DC: World Bank; New York: Oxford University Press.

World Bank (2007). *World Development Indicators 2007*. Washington, DC: World Bank.

Index

Figures are indicated by **bold** page numbers, tables by *italic* numbers.

E

F

R

9781032923741